# State College

## at

## Framingham

5M-6-65-940607

*An Experimental
Approach to Projective
Techniques*

# JOSEPH ZUBIN
*Chief of Psychiatric Research (Biometrics)*
*New York State Department of Mental Hygiene, and*
*Professor of Psychology, Columbia University*

# LEONARD D. ERON
*Director of Graduate Training in Clinical Psychology, and*
*Professor of Psychology, University of Iowa*

# FLORENCE SCHUMER
*Senior Research Associate, Wiltwyck School for Boys*
*Formerly Adjunct Assistant Professor of Psychology, Barnard College*

# An Experimental
# Approach to Projective
# Techniques

John Wiley & Sons, Inc., New York · London · Sydney

10/66

To a pioneer in projective techniques,
David Mordecai Levy

# Preface

This book deals with experimental approaches to projective techniques and is a companion to a book still in preparation dealing with experimental abnormal psychology. The material on projective techniques was prepared first, but the lack of scientific sophistication in this area forced us to retrace our footsteps and explore scientific methods in the field of abnormal psychology. It then became easier to see the procedures required for objectifying projective techniques. Whether projective techniques will continue to remain unaffected by objective approaches will largely depend on the willingness of experimental psychologists to accept the challenge.

Projective techniques originated as a revolt against the rigid framework which grew up around mental testing. The first revolt was led by experimentalists in the field of child psychology, who introduced observational techniques to offset the static results yielded by testing. The second revolt came from clinical psychologists who needed more than an IQ with which to understand their patients. As in the aftermath of many revolutions, the rebels kicked over their traces completely; they now wander over the still uncharted areas of psychopathology without much guidance.

The present book is an attempt at returning projective techniques to the scientific fold. It provides methods for testing the hypotheses and hunches emanating from the clinic and in this way permits an evaluation of present-day methods in projective techniques.

In the following pages, a methodological review of some problems pertaining to projective techniques will be presented, especially with reference to the Rorschach and the Thematic Apperception Test (TAT). Methods will be presented in subsequent chapters for evaluating these instruments. This book is not intended to be a skills book or a clinical manual; the clinical and applied uses of projective instruments—rules-of-thumb, skills, and clinical experience—are described elsewhere. The reader, it is assumed, is familiar with projective instruments and their administration and has at least some knowledge of their importance in the clinic, school, psychiatric setting, counseling center, etc.; their status among assessment techniques will not be spelled out in detail. Whenever relevant, however, at least a few clinical references will be cited.

Moreover, this book is not intended to be a systematic and complete review of research and clinical findings. The literature on projective techniques is voluminous—especially that pertaining to the Rorschach. From time to time, various reviews, compendia, and source books appear. These will be referred to, so that the reader can turn to them for an exhaustive, general bibliography. With respect to both the Rorschach and the TAT, however, there will be some presentation of the history of the method, methodological problems, and most recent advances in theory, research, and general perspective. In this review, "typical" findings and research reports will be provided. Our review will undoubtedly raise more problems than it will solve; but this is dictated by the present status of the fields covered. The problems raised serve as a springboard for the presentation of research and methodological procedures which have been developed for solution of some of these problems. But this is not the goal. It is hoped that by making explicit some of the dilemmas, contradictions, and blind alleys, as well as advances and achievements of the field of projective techniques, the young clinician will begin to develop an interest in constructing research hypotheses and designs of his own. Even more optimistically, it is hoped that clinicians and clinical students *without* research interests and *without* the healthy skepticism and questioning attitudes which nourish any science will be stimulated to evaluate their tools and make explicit their assumptions. In short, to call attention to the unsubstantiated but taken-for-granted attitudes in the area of projective techniques should be regarded as an important goal of this book.

The reader may well wonder why the Rorschach and TAT serve

as the framework for this book. The answer is twofold. The first reason has to do with economy of time and space. A more extensive, ambitious review which would include other projective techniques is not possible if an intensive examination of problems is attempted. Second, the Rorschach and the TAT are among the most widely used instruments. The systematic scaling procedures presented in this book can, however, with some modifications, be applied to the evaluation of other projective instruments. Moreover, the research clinician, to whom this book is ultimately addressed, will undoubtedly conclude that some of the theoretical, methodological, and statistical problems raised about the Rorschach and TAT are applicable to other instruments.

Chapter 1 is devoted to a general survey of the projective field, beginning with a review of some definitions, classificatory systems, and assumptions. The relationship between projective and psychometric approaches will be discussed, as well as the direction taken by projective theory. Some general psychometric problems will be raised, relevant, it is hoped, to all testing including the projective variety.

In Chapters 2 and 3 a systematic review of theories of perception is presented—with a specific orientation. This orientation can be reduced to the following question: Has the link between personality and perception been definitely established? The focus of Chapter 3 is on directive-state * theories of perception, but an attempt is made to survey other major theories, particularly those which provide perspective to directive-state theory.

The Rorschach and related instruments seem to be the foci for the personality-perception approach, the TAT, and related instruments being viewed more flexibly as tests of cognition, imagination, fantasy, and *ap*perception. In the general zeal to "elevate" the Rorschach to the level of other perceptual tasks, cognitive elements, language factors, content considerations, and examiner-subject interactions are often brushed aside. But is perception directly and unitarily involved in projective processes? Many psychologists also make an implicit assumption that almost all behavioral processes are perceptual in nature. Is the type of perception which is considered in social psychology, such as that involved in attitudes, sociometric choice, social scaling, etc., the

---

* *Directive-state* is the term used to describe those approaches, theories, and viewpoints in perception which claim that needs, tensions, motives, etc., and/or "central" and stable aspects and characteristics of the organism's personality, and/or past experience, that is, a *central directive state*, enter into and affect perceptual organization. This term will be used, especially in Chapter 3, to refer to all such theories and approaches to perception, as opposed to a variety of other theories which involve a different set of assumptions.

same as the type of perception involved in projective behavior? And are these the same types of perception (in terms of neurological and physiological processes) as would be involved, say, in the matching of red patches in a psychophysical experiment? There are no simple answers, but some of the material in Chapters 2 and 3 is relevant to these considerations.

Chapter 4 is devoted to an historical review and methodological survey of the Rorschach method. Here again, psychometric and theoretical problems are raised. Despite the essential differences between the Rorschach and TAT in the nature and degree of cognitive elements in the response, structure and content of stimuli, etc., many problems raised in Chapter 4 are directly relevant to both the Rorschach and the TAT.

Chapter 5 is a presentation of an analysis of the Rorschach technique as an experimental situation. The discussion is placed in a framework consisting of the following variables: ($a$) hypothesis; ($b$) experimenter and subject; ($c$) apparatus and stimulus; ($d$) the task and its administration; ($e$) acceptance of the task; ($f$) carrying out of the task by the subject; ($g$) recording of results; and ($h$) analysis and evaluation of the responses. In each section, evidence is reviewed as to the status of our knowledge about relevant variables and the problems and "unknowns" which are still present. A psychometric approach to the evaluation of the Rorschach technique is presented in Chapters 6 and 7, with scales for the evaluation of various formal factors appearing in Chapter 6, and content factors in Chapter 7. Chapter 8 presents some material pertaining to certain derivatives of the Rorschach technique.

Attention is next turned to an evaluation of the TAT. The ground covered in Chapter 9 is roughly equivalent to that covered for the Rorschach in Chapter 4 (some historical perspectives, current status, and methodological problems). Chapter 10 contains a review and evaluation of some of the major derivatives of the TAT and cognate techniques, Chapter 11 consists of an analysis of the TAT as an experimental situation (following the same framework utilized for the Rorschach), and Chapter 12 presents a psychometric approach to the evaluation of the TAT.

A supplement to this book contains material which implements the clinical and research use of the scales for the Rorschach and the TAT. The *Supplement* has been deposited as Document number 7955 with the ADI Auxiliary Publications Project, Photoduplication Service, Library of Congress, Washington 25, D.C. A copy may be secured by citing the Document number and by remitting $21.25 for photoprints, or $6.25 for 35 mm. microfilm. Advance payment is required. Make checks or money orders payable to: Chief, Photoduplication Service, Library of Congress. Separate parts of the material may also be ordered. Fees must be determined through written inquiries in advance, however.

The *Supplement* consists of the following parts: I—Tables of inter-scorer and split-half reliability of various Rorschach scales; II—Topographical charts for locating Rorschach responses; III—Rorschach stimulus area attributes; IV—Scales for the Levy Movement Blots; V—Norms for the Communality (popularity-originality) Scale; VI—Sample of psychometric scoring of a Rorschach response; VII—Sample Rorschach record and demonstration analysis; VIII—Tables for use in psychometric scoring of TAT protocols; and IX—Demonstration analysis of a sample TAT protocol.

We thank the many colleagues and students who have helped in the development of the techniques included in this book. We are especially grateful to Drs. E. I. Burdock and S. Zelen who provided the systematic method for locating Rorschach responses; to Dr. Dorothy Park Griffin for improving the Communality Scale; to Dr. R. McCall for much counsel and for helping to formulate the psychometric scales; and to Dr. R. M. Rust for his work with the Levy Movement Blot Scales. Drs. E. E. Baughman, I. E. Farber, J. J. Gibson, W. H. Holtzman, R. L. McFarland, S. Sarason, and Dorothy Terry read parts of the manuscript and made many valuable suggestions. Mrs. Florence Sultan suggested numerous practical uses of the scales in research and practice. To the various students at the University of Wisconsin, University of California at Los Angeles, Columbia University, Yale University, and the Post Doctoral Institutes at Pennsylvania State College, Kent University, Stanford University, University of Chicago, and Long Island University, and especially to Jean Andersen and Harrington Gosling, we are most grateful for the many valuable suggestions which emerged from the discussion of the material in this book. Thanks are due the Psychoanalytic Clinic for Training and Research, Columbia University, for the use of certain test data, and to Dr. David M. Levy for much advice and guidance, and permission to use the data on the Levy Movement Blots. Partial financial support in the analysis of the data included in this book was provided by the Foundations Fund for Research in Psychiatry and by Research Grant M-586 from the National Institute of Mental Health of the National Institutes of Health, Public Health Service.

We wish to acknowledge the secretarial help of Mrs. Susan Henry (Yale University), Mrs. Irene Quinn (Rip Van Winkle Foundation),

Mrs. Judi Bulgarelli (University of Iowa), and Mrs. Madeline Misar (Biometrics Research). Finally, we would like to mention, with gratitude, the patience and understanding of our families during the preparation of this book. Special thanks are given to Leo Schumer for reading parts of the manuscript and making many helpful suggestions about style and grammar.

JOSEPH ZUBIN

LEONARD D. ERON

FLORENCE SCHUMER

*New York,*
*December 1964*

# Acknowledgments

We would like to express our appreciation to all the authors whom we have quoted in this book. We would particularly like to mention the following people, publications, and companies who have graciously granted us permission to reproduce lengthier sections of their material: Drs. S. Feshbach, J. R. Grassi, J. Hochberg, L. M. Kendall, G. Lesser, E. Shapiro, and Mrs. George Jean Nathan; also, Alfred A. Knopf, Inc., *American Journal of Psychiatry*, Appleton-Century-Crofts, *Audiovisual Communication Review, British Journal of Animal Behaviour*, Charles C Thomas, The Clarendon Press, Clinical Medicine Publications, Inc., *Daedalus*, Duke University Press, D. Van Nostrand, Co., Inc., Grune and Stratton, Inc., Hans Huber, Harcourt, Brace and World, Inc., Harper and Row, Inc., Harvard University Press, *Journal of Clinical Psychology*, The Journal Press, *Journal of Projective Techniques*, The Macmillan Company, Oxford University Press, Inc., Paul B. Hoeber, Inc., Prentice-Hall, Inc., *The Psychoanalytic Review, Quarterly Journal of Experimental Psychology*, University of California Press, and University of Nebraska Press.

# Contents

*Polonius*  My Lord, the queen would speak with you, and presently.
*Hamlet*  Do you see yonder cloud that's almost in shape of a camel?
*Polonius*  By the mass, and 'tis like a camel, indeed.
*Hamlet*  Methinks it is like a weasel.
*Polonius*  It is backed like a weasel.
*Hamlet*  Or like a whale?
*Polonius*  Very like a whale.

HAMLET, Act III, Scene ii

# 1 THE CHALLENGE
# OF PROJECTIVE TECHNIQUES

Like many innovations in psychology, projective techniques arose as a protest. What was the *status quo* which gave rise to the projective revolution? Apparently, the testing movement, so successful in objectifying the measurement of that part of personality which dealt with intelligence, achievement, attitudes, and interests was quite unsuccessful in its dealings with the area of emotions, motivations, and values. Although personality inventories, sorting tests, and even handwriting analysis and other expressive techniques had tried to fill the existing gap, they were not received with universal approval on the part of the practicing psychologist.

The promise of projective techniques proved a strong lure, and today there is hardly a clinic in this country that is not well equipped with Rorschach cards, TAT cards and similar materials. Projective techniques have been the favorites for two decades. It is time to assess their contribution and to see whether they have lived up to their promise. It is also interesting to note whether a new revolution is in the making which might eventually displace them. This is the task with which this chapter and succeeding chapters will deal.

The current interest in and use of projective techniques present the research psychologist with two challenging questions: (*a*) how valid are the conclusions obtained by these methods?; and (*b*) if valid, how

1

can the results be related to the rest of psychology? The first challenge is one which faces all users of tests, instruments, or measures, in or outside clinical psychology. The second challenge derives from the fact that the assumptions, working hypotheses, and conclusions germane to the area of projective techniques stem from sources foreign to the field of traditional psychology. Methods, vocabulary, and even scientific requirements in this area have traditionally differed from those, for example, in psychometrics or in experimental psychology. More than a decade ago, Thurstone (1948) outlined some of the reasons why one of the projective techniques—the Rorschach—remains outside the fold of psychological science. He noted the prevalent misconception in Rorschach circles that a projective technique is basically, by its very nature, not amenable to objective scoring. He also noted that for some unknown reason, high-level scientific demands are not made of the Rorschach in the way they are made of other psychological procedures. These comments are still relevant today and are applicable not only to the Rorschach but to many other projective instruments. Since projective instruments (and one or two individual intelligence tests) are among those tools most frequently used by clinicians, we feel that projective techniques deserve scientific treatment and appraisal.

## PROJECTIVE METHODS

***Brief History of Projective Methods; Concept of Projection.*** The chapters on the Rorschach and TAT contain specific historical accounts of each of these instruments. The reader is also referred to several volumes for surveys of the field of projective techniques: Abt and Bellak (1950); Anderson and Anderson (1951); Bell (1948); Brower and Abt (1956); and Rabin and Haworth (1960). These works cover a variety of projective tests and techniques.

Rorschach began his "experiments" with inkblots before World War I. About 30 years ago, Morgan and Murray published a note on the Thematic Apperception Test (1935). A year later, Cattell (1936) described a test of projection which, if standardized more thoroughly, would be a highly objective instrument.[1] This test consisted of 74 incomplete sentences each followed by three alternatives which would complete the sentence. S was required to choose one of the alternatives, on the assumption that he would "project" his own needs and motives by making this choice.

---

[1] See section on p. 19 in this chapter which stresses the point that objectivity is not necessarily restricted to tests of a strictly nonprojective nature.

Three years later Frank (1939) stated his "projective hypothesis," which unleashed a torrent of research, test construction, and clinical speculation. Because of their "dynamic" and "field theory" qualities, Frank's notions were enthusiastically received by clinical psychologists as well as by many workers outside psychology, such as social workers, psychiatrists, psychoanalysts, and anthropologists, whose background and orientation were different from that of the more objectively minded test constructors. Clinical psychologists responded to the demand for psychological testing of a projective nature, and reports and test findings quickly became geared in language, concepts, and organization to this new, enthusiastic audience. Workers in these fields assumed that since projective techniques were constructed by psychologists, they must be, like other psychological tests, reliable and valid; under this blithe assumption, they carried these techniques to the far ends of the world in their field investigations. On the other hand, psychologists, overwhelmed by their *Pandora's Box*, began to believe that the findings in the hands of otherwise reliable field workers demanded attention. Thus, once the techniques crossed disciplinary boundaries, they began to be accepted in a way similar to the unwarranted acceptance of the normal distribution curve as characteristic of all natural distributions—psychologists assuming that mathematicians had proved its relevance, and mathematicians thinking that psychologists had demonstrated the point.

From the beginning, a number of experienced test experts regarded projective instruments as potentially useful not only for assessment of individual differences, but also for experimental psychology. Sharp differences appeared between these experienced test developers and their enthusiastic colleagues from the clinical fold regarding the use and interpretation of these tools, but neither group influenced the other very much until recently.

It has been pointed out that full-fledged acceptance of and belief in projective techniques arose during World War II from the forced alliance between psychiatry and psychology. This offspring, claimed by neither parent, grew up without much guidance and has since broken all the rules and regulations by which normal tests live. It is to be hoped, however, that when projective techniques finally grow up and settle down, like the prodigal son, they will begin obeying the laws of reliability and validity and become solid citizens in the field of measurement.

The concept of *projection* in relation to projective techniques is widely and often rather loosely used. Various connotative and denotative meanings have become associated with this term; there is a "catch-all" quality in many attempts to define projection and many difficulties and disagreements (Chase [1960]; Murstein & Pryer [1959]).

The concept of projection in personality theory is generally credited to Freud, who used it as early as 1896 (Freud, 1950). Later he elaborated some of his earlier ideas and defined projection as a tendency to ascribe one's own drives, feelings, and emotions to other people or to the outside world, in such a manner as to defend oneself against awareness that these are part of oneself. The defensive nature of projection—as in the paranoid process—is the essential element; that is, there is an externalization of impulses unacceptable to "agencies" like the ego or superego. Thus, projection, subsequently elaborated again by Freud and others, is, in this context, a defensive process in which impulses, wishes, and ideas are externalized because their conscious recognition would be too painful to the ego.

Murray (1951) analyzed the essential elements in Freudian projection, and noted how projective workers in their everyday parlance have confused the meaning of this term. The essential criteria in Freudian projection, according to Murray are:

(1) The occurrence of a *veritable* delusion or misbelief (misapperception, misinterpretation). The patient *really believes* something about another person that is not true, not justified by the observed facts. . . .

(2) The subject (projector) ascribes to the object (projectee) either a tendency directed toward another object (as in pathological jealousy based on homosexuality) or a tendency directed toward himself (as in paranoid states).

(3) The ascribed tendency is a significant constituent of the projector's own personality.

(4) The projected constituent is unacceptable (seems shameful or blame-worthy) to the subject, and is therefore repressed or suppressed. The subject is unconscious (or only half-conscious) of its existence in himself.

(5) The goal of the projective process is the maintenance of self-esteem, and freedom from intolerable admissions of inferiority or guilt (p. xii).

Murray noted that despite the commonly held assumption that projection in projective techniques is of the same *genre* as defensive projection in the Freudian sense, projective protocols simply do not satisfy all of these criteria, nor do most projective interpretations assume their presence. Many subjects, for example, attest to the conscious nature of their responses, sometimes even consciously admitting that the ascribed, unacceptable tendencies occur in *themselves;* often, ascribed tendencies are favorable. Thus, projections in a projective protocol may be unrepressed, conscious, acceptable, or even admirable. The picture is further complicated by the fact that (in the TAT, for example) projections are now extended to include qualities, descriptions, characteristics of figures, etc., *not* pertaining to self, but to others, such as mother, father, and sibling. Murray concluded:

A simplification that has clarified the problem for me is this: Projective techniques are ways of stimulating the imagination, of evoking and exposing single images, fantasies of interactions, and dramatic improvisations. These stimulated fictions constitute one of several forms of behavior (in the largest sense) and are of interest in themselves, especially in respect to their formal properties. But only certain parts of these representations can be called projections, *grain* for the analyst of personality. The rest is *chaff*. To call something a projection one must demonstrate that it is similar to a "relevant" constituent of the subject's personality. A relevant constituent is one that should be included in the final formulation of the personality. The distinction is important because chaff is capable of misleading us most grievously. Hence, the great question is this: By what signs can one differentiate grain from chaff? (p. xiii–xiv).

Generally, then, projection, as applied to projective techniques, seems more likely to be a process by which S, when he is presented with a number of ambiguous or semi-ambiguous stimuli and asked to make "sense," order, or to give meaning to these stimuli, does so while drawing on a reservoir of his own needs, emotions, feelings, or even level of knowledge. Projection does not necessarily have to include defensive, unconscious, unacceptable, or anxiety-avoidant components. Projection, in the sense used by projective workers, is normally displayed by Ss when asked to assign meaning, cognitive content, order, etc., to certain types of stimuli. Delusions, extreme distortions of reality, hallucinations, and other abnormal manifestations (as in paranoid thinking) are presumably also manifestations of projection; the projective worker's view of projection, however, is considerably broader than would be subsumed by these abnormal manifestations. Normal projection apparently differs from abnormal projection in degree as well as in kind, and the differentiation between them is itself a problem of differential diagnosis, which, clinicians say, projective techniques can clarify.

*Projective "Theory."* Projective workers, by and large, seem to be in favor of theory-making; however, they often do not embed their thinking in *general* theory. Instead, they propose specific theories to explain the significance of various Rorschach determinants or TAT factors. These specific theories do not concern us now. We shall instead discuss some general theories attempting to explain projective techniques.

According to Warren (1934), all perception appears to be projected, since the inner experience of perceiving an object, tasting a substance, feeling a pain, or hearing a sound is probably a subjective correlate of neural impulses occurring in the cortex, which are projected to locations where the original source of stimulation is believed to lie.[2] Adrian (1947), for example, has noted that the usual sequence of events in perception is that some stimulus to a receptor organ causes the discharge of impulses along afferent nerve-fibers which are synaptic relays evoking specific spatio-temporal patterns of impulses in the cerebral cortex. This specific spatio-temporal pattern gives rise to the experience of a sensation (or when more complex, a perception) which is "projected" (believed to occur) somewhere outside of the cortex, that is, the surface of the skin, within the body, or at a distance from the body.

How this "projection" develops is still a moot question. Stern (1938), Piaget (1950), and Eccles (1953) have given much thought to the development of "projection" in infancy and early childhood. It is at least a tenable hypothesis, even though the evidence for it is sparse, that in earliest infancy the observing infant experiences a private, noncommunicable perceptual world which is a highly individualized "interpretation" of the specific events in his nervous system, especially the brain.[3] Perhaps the very first experience of stimulation is a feeling of "difference," some alteration from the previous unstimulated state. The diverse patterned sensory inputs are finally conventionalized through observation, communication, and perhaps inherent maturation so that they become a part of the microstructure of the nervous system. The perceptual world of each observer may be regarded (following Eccles) as a kind of map developed from the experienced spatial relations between objects of the external world and the inner neural and cortical experiences. Gradually this map is filled in; the subjective experiences begin to correspond more and more to the externally conventionalized objects and events. Secondary qualities of a symbolic sort are also attached to these spatial localizations, as is customary in conventional maps with their symbols for rivers, mountains, railways, and towns. Thus, colors, sounds, and smells, although they belong to the private world of the observer, and are merely symbolic of events in the physical world, which they do not resemble in the least, finally become attributed to the public world and can be subjected to such rigorous testing as psychophysical experimentation.

---

[2] This section is based almost entirely on material taken from an earlier work by Zubin (1956, pp. 180–182).

[3] This is the type of mental content which is neither inwardly nor outwardly reportable (see p. 41 in this chapter).

There is by no means agreement among theoreticians and experimentalists as to the development of the mechanics of perceptual experience; such phenomenological questions have puzzled philosophers and perceptionists alike for centuries; even today, not only are there vast theoretical differences in various approaches, but also there is little advance of knowledge as to the precise nature of the physiological, neurological, cortical, and sensory events which occur during an act of perception.[4]

This idiosyncratic, personal, perceptual world somehow or other is brought into correspondence with the personal perceptual world of others, so that eventually the existence of a physical world common to the personal individual worlds is agreed on. Personal experience from earliest childhood and communication with other observers are the standard procedures by which we learn to interpret a part (and only a part) of our private perceptual world as events in a single, physical world common to other observers. In this way the private worlds of most individuals overlap, and this common overlap is called the public, physical, or real world. Just how far the personal world corresponds with the "common" world of reality varies from person to person. Private experiences of colors, tones, warmth, sizes, and shapes seem to be more amenable to conventionalization than other experiences such as aesthetic experiences.

The residual, nonpublic world remains an idiosyncratic world which only the individual himself had access to, it was believed, until projective workers claimed to hold the key which could unlock the private chambers of these inner worlds and open them to public scrutiny. Thus, in essence, the "projection" in projective techniques differs from the "projection" that takes place in ordinary perception, not in kind, but in the type of material it aims to unfold. Projective techniques, it is claimed, provide the avenue by which material is "projected," which in ordinary life experience never becomes projected externally but remains enclosed in the personal life of the individual.

Just how projective techniques attain this end is not demonstrated, and whether or not they have accomplished it is still being debated. But to reduce these implicit hypotheses to public investigation, a modification of some of the foregoing assertions might be suggested. Instead of concerning ourselves with the inner sanctum of personal experience, which by definition is incommunicable, we can limit ourselves to deviations from what is expected in the communicable portion of the personal world, that is, to the type of unique (deviant) perceptual

---

[4] Chapters 2 and 3 present a more detailed discussion of these disagreements.

response pattern which characterizes the individual. In other words, although elements common to most personal worlds become the data for examination, special attention is paid to deviations from the commonly expected responses. In this context, then, projective techniques could be regarded as an attempt to study the personal deviations from the patterns of response that emerge as common elements in most people's personal worlds. What the cause of these deviations may be and whether they are produced by the still "unprojected" parts of the private world remain unsolved problems.

Murstein (1959) has suggested, following Helson, that responses to projective techniques can be considered in terms of three classes of stimuli: (a) the stimulus in the focus of attention; (b) all stimuli in the field forming the context or background; and (c) residuals from past experience. Murstein translated these classes of stimuli into the field of projective techniques as follows: (a) stimulus properties of tests; (b) background (both physical and psychological) of testing situations; and (c) personality characteristics of S (organismic needs and acquired needs).

Murstein illustrated his approach by a detailed analysis of the TAT, essentially with respect to the first of his designations—stimulus properties. He reviewed studies in which the stimulus properties of the TAT cards were modified, for example, amount of illumination, duration of exposure, background of pictures, nature of central figures (animals, Negroes, etc.), and ambiguity of the cards. Following this analysis, he listed a wide variety of conclusions, for example, similarity between S and the central figure does not necessarily expedite projection.

Murstein's rationale was based, in part, on dissatisfaction with Frank's projective hypothesis. In that hypothesis, stimulus properties of the various techniques as well as such background characteristics as E-S interaction were not sufficiently emphasized. Although Murstein indicates that he has based his approach on the adaptation-level theory of Helson, his direct "translation" of Helson's theory to an analysis of the important variables in accounting for the projective response, unfortunately does not add up to what it might, on the surface, purport to be—a highly quantified, systematic and controlled theoretical system which actually is predictive of behavior, as is Helson's system. On the other hand, Murstein's interest in analyzing the projective response from the point of view of other than a mere direct reflection of S's need, as well as his recognition of an interactional relationship among several variables in determining this response, is a useful framework by which TAT material can be evaluated. As a matter of fact, our own analysis of the TAT has followed a similar model. This approach can be utilized to examine more than just TAT-type responses. Rorschach responses, as well as other projective responses, may be regarded as determined by these three classes of stimuli.

An illustration of a "typical" eclectic approach to "projective theory" is illustrated by some of the writings of Abt (1950), who proposed a holistic and functional theory of personality, as opposed to a behavioristic one. He felt that his theory was useful for the clinician as a framework for the understanding of projection. His general point was that all behavior is active, purposeful, and goal directed, and that to assess or understand it, a holistic approach is necessary—an approach necessitating the use of not one, but many different types of projective techniques. Abt drew heavily on psychoanalytic thinking and gestalt psychology for some of his personality tenets, and stressed the fact that the projective worker's approach to his material should also be derived from these points of view. (His formal analysis and content approach to projective techniques can be said to draw heavily on both psychoanalytic and gestalt thinking.) Abt has emphasized the fact, along with Gordon Allport (1937), that psychological causation is uniquely personal and never actuarial. This would, of course, apply to the projective response, according to Abt. In reviewing the projective climate of opinion as to "personality," Abt has outlined the following points: (a) personality is viewed as a dynamic and motivational process; (b) this process is a constant interaction between the physical and social (cultural) environment, and the state and intensity of needs; (c) field theory, psychoanalytic thinking, and an historical-genetic approach seem most appropriate for the study of this process; and (d) personality should be viewed as a "whole."

Utilizing the triad of directive-state (see Chapter 3), psychoanalytic, and gestalt points of view, Abt has offered an overview which he called projective theory, but which is generally typical of the overview of other workers in personality including those with nonprojective approaches. On the other hand, Abt felt that the *methodology* of projective tests is quite unique: "I am of the belief that projective tests have developed from a climate of opinion so radical from that which made possible other personality assessment procedures that their validity and reliability can never be established in the same ways. To demand these things of projective methods is to require something that simply cannot be met" (1950, p. 64). It is difficult to follow Abt's reasoning; his leap from the "climate" from which projective tests emerged to their inability to be evaluated (which is in effect what he is saying) or validated by standard procedures is a *non sequitur* which he fails to justify.

An out-and-out psychoanalytic view toward constructing a "projective theory" is illustrated by Hutt's note on projective testing (1954). Although this will not be described in detail here, it is mentioned as an example of the vagueness of terms, the "borrowing" of psychoanalytic phrases and the analogical thinking applied to projective responses, which defy methodological analysis and an operational approach. Hutt has nowhere indicated how validation of some of his concepts could proceed. The shift from "projection," the Freudian mechanism, to projective testing is made, but the logic in this transition is not clear. One wonders what would have happened if another term had been used (by Frank, say) in describing these instruments when they were becoming popular—the "no-right-or-wrong-answer" tests, or the "semi-structured" tests. Would standardization, rationale, scoring and validation procedures, as well as theorizing and research have proceeded differently? Would there have been a need for a "projective theory"?

Frank (1939) is generally credited with the first statement of the projective hypothesis and with the labeling of projective methods, as such. His views of personality are so embedded in the field of projective techniques that a brief review of some of his thoughts seems worthwhile. He has stated, "We may therefore look upon the personality as a dynamic process, the continual activity of the individual who is engaged in creating, maintaining and defending that 'private world' wherein he lives" (1948, p. 8). After a general review of the early experiences of the individual in his psychocultural environment, through which the individual incorporates and interacts with his culture, Frank said:

What is of major significance for understanding individual personality is that the individual organizes experience as he warps, twists, distorts and otherwise fits every situation, event and person into the framework of his private world, giving them the affective significance which they must have for him in his private world. Moreover, the individual may attempt to impose his personal beliefs and feelings upon the world of people and events or carefully guard his private world from any public disclosure that might reveal his own ideas and feelings (1948, p. 15).

The following statement pinpoints the role that projective techniques can play in the assessment of personality:

. . . we may approach the personality and induce the individual to reveal his way of organizing experience by giving him a field (objects, materials, experiences) with relatively little structure and cultural patterning so that the personality can project upon that plastic field his way of seeing life, his meaning, significance, patterns, and especially his feelings. Thus, we elicit a projection of the individual personality's *private world* because he has to organize the field, interpret the material and react affectively to it (1939, pp. 402–403).

The types of material or stimuli required to elicit responses which will reveal personality seem to be unimportant. There is almost a complete denial of the importance of the objective properties of the stimulus in eliciting the response; not only does each stimulus have nothing more than almost a wholly private significance for the individual, but, in projective testing almost any stimulus can be substituted for another. This point of view is clearly one which refutes the possibility of an objective instrument which can be used in an independent assessment of personality.

Frank's discussion of reliability and validity (these, according to him, are for *groups*, not for individuals, therefore how can we judge reliability or validity for an individual?) is not thoroughgoing or detailed. Yet in it he shows his distaste for all such procedures. His discussions have undoubtedly influenced many clinicians *away* from quantitative research, psychometrics, etc., almost as if some basic principles would be violated if such procedures were adopted—much in the way an experimentalist would stay away from a ouija board!

Despite Frank's generally optimistic outlook regarding projective techniques, he has pointed out some dangers (1960). First, he raised some doubt concerning the assumption that projective material is an expression of psychoanalytic projection and of the unconscious; he is of the belief that the interpretation of projective material is tied in too closely with psychoanalytic views, and that cognitive processes have not been sufficiently stressed. He also feels that there has been too much stress on the use of projective techniques in psychopathology. As a consequence psychopathology is attributed, without sufficient reason, to responses that are found quite frequently in normals.

The foregoing approaches to "projective theory" illustrate from various points of view several different avenues projective workers have taken toward building a theory. Is there a separate projective psychology? It seems that attempts to construct such a separate psychology result in borrowing, lifting, and transliterating concepts, phrases, etc., from their older, more respectable, traditional cousins. And yet, is there an adequate theory of personality, diagnosis, nosology, etc., to which projective workers can turn? There are no simple answers to this question. One point of view holds that lack of theoretical orientation should not be an obstacle for the psychometrically oriented clinician, and that projective workers should be able to predict with, and empirically justify, their instruments without a "sound" theory. On the other hand, there are those who believe that until a sound theory is provided, testable hypotheses cannot be deduced for experimental investigation.

*Some Assumptions of Projective Techniques.* One basic assumption which projective techniques have in common with the rest of psychology is that response to stimulation is determined and predictable and not accidental. Behaviors that appear chaotic, even in abnormal individuals, usually become understandable and predictable when more of the underlying conditions are understood. Workers in the field of projective techniques often do not seem to have the patience for unraveling the web of circumstances which give rise to a given behavior. Instead, they attribute the behavior to "personality." As a result, since the major determinant in the response is not the stimulus, but the "personality" of the responder, the role of the stimulus is minimized.

To obtain an evaluation of personality through projective techniques, the following must be further assumed (MacFarlane & Tuddenham, 1951): (*a*) ". . . a protocol is a sufficiently extensive sampling of the subject's personality to warrant formulating judgments about it"; (*b*) ". . . the psychological determinants of each and every response are basic and general"; and (*c*) ". . . projective tests tap the durable essence of personality equally in different individuals" (p. 34).

Many projective workers assume, further, that the test behavior is not only a small sample of lawful behavior (rather than a random, inexplicable performance), but that this lawful behavior *directly* reflects inner personality and behavior in other situations. This assumption implies an "isomorphic" process. Thus a person who has a pedantic approach in a test situation will also be pedantic in his approach to other situations; a person who approaches the test material practically is a practical-minded person in everyday life; a confused approach in the test situation reveals a confused inner state in the mind of the patient.

Another assumption is that the indirect approach characteristic of these tests insures a spontaneous and representative response. Since the material is entirely "unstructured," or, at best, only semistructured, any response given will be a spontaneous reflection of S's own creation, and will not reflect the conventional and cultural forces which are so evident in other types of tests. S cannot put his best foot forward, since he does not quite know which is his best foot.

Still another assumption, probably quite implicit, is that a basic personality structure exists within the individual and expresses itself as the underlying unity of all his behavior. This basic personality structure finds expression in the patient's private world as opposed to the external world, which is overladen with other factors and forces that interfere with the true expression of his inner life. This personality structure cannot always be the basis for a correct prediction of future behavior, but it can form the basis for explaining or interpreting observed behavior.

The foregoing assumptions, although probably useful in the clinical field, need not be accepted entirely, and, as a matter of fact, they are not all accepted by many research workers. At best, they are working hypotheses which require proof before their tenability can be established.

*Some Classifications.* Many projective workers have been lured by the "call to classify." Unfortunately, in the case of projective techniques, so many different *genre* are included that classifiers often find it impossible to find categories that will include all the techniques. Some classification systems stress materials used in the test; others, the type of behavior or response that S produces.

Some projective workers find "projection" in almost all behavior. Thus a return to the traditional disciplines in psychology may offer the most realistic classification system: projection through memory, projection through perception, projection through social behavior, and projection in the learning situation. The reader is urged to consider some of the merits such a system possesses. Workers in these respected fields might be tempted to consider projection as part of their everyday thinking. (Bartlett [1932], it will be recalled, did this in the field of memory.) Another possible advantage lies in the fact that "projective psychology" might then be eliminated as a separate field with its own laws!

Since projective techniques may be regarded as personality tests, a brief note on some overall classification systems of personality tests in general might be the springboard for reviewing classifications of projective techniques.

*Personality Tests.* Watson (1959) has reviewed some of these classifications: Rosenzweig (1950), for example, classified personality measures into objective or overt; subjective or covert; and projective or implicit levels of reference. These measures are not uniquely associated with one or another of various tests since some tests tap all three levels. Campbell (1957) listed three sets of dichotomies: objective tests (S understands that there are correct responses) vs. voluntary tests (S understands that there are no right or wrong responses); direct (S understands purpose of test) vs. indirect; and free-response vs. structured response. In this system, the Rorschach and TAT are voluntary, indirect, and free-response tests; the MMPI is a voluntary, direct, and structured test. George Kelly (1958) once remarked, "When the subject is asked to guess what the examiner is thinking, we call it an objective test; when the examiner tries to guess what the subject is thinking, we call it a projective device" (p. 19).

The following scheme, a more detailed one than some of the foregoing, offers a rough classification (by content, as well as structure) of various personality tests and techniques, and although there is considerable overlap among areas the classification nevertheless offers an overview of available tests from which a clinician usually draws his personality battery.

1. Projective tests. These tests deal with material that is usually unstructured or ambiguous, supposedly permitting S to project his own wishes, desires, and needs into the unstructured stimulus. Examples are Rorschach, TAT, and their derivatives. Other tests with varying degrees of structure belong in this category too, such as figure drawings, Rosenzweig P-F Study (1945), and sentence completion tests.

2. Tests of expressive movement. In this group, the "style of behavior" of the individual is tapped. Examples are techniques such as handwriting analysis, speech analysis, and the analysis of gestures, facial expressions, and the like.

3. Aesthetic preferences. The type of aesthetic preference made by S is considered to be related to the particular temperamental type to which he belongs.

4. Perceptual tests. In this group are techniques and tests intended to tap the capacity of S to organize and reproduce visual stimuli. Examples are Bender-Gestalt Test, Street Gestalt Test, Bolles Progressive Completion Test, and Benton Visual Retention Test.

5. Tests of abstract behavior. Tests in this group attempt to measure the capacity of S to utilize abstract and conceptual thinking. Strictly speaking, these tests may perhaps be tests of capacity rather than of personality, but some of them have proved to be useful in diagnosis and prognosis, so they can also be placed among tests of personality. Examples of such tests are sorting tests of varying types and tests of concept-formation.

6. Refined questionnaire and interviewing techniques. The MMPI, which provides separate scoring scales for various diagnostic categories, and the Kinsey Interview would be examples of these methods. The

latter technique, which is a compromise between a questionnaire and an interview, can be easily adapted to areas other than that of psychosexual development and behavior. Similar procedures could be evolved for vocational interests, educational interests, and such clinical variables as anxiety, obsessive thinking, compulsions, and personal values.

7. Verbal reinforcement techniques. A new way of assessing personality variables is to utilize the operant conditioning paradigm. In assessing the level of affect of schizophrenics, Salzinger found that by utilizing verbal reinforcements such as "yes," "I see," and "mhm," whenever the patient uttered a self-referred affective statement during an interview, the frequency of such statements increased.[5] By comparing the number of affective utterances in the operant period (before reinforcement), during the conditioning period (when reinforcement was given), and in the succeeding extinction period (when reinforcement was discontinued), the capacity of the patient to display affect could be gauged. This technique could be applied with equal effectiveness to other aspects of personality.

8. Techniques involving assessment of total behavior. An example would be that used by the OSS (1948) in evaluating the personality of men applying for foreign service in the intelligence corps. This technique involved the use of actual life situations; S was under continual scrutiny for several days in various trying and experimentally contrived situations. Such methods are at present probably beyond the possibilities of most ordinary clinical situations, but they offer rich possibilities for tapping important personality variables.

*Projective Techniques.* The classification of projective techniques was undoubtedly spurred by Frank's monograph (1939) in which he classified projective techniques into the following scheme.

1. Constitutive methods. These methods require S to provide some structure or organization of unstructured (ambiguous, plastic) materials or semistructured materials. The best example of this method would be the Rorschach, but other sensory modalities could be utilized, as in the case of working with clay, plasticine, or cold-cream. Free, spontaneous "doodlings," finger paintings, and drawings would also fall into this classification. Frank noted that ambiguous sounds or patterns, and sequence and rate of S's language, regardless of content, would also fall into this category.

2. Constructive methods. These methods require S to sort or arrange

---

[5] The section *The Task and its Administration* in Chapter 11 (TAT) contains a description of some of the work of Salzinger and his associates.

materials of a definite size and shape into larger configurations, for example, miniature life toys or colored units for making a mosaic. S is asked to make a house, construct a scene, put them in order, or simply play with them. Dramatic play, role-playing, psychodrama, finger painting, and drawing are considered constructive methods, provided that in the case of drawings and paintings, S is specifically asked to do or draw *something*—a man, a woman, etc., rather than to produce a free and spontaneous product.

3. Interpretative methods. S is required to interpret a situation or action in which he finds some personal meaning or affective experience. The TAT, creative writing, Rosenzweig Picture-Frustration Study, reactions to a puppet show, completion of unfinished sentences, and free-association to music, are examples of this method. Content analysis of S's productions is the chief method used to analyze this material—the systems differing from worker to worker.

4. Cathartic methods. Although Frank suggested the possibility that all projective methods permit the possibility of release of emotional and affective reactions, he felt that some techniques were specifically designed for this purpose. The therapeutic doll (David M. Levy), clay modeling and its later destruction or distortion, or the audience participation in a movie, and stageplay, are examples of this method.

5. Refractive methods. These methods provide clues to S's personality process by his idiomatic manner of modification of a conventional medium of communication, as in language, handwriting, etc. The individualized manner of S—tone of voice, handwriting idiosyncracies, gestures, expressive movements—fall into this classification.

Although Frank felt that his system was based essentially on mode of response of S, that is, what he is asked to do, it is clear that he also included references to the nature of material used and hinted at different types of analysis which might be appropriate. He felt that a system based on types of materials could also be used (1948, p. 47). Frank stressed the fact that the essential element in projection is not the ambiguity of the situation, but rather the opportunity to make an idiomatic, personalized, individualized response. For Frank, all situations are potentially projective. As already noted, Frank's point of view is antistatistical; he is opposed to normative and standardized procedures ([1939]; [1948]; especially the latter, pp. 36–37). But these procedural conventions are indispensable, for how else are we to determine *what* is idiomatic (as in item- or pattern-analysis) if no norm is used? What is presumably individual may, after all, be not individual—it may even be accidental, fortuitous, or a mistake in the recording of the response (reliability) or not significant in the way the clinician thinks it is (validity). Thus, even the most staunch, idiographic projective worker must at some time face these essentially psychometric questions.

Other classification systems have been proposed. Lindzey (1959) has listed six different schemes of classification. These included: (a) attributes of the test material itself; (b) techniques employed in constructing the test (rational vs. empirical); (c) manner of interpreting the test (i.e., formal analysis vs. content analysis); (d) purpose of the test; (e) administration of the test (i.e., group vs. individual); and (f) type of response it elicits (i.e., story construction, association, etc.). He felt that the last classification system was the most appropriate, since the actual psychological process involved in the test situation is what is subsumed in this system. Still other classifications are based on such factors as the sense modality involved and degree of rigidity or specificity of directions.

Most of the instruments and techniques falling into these categories have had a long history of laboratory and experimental manipulation. Inkblots, for example, have had an experimental history, preceding Hermann Rorschach, in the investigation of imagination as a function of intelligence. Pictures of a somewhat ambiguous nature (as those used in the TAT) had been used during the early decades of the twentieth century by Stern (1938) and others for the investigation of testimony (Aussage) and by Binet and Simon (1905) for measuring intelligence. Incomplete sentences had been used by Ebbinghaus (1897) and Ziehen (1923) for measuring intelligence. Word association techniques, a familiar clinical tool, had their day in the laboratory as a means of investigating association, will, and imagination; picture completion tests had also been utilized for the measurement of intelligence.

The adaptation of these techniques for the measurement of personality was accompanied by a move away from the rigorous framework demanded by intelligence and achievement tests. The requirement of scoring of responses as correct or incorrect was abandoned, and specific instructions for performance in a prescribed manner was replaced by instructions calling for freedom and choice in the performance. Greater freedom was also introduced in the scoring of responses, and the style and manner in which the performance took place assumed greater prominence. As a result of this increased freedom in performance, scoring, and interpretation of results, many of the scientific values achieved in the field of intelligence tests were sacrificed.

There is, currently, a swing-back toward the more rigorous and systematic procedures and scoring systems of earlier days; the systems of scoring and interpretation which are now emerging are more amenable to scientific scrutiny. Hopefully they are based on and will profit by the rich experience which these techniques have acquired during the course of several decades of almost complete anarchy!

*Modifications of Existing Techniques.* Some of the projective literature has introduced modifications of the traditional and existing techniques. A few of these reports have resulted in new techniques, useful or potentially useful as clinical instruments in their own right. Most of these instruments were introduced because of dissatisfaction with the available tests, or because of a theoretical interest in one particular aspect of the instrument. Examples of such instruments are the Holtzman Inkblots (Holtzman, *et al.*, 1961), the Levy Movement Blots (Rust [1948]; Levy, Schumer, & Zubin [1964]), the Blacky Test (Blum, 1949), the O'Reilly Objective Rorschach Test (O'Reilly, 1956), and the Howard Ink Blot Test (Howard, 1953).

Some of these tests, such as the Levy Movement Blots, are explicitly concerned with testing a particular hypothesis or theory (e.g., with respect to human movement); others, such as the Holtzman Inkblots, are concerned with constructing a more reliable and objective instrument for certain specified factors in the Rorschach response; still others, such as the Howard Ink Blots, are predicated only on the basis that another instrument similar to the parent instrument would be useful to have. No matter what the rationale, however, as long as such tests are offered to the clinician as *instruments* for use with clients, they must stand the test of all such instruments. Questions of standardization, norms, reliability, validity and objectivity of scoring must be answered anew, notwithstanding the purported relationship of the offspring to the "parent" test which served as a model. Further details as to modifications and derivatives of the Rorschach and TAT will be presented in subsequent chapters.

In addition to these deliberate innovations there are modifications of administration, instruction, and scoring procedures, as well as changes in stimulus structure, material, and response of traditional techniques, *without* the intent to offer such modifications as new instruments. An excellent discussion of these procedures can be found in Lesser (1961). Clinicians are wont to attack these modifications, suggesting that they are a departure from the usual methods, have little generalization value, and are a negation of the original standardization. Research of this sort, however, when the technique itself is examined as the research problem, often sheds light on the basic process of projection and permits tests of hypotheses about the stimulus, instructions, scoring procedures, and the like. As a result, new instruments may emerge, but this is not the original goal of such researches. Rather, they are intended to illuminate basic principles and test constructs, and to gain insights about E-S relationships, stimulus conditions, and productivity, cutting across many projective techniques. They have added to psychometric knowledge and brought refinement and sophistication into an under-developed area. Such research does not necessarily add to a more precise knowledge of psychological process unless (and often this is precisely the context of such modification) the variations are specifically geared to the measurement needs of an hypothesis or research problem. Such use of projective techniques is "old hat" for the experimentalist, who has long been accustomed to constructing measures in terms of the specific hypothesis being studied. This type of research is not test oriented, but theory oriented, and modifications of available techniques, if relevant, are justified within the framework of the particular study. The researcher must, of course, face the problem of reliability and validity of his measure, and questions concerning construct validity are particularly relevant.

Thus modifications of projective instruments can shed light on the nature of the instrument itself, on testing procedures, projective theory, clinical diagnosis and clinical problems, if the test modifications are clearly understood and made explicit and if attention has been paid to test construction problems. Specific relevance to personality theory or other research problems should be made explicit in the research report.

*Objectivity, Projective Techniques, and Psychometrics.* Many psychologists assume that projective techniques deal with idiomatic responses, reflections of the "inner world," whereas standardized tests do not. Another shibboleth is that only psychometric instruments may yield an obtained score which reflects a "true" (hypothetical) score for which the likelihood of error can be estimated. Projective techniques, properly treated, however, may fulfill many of the same requirements. Reliability of scores, objectivity of methods, item validity, construct validity, even the estimate of error from a true score, may apply not only to a single score but to various patterns and interactions among scores, as would be appropriate in projective techniques. Configural scoring, pattern and profile analysis, and use of nonlinear scales are all subject to psychometric analysis without violating the projective principle.

As Holtzman (1959) has indicated, a psychometric assumption is actually made by almost all clinicians:

In most instances, the projectivist has tried to preserve the qualitative, idiographic essence of the projective method while searching for ways in which to categorize, quantify and standardize the response variable underlying test behavior. When he classifies and enumerates any of S's responses to a projective technique, he is adopting, even if crudely, a psychometric frame of reference. When he counts such responses, he is implying a crude ordinal scale by which 10 M means more of something than 1 M (p. 121).

Clinicians who wish to adopt a psychometric approach to their projective instrument must consider many difficulties, however. Problems of scorer reliability, standardization, cross-validation, item validity and reliability, etc., are not easily solved in the projective area. Test-retest reliability is itself virtually impossible to estimate, and the nature of S's verbal productivity and ability to "express" himself is constantly confounded with the response, as is the complicated interaction between E and S. The configural relationships between scores and variables, their relevance, linearity and/or unitary nature (or lack of it) are all variables difficult to assess and evaluate. Yet, we are beginning to make attempts to understand these variables.

Today, a trend toward greater objectification of projective instruments seems to be emerging. Since objectivity is a goal of science, discussion of this criterion seems appropriate. As a matter of fact, almost all assessment procedures must answer the question: how objective is this instrument? Although workers are not in complete agreement as to what objective means (Watson [1959] provides a review of some different interpretations assigned to this term), it is generally agreed that an assessment procedure is objective to the degree to which it lends itself to agreement of observation among scorers, judges, observers, etc. In addition, some quantitative measure is implied when the term "objective" is used.

One implication of the term objective is that there is a minimum of intervening interpretation, subjective inferences, etc., between the behavior of S and the score assigned to this behavior, that is, examiner effects are at a minimum, and scoring procedures are rigorously defined. From this it may be assumed that tests which encourage or permit interaction between E and S as part of the response variance (and score variance) would be relatively less objective than tests which do not.[6]

Some workers feel that true objectivity in a test can be achieved only when the stimulus situation has the same significance for all subjects—and that agreement in scoring (as well as lack of subjectivity on the part of the scorer) is only part, albeit an important part, of the picture. Projective material, it is claimed, would not satisfy this require-

---

[6] Sarason (1954) presents a discussion of this particular problem.

ment, but even objective tests cannot make this assumption. As a matter of fact, it is the inability of the subject to attach the proper meaning (the one which the examiner has prescribed) that results in errors on his part. It is not the significance or meaning of the stimulus for the responder which is at stake, for this can be inferred only from the response. It is rather the interpretation of the response by the examiner which is the core issue. Granted, however, that there might be a difference between subjects in this regard, there also are elements in projective tests, including the Rorschach, which apparently *do* have similar meaning for certain groups of Ss (subsequent chapters discuss this further). Teasing out these elements and identifying them clearly would certainly seem part of the task of objectifying these instruments.

This discussion should certainly suggest that the so-called sharp dichotomy between "projective" and "objective" is misleading. Many objective tests sometimes involve considerable subjectivity in their scoring procedures. On the other hand, some projective devices could be scored quite objectively and are not necessarily at the other end of the continuum from objective tests, as is commonly felt. Both projective and nonprojective tests range along a continuum of objectivity—and cannot be labeled dichotomously, as objective or nonobjective.

*"Deviation Hypothesis."* It has been mentioned that deviations from the common or expected response in projective protocols may be potentially useful data for analysis. Ritter and Eron (1952) employed such an approach in using the TAT to differentiate normal from abnormal groups. This subject is developed in Chapter 12.

Perhaps the earliest use of deviations as criteria in scoring test performance are the two instances recorded in the Bible: (a) Gideon's use of kneeling vs. bending at the shores of the Jordan to drink water, as a screening test; and (b) Jephtha's rather crucial "shibboleth" test for distinguishing the Ephraimites from the rest of the Israelites. In modern times, Kraepelin was perhaps the first to point out deviation as a criterion for mental health. He said (1896):

As soon as our methodology has sufficiently proved itself through experience with healthy individuals, it would be possible to approach the actual ultimate goal of these efforts, the investigation of the sick personality, especially of the inborn pathological disposition. In an investigation of many individuals we will always find some who deviate profoundly from the behavior of the vast majority in one or another aspect. If this deviation appears to be damaging to the mental life, and if it reaches a certain degree—which admittedly can only be arbitrarily determined—then we tend to regard it as an illness. Experience teaches us that persons with pathological traits of this kind are, on the whole, in greater danger of a general mental disturbance than those personalities (natures) whose characteristics are in the middle range. We therefore have first of all to investigate whether it is possible by means of psychological tests to determine individual deviations, which cannot be recognized by ordinary observation. If that succeeds, we would be in the position, through quantitative determinations at our disposal, to establish the borderline between health and disease much more precisely and more validly than has been possible so far (p. 77).

An interesting expansion of these notions, with a psychometric orientation, was suggested by Berg (1959), whose general thesis is that the content of test items is not important, and that any sense modality should be suitable for a test situation. He claims that the factors underlying this assumption can be explained by the "deviation hypothesis." This hypothesis is concerned with responses which are departures or deviations from a determined pattern. These deviations are felt to be representative of critical aspects of behavior for a given individual. Furthermore, according to Berg (1957), the tendency to produce deviant responses is a general characteristic of the individual; therefore the tendency to deviate will reflect itself in various critical as well as noncritical (everyday) areas of behavior.

Berg did not theorize about the origin of deviant responses. He suggested, however, that these may be inherited, learned, or reflections of organic or physiological states, singly or in combination. For Berg, any stimuli which would elicit deviant responses are relevant, independent of content. These could be found in language behavior, drawings, judgments of sounds, and the like. Deviations themselves, of course, should be statistically established. The pattern and *number* of deviant responses are also important.

Berg supported his contentions by citing evidence in many diagnostic fields and in psychopathology, where seemingly unrelated aspects of behavior were found to be significantly related to diagnostic grouping. It might be noted, however, that the "baffling" findings that Berg has mentioned (such as autokinetic movement estimates being related to diagnostic groups) might only be baffling because of our lack of knowledge about psychopathology, perception, subjective estimates, etc. Ultimately, theoretical explanations are necessary for predictive purposes; otherwise Berg's position remains self-limited and self-contained—a positivistic search for correlations of deviant responses with population labels—useful only for classification or diagnostic purposes.

Another point might be raised. As noted, Berg has implied that the *number* of deviant responses as well as their pattern is important. Here we get into the problem of weighting. How do we know whether or not 100 deviant responses (all correlated with each other) suggest more deviation than several deviant responses not correlated with each other. It is questionable, also, whether his notions should be labeled "The Deviation Hypothesis," with the implications that it is an experimentally testable construct of theoretical import. It is undoubtedly true, however, that many different types of material could prove to be useful to elicit individual variations of response. Thurstone (1948) recognized this when he made an analogy between the Binet test and the Rorschach: both are constantly used as a criterion and a baseline by which *other* tests are measured. About the purported uniqueness of the Rorschach, he said: "It [Rorschach] is regarded as if it were something scientifically unique. Whatever it is that makes the Binet test useful, or whatever it is that makes the Rorschach test useful, we can be pretty sure that the same results can be obtained with different methods and with entirely different tests" (p. 471).

*Validation of Projective Techniques.* There is little agreement as to the meaning of the term validity, although many research workers assume a common ground of understanding when the term is used. Most workers have stressed those aspects of validity concerning the calculation of a validity coefficient. This definition places great faith in the criterion measures as the "true" and reliable indicators of the attributes being measured. External criteria such as chronological age for mental measurement and expansion of mercury for temperature have proved to be most useful in widening the service which tests perform. Whether such external criteria can be provided for measuring personality via projective techniques remains an open question.

The burden placed on the criterion measure is as heavy as that placed on the test. How does a criterion develop properties so that it can be viewed as the "true" measure of what a test is designed to measure? Obviously the same questions can be asked of the validity criterion as are asked (or should be asked) of the test itself. Is it reliable? Does it measure what it purports to measure? Of course some criterion measures have face validity and on a common-sense basis appear more "valid" than others. These are the direct measures of performance—for example, on-the-job measures of productivity. The question of the criterion used to "validate" personality, however, is certainly more complex.

In a large group of homicide cases—a rather "specific" behavioral entity—Shneidman (1959) has noted that there is a wide variety of personality pictures. Hooker (1959) has discussed the failures of the Rorschach (and other instruments) in connection with the diagnosis of homosexuality. Although we might suspect on an a priori basis that homosexuality represents a distinct personality syndrome with clear-cut behavioral manifestations, Hooker's presentation, based on extensive research, dispels this notion rather quickly! Her discussion is relevant to the concept of construct validity and to the general problems involved in validation research which uses nosological criteria. In this area (homosexuality) she has presented an alarming array of problems which disclose the difficulty in oversimplifying research designs involving validation against a simple diagnostic statement. Who is a homosexual? Is he anxious to hide this fact? Does he practice homosexuality openly? With what frequency? She has shown with clarity that the term homosexuality subsumes a wide variety of personality variations. How, in fact, can a validation study be conducted even in this presumably clear-cut area?

To test the validity of an instrument, however, some criterion must be provided. One criterion is prediction of future behavior. If the technique yields predictions which are later verified, the prognostic validity of the instrument can be established. Another criterion that may be employed involves estimates of concurrent validity. If other measures of current behavior are available, the degree to which the behavior on the projective technique corresponds to the behavior on the other technique can be taken as a measure of concurrent validity. A third criterion relates to construct validity, which refers to the correspondence between the results of the technique and certain expectancies based on a theoretical construct. Thus, if certain scores on the Rorschach reflect anxiety, will the introduction of an anxiety producing load raise the scores? A fourth criterion is employed in content validity. If we could specify the types of behavior to be expected from, say, a schizophrenic, will the application of the technique give a fair estimate of how many of the schizophrenic traits are exhibited by the patient?

The first three criteria have been employed in Rorschach and TAT validation. The fourth type—criteria relevant to content validity—is difficult to apply because of our uncertainty of what type of behavior to expect.

Procedures used in ascertaining prognostic validity seem to offer some promise, since a test which can predict behavior at some future time has an operationally testable validity. Unfortunately, the attempts to utilize the Rorschach and the TAT prognostically have yielded as many negative as positive results (see Chapters 4 and 9).

The procedures involved in measuring concurrent validity can be illustrated in the correlation between Rorschach results and clinical diagnosis. If clinical diagnoses themselves were based on objective criteria independent of the clinician, concurrent validation of projective techniques against diagnoses would be an acceptable procedure. Unfortunately, the lack of reliability in the diagnoses themselves prevents placing too much credence on either agreement or disagreement between projective techniques and diagnoses. To go to the opposite extreme, however, and claim diagnostic validity for the Rorschach because clinical diagnoses are unreliable, as some clinicians do, is a travesty on scientific method.

Construct validity involves coordination with a theory. A demonstrated relationship of test scores to a single criterion would not satisfy this approach. The worker validating an instrument must be concerned with all the inferences and implicit qualities underlying the trait which he claims is being measured, not just the operationally defined measure he is using. He must show (and indicate why he feels so) that his measure is related to a broader usage of the trait or behavior he claims he is measuring.

Cronbach and Meehl (1955), in their detailed discussion of construct validity, stated that "construct validation is involved whenever a test is to be interpreted as a measure of some attribute or quality which is not operationally defined" (p. 282). The worker who brings the concept of construct validity into his test development procedures goes beyond the simple statement of a validation coefficient. He brings in other evidence to support his statements as to what he thinks his test is measuring, and he is concerned with the effect of other variables on his test scores, such as intelligence, cultural background, reading ability, and the like. He looks for alternative explanations of some of his findings. A score presumably is interpreted to reflect some attribute of people. This attribute could be regarded as a "construct," and construct validation involves the amassing of evidence to show that the test score does indeed reflect this "construct" or attribute in a variety of situations.

Many test developers have in the past utilized a kind of "construct validation" in their approach to validating their instrument, without necessarily making explicit their choice of technique as opposed to "single criterion" validation. Levy, Schumer, and Zubin (1964), for example, in their validity study of the Levy Movement Blots were concerned with the testing of various hypotheses and assumptions concerned with the construct "empathy," on the assumption that Levy Movement scores reflect this attribute. The testing of this general thesis was done with respect to a variety of groups, utilizing several types of "validity approaches." A single criterion approach had been deemed inappropriate for adequate exploration of the overall hypothesis. A section of Chapter 8 describes this research in greater detail.

There has been some recent attention to the application of principles of construct validation to the Rorschach technique (e.g., Harris, 1960). Some Rorschach workers, however, might claim that the search for constructs and for Rorschach theory is, after all, what they have been doing for years. The systematic exploration, however, of evidence for *each* of the many purported "hypotheses" in a variety of contexts and situations has not been the prevailing research technique. Loevinger (1959) has noted that despite the theoretical acclaim the concept of construct validity has provoked, it "has by no means carried the day; prediction to a single criterion remains a major line of research and the chief method of test construction" (p. 291).

Construct validity recommendations are aimed precisely at those test developers who go beyond their validity coefficients and imply or state that their test is useful for a specific purpose, or suggest that a specific attribute, trait, characteristic, behavior or personality pattern is being measured by their instrument. To choose one example from the literally hundreds of interpretive statements and "hypotheses" made with respect to the Rorschach, we might mention the typology that underlies Rorschach interpretive thinking. That personality is essentially typological and that this typology is reflected by the "experience balance" (EB) on the Rorschach, is indeed a construct. Do we find such a distribution of behaviors in real life, or on other tests? Can we predict from EB on the Rorschach, other test behavior, personality diagnosis, or behavior in a variety of situations? Palmer (1956), for example, found no relationship between four EB types (30 Ss in each group) and MMPI scores, and a test of social introversion. Palmer's study would be only one of a systematic attempt to amass evidence to show that EB scores on the Rorschach do or do not have the meaning assigned to them.

Can we talk about the validity of the Rorschach technique as a whole? Can we validate a test as a whole? Those who are proponents of construct validation say no. In this connection, Cronbach and Meehl (1955) have noted that an incorrect conclusion would be that since *some* correct predictions can be made from the Rorschach, the test as a whole can therefore be regarded as valid. They have warned:

This conclusion overlooks the negative evidence. Just one finding contrary to expectation, based on sound research, is sufficient to wash a whole theoretical structure away. Perhaps, the remains can be salvaged to form a new structure. But this structure now must be exposed to fresh risks, and sound negative evidence will destroy it in turn. There is sufficient negative evidence to prevent acceptance of the Rorschach and its accompanying interpretative structures as a whole. So long as any aspects of the overriding theory stated for the test have been disconfirmed, this structure must be rebuilt (*Ibid.*, p. 299).

There is by no means common agreement in the conviction that construct validation should accompany the more traditional forms of obtaining validity evidence. Shneidman (1959) is of the opinion that construct validation is much like validating a theory itself, and thus has little value until personality theories "that give them (psychological tests and projective techniques) their intellectual permissiveness themselves gain greater construct validity" (p. 260).

In a critique of the concept of construct validation, Bechtoldt (1959) raised serious objections to the usefulness or appropriateness of "construct validity" in psychological science. His is an operational approach employing the terminology of logical behaviorism, and in this sense both his views, as well as the views of those who support the principles of construct validation, represent a departure from the strictly clinical and traditional approaches to Rorschach validation. Bechtoldt was of the belief that adherence to principles of construct validation creates "unnecessary confusion" and a "nonempirical, nonscientific approach to the study of behavior" (p. 628).

Bechtoldt's critique was challenged by Campbell (1960), who in defending the principles of construct validation at the same time clarified their meaning. Campbell noted that certain "institutional decision situations" require studies of predictive or concurrent validity, which must make use of a single validity criterion.

Most test research, however, is not of this practical "decision-making" nature. More often than not, tests have been developed to measure some trait or personality syndrome, and although research along these lines may be vague or even unproductive, it can really be labeled construct validity research. The single criterion, the "true" measure for the trait in question, is not a tangible, palpable, available bit of datum; the test developer somehow has to "show" that his test is indeed a measure of that hypothetical trait. This aspect of construct validity Campbell has labeled *trait validity,* and it is with respect to trait validity, that he has chosen to address his clarificatory comments. (A second type of construct validity which Campbell labeled *nomological validity* had been advocated by Cronbach & Meehl [1955]. This involves the coordination of test development within the context of a particular theory, and to date, is a rarely used but important validity procedure.)

As for distinctions between trait and practical validity, some differences might be noted. In trait validity there is no "true" measure or operational definition of the criterion, and the score may be checked against another independent measure which the validator thinks is measuring the same trait in which he is interested. But criterion and test are both equally fallible, and the criterion has no higher "status" than the test itself. Cumulative evidence may indicate the worth or lack of worth of a test, but a single "crucial" correlation coefficient is not sufficient. Trait validity involves some information concerning *discriminant* validity (Campbell & Fiske, 1959)—"the requirement that a test not correlate too highly with measures from which it is supposed to differ" (Campbell, 1960, p. 548). A test can sometimes be invalidated by a *high* correlation. Thus, results which show that variance in scores of a personality assessment technique can be attributed to response sets, reading ability, social desirability factors, or even intelligence serve to *invalidate* that instrument. Campbell has suggested several additions to the list of the American Psychological Association's technical recommendations regarding validity (1954). These include, among others, the recommendation that all tests, regardless of content, should be correlated with an intelligence test, measures of social desirability, various types of response sets, etc., and that the test developer must show that the new test predicts criterion or trait-relevant measures better than the aforementioned trait-irrelevant factors. Moreover, he suggests that test validators show that their tests predict the trait better than self-ratings. Implicit in some of Campbell's comments is the necessity in any validational procedure of including several methods of measuring a trait, as well as the measuring of several traits. Perhaps Campbell has gone too far in his requirements. It is not necessary that the new test predict the criterion better than the trait-irrelevant factors; it is sufficient that it predict *independently* of the other traits. Similarly, although self-ratings are a good criterion to have, if a test can attain the same result as a self-rating, it is to be preferred, since self-ratings are notoriously unreliable and subject to bias.

Campbell has further stated that construct validity is really not a new concept, nor, as is believed by many psychologists, should it be introduced only in the context of formal theory. He continued his discussion of some of the criticisms of construct validity by noting that the concept does not confuse reliability and validity, nor does it call for a departure from operationalism. These, plus other clarifying statements about what construct validity is, and what it can do and cannot do, seem to add up to a rather favorable impression in general, but serve to illustrate the complex, detailed, methodologically laborious job involved when one sets out to do what on the surface might appear to be a relatively simple task—establish the validity of an instrument.

*Cross-validation: Base Rates; General Applicability of Results.* Even instruments that have very high reliability do not always produce consistent results when an experiment is replicated. Failure to replicate results with a reliable test often leads to the discovery of differences either in the method of applying the test or in the two or more samples under investigation. Thus Lesser (1959) and Riessman and Miller (1958) explain failures in replication on the basis of sample differences. The finding of population differences is itself subject to cross-validation, however, and not every discrepancy should be attributed to population differences without cross-validation of this factor. Other factors may be involved, for example, conditions of the experiment, role of *E-S* relationships, expectancies of the subjects even when drawn from the same socioeconomic status, and finally, the possibility that the difference originally observed was due to chance.

Examples of failures in cross-validation studies with projective techniques are not difficult to find. Corsini and Uehling (1954), for example, tested the Davidson Rorschach Adjustment Scale in a cross-validation situation. Probationary prison guards ("normal") were contrasted with prison inmates ("abnormal"). Even when the cutting score of the Davidson Scale was adjusted to maximum efficiency, it did not discriminate sufficiently well over chance to warrant its use in separating adults in terms of personality adjustment.

It stands to reason that the results of studies that have never been cross-validated should be regarded with skepticism. This is especially true where the study is a ground-breaking undertaking in a new area and where the findings resulted from a comparison dictated by the data after they were collected. An exception may be made where a hypothesis based on previous findings is tested. Another exception is a longitudinal study in which the same individuals are followed up for a long period. We must be careful, however, not to generalize such findings to samples and situations different from those which obtained in the original study.

This raises the question of parameters that should be controlled in making generalizations. Among those likely to influence responses to projective techniques are age, sex, physiological maturation, mental and educational level, socioeconomic level, and the interactions of these factors. In any study comparing groups, the foregoing variables represent the minimal required controls. If norms are to be established, it becomes necessary to study a stratified sample of the entire population in which these factors are duly represented.

Another question to be considered is: how much better than chance is a particular prediction? Would it have been better to make choices on the basis of knowledge of base rates [7] in a particular population? Base rates, diagnostic fads, etc., differ from clinic to clinic and population to population. Each clinician can determine the base rates of the population with which he is working, and reports of successful predictions or differentials in terms of cut-offs, scores, etc., should be based on these rates.

According to Meehl and Rosen (1955) ". . . a psychometric device, to be efficient, must make possible a greater number of correct decisions than could be made in terms of the base rates alone" (p. 194). It is insufficient merely to cross-validate when testing the efficacy and applicability of signs.

Failure to consider the distribution of the measures of the criterion in the sample being studied may lead to spuriously optimistic interpretations of a given finding, as well as a more favorable (erroneous) view of the test as a predictor in one sample as opposed to another sample. Fulkerson and Barry's discussion (1961, especially p. 178) of these considerations with respect to the prognostic use of psychological tests illustrates this point.

According to a worker like Meehl, the ability of a test to predict for *all* populations, that is, to possess cross-situational power, is a research consideration for the *long* run. Concern with the construct validity of a test and/or its basic theory does not meet the clinical needs of today. For efficiency now, procedures relative to a specific clinic and a clinic population should be adopted.

This approach is reasonable. It is questionable, however, whether or not in the short run it is efficient to expend time and energy in an endeavor which will constantly be shifting ground and demanding change after change. The writers do not agree that it is inefficient to look for construct validity and for general principles in diagnostic procedures. But, and this is stressed, concern with base rates and efficiency of prediction procedures (see the next section) is relevant and should be an important aspect of clinical work and research.

*The Clinical Procedure—Some Problems.* Hathaway (1959) has noted, as have others, that many clinicians, despite their dogged use of tests, use them only as a jumping-off point and that their ultimate reports are not based on objective material. Clinicians, he pointed out, feel more confident when they can quote test material and base inter-

---

[7] A clinician who concerns himself with this question is asking, essentially, "Have I (or has this test) done better than if a choice (or rating, diagnosis, judgment, etc.) were made by chance, or by sheer knowledge of the proportion of cases coming for testing, who have the characteristic I attribute to the case before me, that is, the base rate for the characteristic under question?"

pretations on test material—even if invalid.[8] He proposed that we differentiate tests and test situations: "The Rorschach provides a good illustration of this contrast. It is a test when it yields scores and profiles, but it is merely a partially controlled interview when the clinician uses unscored and unstandardized data to describe the patient's personality, no matter how much authority and experience lie behind the interpretations" (pp. 193–194). Are projective techniques to be thus categorized as semicontrolled interviews? Can they achieve greater objectivity? [9]

Meehl (1954), in his monograph on clinical vs. statistical prediction, agreed with Hathaway on what constitutes a clinical judgment: these are never actuarial—essentially they are idiographic and nonexplicit. But once a clinical statement (prediction, judgment) is made, it is open to empirical confirmation. The skill involved is nonactuarial, but the confirmation of predictions which a clinician makes, that is, his actual success, can be empirically determined. The clinician's judgments can thus be compared to actuarial (mechanical) judgments in terms of success of prediction. After reviewing some relevant studies, Meehl concluded that the evidence seems to favor actuarial (mechanical) predictions.

Thus, despite the fact that almost everyone (including Meehl) is convinced that something *is* involved in clinical work which mechanical activities cannot tap, predictions from projective tests to overt behavior, as in forecasting outcome of therapy (Meehl, 1959), are not very successful. Yet clinicians do differ. Despite the fact that clinical intuition is nonstatistical and nonactuarial, the hits and misses, that is, frequency of correct predictions, *are* statistical, and actuarial information of this sort is essential. Even if the clinician says that this time he feels confident, it would be helpful to know the frequency of his successes when he feels this way.

W. A. Hunt (1959) concurred with this viewpoint, but did not agree with Meehl that the idiographic-clinical and the nomothetic-actuarial approaches are irreconcilable. He felt that clinical procedures are probably more efficient than Meehl would believe. Yet Hunt suggested, as did Meehl, that the actuarial locus should be transferred to the clinician

---

[8] A most ingenuous reason for continuing the use of projective techniques comes from an otherwise competent clinician who points out that for such tests as the Porteus, for example, once the obtained score and MA or IQ are noted, nothing more can be added, whereas there is no limit to what can be said about projective protocols!

[9] On the other hand, it may be pointed out here that viewing the Rorschach as an interview may have more merit than Hathaway allows. Zubin (1954) has suggested that if the protocols are analyzed for their interview content, a highly reliable result can be obtained which correlates with other estimates of personality.

himself as an instrument. He summed up his position thus: "We can evaluate the success of each individual prediction and arrive at an over-all actuarial expression of how often any clinician has been correct in a past series of unique predictions. The probability weighting which results can then be transferred to any future prediction for estimating its probable correctness" (p. 173). For an earlier statement of this approach, see Horst (1941).

The essential fallacy inherent in the question as to which is better— actuarial or clinical prediction—was pointed out by Zubin (1955). Whereas practically, at any given moment, the two methods can certainly be contrasted in the prediction of the outcome of a given case, the data used by the two methods are so interlaced that it is difficult to generalize from any given set of circumstances. To be sure, a poor clinician who is unaware of the facts already unraveled by previous clinical and actuarial studies on the relationship between presenting symptoms, personality, and outcome, will fare worse than an up-to-date actuarial equation in prognosis. By the same token, an old, dated equation will fare worse than an up-to-date clinician. Given the most sagacious clinician and pitting him against the most up-to-date actuarial equation, we can predict either a draw or an advantage for the clinician, if he has knowledge not yet contained by the actuarial equation, or vice versa. In the comparison of average clinicians with average actuarial equations, we would be inclined to give the advantage to the actuary, since his rigor may be superior to the insights of the average clinician.

## PROJECTIVE TECHNIQUES IN CROSS-CULTURAL RESEARCH [10]

The increasing concern with cross-cultural studies and the parallel stress on a culture-personality approach in anthropology have been accompanied by a growing use of projective techniques in anthropological field studies. Projective methods have also been applied with considerable frequency to the study of complex subgroups within literate cultures and to the study of the "national character" of various industrialized, contemporary civilizations. Thus, projective techniques, whether administered by a clinical psychologist as part of an interdis-

---

[10] Some of the following sections make use of material provided by Dr. Bert Kaplan, in a chapter prepared for an earlier draft (1958) of the current book. We are indebted to Dr. Kaplan for the time and energy he put into the preparation of that draft, and wish to acknowledge his generous contribution to our thinking and orientation.

ciplinary field team or by the anthropologist himself, have been used in the study of cultural processes, "modal personalities," personality change and acculturation, modifications in motivations and adjustments under the impact of varying types of cultural change,[11] etc.

Earlier studies—those, say, of a quarter of a century ago—were concerned with whether or not projective techniques such as the Rorschach reflected "racial" and biological characteristics (for example, Vernon [1935]; and Bleuler & Bleuler [1935]) on an assumption that such techniques were essentially "culture free." More recent approaches have moved in an opposite direction, toward the study of specific cultures and subcultures, whether literate or nonliterate, through the nature of projective material produced by the individuals who were "socialized" in a given setting, as well as the study of their personalities as a result of the types of socializations they received. Moreover, the expectation grew that projective material would change accordingly, as the given setting changed, or as the individuals themselves moved about in a fluid society or into another culture through immigration, or as other cultures were introduced into a specific culture.

For political and military purposes, as well as in the interests of science and human welfare, the more developed nations of the world became vastly interested in improving the communication, transportation, educational level, and health of many underdeveloped areas of the world. The industrialization, colonization, mechanization (and unfortunately, exploitation) of many of these areas have provided not only innumerable opportunities to study culture and personality in a changing world, but also to demonstrate the aridness of and lack of evidence for approaches claiming an inviolate relationship between racial and biological factors and culture and/or personality.

Although a review of such studies and their use of projective techniques is not the purpose of this section, the reader is referred to the following if such reviews or surveys are desired: Henry and Spiro (1953); Honigmann (1954); Inkeles and Levinson (1954); Kaplan (1957); Kluckhohn (1954); and Lindzey (1961). Reference might be made, too, to Kaplan's volume on studying personality cross-culturally (1961), and especially to Henry's chapter in that volume which raises certain problems pertaining to the use of projective techniques in cross-cultural research. Special reference might also be made to an excellent review and bibliography in Hallowell's report (1956). For the "classic" and pioneer study which stimulated much subsequent research, refer-

---

[11] Cross-cultural research using projective techniques has even been used to demonstrate that there is a correlation between constitutional and psychological variables (e.g., Adcock, McCreary, Ritchie, & Somerset, 1958).

ence should be made to the study of the Alorese (see DuBois [1944]; and Kardiner [1945]); and for a more recent study, utilizing projective material which was analyzed in great detail, reference might be made to Gladwin and Sarason (1953) and their study of the people of Truk.

Projective techniques were "adopted" by anthropologists to supplement their usual methods of exploration in the field: participant observation, passive observation, interviewing, films, recordings, and the like. In the rush to absorb projective techniques into the array of tools used by the anthropologist, however, there were some dissenting opinions. Thus, Henry (1955) had suggested strongly that interviewing and observational techniques should be perfected instead of placing faith and stress on projective tests in anthropological research.

For the reader not too familiar with some of the relevant literature, some illustrative studies will be noted, not in the context of a review, but by way of demonstrating some of the uses of projective techniques and some of the problems which have thus arisen. Some studies were naively planned and executed, whereas others were considerably more complex. Complexity, however, does not guarantee that all problems of design have been solved.

Cheng, Chen, and Rin (1958) reported a personality study of the Ami, one of the aboriginal Formosan tribes, based on 249 Rorschach protocols. Borrowing from traditional Rorschach interpretation, without concern for validity of constructs and with failure to cross-validate their findings, they described the Ami as having imaginative and introversive tendencies, anxiety and hostility in interpersonal relationships, and the like. Similar criticisms could be raised with respect to Rosenblatt's study (1960), which used the TAT in an exploration concerned with responses of former Soviet citizens. Rosenblatt, however, did use a control group consisting of an American sample. Another failure to cross-validate findings is found in a study reported by Caudill (1952), which was concerned with values and acculturation. This study, however, was methodologically more sophisticated and complex than those just cited and illustrates an attempt to establish a special framework by which the projective material could be explored. Caudill hypothesized that the similarity of the value systems in the culture of Japan, to those of American middle class culture, suggests that there would be similar adaptive mechanisms (as defined psychologically) between Ss from these different national backgrounds. He compared TAT material of both Issei (first generation Japanese immigrants) and Nisei (their second generation children) with that of white American lower-middle class and upper-lower class Ss. He found that both Issei and Nisei showed much more similarity to the middle class than to the lower class group, thus confirming his hypothesis. Would a different scoring system yield the same results? Would cross-validation with a sample of first generation immigrants and their second generation children of *another* national background reveal a similar "middle-class" value-orientation? Because of the nature of the study, the findings are, in a sense, inconclusive. Dana (1959) found, for example, that China-born *Chinese* students attending an American university, also had similar personality characteristics compared to Americans of equivalent social and educational background.

Another study which not only failed to cross-validate findings but which made some basic assumptions as to developmental Rorschach findings in European and North American cultures, was reported by Newman (1958). This research also illustrates the "modal personality" approach of many workers. Newman, in an investigation of Rorschach records of adolescent Otomi Indians, delineated basic personality structure through use of a medial personality profile. He concluded that the "storm-and-stress" of adolescence in our own cultures was absent in this culture and that there was probably little developmental change in the second decade of life in cultures other than our own.

A study by Hanks (1956), utilizing the TAT with agricultural workers from Thailand, resulted in a striking sparseness and lack of productivity of TAT material. The author recognized the possibility that the test situation itself had created anxiety in his Ss and did not conclude, therefore, that the sparseness was a direct reflection of deep-seated personality characteristics of the Thai. Other interpretations might relate to a possibility that the Thai did not understand what was required, or did not know how to meet these requirements. Carstairs (1956a; 1956b), in Rorschach studies of Indians in Delwara Village in Udaipur and of the Bhil tribe, also in Udaipur, found markedly contrasting productivity in the two groups. The Bhils, for example, despite their seeming enjoyment of the test, readiness to respond, and good relationship with the E, were extremely unproductive. The Hindus from Delwara Village, on the other hand, despite considerable caution and anxiety, were extremely expressive. It seems quite likely that not only were "basic" personality factors involved, but also many cognitive elements, such as interpretation of the testing situation and instructions, preferred "modes" or types of expression, and attitudes toward testing.

A considerable amount of research concerned with acculturation of the American Indian, especially of the Ojibwa, has been described. The reader is referred to Barnouw (1950, 1957); Caudill (1949); Friedl (1957); Hallowell (1957); Kerckhoff (1956); and Watrous (1956).

Much of this research has demonstrated marked changes in projective performance. Kaplan (1954, 1955), in a study of differences in Rorschach performance of war veterans and non-war veterans in four cultural groups in the American southwest, also found that the acculturation process resulted in striking changes in Rorschach performance. Kaplan (1958) however, raised some interesting questions which have some bearing on acculturation studies which use projective techniques. He wondered:

. . . whether the Rorschach changes necessarily reflected personality changes or could equally well be caused by more superficial attitude changes. It does seem plain from recent Rorschach research that Rorschach changes can be effected by these more superficial factors and that the assumption that profound personality patterns have been affected in these studies is a very hazardous one. The Kaplan study and perhaps some of the others as well suggest that acculturation is related to the problem of how personality can best be studied in societies other than our own. One obvious point is that as non-literate peoples become more and more influenced by western culture and become more like the population for whom the tests were devised, the tests will work better, in the sense of yielding richer and more valid data (p. 15).

The foregoing material suggests that the marked changes found in projective data in acculturation studies may not be a reflection of personality changes, but of changes in cultural, cognitive, and motivational attitudes toward this type of testing.

What, then, are some of the pitfalls and problems in the wholesale and sometimes indiscriminate use of projective techniques in anthropological research? The illustrative material noted previously highlights some of the following points:

1. Culture has sometimes been used almost interchangeably with personality; thus, "culture-in-personality," "personality-in-culture," and the like. Projective techniques have been used to study both culture and personality. Are projective techniques so culture free that they can be used in the study of "modal personality" and national character, with relative independence from factors related to attitude, motivation, test interpretation, and various other cognitive variables? If so, what is the justification then of using projective techniques to describe cultural change and processes? Implicit in this use of projective techniques is the belief that projective material is *not* culture free, and that, as a matter of fact, it reflects cultural processes in a most sensitive manner.

2. Related to the questions under (1) are certain recent findings concerning: (a) cultural variations in the degree to which individuals are willing to reveal themselves; (b) cultural variations in the "style"

preferred when an individual *does* yield information about self; (*c*) cultural variations in the interpretation of a test situation, attitude toward the examiner, and fluidity and productivity of language. It may be argued that these and related factors are ingredients in basic personality structure, and that when these variations are found, they are clues to personality variations from culture to culture. It is perhaps more feasible, however, to suggest that the influence of various motivational and cognitive factors on test performance and the interpretation of these features of performance are still not clear—especially in their relationship to basic personality structure. It has taken a long time to discover the importance of the effects of examiner–subject interaction and various other factors, such as nature of instructions and test situations, on projective performance in our own culture!

3. Often there is little attention paid to basic problems of reliability of scores and of scoring, and of validity (especially construct validity) of the interpretations assigned to records obtained from various ethnic groups. Too often, traditional meaning and interpretations are simply transferred to the new population with little regard for the ethnocentrism of such a procedure. This is one of the chief problems in anthropological research using projective methods: these techniques are accepted by many workers as a final, trusted yardstick (much in the way an IQ was accepted in the twenties). Moreover, the design of many of these studies is crude, overly simple, and shows little regard for sampling problems and cross-validational procedures.

4. There is recent evidence, too, that wholesale use of either the Rorschach or Thematic Apperception techniques is not justified and that for many populations and cultures, other techniques yield more productive and more expressive material. Thus Kaplan (1958) reported that in a series of informal studies of young Navaho men, the Rosenzweig Picture-Frustration Study was much more productive than either the Rorschach or TAT. Moreover, despite considerable difficulty with written English, *written* accounts of life histories were considerably more lengthy and more detailed than oral accounts.

5. The concept of modal personality involves certain judgments and decisions which are often made on tenuous grounds. For example, the variability of personality scores within a group must be considered, as well as how narrowly or widely the limits which define the modal type should be set. Kaplan (1954) found that although Rorschach records for four cultures in the American Southwest (Navaho, Zuni, Mormon, and Spanish-American) were different from each other, the variability within groups was very high whereas the differences between groups were rather low.

6. Some studies utilize a technique of matching or a search for "congruence" between anthropological data, such as child-rearing practices, and projective material. In this procedure, each expert presumably arrives at certain judgments independently before the extent of agreement is determined. In addition to the general question as to whether or not projective material is useful in "predicting" day-to-day behavior and other overt behavior in general, the methodological problems and difficulties in matching procedures should also be considered. In a discussion of some of these problems, Kaplan (1958) raised some questions concerning the Gladwin and Sarason study of the Trukese (1953). Of the famous study of the Alorese (DuBois [1944]; and Kardiner [1945]), Kaplan had this to say:

Although Kardiner claimed that the personality constellation of the Alorese which he inferred from DuBois' description of their child-rearing practices was found in the autobiographies he examined and was "almost identical in essence" to the constellation Oberholzer found in the Rorschachs, he did not support this judgment with the appropriate objective analyses. At a number of points where Kardiner or Oberholzer found close agreement, we could hardly see any similarity whatever. Also a number of the agreements were instances where the adult constellations in the Rorschach were linked to dynamic factors in the child-rearing pattern such as maternal deprivation, from which a wide variety of different adult constellations might be derived. In any case it does seem that this study, one of the most influential in the social sciences in the last quarter century, failed to utilize ordinary standards of scientific rigor (p. 22).

7. Because of the special circumstances in which much projective testing with many societies and subcultures is conducted, frequent modifications in stimulus materials, instructions, scoring frameworks, and interpretations are introduced. A previous section has already noted some of the problems involved when such modified instruments are used. But it might be mentioned again that when the goals of such "custom made" instruments are more than the testing of an "instrument-oriented" hypothesis (such as the optimum number of cards to use, or the most efficient type of instruction)—that is, when the purpose of such modification is to use the stimulus material as an *instrument* to elicit relevant data about an individual—the modified instrument must meet particularly rigorous standards of reliability, objectivity, and validity. The exigencies of a field study, unfortunately, often do not permit the time and expense involved in such test construction procedures. For an interesting symposium concerned with some of these problems, the reader is referred to Forer (1961); Goldstein (1961); Lesser (1961); and Rabin (1961).

In summary, the projective worker should be aware of the many problems and pitfalls associated with cross-cultural research. This is true despite the fascination, importance, and tremendous achievements of cross-cultural research which utilizes projective techniques, and especially because of the interdisciplinary aspects of such research. Besides the "ordinary" methodological problems most projective workers face, a psychological "expert" working in the cross-cultural area must tangle with innumerable others, including the cultural variables (motivations, for example, and customs and cognitive attitudes) which he has been asked to shed light on in the first place.

The hope that projective techniques would provide culture-free evaluation of personality did not materialize. Can projective techniques provide us with culture-fair results, that is, results dependent on cultural influences but invariant nevertheless from culture to culture in their significance? To answer this question, a knowledge of cultural forces, their equivalence among cultures, and their interaction with personality is prerequisite. If these were known, however, what would we need projective techniques for?

## THE FUNCTION OF PROJECTIVE TECHNIQUES [12]

Projective techniques are widely used by clinicians in the evaluation of personality for diagnostic and treatment purposes. In addition, they are commonly used in educational planning, vocational placement, vocational counseling, etc. Why are these techniques viewed as contributing something *special,* above and beyond the information gained from inventories, interviews, and the like, in the proper understanding and evaluation of personality? To answer this question, it would be well to determine the types of content which have been reliably sampled by available tests, as well as the content which has been hitherto more or less untapped.

The "mental content" or "mental life" of the individual, consisting of cognitive, emotional, volitional, and attitudinal areas, may be, roughly and descriptively speaking, classified into four "levels" in terms of its accessibility to the individual as well as to the external world. If we designate by *internal accessibility,* the awareness of a given "mental content" or behavior, and by *external accessibility* the manifes-

---

[12] The following paragraphs are based, with slight modification, on an earlier exposition by the senior author in his chapter, Test Construction and Methodology, in *Recent Advances in Diagnostic Psychological Testing,* Springfield: Charles C Thomas, 1950. These notions are offered as suggestive and descriptive, rather than as rigorous and testable constructs.

tation, expression, communication, or reporting of such content, either directly or indirectly, a double dichotomy can thus be established.[13]

The four levels would consist of material which is both (a) inwardly accessible and outwardly reportable or manifested or observable; (b) inwardly accessible but outwardly not reportable or communicable; (c) inwardly inaccessible but outwardly apparent; and (d) neither inwardly accessible nor outwardly reportable or communicable. Of course there is overlap among these categories, and for some individuals "similar" material may not fall into the same category. Cultural pressures and practices, individual characteristics, and familial patterns may determine what is reportable, or even observable. But by and large, the following data can be found in each of these categories:

1. Inwardly accessible and outwardly reportable. These data would include the everyday facts about oneself, family, capacities, interests, attitudes, etc., and constitutes to a large extent one's normal conversation with family, friends, or congenial strangers. Questionnaires, interviews, etc., can elicit information on this level.

2. Inwardly accessible but outwardly not reportable or communicable. These data would include daydreams, secret wishes, weaknesses, humiliations, and embarrassing situations, as well as other experiences and fantasies by which one "shows his hand," albeit reluctantly. This material, often suppressed, may be probed through psychoanalytic and hypnotic techniques and through the use of drugs. Since these techniques are rather expensive in time, energy, and prerequisite training, projective techniques might, hopefully, be used in their stead.

3. Inwardly inaccessible but outwardly apparent. These data would include material, which, although inaccessible to the individual himself, are more or less accessible to the trained observer. Among these may be included indirect signs and symbols of underlying conflicts in the personality, unacknowledged ambitions, strivings, and other repressed material which would cause too much pain and anxiety if they were allowed to come into consciousness. Among such signs may be included blushing, fidgeting, tics, changes in breathing, and exclamations. There is some evidence that such mental content, although "sub-

---

[13] Dostoyevski (1821–1881), in his *Notes from the Underground,* wrote: "In every man's memory there are things which he does not reveal to everyone, but only to his friends. There are also things which he does not reveal to his friends, but at best to himself and only under a pledge of secrecy. And finally there are things which man hesitates to reveal even to himself, and every decent person accumulates a considerable quantity of such things. In fact, you might say, the more decent a person is, the greater the number of such things that he carries around with him."

ceived" rather than perceived, nevertheless does affect autonomic function perceptibly, and can be detected by the psychogalvanic response, breathing rate, heart beat, temperature, and other physiological indicators. Even when no direct autonomic indicator is available it is likely that some day the corresponding electrical activity pattern of the brain may be detected instrumentally. Such material might well be explored through psychoanalysis, hypnosis, and the use of drugs; projective techniques, it is hoped, may be a short-cut method to "get at" these data.

4. Neither inwardly accessible nor outwardly reportable. How do we know such "mental content" exists? It might be well to leave this final rubric uncharted. Perhaps the still undeveloped potentialities of the individual belong in this area.[14] Operationally speaking, however, unless some indicator like electric brain potentials becomes available, we might regard this rubric as a still unfilled gap in our fourfold categorization. Also falling into this category would be content which apparently existed within the individual at a given time, but is revealed only by later reports and is at the time of its occurrence neither accessible to the individual nor reportable to others. Among these are included such situations as emotional dependence of such a degree that the individual has no idea of its existence, and other phenomena for which he has no grounds for comparison and no framework for reporting. Delusions and hallucinations of which he is unaware and memories of experiences of early childhood before concepts were available are further examples.

Thus it is seen that projective techniques may well supply the answer to questions relating to a wide variety of data. Are projective techniques suited for the task? Can we rely on their data? Have they fulfilled their promise? These are the questions which are being raised currently, not from the point of view of dismissing such techniques, but rather from a position which fully recognizes their importance.

The survey of projective techniques given in the succeeding chapters includes an assessment of their achievement during the last two decades, which have seen them rise to top popularity among testing devices. A sober evaluation of their achievement can be epitomized by saying that they are still promising but have not yet delivered. Why this is so is given in greater detail later. At least in the mental hospitals where they grew up and where they have had their maximum use, projective techniques are gradually declining in usefulness. What the revolution that is brewing against them will bring forth is not yet clear

---

[14] See p. 6.

—perhaps observational techniques utilizing behavior inventories, or interview techniques, under the new guise of objective investigations of verbal behavior. Meanwhile, let us see what the character of these projective techniques is and how they can be improved.

## SUMMARY AND CONCLUSIONS

Chapter 1 surveys the history and methodological problems of projective techniques. We have briefly surveyed the history of projective methods and have considered the concept of projection, several "projective theories," and a variety of assumptions made by the projective worker. Various classificatory systems were examined and modifications of traditional techniques discussed. We have compared the objectivity of psychometric and projective techniques and have considered the deviation hypothesis. We have presented problems pertaining to validity, especially to construct validity; and considerations concerning cross-validation procedures, base rates, and general applicability of results were also discussed. Finally, the use of projective techniques in cross-cultural research was evaluated.

Clinicians who use projective techniques, whether they are research oriented or not, must ask themselves, if only on a common-sense level, certain questions concerning the validity and reliability of their findings. Investigators in this field have answered some of these questions rather pessimistically. Their comments tend to dismiss projective instruments (and especially the Rorschach) as unworthy of the time and effort put into them. For example, questions are raised relating to economy, the general point being that it is unreasonable to use the Rorschach to obtain information which is available more directly and quickly by other methods and from other materials—such as interviews, case histories, direct observations, or psychiatric judgments.

Super (1959), in an evaluation of projective techniques, examined some of the comments contained in *Annual Reviews* over a period of several years. He quoted from Lowell Kelly (1954), Cronbach (1956), George Kelly (1958), and Eysenck (1955), among others, all of whom were most pessimistic. Eysenck, for example, reported that the Rorschach has been abandoned as a clinical tool at the Maudsley Hospital, and Lowell Kelly noted, in connection with projective techniques: "The curious state of affairs wherein the most widely (and confidently) used techniques are those for which there is little or no evidence of predictive validity is indeed a phenomenon appropriate for study by social psychologists" (p. 288). Super himself noted that the elimination of the skills course in projective techniques at his own institution was under consideration; it was not dropped for three reasons: psychologists are *expected* to possess these skills, they may learn something useful about clinical interaction, and knowledge of these skills may be useful for research in the field of personality assessment.

It is felt, nevertheless, that the enthusiasm for projective techniques, the reliance placed on them by responsible and mature clinicians, and the frequent (if not consistent or reproducible) reports of positive findings, are such that projective techniques not only deserve a hearing, but should be evaluated in the most objective way possible.

Projective methods have been influenced by a number of disciplines outside of the mainstream of psychology. As a result, confusion exists between the psychoanalytic concept of projection as a defensive, unconscious act, and projection as displayed in projective instruments. Furthermore, the standards, language, methodology, and general approach to validity and test construction problems in the projective field differ considerably from those in experimental psychology or in psychometrics. Moreover, although many projective workers are interested in theory making, their attempts generally result in a direct transliteration of concepts, phrases, and terms from other sources, such as psychoanalytic theory; or an in-bred, "special" approach containing technical terms related only to the particular instrument; or an eclectic, general, and often vaguely stated approach, borrowing from "general personality theory." There is little agreement as to "projective theory." We feel, however, that the separatism involved in attempts to construct a special projective theory, applicable only to projective behavior, is not warranted. The lack of refinment and reliability in nosology and personality theory in psychology in general, further complicate the picture. Research clinicians would do better to direct some energy into the latter area, rather than to attempt to construct a separate projective psychology. Nevertheless, the writers feel that evaluation of projective instruments can and should proceed with the help of psychometric criteria.

Assumptions of projective techniques were reviewed and the notion raised that many of these should not be accepted entirely without further proof. On the other hand, a review of the concept of objectivity, in relation to psychometrics and projective techniques, has suggested that "objective" need not be regarded as the opposite of "projective." Projective workers do make psychometric assumptions, implicitly or explicitly. It is felt that testing these assumptions, as well as objectifying projective instruments, are possible despite the difficulties involved.

In this light, it is proposed that a systematic procedure for rating responses to projective techniques be utilized. Such a scoring method would provide a uniform system for rating and evaluating a variety of projective materials; and, moreover, its reliability could easily be established. The task is first to determine and define the different dimensions which clinicians use today in evaluating and scoring projective protocols and then to provide scales for evaluating each of these dimensions. In this way the overall problem of evaluation becomes amenable to experimental and statistical treatment.

The chapters ahead attempt this survey; later, experimental and clinical approaches to projective techniques will be integrated by providing scaling devices for evaluating performance on these techniques. Systematic research will thus be possible, enabling the research clinician to explore the "no-man's land" between experimental psychology, clinical psychology, personality research, and psychopathology. When the experimental roots of projective techniques are discovered and analyzed, they will enable the research worker to integrate all these fields in the light of systematic experimentation.

## REFERENCES

Abt, L. E. A theory of projective psychology. In L. E. Abt and L. Bellak (Eds.) *Projective psychology.* New York: Alfred A. Knopf, 1950, 33–66.
Abt, L. E., & Bellak, L. (Eds.) *Projective psychology.* New York: Alfred A. Knopf, 1950.
Adcock, C. J., McCreary, J. R., Ritchie, J. E., & Somerset, H. C. A. Personality and physique. *Victoria U. Wellington Publ. Psychol.,* 1958, No. 12.
Adrian, E. D. *The physical background of perception.* Oxford: The Clarendon Press, 1947.
Allport, G. W. *Personality: a psychological interpretation.* New York: Holt, 1937.
American Psychological Association, Committee on Psychological Tests. *Technical recommendations for psychological tests and diagnostic techniques.* Washington, D.C.: APA, 1954. (Reprinted from: *Psychol. Bull., Suppl.,* 1954, **51,** 201–238.)
Anderson, H. H., & Anderson, Gladys L. (Eds.) *An introduction to projective techniques.* Englewood Cliffs, N.J.: Prentice-Hall, 1951.
Barnouw, V. Acculturation and personality among the Wisconsin Chippewa. *Amer. Anthrop.,* 1950, **52,** Part 2, Memoir 72.
Barnouw, V. Rorschachs of 18 Chippewa (Ojibwa) men and women. In B. Kaplan (Ed.) *Primary records in culture and personality,* Vol. 2. Madison: The Microcard Foundation, 1957.
Bartlett, F. C. *Remembering.* Cambridge: Cambridge University Press, 1932.
Bechtoldt, H. P. Construct validity: a critique. *Amer. Psychologist,* 1959, **14,** 619–629.
Bell, J. E. *Projective techniques.* New York: Longmans, Green, 1948.
Berg, I. A. Deviant responses and deviant people: the formulation of the Deviation Hypothesis. *J. counsel. Psychol.,* 1957, **4,** 154–161.
Berg, I. A. The unimportance of test item content. In B. M. Bass and I. A. Berg

(Eds.) *Objective approaches to personality assessment.* Princeton, N.J.: D. Van Nostrand, 1959, 83–99.

Binet, A., & Simon, T. Application des méthodes nouvelles au diagnostic du niveau intellectual chez des enfants normaux et anormaux d'hospice et d'école primaire. *Année psychol.*, 1905, 11, 245–336.

Bleuler, M., & Bleuler, R. Rorschach's ink-blot test and racial psychology: mental peculiarities of Moroccans. *Charact. & Pers.*, 1935, 4, 97–114.

Blum, G. A study of the psychoanalytic theory of psychosexual development. *Genet. Psychol. Monogr.*, 1949, 39, 3–99.

Brower, D., & Abt, L. E. (Eds.) *Progress in clinical psychology,* Vol. II. New York: Grune and Stratton, 1956.

Campbell, D. T. A typology of tests, projective and otherwise. *J. consult. Psychol.*, 1957, 21, 207–210.

Campbell, D. T. Recommendations for APA test standards regarding construct, trait or discriminant validity. *Amer. Psychologist*, 1960, 15, 546–553.

Campbell, D. T., & Fiske, D. W. Convergent and discriminant validation by the multitrait-multimethod matrix. *Psychol. Bull.*, 1959, 56, 81–105.

Carstairs, G. M. Rorschachs of 22 Bhil men from Udaipur, India. In B. Kaplan (Ed.) *Primary records in culture and personality,* Vol. 1. Madison: The Microcard Foundation, 1956. (*a*)

Carstairs, G. M. Rorschachs of 40 high caste Hindus and 10 Moslem men from Delwara, Udiapur, India. In B. Kaplan (Ed.) *Primary records in culture and personality,* Vol. 1. Madison: The Microcard Foundation, 1956. (*b*)

Cattell, R. B. *A guide to mental testing.* London: University of London Press, 1936.

Caudill, W. Psychological characteristics of acculturated Wisconsin Ojibwa children. *Amer. Anthrop.*, 1949, 51, 409–427.

Caudill, W. Japanese American personality and acculturation. *Genet. Psychol. Monogr.*, 1952, 45, 3–102.

Chase, P. H. A note on projection. *Psychol. Bull.*, 1960, 57, 289–290.

Cheng, F., Chen, C., & Rin, H. A personality analysis of the Ami and its three subgroups by Rorschach test. *Acta Psychol. Taiwanica*, 1958, 1, 131–143.

Corsini, R., & Uehling, H. A cross-validation of Davidson's Rorschach Adjustment Scale. *J. consult. Psychol.*, 1954, 18, 277–279.

Cronbach, L. J. Assessment of individual differences. *Annu. Rev. Psychol.*, 1956, 7, 173–196.

Cronbach, L. J., & Meehl, P. E. Construct validity in psychological tests. *Psychol. Bull.*, 1955, 52, 281–302.

Dana, R. H. American culture and Chinese personality. *Psychol. Newsltr.*, 1959, 10, 314–321.

DuBois, Cora. *The people of Alor. A social-psychological study of an East-Indian island.* (With analyses by Abram Kardiner and Emil Oberholzer.) Minneapolis: The University of Minnesota Press, 1944.

Ebbinghaus, H. Über eine neue Methode zur Prüfung geistiger Fähigkeiten und ihre Anwendung bei Schulkindern. *Z. Psychol., Physiol.* 1897, 13, 401–459.

Eccles, J. C. *The neurophysiological basis of mind.* Oxford: The Clarendon Press, 1953.

Eysenck, H. J. La validité des techniques projectives. *Rev. Psychol. appl.*, 1955, 5, 231–233.

Forer, B. R. Custom-built projective methods: a symposium. *J. proj. Tech.*, 1961, 25, 3–5.

Frank, L. K. Projective methods for the study of personality. *J. Psychol.*, 1939, 8, 389–413.

Frank, L. K. *Projective methods.* Springfield, Ill.: Charles C Thomas, 1948.

Frank, L. K. Toward a projective psychology. *J. proj. Tech.*, 1960, 24, 246–253.

Freud, S. Further remarks on the defense neuro-psychoses (1896). *Collected papers,* Vol. 1. London: Hogarth Press, 1950, 155–182.

Friedl, Ernestine. Chippewa (Ojibwa) Rorschachs from 72 women and 25 men. In B. Kaplan (Ed.) *Primary records in culture and personality,* Vol. 2. Madison: The Microcard Foundation, 1957.

Fulkerson, S. C., & Barry, J. R. Methodology and research on the prognostic use of psychological tests. *Psychol. Bull.,* 1961, 58, 177–204.

Gladwin, T., & Sarason, S. B. *Truk: man in paradise.* New York: Wenner-Gren Foundation, 1953.

Goldstein, F. J. Custom-made or store-bought projective techniques: what do they represent? *J. proj. Tech.*, 1961, 25, 11–20.

Hallowell, A. I. The Rorschach technique in personality and culture studies. In B. Klopfer, *et al. Developments in the Rorschach technique. Vol. II. Fields of application.* Yonkers-on-Hudson: World Book Co., 1956, 458–544.

Hallowell, A. I. Rorschachs of 151 Berens River Saulteaux (Ojibwa) adults and children and 115 Lac du Flambeau adults. In B. Kaplan (Ed.) *Primary records in culture and personality,* Vol. 2. Madison: The Microcard Foundation, 1957.

Hanks, L. M., Jr. Modified TATs of 47 Thai children and adults. In B. Kaplan (Ed.) *Primary records in culture and personality,* Vol. 1. Madison: The Microcard Foundation, 1956.

Harris, J. G., Jr. Validity: the search for a constant in a universe of variables. In Maria A. Rickers-Ovsiankina (Ed.) *Rorschach psychology.* New York: John Wiley and Sons, 1960, 380–439.

Hathaway, S. R. Increasing clinical efficiency. In B. M. Bass and I. A. Berg (Eds.) *Objective approaches to personality assessment.* Princeton, N.J.: D. Van Nostrand, 1959, 192–203.

Henry, J. Symposium: projective testing in ethnography. *Amer. Anthrop.,* 1955, 57, 245–270.

Henry, J., & Spiro, M. E. Psychological techniques: projective tests in field work. In A. L. Kroeber (Ed.) *Anthropology today.* Chicago: University of Chicago Press, 1953, 417–429.

Henry, W. Projective tests in cross-cultural research. In B. Kaplan (Ed.) *Studying personality cross-culturally.* Evanston, Ill.: Row, Peterson, 1961, 587–596.

Holtzman, W. H. Objective scoring of projective techniques. In B. M. Bass and I. A. Berg (Eds.) *Objective approaches to personality assessment.* Princeton, N.J.: D. Van Nostrand, 1959, 119–145.

Holtzman, W. H., Thorpe, J. S., Swartz, J. D., & Herron, E. W. *Inkblot perception and personality: Holtzman Inkblot technique.* Austin: University of Texas Press, 1961.

Honigmann, J. J. *Culture and personality.* New York: Harper and Brothers, 1954.

Hooker, Evelyn. What is a criterion? *J. proj. Tech.*, 1959, 23, 278–281.

Horst, P. *The prediction of personal adjustment.* New York: Social Science Research Council, 1941.

Howard, J. W. The Howard Ink Blot Test: a descriptive manual. *J. clin. Psychol. Monogr. Suppl.,* 1953, 9, 209–254.

Hunt, W. A. An actuarial approach to clinical judgment. In B. M. Bass and I. A. Berg (Eds.) *Objective approaches to personality assessment.* Princeton, N.J.: D. Van Nostrand, 1959, 169–191.

Hutt, M. L. Toward an understanding of projective testing. *J. proj. Tech.,* 1954, 18, 197–201.

Inkeles, A., & Levinson, D. J. National character: the study of modal personality and sociocultural systems. In G. Lindzey (Ed.) *Handbook of social psychology,* Vol. II. Cambridge: Addison-Wesley, 1954, 997–1020.

Kaplan, B. A study of Rorschach responses in four cultures. *Pap. Peabody Museum of Arch. and Ethnol.,* Harvard University, 1954, Vol. 42, No. 2.

Kaplan, B. Reflections of the acculturation process in the Rorschach test. *J. proj. Tech.,* 1955, 19, 30–35.

Kaplan, B. Personality and social structure. In J. Gittler (Ed.) *Review of sociology.* New York: John Wiley and Sons, 1957, 87–126.

Kaplan, B. Projective techniques in cross-cultural research. Unpublished report, prepared for earlier draft of current volume, 1958.

Kaplan, B. (Ed.) *Studying personality cross-culturally.* Evanston, Ill.: Row, Peterson, 1961.

Kardiner, A. (with the collaboration of R. Linton, Cora DuBois, and J. West). *The psychological frontiers of society.* New York: Columbia University Press, 1945.

Kelly, E. L. Theory and techniques of assessment. *Annu. Rev. Psychol.,* 1954, 5, 281–310.

Kelly, G. A. The theory and technique of assessment. *Annu. Rev. Psychol.,* 1958, 9, 323–352.

Kerckhoff, A. Modified TATs of 54 Chippewa (Ojibwa) children. In B. Kaplan (Ed.) *Primary records in culture and personality,* Vol. 1. Madison: The Microcard Foundation, 1956.

Kluckhohn, C. Culture and behavior. In G. Lindzey (Ed.) *Handbook of social psychology,* Vol. II. Cambridge: Addison-Wesley, 1954, 921–976.

Kraepelin, E. Der psycholigische Versuch in der Psychiatrie. *Psychol. Arbeiten,* 1896, 1, 1–91.

Lesser, G. S. Population differences in construct validity. *J. consult. Psychol.,* 1959, 23, 60–65.

Lesser, G. S. Custom-making projective tests for research. *J. proj. Tech.,* 1961, 25, 21–31.

Levy, D. M., Schumer, Florence C., & Zubin, J. *The Levy Movement Blots: a study of correlates and validity.* In preparation, 1964.

Lindzey, G. On the classification of projective techniques. *Psychol. Bull.,* 1959, 56, 158–168.

Lindzey, G. *Projective techniques and cross-cultural research.* New York: Appleton-Century-Crofts, 1961.

Loevinger, Jane. Theory and techniques of assessment. *Annu. Rev. Psychol.,* 1959, 10, 287–316.

MacFarlane, Jean, & Tuddenham, R. D. Problems in the validation of projective techniques. In H. H. Anderson and G. L. Anderson (Eds.) *An introduction to projective techniques.* Englewood Cliffs, N.J.: Prentice-Hall, 1951, 26–54.

Meehl, P. E. *Clinical vs. statistical prediction.* Minneapolis: University of Minnesota Press, 1954.

Meehl, P. E. Some ruminations on the validation of clinical procedures. *Canad. J. Psychol.,* 1959, 13, 102–128.

Meehl, P. E., & Rosen, A. Antecedent probability and the efficiency of psychometric signs, patterns, or cutting scores. *Psychol. Bull.*, 1955, **52**, 194–216.

Morgan, Christiana D., & Murray, H. A. A method for investigating fantasies: the Thematic Apperception Test. *Arch. Neurol. Psychiat.*, 1935, **34**, 289–306.

Murray, H. A. Foreword, in H. H. Anderson and G. L. Anderson (Eds.) *An introduction to projective techniques.* Englewood Cliffs, N.J.: Prentice-Hall, 1951, xi–xiv.

Murstein, B. I. A conceptual model of projective techniques applied to stimulus variations with thematic techniques. *J. consult. Psychol.*, 1959, **23**, 3–14.

Murstein, B. I., & Pryer, R. S. The concept of projection: a review. *Psychol. Bull.*, 1959, **56**, 353–374.

Newman, R. E. Personality development in a primitive "adolescent" group. *Z. diagnost. Psychol.*, 1958, **6**, 241–253.

Office of Strategic Services (OSS). *Assessment of men: selection of personnel.* New York: Rinehart and Company, 1948.

O'Reilly, P. O. The objective Rorschach: a suggested modification of Rorschach technique. *J. clin. Psychol.*, 1956, **12**, 27–31.

Palmer, J. O. Attitudinal correlates of Rorschach's experience balance. *J. proj. Tech.*, 1956, **20**, 207–211.

Piaget, J. *The psychology of intelligence.* New York: Harcourt, Brace, 1950.

Rabin, A. I. Devising projective methods for personality research. *J. proj. Tech.*, 1961, **25**, 6–10.

Rabin, A. I., & Haworth, Mary R. (Eds.) *Projective techniques with children.* New York: Grune and Stratton, 1960.

Riessman, F., Jr., & Miller, S. M. Social class and projective tests. *J. proj. Tech.*, 1958, **22**, 432–439.

Ritter, Anne, & Eron, L. D. The use of the Thematic Apperception Test to differentiate normal from abnormal groups. *J. abnorm. soc. Psychol.*, 1952, **47**, 147–158.

Rosenblatt, D. Responses of former Soviet citizens to selected TAT cards. *J. gen. Psychol.*, 1960, **62**, 273–284.

Rosenzweig, S. The picture-association method and its application in a study of reactions to frustration. *J. Pers.*, 1945, **14**, 3–23.

Rosenzweig, S. Levels of behavior in psychodiagnosis with special reference to the Picture-Frustration Study. *Amer. J. Orthopsychiat.*, 1950, **20**, 63–72.

Rust, R. M. Some correlates of the movement response. *J. Pers.*, 1948, **16**, 369–401.

Sarason, S. B. *The clinical interaction.* New York: Harper and Brothers, 1954.

Shneidman, E. S. Symposium: current aspects of the problem of validity: suggestions for the delineation of validational studies. *J. proj. Tech.*, 1959, **23**, 259–262.

Stern, W. *General psychology from the personalistic point of view.* Translated by H. D. Spoerl. New York: Macmillan, 1938.

Super, D. E. Theories and assumptions underlying approaches to personality assessment. In B. M. Bass and I. A. Berg (Eds.) *Objective approaches to personality assessment.* Princeton, N.J.: D. Van Nostrand, 1959, 24–41.

Thurstone, L. L. The Rorschach in psychological science. *J. abnorm. soc. Psychol.*, 1948, **43**, 471–475.

Vernon, P. E. Recent work on the Rorschach test. *J. ment. Sci.*, 1935, **81**, 894–920.

Warren, H. C. (Ed.) *Dictionary of psychology.* New York: Houghton Mifflin Company, 1934.

Watrous, Blanche. Rorschachs of 103 Ojibwa children. In B. Kaplan (Ed.) *Primary records in culture and personality*, Vol. 1. Madison: The Microcard Foundation, 1956.

Watson, R. I. Historical review of objective personality testing: the search for objectivity. In B. M. Bass and I. A. Berg (Eds.) *Objective approaches to personality assessment.* Princeton, N.J.: D. Van Nostrand, 1959, 1–23.

Ziehen, T. *Die Prinzipien und Methoden der Begabungsinbesondere der Intelligentzprüfung bei Gesunden und Kranken.* Berlin: Karger, 1923.

Zubin, J. Failures of the Rorschach technique. *J. proj. Tech.*, 1954, 18, 303–315.

Zubin, J. Clinical vs. actuarial prediction: a pseudo-problem. In *Proceedings of the 1955 invitational conference on testing problems.* Princeton: Educational Testing Service, 1955, 107–128.

Zubin, J. The non-projective aspects of the Rorschach experiment: introduction to the symposium. *J. soc. Psychol.*, 1956, 44, 179–192.

# 2 PERCEPTION:

## *an approach to personality?* PART I

Although workers in the field of projective techniques differ in many of their aims, assumptions, and approaches, they hold one purpose in common—delineation and measurement of personality—and one assumption in common—that perception is the medium through which personality can be assessed. Zubin (1951),[1] in calling attention to this assumption, felt that despite their theoretical link there was little integration between projective techniques and experimental studies of perception. Unfortunately, this is still the case, not only because of apathy on the part of projective workers and the undeveloped status of perceptual theory, but also because the search for a direct link between perception and the Rorschach technique, for example, has not yet succeeded, and may indeed turn out to be fruitless.

The early formulations as to the relationship between perception and personality (e.g., Klüver in Murphy [1929]) are convincing because they are simple, and seem to make intuitive sense. One such formulation follows: optical perception can be divided into three aspects— retinal image, gestalt disposition of sensory impulses, and ongoing stimulation of the cortex from other sources at the time when the external stimulus impinges on the retina, such as anxiety, fears, and mental sets. In persons with intact vision and no organic involvement

---

[1] The bibliographic references of this chapter are contained in the list at the end of Chapter 3.

of the optical system, neither the retinal image level nor the gestalt structure level could explain the multiplicity of responses arising from the same stimulus, as is the case in projective techniques. According to this analysis, only the third level, the ongoing stimulation from other cortical centers, could be the source of the wide variety of responses. The relationship between and among these levels remains a problem, however; different theoretical approaches stress one or the other of these levels, and the total picture is still unclear.

Chapters 2 and 3 attempt to summarize some of the unsolved problems in the field of perception, especially as related to the hypothetical link between perception and personality. Unfortunately, this is by no means a straightforward task from which logical conclusions can be drawn. All that can be done now is to present the reader with a representative selection of material which he can begin to sift and sort for himself. To explore the entire problem would take a book in itself. The plan is to present the complexity of the area by first discussing some definitions of perception and personality, as well as the perennial kinds of problems which workers in perception and personality face; most of this chapter and the next, however, is devoted to describing various theoretical approaches to perception. Some of the experimental findings to which this literature has given rise is summarized in the context of their relevant theoretical frameworks. In Chapter 3 (a continuation of this chapter) special reference is made to directive-state theories of perception—the so-called "New Look" in perceptual theory which has fostered, encouraged, and focused attention on studies assuming a link between perception and personality.

### Some Definitions

*Personality.* Definitions of personality, as the reader undoubtedly already knows, can be found in abundance, and they are often expressed in terms of the language and concepts of the particular theoretical system to which each author subscribes. Lewin, for example, described the personality as a "more or less unitary and more or less closed" organization of interrelated psychical systems (1935), or as a "differentiated region of the life space" (1936). Learning theorists express themselves in terms of systematic, learned ways of behaving and families of habits. Trait psychologists, concerned with measuring individual differences, define personality as a summation or aggregate of traits and dispositions. Gordon Allport (1937), in summarizing a vast amount of material pertaining to the definitions of personality through the ages, described fifty different meanings attributed to the term "personality." He himself stressed the *uniqueness* of the personality of each individual in his definition: "Personality is the dynamic organization within the individual of those psychophysical systems that determine his *unique* adjustments to his environment" (*Ibid.*, p. 48).

Before launching into an examination of the relation between perception and personality, the need for such a concept as personality might be raised. Zubin and Katz (1964), in a discussion of the relation between drugs and personality, stated, "As everyone would agree, the concept of personality, as representing the unique pattern of behavior of the individual, is no more than a scientific model. If it has ceased being a useful model, we ought to discard it. If it is still useful in the study of behavior, it ought to be retained" (p. 368). Viewing the matter historically, personality is apparently another example of a shrinking universe which contracts as measurement expands. As we all know, in the beginning, personality as a field of study had everything; then it lost its intelligence, and before it could recover, it lost its interests and its attitudes. It still feels, aspires, and has sentiments as long as they remain unmeasurable. Once they too fall under the psychometrician's ax, personality will be extinct, or will it?

The one thing that keeps motivation, feeling, and sentiment out of the psychometrician's reach is the absence of an external criterion, independent of subjective, self-referred judgment. Had not Binet utilized the criterion of chronological age to develop the concept of mental age, we would still be classifying people as "intelligent" and "unintelligent." Such subjective, self-referred judgments characterize all primitive measures. Height, weight, time, and warmth were evaluated subjectively long before objective measuring devices became available. Invention of such impersonal external criteria as yardsticks, balances, clocks, and thermometers permitted science to transcend self-reference as a criterion. We have not yet found external criteria for measuring motivation, feeling, and sentiment, which is why they, as well as certain of their aspects which remain unanalyzed, are still unmeasurable. When external criteria are found by which to measure them, they can be set apart from the total impression of personality, to be studied as separate entities and (to be studied) in relation to other factors.

Even if we were to vote personality out of existence, it would return to haunt us in some other form, as Knight Dunlap once said would happen if we exorcised the concept "emotion." Personality, it would seem, is here to stay. Let us look for a suitable model for it, from which testable hypotheses can be drawn. As Zubin and Katz (1964) have noted:

No matter what organizational principles may be postulated (needs, traits, etc.), personality is inferred from behavior. It might be interesting to classify observable behavior into its parts to recognize that sector for which a concept of personality is useful. Behavior includes parts which are overdetermined by biology and hence highly predictable, e.g., reflex action, imprinting, and other natively endowed behaviors. It also is composed of parts that are over-determined culturally, e.g., language, food habits and dress. While these two types of overdetermined behavior are highly consistent and characteristic, they do not differentiate among individuals in the same social-cultural and biological subgroup. There is a third class of behaviors, which may be re-garded as accidental or erratic and unsystematic, which are not useful in prediction. The rest of behavior may be sampled for its usefulness as measures of personality (pp. 368–369).

In the past few years, experimental psychologists have been less concerned with defining personality than with its measurement. Stress is being placed on the development of adequate instruments which can reliably measure this or that aspect of adjustment, motivation, need, trait or behavior, alone or in various combinations, and in testing the validity (against an outside criterion) of the measurement being used. Thus, Pepinsky (1959), in summarizing a volume (Bass & Berg, 1959) which contained various chapters on objective methods of per-sonality assessment, noted that "none of the authors has stopped to define the term 'personality'" (p. 223).

Zubin and Katz (*Ibid.*) noted that the present ambiguous status of the concept of personality is making difficult the exploration of rela-tionships between various experimental factors and personality change. Continuing their discussion of how they view personality, they have noted that personality deals only with certain systematic ways of behaving which have a generality over many situations and at different times and which allow some predictions as to an individual's future behavior which could not be made from knowledge of any group to which he belongs. These authors thus recognize that their concept of personality must be limited by the kind of problem with which they are working; the scope or generality of what they can subsume under "personality" is deliberately restricted to measurable responses relevant to their purposes. This is not unlike the state of affairs in intelligence testing giving rise to the old cliché, "intelligence is what the intelligence test measures." The reader will note that our survey of perception-personality research places a parallel limitation on the scope of the concept "personality."

*Perception.* Koffka's famous question (1935), "Why do things look as they do?" is, at first blush, a relatively simple expression of what the field of visual perception seems to include. Floyd Allport (1955) has suggested expanding this query by substituting "seem" or "appear" for the word "look," thereby including sensory modalities other than vision.

By adding "occurrences" to the "things" in Koffka's question, we can imply that perception has to do with complex situations, rather than just simple objects. A review of some of the earlier as well as more recent attempts to define perception suggests that there are common elements that man has utilized from time to time through history in answering this question. Some of the more important of these elements include references to: (a) external reality—the world of objects, people, scenes, topography, etc.—which presumably exists independent of any observer; (b) man's "knowing," "sensing," or being "aware" of the reality around him; (c) the real world making its impact only through the receptors of the organism; (d) what have been called cognitive factors—judging, thinking, etc. Sometimes a distinction is made between the conceptual processes (which may arise spontaneously) and the process of perception (which is dependent on external stimulation), but this is not always explicit; frequently there is reference to the "immediacy" of the subjective (phenomenal) experience.

Some definitions have stressed behavioral aspects of perception, which is viewed as a mediating event leading up to behavior. The reader will find, in later sections, that many recent authors have stressed the "motor" aspects of the perceptual event, unlike some of their more sedentary arm-chair forbears. Other workers have used so broad a definition of perception that judgments of people, situations, and circumstances, as in studies in social psychology, are subsumed under the general heading of perception.

What are some of the specific definitions which have been offered? A few will be noted to draw attention to some of the problems in this complex field. Gibson (1959) defined perception as a "process by which an individual maintains contact with his environment," that is, keeping in touch with the world. Dreger (1961) defined perception "as the immediate response of the organism to the impingement of energy upon the sense organs." Gibson does not mention sensory experience, but implies it. At the same time, Dreger's definition does not rule out various classes of experience and behavior, such as reflexes, adaptation, imagery, and thinking. The same comment applies to Bartley's definition, "Perception is the overall activity of the organism that immediately follows or accompanies energistic impingements upon the sense organs" (1958, p. 22). Awareness and meaning are stressed in Helson's definition, ". . . perceiving involves the apprehension of and reaction to the qualities and properties of objects and events as they interact with the organism" (1951, p. 348).

Since there are so many problems attendant to defining perception, a fruitful approach to understanding the scope of the field may be to discuss some of these problems and dilemmas rather than to dwell on the various tentative answers. We know that throughout the ages, man has sought answers to the general question: How are we made aware of the world around us? Philosophers have long delighted in the complex epistemological issues involved in this question. Psychologists have not been satisfied with the philosophers' elegant and eloquent solutions to various problems, which have ranged from final and ultimate reference to superhuman beings, to the positing of particles or faint images given off by objects which act on the organism, especially on his mind, thus causing "awarness." But psychologists, too, have found no final solution and instead have come up with confusing, conflicting, and often contradictory answers.

*Problems in Defining Perception.* One of the problems relates to a traditional distinction between sensation and perception. Sensation was and is commonly felt to refer to the physical energies impinging on one or another of the sense organs, but without experiential "awareness" and "meaning." When meaning accompanies sensation, it is no longer pure sensation but perception. The sensory data form the raw material for the ultimate perceptual experience. The perceptual experience has been linked with cortical activities, such as memory, judgment, and insight. There is no agreement, however, even on the existence of "pure sensation." There are some who feel that all sensory experiences are perceptual in nature, whereas others stress the judgmental and cognitive aspect of perception to such an extent that perception is made almost synonymous with learning, thinking, and consciousness itself. The very immediacy and spontaneity of a perceptual act is thus denied.

An additional problem workers in perception face, especially when experimental results from a particular study are generalized, is the delimitation of the boundaries of the concepts with which they are working. Recent usage of the term "perception" is so broad that it includes almost all of cognition and judgment. The reader is referred, for example, to Dreger (1961) for an illustration of how the terms "perception," "roles," "social perception," "conception," "personality," etc., are used almost interchangeably. (This particular report, incidentally, is a good example of the "New Look" or "directive-state" approach in perceptual theory—an approach which is described at length in Chapter 3.) In this connection, Floyd Allport (1955, pp. 364–369) described a general "cleavage" in perceptual theory. On the one hand, perception is defined so broadly, especially by social psychologists, as to include almost all of cognition, and on the other hand, it is defined rather narrowly and specifically, in the classical sense. As Hochberg (1956, p.

400) once observed, "So loose has the term become that today Murray might call his battery the Thematic Perception Test, and not arouse any great comment." Are social psychologists, when they talk of social perceptions, considering the same set of processes as the perceptionist when he talks about size constancy, color perception, and the like? Is the social perception involved in prejudiced attitudes, judgments of traits, or sociometric choice, based on the same psychological processes as when S perceives one object to be farther away from him than another? Perhaps there are general principles which apply to all of these behaviors; if so, these principles would have to be demonstrated and the limits of their application noted.

As already suggested, a difficulty in defining perception relates to the immediacy of perception and the perceptual experience. Does S actually *see* what he verbalizes? When he responds verbally to a given stimulus, is he being influenced by memories, motivational and cognitive factors in the *expression* of his response, or do these variables actually influence the perception itself? One criterion some workers have found useful in this connection is that of *immediacy*. There are several possible definitions of the term. First is "nonmediated," that is, the perceptual response follows directly upon the stimulus without the intervention of any intermediate processes such as cognition and awareness. Secondly, it may refer to the immediate rather than delayed effects. How long is the duration of "immediate"—microseconds, milliseconds, or seconds? If perception is viewed as an immediate, direct response to the stimulus, that is, to energy impinging on the receptor(s) of the organism, any behaviors or experiences which are not immediate, that is, which can go on *after* there is no longer any demonstrable stimulation, or in the absence of a stimulus all together, are excluded from the definition. Thus, memory, imagination, judgment, and other cognitive activities would not be regarded as perceptual acts. The reader is referred to Bartley (1958, especially Chapter 2), as well as to Hochberg (1956) for further clarification and expansion of this line of reasoning. It should be noted here, however, that the criterion of immediacy for the perceptual response is not completely accepted by all investigators.

The concept of immediacy raises more problems. Are certain physical and biological reactions and responses, such as reflexes which are immediate and direct responses to energy impinging on the organism, therefore also to be regarded as perceptions? Bartley (*Ibid.*) answers this question by introducing the concept of discrimination into his definition of perception. We may assume that some type of awareness, the ability to behave differentially when changes in stimulation take place, and some cerebral involvement occur when perception is involved.

As the problem of perception is probed further, a subtle and puzzling feature emerges. If perception is something other than judgment, memory, and thinking, that is, something not to be confused with strictly cognitive processes which can take place without concurrent external stimulation, can a perceptual event be said to be devoid of meaning? Obviously not. Most workers agree that the very essence of perception is the "knowing" or becoming aware of the world around us. Meaning seems to be intrinsically and essentially involved in all perceptual acts. Moreover, the evidence suggests that selective processes, interpretation, classification, expectancies, etc., are also involved —precisely the kinds of cognitive activities which, it would seem, we have excluded from our definition of perception. Yet perceptual theories have tended to neglect a consideration of how meaning is "assigned" to energy impinging on the receptors. (Note that the energies, and the neural impulses into which they are translated, in no way are similar to or "mirror" the distal source, that is, the object or scene.) Nor have they adequately dealt with the way in which critical events give rise to the experiencing of the object "out there." This may well be because our ignorance is great in this area and especially because methodology for examining the "experiences" of the S is limited.

Note should also be made of the fact that perception is essentially an event in which the structure and make-up of the individual "does something" to, and with, the neural impulses activated by energy sources from the outside. This has to do with the neurophysiology of the organism. There are many who feel that such content is best left to the neurophysiologist—the psychologist is busy enough trying to understand and predict behavior! Unfortunately, perceptual events are so delicately and yet so firmly rooted in the very physiological and neurological structure of the individual, and especially his brain processes, that a full understanding of perception will probably not take place until more flexibly oriented psychologists are willing to get "into" the organism—under his skin, as it were. Many will not agree with this notion, suggesting that disciplines can function on their own "levels," using their special sources of data, and that ultimately all disciplines should agree on the types and outcomes of predictions made, despite differences in constructs, orientation, methodologies, and even the raw datum used. This may well be a logical and acceptable notion; but then, it does seem that perception has never really been a truly "psychological" discipline. Workers in perception *have* worked with physiological concepts concerning sensory thresholds, receptor mechanisms, neural impulses, and the like. Failure to go further "inside" the organism may not be based on scientific bias or preference, but on hesitancy because of limitations of techniques and a recognition that the neurophysiologist himself does not have the techniques (or answers) either. Fortunately, theorists of various types have been moving away from the "empty organism" approach, as we shall soon see. There are many questions with answers that seem to require neurophysiological considerations, such as, how do mental (neural) and external energies impinging on receptors interact and give rise to the experience of a percept? How, also, do memories, judgments, and experiences enter into this perceptual act? What is the role of learning in a perceptual event? How does the prevailing set (motivational, attitudinal, or motor) affect incoming neural impulses and, since there is evidence for interaction between and among various sensory modalities, how do all these afferent impulses feed back to the organism's efferent mechanisms causing motor adjustments, adaptations, and various postural and positional changes?

Then, of course, there is the problem of "innate vs. learned factors" in perception, for the empiricism-nativism controversy is still quite lively and spirited. According to Hochberg (1957), who summarized a Cornell University symposium on perception dealing with diverse and opposing viewpoints, there seems to be an empiricist "explanation" for practically all perceptual phenomena. We might add that the nativists have not been shy with explanations either. Subsequent sections will discuss this in greater detail. For a general presentation of this controversy, the reader is referred to Floyd Allport (1955, pp. 86–89, 299–303).

Another problem relates to the nature of the response used to indicate the presence of a particular perception. Since perception is an immediate, subjective, and phenomenological *experience*, how can E ascertain that he is getting at what he really wants to know? This is an important methodological problem which is not too frequently handled by psychologists working in this or other areas. E must use some type of *response* indicator as a measure; S must communicate, by verbal, motor or other means, to E. For example, verbal indicators of an either-or, yes-no type, or responses involving memory or recall are often employed to indicate the presence or absence of a perception. The adequacy or reliability of this type of measure, as well as its validity as an indicator of the perceptual event, cannot be taken for granted. Such measures may well provide a distorted picture of what is actually happening. Our dependence on these indicators for experimental results in the area of perception has serious limitations. But neurophysiological indicators such as evoked potentials, even if they could be obtained in humans, are also incomplete as indicators. Goldiamond (1958) has summarized this problem, particularly with respect to traditional experiments in subception and subliminal perception. In his extensive review, he explained many of the subliminal effects in terms of methodological problems inherent in the design of various types of experiments and demonstrations. Subjects may, for example, say that they did not see the stimulus, but they may, in fact, simply not have *reported* that they had seen it, perhaps because they did not feel absolutely sure. "Explanations" for these effects included: response to partial cues, nature of instructions, manner of scoring, and certain problems in the use of ascending and descending series of stimuli.

*Problems in Defining the Stimulus.* That stimulation is essential in the occurrence of a perceptual event is generally accepted, but the implication of this fact raises interesting problems. Is the stimulus-thing (or object) itself to be regarded as the stimulus, or would it rather be the energy change which the stimulus gives rise to, for example a change in light rays impinging on the visual receptors of the organism? The difficulties in working with distal or proximal concepts of stimulation at the same time are enormous—and each set of concepts seems to yield differing theoretical structures, requiring special terminology and a different set of predictions.

Furthermore, many workers in perception have devoted most of their attention to problems of exteroceptive stimulation—that is, energies falling on the *exteroceptors* which have to do essentially with *external* events. There is much less evidence and knowledge concerning the role of interoceptive stimulation—that is, stimulation of *interoceptors inside* the organism, which has to do with essentially nonexternal events. These events would include various physiological and organic kinds of stimulation which may or may not give rise to focused perception. Some theoretical positions stress the interaction and equivalence of "sensory" and "tonic" states (see later sections); others have suggested that when "interoceptive" elements dominate the scene, the final percept will be less veridical and more subjective. In any event, S is constantly being subjected to both exteroceptive and interoceptive stimulation, as well as proprioceptive stimulation (arising from the kinesthetic and vestibular senses). Exteroceptive stimulation is more easily demonstrable through various measurable response indicators, whereas proprioceptive and, especially, interoceptive stimulation is more likely to be inferred. It is perhaps because of this fact that interoceptive stimulation has been slighted, in a sense, in many perceptual theories. Yet, the interaction, interdependence, and ultimate integration of various types of stimulation in producing the final percept are probably crucial aspects of the answer to the question, "Why do things look as they do?" That our knowledge of the parameters of interoceptive stimulation is now extremely limited, but need not necessarily remain so, is indicated by Razran's detailed and extensive review of research in psychophysiology in the Soviet Union (1961). A major portion of this review was devoted to work on interoceptive conditioning, an area which represents almost a unique and unduplicated research domain in psychology, dominated by Russian psychologists. It is concerned primarily with classical conditioning, in which either the conditioned or unconditioned stimulus or both, are delivered directly to visceral loci of the organism. Such attempts to develop laws and extensive knowledge about visceral action and learning, according to Razran, have widespread implications for the study of the "observable unconscious."

Another aspect of stimulation is its appropriateness or inappropriateness for inducing effective physiological excitation. For example, light falling on skin receptors is inappropriate for effective stimulation of the visual system. With sufficient increases in intensity, however, the light energy for stimulating the temperature receptors will be reached, thus becoming an appropriate stimulus for temperature perception. Hence, in effective stimulation the energy exchange must not only be enough to induce physiological excitation in the cells of a receptor organ but must also fall on the appropriate organ for excitation spread to occur. When both of these conditions are fulfilled, sensation or perception may follow.

The definition of the "stimulus" acting in a given situation is often beset with great difficulty. Boring (1952) has indicated that finding the stimulus which gives rise to a given response is one of the major tasks of psychology. (This search is embarrassingly lacking in the field of projective techniques and may account for much of the difficulty that projective techniques are experiencing in their quest for scientific respectability. Not until more effort is expended in this direction will the scientific acceptance of projective techniques become a possibility.) In a paper concerned with the concept of the stimulus in psychology, Gibson (1960) noted the confusing number of definitions of the stimulus and the lack of a "theory of the stimulus." He indicated a number of questions about which there are disagreements between various schools in defining and understanding the role of the stimulus in behavior:

1. Do all stimuli impel to action? Does a stimulus motivate the individual or arouse a sense organ?

2. Can a stimulus alone cause only a sensory response but not a perceptual response, since the organism contributes to the latter? Or, as Gibson inquires, is the percept "in very good correspondence with the physical variables of the stimulus?" (p. 695).

3. Is physical energy a stimulus only when some response is observed? Can a stimulus be regarded as a *potential* activator of a sense organ, that is, as a *potential stimulus?* Gibson believes that physical energy or stimulus energy may be present even when it does not elicit a response. Moreover, the same stimulus energy may be effective in terms of the organism's response at one time, but not another. This raises some ancient epistemological questions which are beyond our immediate concern, e.g., when something crashes with no one to hear it, is there sound? There are certainly disturbances of air particles described as waves with amplitude, frequency, etc., even though there is no S subjectively experiencing sound, as such; but if there is no one to observe them, do they exist? The general question can be stated: can a stimulus be defined independently in physical terms or must it always be in terms of S's behavior or sensory processes? The circularity in defining the stimulus–response sequence is still an unsolved problem.

4. Traditionally, in experimental psychology, almost anything can be called a stimulus. Things "out there" are called stimuli, especially by S-R psychologists; stimuli include any and all things an ingenious experimentalist uses—bells, tones, pictures, tachistoscopic slides, etc. Gibson reminds us that only receptors at the skin of an individual can be stimulated, and that, in this sense, stimuli are not objects or things—only physical energies. He noted that Koffka, especially, has cautioned us about this paradox; although both behavior and perception *seem* to be in response to the distal object, they are, as a matter of fact, aroused only by proximal stimulation. Such proximal stimulation is constantly changing, almost never the same. How does a perception with respect to one object or thing appear stable and unchanging? This raises the problem of perceptual constancy, which also remains unsolved.

Gibson has raised further questions concerning the patterning and relationships of stimuli. Are these patterns to be conceived of as single stimuli, or as consisting of separate stimuli? Other questions are raised about temporal aspects of stimuli. Furthermore, he has noted that the concept of lack of structure as applied to certain stimuli is meaningless. All stimuli have structure although we may not assign words, meaning, etc., to that structure. Only film-color or the cloudless, blue sky lack structure. Another puzzling problem to Gibson is how distal objects, through the mediation of physical energies impinging on receptor organs, convey information about themselves. Traditionally, this touches on the dichotomy between sensation and perception. Most psychologists have believed that physical energies (sensations, after they activate receptors) are meaningless, raw data, devoid of content, and do not give rise to perceptions immediately. Gibson believes that stimuli *do* provide information about their sources, and are not completely empty of meaning. He is not referring, of course, to words, symbols, etc., which he terms *coded stimuli* and which he suggests carry information in a different manner. The question he raises is how do stimuli "carry information about their sources in the world, and how do they specify them?" (p. 700).

Gibson completed his discussion with a plea for recognition and study of stimuli in terms of concepts which are not usually handled either by the psychologist or the physicist:

1. *Molar stimuli* are conceived of as complex arrays of a higher order to which we are always responding, rather than pinpoints of light or amplitudes of sound. Gibson feels that psychologists should explore that aspect of stimulation to which S is responding—not what excites "all the little receptors." Our concern with molar *responses* should have a corresponding parallel in stimulation. Such an exploration would involve the concept of higher-order stimulation. Gibson quotes Holt (1915) who suggested that the effective stimulus "recedes" as one goes from reflexes to behavior. "By the *recession* of the stimulus he meant that it seems to be located far out in the environment rather than close by in the receptors. And he also meant that as cognition develops, the stimulus of which it is a function recedes more and more" (Gibson, 1960, p. 700).

2. *Potential stimuli* are conceived of as consisting of possible stimuli for both perception and action, and offer a wide possibility for study which departs from that of the traditional physics—or psychology—textbook. He offered several examples to illustrate the types of potential stimuli not traditionally classified or listed (such as optical texture).

3. *Effective stimuli* are defined as those which activate receptor activity, or various response indicators. There are no fixed innate thresholds of sensation. Potential stimuli become effective stimuli depending on a variety of factors. "In short, whether or not a potential stimulus becomes effective depends on the individual. It depends on the species

to which he belongs, on the anatomy of the sense organs, the stage of maturation, the capacities for sense organ adjustment, the habits of attention, the activity in progress, and the possibilities of educating the attention of the individual" (p. 701).

Gibson, in line with his theoretical orientation, has noted that the crucial area for study is how experience is related specifically to molar stimuli because of the information such stimuli carry. Such information he has suggested can be described in completely physical terms. Stimuli are not intrinsically "meaningless," as the sensation-perception dichotomy would imply and as traditional Rorschach-ers, for example, have insisted in regard to inkblots. He designated the laws by which stimuli specify their sources as crucial for study. The meaning of words or pictures would be called *mediated* perception, which probably has its own laws.

The absence of consensus in defining perception, and the lack of precision in such definitions as do exist, may lead the reader to wonder why psychologists persist in working in this area and why the authors of this book did not decide to give up at this point. As a matter of fact, one of the authors, who began the writing of this manuscript in 1948, did give up for a while and permitted the book to lie fallow for 15 years. His decision to resume came after reading Julian Huxley's distinction between the "precision" and the "utility" of a concept in science (1940). Huxley pointed out that even such well-entrenched concepts as *species* in biology have no rigorous, precise definitions:

Morphological differences; failure to interbreed; infertility of offspring; ecological, geographical or genetical distinctness—all of those must be taken into account but none of them singly is decisive. . . . A combination of criteria is needed with some sort of *flair*. With the aid of these, it is remarkable how the variety of organic life falls apart into biologically discontinuous groups. In the great majority of cases species can be readily delimited, and appear as natural entities, not merely convenient fictions of the human intellect (p. 11).

Thus the utility of a concept is not limited by the preciseness of its definition. The final conclusion reached by Kaplan ([1946]; Kaplan & Schott [1951]), is that the specification of meaning of a term must acknowledge its vagueness. The term is represented not by a well-defined area, but by an open set of regions, overlapping to a greater or lesser degree. The meaning of a term corresponds neither to the logical sum nor the product of these regions but to the pattern as a whole.

For this reason, perception, loosely defined as it is, is still a useful concept. Some experimenters can eliminate at least part of the controversy regarding its definition by viewing its various aspects as limiting states. Thus, sensation can be defined as the limiting state in which only the sensitivity to the impinging energy of the stimulus is our concern; past experience, meaning, etc., are for the moment excluded and only the ability to detect the presence or absence of the stimulus is the experimenter's goal. When discrimination between stimuli in space or in time is demanded, perception enters, and when, in addition, the stored memories of the organism are involved, conceptual activity is involved. Thus, depending on the experimenter's desire, either sensory, perceptual or conceptual activity can be elicited and measured, regardless of whether the other levels are involved.

It may be questioned whether even in the limiting state there can be a pure sensory response. Perhaps only the newborn's first experience with a stimulus can be regarded as purely sensory, whereas the second experience with the same or similar stimuli is already flavored with the past and hence no longer a pure sensation. When the experiment is focused merely on detecting the presence or absence of a stimulus, however, the role of past experience may influence the criterion on the basis of which S responds with "yes" or "no," but will not influence the sensitivity of S to the stimulation in question (see discussion of "detection theory" in Chapter 3, p. 141). An experiment which is focused on *recognition* rather than on *detection* of a previously experienced object or event, depending as it does on discrimination between objects rather than on discrimination between presence or absence of any stimulation, elicits more than a sensory response and is regarded as a perceptual response. Detection of presence or absence of a stimulus need not inevitably involve discrimination between figure and ground as some would have us believe, since we can contrive a *Ganzfeld* in which there is no ground, and the responses to such stimuli do approximate sensory responses quite closely. But the kind of temporal rather than spatial "ground" provided by the sequence of absence vs. presence of the stimulus is impossible to eliminate. (For a further discussion of the difference between sensory and perceptual responses, see Burdock & Zubin [1957].)

*Other Aspects of Perception.* Certain aspects of perceptual research are not within the framework of Chapters 2 and 3; yet, a study of these might be helpful and relevant to a reader who wishes to go further into areas not touched on in any detail in these two chapters.

Some comments will be made about some of these areas, and a few references will be cited.[2]

Wohlwill (1960) has presented an excellent review of developmental studies of perception. His review of age changes in various perceptual processes covered several "classical" aspects of perception such as sensory thresholds, spatial assimilation, contrast, illusions, spatial localization, and the constancies. An overall "trend" in the many findings reported seemed to suggest that younger children required more "information" to perceive a stimulus correctly; as they get older, fewer cues are necessary for veridical perception.

Cultural as well as developmental aspects of perception were reviewed by Dennis (1951), who presented evidence from our own as well as other cultures which suggested that perceptual events are modifiable as a result of cultural experience. It is not clear, it might be noted, as to whether or not cultural factors have a *direct* influence on perception or whether or not more cognitive and interpretive elements are primarily, if not wholly, involved.

Beach (1951) has reviewed an extensive body of knowledge concerning various alterations in body chemistry and their correlations with changes in behavior (under which, apparently, perception is subsumed). Factors such as dietary deficiency, vitamin deficiency, metabolic dysfunction, oxygen deficiency, drugs, alcohol, hormonal secretions, etc., are discussed with respect to both humans and animals, with a general overall conclusion that chemical changes can dramatically affect and influence behavior. Beach's contention was that *neural* changes actually alter the behavior, since "a particular chemical change might result in the destruction of certain groups of nerve cells and thus interfere with the behavior they normally mediate" (p. 81). In addi-

---

[2] The reader is also referred to work on *cognition*, the process by which knowledge is acquired—an often neglected field, but which has a decided relevance and relationship to the field of perception. Using language behavior and an analysis of the grammar of language as a specific instance, Osgood has, in great detail, elaborated a behavioristic theory of cognition (1957), which has made an attempt to get "inside the organism" and which has much relevance to the fields of perception and meaning. Reference might also be made to a symposium on *cognition* (Bruner, et al., 1957).

For those who are interested in general references to the field of perception, especially works containing summaries, comprehensive coverage of a specific area, surveys of theories, etc., the following works are cited: Floyd Allport (1955); Bartley (1958); Beardslee and Wertheimer (1958); Bevan (1958); Blake and Ramsey (1951); O'Neill (1958); and Solley and Murphy (1960). More specific references and summaries will be noted in the sections which follow.

tion to changes in the structure of the nervous system, blood chemistry might affect activities of the organisms, peripheral receptors, etc.

Brain (1951) and Hirst (1959) have discussed the philosophical, logical, and epistemological problems involved in the field of perception, especially in terms of certain logical dilemmas and paradoxes. Hirst, a logician and philosopher, discussed illusions and hallucinations, the relativity of perception, the time-lag involved in perception, and the general consideration that nerve impulses and neurological processes involved in perceptual acts are always the *same*, despite enormous differences in receptors and sensation. He has suggested that the brain is the "necessary and sufficient condition" for perception, and has thrown open for inspection a variety of assumptions and implicit premises that psychologists might do well to recognize. Additional fascinating and complex issues were raised by Brain, a neurologist—issues not often raised by psychologists but which are relevant to methodological and scientific issues. For Brain, who has long been puzzled by the events of perception, the phenomenon of consciousness, and the problems involved in the question of how we ever get to know "externality," only a central, cortical "explanation" will suffice. He has insisted that experiences of awareness of the world are constructed only out of cortical events. In short, there is one "reality," consisting of cortical events within each of us; the other, external reality, is never "known" by us in terms of our percepts. We receive sensory input only on the basis of energy which has taken time to reach us, for example, light energy from stars known to be extinct or sound energy from a moving object which reaches us when the object is no longer in the same position. We "know," therefore, only past events. Brain, like Hirst, also stressed the fact that the nature of the neural impulse is the *same*, no matter what the source of energy. Neural impulses, in turn, differ from the cortical events and also from our awareness of these events. How does this happen? Central processes alone "reconstruct" these impulses and give rise to consciousness, creating an experiential world which is individual and subjective, for we can never really "know" the world out there.

## THEORIES OF PERCEPTION

Our basic question is: Does personality influence perception? Furthermore, what do we know of the field of perception, anyway? Is there general agreement about the influence of past needs, events, and experience on contemporary perceptual events? Are the projective techniques tests of perception? To answer these questions we need to survey various theories that have been proposed.

*Core-Context Theory.* This is one of the classical theories of perception which will be described briefly to set the stage for some of the other approaches to be described subsequently. Core-context theory (see Boring, 1942) grew out of an historical orientation in which "awareness" and consciousness were considered to be the basic subject matter of psychology and introspection was the chief methodological tool.[3] Phenomenology (reported experience) had also been the primary indicator in the earlier period of psychophysical experimentation. These earlier researches studied the relationship between reported perceptual experience and variations in stimulus energy, a parallelism which circumvented the question of brain processes and neurophysiological mechanisms. Core-context theorists, as did the psychophysicists, assumed that "something" was happening inside the organism which somehow or other ran "parallel" to both stimulation and conscious experience; what this was, was left to the physiologist. As we shall see, various perceptual theories handle this problem in different ways. Many theoreticians believe that a theory may be adequate to explain the same phenomena on various levels; and that the test of the theory is not its applicability to molecular problems, when it is, after all, a molar theory.

An introspective, "active" approach on the part of S was the essential means by which a perceptual event was analyzed into its components (elements), later to be synthesized again. These elements were felt to be the essential aspects of the mind; laws of attention and association were constructed to explain how these elements were combined. Titchener, whose name is associated with this theory (along with Wundt and Külpe) had early in the twentieth century isolated sensations, images, and feelings as basic elements, with sensations being the es-

---

[3] A contemporary approach to perception utilizing a decidedly introspectionistic procedure can be found in the work of Zener and Gaffron (1962). These authors have developed an approach to pictorial perception which utilizes the phenomenological experiences of the observer as the basic data for study. In this approach, the type of "looking behavior" employed by the observer is thoroughly analyzed. The authors have attempted to demonstrate the significant role these variations in "looking behavior" play with respect to the kinds of perceptual experiences reported. One feature of this orientation is a stress on sociocultural variations in "looking behavior" which are thought to result in concomitant variations in reported perceptual experience with respect to certain types of pictorial material.

sential ingredient of mental activity. Further study of sensation into *its* component elements yielded various dimensions, such as quality, intensity, duration, clearness. This dimensionalism, however, failed to account for the association between, or the linking of elements, into larger aggregates, that is, perception. For Titchener, this was accomplished by means of various laws which connected sensory dimensions to each other, and through various laws of attention. But, since perception (as well as ideas) had meaning, Titchener became concerned with how meaning becomes associated with sensations, for he felt, as did many others, that a perceptual event was more than the passive reception of a stimulus. Thus, for Titchener and Wundt, sensationalism had to be transcended to explain how sensory components acquired meaning, that is, became a perceptual event. Floyd Allport (1955) has indicated in great detail how this question plagued philosophers for many decades in the eighteenth and nineteenth centuries; there were no analytic "tools" by which experimental approaches into this problem could be made.

The core-context theory, as outlined by Titchener, consisted of the way in which meaning became fused with sensations (which were grouped together according to laws of attention and connection) and images (residuals from past sensations); this was accomplished by the positing of a *context*, which served as the background of meaning which "surrounded" the "core," which was the focal group of sensations. Thus, the sensory core would be the same for individuals in similar situations; but the *context* would differ, thus explaining individual differences. Kinesthetic impulses, memory of names, words, etc., would form differing contexts for similar cores.

The perceptual aggregate, then, was thought to be comprised of elements of sensations and images, combined in various ways into a core, the context of which (also comprised of elements) provided the ultimate meaning. How this process occurred physiologically was not the concern of psychologists at that time. Analytic, introspectionist methods were the keynote of the day, however, and the problem of meaning, since its origins were not clearly understood, was never fully attacked.

*Gestalt Theory.* Gestalt theory (Ellis [1938]; Koffka [1935]; Köhler [1929]; and Wertheimer [1912]) offers a view of perception which is in direct opposition to associationist, atomist, and empiricist views of perception. Broadly philosophical in nature, with many ramifications for questions of meaning, memory, thinking, and problem-solving, the gestalt theorists offer a "point of view" as to how phenomena should be interpreted in a variety of psychological areas. Our summary will survey briefly some of the gestalt principles pertaining to perception, noting, in this connection, that the raw "datum" for the gestaltist is essentially phenomenological in nature. Intrinsic to this approach is a set of assumptions concerning cortical and central processes. These are not so much explicitly and specifically neurophysiological in nature (as is Hebb's approach, for example) as they are, once again, broad, "functional" constructs requiring more detailed exposition and clarification before they can be tested directly. Some comments will later be presented concerning the gestalt "trace" theory and the "satiation" hypothesis.

The influences of gestalt thinking have been profound and sweeping in almost all areas of psychology. Theorists such as Gibson and Hebb have been strongly influenced by the gestalt orientation despite their ultimate departure from it. Moreover, the many ingenious, inventive, illustrations and perceptual experiments which form the nucleus of gestalt demonstrations have not only contributed to clinical diagnosis, psychological testing, concepts and constructs in social psychology, etc., but have served well to highlight the complex, many-factored, puzzling nature of sensory and perceptual events.

Floyd Allport (1955) noted that 114 laws of *Gestalten* have been formulated by various writers and that many attempts have been made, including one by Boring (1942) who reduced the list to 14 basic principles, to edit these laws into a more parsimonious statement. Allport himself collapsed a bewildering array of "laws" into six basic generalizations. These can be briefly summarized as follows:

1. All experience, including perceptual experience, has *form* properties, that is, *Gestalten;* the gestalt quality of experience is paralleled by the gestalt or form qualities within the central nervous system (brain), that is, the configurational qualities of brain processes are *isomorphic* to those of the perceptual experience which accompany them. The form-qualities of a perceptual experience are independent of, and may persist independently of, the external stimulus, for they are a function of the perceiving organism, rather than the isolated parts of the stimulus.

2. The gestalt qualities of the experience (or of the brain process) are not based on a linking together of isolated parts, an interaction of elements, or in any way an additive function of parts; rather, the *whole-quality* of the experience (or of the isomorphic physiological counterpart) and the relational quality of the parts are stressed. These cannot be built up from an analysis of the parts, since the whole possesses

unique qualities which must be viewed as a whole, and which cannot be broken up, for then it becomes something else.

3. Field forces, and the concept of "field," are essential ingredients to the gestalt orientation. These are influences, continuous in nature, which maintain the equilibrium of the "whole" and which operate in terms of both perceptual experience and the physiological state of the organism.

4. The pattern of stimuli received by the organism from an external stimulus does not bear a one-to-one relationship to the perceptual experiences of the organism. Transformations and transpositions may take place which follow certain "laws." Relationships, configurations, and "whole" qualities may be preserved experientially by S, even if the parts and elements of the stimulus pattern undergo various changes.

5. Figures or configurations which are perceived (as well as underlying brain processes) tend to follow certain laws of "good form." The organism tends to organize his perceptions so that "good form" is maintained in terms of balance, symmetry, simplicity, closure, articulation from the ground, etc.

6. The organism tends to organize the field and the configuration into groups, combinations, etc., that is, to give it "structure"; there are laws of organization which determine this structure, for example, similarity, good continuation, common fate, and proximity.

As noted earlier, the early gestaltists such as Köhler and Koffka reacted against the elementarism of the associationists, behaviorists, and empiricists. How could the empiricists explain, for example, a wide variety of perceptual events, such as the whole character and stability of some perceptual experiences despite changes in proximal stimulus pattern? They vehemently introduced the notion that perceptual experiences were not learned, and that "interpretations" from past experience were irrelevant. Many perceptual phenomena such as the constancies are innate, in that they cannot be reduced to more basic elements of time or space, nor are they explainable by peripheral (such as retinal) events; cortical rather than proximal events are the essential substance of the perceptual experience. Although many of the gestalt examples are given in the field of vision, their theory applies to other sensory modalities as well.

Intrinsic to and necessary for some of the gestalt tenets is a trace theory of brain excitation. Forms which are experienced tend to persist through time and are subject to retention and recall; *traces* are residuals in the brain of earlier stimulations and retain, isomorphically, some of the properties of the original perceptual event. Temporal successions of stimulation are translated into *spatial* properties in the brain via traces; and through time, traces themselves tend to follow certain laws of organization—they become simpler, better organized, and tend toward "good form." It should be noted that phenomena such as memory, learning by insight, and the like, have been explained by this trace theory. In an experiment on the perceptual conditions of association, in which they demonstrated the importance of the structure of the stimulus and the coherence of its parts in memory and recall, Asch, Ceraso, and Heimer (1960) utilized the trace theory of the gestaltists to explain their results.

For an interesting, earlier use of the gestalt-trace concept to explain the relationship between cognition and perception, and especially their temporal relationship, see Wallach (1949). His view, simply stated, is that memory traces—on a very complex level, rather than a simple associationistic level—are brought into play in a perceptual event, and these may contribute to new perceptual qualities. The influence of needs on perceptual events would be explained according to Wallach by the arousal of memory traces *after* simple perception occurs, which in turn may invoke a need which then affects the more complex perceptual event. Wallach stressed the notion that sensory organization takes place first, in accordance with gestalt principles, before the memory trace is affected. There has been some criticism of the notion that a primary perceptual process can occur before there is contact with a memory trace. In this connection, Murphy (1949) noted that perception is immediate and that an interaction between perception and trace is immediate.

Another aspect of gestalt theory which will be noted only briefly, was developed by Köhler (1940), who posited several hypotheses about the brain, especially with respect to its electrochemical processes and states. These concepts are consistent with a field-theoretical approach and will not be described currently. One implication of Köhler's postulate, however, is that electrical current passing through brain tissue *alters* that tissue and creates an obstructing effect, which he called "satiation." Implications of the satiation hypothesis for perceptions of "old" and "new" figures, figure-ground reversals, and figural after-effects have been tested experimentally and in some instances confirmed (Köhler [1940]; Köhler & Wallach [1944]). In a recent survey, however, McEwen (1958) concluded that although the Köhler-Wallach hypothesis has given rise to more research than any of its competitors, the satiation effect cannot yet be measured with sufficient precision to test any one of the orthodox or new hypotheses.

Finally, to pull together some important implications of gestalt theory, two further reports will be mentioned. One is in connection with the gestalt view that perception is innately determined. For a lucid and direct statement of this position, the reader is referred to Pastore (1960), who claims that all the significant aspects of perceiving are unlearned, that is, the major features of perception are determined by the intrinsic properties of the nervous system. Learning can *modify* a perceptual act, but the origin of perceptual acts is innate. Empirical factors in perception relate to modifications, not origins of perceptual responses. The fact that such acts are modifiable is a fallacious argument on the side of empiricism, he noted. "Environmental modification of a trait does not preclude its genetic determination" (*Ibid.*, p. 94). Pastore then claimed the following points to support his thesis: perceptual functions in man and in lower animals are similar; in some species many important perceptual functions are present shortly after birth or hatching; "deprivation" studies may hamper maturational development in some species, therefore such studies provide no "proof" that learning and experiential variables determine perception; furthermore, the discrepancy between proximal stimulation and the perceptual experience as in depth perception and in the constancies can be explained not by unconscious inference, knowledge, experiential factors, probabilistic weighting of cues, etc., but by gestalt postulates—central, cortical transformations of peripheral impulses.

In the late 1940's the gestalt viewpoint came in for much criticism, mainly from the camp of the "New Look" perceptionists.[4] Luchins (1951), in answering these criticisms, highlighted the essential orientation of the gestaltists. He claimed that gestalt psychology *is* dynamic, but that motivation is not always from within, and that perception is not always social, defensive, and psychoanalytic. He opposed the limits set by the overly simple New Look splitting of forces into those from within (needs, often with disruptive or maladaptive results) and those from without. In addition, structural and autochthonous factors vs. functional factors, as a dichotomy, results in separatist thinking; perception is a unity, not a composite of elements. He claimed, in opposition to the critics, that past experience *is* considered in the gestalt viewpoint, although not necessarily sheer frequency.

*Topological Field Theory.* Topological field theory is derived essentially from the works of Lewin (see Brown [1936]; Leeper [1943];

---

[4] The term "New Look," as already noted, refers to a school of perceptual theory, otherwise known as the directive-state approach, which states that needs, past experience, and personality are powerful determinants of perception. A large portion of Chapter 3 is devoted to a description and evaluation of this approach.

Lewin [1935], [1936], [1951]; and Nash [1959]), but has its roots in gestalt psychology, insofar as it stresses the dynamic structure of the field, a wholistic approach, and opposes elementarism, associationism, and learning, as explanations or descriptions of behavior. However, gestalt psychology has always stressed neurophysiology, making an attempt to bridge the gap between so-called sensation and perception in terms of what is going on in the organism, and in addition, has posited isomorphic principles of brain processes. Lewinian thinking, on the other hand, eschews this approach and is concerned primarily with molar forces, fields and "life space"—constructs which are not rooted in neurophysiology.

Lewinian topology is concerned only with phenomenological data. As will be seen later, some of its terms and concepts, although borrowed from physics, apply only to psychological and subjectively perceived aspects of the world, rather than physicalistic ones. It has been criticized precisely on this basis, for there is confusion in terms as well as in constructs and concepts. Moreover, little attention has been paid to the "inside" problem of the organism and the questions concerning the "how" of perception. As a descriptive system, Lewinian concepts have influenced the methodology, thinking, and hypotheses of many aspects of social psychology as well as the application of projective techniques. Studies of group atmosphere, group decision making, and group processes; attitude change; level of aspiration; interrupted activities (Zeigarnik effect), etc., have been either originated or stimulated and facilitated by Lewinian thinking. In addition, problems of cognition and motivation have been approached using Lewinian methods. Perception plays a key role in topology and as such, topological field theory is included with the other theoretical systems described. Field theory, however, is not a theory of perception *per se.*

One way of conceptualizing the "field" in field theory is to view the "life space" of the individual as a spatial construct, rather than in terms of quantitative units, and in terms of the experiences and perceptions of S, rather than physically or "realistically." The life space of the individual is seen as a region or field (with the individual conceived of as a point within this field). This field consists of the goals of the individual, who is regarded as showing locomotion toward these goals. Locomotion does not necessarily involve physical direction or distance, however, and activity toward a goal does not refer to physical movement.

The life space may contain subregions, barriers, and boundaries; moreover, consistent with field theory is the concept of forces and vectors which "push" the individual with varying degrees of intensity toward his goals. Perceived objects have "demand character" in varying degrees, repelling S or "inviting" S. These are described as "valences" —negative or positive. Various "tension" systems exist within a field, which seek to maintain equilibrium. Vectors and valences, it would seem, operate on S externally; but presumably, needs, internal motivations, etc., become conceptualized as external to the extent that they are part of the life space of the individual. Various regions of a field interact and affect each other until the field achieves equilibrium, that is, until field-tensions subside, and S has presumably reached his goal or resolved "tensions" by "leaving the field."

Conflict, approach-avoidance situations, etc., have been described in Lewinian terms, and clinical psychologists have often used these concepts to describe their patients' behavior or means of handling conflict. What is relevant to our survey of theories of perception is that Lewin fully recognized, and has persuaded many other psychologists to recognize also, the importance of considering the phenomenological world of the organism itself, that is, *his* way of viewing things, and *his* structure of the world around him, rather than only the physical world, with "barriers," "goals," and "valences" as seen by *others*. The popularity of this approach with psychologists searching for a projective theory is understandable since Lewinian concepts are strictly psychological and behavioral, with little implication for or interest in physiology, sensory perception, or brain processes.

*Gibson's "Psychophysics."* A provocative and inventive derivative from the gestalt position which has produced interesting methodological innovations as well as important departures from traditional thinking in this area, is that of Gibson. In the various studies executed by Gibson and his co-workers is a single, common thread: perception is a function of stimulation—and there is always some variable in stimulation which can be related to the perceptual process.

Although some reviewers have not assigned to this group of related studies and papers the status attached to the term "theory" (Floyd Allport [1955, p. 147], for example, described Gibson's approach in a footnote, whereas the approaches of other perceptual workers were exhaustively presented and appraised in hundreds of pages), the work of Gibson and his colleagues certainly seems to us to be characterized by some of the important requisites of a "theory." The narrowness of the area in which predictions stemming from Gibson's approach are possible, the concern with stimulation, defined specifically and mathematically as psychophysical, rather than physiological, the stress on *visual* perception and retinal events, and the exploration and solutions offered to problems concerning essentially *veridical* perception of things and objects in what he calls the "visual world" certainly represent a departure not only from the gestalt viewpoint but from tradition. The uniqueness of Gibson's approach should not, however, be a factor in either its description or its evaluation.

Gibson's viewpoint is best illustrated by an early work (1950) and a more recent one (1959), in which several essential elements in his approach were described. Refinements, modifications, and confirmation of basic tenets found in a series of studies over the past decade will be briefly touched on or noted. His specific views as to the need for a theory of stimulation were described earlier. Essentially, Gibson's approach rests on the following, but it should be noted that only highlights rather than complete details will be presented:

1. The chief problem in visual perception is how to account for the fact that the complex world of objects—which has depth, solidity, and distance and is three dimensional—is shown to us by projection of light on the retina, a light-sensitive, two-dimensional surface. In perception, how is the third dimension which has been "lost" in the process, "restored"? To solve this dilemma, variables of stimulation not previously stressed are emphasized. Visual space is conceived of as a continuous or adjoining surface, not as a series of discrete objects, thus constituting a complex array of continuous variations of light transmitted to the retina. Surfaces and edges are the simple, primary constituents of the visual world.

2. Even complex perceptual (phenomenological) experiences must have some correlate in stimulation. Thus, impressions of surfaces are probably textured retinal images; impressions of distance or depth may be related to increases or decreases in the density of the texture of the image. Similarly, impressions of depth at an edge of a surface, or even the edge itself, may be correlated with jumps in the gradient of the retinal image. However these correlates are explored, and whatever they may be, the basic point in Gibson's approach is that qualities of experience are in correspondence with physical stimulation, and that we need not go beyond the ocular system to demonstrate the lawfulness and orderliness of the relationship. However, and this point is stressed, the physical stimulation or stimulus-variable within the ocular system is a *correlate*, in a complex mathematical sense, not a *copy* or replication of the property in visual space to which it corresponds; neither is it a copy but only a correlate of the experience to which it gives rise. Gibson does not concern himself with so-called "inside" problems of a neurophysiological nature; just *how* the experience or aware-

ness of the three-dimensional world of real objects arises in consciousness, and by what mechanisms, do not enter into his approach. He is much more specifically oriented in a direction which implies that central and cortical processes (the cortical organization of the gestaltists) are less important than previously believed. That is, the real world around us is "specified" through variations of light of a continuous nature on the retina in such a way that the important "information" or "input" *at that level* is sufficient to "specify" the so-called higher-order perceptual experiences or qualities. Transformations, in a complex mathematical sense, of variations in the physical world (including the so-called "lost" third dimension) are found in the retinal image, which can account for any and all variations of light, dark, texture, etc., found in the real world. The complex pattern found in retinal images, thus, can be conceived of as stimulation which can be analyzed in geometric and mathematical terms. This pattern itself is a stimulus and consists of various gradients which are in correspondence to the texture, contour, and density of texture found in the visual world.

3. Gibson is furthermore concerned with what he terms "literal" perception which has to do with the visual world of color, texture, surface, edge, etc. In addition, he now distinguishes between the meaning of objects and places and that of signals and symbols, a modification of his earlier position. Furthermore, he distinguishes between the "visual field" and the "visual world." The former is the visual scene when we introspect and analyze what we see (standing upside down and analyzing the visual scene is helpful—or closing one eye with a finger before it, the way a painter does). The visual field has boundaries, a kind of flatness or certainly less depth than the visual world; parallel lines meet, objects at a distance are strikingly smaller than objects close by, objects eclipse each other, deformations and disconcerting changes in shape, size, and perspective occur with head and eye movements and visual scanning. The visual world, on the other hand, is not distorted constantly by head and eye movements. There is stability and orientation; there are no boundaries and there is depth. Objects do not eclipse one another, but are instead seen as behind or in front of each other. There is constancy of size, with distance and form and shape retaining stability despite changes in the observer's position. Gibson is primarily interested in studying the visual *world*—the experience of the world around us. He is interested in *veridical* perception, the ability of man to be aware of things as they really are—in which parallel lines do not converge, objects remain the same shape despite the position of the observer, and men remain the same size, no matter how far away they are from an observer. In this sense, his foci are different from those of

traditional perceptionists who have long been concerned with problems of the visual *field,* and who have focused attention on *non*veridical perception.

4. There follows, then, as a result of the foregoing framework, a series of more specific propositions, hypotheses, and empirical statements, some of which have to do with the nature of retinal stimulation and others with the relationship between the world "out there," the three-dimensional world, and its retinal correlates. The obscure and subtle variations of the retinal image become the chief concern of Gibson's experimental approach.

The retinal image consists of color points which may or may not be patterned. When these points are identical, the perceptual correlate is film color (as in a cloudless, blue sky or in dense fog). Gibson and Waddell (1952), for example, placed translucent half-globes over the eyes of Ss, producing homogeneous distribution of light points (*Ganzfeld*) on the retina, and found, by and large, that the absence of textures, light and dark blotches, etc., in stimulation produced the experiential or phenomenological attribute of color film—"pure" space, seen at an indeterminate distance.

On the other hand, changes or transitions in the light array of the retinal image give rise to the attributes of lines or contours; perception of surfaces arises from the quality of "texture" in the retinal image, that is, lack of homogeneity of color points in the retinal image; gradients of texture in the retinal image give rise to impressions of distance and depth (surfaces nearer to S have corresponding coarser textures in the retina than those which are farther).[5] As a matter of fact, gradients in the retinal image in general—whether or not they are abrupt or gradual, be they of texture, retinal disparity, shading, or deformation when S moves, etc.—may all be involved in the impression of distance, slant, edges, slopes, etc.

Even perception of a moving object, the perception of the motion of an object which is fluid and elastic but not in motion through space, and the perception of a stable, nonelastic object while S is moving have corresponding correlates in the retinal image which give rise to verid-

---

[5] A study which has appeared since Gibson's book (1950) has suggested that in some instances the author has overstated the simplicity of some of his original notions. Gibson, Purdy, and Lawrence (1955) worked with an "optical tunnel" which produced *synthetic* perceptions of space in order to explore assumptions about *natural* perception of space. Although visual perception did seem to have a complete basis in the nature of stimulation, fixed single point perception of gradients of texture density alone did not yield phenomenal slant and recession, i.e., the case for fixed monocular depth perception was probably initially overstated.

ical perception. These are analyzable geometrically and through an analysis of invariants in transformation. Although various geometric and mathematical transformations take place when the physical, real world is "transferred" through light energy, to the retina, that is, when three-dimensional characteristics are transformed into a two-dimensional array, certain invariant properties are present. Furthermore, *succession* of stimuli, through time, as in motion perception, is a significant feature of stimulation. The motion of S is also a variable to be considered, since, in a sense he "samples" successive families of arrays while doing so. Thus continuous sequences of textured arrays involve continuous transformations (and there are, in binocular vision, a *pair* of such continuous transformations). Gradients of density which remain invariant despite size transformations seem to be the stimulus for depth perception, as well as various gradients of motion disparity. The "constancies" of shape, velocity, etc., are similarly explained by this approach. For familiarity with some of the recent thinking and approach with regard to the question of perception of motion, depth, etc., the reader is referred to Gibson and Gibson (1957), Gibson, Gibson, Smith, and Flock (1959), and von Fieandt and Gibson (1959).

To illustrate some of the premises and foci of this approach, brief attention will be given to a few related experimental reports. Gibson and Gibson (1957) were interested in exploring the perception of a rigid surface moving in one of six ways. They studied the changes and transformations, in a geometrical sense, of various stimuli, hypothesizing that, ". . . any continuous sequence of perspective transformations is the correlate of perceptually rigid motion" (p. 129). The *form* of the changes in form, not the form itself, in the pattern of retinal stimulation focusing on a rigid, moving surface, gives rise to the perception of it. They concluded that, the "eye appears to be very sensitive to a continuous perspective transformation in the optic array. Psychophysical experiments are possible if the parameters of this stimulus are isolated and controlled" (*Ibid.*, p. 138). For a general analysis of how we see motions of objects from a Gibsonian point of view, the reader is referred to Gibson (1957).

Consistent with the approach already noted, Gibson's thesis involves the translation of motion into energy arrays on the eye, that is, the projection of physical motion which is three-dimensional into a two-dimensional array. His method is geometrical and involves an analysis of various types of perspective transformations of a continuous nature. Gibson has been able to illustrate, by use of a screen, the various parameters and types of perspective transformation adequate to give rise to impressions of a rigid surface moving in depth. He suggests that such continuous perspective transformations are precisely the stimuli, in the retinal image, for the perception of motion of a rigid surface. When transformations are *non*perspective continuous transformations, the perception is that of elastic motion ("tapered stretch"; "rubber sheet geometry"). Separate or noncontinuous transformations of a connected pattern yield a perception of two surfaces, etc. The point is, therefore, according to Gibson, that our eyes are so constructed as to be sensitive to various types of optical transformations; we do not *learn* to associate certain types of motion in the world with retinal stimulation nor does our brain organize sensory data this way. Our ability to perceive rigid, elastic, or multiple-moving things is based on the fact that three-dimensional motion can correspond geometrically to retinal two-dimensional images through transformations in the energy array.

In a series of experiments, Walk and Eleanor Gibson (1961) explored the visual factors involved in depth perception. Theirs was a comparative study of various terrestrial animals, such as hooded rats, albino rats, baby chicks, adult chickens, kids, lambs, pigs, turtles, cats, monkeys, and human infants. Their basic procedure involved the use of a "visual cliff"—an apparatus which provides for "drop-offs" of graduated heights, with a short drop at one and a steep drop at the other side, covered by transparent glass so that though the animal sees the cliff, it will not fall. Animals, if responding to visual cues, should prefer the short drop-off to the long one. The apparatus and general experimental procedure controlled or eliminated all nonvisual cues which could permit distinction between the deep and shorter drop-offs; pretraining was not required; and all Ss were tested with essentially the same apparatus. According to Walk and Gibson, evolutionary theory suggests that by the time animals are ready for independent locomotion (and this occurs at different ages for the different species) unlearned discrimination for perception of depth at a drop-off would be present and effective. Obviously, lack of such discriminative ability is dangerous and maladaptive for terrestrial animals. The optical cues explored, which proved to be effective in this type of discrimination, were: differences in density in optical texture (both sides of the visual cliff were patterned in a similar way); motion parallax (differential velocity of elements in the optical array); and binocular parallax (there are overlapping visual fields in the species tested).

Walk and Gibson wondered whether or not this type of discrimination is present in animals from various species and at various ages; would there be a tendency to avoid a drop-off? What optical cues contribute to effective discrimination? Does visual experience play a role in effecting this type of discrimination? Their results showed that all the animals studied did display capacity for discrimination of depth "at the visual cliff" in varying degrees of accuracy. The chick and the goat, as a matter of fact, displayed excellent discrimination only a few hours after they were born. Monkeys, human infants, and kittens, on the other hand, were "late maturers," but the first two are carried by their mothers for a considerably long time before locomotion is independent, and the last ordinarily remain hidden in a dark place for some time before getting about.

Thus, by the time locomotion is present, all the animals displayed discrimination of visual depth, although the time for independent locomotion varied from species to species. The various studies reported by Walk and Gibson also indicated that motion perspective is probably more effective than density perspective in making this kind of discrimination. The authors, on the basis of additional findings, concluded, "The results in general support a hypothesis of innate depth perception, though the presence of certain kinds of environment during growth may be important for late maturing animals. Furthermore, it has been shown that innate mechanisms for discriminating depth may be supplemented by the acquisition of a learned cue" (p. 42). In general, studies such as these illustrate the overall Gibsonian approach: various aspects of visual impressions are paralleled by analyzable and specific components of the visual environment. Visual experience is directly traceable to stimulation. The components of such stimulation can be simulated in the laboratory, giving rise to the same visual impressions as are experienced in the visual world.

The Gibsonian viewpoint, thus, involves a kind of nativism as well as an isomorphism, but of a different nature from that of the gestaltists. The isomorphism is, of course, a kind of "identity" (or parallelism) between the real, physical world, retinal images, and the experiences to which they give rise. Transformations occur in an analyzable, mathematical sense, however.[6] In Gibson's approach to veridical perception, there is a de-emphasis of central factors, learning and subjective need-states, and a corresponding stress on stimulation, that is, on retinal stimulation.

As is already evident, Gibson has some interesting views about the role of learning in perception; his views are anti-associationistic. Learn-

---

[6] The reader is advised that the foregoing presentation of Gibson's theoretical structure is sketchy; important areas have been excluded in our presentation. For example, the *type* of geometrical analyses (non-Euclidean) of transformations that take place is not discussed; the principles involved are not completely worked out, however.

ing in perception, according to Gibson, is of a different order than commonly believed. Even if *cues* are coded in accordance with social agreement, incoming data from the *sensory* level are not. Although effects of earlier stimulation on later stimulation can be viewed, in a sense, as learning, they may actually be instances of continuous changes in the stimulation pattern to which S is responding. Gibson raises the question: how far back in the past must an event be in order to be regarded as past experience? Gibson (1959) believes that repetition of stimulation may result in "learning" in the sense that the organism "adjusts" to or discovers new ways of fixating, listening, etc., that is, he is attending to more and more detail in the complex stimulation around him. Thus, discrimination is increased.

Although Gibson does not deny the importance of memory, recall, etc., these, not being a function of external stimulation, are for him outside the realm of perception. Moreover, he stresses the fact that the sensory equipment of an organism determines and limits the kind of perception that can occur; set and attention are similarly significant, since what S is responding to may differ from individual to individual. Defects of a sensory or central nature, failure in discriminatory responses, etc., may also reduce veridical perception.

The Gibsonian approach, then, stated quite simply, is that perception can be viewed as a function of the environment, since perception is a function of stimulation and stimulation a function of the environment. As is already obvious, this represents a departure from the mainstream of perceptual theory. Central and neural processes are not stressed; the role of learning, memory, and association in forming percepts is minimized; and the traditional distinction and dichotomy between sensation and perception fades away. Methodologically, Gibson suggests the exploration of special techniques for studying the relevant aspects of gradients, ratios, rates, etc., in the energy array that is found in natural stimulation. He suggests producing these artificially in the laboratory in order to explore psychophysical relationships. The basic assumption is that for every phenomenal attribute with which the organism endows objects in the environment (solidity, surface, distance, movement, etc.) a correlate or corresponding variable, albeit complex, can be found in the "energy flux" at his receptors.

This general approach, then, has stressed the importance of stimulation in perception, especially veridical perception. Although limited in what perceptual phenomena it covers (illusions, perceptions of verbal meanings, attention, selective processes, etc., are not completely covered), its rich detail, as well as special focus, provide lessons to be learned and an approach to be considered in working with projective techniques. For the Rorschach in particular, a question emerges. Do not the *content* and *meaning* (i.e., cognitive) aspects offer, after all, the significant areas of deviation which can be analyzed psychometrically and used for the prediction of individual differences? Perhaps we all "see" the Rorschach blots in a similar way; norms for communality are essential, then, in this sense. The S's task is to *interpret*, however. What are the significant features for clinical prediction, of this interpretive process? Which responses can be attributed almost directly, in the Gibsonian sense, to what the stimulus array specifies? Chapter 5 raises some of these questions again.

*Sensory-tonic Field Theory.* Werner and Wapner, in the 1940's, introduced an approach to perceptual phenomena which they labeled the *sensory-tonic* theory. (See Floyd Allport [1955, pp. 184–194]; Crandell [1961]; Goldman [1953]; Krus, Werner, & Wapner [1953]; and Werner & Wapner [1949], [1952], [1956].) Their dilemma, out of which grew a series of experiments all within the same theoretical framework, was how to integrate within a single approach the "paradox of interaction." How, in a perceptual event, do the sensory processes in the visual or tactual areas become fused or integrated with presumably alien elements such as emotion or motivation? For Werner and Wapner, consideration of such "broad" constructs as personality, attitudes, and emotions was not the primary element in their theoretical approach. Rather (and in this respect, note the similarity to Freeman's perceptual theory of set and motor adjustments—see later section), this integration was achieved by postulating the "equivalence" of tonic and sensory elements in the perceptual event.

(The interaction between tonus and sensory stimulation had already been demonstrated by Magnus [1924], Metzger [1931], Sherrington [1906], and Stein [1910]. For example, strong illumination of one eye causes a one-sided increase of body tonus, which can be measured by the tendency to fall to the illuminated side. Similarly, auditory stimuli have a tonus-producing effect. On the other hand, tonus can produce effects on sensory organization. One of the earliest demonstrations of the influence of tonus on perception was made by Mach. He fixated the eyes of his subject to one extreme side by means of putty. With their eyes thus immobilized they were asked to look toward the other side. They reported that objects looked displaced in that direction. It was concluded that space perception emerges from the impulse necessary for the execution of eye movements.)

Werner and Wapner have gone "inside" the individual, not from a neurological or even a physiological point of view (as in Hebb's theory) but, nevertheless, for a consideration of all motor events within the organism. Tonic states are broadly defined. They include motor activity, postural states, proprioceptive impulses, skeletal movements, and muscular activities. Emotional states, drives, motivational sets, and the like, presumably affect the organism's sensory-tonic state.

The authors are opposed to the traditional separation of sensory and motor functions. They and their co-workers define perception as a total dynamic process that can be empirically broken up into contributing factors that are both tonic and sensory. Tonic and sensory factors are dynamically equivalent, and evidence is cited from the neurophysiological area to support the notions of equivalence and interaction.

From a wide and ingenious group of experiments, certain postulates and generalizations have emerged: (a) any stimulation, whether from extero-, proprio-, or intero-ceptors is sensory-tonic in nature; (b) the percept, or properties of an object, is a resultant of stimulation from that object and its affect on the existing sensory-tonic state of the organism and the subsequent manner in which the organism reacts to it; (c) the organism always reacts to establish equilibrium between body and object; (d) there is a functional equivalence between sensory and muscular (tonic) factors; and (e) from the preceding postulate, the notion of *vicariousness* emerges—that is, equivalent functions may serve as substitutes for each other with respect to an end product. A corollary of postulate (e) is that sensory-tonic energy is available which not only may be released through different channels, but, if one channel is not utilized, substitute channels will be.

From the latter postulate a large group of laboratory demonstrations and experiments have accumulated which show that inhibition of one aspect of the sensory-tonic field has resulted in an increase of channelized energy into the other. For example, Krus, Werner, and Wapner (1953) demonstrated that motor activity of Ss prior to a perceptual task resulted in a significant decrease of perception of movement in a static visual field, as measured by verbal responses to pictorial material. Vicarious channelization of energy was also demonstrated by Goldman (1953), who utilized the autokinetic effect. In Goldman's study, greater amounts of motor involvement in Ss were accompanied by reduction of the autokinetic effect as measured by reaction time, duration, and complexity of pattern. The postulated inverse relationship between amount of perceptual movement and motor activity was also tested and generally confirmed in a large group of related studies which utilized Rorschach M and Rorschach experience-type. (See Levine & Meltzoff [1956]; Meltzoff & Levine [1954]; Meltzoff & Litwin [1956]; Meltzoff, Singer, & Korchin [1953]; Singer & Herman [1954]; Singer, Meltzoff, &

Goldman [1952]; Singer & Spohn [1954]; and Werner & Wapner [1956].)

Werner and Wapner (1956), in reviewing some of the foregoing studies, noted that in light of the release or inhibition of motor activity and its consequent effect on movement perception, it was important to conclude that Rorschach performance is strongly affected by *other* than basic characteristics of personality. Yet they did not overlook the possibility, even early in the development of their theory (although their experimental work did not directly stress this), that their approach contained rather direct implications for directive-state theory, that is, sensory-tonic theory offered possibilities for explanations of higher or more complex levels of behavior:

It might not be too bold to assume that attitudes and motivations affect the "sensory-tonic" (particularly viscerotonic) state of the organism, and it is through these basic mechanisms that attitudes or motivations may "project" themselves into perceptual objects. Thus somatotonic and viscero-tonic events may be specifically expressed, projected or channelized at a higher level in accord with the specific—transient or enduring—need structure of the individual (Werner & Wapner [1949], p. 104).

Other basic postulates of sensory-tonic field theory have also been supported by a large number of experiments and demonstrations. For example, many studies have shown that both sensory (e.g., auditory) and tonic (direct muscular) factors have affected S in identical ways, resulting in similar perceptual changes. The equivalence of sensory and tonic events has been demonstrated in various studies of space perception, size and form; bodily tilt has been shown to affect visual perception of verticality in an opposite direction (Werner, Wapner, & Chandler [1951]); and the same has been found for the influence of acceleration in bodily rotation (Wapner, Werner, & Morant, 1951). Additional evidence for the effectiveness of sensory-tonic theory as an explanatory principle has been claimed on the basis of perceptual studies with subjects of various ages. Developmental changes in perceptual processes were explained in terms of sensory-tonic theory.

Despite the ingeniousness and inclusiveness of sensory-tonic theory in explaining many perceptual events, Werner and Wapner have failed to show *how* the interaction between sensory and tonic factors takes place. Moreover, the notion of functional and dynamic equivalence of sensory and tonic factors is probably *descriptive* of events rather than a direct statement of neurophysiological happenings and processes. Yet the importance of this approach should not be minimized. The influence of motor states, intersensory effects, tonic states, and set, on the perceptual event, has been more than adequately demonstrated by these authors through a series of related, well-controlled, and well-designed experiments with clear-cut terms, definitions, and predictions.

*Adaptation-level Theory.* Helson's theory (see Floyd Allport [1955, pp. 243–246]; Helson [1948], [1951], and [1953]; and Helson & Nash [1960]) is concerned with a generally accepted notion that individuals, in their perceptions, tend to utilize some sort of subjective frame of reference by which they judge objects as to dimensionality—size, weight, value, etc. For Helson, this frame of reference is based not only on the experiences of S in the past, but on all stimuli affecting him in the present.[7] But Helson's notions do not stop here. He has conceived of a quantitative model to explain how this process works—a model in which the concept of adaptation level is of prime importance.

All individuals *order* their experiences on the basis of a neutral zone, which varies for each individual. This neutral zone, to which the individual is adapted, is called the adaptation level. Adaptation level is conceived by Helson to be a kind of average—a weighted mean function not only of present stimuli but of all past stimuli, around which S can judge or order dimensionality of the stimuli to which he is responding. In terms of Helson's actual experiments, adaptation level is given the value of the stimulus (in a series) to which S responds neutrally (e.g., neither large nor small, but medium), when he is qualitatively or quantitatively rating stimuli. These judgments or ratings are bipolar: large and small, good and bad, heavy or light, etc. Adaptation levels change according to changes in the background, stimuli, etc., and this neutral category is never at the center or the arithmetic mean of a series. Helson further indicates that preponderant stimuli—because of their intensity, emotional significance, impact, and the like—should not be regarded as the sole determiners of adaptation level. He stresses the importance of considering *all* stimuli:

Actually numerous experiments indicate that the adaptation-level is determined by all stimuli attended to in the field, by background stimuli, and by residuals from past experiences with similar stimuli, so that the effect of preponderant stimuli, while tending to raise or lower the level in their own direction, depends upon the way they are figured against the general level (Helson, 1953, p. 36).

Helson's view of crucial stimuli as determinants of S's response (and essentially, he is interested in S's *ordering* or scaling of responses) is

---

[7] Note the similarity—in a general sense—to some of Sherif's concepts concerning social norms and frames of reference (Sherif & Sherif, 1956).

rather broad; he feels that automatically acting forces as well as rational and cognitive factors determine adaptation level. Stimuli to which S is responding, background stimuli and residuals from previous stimuli affect S's response. Moreover, frequency, nearness, spacing, etc., all enter into the picture. All these factors are "pooled," and the pooling is accomplished quantitatively. "Pooling" is not a conscious process and is physiological as well as psychological.

As seen by the foregoing brief account, Helson is puzzled, as are so many of the perception theorists, by how past experience influences contemporary behavior. He has described a model which *does* seem to work, when judgments of a set of pitches, weights, sizes, heights, and the like, are considered. But Helson has indicated (see especially [1953]) that his concepts of "pooling" and adaptation level also are applicable to an understanding of how residuals from past experience, needs, ego-involvement and various cognitive states (e.g., "personality") enter into S's contemporary judgments and percepts.

Some methodological problems and difficulties in the statistical treatment of data arising from studies using absolute judgments (single stimuli) and shifts in these judgments as a result of anchor and social stimuli were discussed in detail by Salzinger (1956). In all, nine statistical methods were discussed in terms of merits, disadvantages, and statistical assumptions, for various types of experimental conditions. Salzinger (1957) also reported a study of differences between a matched group of normals and schizophrenics in an experimental situation employing a modification of the method of absolute judgments of weight. Two conflicting "anchor" stimuli were used: a verbal stimulus (E's instructions) telling S not to shift; and a physical weight stimulus (very heavy or very light) preceding the test stimulus in the series. Salzinger hypothesized that if the verbal stimulus is viewed as abstract, and the physical stimulus as concrete, following Goldstein's thinking (1944), schizophrenic Ss would shift more than the normal Ss. Furthermore, he hypothesized that schizophrenics could not maintain constancy of judgment (with and without the physical anchor) as well as normals. Another hypothesis (following Rado [1953]) was that proprioceptive difficulties are innate schizophrenic traits; therefore, in judging weights, there would be more errors in absolute judgments among schizophrenics than among normals.

When results of both a test and a retest condition were combined, schizophrenics were found to have shifted significantly more in the "heavy anchor" condition than normals, but not in the "light anchor" condition. An examination of the data suggested that differences between normal and schizophrenic reactions to the experimental conditions in the second session were less dramatic than in the first session. Salzinger's second hypothesis as to poorer kinaesthetic sense in schizophrenics as compared to normals was not confirmed. He concluded that this study provided "evidence for the theory that schizophrenics are more prone to react to concrete than to abstract stimuli, as well as for the theory that schizophrenics are less able to maintain constancy in weight judgment than normals" (1957, p. 48).

Although there is much laboratory support for Helson's model, this evidence comes especially and essentially from experiments on sensory dimensionality. The extent to which Helson's concepts are applicable to broader aspects of perception and to the perception of complex patterns and figures is not clear; moreover, just *how* pooling takes place, neurologically and physiologically speaking, that is, how all the elements in the background, residuals from the past, and in the stimuli to which S is responding combine and interact, is not within the scope of the theory.

*Cell Assembly Phase Sequence Theory.* Hebb, in his book, *The Organization of Behavior* (1949), presented an approach to perception which is also concerned with past experience. Unlike Helson's theory, however, his approach is more associationistic. Hebb is specifically concerned with *how* behavior patterns are built up. Even more important, his approach goes "inside" the organism, for he has definite views on neurophysiological process.

Hebb feels that initially, perception is not a complete, "given" event, as the gestaltists have claimed; perception is a learned affair. Infants, he states, probably go through a complex, piecemeal learning process which is not apparent when the adult, spontaneous, simple perceptual response is studied. Eye movement and excitations from parts of the stimulus figure are important aspects of the learning process; after perceptions are learned, these become extremely rapid and unconscious. Wholes, for Hebb, are built up from the parts, through a process of learning, an associationistic process—a view which is in marked contrast to that of the gestaltists.

Hebb's major theoretical contribution is a model, in terms of brain processes, of how this learning takes place. He does not concur with Lashley's earlier views and those of others, as to brain "equipotentiality," that is, a view of brain process which suggests that the amount of cortical activity involved rather than the specific localization is important, and that different parts of the brain may serve equally well as others in the formation and "storage" of a habit. Hebb, on the contrary, feels that a perceptual event is quite specific to the excitation of particular cells in a particular part of the central nervous system (CNS). Specifically, the short-lived excitation of cells in the cortex activate neighboring cells, and when this is repeated sufficiently an association will occur between these cells (explained neurologically) as well as more distant cells, so that a long-lasting *cell-assembly* emerges. A cell assembly is a group of cortical neurons functionally connected to each other, not initially but through learning, in the sensory-sensory or sensory-motor context. As a unit of perception, the cell-assembly is defined by Hebb in specific neurological terms as to function, structure, and process; the cell-assembly represents the neurophysiological basis for the most simple percepts. More complex percepts are built up from the cell-assemblies in a similar manner. The neurological structure and basis for more complex percepts are called *phase sequences.*

On the basis of a rather complex, detailed, and lengthy utilization of these two basic constructs, cell-assembly and phase sequence, Hebb explained how perceptions of various types of figures are built up, for example, a triangle. Eye movements and specific, localized cortical excitations are intrinsic aspects of this process, and the simple perceptual event, the seeing of a triangle, is built up only after a process of extremely complex and gradual cortical associations.

Hebb's theoretical approach is designed to subsume much more than perception. Constructs such as attention, motivation, learning, and emotion, are also explained by Hebb, in terms of excitation, activation, disruption, etc., of cell-assemblies and phase sequences.

Hebb's theory is connectionistic, involving *specific* cortical associations. As such, it stands in contrast to many beliefs of the gestaltists, as well as of those who point to evidence which suggests brain equivalence and equipotentiality. Yet, Hebb, unlike many of his fellow theorists, has made an attempt to bring neurophysiology and the cortex into perception, not as an intervening variable, but as the primary and crucial aspect of the perceptual event.

*Set; Freeman's Theory.* This section will serve to introduce the question of set and "preparatory" variables in the perceptual event. Specifically, Freeman's approach will be presented. Another important theory of set, Bruner's "hypothesis" or "expectancy" theory, will be presented in a subsequent section in a review of directive-state studies. Bruner's theoretical approach could also be described in the current section, and the comments and rationale for a theory of set apply also to his position.

The student of psychology knows the importance of set (or prevailing state or attitude) in almost all phases of behavior—memory, learning, motor behavior, and the like. He utilizes certain principles of set in the instructions he gives to his Ss when he tests or experiments. There is much experimental evidence to show that the organism is "tuned" to react before it reacts, and that this, in part, determines the reaction. Some of this literature has disclosed that preparatory set often facilitates the act it is accompanying, and may sometimes precede, or even outlast that act. This facilitation might involve temporal factors, magnitude of the behavior, energy involved, etc. Sets also act selectively, in that other acts will be excluded or inhibited. They involve the "attentive" aspects of the organism and contain sensory, as well as motor elements. Thus Ss can be prepared or "tuned" to expect a certain stimulus or to react in a certain way. It seems likely that in perception both aspects are involved. Many other principles of set that have been described but which will not be presented here in detail include facts such as: sets can be generalized, getting set may either be voluntary or involuntary, and sets can be instituted in a variety of ways—through instruction, implicit expectation, needs, and motivations. Sets may be one way of "explaining" the influence of past needs and current motivational states on a *contemporary* perceptual event and thus are important in the understanding of responses to projective techniques.

In a series of experiments which, when grouped together, contribute to his motor-adjustment theory, Freeman (1939, 1948) outlined many of the principles governing "set" and their applicability to perception. His point, in general, is that motor adjustments play a significant part in perception, especially meaning. Muscular reactions are involved in all perceptual responses, and "backlash" from muscular tensions into the CNS contributes to the state of the CNS when it is receiving impulses from exteroceptive sources. Thus, motor adjustments, which include not only generalized and diffuse muscular tension but also specific muscular tensions, contribute to the final perceptual integration.

The similarity between sensory-tonic theory and Freeman's theory should be noted; both stress the relevance of muscular tension, tonicity, and "backlash" in the final integration of the percept. Freeman's theory, however, as well as that of Werner and Wapner, fails to show us *how* the motor and sensory finally become fused and integrated. Freeman's work, nevertheless, is particularly important in highlighting the pervasiveness and importance of set in terms of behavior—an area which many theorists have ignored or failed to account for adequately.

*Cybernetics.* Cybernetic theory is an attempt to further our understanding of central brain processes through use of models derived essentially from machines involving steering or regulatory feedback mechanisms.

Engineers, physiologists, and mathematicians rather than psychologists have been largely responsible for developing this approach. In the 1940's, workers such as Wiener (1948) and McCulloch and Pitts (1948) wrote about the vast implications for human behavior found in the study, operation, and design of electronic computers. Since that time many other workers have become fascinated by the theoretical possibilities which the analysis of electronic computers offers with respect to the operations and functions of the brain, and to the regulations, controls, and communications that take place in that system.

Cyberneticists, in their study of various systems, open and closed, have been struck with similarities to actual brain processes. They have stressed the importance of examining and studying various processes of the brain such as input, output, information (stimulation), "noise" (random, irrelevant stimuli), decisions, choice, and processing and transmission of information. In other words, the types of internal, regulatory mechanisms of the brain are examined in terms of the principles already known about electronic machines.

In terms of perceptual theory, an important contribution of the cyberneticist is the concept of feedback, both positive and negative. This concept stresses the interdependence and circularity of the parts of the perceptual process, although others (such as Freeman, Werner, and Wapner) have also long been aware of this aspect of perceptual functioning. Feedback further describes how a system can have internal controls and regulatory mechanisms, so that deviations from a desired goal are constantly being eliminated in the execution of a process. Neurophysiologists also have been aware of this process for some time despite the fact that perceptual theorists have not always accounted for this kind of regulatory circularity ("steering").

Von Holst (1954) for example, illustrating with experiments and observations of lower and higher animals as well as man, outlined a theory of perception which makes use of "feedback" from CNS activity. He noted that motor impulses from the CNS as well as from the "outside" affect sensory receptors; those impulses arising from the CNS he called re-afference; the latter he called ex-afference. In other words,

The same receptor can serve both the re- and the ex-afference. The CNS must, however, possess the ability to distinguish one from the other. This distinction is indispensable for every organism, since it must correctly perceive its environment at rest and in movement, and stimuli resulting from its own movements must not be interpreted as movements of the environment (*Ibid.*, p. 89).

A paraphrased and considerably reduced version of von Holst's position would be this. He is simply suggesting that the CNS makes comparisons between an effector *command* (motor impulse) and the actual stimulation of a sensory receptor by the effector *movement* (re-afference) made in carrying out this command. This comparison yields "information," utilized by the CNS, which can account for various previously unexplained phenomena. In fact, he has specified the manner in which discrepancies or lack of discrepancies can affect behavior.

Many phenomena in lower animals are explained by von Holst's hypothesis, but the specific assumption of an "efference copy"—an image in the CNS as a result of a motor command and matched by the re-afference, is proven, according to the author, by certain specific demonstrations with humans.

One illustration refers to the well-known phenomenon that individuals with paralyzed eye muscles experience the perception of the surroundings jumping or moving in the direction of the intended (but not fulfilled) movements. In this instance, the efference copy (EC) is produced, but the lack of muscular movement in the eye does not produce a matching re-afference. The efference copy is thus not canceled, but is transmitted to higher centers, producing a perception. "Since here *nothing* happens on the afferent pathways, this false perception can only result from the activity, originated by the intention of the eye movement, being returned to higher centres. This is another way of saying that the unmatched efference-copy causes the perception" (*Ibid.,* p. 93).

Now if the paralyzed eye is mechanically turned to the right, the surroundings jump or move to the left—a false perception. This would be consistent with von Holst's expectations, that is, the motor intention and efference copy are not present (the eye was mechanically moved) but there is afference, now unmatched with an efferent copy, and a "minus" false percept of movement in the opposite direction results.

When the first and second conditions are met, the following should occur according to von Holst's reasoning, and indeed it *does* occur! If the eye is moved mechanically to the right at the same time that there is an *intention* of movement, the two "false perceptions" noted above cancel each other—and there is no perception of anything moving. This is exactly what happens in normal vision, and although this results in a correct perception, it is based on two false perceptions. Constancy effects are thus explained by this worker.

Von Holst presented other illustrations of the role that re-afference plays in behavior. Various perceptual experiences can result without ex-afference. Motor impulses which initiate a muscular movement can have an effect on sensory receptors, and can limit the magnitude of a movement or insure constancy in the perceived surroundings during movement; real and apparent motion of objects can be differentiated, and various false perceptions can be explained. The circularity of efferent and afferent impulses and their interdependence were thus stressed by von Holst.

The problems of constancies in perception were handled by Pitts and McCulloch (1947) through use of rather complex models and concepts such as transformations, storage of information, invariants, and scanning. An example of the use of probability theory and information theory in application to problems in visual perception might be found in the work of Fitts, Weinstein, Rappaport, Anderson, and Leonard (1956), who worked with a variety of visual samples of a "parent" population to get sets of figures. They used a probability approach based on information theory and statistical learning theory (Attneave, 1954), with precise control over the probability characteristics of the stimuli they used. They were able to develop a system whereby an almost unlimited number of stimuli with controlled and known characteristics could be produced. (Note relationship of this to Brunswik's ecological sampling—see p. 97.) These characteristics could be described (and were) in terms of redundancy, information necessary to specify them, noise (any source not coherent with the "signal or message," i.e., interference with maximum communication, as in audition), complexity, etc. Experiments based on these controlled stimuli, that is, recognition, were offered as a model to indicate how some of these communication and information variables can be related to S's response.

Cyberneticists, thus, have much to say, on a microscopic, neurophysiological level about the operations and processes of the brain. According to Floyd Allport (1955), much of this material is in agreement with known facts of neurophysiology; yet, the contrast between the organism and the machine is great, and the problem of meaning has not been attacked by cyberneticists. Furthermore, cyberneticists offer a contribution to the study of brain processes primarily, rather than of the organism and the interdependence of its parts (including the brain). This is a serious limitation on the applicability of their work to the interests of most psychologists.

*Allport's Theory of Event Structure.* Floyd Allport (1955) not only wrote a remarkable and extensive review and critique of current perceptual theories, but on the basis of common threads and findings cutting across all theoretical fields, he constructed a theory of his own. His theory is essentially a model which describes processes within the organism in terms of "ongoings" and "events." It is nonquantitative, dynamic, and yet quite concerned with structure, albeit complex. Processes are cyclical; there is attention to motor adjustments, set and the state of the organism at the time of a perceptual event. Each "ongoing" consists of lower-order ongoings and they, in turn, of still lower-order ongoings. Events "happen" when ongoings "touch" each other. Allport's system will not be described. Suffice it to say, however, that he has attempted to account for set, native dispositions, the operation of personality and even society, in his all-inclusive system of event structure. In his system, he has been influenced by cybernetics, advanced thinking in physics, as well as some of the biological sciences. It is too early to evaluate his system, and Allport himself has not proposed or even stated his theory in terms of testable hypotheses.

*Perception and Behavior Theory.* Before we review directive-state approaches, a brief presentation will be made of the views of the behaviorist. Behaviorism today is chiefly expounded by the learning theorist. We will make no attempt to describe the *specific* views of the major "schools" of learning theory, nor of the specific writings of some of the exponents of various positions. In a section on Perceptual Learning in Chapter 3, some relevant material will be raised again. In our discussion at the end of Chapter 3, attention will be drawn to the views of Schoenfeld and Cumming (1963), not only as a "model" of a behavioristic approach, but also for some of the lessons that can be learned for our purposes. Indeed, the paradigm offered by these workers will be utilized as a framework for some of the discussion at that time.

As obvious as it may be, we might state at the risk of oversimplification, that one behavioristic view of perception is that it is a response, and as such, no different from other classes of response. The laws and principles of learning apply equally well to this class of response as to others—and *should* be applied. For the learning theorist, perceptual research, theory, and explanatory constructs have been clouded with mysteries, vagueness of terms, and phenomenology, but this may have been the result of misplaced zeal in constructing "separate" theories of perception; "theories of perception," as such, are deemed unnecessary by many behaviorists.

From this vantage point, phenomenology fades away. This is a sorry plight for introspectionism, "subjective experience," "awareness," etc. —these being irrelevant as either sources of data or meaningful content for psychological study. True, verbal responses, motor responses, muscular responses, etc., may be viewed by some *E*s as indicating the perceptual event, but in the last analysis the laws of behavior are laws of *responses*, and any inferences about perceptual events or occurrences may be invalid.

As a matter of fact, perception plays a secondary role in the behaviorist's theater, occupying at the very best only a small part of the stage. Along with perception, goes the sensation-perception dichotomy. Attention to "inside" neurophysiological variables is minimized, "upstaged," as it were, by a troupe of intervening variables.

Many contemporary behaviorists view the constancies, figure-ground perception, indeed the entire gamut of the classical perceptual domain as instances of learning—that is, as learned responses. Nativism, either of the gestalt variety or of the Gibsonian, is viewed with skepticism, if not alarm, and learning theory in its various forms dominates the scene. Stimuli are distal. They can be any or all "things" which $E$ can manipulate experimentally (independent variable) and by doing so produce change in the response (dependent variable).

# 3 PERCEPTION:

*an approach to personality?* PART II

Chapter 3 continues our survey of perceptual theories with special attention to those probably more directly related to the interests of workers in the fields of personality, clinical psychology, and projective techniques.

*Functionalism.* Functionalism, in perceptual theory, derives its name from a viewpoint which stresses function (purpose or result) of the process under consideration, rather than structure. As a corollary, functionalism is not necessarily concerned with defining and describing the details and processes of an event *inside* the organism; rather S is regarded as an *agency*, the doer or perceiver, in the molar sense. The current functional approaches to be described have historical roots in the nineteenth century concept of unconscious inference (Helmholtz), which described perception as an event based on expectations owing to past experience—an unconscious inference derived from sensory data. (See Vernon [1957] for an example of an explicit, contemporary statement concerning the important role of cognitive inference in perceptual activity.)

*Transactional Psychology.* Transactional psychology yields a school of functionalism in perception which claims that perception is a process used by man in a purposive manner, not as a response to the environment but rather as a "transaction" with the environment. The meanings and significance we attribute to the world around us are built up through our past experience and are not "given" in the stimulus, as Gibson would hold. According to Ames, and his colleagues who share his theories, the world we know is determined largely from our experiences in dealing with our environment. (For a more detailed description of this viewpoint, see Ames [1951]; Cantril [1957]; Ittelson & Kilpatrick [1951]; Kilpatrick [1952]; and Kilpatrick [1955].)

Through ingenious experiments (using balloons, distorted rooms, etc.), in which size and distance judgments conflict with reality, investigators in transactional research have suggested that evidence has been found to show that we weigh probabilities and guess as to the nature of the external world, as well as what our actions should be. In other words, we make assumptions about the real world, assumptions based on and serving our needs for self-protection and for "getting along." (Brunswik's viewpoint, although developed independently, is related to the foregoing—see next section.)

The crux of many of the Ames-type experiments is that a given retinal pattern may be interpreted in a variety of ways and that the chosen way apparently depends on the previous experiences of the organism, that is, he assumes that what has been most probable in the past is also most probable in the present. Thus, our perceptions are not absolute judgments but rather probabilities based on past experience. These probabilities or predictions are, therefore, not always veridical. The predictions are also based on the best course of action coordinating with the purpose of the organism. Two implications follow from this viewpoint. When an unfamiliar external stimulus yields a retinal pattern with which the organism is familiar, he will interpret or judge the external stimulus to be the one with which he is familiar; and when the organism, acting on this percept, finds that he is wrong, his percept will change accordingly, even though the retinal pattern is the same. Perception is regarded, therefore, as a functional affair, based on action, experience and probability; the thing (which is perceived) and the percept are part of the same process. "Constancies" in perception are what *we* contribute, because they make us more sure of the world around us; these constancies are always being tested against our experiences.

Transactional psychology has a great deal to say, of a philosophic, broad nature, concerning the "reality world," a world not just of physical things, but of our own wishes, anxieties, etc. Moreover, as has often been noted by others, a towering theory is offered on the basis of some very striking and dramatic, "rigged" experiments in the laboratory—a theory which eventually has things to say concerning social perception, social constancies (as in typing people), etc., a leap which may well be hazardous.

*Probabilistic Functionalism.* This section presents Egon Brunswik's viewpoint, based largely on his work with the constancies of perception (Brunswik, 1943; 1944; 1956; 1957). In his writings, Brunswik has stressed a psychology of *objects* (see especially, *Perception and the Representative Design of Psychological Experiments* [1956]). For Brunswik, only *ecological* variables are open to control, not central, organismic variables; he is concerned with stimulus representativeness— a sampling of objects and situations, not just Ss, as in traditional experimentation. The status of subjects and objects are equal; the latter have to be *sampled*, much in the way we use sampling procedures with populations of subjects.

Brunswik's perceptual theory, based on this ecological approach, is concerned with distal factors—how cues are utilized in judging or perceiving things and objects. Cues (such as traditional constancy cues) are utilized probabilistically, according to their ultimate validity, expressed as probabilities, rather than certainties. Brunswik is not concerned with physiological explanations, consciousness, or phenomenology. His point is simply that the achievement or attainment of results, falling short of precision, in the judging or utilization of the environment, is the nature of the perceptual process. The perceptual system accumulates and combines cues; a "cognitive wager" is involved, or "uncertainty-geared probabilistic strategy." The object, as perceived, is actually constructed by the organism on the basis of available data (cues) as an approximation, a probability model, of the "real" thing.

According to Brunswik, the organism and the environment are both systems, each with properties of their own, but equal partners. Both have to "come to terms." Perception is subsumed in cognition, but is a more intuitive kind of cognitive process, and is the mediation between the organism and his environment (note the similarity to transactional psychology) based on the frequency of association of cues with its significate.

As for ecology, Brunswik has criticized many of his co-theorists such as Gibson, even Ames, for not being representative, for working with single cues and only under certain conditions. His views are best expressed in his own terms:

Ecological validity is a statistical concept based on the principle of contingency or correlation and requiring the coolheaded gathering of a representative array of information. In the general case, it involves the integration of both positive and negative, confirming and disconfirming (misleading) instances of concomitance of the distal variable with the cue variable (Brunswik, 1957, p. 16).

And finally, as for perception itself:

Perception, then, emerges as that relatively primitive, partly autonomous, institutionalized, ratiomorphic subsystem of cognition which achieves prompt and richly detailed orientation habitually concerning the vitally relevant, mostly distal aspects of the environment on the basis of mutually vicarious, relatively restricted and stereotyped insufficient evidence in uncertainty-geared interaction and compromise, seemingly following the highest probability for smallness of error at the expense of the highest frequency of precision (1956, p. 146).

The theories of Ames and his co-workers and of Brunswik can be placed in a decidedly molar framework. As such, there is no concern with "inside" problems. S is viewed from the "outside" as a purposive being; although functionalism is a theory of perception, there is little relevant material in terms of perceptual processes, mechanisms, or neurophysiological correlates. Brunswik's views, in particular, are methodologically rather than perceptually oriented.

*Approaches to Personality through Perception—Typologies.* The following sections describe several dominant or major approaches—probably the word "theories" should not be used in this context—which are more directly relevant to the task of the current book. These approaches, although developing independently of each other, suggest that the study of perception is of interest not necessarily *per se*, but as an approach to the understanding, exploration, and perhaps even diagnosis of personality. If, in the long run, relationships are clearly established, and if these relationships prove to be useful to the worker in personality for prediction, prognosis, and evaluation, then not only will some of the "rationale" for a technique such as the Rorschach be more acceptable, but perhaps traditional projective techniques will be supplanted by the more simple tasks used by workers in the perceptual area. Needless to say, we are a long way from this.

As early as 1944, Thurstone, in his monograph, *A Factorial Study of Perception,* described an extensive factorial exploration of various perceptual tasks in order to isolate underlying variables which could be used to account for individual differences. Since that time there have been many attempts to relate various diagnoses and/or personality variables to differences in performance on perceptual tasks. Innumerable perceptual tasks have been studied; significant correlations have frequently been reported. For example, to mention only a few studies, Johansson (1955), in a study of motion perception and personality, constructed a perceptual measure based on the fact that the perceived velocity of a single object moving in a visual field increases considerably when a second object, moving with the same speed in the opposite direction is introduced. Ss with extremely slow "velocity synthesis" (affected little by the relativity effect introduced by the other object in the motion percept) were found to be autistic, withdrawn, and to possess self-isolating attitudes. Schumer (1949) found marked differences in the quality of phi phenomenon experiences reported by 100 college men. These differences were found to be significantly related to productivity of human movement on the Rorschach.

Eysenck, Granger, and Brengelmann (1957), in a study of perceptual processes and mental illness, explored a wide variety of noncognitive behaviors in and attempt to find relationships to personality. Working with samples of 100 normal, 20 psychotic, and 20 neurotic males, they did an extensive factor analysis which included 29 simple perceptual measures, such as visual acuity and simple closure, and more complex measures, such as after-images, tachistoscopic performance and various autonomic tests. The perceptual tests, as well as a questionnaire which was used, held up well, that is, normals, neurotics, and psychotics were differentiated. The physiological measures did not differentiate, however. The authors' hypothesis that normality was associated with "integrative," "wholistic," and "synthetic" attitudes, was, according to them, generally confirmed. Vandenberg (1959), in reanalyzing some of Eysenck's results, generally confirmed his findings, especially with respect to his "bi-factor" theory of neuroses vs. psychoses. It seems strange, however, that in these studies, insufficient attention was paid to questions of set, attention, and motivation which plague workers in psychopathology.

Granger (1953), in an extensive review of research on personality and visual perception, included studies on dark adaptation, color vision, visual acuity, visual fields, flicker-fusion, autokinetic effect, pupillary reactions, ocular movements, accommodation, response time, and perceptual attitudes such as color-form attitude and analytic-synthetic attitude. On the basis of this review, he reported conflicting but sufficiently positive evidence to show the existence of individual differences in perception. But he deplored the absence of consideration to questions of attention, set, motivation, motor factors, and autonomic functioning, as well as the lack of theoretical framework for the correlations which did appear. Moreover, he has suggested that in many of these studies, the level of experimental control and rigor had dropped in comparison to the earlier experimental studies in physiology and psychology from which so many of the perceptual tasks had been derived.

*The Approach of G. Klein, et al.* Klein and his co-workers (Klein [1951], [1953], [1954]; Klein, Holzman, & Laskin [1954]; Klein & Schlesinger [1949], [1951]; Klein, Schlesinger, & Meister [1951]) have long felt that insufficient attention has been paid to the perceiver in perceptual theory. Their research is typical of an approach which regards perception and the study of perception from a strictly personality-oriented viewpoint, not as an attempt to understand perceptual processes, but personality processes. They criticized some of the work of Postman, Bruner, etc., stating that all need states do not affect *generalized* perception in the same ways.

Their position, briefly, is that the individual must maintain equilibrium between inner strivings and the demands of reality; this results in defenses which emerge as stable, pervasive, and autonomous features of the personality, reflecting themselves in all situations where some sort of adaptive response is made. Since perception can be regarded as an adaptive response (motor processes, thinking, etc., are also relevant), perceptual situations and tasks should reflect the individual's particular defensive pattern.

Thus, the authors were concerned with examining traditional perceptual parameters such as thresholds, speed of response, etc., in order to search for "typical adaptive solutions" of the individual. Their concept of "mode" relates to what they have regarded as the "typical" response pattern of S with respect to a particular perceptual task. Various patterns of "modes," empirically determined, have been called "syndromes"; syndromes presumably indicate the perceptual attitude of the individual, that is, his preferred style or expression.

From these preferred styles or expressions, the individual's central controls can be inferred. Thus Klein goes further than the functionalists, who say that perceiving is adaptive. Klein feels that the adaptive process actually reveals, for each individual, his *Anschauung*—his solution which reflects his ego control system. Klein is thus more "clinical" in approach than most of the perceptionists discussed previously. Moreover, as will soon be seen, his thinking illustrates, as does that of the two workers to be described, an implicitly typological approach, wherein perception and personality are classified jointly, as expressive or indicative of stable *types*. (As noted, Klein feels that *Anschauungen*, distinctive ways individuals meet reality, are demonstrated in various neutral and cognitive situations, too.) Thus, in an experiment in which Ss judged the size of squares of varying dimensions (Klein, 1951), the Ss were classified as levelers (those who minimized differences) and sharpeners (those who maximized differences); these Ss were found to be consistently levelers or sharpeners in other tasks, too. In other experimental situations, particularly with respect to the phi phenomenon, Ss were classified as tolerant of, or resistant to, the unstable (Klein & Schlesinger, 1951); "form-boundedness" and "form-lability" on the Rorschach were significantly related to the types found in the phi situation. The authors concluded that similar perceptual attitudes toward instability were operating both in the phi situation and the Rorschach.

Klein (1954) described additional experiments which differentiated Ss in terms of ability to disregard irrelevant or interfering stimuli in the solution of a task; high-interference and low-interference groups (depending on ability to ignore irrelevant stimuli) were further shown to possess tightened, suppressive controls (high-interference group) and flexible, nonconstrictive controls (low-interference group). Klein, Holzman, and Laskin (1954), in summarizing part of their work to date, delineated some of the typological dichotomies disclosed by their studies. Their Ss could be described as tolerant or intolerant of unstable or ambiguous stimuli; they could be called levelers or sharpeners (see earlier); they could be dichotomized in terms of method of handling intruding stimuli; they were labeled as focusers or nonfocusers (focusers could disregard distractions and irrelevancies from tasks at hand), etc. The authors did recognize the need, however, to measure the relation of these cognitive styles to each other as well as to different "modes" of behavior popular with other investigators (such as the field dependence and field independence of Witkin—see next section).

Klein (1954) further distinguished between needs and cognitive controls. Although similar in many respects, the latter does not impel action for gratifications, but may, in fact, delay gratification. Such restraints serve a reality function and are similar to constructs of delay in ego functions posited by Freud. Behaviorally, they are manifested in a consistent manner in terms of the individual's perceptual, memory, and thinking activity—the *Anschauungen* noted previously. Cognitive controls need not be defensive in nature, since they appear with respect to neutral stimuli, too. As a matter of fact, these authors (Klein, Schlesinger, & Meister, 1951) generally and specifically have indicated their belief that the "personal values" and "perceptual defense" interpretation of the early Bruner and Postman perceptual studies is incorrect; they have rather interpreted some of these findings in terms of "preferred perceptual attitudes" and "individualized styles," in the context of less than optimal visual conditions.

*The Work of Witkin and His Colleagues.* Witkin, in a series of re-

searches (Witkin [1949]; Witkin & Asch [1948a], [1948b]; and especially, Witkin's book, *Personality Through Perception* [1954], written
with Lewis, Hertzman, Machover, Meissner, & Wapner), explored exhaustively the perception of the upright, examining the various parameters of this function. These studies in space orientation involved several experimental situations in each of which S was asked to determine
the vertical or upright orientation, and to indicate this judgment by adjusting his body, the visual field, or a rod. In doing so, S could rely
chiefly, or in part, and in various combinations, on cues from his own
body or from the visual field. The three tests of space orientation were:

1. *The rod-and-frame test.* This test, originally used by Aubert
(1886), was designed to measure perception of the upright in a limited
visual field. It consists of a luminous square frame, which encloses
(without apparently touching) a luminous, movable rod, which S is
asked to adjust in a completely darkened room. The frame surrounding
the rod is tilted, and during some trials S is erect, at other times tilted
to the same side as the frame and in still other trials to the opposite
side. To achieve the "true" (gravitational) upright, S is required to
rely less on the visual cues supplied by the luminous frame and more
on the cues provided by his body.

2. *The tilting-room-tilting-chair test.* This test involves perception of
the upright of the entire visual field and of the position of S's body
within this field. It consists of seating S in a tilted visual field and requiring him to adjust his body (which is in an adjustable seat) to the
"true" upright position. The visual field—the room in which he is seated
—is also adjustable, and S is asked to adjust the tilt of the room to the
true upright position. In adjusting his body, S may do so in the direction of tilt of the upright room, or he may ignore the influence of the
visual field. Similarly, S may adjust the position of the total visual field
(the tilted room in which he sits) relying chiefly on bodily cues (felt
position of own body) or, in varying degrees (up to complete acceptance of the vertical axis of the tilted room as the true upright) may be
influenced by the visual field.

3. *The rotating-room test.* In this test, instead of distorting or altering the visual field, bodily and postural factors are altered by rotating
the room in which S is seated around a circular track so that in addition to gravitational pull he is also influenced by centrifugal force. Under these conditions, S is required to adjust his body or the room to
the true upright (gravitational upright). Since the room and the chair
are upright, initially, Ss who determine the upright in accordance with

this are relying essentially on the visual field. If, on the other hand, S's alignment of the upright is in accordance with the forces exerted on his body, he will be ignoring the visual field.

Using various normal male and female Ss of different age groups and hospitalized diagnostic groupings, Witkin and his associates conducted a massive correlational study which included additional perceptual tests, such as the embedded-figures test, auditory-visual conflict test, and brightness-constancy tests (designed to "get at" S's ability to extract an item from its context); tests of "body action," which attempted to measure the influence of the visual field upon body steadiness, balance, etc.; and various tests and procedures designed to assess personality variables—a personality questionnaire, sentence-completion test, clinical interview, figure-drawing test, Rorschach technique, TAT, and a word-association test. The complete battery of tests could not be, for various reasons, given to all Ss.

In addition to exploring their data from the point of view of sex and developmental differences, Witkin and his associates were concerned with the consistency an S showed from test to test and *within* parts of each test, as to his preferred mode of perception, that is, does S rely primarily on the visual field or on bodily and postural factors, and is this reflected in various tasks with any degree of stability? Although marked consistency was found in and among the tests of space orientation, there was somewhat less consistency when the nonorientation perceptual tasks were considered. When the structure and nature of the tasks were examined, however, greater consistency was revealed—for example, when degree of separation of an item from context was regarded as a factor. From the mass of findings, it was concluded that marked individual differences exist and are definable in accordance with the degree to which S is dependent on or independent of the "prevailing visual field."

These perceptual types, such as those with the ability to "resist the pull of the visual field" or "the field dependents," were utilized as the basic variables in the vast correlational analysis of the personality data, in an attempt to evaluate whether or not material from the personality area bore any relationship to S's perceptual mode, based on indices derived from the three orientation tests and the embedded figures test.

After extensive treatment of the clinical and personality-test data by separate authors, with a wide variety of "systems," hypotheses, and procedures for data analysis, Witkin (1954, Chapter 21) summarized the major findings as to the relationship between perception and personality, always, of course, in terms of correlates of the two modalities with which he was concerned. For example:

. . . field-dependent persons tend to be characterized by passivity in dealing with the environment; by unfamiliarity with, and fear of, their own impulses, together with poor control over them; by lack of self-esteem; and by the possession of a relatively primitive, undifferentiated body image. Independent or analytical perceptual performers, in contrast, tend to be characterized by activity and independence in relation to the environment; by closer communication with, and better control of, their own impulses; and by relatively high self-esteem and a more differentiated, mature body image. These are the relationships that were revealed in our intensive study of a group of young, normal adults, and confirmed in studies of children and of hospitalized psychiatric patients (*Ibid.*, p. 469).

In general, the authors were satisfied that particular ways of perceiving were congruent with certain personality characteristics, although they did suggest that the degree to which a task facilitated or inhibited "field dependence" was also an important variable, in terms of whether or not S's usual perceptual mode was elicited.

Unfortunately, in reviewing the volume by Witkin and his associates, some important methodological limitations arise regarding the conclusions relating perception to personality. These will be briefly noted, not for the sake of carping criticism, for their ingenious approach to perception is most productive, but as an evaluation of the personality-perception link they claim to have established.

Briefly, then, their work, judging by their report, appears to be neatly divided, methodologically, into clean-cut, operationally defined, carefully controlled, standardized laboratory procedures with objectively defined, quantitatively reliable, and carefully pretested scoring procedures and measures, on the one hand (the orientation and perceptual tasks and tests); and on the other hand, into clinical material evaluated crudely, unreliably and quite subjectively (the personality material, especially the projective tests). There is the feeling that the high standards used in the laboratory were suddenly and inexplicably dropped when the clinic was entered. Why, for example, when using rating scales with the personality material, was the question of their reliability never explored? Why was it necessary to "explain" clinical findings and interpretations by a wide variety of undefined and subjective "rationales"? Why, moreover, were "discriminating" signs based on the clinical instruments derived from a sample and then reapplied to the same sample with a consequent report that the signs differentiated perceptual modes? Signs were used frequently in this manner with no attempt to cross-validate. (Indeed, when the signs were applied to the hospital group, discrimination dropped.) Generalizations as to personality findings often paid little attention to the important consideration of sampling problems—a particularly important feature of the hospital group data, especially since *ex post facto* interpretation of results was the order of the day. Witkin's brilliant investigations of the perception of the upright fail to generate equally brilliant hypotheses when he attempts to relate his measures to personality considerations. His work illustrates some of the general methodological problems and difficulties in the clinical-personality area. Certain procedural checks, controls, pretesting of operations, measures and signs, and assessment of scorer and score reliability might have been introduced, however. His answer to the basic questions concerning the relationship between perception and personality would then have been more effective and definitive.

*The Work of Frenkel-Brunswik.* Else Frenkel-Brunswik's approach to perception is still another example of perceptual research which is almost entirely personality oriented (1949, 1951); that is, a branching out from traditional perceptual research in order to throw light on personality factors as well as social and emotional variables.

Frenkel-Brunswik became interested in perceptual variables in connection with the well-known research at the Institute of Child Welfare of the University of California, which dealt with prejudiced and nonprejudiced attitudes and their motivational and cognitive correlates (Adorno, Frenkel-Brunswik, Levinson, & Sanford, 1950). Generally speaking, ethnocentric attitudes, as disclosed in a large-scale correlational study, were found to be related to authoritarian personality structure.

Frenkel-Brunswik soon discovered that many of her Ss were less able to tolerate "emotional ambiguities" than others. She became interested in whether or not this "intolerance" extended also to the more traditional field of perception. As a result of some of her explorations, she was able to offer rich evidence, on the basis of interviews, clinical evaluations, etc., that in emotional attitudes toward values, parent figures, other children, and the like, there is often a dichotomy; but some children are simply unable to accept "coexistence" in the form of good and bad, right and wrong, or sheer complexity in any event or interpersonal relationship.

She showed that in memory (recall of a story) as well as in various traditional, experimental, perceptual situations in which some ambiguity is "built into" the stimuli, the more prejudiced Ss tended to be more rigid and perseverative. She was concerned with the relationship of the perception of self and others and various social attitudes with the more traditional perceptual responses—a "unity of style" approach, which is decidedly similar to the approach of Klein and his co-workers, although apparently her work developed independently of that group.

Else Frenkel-Brunswik's work in the perceptual area must be evaluated, for our purposes, separately from her work in other areas. In this connection it should be noted that she offers no theory of perception or of the relationship between personality and perception; there is also some difficulty in distinguishing between perception, cognition, and social attitudes. Her work is largely correlational in nature, albeit rich and suggestive; furthermore, the mechanisms as to how or why relationships exist are not offered although there are "explanations" of a broad, clinical, largely psychoanalytic nature.

*Directive-State Theory.* In the late 1940's, a "New Look" in perceptual theory emerged. The approach of the workers doing the early studies within this framework can be regarded as the single most important influence in the swing toward the belief that perception is essentially a personality-oriented phenomenon. Everyone seemed to be jumping on the bandwagon; there were innumerable reports of research, some opposing, some defending the conclusions of the original classic studies; bitterness, criticalness, and deep conviction pervaded the literature. Opponents and proponents alike, aware of the rifts and controversies involved in such a departure from tradition, looked elsewhere for an apt, succinct label to apply to this movement, and found one custom-made, in the fashion world. The "New Look" is a phrase (as some of our readers will recognize) borrowed from the publicity releases from *Maison Dior* in Paris, which described some startling changes in fashion—changes incidentally, which were rather short lived.

The great discovery of the "New Look" was that the perceiver also counts. In some ways, the introduction of the perceiver into the process of perception can be likened to the introduction of the observer into the measurement of velocity in the theory of relativity. Einstein's great contribution emerged when he introduced the velocity of the observer or his frame of reference into the measurement of the velocity of an object. In the same way, the New Look hoped to revolutionize perception by introducing the characteristics of the perceiver, that is, his personality (drives, needs, etc.). Unfortunately, the revolution in psychology did not go off as successfully as the revolution in physics, but fizzled, more like the revolution in fashion.

The New Look perceptionists, although recognizing autochthonous or structural factors in perception—the stimulus, mechanisms for perceiving, the organization of the nervous system, the so-called formal factors—stressed primarily other determinants. These determinants have to do with the previously neglected "inside" factors, not associated with the stimulus, for example, need states, values, past experience, and expectancy. Adherents of this position began with simple *functional* interpretations, such as we perceive what we *need* to perceive or *expect* to perceive, but later embraced a large variety of principles and generalizations. In short, values, motives, and even "personality" —a "central directive state"—influence our perceptions. A more formal label for this movement thus emerged: directive-state theory. Attention was dramatically turned to factors having to do with the perceiver as a whole, his attitudes, beliefs and motives. It might be noted that directive-state theory actually subsumes several positions; it is not a theory in the formal sense, and arguments *within* the movement were as vivid as those coming from without. A review of some of the earlier studies seems appropriate, in order to set the stage for the lively controversies which followed.

Before we attempt this review, however, it might be noted that Gardner Murphy and his colleagues, who had devoted considerable attention to the investigation of perceptual learning, anticipated much of the work to be described. They conducted a group of studies which aimed to show the relationship between perception and certain organismic motivational states. Levine, Chein, and Murphy (1942), for example, demonstrated that verbal associations to ambiguous drawings of objects contained many more food responses in groups deprived of food than in the control group. Schafer and Murphy (1943) demonstrated that reward and punishment had a sizable influence in determining which alternative of reversible (figure-ground, ambiguous) stimuli would be subsequently perceived, that is, that Ss would "learn" what to perceive. And Proshansky and Murphy (1942) demonstrated a similar effect of training with reward or punishment on the estimates of lengths of lines.

One of the earliest of the "classical" studies was that of Bruner and Goodman (1947), who studied the effect of values on judgments of apparent size. The purpose of this research was to investigate the hypothesis that judgments of the size of objects and some of their other properties are dependent not only on the physical size, but on the values attached to these objects. The Ss, 30 ten-year-old children of normal intelligence, were shown a rectangular wooden box through which different objects were exposed. The child was told that this was a game, and that he was to make the circle of light in the box the same size as the various objects he was shown or told about. The results indicated that when discs the same size as the five coins, namely the penny, nickel, dime, quarter, and fifty-cent piece were presented, no great deviation occurred between the observed size and the actual size of the disc, the per cent deviation from the actual size varying about zero without any large outstanding differences. When the coins were presented, however, the settings deviated considerably from the actual sizes in a positive direction. In other words, the coins were regarded as being larger than they really were and this discrepancy increased with the size of the coins so that the quarter and fifty-cent piece were regarded as much larger than their actual sizes by nearly 30 per cent.

When the same comparison was made for rich and poor children, it was noted that the increase for the poor children was much greater than for the rich. Whereas the rich children showed no great variation in their size judgments for the coins, the poor children showed the same general tendency that was noted before, namely, for the overestimation in size to increase with the value of the coin. In another experiment the size of the perceived coin was compared with the size of the memory image of the coin. It was noted that among the poor children, the presence of the coin always tended to increase the perceived size, whereas, with the rich, the converse held true, the presence of the coin tending to serve as a check on its size. The authors tried to explain this divergence on the basis of the weakened fantasy of the deprived, poor children as compared to the strong, active fantasy of the rich children. In a follow-up study by Carter and Schooler (1949) however, this finding was not confirmed. When their Ss had the coins before them, there was no accentuation. Only when the sizes were estimated from memory did such accentuation occur. Apparently the accentuation effect is eliminated by the reality testing that the presence of the coins makes possible.

Further evidence for "accentuation," that is, the effect of value on perceived size of an object, but this time when the object had *symbolic* positive or negative value, was reported by Bruner and Postman (1948). Ss were asked to estimate the size of discs which bore a dollar sign or the swastika. Estimates for the discs bearing the positively-valued symbol were larger than for the negatively-valued symbol, but these, in turn, were estimated to be larger than discs with a neutral symbol. The authors concluded that whatever is significant for S, whether positive or negative, is "accentuated" in perception.

In another early research, Bruner and Postman (1947) studied the influence of emotional selectivity on perception. The purpose of their experiment was to analyze the relationship between reaction time and correct recognition of words that are emotionally loaded or complex bound for an individual. That is, will an individual recognize an emotionally surcharged word as readily as he would a word not emotionally charged? The selection of the emotionally charged words was made through the use of a word-association test and two weeks later the words were exposed tachistoscopically to determine both the amount of time required for correct recognition as well as the various misrecognitions that occur during the presolution period. The relationship between the original association reaction time and the time required for later recognition of the emotionally surcharged words was obtained. In general, the words with an initially long association reaction time tended also to have longer recognition times, but the relationship was curvilinear. The words with the shortest association reaction time and those with the longest association reaction time both required rather short recognition times for their correct recognition, whereas the words of medium original association reaction time showed the highest recognition time. To explain this phenomenon two effects were postulated, a defense process and a sensitization process. The defense process was indicated by the fact that as a word increased in emotional tone it took longer to recognize it correctly. This, of course, involves the assumption that the original reaction time was truly an indicator of emotionality. The second factor, that of sensitization, was introduced to explain why certain words, despite the fact that they had a rather long reaction time originally, were recognized in rather short order. These words were regarded as emotionally surcharged words to which the individual had become sensitized and hence dropped them like "hot potatoes" the moment they appeared.

In an attempt to demonstrate the process of selectivity—the "differential tuning" of S to the stimuli in his enviroment—Postman, Bruner, and McGinnies (1948) reported an experiment which explored the relationship between personal interests or values and the speed of recognition of preselected words, exposed tachistoscopically. The words used, each of which represented one of the six Spranger values, were equally distributed over the range of values.[1] For each S, time of recognition for each of the exposed words was obtained, as well as their attempted solutions (precognition solutions), and this information was compared to the scores of S on the Allport-Vernon Study of Values which indicated for each S his highest and lowest values. The results of the study indicated that Ss recognized the words representative of their own high values more rapidly than other words. In an

---

[1] The six Spranger values are: theoretical, economic, aesthetic, social, political, and religious.

analysis of the presolution responses, the authors found evidence which suggested to them that values even had affected the *type* or *content* of the wrong response. In their discussion of the findings, the authors spoke of values as "sensitizers" which could apparently lower perceptual thresholds; values could also *raise* perceptual thresholds, and this was regarded as *perceptual defense*. *Value resonance* was the label they used to describe the finding that presolution responses were not just "haphazard guesses" but also reflected S's value-orientation.

Further support for the concept of *perceptual defense* was claimed by McGinnies (1949) in his discussion of a study which examined differences between recognition thresholds for emotionally toned and neutral words. GSR data prior to the response to the emotionally toned stimuli were also recorded. The findings confirmed the notion of perceptual defense, according to the author, in that thresholds were higher for the emotionally toned words; incorrect responses preceding such words tended to show avoidance of recognition of such words; and GSR's before recognition of these words were considerably higher than those for neutral words. This particular research report was the center of a storm of controversy which will be summarized shortly, but first, several additional relevant reports will be noted, as well as a brief summary of some of the major contentions of directive-state theorists.

Bruner and Postman (1949b), in a study of the influence of incongruity on perception, suggested on the basis of their findings that most people depend on a stable, constant environment and that they tend to ward off deviations from their expectations. In their study, they showed that recognition thresholds for tachistoscopically exposed "trick," incongruous cards such as a red six of spades or a black seven of hearts, were significantly higher than the thresholds for normal cards. They also classified individual differences in content of responses to incongruity, for example, dominance, compromise, or description. They concluded that our expectations based on past experiences with our environment are extremely important determinants of our perceptual organization.

Another example of the "disruptive" effect of incongruity on perception was provided by Siipola (1950). She compared response time and response content of matched pairs of chromatic and achromatic blots derived from the Rorschach stimuli. The element of hue in the blots interfered with perception only when there was some incongruity present between the form of the blot and its hue. One of the stimuli to which the normal group of subjects studied by Siipola responded with the greatest difficulty was the portion of Card VIII usually interpreted as "pink animals." Since the color is unexpected and incongruous with the form, great difficulty was experienced by a considerable number of the subjects in responding to this stimulus.

A study frequently cited by the supporters of the directive-state approach is one by McClelland and Atkinson (1948). This particular study provides a good example, however, of one of the problems persistently raised by the "enemy camp." The question is simply this: Are we talking about imagery, judgment, guesses, and various other cognitive factors, or are we talking about perception? It might be noted, too, that although this question applies even to some of the studies already noted in this section, these seem to be more "convincingly" dealing with perception—or are they? McClelland and Atkinson (1948) conducted a study of the influence of the hunger drive on perception. The purpose of this study was to investigate the influence of varying strengths of the hunger drive on the visual "percepts" which emerged when the subjects were asked to look at a blank slide. Of the 108 Ss who participated in this experiment, 44 took the test from one to two hours after eating, 24 four to five hours after eating, and 40 from sixteen to eighteen hours after eating. Their reactions were analyzed into frequency of food-related responses and comparative size and number estimates of food-related and neutral objects. The findings were: (a) the frequency of food-related responses increased reliably as hours of food deprivation increased; (b) the increase in food-related responses was more prominent for instrumental objects related to food, such as knives and forks, than it was for goal objects, such as apples or bread; and (c) the food-related objects were judged larger in comparison with neutral objects by the hungry Ss but not by the satiated Ss.

The first half of the 1950's was devoted to a lively and spirited controversy which centered around some of the findings in these earlier reports. The authors of the original articles themselves participated actively, along with others, in modifying and even repudiating their own earlier concepts. Bruner and Postman, for example, came up with some new concepts and theories because of dissatisfaction with "explanations" for previous experimental results. But is *perceptual defense* as a concept, dead? By no means! Research reports on perceptual defense, subliminal sensitivity to certain words with "taboo" qualities, etc., are still being published with considerable zeal and emotional fervor. Here are some examples: Chodorkoff and Chodorkoff (1958) attempted to "pull together" findings from psychological, physiological, and psychoanalytic sources to explain perceptual defense. Largely from a review of physiological studies, the authors concluded that, "If we can assume that fear and/or threat involve autonomic activity and that there exists a negative feedback loop between autonomic discharge and perception, then these research findings strongly suggest that when threat is present, the feedback system can act to prevent panic by reducing the magnitude of the perceived threat. This would be accomplished in terms of decreased awareness of, or reactivity to the threatening stimulus" (p. 77).

Spence (1957) demonstrated the effect of anxiety on recognition thresholds of tachistoscopic stimuli, but indicated that both increases or decreases of threshold (defense *and* vigilance) may be parts of the same process. On the basis of experimental findings, Levy (1958) has claimed evidence for perceptual defense in tactual discrimination. Walters, Banks, and Ryder (1959) reported a study in which perceptual defense was accounted for in terms of learning, that is, responses exemplifying perceptual defense were regarded as instances of conditioned avoidance responses. Their study demonstrated that nontaboo words which followed subliminally presented taboo words were correctly identified less frequently than nontaboo words that did *not* follow subliminally presented taboo words. In other words, the perceptual defense was "generalized," influencing the response even to neutral words. The authors, however, were "baffled" by their findings: "Possibly at the present time we can predict correctly even when we cannot explain" (p. 54). Blum (1957), who is the author of the Blacky Pictures (1950), reported evidence which suggested that Ss who showed avoidance reactions to the Blacky Pictures manifested increased thresholds when tachistoscopic presentation of the pictures at levels below awareness was made. Blum's explanation attempted to link psychoanalytic theory to perceptual processes.

Freeman (1955) explored the hypothesis that parsimonious explanations could be found to explain the effect attributed to perceptual defense in tachistoscopic presentations of taboo and nontaboo words. He was particularly interested in whether or not "set" could explain the perceptual defense effect. His experimental instructions asked the Ss to "feel perfectly free to respond with whatever word they thought they saw" (p. 711). Ss were encouraged  to report taboo words. In another experimental condition Ss were told to identify words as quickly as possible and that their performance was related to academic success and aptitude ("ego-involving" instructions). The author felt that his findings generally supported his hypothesis that ego-involving instructions and the general factor of set could account for some of the perceptual defense effects he found. Sex differences in the "effect" were also found, it might be noted. On the other hand, Mathews and Wertheimer (1958), also exploring a more parsimonious explanation—in this instance, response suppression—found no evidence that perceptual defense effects could be accounted for completely by the "simpler explanation."

In another study, Hatfield (1959) explored the relative merits of word frequency, set, and motivational factors in explaining subliminal sensitivity.[2] The author hypothesized that there is a relationship between motivational factors and perception—but the direction of relationship was not predicted. His experimental procedure involved the induction of anxiety, through electric shock, in relation to certain meaningless disyllables, and a study of the subsequent changes in speed of tachistoscopic perception of these stimuli. The variable of word frequency was controlled by the use of these disyllables. Significantly lower thresholds were found for shock than for nonshock syllables—implying a kind of "vigilance," or "overalertness" rather than defense. The reader, at this point, may well wonder, as do many workers even from *within* the directive-state school, why sometimes perceptual defense and sometimes vigilance affect recognition thresholds. Also, is the threshold for shock syllables *actually* lower, or does the verbal reporting by S, his set, etc., affect the situation so that quicker reactions result?

For a detailed summary and review of "perceptual defense" as a concept, the reader is referred to an excellent monograph by Brown (1961). Here can be found not only an historical survey of the experiments and researches in this area, but a comprehensive discussion of the unresolved problems this concept presents, as well as of the validity and reliability of the various measurements used. Brown is of the opinion that the concept is valid, but that the theoretical explanations for the phenomena of perceptual defense have been inadequate. To explain some of the contradictory results concerning sensitization and defense, he has offered an hypothesis, with some experimental evidence to back it up, that, "recognition thresholds at first rise with increases in stimulus emotionality" (p. 39). On the basis of further evidence, he hypothesized that, ". . . the amount of stimulus emotionality required to bring recognition thresholds to their peak is directly related to the degree of extraversion of the subject" (p. 55). Furthermore, after a thoroughgoing description and evaluation of various theoretical viewpoints, both critical and noncritical, he has derived his own theoretical "explanation" of this concept by extending certain aspects of Hullian learning-theory, especially from Dollard and Miller's analysis of repression and approach-avoidance conflict behavior.

---

[2] See pp. 133–141 in this chapter for a review of this controversy and for a discussion of these as well as other variables.

The major tenets [3] of directive-state studies can be briefly summarized as follows:

1. Bodily needs (such as hunger and thirst) influence the perceptual event, that is, *what* is perceived.

2. Past learning, or more specifically, rewards and punishments associated with the perceiving of a stimulus, determine subsequent perception of that stimulus; past experience and memories are presumably involved through the availability of trace systems.

3. Values, as determined by some outside criterion, are related to the speed with which certain words are recognized, and to estimates of size and brightness of objects (selective sensitization). Analyses of precognition (incorrect) responses have suggested a construct of *value resonance*.

4. Threatening stimuli (usually in the form of tachistoscopically presented words) are recognized after a longer time interval than neutral words (perceptual defense), and they are misperceived (precognition response) before they are recognized in accordance with a tendency to ward off the threat they pose. An effect opposite to perceptual defense (*sensitization* or *vigilance*) is found in certain experimental conditions.

5. Certain groups of workers, for example Klein and his associates, although differing from the directive-state workers in many respects, have concentrated on the *perceiver* rather than on types of perceptual responses, and have suggested that broad personality characteristics of the individual are related to his "style," "mode," or "manner" of perceiving.

6. Some investigators, Murphy and his associates, for example, have posited "autism" as the mediating mechanism between the central motivational state of S and his perceptual response. Other workers have not felt that a mediating mechanism was necessary. Still others have elaborated theories (see Bruner, below, for example) to account for the mediating mechanisms. In general, the mediating constructs offered comprise a lengthy list which includes perceptual defense, as well as constructs such as accentuation, compromise, degree of personal relevance, or hierarchy of thresholds. Some of these mechanisms how-

---

[3] The numerical sequence does not imply mutually exclusive principles or arguments, nor an order of importance, but is introduced for convenience in reading. The reader is referred to Floyd Allport (1955, especially pp. 304–361); Bruner and Postman (1949a); Jenkin (1957); Postman, Bronson, and Gropper (1953); and Prentice (1956), for a detailed history, review and/or critique of relevant material in this area.

ever, are nothing more than descriptive phrases which serve as *ad hoc* explanations of experimental results.

7. Evidence has been suggested for discrimination without awareness (e.g., Lazarus & McCleary, 1951), that is, subception, which is probably a necessary corollary for the concepts of defense, vigilance, etc. The question of "two" perceptual processes, subliminal and supraliminal, is a controversial one, indeed. Essentially the question is: is it possible for "recognition" of a stimulus to take place *before* its conscious identification is made, or for recognition to be absent, after identification has apparently been made? Some aspects of the case for and against subception will be presented in a later section.

*Directive-State Theory* (*continued*)—*the Controversy; Re-evaluation.* McGinnies' study (1949), described previously, which reported increased thresholds for recognition of emotionally toned, taboo words, was regarded as strongly supportive of perceptual defense as a special mechanism. This specific study stimulated much controversy, which will be briefly summarized. Howes and Solomon (1950; 1951) advanced the notion that McGinnies' results could be explained in other ways. Using the Thorndike-Lorge word count, they noted that McGinnies' taboo words were much less familiar than the neutral words. They demonstrated that the more familiar a word is, the briefer is its recognition threshold—thus explaining the increased recognition thresholds (perceptual defense) for the taboo words. Moreover, Howes and Solomon suggested that McGinnies' Ss may not have produced as quick a verbal report to a taboo word until absolutely sure that they recognized it correctly because of its social unacceptability. Although McGinnies defended his original interpretation (McGinnies [1950]; McGinnies & Sherman [1952]), the cogent criticisms of Howes and Solomon were picked up and elaborated by others; in general, the concept of perceptual defense began to lose status, even among directive-state workers themselves.

McGinnies' defense consisted of noting that increased recognition thresholds for neutral words were found when they followed immediately after taboo words—constituting evidence for "generalization" of the avoidance (defensive) reaction; furthermore, the analysis of pre-cognition responses suggested that for neutral words there was a greater resemblance to the stimulus words than there was for the taboo words. This was interpreted as an indication that S attempted to *delay* seeing danger signals or threatening stimuli as much as possible. Postman, Bronson, and Gropper (1953), in a discussion of their experimental findings, strongly contested these explanations, suggesting that uncontrolled variations in familiarity of words could account for most of the perceptual defense effect. In a well-controlled experiment, they found that instructional set, selective verbal report, word frequency, and E-S relationship had demonstrable effects on recognition thresholds. They concluded, "The experimental results thus fail to provide any support for a mechanism of perceptual defense. The discussion stressed the inadequacy of *ad hoc* mechanisms for the analysis of motivational factors in perception. The effects of such factors are most economically treated in the framework of a general theory of perception" (p. 223). Solomon and Postman (1952) had already reported a study which showed that recognition thresholds varied inversely with frequency of past usage. They interpreted their findings within the context of general verbal learning theory, rather than in terms of perceptual defense, or perceptual sensitivity.

In general, Postman (Postman [1953*a*]; Postman [1953*b*]; and Postman, Bronson, & Gropper [1953]) strongly criticized his own earlier formulations with Bruner, concerning "defense." He raised the general notion (1951) that interference by competing responses might be involved and that this mechanism does not operate only with emotionally-tinged material. He also noted that stimuli purported to be emotionally toned cannot be shown to elicit perceptual defense until and unless they are equated for familiarity and structural characteristics with neutral stimuli.[4]

Postman (1953*b*) agreed with Howie (1952) that there is little justification for the concept of perceptual defense, but did not go along with Howie's contention that the basic issue was the antithetical nature of perceptual defense and perceptual vigilance: how can both be operant at the same time in a theory of perception? Postman agreed, however, that a paradox was involved in the concept of defense in that a stimulus must *first be discriminated before there is a delay or avoidance of its discrimination,* but suggested that perhaps there is more than one kind of discrimination. This question, incidentally, as to whether there are two different perceptual thresholds (perceiver within the perceiver—sometimes called the "homunculus" approach) is one of the most cogent ones raised by many of the critics of directive-state theory. That is, before a stimulus can be defended against, and

---

[4] A similar suggestion has been made with respect to the validity of color or shading "shock" on the Rorschach test (Siipola, 1950). Should not the structural complexity or unfamiliarity of the stimuli be explored first, and comparisons made with other cards of like complexity or unfamiliarity, before accepting the assumption that delayed reaction times reflect emotionality?

its perception delayed or avoided, it must be *perceived*. This presents a dilemma and a basic fallacy, many perceptual theorists believe. Postman, in general (1953*a*), argued that the former, earlier concepts of the direct influence of motivational factors in perception were oversimplified, and although agreeing still that central motivational states affect perception, he felt that just how this is accomplished is still unknown.

An "explanation" for some of the experimental effects being considered was offered by Lawrence and Coles (1954), who explored the hypothesis that perception, as defined by activity during the actual stimulus presentation, is not influenced by motivational states. The effects noted by directive-state workers, they argued, are not those relating to perception *per se*, but to memory traces and to availability of responses because of competition with other responses. Their ingenious experiment evaluated the relative roles of perceptual modification, memory trace modification, and availability of responses in the accuracy of recognition of tachistoscopically presented stimuli; their findings supported their hypothesis.

And so the critical argument and discussion went—sometimes stemming from within the camp of directive-state psychologists, and sometimes from without. By way of indicating that the discussion is still alive, a few additional reports might be noted. Brown (1960) studied the question of whether or not instructions and experimental procedures affected the actual *perception* of a stimulus or its subsequent recall or retention (similar to the question raised by Lawrence and Coles). Although his results were not clear cut, he did raise a trenchant question: does set have a *direct* influence on perception, or on other intermediate variables such as retention or recall which in turn influence the perceptual response?

Johnson, Thomson, and Frincke (1960) have revived the presently old controversy as to values, word frequency, and lowered visual thresholds. In a series of related and interesting experiments, they have demonstrated the fact that word frequency is directly related to word value—that is, the more frequently a word is used in the English language, the *better* it is rated on a good-bad scale. When frequency of nonsense words was manipulated, a concomitant variation in ratings on a good-bad scale occurred, with more frequent words being more likely rated as better words. With tachistoscopic presentations of words to Ss under various conditions, the following results were obtained: when good and bad words matched in frequency were presented, *good* words had lower visual thresholds; when frequent and infrequent words matched in goodness were presented, *frequent* words had lower visual thresholds. The authors felt that both frequency and value operate in differential visual thresholds.

Special attention might be given to a report by Eriksen (1964), who comprehensively summarizes research on the perceptual defense effect. Eriksen's viewpoint, based on much of his own research as well as an examination of the studies of other workers, is that the familiarity or frequency factor cannot adequately explain various experimental findings. *Reinforcement* rather than frequency as an explanatory principle must be introduced, since perception is essentially a learned response. In addition, the defensive nature of these learned responses may differ among different individuals, that is, threatening stimuli do not automatically elicit repression from all individuals, nor do individuals who repress responses at some time, repress responses to *all* threatening stimuli.

Eriksen indicates that perceptual defense effects can be adequately demonstrated in the laboratory, provided that we independently show that the stimuli for which the defense is expected *are* anxiety arousing, and that we independently show that the S uses avoidance-type defenses. Most early experiments failed to meet one or both of the criteria. When, as in his experiments, these criteria are introduced, the findings can be used to shed light on clinical defenses, in general.

According to Eriksen, the perceptual defense effect is genuine, but its explanation should apply to defense mechanisms in general. Having ruled out as explanations, frequency, subception, and hypothesis theory (see later sections), he proposes his own explanation, which in essence states that the defense effect does not have to do with perception, but rather, with response variables and response effects. Drawing heavily on the learning approach of Miller and Dollard, Eriksen proceeds to show how the habit strength (based on reinforcement) of the response to partial cues is the significant variable in perceptual recognition experiments.

As already noted, implicit throughout the New Look approach is a belief that there are two kinds of perception—one that takes place "before" another. This "manikin" or "homunculus" problem can be expressed by the question: who does the (veridical) perceiving in order to screen the percept so that the organism is misperceiving? Floyd Allport (1955) succinctly summarized the problems involved when he stated:

If the defending agent is something inside the individual that controls perceptual activity, we have a manikin-theory. If the defense is carried out by the perceptual process itself, we would have to believe that a physiological process operates in such a way as to prevent itself from operating. Critics have not been slow to point out the inconsistency involved in perceiving something before one perceives it. Behind the perceiver we must postulate a "preperceiver." . . . Hochberg and Gleitman charge that this kind of interpretation implies a "Pure Ego," one who "initially cognized the percept, then rejected it," and that "the need theorist can unify his battalion of needs only by placing them at the disposal of a small simulacrum of the organism, almost an organism in miniature, placed somewhere within the 'personality.'" Such an approach seems to reduce psychology to an "homunculus situation," with a tendency to relegate problems to a "never-ending, concentric series of homunculi." Bruner and Postman are themselves aware of the difficulty. The experiments, they say, "suggest to the guileless investigator the image of the superego peering through a Judas eye, scanning incoming percepts in order to decide which shall be permitted into consciousness" (p.322).[5]

Earlier, Allport (*Ibid.*) had said in describing McGinnies' experimental subjects, "It was as though they had recognized the words in exposure-times too short for them to be recognized" (p. 321).

As for a brief summary of additional critical points made by many authors, the following might be noted: [6]

1. Although many correlations between needs and perception have been demonstrated, there is a general failure to explain *how* or *why* these take place, that is, the mechanisms or mediating factors are not clear.

2. In many studies which have purported to show the relationship of needs and perception, cognitive and judgmental elements are used as measures of perceptual response. These studies have failed to distinguish between perception and judgment. As a matter of fact, in some studies a physical stimulus is not even present! Estimates based on memory are sometimes the crucial variables studied. If perception is defined as an event which requires the presence of a stimulus, and if some of the cognitive variables noted earlier are eliminated experimentally, would the same effects be found? If motivational states influence perception *per se*, this should probably be demonstrated in experimental designs which control for factors such as attitude, set, memory, attention, and familiarity.[7]

---

[5] The Hochberg and Gleitman remarks, as well as those of Bruner and Postman, are to be found in Bruner and Krech (1950; p. 184 and 25, respectively).

[6] Once more, the reader should note that these points are not stated in order of importance, nor are they mutually exclusive.

[7] In this connection, note might be made of a well-controlled study by Gilchrist and Nesberg (1952), which demonstrated perceptual changes occurring as a result of need, and of Floyd Allport's critical summary (1955, pp. 328–329) of this experiment which lucidly suggested that memory quite specifically is involved in the effects noted, rather than perception. In their study, Gilchrist and Nesberg found that apparent brightness of the stimulus was related to need. But apparent brightness was determined by matching from memory, rather than by direct matching!

3. Most of the effects have been demonstrated with marginal, ambiguous stimulus conditions. *Most* perception, however, is veridical and stimulus bound. How do directive-state theorists account for perception, in general? Are needs and motivations as powerful and influential in "everyday" veridical perception as they are under marginal stimulus conditions?

4. Perceptual modifications as a result of motivational states should be demonstrated through immediate perception, rather than in more complex, cognitive, and social situations. Perhaps the effects shown are social responses to complex social situations, rather than actual perceptual modifications.

5. A large number of studies on thresholds, values, and words used Allport-Vernon's Study of Values as a measure of S's value-orientation. Effects demonstrating the relation between perception and needs should probably not only be shown with other measures, but with other experimental procedures, and other perceptual events and situations.

6. Effects suggesting both vigilance and defense have been demonstrated. But when and how one or the other takes place, and the relationship between these effects have not been adequately handled.

7. Word frequency and word familiarity in the perceptual defense studies seem related to the perceptual defense effect; as a result, "defense" as a concept has been severely criticized.

8. Some experiments which require S to verbalize associations to ambiguous material may not involve perception at all, that is, what S actually sees!

9. Whether or not simple *inhibition* of verbal reports is involved in the effects demonstrated should be explored further. In the demonstration of relationships between learning and perception, does S learn to *communicate* differently rather than to *perceive* differently?

10. The question of *set* has not been adequately ruled out as an explanation of some of the effects, especially with respect to judgments of size.

11. The role of motor adjustments, competing responses, and the availability of responses has not been adequately considered.

12. The question of "subception" and discrimination without awareness—crucial to much of directive-state theory—creates many problems. (A summary of some of these problems is given in a later section.)

13. The role of "preferred perceptual attitudes" (in the manner of Klein and co-workers) in tendencies to underestimate or overestimate, as well as various other effects noted earlier, is not clear. Apparently

there are many individual differences which come into play, especially under conditions of poor vision, which are not completely accountable for by a concept like perceptual defense or vigilance.

The basic question thus may still be unanswered. Prentice (1956) wondered whether or not sensory experience was more plastic than it seemed to be. "We run the risk of making of the field of perception what has been made of 'extrasensory' perception: an area in which more and more demonstrations are carried out but in which theory and understanding never progress because certain kinds of systematic questions are not asked, because students are satisfied with analogies instead of with laws binding the phenomena to other known facts" (p. 37).

Some of the considerations noted previously caused the "elders" of directive-state theory to reformulate their beliefs. The next section presents one such reformulation which has received considerable attention and has stimulated much new research.

*Hypothesis or Expectancy Theory.* This directive-state approach, as noted, grew out of earlier New Look studies as a result of some of the methodological problems and dilemmas associated with earlier studies; moreover, there was an increasing feeling that some of the New Look tenets were descriptive rather than explanatory concepts. Both Bruner and Postman had revised their earlier thinking considerably. For a more detailed statement of hypothesis or expectancy theory the reader is referred to Bruner (1951); later refinement of this approach can be found in a report by Bruner (1957); an overall review and evaluation is presented by Floyd Allport (1955, pp. 375–406).

Essentially, this approach suggests that perceiving is always based on an expectancy or "hypothesis" on the part of the organism, that is, he is "tuned" to some aspect of his surroundings. (This view of perceiving is of course related to the approach of various *set* theories; as a matter of fact, this entire section could well appear in connection with a theoretical approach already described, that pertaining to sets.)

Perception involves the input of information from the environment. Input, in this theory, is not specified in terms of stimulus energy, but rather in terms of its signal value, as cue or clue. The next process involves the checking or confirmation of the organism's hypothesis; if there is confirmation, the hypothesis is strengthened and its arousal will be "easier" in the future when similar "information" from the environment is received. If the hypothesis is not confirmed, the organism will introduce new hypotheses, until one of them is confirmed.

There are many principles governing the process by which hypotheses become confirmed or infirmed. Frequency of confirmation strengthens an hypothesis; the stronger it is, the greater is the likelihood of its arousal, the *less* information is necessary for its confirmation, and the *more* inappropriate or contradictory information is necessary to infirm it. The arousal of an hypothesis is dependent also on *monopoly* (the number of hypotheses extant), as well as on cognitive, motivational and social consequences, such as integration with past experiences, relationship to the goal-strivings of the organism and agreement with others (when information is weak). Cues can be reliable or unreliable and the information provided by them can be used to confirm or infirm the organism's hypotheses.

Strong hypotheses may be confirmed by even "unreliable" information. Thus, in directive-state studies, when ambiguous or impoverished stimuli are used, the informational input is weak, and S is thrown back on utilizing his own hypotheses—characteristic of his own experiences and motivation. However, stimuli around us tend to limit the degree to which our past experience and needs enter into the perceptual event, for when the input is simple and reliable (overdetermined), the organism is no longer in a situation of "poor perception." Bruner insisted, however, that most complex perception, especially of a social nature, involves less reliable cue value and information than we like to think, and that we do indeed, in daily life, fall back on hypotheses and expectancy derived from our own past experience.

Bruner and Postman have suggested that there are any number of differences in the kinds and strengths of hypotheses individuals utilize as a result of motivational factors, past experience, and personality structure. As a matter of fact, hypotheses with strong motivational and cognitive support need *less* stimulus input for confirmation and more contradictory input for infirming them. Thus there is an ample framework in this approach for accounting for set, individual variables, individual differences, and obvious differences between, on the one hand, clear-cut and direct and, on the other hand, impoverished stimulation. Moreover, there is an appreciation of the role of the stimulus, as well as an attempt to state more specifically how and under what conditions "central states" influence perception.

It should be noted that in their reformulation Bruner and Postman argued against the simple statement that motivational factors have a *direct* influence on perception. They indicated that inferences, cognition, and a process of categorization are directly involved in all perceptual events, and that these are essentially learned processes. Moreover

(Postman, 1953a), they deplored the fact that nonmotivational variables, such as stimulus characteristics and S's verbal response habits were virtually ignored in earlier studies. Postman, especially (*Ibid.*), suggested that there was much to consider in the argument that perception *per se* was *not* affected by motivational elements, but that verbal and motor responses used to indicate perception *were* subject to motivational effects. He felt that earlier directive-state studies, since they were based on conditions of reduced stimulation, were unrepresentative.

In general, Postman has turned to association and learning theories as an explanatory concept for some of the earlier results, and has suggested that a separate perceptual theory is not crucial. Many of these results, he felt, were satisfactorily "explained" by laws of frequency, effect, selective verbal reporting, subjective "instructions" resulting in inhibition of certain responses, etc. Thus he questioned whether or not perceptual discrimination itself was influenced:

Motivational selectivity in perceptual discrimination is often mediated by and is a consequence of, the operation of (these) general principles of learning. There is little evidence for direct sensitizing effects of motivational conditions on perception. Apparent motivational selectivity may sometimes be produced by artifacts of performance. The analysis of performance variables represents a major methodological problem in the investigation of motivational factors in perception (*Ibid.*, p. 99).

Thus, hypothesis theory states that perception is inferential in nature and yet, to varying degrees, represents reality in a predictive and adaptive sense. We learn to perceive, and this learning involves learning how to make predictions and how to confirm our expectations about the world around us. In other words, perception involves a process of inference or categorization from cues as to the identity of things around us and the nature of the physical world in which we live. Category systems may be more or less adequate, and this will determine the veridicality of the perception that results.

Bruner's later reformulation of hypothesis theory (1957) introduces terms such as categorization, cue-search, confirmation check, and confirmation completion; perception is now regarded by him as a decision process which involves probabilities of events, coding of stimulus input into appropriate categories, etc. "Gating" is also introduced (increase or decrease of sensitivity to incoming stimuli at the peripheral level), as well as "noise" (masking of cues that could be used to discriminate an environmental event). Thus learned probabilities are introduced as an "explanatory" factor, but the hypothesis theory of perception as such is only restated in more contemporary language, rather than really modified or replaced. For example, what is now called accessibility of categories had formerly been called "arousal of hypothesis."

The formulation just presented has certain limitations, chiefly arising from the fact that there is little specific tie-in with data or knowledge from neurophysiology. As a nonphysiological system, however, it organizes many facts about nonveridical perception within its scope; it ties in with many facts already known concerning set; and it has the distinct advantage of being coordinated with the mainstream of psychology, specifically because of its utilization of some of the laws of associative learning. Although still essentially a directive-state approach, this reformulation has ironed out many of the "kinks" and inadequacies of earlier formulations. According to Floyd Allport (1955, pp. 402–406), who, in his review of theories of perception, was rather favorably impressed with this reformulation, there are, nevertheless, some serious limitations, including the failure to stress or give equal status to problems of veridical perception. Yet Allport seems willing to concede the fact that by expanding the aspects of this approach that specifically relate to set, and by further refinements and research along these theoretical lines, many known facts as well as mysteries about the perceptual process, even those of a physiological nature "inside" the organism, might be better understood.

## SOME ADDITIONAL PROBLEM AREAS

The following sections describe some special areas of perceptual research, methodology, and concepts. These areas, although of marked theoretical interest, can best be described outside the context of the review of the theories in the previous sections, but could be included here only after the consideration of theories. Some of these areas have important implications for one or more of the theoretical systems just described, and when this is the case, it will be indicated.

*Perceptual Learning.* The stress on learning in different theoretical approaches varies considerably. Some approaches, such as functionalism, suggest that learning is the key to the perceptual event; other approaches (such as the gestaltist's) deny the associationistic approach; still others (Hebb's approach, for example) regard associationism as the key to an understanding of how the perceptual aggregate is built up. This section attempts to illustrate the nature of some of these controversies. It might be noted that the nativism-empiricism argument is by no means dead.

One aspect of the controversy centers around the origin of perceptual acts and their initial wholeness and completeness, as opposed to the notion that there is a gradual building up on an associationistic basis of the mature perceptual act. But this is not the whole picture. Whether or not an innate approach is accepted, there are additional controversies concerning the modifiability of a perceptual event, the laws concerning this modifiability, and even whether or not central or peripheral processes are involved. For example, Platt (1960) illustrated with clarity, through an examination of how straight lines are perceived, that peripheral, retinal elements—not even motor elements—eventually become associated, through frequency, with the perception of straightness. After learning, new lines need not be scanned afresh, whereas originally, in order to perceive a line as straight, rotations of eyeball in scanning movements are involved.

As already noted, although the learning theories of many workers attempt to embrace all behavior under the rubric of learning, specific attention to perception *per se*, has been minimized. The perceptual event, since it is a phenomenological bit of datum, is usually classified with other intervening variables and is by-passed in the attempt to formulate testable, operational laws of S-R associations. For this reason, the rich theoretical and experimental products of the various learning theories will not be described. On the other hand, learning theories of various kinds suggest and logically imply that perceptions are learned acts. Thus perceptual responses will follow the same laws as other responses, and this can be experimentally tested. For many learning theorists, reinforcement (drive-reduction), discrimination of cues, generalization, level of drive, acquired drives, habit strength, goal-gradients, anticipatory goal responses, and the like, would apply as much to a perceptual act, and the *learning* of the act, as they would to a motor or verbal response. Since the discrimination of cues is an essential aspect of most learning theories and responses are elicited (according to strength of habit) by various stimuli, the perception of such cues, we would think, should be of more concern to learning theorists.

The degree to which perceptual events are subject to various laws of learning is still another aspect of the perception-learning problem. Thus nativists may well claim (as they do) that the origin of a perceptual act is essentially unlearned, although they are willing to admit that the act itself is subsequently modifiable through various operations. This problem has direct bearing on the problem of perception as a clue to personality and motivation, since if perceptual acts *are* modifiable, the direction in which they become modified may well be an indication of the past experiences, expectations, and motivations of S.

Thus, by the direct study of perception in the laboratory, with attempts to modify perception through various principles of learning, the question of the effects of past experience on the perceptual act can be explored—with direct relevance to notions raised by the directive-state theorists. A complete review of this problem, that is, learning and perception, will not be attempted. Rather, three viewpoints will be discussed—each directly relevant to three theoretical positions described earlier. These viewpoints are: gestalt approach, Gibson's approach, and directive-state approach (and associationism).

1. Gestalt researchers pay tribute to the role of the past in perception through the arousal of memory traces which, as previously noted, occurs after the perceptual event. Memory traces, residuals of previous perceptual events, follow the same isomorphic laws of organization as does the phenomenological experience. The reader is referred once again to Pastore (1960), who lucidly stated the gestalt view of the innateness of perception. Over a decade ago, Pastore (1949) attacked some of the work of Murphy, Bruner, Postman, and their co-workers, suggesting that the marginal perceptual situations they used were inadequate and that an overly flexible use of the term perception had been made, that is, judgments, rather than perceptions were probably involved. Moreover, he noted, perceptual selectivity should not imply that perception is actually modified. Later Pastore (1956) expanded some of these points and made the additional point, with dismay, that experience-oriented theorists even imply that shape, size, and depth perception are learned. According to the empiricists, initially there is a random perceptual response to a given stimulus, that is, the relationship between a stimulus and a perceptual event is a fortuitous one, and any particular perceptual process may lead to a random number of motor responses. Pastore argued, however, that initial perceptual and motor randomness is an impossibility, since it is incompatible with the fact that learned behavior, that is, learning, as with motor responses, *does* take place, and to a specific visual stimulus, so that the *perception* of that stimulus must have been present from the beginning.

2. Gibson is concerned primarily with *veridical* perception, whereas the position of the "New Look" people is demonstrated primarily with respect to nonveridical perception. Nevertheless, Gibson and some of the directive-state workers have been engaged in a controversy which might be interesting to sketch briefly. The Gibson group, despite an approach which is essentially nonempiricist, has recognized the fact that perceptual learning occurs under many conditions. Improved skills in perceptual judgments as a function of training (discrimination learn-

ing), seem to be an important feature of this learning (Eleanor Gibson, 1953). In a statement about social perception and the psychology of perceptual learning, Gibson (1953) noted, after a discussion of some of Sherif's work, that *words* are involved in social conformity, rather than perception; perception changes only the amount or detail of stimuli differentiated. Empiricists can only say how learning creates misperception, not veridical perception. He stated,

Perception is selective. It is also true that the percept of one person is that which his characteristic motives make relevant. Perception will differ among different individuals in the same situation. But in all cases the percept is in correspondence with some variable or set of variables in the vast and complex flux of stimulation explored by our sense organs. . . . The progress of learning in perception is not in the direction of becoming *independent* of stimulation but, on the contrary, in the direction of becoming *more dependent on higher order variables of stimulation.* . . . Perhaps learning is not the ability to summon up memory-traces but the ability to experience stimulation in a new way, and the former ability is only incidental to the process (*Ibid.*, p. 135).

Gibson's position (Gibson & Gibson, 1955*a;* 1955*b*), stated in connection with specific questions raised by Postman (1955), is the following. The traditional distinction between sensation and perception is obsolete. Information about the world is registered only through variations in energy which come through the senses. Nothing is added through learning, and enrichment as a result of learning does not take place—only further differentiation of previously vague impressions. The empiricists suggest that perception becomes "more imaginary" and further removed from sensory input. Gibson feels, however, that through learning, perception becomes more discriminatory and in *greater* correspondence with stimulation, that is, in *closer* touch with the environment. Stimuli are complex and do not function as cues until they are a matter of energy falling on the receptors; learning enters into the situation when the complexity is differentiated and S can respond to complexity as a cue. Learning helps us to discriminate more of the energy variables around us, that is, helps us to respond with increasing sensitivity to the stimulus array. Learning is not so much a change in the perceptual response as it is a change in what the organism is responding to.

3. Postman (1955) attempted to refute Gibson's position. He argued for a psychological associationism, eschewing any particular physiological constructs, and indicated that Gibson's approach did not allow for testable hypotheses. In general, he went along with Titchener in stating that, with perceptual learning, more is associated and eventually "perceived" than is "put in"—a position in marked contrast to that

of Gibson. Postman's approach and argument were based essentially on learning theory: perceptual learning occurs when there is a change in stimulus-response relationships, and the process would follow the usual laws of frequency, recency, effect, etc. The same principles which apply to verbal and motor learning would be effective here. Memory and association *are* involved, and perception, treated as a response, would therefore be subsumed in the broader context of associative learning. Although he agreed that learning theories in general have little to say about physiological and neurological aspects of perceptual learning, this is no reason to reject them as irrelevant.

Another refutation, this time of the gestalt position (especially that of Pastore [1949]), can be found in a note by Chein, Lane, Murphy, Proshansky, and Schafer (1951). These authors, who have defended the directive-state position with much feeling, have argued that past events and motivational factors *are* extremely important determinants of perception. For a more eclectic, "functional" position see Hilgard (1951), whose position is representative of that of many psychologists, particularly those with a learning orientation. This position can be summarized as follows. Although there is much evidence to suggest that structural, anatomical, and chemical factors modify perception, and that there are probably innate preferences, such as for patterned stimuli, learning *does* play a role in perception. The empiricism-nativism controversy is still raging, and the same experimental evidence is often used to support either side of the argument. But perception, treated as a response, is goal oriented—the achievement of environmental stability and definitiveness in the world around us may be regarded as a secondary, learned drive, essential for the achievement of other goals. Thus, not only may a perceptual event be influenced by learned needs, motives, sets, and the like, but the perceptual achievement itself and the *way* we perceive is also learned. Thus, briefly stated, we have the very antithesis of the gestalt position.

The reader is referred, finally, to a volume by Solley and Murphy (1960) which is a general survey of relevant experimental and theoretical material. Much of the experimental work surveyed was done in the laboratory of Gardner Murphy and his co-workers, and was based on experimental situations using impoverished stimuli, or ones in which $E$ forces $S$ to perceive in opposition to "natural" perceiving. Perceptual changes as a result of learning have been amply demonstrated.

For example, the influence of reward and punishment on perception was investigated by Proshansky and Murphy (1942). The purpose of this experiment was to build up, by means of rewards and punishments, a tendency to perceive in a predetermined manner; in other words, to induce autistic thinking in the individual. Eleven college students served as Ss. The experiment was divided into three periods: a pretraining period in which lines and weights were estimated; a training period in which a money reward was given in association with certain percepts and taken away in association with other percepts; and a post-training period physically identical with the first pretraining period. The experimental Ss showed in the post-training series significant shifts in the direction of the rewarded percepts. Control Ss showed no significant shifts in perception. The authors concluded that by suitable rewards and punishments the nature of the percept can be altered even though the stimulus remains the same.

Note should also be made of a general discussion by Murphy (1956) of the role of affect in perceptual learning. The particular aspect considered was pleasantness-unpleasantness with the general hypothesis being that ". . . given two or more aspects of a perceptual whole and repeatedly associating one of these with positive affect, will tend, when these various perceptual aspects are simultaneously presented, to lead the dominant role to be taken by that which has been associated with positive affect" (p. 3). Murphy's presentation surveyed various historical, theoretical, methodological, and experimental aspects of this general thesis, and his conclusions suggest that there is much evidence to support his notions.

According to Solley and Murphy, drive reduction in the usual sense is not necessary for perceptual learning to take place. Reinforcement is present in all perceptual acts, however, since they postulate that structuring or making "sense" out of sensory input is itself reinforcing.

Following a generally eclectic approach, but one which acknowledges "inside" factors, Solley and Murphy state that all of the following may be involved in a perceptual event: feedback of proprioceptive, motor, memory and sensory impulses, expectancies, memory factors, and energic input to the brain. The authors feel that this restatement of the directive-state approach is an improvement over S-R theory, wherein the stimulus is sometimes outside the organism, sometimes sensory and at the proximal level, sometimes social, etc., and E, in most cases, is never really sure that the stimulus is what he thinks it is. The authors describe perception as a process extended in time, taking due account of preparatory sets, expectancies, and sensoritonic states; incidental and surrounding stimuli the moment before stimulation; attending; reception; "inside" factors and the nature of the brain structure; autonomic and proprioceptive arousal and feedback; trial-and-check of the organism (there is a time lag between reception and the final product); and consolidation of stimulus traces into a percept. Solley and Murphy, it might be noted, have considered the viewpoints and research arising from many of the differing theoretical positions already described.

A perceptual act is thus analyzed into temporal phases. Any of these phases can become altered through learning; various types of perceptual responses and deviations can be thus explained. Autism, for example, utilizes feedback and "inner" stimuli more than "outer." Failures in veridical perception, bizarreness in perception, lack of productivity, pathological perception, and the like, may similarly be explained by "noise" at any of these temporal phases.

In their extensive review of related research in this area, much of it their own, the authors have summarized general principles of perceptual learning research. For example, positive reinforcers (external) are most efficient when the percept is poorly structured; negative reinforcers have a disruptive effect if given at the moment of the perceptual act. Gardner Murphy has come to believe that almost all aspects of the perceptual act belong in the same class and are subject to the same laws as the type of responses studied by learning theorists; his co-author, incidentally, did not completely agree with his formulations.

By way, not of summary, but of a general summarizing *question*, it might be said that the general problems do not seem to be resolved. Are we sure that learning has a *direct* effect on the perceptual act and that it (learning) does not operate through the altering of competing responses, attention, expectancies, set, "style" of response, motor or verbal behavior rather than on the perceptual act itself?

*Sensory Deprivation.* Hebb's contribution to theories of perception has already been noted. His theoretical orientation has stressed the importance of early experiences in our perceptual responses. A body of experimental work has recently emerged which, although spurred by Hebb's theory, has significance by itself for our purposes. Specifically, recent evidence concerning sensory deprivation and "perceptual" or "social isolation" indicates once again the complex relationship between perception and central states. Further, the delicate, interdependent balance between and among factors of stimulation from without, activity of the central nervous system, and perceptual experiences is also indicated by these studies. For a good overview of the field the reader is referred to a report (Solomon, *et al.*, 1961) which summarizes a symposium concerned with sensory deprivation.

The various studies and accumulated data in this area do not examine the organism's behavior from the point of view of how changes or modifications in values, needs or existing "states" (such as personality) of the organism have influenced the perceptual event. They are concerned, rather, with the changes in the organism's behavior which occur when he is placed in a situation where there is reduced or virtually no stimulation from without, and/or reduced patterning of sensory input, or monotony of sensory input—these conditions being achieved in social isolation. By manipulating sensory input, novel approaches to the study of perception, individual differences in isolation, and the central nervous system have been made possible.

Although literature is available on the effects of isolation written by shipwrecked sailors, prisoners, etc., most of these are anecdotal. Even so, clear-cut and vivid accounts of incapacitation in judgment and reasoning, hallucinatory experiences, bizarre imagery, emotional changes and perceptual distortions have been reported. These reports are not unlike those by (or were observed with respect to) people in psychotic states and under the influence of varying types of drugs, narcotics, and anoxic conditions or with certain organic brain involvements. It was not until Hebb became interested in these phenomena that systematic experimental research was undertaken on a large scale. It might seem that the space age with its astronauts and extended journeys into the universe has spurred interest in this area, in view of the fact that man-in-space is being subjected not only to the rigors of radiation, weightlessness, excessive heat, "g," lack of atmospheric pressure and oxygen, etc., but to the even more formidable array of problems presented by isolation, sensory deprivation and loneliness-over-time. Actually, however, the work of Hebb and his associates in the early 1950's was motivated by some of the problems posed by the "brainwashing" of prisoners of war, and its effect on subsequent judgment and perception. Since, as already noted, Hebb's particular approach to the neurophysiology of perception involves a belief that central processes and early learning experiences are important aspects of the mature perceptual event, it was logical that he should turn to an exploration of early deprivation experiences and their subsequent effects on the development of the central nervous system.

The general procedure for many of the experiments in this area (with animals as well as humans) is to isolate S in a cubicle in which sensory input—visual, auditory, tactile stimulation—is at a minimum (all or one of various sensory areas might be manipulated in a given experimental setting) or so diffuse and undifferentiated that S is unable to "perceive" anything. The sensory input might be monotonous or repetitive, without sensory reduction. Tests are administered and behavior observed during, before, or after experimental exposure in a variety of areas: perceptual, cognitive, spatial, motor, intellectual, physiological, electroencephalographic, etc. Apart from "breaks" for toileting and feeding, Ss could be in these conditions of sensory deprivation for stretches ranging from several hours to several days.

During the period of isolation itself, many important individual differences emerged as to tolerance for isolation, anxiety, and content of reactions. These differences have been regarded by some workers as important evidence for demonstrating the role of central states and individual differences in perception. In the main, however, the general reports of hallucinatory experiences, acute unpleasantness, and disorganization of thinking and judgment on the part of Ss, have been interpreted so as to highlight the relevance and importance of patterning and stimulation in the environment, that is, the need for a certain type of afferent input to maintain a steady, normal, and functioning central nervous system state. For example, on the basis of experimental work with mammals, Riesen (1961) reported that after prolonged early sensory deprivation, his experimental animals manifested severe perceptual and emotional disturbances as well as hyperexcitability and susceptibility to convulsions with a sudden increase of stimulation. As a result of tests with human Ss, other workers have demonstrated that severe disruption and disorganization were found in various motor, perceptual, and cognitive tasks; disturbances in EEG records, etc., were also noted.

Although it is not feasible to summarize in detail the implications these experiments have for central nervous system functioning, it seems that a certain level of excitability and frequency of neuronal discharge as a result of varied and patterned stimulation is necessary for the efficiency and stability of the brain. Others have spoken of a central regulating system which is "upset" or put into imbalance under various sensory conditions—deprivation, overload, or distortion. Stimulation which is consistently repeated may have similar neurophysiological effects to those correlated with the absence of or low sensory input.

Various workers from different disciplines such as psychiatry, neurology, and physiology have offered a number of different "explanations" for the phenomena just noted. The perceptionists with an essentially "functional" orientation tend to regard these experimental results as suggesting that in his perception of his environment the organism is constantly seeking "meaning," order, and orientation in time and space—if this is not possible, emotional disturbance as well as other behavioral disorganization will result. Even more specifically, Bruner (1961) has interpreted the disorganizing effects of early sensory deprivation in terms of inadequate opportunities to test hypotheses about reality and to manipulate the environment, with a resulting impoverishment of ability to handle the environment later on. No matter what the theoretical orientation, however, most workers seem to be agreed that stimulation of a patterned nature is essential for normal brain functioning, emotional stability, and perceptual organization. If deprivation occurs in early stages of development, damage may be irreversible. Early learning experiences, therefore, seem to be crucial for development.

The personologists have in addition stressed the wide array of individual differences in response to sensory deprivation or social or perceptual isolation conditions. Is there support as a result of these studies for the directive-state approach? It is too early to tell. There are methodological problems, inconsistencies in experimental approach, confusion of terms, conflicting or inconsistent "explanations," and ambiguities in the operational definition of sensory deprivation. What is the role, for example, of afferent impulses arising from S's own body? The reader is referred to Kubzansky and Leiderman (1961) for a statement and overview of some of these problems. Attention should also be drawn to a report by Schaefer (1964), who on the basis of experimental findings, put forth the notion that suggestion or expectancy is a sufficient condition to elicit the sorts of subjective reports described by workers in this area.

Suffice it to say that for our purposes an important lesson is learned: a study of the organism, particularly of his perceptual experiences, must be placed not only in the context of neurological organization but also in the context of the continuous flux of stimulation in his surrounding environment and that arising from his own body. A few theorists have stressed one or another aspect of this "unity"; only rarely have there been attempts to integrate data and material from all the disciplines and observational levels involved.

*Subception: Discrimination without Awareness.* Essential to most directive-state theories, as well as to many assumptions underlying the often taken-for-granted relation of needs and motives to perception, is the presence of some underlying unconscious process, involving a "preperceiver," subliminal response, or more commonly, subception, or discrimination without awareness. Simply and briefly, the subliminal effect is this: a stimulus, presented to Ss below recognition thresholds (i.e., before awareness of that stimulus is reported) can be shown (it is claimed) to elicit a response despite S's lack of awareness of that stimulus. Recognition thresholds—the level at which S is aware of a particular stimulus—may vary from subject to subject; there are many procedures used to determine such thresholds, but often, the methods of traditional psychophysics have been used.

Most of the experiments in this area have utilized visual stimuli, tachistoscopically presented with varying exposure-times (measured usually in milliseconds). However, subliminal effects have also been obtained by varying brightness or vividness of the stimulus, its clarity or delineation, illumination of surroundings, distance of stimulus from the observer, size of the stimulus, etc. In short, almost any paremeter which can be manipulated in the stimulus by successive decreases or increases of, for example intensity, size, or duration, may be utilized to demonstrate the effect. Moreover, effects can be found with respect to other sensory modalities. Tactile, olfactory, and auditory (even taste) stimuli have also been presented, either so rapidly or at such a low intensity, that although S has not recognized the stimulus or has had no awareness of its presence, some response has been elicited. Of course for any of the stimuli used, if exposure-time is too rapid or intensity too low to elicit excitation, there will be no response at all.

The demonstration of subliminal or below-threshold discrimination is "old hat" in traditional psychology. Experiments demonstrating the effect were described as far back as a century ago. In 1863, for example, subliminal electrical stimulation was reported to have had an effect on the Ss' responses (see Miller [1939], and Adams [1957] for a review of some of these studies, which were often concerned with the discrimination of weights, geometric designs, or even whispers; other reviews have been written by Eriksen [1960]; Jenkin [1957]; McConnell, Cutler, & McNeil [1958]; and Miller [1942]). Pierce and Jastrow (1884) demonstrated that Ss could make correct judgments (on a basis which exceeded chance expectancies) of which weights were heavier or lighter, without any awareness that the weights differed in any way, and with absolutely no confidence in the way they were making a decision except on the basis of a sheer "guess."

More recently, Williams (1938) presented one of three geometrical figures on a screen, below threshold, and had his Ss guess which of the figures was being projected. Results were much more accurate than could be expected on a chance basis. Miller (1939) similarly projected one of several geometric figures at varying degrees of illumination, all below threshold, and reported better than chance "guesses" as to the identification of these figures, although Vinacke (1942) could not replicate these results. King, Landis, and Zubin (1944), however, reported success in demonstrating subliminal effects with respect to "guessing" (better than chance) the forms of a circle, square, or triangle which were projected on a screen with visibility obscured by "flooding" with strong illumination. The authors also reported that intensity of the subliminal stimuli, the particular form, and the "distance" below threshold did not affect the accuracy of the response.

Coyne, King, Zubin, and Landis (1943) have described a study demonstrating subliminal recognition of auditory stimuli; Miller (1940) demonstrated that subliminal responses are modifiable through learning; and Davis (1950) has done research based on the well-known fact that moderate auditory stimuli produce muscular tension responses (increased action potentials). On the basis of a study in four body areas, Davis reported that muscular responses were recorded whether or not the stimulus was reported heard, although subliminal auditory stimuli produced smaller increases in action potential than supraliminal stimuli.

The recent literature claiming evidence for subliminal effects continues to be substantial. A previous section which summarized the New Look studies, especially those pertaining to perceptual defense, describes some of the "classical" studies, such as McGinnies (1949), who used meaningful words—taboo and nontaboo—tachistoscopically exposed, to demonstrate the effect. Meaningful words are not necessary to demonstrate a subliminal effect, however. McCleary and Lazarus ([1949]; also Lazarus & McCleary [1951]) worked with ten nonsense syllables of five letters each. They exposed these stimuli for one second (above recognition threshold), but for five of these nonsense syllables, the exposure was accompanied by an electric shock, thus creating an unpleasant association with those five syllables. After some repetition, a galvanic skin response was conditioned to the five syllables, so that anyone of these critical stimuli could elicit a galvanic skin response without an accompanying electric shock. All ten nonsense syllables were then tachistoscopically exposed at varying speeds below threshold, without shock. For the syllables which had previously been accompanied by shock, there was a greater galvanic skin response than for the other syllables. Ss, in other words, were still making a discrimination, measurable through their GSR, but below the level of awareness.

Hatfield (1959), by verbal means as well as by use of electric shock, conditioned negative associations to certain nonsense syllables. When these syllables, along with others which had not been negatively conditioned, were presented to the Ss below recognition thresholds, the syllables which received the negative associations were recognized more quickly than those which did not.

Rubenfeld, Lowenfeld, and Guthrie (1956) reported another study concerned with GSR, but this time conditioned to stimuli which could not be verbalized. The authors were concerned with the generalization of GSR to similar stimuli. Working with geometric designs, eight of which were basically rectangular and four of which were basically triangular, they presented these figures tachistoscopically to their Ss. Some of the "square" stimuli had been previously associated with shock and a GSR had been conditioned to them. Subsequent tachistoscopic "subliminal" exposure of various stimuli showed that GSR responses were generalized to similar figures but not to dissimilar figures.

Smith (1957) described experimental work in which a short tachistoscopic presentation of stimulus A, of which S was unaware, was followed by an above threshold presentation of stimulus B. Reports on B were demonstrated to be significantly influenced by A when B was preceded by A; but when not preceded by A, this effect was absent. (See also Smith & Henriksson [1955].) Jenkin (1955; 1956), working with ambiguous picture material exposed at various levels of illumination, found decidedly characteristic and classifiable responses when "guesses" as to the nature of this material were obtained. Not only were responses at the prerecognition level classifiable, but they bore a definite relationship to personality characteristics of the Ss. This work is related to a study by Stein (1949) who utilized tachistoscopic exposure of Rorschach stimuli, and is also related to some of the research of "microgenetic" investigators (see next section).

Another recent experiment is that of Eriksen, Azuma, and Hicks (1959), who tachistoscopically presented to their Ss two sets of words which had previously been judged to be pleasant or unpleasant. Ss were asked to guess the identification of the words and whether or not the words were pleasant or unpleasant. Although the identification of the words was incorrect, Ss' judgments of the tone of the word were more often correct than could be attributed to chance. Spence (1957) found that when Ss were asked to identify tachistoscopically presented words, half of which had been previously associated with anxiety and failure, they had either markedly raised or markedly lowered thresholds for the recognition of these words, in contrast to the thresholds for the nonfailure and for the nonanxiety words. Newton (1955) equated words in terms of frequency of usage, and, after presenting them tachistoscopically, found that there were fewer errors in identifying pleasant as compared to unpleasant words. And Aronfreed, Messick, and Diggory (1953) also found increases in GSR when unpleasant words, as contrasted with pleasant or neutral words, were encountered in tachistoscopic presentations below threshold.

Dixon, a British psychologist, has written extensively in this area. On the basis of experimental results (1956), he has suggested that responses made to subliminal presentation of certain stimuli are symbolic associations (in a Freudian sense). In working with subliminally presented visual or auditory stimuli, he described three experiments in which Ss were required to make verbal guesses as to the identity of words presented subliminally. In one experiment, Ss "guessed" at one of fifty words each time a light went on, the words being presented below their auditory thresholds. Some of these words were of emotional interest—with or without sexual meaning—others were neutral, and still others were of a sexual or taboo nature. The Ss responded with increased reaction time to all the emotional words. An examination of their guesses also disclosed, the author noted, that their responses were associations to the stimuli—a number of which were Freudian symbols, rather than ordinary associations.

Dixon's second experiment (*Ibid.*) was like the first, only this time the Ss were requested to select their "guess" word from a list of twenty words. The findings disclosed that there was a tendency to select a symbol whenever one of the three sexual words was subliminally presented, and, in addition, other emotionally laden, subliminally presented words received a corresponding "guess" which had associative meaning to the stimulus word.

Dixon's third experiment (*Ibid.*) was concerned with whether or not these effects could be repeated with a visual stimulus, and whether or not an emotional disturbance was created of which S was unaware. The procedure was similar to that just noted, except this time words were flashed on an illuminated screen at subliminal intensities. GSR's were used as measures of emotional response. The results, which were statistically significant, showed that all Ss responded with heightened galvanic skin responses when "emotional" words were presented as compared to the neutral words.

Dixon (1958) reported a study which attempted to account for some of the criticisms advanced by many workers who have sought for alternative explanations for the subception effect. This particular study has been regarded as strong evidence and support on the side of the subceptionist. The author's experimental approach eliminated the use of *verbal* indicators of a subliminal effect; furthermore, he was concerned with absolute thresholds of awareness of light exposed to the left eye, while verbal material of varying degrees of emotionality was subliminally presented to S's right eye. Voluntary suppression of response is eliminated, since S is unaware of the presentation of verbal material, it might be noted. Dixon tested the following hypotheses among others: "That the differential visual threshold for the left eye would be raised when 'emotional' as opposed to neutral stimulus material was presented to the right eye, at subthreshold intensities; . . . and that threshold changes brought about by 'emotional' stimulus material would to some extent be a function of the sex of the percipient" (p. 213).

His main results indicated that higher thresholds were obtained during exposure of "emotional" words than neutral words. For individual subjects, however, trends were found which indicated consistently raised or consistently lowered thresholds for the emotional stimuli, that is, individual Ss were consistently "vigilant" or "defensive" with respect to their responses. Some sex differences in threshold were found, too. Although his findings, in the main, supported his hypotheses, he noted some methodological difficulties in the design of his experiment. These included the fact that the "familiarity" factor of the stimulus words was not controlled, nor was sufficient attention paid to the possible factor of "waning attention" in accounting for higher thresholds.

As a result of the foregoing methodological considerations, Dixon and Haider introduced some additional controls in a basically similar research study, reported a few years later (1961). One important control was that emotionally tinged words were selected with a *higher* frequency value than the neutral words; raised thresholds for such words could therefore not be accounted for in terms of their relative unfamiliarity, as compared to the neutral words. The four words used (cancer, breast, recant, and stance) were more or less equivalent in terms of brightness, length, and as far as possible, for letter content. Ss were subsequently asked to report the degree to which the words held an unpleasant association for them. Ruled out, by preliminary analysis, was a subliminal effect due to the *light* being transmitted rather than word content and meaning. The word "cancer" not only showed the highest thresholds, but was subsequently reported to hold the highest rank in terms of degree of unpleasant association. Among some of the author's conclusions, are the following:

The results support the conclusion from an earlier research (1958) that anxiety provoking stimuli presented below threshold to one eye will evoke a rise in the visual threshold as measured for the other eye. They indicate moreover that the relative familiarity of the stimulus items does not constitute a decisive factor. In the previous experiment those stimulus items which appeared to evoke higher thresholds were less familiar than the other and neutrally toned items. In this experiment the reverse held good. A further point of significance regarding the present experiment is that it showed a relationship between conscious judgments regarding the emotionality of the stimulus words and the effect of these same words upon the threshold (p. 234).

There has been some lively controversy as to the validity of the "subliminal effect." Those who have claimed reliable evidence for this concept include Klein (1959); Klein, Spence, Holt, and Gourevitch (1958); Lazarus (1956); Lazarus and McCleary (1951); and Solley and Murphy (1960). Workers who have challenged certain methodological and theoretical aspects of the concept include Bricker and Chapanis (1953); Eriksen (1956a, 1960); Goldiamond (1958); Hochberg and Hochberg (1953); and Wiener and Schiller (1960). The position of the subceptionist is clearly being challenged with considerable vigor.

One of the challenges is aimed at the assumption of an underlying unconscious process in the perceptual act. This challenge can be summarized as follows: "Unconscious process" is one of the most loosely defined, yet almost always revered, constructs in personality theory. Few adequate methodological and experimental studies are concerned with defining this process; and there are still fewer studies of a theoretical or of a hypothesis-testing nature. Most of us "take on faith" the belief that the data (or demonstration of evidence) show the working of the unconscious. In many of the studies concerning perceptual defense, sensitization, etc., discrimination without awareness is taken for granted. In such studies, lack of awareness is often equated with S's failure to produce a verbal report—at best, a highly tentative assumption—since verbal reports are subject to many factors which might often prevent a complete verbalization of something of which S might well be aware.

Some workers have suggested that the subliminal effect is probably a reflection of response to partial or incidental, or to peripheral cues; a "two-way" process of perception—subliminal and supraliminal—is thus eliminated (Bricker & Chapanis [1953]; Jenkin [1957]; and Wiener & Schiller [1960]). Even Klein et al. (1958), who with an ingenious experimental design studied cognitive effects of stimuli that do not give rise to conscious percepts, admitted the possibility that their experiment did not aim explicitly to explore the possibility that their "subliminal" stimuli may, in fact, have been partly discriminable.

Still another challenge relates to the New Look position that some sort of "preperceiving" process is at work. The New Look position asserts that recognition of the stimulus and its meaning occurs before perceptual organization takes place, and that this "preperception" elicits certain "defenses" which may prevent conscious perception of that stimulus. Who does this preperceiving? (Floyd Allport [1955] gives a general criticism of this "homunculus" approach.) Hochberg and Hochberg (1953) further noted a methodological criticism of "preperceiving" studies: "Experiments which permit or even encourage subsequent modification of earlier responses before final measurement is made do not constitute convincing evidence of the inferential nature of the first responses" (p. 343).

Set, instructions, and many other variables (planned and unplanned in an experimental situation) such as social factors, competing responses, even irrelevant responses, might well help to hinder, distort, inhibit, or even block a concise verbal report from being rendered. In other words, there are alternative interpretations for many of the results cited. Hochberg, Haber, and Ryan (1955) have suggested that competing and alternative responses are evoked simultaneously by a stimulus. If an emotional or autonomic response does occur, it may be so strong as to interfere with the evocation of the verbal report, thereby giving the impression that a "subliminal response" has occurred. Adams (1957), in his extensive review, concluded that demonstrations of discrimination without awareness are based on the fact that S does not know that he is discriminating because of the absence of the usual sensory experiences he has become accustomed to expect. Adams believes that the effect has been best demonstrated in circumstances in which S knows *what* he is supposed to discriminate, but not *that* he is discriminating at any particular time. This would suggest that foreknowledge or familiarity with certain stimuli exposed at above-threshold levels would enhance a subliminal effect when these same stimuli are exposed subliminally.

Eriksen (1960) also felt that lack of awareness of *above*-threshold cues, competing responses, etc., could account for the subliminal effect, and that so-called below-threshold cues are not below threshold at all. He did not believe (1956a; 1956b) that affective and emotional judgments are "earlier" or more simple responses than verbal responses and therefore more liable than a conscious, verbal report to occur to a subliminal stimulus. He felt that both types of response may occur at the same time, and that the emotional response may be correct whereas the verbal response may be incorrect and vice-versa. This would explain, he felt, many experimental findings in this area. In other words, he does not agree with the assumption that affective responses can occur temporally prior to verbal identification, and that there are two perceptual thresholds, one for affective discrimination and the other for verbal identification (see also Fuhrer & Eriksen [1960]).

Finally, note should be made again that the question of the validity of the indicator used as the criterion for the "subliminal" effect is an extremely significant one. A previous section has already discussed this problem, and reference has been made to Goldiamond (1958), who reviewed the relevant literature extensively and explained many of the subliminal effects in terms of methodological problems inherent in the design of a large group of these experiments. Ss may, for example, say that they did not see the stimulus, but they may, in fact, simply not report that they had seen it. Partial cues, instructions, manner of scoring, certain problems in the use of ascending and descending series, etc., may also in part explain the effect.

Another question that needs to be considered arises from the newly developed area of "detection theory" (Swets, Tanner, & Birdsall, 1961). This approach grows out of an attempt to deal with threshold determinations from the point of view of the signal to noise ratio in which the signal is to be detected despite the ever present "noise" in the sensory system. By introducing blank trials (absence of signal) and noting the frequency with which S responds with "yes" to these trials (false alarms) and the frequency with which he responds "yes" to the presence of the signal (hits), the subjective criterion by which he detects the presence of the signal can be established. This will vary with such parameters as frequency of blank trials, value system as determined by pay-off ratios of hits to misses, and other subjective criteria. On the other hand, the sensitivity of the S to the signal, which can be determined independently of the subjective criterion, may remain constant, and may be regarded as the basic measure of responsiveness to threshold or supra-threshold values of the stimulus.

Let us now examine some of the results of subception demonstrations from this point of view. Take for example, the King, Landis, and Zubin (1944) or Coyne, King, Zubin, and Landis (1943) studies in which S was able to guess the identity of the stimulus with better than chance probability even though he reported that he did not "perceive" it. We need not invoke any subliminal perception here. We only need to recognize that under the set to guess, his criterion for reporting the identity of the stimulus has been eased, and he is willing to act on lesser cues. Since no set for guessing was given when he was tested for the presence vs. absence of the stimulus, his criterion for this judgment demanded more cues than the guessing set.

In summary, then, it is suggested that the evidence for a process of subception or subliminal perception is by no means convincing. The outcome has not been decided, however. Those who suggest that there are *two* perceptual processes, may well exploit the possibility of convincingly demonstrating their beliefs.

*A "Microgenetic" Approach.* The term "microgenesis," first coined by Heinz Werner (1956) from the German, *Aktualgenese,* refers to stages of events which presumably take place between the time a stimulus is presented and S produces a percept (or cognitive response). Actually, many researchers before this date had experimentally and theoretically employed some notion which suggested that a perceptual event takes place over a period of time, and that a study of the early stages of a single perceptual event, that is, before the final organization of the percept took place, might be a fruitful and provocative area of exploration. The Rorschach inkblots, for example, have been regarded by some workers as essentially "impoverished" stimuli which permit the emergence of a microgenetic process. Thus, Stein (1949) employed successive tachistoscopic presentations of Rorschach stimuli in a study which attempted to shed light on how a final Rorschach percept is built up. Zubin (1951) utilized tachistoscopic exposure of emotionally tinged words obtained from case histories to elicit word associations, in order to examine presolution responses before and after psychosurgery. Jenkin (1955; 1956) exposed ambiguous pictorial stimuli at various levels of illumination to a group of Ss, and classified their attempts to identify these stimuli into five categories. Although such studies are designed to explore the nature of "precognitive" perceptual responses, their point was to find correlations and parallels with personality characteristics in terms of the different types of precognitive perceptual responses. These workers (also Smith, 1957), using tachistoscopic methods, have suggested that, since the preoptimal perceptual events are part of a perceptual process which takes place over time, their study is important for an understanding of the perceptual event. Thus, so-called subliminal perceiving is an aspect of the perceptual process, and has a demonstrable and significant role in our perceptual experiences.

In a comprehensive review of the microgenetic approach to perception and thought, Flavell and Draguns (1957) were more specifically interested in cognitive processes and the pre-stages of such processes, as useful for understanding pathological thought or normal thought under abnormal conditions (such as drugs, semiwakefulness, etc.). In their review of the German literature, mostly from the 1920's, they shed much light on what aktualgenetic psychology is.

The German literature of the 1920's in perception is replete with studies falling within the aktualgenetic framework. The work of Sander (1928; 1930) is representative, and can be used as an illustration of this approach. Sander believed that perception is a developmental process involving distinct phases, each of which could be isolated and described, by exposing various stimuli under inadequate conditions—usually through tachistoscopic exposure. These precognitive stages are "unconscious." The first stage would be a diffuse, undifferentiated whole. Then figure and ground achieve some differentiation. But details remain vague. There is then a third phase in which contour and content achieve some distinctness but it is accompanied by lability. Finally, the cognitive gestalt is formed. The third stage is said to be emotionally-charged. Ss during this stage report feelings of tension and unpleasantness.

Flavell and Draguns, despite their interest in this general approach, have indicated that most of this early work was based on poorly controlled, crude "experiments." They noted that the aktualgenetic "theory" is vague, poorly structured, and loose, which may account for all the different facts it can "subsume" (and indeed, they have described many such reports from the field of pathology, creative thinking, problem solving and from work with normals under varying conditions). "It could be argued, for instance, that the fact that an S might, under time pressure, produce responses classified within the theory as microgenetically undeveloped does not prove conclusively that such responses really 'occur' but are suppressed in the normal, unhurried associative process" (*Ibid.,* p. 212). Furthermore, the tachistoscopic method may not be an accurate reflection of the natural process of perceptual development. Although much of the early and even recent literature in the "microgenetic" area might be criticized from various methodological points of view, on the whole, the interest of contemporary workers using this approach is in perfecting a methodologically sound technique and a framework by which the processes involved in a perceptual event could be understood (e.g., Pollack, 1961).

This general framework and methodology have been utilized recently, in rather a different context and from the point of view of a parallelism in perception-personality thinking. This work, largely illustrated in recent reports by Kragh (1960a; 1960b; 1960c), makes such unwarranted leaps and so many implicit, largely untestable assumptions, that it will be described in moderate detail in order to illustrate some of the pitfalls that are present when an experimental methodology is borrowed for use in the clinic with wholesale disregard for the need for controls, good design, etc.

Briefly, then, Kragh, through a series of analogical steps, attempted to demonstrate that different precognitive stages of perception, as determined by tachistoscopic exposure of various pictorial material (including variations of TAT cards), bear a direct relationship to trauma, events and interpersonal experiences in the early childhood of that subject. Kragh noted that perception and personality are a unit, and that from a study of any S's precognitive responses, dramatic insights and understandings into the S's early history may be obtained. He used case history material to demonstrate this relationship, but he depended on verbal reports and drawings as precognitive responses, which of course, must certainly have had an effect on S's subsequent reports and drawings—a methodological factor Kragh did not consider.

Kragh stated that successive precognitive percepts run parallel to developmental aspects of S's early life history, and that there is a direct parallel from these percepts to changes in the S from early infancy to maturity. In demonstrating these parallels, when unable to find literal translations from the percepts to events and people in S's early life, Kragh spoke of transformations. His demonstration is thus "foolproof." He felt that his analysis of precognitive stages demonstrated quite adequately the oral-sadistic components, primal scene, repression of anxiety, regression to the oral-sadistic level, and primal scene organization of his S's life history. (The case he chose to illustrate his method, was that of a "dipsomaniac.")

After reading Kragh's account to the end, one is convinced that he could do a "foolproof" job of "correlating" his S's precognitive reports and drawings with a completely fictional or random case history! The time spent on this account is of course no indication of the significance of Kragh's method. But there is, perhaps, a lesson to be learned. And that is, that in the zeal to apply a perception-personality approach to clinical and projective material, even with so-called respectable techniques borrowed from the laboratory, it becomes tempting to use analogy, speculation, ill-defined terms, and to eliminate the necessity of proper statistical and experimental controls. After all, it is easy to reason: perception and personality *are* related; it only suffices to demonstrate dramatically how close the relationship really is.

## PERCEPTION AND PROJECTIVE TECHNIQUES

In terms of the status of Rorschach theory, Bruner (1948) noted the need for integration between the Rorschach technique and a perceptual approach: ". . . inkblots are no separate species of perceptual stimulus. There cannot be an independent theory of the perception of inkblots any more than there can be independent theories of the perception of Picasso collages, the phi phenomenon or autokinetic movement" (p. 158). Yet he did not offer an adequate "explanation" of why or how personality influences Rorschach "perception," except in the most general terms by using principles such as perceptual defense. In addition, although he recognized the difference between perception and interpretation, he continued to discuss the problem without adequately handling this difference.

Bruner's comments were made in the context of the historical fact that although Hermann Rorschach described his instrument as a test of perception, users of this technique turned to existing personality theories and terms to construct a framework for their instrument, rather than to the perceptionist and to theories of perception. As a result of the New Look approach in the late 1940's, however, it became increasingly popular to regard the Rorschach as a test of perception. Not only were attempts made to "bring in" principles of perception derived in the laboratory to what had been almost totally a clinical field, but some of the enthusiasm for this point of view spread over even into the TAT field.

The perception-personality marriage, however, so lovingly encouraged by the New Look researchers, yielded little clarification and few new concepts or promising leads. There was frequent reiteration of principles such as perceptual defense, and of the relationship between perception and personality, followed by case reports or illustrative material. For example, Hartman (1959) described an instance of perceptual distortion on the TAT as an illustration ". . . that perceptual distortion is the pathological instance illustrating the general principles of the interaction of personality and perception" (p. 188). In general, as a matter of fact, clinicians attracted to the personality-perception, New Look approach, were wont to review again and again the research of Witkin, Frenkel-Brunswik, McGinnies, etc., to confirm their own belief (and to convince others) that personality and perception are related (see Marsh & Worden [1956] as a good example); they were less successful (and convincing), however, with respect to demonstrating how their specific clinical instruments were related to these general principles.

An exception to this general statement is provided by some of the thinking of Kenny (1961), who was primarily concerned with the relationship of the ambiguity of TAT stimuli with the "level" or "layer" of personality revealed by story-content elicited by these stimuli. Drawing heavily on Bruner's formulations (1957) as well as on those posited by other workers, Kenny's thesis was that, "changes in sensory input are assimilated into a schema after a hypothetical process of differentiation or categorization of the stimulus has taken place" (p. 292). The stimuli play an important role in the "fantasy" content elicited, and "within this model, perception of the picture stimuli is not passive reception, but is an active process of categorization or differentiation" (*Ibid.*, p. 292). S "codes" stimulus input from the TAT cards into categories, which, after being assimilated into schemata, determine his verbalized responses. Stories thus will vary according to individual factors, but in varying degrees, depending on considerations concerned with the structure of the stimulus, such as ambiguity. Kenny made a distinction between categorizations (perceptions) and schemata ("fantasy" story), the latter being more influenced by experience, set, drives, etc., than the former. Although no attempt will be made here to describe the experimental and research suggestions flowing from this general model, Kenny's approach illustrates an attempt to relate the projective method with perceptual theory.

Perceptual approaches to projective material flowing from a theoretical orientation antithetical to that of the New Look movement have been more successful than those stemming from the New Look—largely because the former were primarily anchored in the gestalt framework, which lends itself rather easily to an analysis of the stimulus properties of projective material. Actually, such an analysis is sometimes based only on an analogy involving a direct translation of gestalt principles of organization to, for example, Rorschach stimuli. Yet reports of this nature have had the important function of calling attention to an oft neglected aspect of projective techniques—the stimulus. Chapters 5 and 11 devote special attention to material concerned with stimulus properties of the Rorschach and TAT. In Chapter 5, especially, some of Gibson's theoretical notions and hypotheses are utilized to analyze the Rorschach stimulus situation. The reader's attention is also drawn to an earlier section in Chapter 2 on the need for a theory of stimulation, as suggested by Gibson.

Meanwhile, illustrations of the "gestalt approach" to the Rorschach will be presented. Secord (1953) presented a view which is consonant with a trace theory of recognition and perception. He noted that object-processes, CNS events deriving from properties of the inkblots, should be distinguished from situation processes: ". . . recognition of a particular form in the blot occurs when the object-process communicates with a trace by virtue of similarity between the two" (p. 66). Individual differences and the fact that some traces are more available than others were explained in terms of familiarity, the personality of the examiner, the attitudes of S, and "ego communication."

Wertheimer (1957), in an attempt to integrate the approach of the Rorschach expert with that of the worker in perception, discussed the Rorschach stimuli from the point of view of autochthonous principles —similarity, proximity, symmetry, good continuation, closure, contours, figure-ground principles, reversals, etc. For example, he noted that since figure-ground reversals are more likely with prolonged fixation, more anxious Ss, taking more time to stare at the blot, may actually produce more white space (S) responses. This was not empirically tested, however, and a question may be raised as to whether or not anxious Ss actually stare longer at the cards, as well as whether or not they actually produce more white space responses.

In general, Wertheimer raised the likelihood that certain types of responses have to do in large measure with the stimulus structure of the card. But he also argued that "inside" the organism, other principles of organization exist, such as set, motivation, and past experience. His chief point, however, is that, despite individual distortions with respect to ambiguous situations, Rorschach stimuli are not without structure, and that this structure has not been sufficiently studied. He asks if the current blots are the best set of blots. Can the autochthonous factors he has noted be weakened so that individual factors are strengthened? He has noted, as have other recent workers, that the Rorschach analysis is based on "an interpretation of S's interpretation," that is, on phenomenology, whereas the modern perceptionist does not rely on this. On the other hand, we might suggest that the perceptionist, too, has his own difficulties with the problem of phenomenology.

A worker such as Gibson (especially, 1960) would assume that the *meaning* carried by the patterns of Rorschach stimulation would vary depending on experiences, age, attention factors, recognition of familiar patterns, etc. Rorschach cards are pictures of "low fidelity," carrying multiple ambiguous stimulus meanings. In verbalizing or expressing meaning, individuals are not necessarily reporting their immediate and direct perceptions. The Rorschach, therefore, is a perceptual test only in a limited sense. Furthermore, with respect to the Rorschach's so-called lack of structure, Gibson had this to say:

Users of the Rorschach test assume that a stimulus field can be either structured or, as they put it, unstructured. . . . A picture has one structure, an inkblot another, but it does not lack structure. . . . The capacity of light to carry structure to an eye may be impoverished or reduced experimentally but it remains. The structure of light may not specify anything familiar to the subject, or to any observer, but it is a geometrical fact. The subject may be unable to register the structure because it is nonsense to him or he overlooks it, or he was not told to look for it, or his eyes are defective, or he is too young, or for a dozen other reasons, but it is still in the light (*Ibid.*, pp. 698–699).

Another way of viewing some of these problems is highlighted by Goldiamond's paper (1958) to which reference has already been made, on response indicators of perception. Since a perceptual response is experiential and phenomenological, E is dependent on various indicators which he has designated (sometimes arbitrarily or as a result of expedience) to indicate the presence of the response he is after. Often such an indicator is a verbal "yes" or "no." There are various physiological and motor indicators that can also be used. The question of the appropriateness of the indicator as a measure of the variable sought, or of the one-to-one relationship of the indicator to the perceptual event, is an important, perhaps crucial one. The author implied early in his article that we are dependent on these indicators in our experimental results, citing the example that if pressing a button every time a light goes on is the perceptual indicator, and that if the button required 25 pounds of pressure, the cessation (through fatigue) of pressing the button could not be interpreted as being relevant to the crucial factor of perception.

And so, along the same lines, an important question would be raised with respect to the Rorschach—especially if this technique is viewed as essentially reflecting *perceptual* factors. The usual response indicators in the Rorschach situation, verbal descriptions, brief verbal responses to the Inquiry, sometimes "yes" or "no" in the testing-of-the-limits, are certainly subject to the intervention of "extraneous" variables, such as pressure to conform, fear of making mistakes, verbal ability, and reinforcement of responses due to overt or covert responses on the part of E. Anthropologically oriented workers have something to say about this. Dennis (1951), for example, tells us repeatedly of the wide number of variations in the verbal expression to the Rorschach, in interpretation of the situation, in attitude toward testing, and even in E's interpretation of S's response, which can be due to cultural and subcultural influences (see also Chapter 1). We also know that interests and attitudes can affect various cognitive aspects of S's response. Verbal reports can be withheld because of embarrassment or "respect" for authority. What, then, is a "pure" indicator of a Rorschach percept, and what is not?

It may be argued that the "impure," contaminated (not in the Rorschach sense) response is precisely what we are after, and is precisely the "projective" nature of the situation. But if we are to assign any meaning to our scores, and continue to search for their correlates *as if* they represented a unitary or complex, but existent, pattern of behavior, we have to be clear as to just what our response indicators *do* reflect. One example can be noted. The semantic indicators noted earlier do indeed have serious limitations, and one of these is especially relevant to the Rorschach situation: as Whorf has indicated (1956), the structure of our language calls for discreteness (either-or; yes-no) when in reality S might not have exactly perceived the situation before him with such polarity.

We have taken a long excursion in our attempt to answer some important questions. Does personality influence perception? We have reviewed the extensive, tortuous, and detailed controversies with regard to this question, and have seen that perceptionists themselves not only cannot come to some agreement, negative or affirmative, but also differ even as to concepts, framework, theoretical viewpoint, methodology, and the manner in which they select and define crucial variables for study. We do know that even the staunchest defenders of the directive-state viewpoint concede the importance of set, attitude, memory, judgment, and cognitive variables in the final *verbalization* of a perceptual event. Just where cognitive factors end and perception begins is a difficult boundary to define. Nevertheless, there seems to be some agreement that a *direct* relationship between perception and personality is difficult to demonstrate.

But the question still remains: is the Rorschach essentially a perceptual situation? Should our approach to projective techniques involve application of perceptual principles and theories? Floyd Allport (1955) raises the same question when he states:

Do the answers in a Rorschach test, for example, reveal actual object-perception in the narrower sense of the term perception; or do they reveal associations, imagery, or interpretation—or do they perhaps reveal a composite of all these processes and others besides? Is not the emphasis here upon meaning—classifications and qualitative considerations rather than upon magnitudes and thresholds? And similarly for tests of thematic apperception: Is the individual who acts as subject merely perceiving, or is he also interpreting? (p. 331)

*Are* projective techniques tests of perception? Even if they are, we would be hard set to defend a viewpoint which suggests that since these techniques are tests of perception, they automatically measure personality. The situation is not that simple, however, for many workers are beginning to feel that a host of variables are being measured by projective instruments, some of which may or may not be perception. We have learned much, however, from our survey of perceptual approaches. From workers such as Gibson and Hochberg as well as from the gestaltists, we have seen the importance of analyzing a response in terms of the stimulus characteristics. Perhaps our approach to projective techniques should at least begin with a systematic analysis of their stimulus characteristics, to see if some responses (and which ones?) bear a direct relationship to the stimulus situation. Once these have been explored, deviations from the expected response may have some meaning.

Is the way we perceive in the Rorschach or other projective situations determined by our personality? Very little is known about our "perceptions" in the Rorschach and other projective situations. Let us, however, develop a model which may help to guide us, and see how far we can get.

The first model that suggests itself is the model provided by the following equation adapted from Graham (1951):

$$R = f\ (S,\ T,\ O,\ E,\ \ldots X_1,\ X_2,\ \ldots X_n)$$

where $R$, the response, is regarded as a function of $S$, the properties of the presented stimulus; $T$, the time of exposure; $O$, the state of the organism, including set, motivation, tonicity, degree of fatigue, etc.; $E$, the past experience of the person; $X_1$, $X_2$, . . . personality characteristics. Now the experimentalists maintain that we should exhaust all the parameters in the first part of this equation before calling on $X_1$, $X_2$, . . . $X_n$, the personality variables. The personologists would have us neglect the first part of the equation completely and maintain that in terms of the amorphous, "unstructured" stimuli dealt with in the Rorschach, only $X_1$, $X_2$, . . . $X_n$ are important. At present it is difficult to settle this question. It may be pointed out, however, that experimentally it is easier to identify and vary the parameters of $S$, $T$, $O$, $E$ than to identify and vary the $X$'s. One way of resolving this conflict is to subject to a crucial test the hypothesis that the first set of parameters —$S$, $T$, $O$, $E$—is sufficient to account for variations in the response. If this hypothesis is maintained, there would be no need for the projective personality variables. Some of the personologists may object that by including such factors as $O$, the state of the organism, including set, motivation, needs, fatigue, etc., and $E$, the past experience of the person, we have effectively included personality parameters in our equation. This indeed is a fact, but we mean to include only the variables that can be systematically manipulated experimentally, or controlled through selection of subjects. For the determination of such factors, more objective, more systematic, and more direct tests are available than the projective techniques afford. For example, we would not need the Rorschach to determine the presence of fatigue or of a strong need for food. A stronger need for security or hostility, however, cannot be measured by any objective means, and if the Rorschach technique can reveal the presence of such needs when the effects of all known parameters of visual perception are kept constant or eliminated, it would indeed be of great benefit to personality measurement.

If the Rorschach measures interests, set, attention, memory, and various other cognitive factors, then these "nonperceptual" factors should assume greater importance and should be the focus of validity studies. But essentially the crux of the situation rests on whether or not projective workers can make their instruments into "tests" in the test-development sense, useful for prediction, and based on the usual reliability and validity evidence.

Perhaps we have been looking to the wrong areas for our solutions. Maybe a "new" field should be launched: the psychology of *verbalizing* and assigning *meaning* to (i.e., *interpreting*) unfamiliar stimuli. We doubt if the field of perception, as such, has all the answers.

## SUMMARY AND CONCLUSIONS

The student of general psychology is probably surprised to note the attention that workers in clinical psychology and personality attach to the formal study of perception, to the exclusion of other psychological functions such as learning or memory. But the reason for this interest is not difficult to find. There has been a viewpoint among clinical psychologists that what people see or perceive in a given stimulus is not determined by the stimulus properties alone. The final percept depends also on the characteristics of the perceiver. This has been accepted not only by psychologists but also by philosophers like Nietzsche, who considered all concepts inspired by needs, and by artists, who point out that no two artists will paint identical portraits of the same individual.

Much of the psychophysical experimentation in perception was until recently stimulus centered rather than individual centered. By stimulus-centered research is meant the tendency to be concerned with variations in the stimulus properties alone and to utilize the perceiver only as an "average" sounding board for stimulus changes. For this type of investigation, situations or stimulus conditions which produce little or no interindividual or intraindividual variation are preferable. The ideal stimulus-centered experiment would call for a total suppression of changes other than those connected with the change in stimulus. By individual-centered investigations is meant experiments in which the stimulus is selected with the express purpose of maximizing consistent individual differences.[8] Such differences which are apparently not connected with the stimulus properties directly must reflect some trends in the individual himself and therefore be connected with personality, it is reasoned. This is the rough-and-ready reason given for investigating personality by perceptual methods. The stimulus-centered method is usually called sensory research whereas the subject-centered method

---

[8] Gibson, in a personal communication (1962) has noted in this connection: "But if the 'stimulus' is often a vast potential complex, there is room for individual differences."

goes under the name of personality research. The view of many clinical psychologists is this: whether or not all individual differences in perception can be finally related to some aspects of the stimulus is an academic question, since only when such physical correlates are demonstrable can we accept them as evidence and discard the personality hypothesis as an explanation.

But is the situation so simple? The status of the so-called link between perception and personality has been the focus of Chapters 2 and 3. Unfortunately, there was no clear-cut method of arriving at an overall conclusion; the method chosen for exploring this general question was to take a hard look at the field of perception itself, especially those approaches which are "personality oriented." This was accomplished by first examining definitions and problems in the field of perceptual research. These included some "hardy perennials" such as the sensation-perception dichotomy; the narrowness or scope of what is subsumed in perception (are social perception and visual perception based on the same principles?); the "immediacy" of perception; distinction between adaptation and reflex behavior and perception; the problem of meaning; the relative disregard of neurophysiological ("inside") processes; the empiricism vs. nativism controversy; the validity of the "response indicator" of perception; and the relative neglect of the stimulus.

The primary focus of these two chapters, however, was on a survey of various theories of perception. This procedure, it was hoped, would not only highlight the fact that there are innumerable unsolved problems, dilemmas, points of view, and controversies within the field, but would allow us a convenient framework in which related, relevant, and classical reports and studies could be discussed. Our survey of theories will have served an even more important function, however, if it has helped to place in perspective the attractive, fascinating, and (to most clinicians) logical approach of the directive-state theorists—to which we have devoted considerable attention.

Our survey covered considerable ground; perhaps we have been unfair to some positions because of the need to move so rapidly from one area to another. Included in the discussion were: Titchener's approach and core-context theory; gestalt theory; topological field theory; Gibson's approach; sensory-tonic theory; Helson's approach; Hebb's theory; set theory (Freeman's); cybernetic theory; Floyd Allport's theory of event structure; the behaviorist's approach; and several schools of functionalism, including Ames' and Brunswik's approach. Attention was then turned to the schools of thought more directly associated with the personality-perception orientation. The "typologies" of Klein, Witkin, and Frenkel-Brunswik were discussed and evaluated. A major portion of our presentation was devoted to discussing and evaluating the directive-state approach, the New Look which has been so important in shaping and directing the orientation of psychologists toward a perception-personality framework.

Finally, additional specific problems and approaches were discussed which were felt to be relevant for our overall purpose: perceptual learning, sensory deprivation, subception, and a microgenetic approach to perception-personality.

This presentation, it is hoped, will spur the reader to draw his own conclusions; however, we will indicate our own point of view. Our basic question was: Is perception related to personality? We are forced to admit that a *direct* relationship between perception and personality has been difficult to demonstrate, even by veteran defenders of the directive-state position. Systematic aspects of perception may exist, but whether these are related to general personality—systematic ways of behaving in a variety of contexts (impulsive, submissive, hostile, anxious, etc.)—remains to be demonstrated. We do all of us live in "different perceptual worlds," but is this fact related to personality? We still do not know.

Our survey of the perceptual field moreover, has led us to believe that projective techniques are not only *not* perceptual tests (in the traditional sense) but would fare better as *instruments* if their advocates looked elsewhere for rationale and methodology, that is, outside the field of perception. Yet we have learned much from our survey: the importance of the stimulus and stimulation and procedures for evaluating the stimulus; the role of cognitive and interpretative factors; the question of the *response*-indicator—these among others present important problems not only in perceptual research, but in research with projective techniques.

We have come to believe that attention, set, and individual differences in *interpretation* of ambiguous stimuli are certainly involved in projective techniques. The same combination of stimulus elements of color, brightness, and their gradients may be interpreted differently by the same person at different occasions depending on his purposes and mental sets. Different individuals may interpret the same stimulus pattern differently either because of variation in purpose and mental set or because of variation in systematic, individual inclinations.[9]

In the interpretation of each of these types of stimuli and situations

---

[9] As D. H. Lawrence (1935) wrote, "Anyone can say boo to a goose, but God alone knows what the goose hears."

the "personal equation" enters. Whereas the problem of the student of visual perception is to uncover the general factors involved in the production of a given percept, the problem of the projective worker is to determine what are the factors that make for differences in the responses of different individuals—*be they perceptual or not.* Why for example, does the same stimulus under seemingly similar mental set produce one type of projective response in one individual and a different one in another? And why do certain projective stimuli—even though "ambiguous" at first blush—produce uniform responses in a group of widely different individuals? There is no way out. The projective worker cannot look to the perceptionist for the answers, for he must handle the general problems involved in the psychology of *interpretation*—assigning meaning (often verbally) to a stimulus. And here, he must not only face the question of the stimulus, but of $E$-$S$ interaction, set, cultural variables, verbal ability, education and background, attitude toward testing, etc. The entire reinforcement history of the person is involved, which is why it is so difficult to disentangle the parameters of the response. But these parameters must be specified if we are ever to develop rigorous projective tests instead of loose projective techniques— instruments which will meet the same exacting criteria required in other areas of psychological testing.

In sum, then, our position in regard to responses to projective techniques is that they are not (or perhaps are "more than") perceptual responses. It is possible to invoke a model drawn from the work of Schoenfeld and Cumming (1963). We are less concerned, for the moment, with the implications for learning theory in their approach to perception than we are with their paradigm for so-called perceptual responses: $S{\rightarrow}R_1{\cdot}R_2$ in which $R_1$ is the initial response to the stimulus, and $R_2$ is a response to, or a function of $R_1$. The point about $R_2$ is that it is the "outer" response, the reporting behavior, measurable and observable (the dependent variable in most experimentation). It may be a verbal response, a gesture, a "yes" or "no," a motor response, or a physiological indicator. The reporting response ($R_2$) is a resultant of the verbal reinforcement history of the subject, his instructional set, his expectations as to what $E$ requires, etc., as well as a function of $R_1$. The "so-called" perception as $R_1$, a function of $S$ (the stimulus) is also a conditioned response, but its characteristics can only be inferred. Although $R_1$ is always present, $S$ may not be aware of it, and the conditioning of $S{\rightarrow}R_1$ is complex indeed. However $E$ can deal with responses of only an $R_2$ nature, and these are *not perceptual responses.* As a matter of fact, they are no different from various other responses, and are treatable and analyzable by the same methodology and rationale as these other responses.

For our purposes, projective responses fall into the $R_2$ category. They are not perceptual but may be a function of $R_1$ which may or may not have perceptual components. Experimentally, we must establish the laws governing the relationship between $S$ and $R_2$, not on the basis of a perceptual exploration, but for psychometric and predictive purposes.

# REFERENCES

Adams, J. K. Laboratory studies of behavior without awareness. *Psychol. Bull.*, 1957, **54**, 383–405.

Adorno, T. W., Frenkel-Brunswik, Else, Levinson, D. J., & Sanford, R. N. *The authoritarian personality*. New York: Harper and Brothers, 1950.

Allport, F. H. *Theories of perception and the concept of structure*. New York: John Wiley and Sons, 1955.

Allport, G. W. *Personality: a psychological interpretation*. New York: Holt, 1937.

Ames, A., Jr. Visual perception and the rotating trapezoidal window. *Psychol. Monogr.*, 1951, **65** (Whole No. 324).

Aronfreed, J. M., Messick, S. A., & Diggory, J. C. Re-examining emotionality and perceptual defense. *J. Pers.*, 1953, **21**, 517–528.

Asch, S. E., Ceraso, J., & Heimer, W. Perceptual conditions of association. *Psychol. Monogr.*, 1960, **74** (Whole No. 490).

Attneave, F. Some informational aspects of visual perception. *Psychol. Rev.*, 1954, **61**, 183–193.

Aubert, H. Die Bewegungsempfindung. *Arch. ges. Physiol.*, 1886, **39**, 347–370.

Bartley, S. H. *Principles of perception*. New York: Harper and Brothers, 1958.

Bass, B. M., & Berg, I. A. (Eds.) *Objective approaches to personality assessment*. Princeton, N.J.: D. Van Nostrand, 1959.

Beach, F. A. Body chemistry and perception. In R. R. Blake and G. V. Ramsey (Eds.) *Perception: an approach to personality*. New York: Ronald Press, 1951, 56–94.

Beardslee, D. C., & Wertheimer, M. (Eds.) *Readings in perception*. Princeton: N.J.: D. Van Nostrand, 1958.

Bevan, W. Perception: evolution of a concept. *Psychol. Rev.*, 1958, **65**, 34–55.

Blake, R. R., & Ramsey, G. V. *Perception: an approach to personality*. New York: Ronald Press, 1951.

Blum, G. S. *The Blacky Pictures: a technique for the exploration of personality dynamics*. New York: Psychological Corp., 1950.

Blum, G. S. An investigation of perceptual defense in Italy. *Psychol. Rep.*, 1957, **3**, 169–175.

Boring, E. *Sensation and perception in the history of experimental psychology*. New York: Appleton-Century, 1942.

Boring, E. Visual perception as invariance. *Psychol. Rev.*, 1952, **59**, 141–148.

Brain, W. R. *Mind, perception and science*. Springfield, Ill.: Charles C Thomas, 1951.

Bricker, P. D., & Chapanis, A. Do incorrectly perceived tachistoscopic stimuli convey some information? *Psychol. Rev.*, 1953, **60**, 181–188.

Brown, J. F. *Psychology and the social order*. New York: McGraw-Hill, 1936.

Brown, J. Evidence for a selective process during perception of tachistoscopically presented stimuli. *J. exp. Psychol.*, 1960, **59**, 176–181.

Brown, W. P. Conceptions of perceptual defence. *Brit. J. Psychol. Monogr. Supplement*, 1961, **35**, 1–106.

Bruner, J. S. Perceptual theory and the Rorschach test. *J. Pers.*, 1948, **17**, 157–168.

Bruner, J. S. Personality dynamics and the process of perceiving. In R. R. Blake and G. V. Ramsey (Eds.) *Perception: an approach to personality.* New York: Ronald Press, 1951, 121–147.

Bruner, J. S. On perceptual readiness. *Psychol. Rev.*, 1957, **64**, 123–152.

Bruner, J. S. The cognitive consequences of early sensory deprivation. In P. Solomon *et al.* (Eds.) *Sensory deprivation.* Cambridge: Harvard University Press, 1961, 195–207.

Bruner, J. S., *et al. Contemporary approaches to cognition.* Cambridge: Harvard University Press, 1957.

Bruner, J. S., & Goodman, Cecile C. Value and need as organizing factors in perception. *J. abnorm. soc. Psychol.*, 1947, **42**, 33–44.

Bruner, J. S., & Krech, D. (Eds.) *Perception and personality: a symposium.* Durham: Duke University Press, 1950.

Bruner, J. S., & Postman, L. Emotional selectivity in perception and reaction. *J. Pers.*, 1947, **16**, 69–77.

Bruner, J. S., & Postman, L. Symbolic value as an organizing factor in perception. *J. soc. Psychol.*, 1948, **27**, 203–208.

Bruner, J. S., & Postman, L. Perception, cognition and behavior. *J. Pers.*, 1949, **18**, 14–31. (*a*)

Bruner, J. S., & Postman, L. On the perception of incongruity: a paradigm. *J. Pers.*, 1949, **18**, 206–223. (*b*)

Brunswik, E. Organismic achievement and environmental probability. *Psychol. Rev.*, 1943, **50**, 255–272.

Brunswik, E. Distal focusing of perception: size-constancy in a representative sample of situations. *Psychol. Monogr.*, 1944, **56** (Whole No. 254).

Brunswik, E. *Perception and the representative design of psychological experiments.* (2nd Ed.) Berkeley: University of California Press, 1956.

Brunswik, E. Scope and aspects of the cognitive problem. In J. S. Bruner, *et al., Contemporary approaches to cognition.* Cambridge: Harvard University Press, 1957, 5–31.

Burdock, E. I., & Zubin, J. Measurement of specific functions. In J. Zubin, *et al. Experimental abnormal psychology.* New York: Columbia University Bookstore, 1957, Chapter 6.

Cantril, H. Perception and interpersonal relations. *Amer. J. Psychiat.*, 1957, **114**, 119–126.

Carter, L., & Schooler, E. Value, need and other factors in perception. *Psychol. Rev.*, 1949, **56**, 200–207.

Chein, I., Lane, R., Murphy, G., Proshansky, H., & Schafer, R. Need as a determinant of perception: a reply to Pastore. *J. Psychol.*, 1951, **31**, 129–136.

Chodorkoff, B., & Chodorkoff, Joan. Perceptual defense: an integration with other research findings. *J. gen. Psychol.*, 1958, **58**, 75–80.

Coyne, J. W., King, H. E., Zubin, J., & Landis, C. Accuracy of recognition of subliminal auditory stimuli. *J. exp. Psychol.*, 1943, **33**, 508–513.

Crandell, D. L. Review of sensory-tonic field theory literature. Unpublished Report, 1961.

Davis, R. C. Motor responses to auditory stimuli above and below threshold. *J. exp. Psychol.*, 1950, **40**, 107–120.

Dennis, W. Cultural and developmental factors in perception. In R. R. Blake and G. V. Ramsey (Eds.) *Perception: an approach to personality.* New York: Ronald Press, 1951, 148–169.

Dixon, N. F. Symbolic associations following subliminal stimulation. *Int. J. Psychoanal.*, 1956, **37**, 159–170.

Dixon, N. F. Apparent changes in the visual threshold as a function of subliminal stimulation. *Quart. J. exp. Psychol.*, 1958, **10**, 211–219.

Dixon, N. F., & Haider, M. Changes in the visual threshold as a function of subception. *Quart. J. exp. Psychol.*, 1961, **13**, 229–235.

Dreger, R. Perception in the context of social and personality theory. *J. gen. Psychol.*, 1961, **64**, 3–30.

Ellis, W. D. (Ed.) *A source book of gestalt psychology.* New York: Harcourt, Brace, 1938.

Eriksen, C. W. Subception: fact or artifact? *Psychol. Rev.*, 1956, **63**, 74–80. (*a*)

Eriksen, C. W. An experimental analysis of subception. *Amer. J. Psychol.*, 1956, **69**, 625–634. (*b*)

Eriksen, C. W. Discrimination and learning without awareness: a methodological survey and evaluation. *Psychol. Rev.*, 1960, **67**, 279–300.

Eriksen, C. W. Perceptual defense. In P. H. Hoch and J. Zubin (Eds.) *Psychopathology of perception.* New York: Grune and Stratton, 1964.

Eriksen, C. W., Azuma, H., & Hicks, Rosalie B. Verbal discrimination of pleasant and unpleasant stimuli prior to specific identification. *J. abnorm. soc. Psychol.*, 1959, **59**, 114–119.

Eysenck, H. J., Granger, G. W., & Brengelmann, J. C. Perceptual processes and mental illness. *Maudsley Monogr. No. 2.* London: Chapman and Hall, 1957.

Fitts, P. M., Weinstein, M., Rappaport, M., Anderson, Nancy & Leonard, J. A. Stimulus correlates of visual pattern recognition: a probability approach. *J. exp. Psychol.*, 1956, **51**, 1–11.

Flavell, J. H., & Draguns, J. A microgenetic approach to perception and thought. *Psychol. Bull.*, 1957, **54**, 197–217.

Freeman, G. L. The problem of set. *Amer. J. Psychol.*, 1939, **52**, 16–30.

Freeman, G. L. *The energetics of human behavior.* Ithaca: Cornell University Press, 1948.

Freeman, J. T. Set versus perceptual defense: a confirmation. *J. abnorm. soc. Psychol.*, 1955, **51**, 710–712.

Frenkel-Brunswik, Else. Intolerance of ambiguity as an emotional and perceptual personality variable. *J. Pers.*, 1949, **18**, 108–143.

Frenkel-Brunswik, Else. Personality theory and perception. In R. R. Blake and G. V. Ramsey (Eds.) *Perception: an approach to personality.* New York: Ronald Press, 1951, 356–419.

Fuhrer, M. J., & Eriksen, C. W. The unconscious perception of the meaning of verbal stimuli. *J. abnorm. soc. Psychol.*, 1960, **61**, 432–439.

Gibson, Eleanor J. Improvement in perceptual judgments as a function of controlled practice or training. *Psychol. Bull.*, 1953, **50**, 401–431.

Gibson, Eleanor J., Gibson, J. J., Smith, O. W., & Flock, H. Motion parallax as a determinant of perceived depth. *J. exp. Psychol.*, 1959, **58**, 40–51.

Gibson, J. J. *The perception of the visual world.* Cambridge: Houghton-Mifflin, 1950.

Gibson, J. J. Social perception and the psychology of perceptual learning. In M.

Sherif and M. O. Wilson (Eds.) *Group relations at the crossroads*. New York: Harper and Brothers, 1953, 120–138.

Gibson, J. J. Optical motions and transformations as stimuli for visual perception. *Psychol. Rev.*, 1957, **64**, 288–295.

Gibson, J. J. Perception as a function of stimulation. In S. Koch (Ed.) *Psychology: a study of science*. Study I, Vol. I. New York: McGraw-Hill, 1959, 456–501.

Gibson, J. J. The concept of the stimulus in psychology. *Amer. Psychologist*, 1960, **15**, 694–703.

Gibson, J. J., & Gibson, Eleanor J. Perceptual learning—differentiation or enrichment? *Psychol. Rev.*, 1955, **62**, 32–41. (*a*)

Gibson, J. J., & Gibson, Eleanor J. What is learned in perceptual learning? A reply to Professor Postman. *Psychol. Rev.*, 1955, **62**, 447–450. (*b*)

Gibson, J. J., & Gibson, Eleanor J. Continuous perspective transformations and the perception of rigid motion. *J. exp. Psychol.*, 1957, **54**, 129–138.

Gibson, J. J., Purdy, Jean, & Lawrence, Lois. A method of controlling stimulation for the study of space perception: the optical tunnel. *J. exp. Psychol.*, 1955, **50**, 1–14.

Gibson, J. J., & Waddell, D. Homogeneous retinal stimulation and visual perception. *Amer. J. Psychol.*, 1952, **65**, 263–270.

Gilchrist, J. C., & Nesberg, L. S. Need and perceptual change in need-related objects. *J. exp. Psychol.*, 1952, **44**, 369–376.

Goldiamond, I. Indicators of perception: I. Subliminal perception, subception, unconscious perception: an analysis in terms of psychophysical indicator methodology. *Psychol. Bull.*, 1958, **55**, 373–411.

Goldman, A. E. Studies in vicariousness: degree of motor activity and the auto-kinetic phenomenon. *Amer. J. Psychol.*, 1953, **66**, 613–617.

Goldstein, K. Methodological approach to the study of schizophrenic thought disorder. In J. S. Kasanin (Ed.) *Language and thought in schizophrenia*. Los Angeles: University of California Press, 1944, 17–39.

Graham, C. Visual perception. In S. S. Stevens (Ed.) *Handbook of experimental psychology*. New York: John Wiley and Sons, 1951, 868–920.

Granger, G. W. Personality and visual perception: a review. *J. ment. Sci.*, 1953, **99**, 8–43.

Hartman, A. A. Personality factors in perceptual distortion. *J. gen. Psychol.*, 1959, **61**, 181–188.

Hatfield, R. O. The influence of an affective set on disyllable recognition thresholds. *J. abnorm. soc. Psychol.*, 1959, **59**, 439–441.

Hebb, D. O. *The organization of behavior*. New York: John Wiley and Sons, 1949.

Helson, H. Adaptation-level as a basis for a quantitative theory of frames of reference. *Psychol. Rev.*, 1948, **55**, 297–313.

Helson, H. Perception. In H. Helson (Ed.) *Theoretical foundations of psychology*. Princeton, N.J.: D. Van Nostrand, 1951, 348–389.

Helson, H. Psychiatric screening of flying personnel; perception and personality—a critique of recent experimental literature. *USAF Sch. Aviat. Med. Proj. Rep.*, 1953, Proj. No. 21-0202-0007 (Rep. No. 1).

Helson, H., & Nash, Myrtle C. Anchor, contrast and paradoxical distance effects. *J. exp. Psychol.*, 1960, **59**, 113–121.

Hilgard, E. R. The role of learning in perception. In R. R. Blake and G. V. Ramsey (Eds.) *Perception: an approach to personality*. New York: Ronald Press, 1951, 95–120.

Hirst, R. J. *The problems of perception.* London: George Allen and Unwin, Ltd., 1959.

Hochberg, Carol B., & Hochberg, J. Familiar size and subception in perceived depth. *J. Psychol.,* 1953, **36,** 341–345.

Hochberg, J. Perception: toward the recovery of a definition. *Psychol. Rev.,* 1956, **63,** 400–405.

Hochberg, J. Effects of the gestalt revolution: the Cornell symposium on perception. *Psychol. Rev.,* 1957, **64,** 73–84.

Hochberg, J., Haber, S. L., & Ryan, T. A. "Perceptual defense" as an interference phenomenon. *Percept. mot. Skills,* 1955, **5,** 15–17.

Holt, E. B. The Freudian wish. New York: Holt, 1915.

Howes, D. H., & Solomon, R. L. A note on McGinnies' "Emotionality and perceptual defense." *Psychol. Rev.,* 1950, **57,** 229–234.

Howes, D. H., & Solomon, R. L. Visual duration threshold as a function of word-probability. *J. exp. Psychol.,* 1951, **41,** 401–410.

Howie, D. Perceptual defense. *Psychol. Rev.,* 1952, **59,** 308–315.

Huxley, J. S. Introductory: towards the new systematics. In J. S. Huxley (Ed.) *The new systematics.* Oxford: Clarendon Press, 1940.

Ittelson, W. H., & Kilpatrick, F. P. Experiments in perception. *Scientific Amer.,* 1951, **185,** 50–55.

Jenkin, N. Some relationships between projective test behavior and perception. *J. clin. Psychol.,* 1955, **11,** 278–281.

Jenkin, N. Two types of perceptual experience. *J. clin. Psychol.,* 1956, **12,** 44–48.

Jenkin, N. Affective processes in perception. *Psychol. Bull.,* 1957, **54,** 100–127.

Johansson, G. Motion perception and personality, I. *Reports from the Psychological Laboratory, University of Stockholm,* 1955, **16,** 1–7.

Johnson, R. C., Thomson, C. W., & Frincke, G. Word values, word frequency and visual duration thresholds. *Psychol. Rev.,* 1960, **67,** 332–342.

Kaplan, A. Definition and specification of meaning. *J. Philos.,* 1946, **43,** 281–288.

Kaplan, A., & Schott, H. F. A calculus for empirical classes. *Methodos,* 1951, **3,** 165–190.

Kenny, D. T. A theoretical and research reappraisal of stimulus factors in the TAT. In J. Kagan and G. S. Lesser (Eds.) *Contemporary issues in thematic apperceptive methods.* Springfield, Ill.: Charles C Thomas, 1961, 288–310.

Kilpatrick, F. P. (Ed.) *Human behavior from the transactional point of view.* Hanover, N.H.: Institute for Associated Research, 1952.

Kilpatrick, F. P. *Recent transactional perceptual research, a summary.* Final Report, Navy Contract, Nbonr27014, Princeton University, May, 1955.

King, H. E., Landis, C., & Zubin, J. Visual subliminal perception where a figure is obscured by the illumination of the ground. *J. exp. Psychol.,* 1944, **34,** 60–69.

Klein, G. S. The personal world through perception. In R. R. Blake and G. V. Ramsey (Eds.) *Perception: an approach to personality.* New York: Ronald Press, 1951, 328–355.

Klein, G. S. The Menninger Foundation research on perception and personality, 1947–1952: a review. *Bull. Menninger Clin.,* 1953, **17,** 93–99.

Klein, G. S. Need and regulation. In M. R. Jones (Ed.) *Nebraska symposium on motivation.* Lincoln: University of Nebraska Press, 1954, 224–274.

Klein, G. S. On subliminal activation. *J. nerv. ment. Dis.,* 1959, **128,** 293–301.

Klein, G. S., Holzman, P. S., & Laskin, Diana. The perception project: progress report for 1953–1954. *Bull. Menninger Clin.,* 1954, **18,** 260–266.

Klein, G. S., & Schlesinger, H. Where is the perceiver in perceptual theory? *J. Pers.*, 1949, **18**, 32–47.

Klein, G. S., & Schlesinger, H. Perceptual attitudes toward instability: I. Prediction of apparent movement experiences from Rorschach responses. *J. Pers.*, 1951, **19**, 289–302.

Klein, G. S., Schlesinger, H., & Meister, D. The effect of personal values on perception: an experimental critique. *Psychol. Rev.*, 1951, **58**, 96–112.

Klein, G. S., Spence, D. P., Holt, R. R., & Gourevitch, Susannah. Cognition without awareness: subliminal influences upon conscious thought. *J. abnorm. soc. Psychol.*, 1958, **57**, 255–266.

Klüver, H. Supplement. In G. Murphy. *An historical introduction to modern psychology.* New York: Harcourt, Brace, 1929.

Koffka, K. *Principles of gestalt psychology.* New York: Harcourt, Brace, 1935.

Köhler, W. *Gestalt psychology.* New York: Liveright, 1929.

Köhler, W. *Dynamics in psychology.* New York: Liveright, 1940.

Köhler, W., & Wallach, H. Figural after-effects: an investigation of visual processess. *Proc. Amer. phil. Soc.*, 1944, **88**, 269–357.

Kragh, U. Pathogenesis in dipsomania. An illustration of the actual-genetic model of perception-personality. Part One. Theoretical frame. Anamnesis. *Acta Psychiat. Neurol. Scand.*, 1960, **35**, 207–222. (*a*)

Kragh, U. Pathogenesis in dipsomania. An illustration of the actual-genetic model of perception-personality. Part Two. Presentation and analysis of the actual-genetics series. *Acta Psychiat. Neurol. Scand.*, 1960, **35**, 261–288. (*b*)

Kragh, U. Pathogenesis in dipsomania. An illustration of the actual-genetic model of perception-personality. Part Three. The retest series. The pathogenic transformations. Repression and regression. *Acta Psychiat. Neurol. Scand.*, 1960, **35**, 480–497. (*c*)

Krus, D. M., Werner, H., & Wapner, S. Studies in vicariousness: motor activity and perceived movement. *Amer. J. Psychol.*, 1953, **66**, 603–608.

Kubzansky, P. E., & Leiderman, P. H. Sensory deprivation: an overview. In P. Solomon, *et al.* (Eds.) *Sensory deprivation.* Cambridge: Harvard University Press, 1961, 221–238.

Lawrence, D. H. *Fantasia of the unconscious.* London: Heineman, 1935.

Lawrence, D., & Coles, G. R. Accuracy of recognition with alternatives before and after the stimulus. *J. exp. Psychol.*, 1954, **47**, 208–214.

Lazarus, R. S. Subception: fact or artifact? A reply to Eriksen. *Psychol. Rev.*, 1956, **63**, 343–347.

Lazarus, R. S., & McCleary, R. A. Autonomic discrimination without awareness: a study of subception. *Psychol. Rev.*, 1951, **58**, 113–122.

Leeper, R. *Lewin's topological and vector psychology, a digest and a critique.* Eugene: University of Oregon Press, 1943.

Levine, M., & Meltzoff, J. Cognitive inhibition and Rorschach human movement responses. *J. consult. Psychol.*, 1956, **20**, 119–122.

Levine, R., Chein, I., & Murphy, G. The relation of the intensity of a need to the amount of perceptual distortion. *J. Psychol.*, 1942, **13**, 283–293.

Levy, L. H. Perceptual defense in tactual perception. *J. Pers.*, 1958, **26**, 467–478.

Lewin, K. *A dynamic theory of personality.* New York: McGraw-Hill, 1935.

Lewin, K. *Principles of topological psychology.* New York: McGraw-Hill, 1936.

Lewin, K. *Field theory in social science.* Posthumous papers. New York: Harper and Brothers, 1951.

Luchins, A. S. An evaluation of some current criticisms of gestalt psychological work on perception. *Psychol. Rev.*, 1951, 58, 69–95.

Magnus, R. *Koerperstellung.* Berlin: Springer, 1924.

Marsh, J. T., & Worden, F. Perceptual approaches to personality. *Psychiat. Res. Rep.*, 1956, 6, 171–176.

Mathews, Anne, & Wertheimer, M. A "pure" measure of perceptual defense uncontaminated by response suppression. *J. abnorm. soc. Psychol.*, 1958, 57, 373–376.

McCleary, R. A., & Lazarus, R. S. Autonomic discrimination without awareness: an interim report. *J. Pers.*, 1949, 18, 171–179.

McClelland, D. C., & Atkinson, J. W. The projective expression of needs. I. The effect of different intensities of the hunger drive on perception. *J. Psychol.*, 1948, 25, 205–222.

McConnell, J. V., Cutler, R. L., & McNeil, E. B. Subliminal stimulation: an overview. *Amer. Psychologist*, 1958, 13, 229–242.

McCulloch, W. S., & Pitts, W. The statistical organization of nervous activity. *Biometrics*, 1948, 4, 91–99.

McEwen, P. Figural after-effects. *Brit. J. Psychol. Monogr. Supplements*, 1958, XXXI.

McGinnies, E. Emotionality and perceptual defense. *Psychol. Rev.*, 1949, 56, 244–251.

McGinnies, E. Discussion of Howes' and Solomon's note on "Emotionality and perceptual defense." *Psychol. Rev.*, 1950, 57, 235–240.

McGinnies, E., & Sherman, H. Generalization of perceptual defense. *J. abnorm. soc. Psychol.*, 1952, 47, 81–85.

Meltzoff, J., & Levine, M. The relationship between motor and cognitive inhibition. *J. consult. Psychol.*, 1954, 18, 355–358.

Meltzoff, J., & Litwin, Dorothy. Affective control and Rorschach human movement responses. *J. consult. Psychol.*, 1956, 20, 463–465.

Meltzoff, J., Singer, J. L., & Korchin, S. J. Motor inhibition and Rorschach movement responses: a test of the sensory-tonic theory. *J. Pers.*, 1953, 21, 400–410.

Metzger, E. Experimentelle Untersuchungen ueber den Lichttonus. *Arch. Opthal.* (Graefe), 1931, 127, 296–346.

Miller, J. G. Discrimination without awareness. *Amer. J. Psychol.*, 1939, 52, 562–578.

Miller, J. G. The role of motivation in learning without awareness. *Amer. J. Psychol.*, 1940, 53, 229–239.

Miller, J. G. *Unconsciousness.* New York: John Wiley and Sons, 1942.

Murphy, G. Interrelationships between perception and personality: a symposium. Part I. Discussion. *J. Pers.*, 1949, 18, 51–55.

Murphy, G. Affect and perceptual learning. *Psychol. Rev.*, 1956, 63, 1–15.

Nash, H. The behavioral world. *J. Psychol.*, 1959, 47, 277–288.

Newton, K. R. A note on visual recognition thresholds. *J. abnorm. soc. Psychol.*, 1955, 51, 709–710.

O'Neil, W. M. Basic issues in perceptual theory. *Psychol. Rev.*, 1958, 65, 348–361.

Osgood, C. E. A behavioristic analysis of perception and language as cognitive phenomena. In J. S. Bruner, et al. *Contemporary approaches to cognition.* Cambridge: Harvard University Press, 1957, 75–118.

Pastore, N. Need as a determinant of perception. *J. Psychol.*, 1949, 28, 457–475.

Pastore, N. An examination of one aspect of the thesis that perceiving is learned. *Psychol. Rev.*, 1956, 63, 309–316.

Pastore, N. Perceiving as innately determined. *J. genet. Psychol.*, 1960, 96, 93–99.

Pepinsky, H. B. Summary and conclusions. In B. M. Bass and I. A. Berg (Eds.) *Objective approaches to personality assessment.* Princeton, N.J.: D. Van Nostrand, 1959, 217–224.

Pierce, C. S., & Jastrow, J. On small differences of sensation. *Ann. National Academy of Science*, 1884, 3, 73–83.

Pitts, W., & McCulloch, W. S. How we know universals: the perception of auditory and visual forms. *Bull. math. Biophys.*, 1947, 9, 127–147.

Platt, J. R. How we see straight lines. *Scientific Amer.*, 1960, 202, 6, 121–129.

Pollack, R. H. The concepts of development in perception. Address, Biometrics Research Seminar, Columbia University, 1961.

Postman, L. Toward a general theory of cognition. In J. H. Rohrer and M. Sherif (Eds.) *Social psychology at the crossroads.* New York: Harper and Brothers, 1951, 242–272.

Postman, L. The experimental analysis of motivational factors in perception. In J. B. Brown, H. F. Harlow, L. Postman, V. Nowlis, T. M. Newcomb, and O. H. Mowrer. *Current theory and research in motivation: a symposium.* Lincoln: University of Nebraska Press, 1953, 59–108. (*a*)

Postman, L. On the problem of perceptual defense. *Psychol. Rev.*, 1953, 60, 298–306. (*b*)

Postman, L. Association theory and perceptual learning. *Psychol. Rev.*, 1955, 62, 438–446.

Postman, L., Bronson, Wanda C., & Gropper, G. L. Is there a mechanism of perceptual defense? *J. abnorm. soc. Psychol.*, 1953, 48, 215–224.

Postman, L., Bruner, J. S., & McGinnies, E. Personal values as selective factors in perception. *J. abnorm. soc. Psychol.*, 1948, 43, 142–154.

Prentice, W. C. H. "Functionalism" in perception. *Psychol. Rev.*, 1956, 63, 29–38.

Proshansky, H., & Murphy, G. The effects of reward and punishment on perception. *J. Psychol.*, 1942, 13, 295–305.

Rado, S. Dynamics and classification of disordered behavior. *Amer. J. Psychiat.*, 1953, 110, 406–416.

Razran, G. The observable unconscious and the inferable conscious in current Soviet psychophysiology: interoceptive conditioning, semantic conditioning, and the orienting reflex. *Psychol. Rev.*, 1961, 68, 81–147.

Riesen, A. H. Excessive arousal effects of stimulation after early sensory deprivation. In P. Solomon, *et al.* (Eds.) *Sensory deprivation.* Cambridge: Harvard University Press, 1961, 34–40.

Rubenfeld, S., Lowenfeld, J., & Guthrie, G. M. Stimulus generalization in subception. *J. gen. Psychol.*, 1956, 54, 177–182.

Salzinger, K. Techniques for computing shift in a scale of absolute judgment. *Psychol. Bull.*, 1956, 53, 394–401.

Salzinger, K. Shift in judgment of weights as a function of anchoring stimuli and instructions in early schizophrenics and normals. *J. abnorm. soc. Psychol.*, 1957, 55, 43–49.

Sander, F. Experimentelle Ergebnisse der Gestaltpsychologie. In E. Becher (Ed.) *10 Kongr. Ber. Exp. Psychol.* Jena: Fischer, 1928, 23–88.

Sander, F. Structures, totality of experience, and gestalt. In C. Murchison (Ed.)

*Psychologies of 1930.* Worcester, Mass.: Clark University Press, 1930, 188–204.

Schaefer, T., Jr. Sensory deprivation and its effect on perception. In P. H. Hoch and J. Zubin (Eds.) *Psychopathology of perception.* New York: Grune and Stratton, 1964.

Schafer, R., & Murphy, G. The role of autism in a visual figure-ground relationship. *J. exp. Psychol.,* 1943, **32,** 335–343.

Schoenfeld, W. N., & Cumming, W. W. Behavior and perception. In S. Koch (Ed.) *Psychology: a study of science,* Vol. V. New York: McGraw-Hill, 1963, 213–252.

Schumer, Florence C. Some behavioral correlates of the Rorschach human movement response. Unpublished doctoral dissertation, Yale University, 1949.

Secord, P. F. An analysis of perceptual and related processes occurring in projective testing. *J. gen. Psychol.,* 1953, **49,** 65–85.

Sherif, M., & Sherif, Carolyn. *An outline of social psychology.* New York: Harper and Brothers, 1956.

Sherrington, C. S. *The integrative action of the nervous system.* New Haven: Yale University Press, 1906.

Siipola, Elsa M. The influence of color on reactions to ink blots. *J. Pers.,* 1950, **18,** 358–382.

Singer, J. L., & Herman, J. Motor and fantasy correlates of Rorschach human movement responses. *J. consult. Psychol.,* 1954, **18,** 325–331.

Singer, J. L., Meltzoff, J., & Goldman, G. D. Rorschach movement responses following motor inhibition and hyperactivity. *J. consult. Psychol.,* 1952, **16,** 359–364.

Singer, J. L., & Spohn, H. E. Some behavioral correlates of Rorschach's experience-type. *J. consult. Psychol.,* 1954, **18,** 1–9.

Smith, G. Visual perception: an event over time. *Psychol. Rev.,* 1957, **64,** 306–313.

Smith, G., & Henriksson, M. The effect on an established percept of a perceptual process beyond awareness. *Acta Psychol.,* 1955, **11,** 346–355.

Solley, C. M., & Murphy, G. *Development of the perceptual world.* New York: Basic Books, 1960.

Solomon, P., et al. (Eds.) *Sensory deprivation.* Cambridge: Harvard University Press, 1961.

Solomon, R. L., & Postman, L. Frequency of usage as a determinant of recognition thresholds for words. *J. exp. Psychol.,* 1952, **43,** 195–201.

Spence, D. P. A new look at vigilance and defense. *J. abnorm. soc. Psychol.,* 1957, **54,** 103–108.

Stein, S. *Schwindel.* Leipzig: Lainer, 1910.

Stein, M. I. Personality factors involved in the temporal development of Rorschach responses. *J. proj. Tech.,* 1949, **13,** 355–414.

Swets, J. A., Tanner, W. P., Jr., & Birdsall, T. G. Decision processes in perception. *Psychol. Rev.,* 1961, **68,** 301–340.

Thurstone, L. L. *A factorial study of perception.* Chicago: University of Chicago Press, 1944.

Vandenberg, S. G. Difference between neurotics, psychotics, and normals on perceptual tests: reanalysis of Eysenck's results. *J. clin. Psychol.,* 1959, **15,** 373–376.

Vernon, Magdalen D. Cognitive inference in perceptual activity. *Brit. J. Psychol.*, 1957, 48, 35–47.

Vinacke, W. E. The discrimination of color and form at levels of illumination below conscious awareness. *Arch. Psychol.*, 1942, 38, No. 267.

von Fieandt, K., & Gibson, J. J. The sensitivity of the eye to two kinds of continuous transformation of a shadow-pattern. *J. exp. Psychol.*, 1959, 57, 344–347.

von Holst, E. Relations between the central nervous system and the peripheral organs. *Brit. J. anim. Behav.*, 1954, 2, 89–94.

Walk, R. D., & Gibson, Eleanor J. A comparative and analytical study of visual depth perception. *Psychol. Monogr.*, 1961, 75 (Whole No. 519).

Wallach, H. Some considerations concerning the relation between perception and cognition. *J. Pers.*, 1949, 18, 6–13.

Walters, R. H., Banks, R. R., & Ryder, R. A test of the perceptual defense hypothesis. *J. Pers.*, 1959, 27, 47–55.

Wapner, S., Werner, H., & Morant, R. B. Experiments on sensory-tonic field theory of perception: III. Effect of body rotation on the visual perception of verticality. *J. exp. Psychol.*, 1951, 42, 351–357.

Werner, H. Microgenesis and aphasia. *J. abnorm. soc. Psychol.*, 1956, 52, 347–353.

Werner, H., & Wapner, S. Sensory-tonic field theory of perception. *J. Pers.*, 1949, 18, 88–107.

Werner, H., & Wapner, S. Toward a general theory of perception. *Psychol. Rev.*, 1952, 59, 324–338.

Werner, H., & Wapner, S. The non-projective aspects of the Rorschach experiment: II. Organismic theory and perceptual response. *J. soc. Psychol.*, 1956, 44, 193–198.

Werner, H., Wapner, S., & Chandler, K. A. Experiments on sensory-tonic field theory of perception: II. Effect of supported and unsupported tilt of the body on the visual perception of verticality. *J. exp. Psychol.*, 1951, 42, 346–350.

Wertheimer, M. Experimentelle Studien über das Sehen von Bewegung. *Z. Psychol.*, 1912, 61, 161–265.

Wertheimer, M. Perception and the Rorschach. *J. proj. Tech.*, 1957, 21, 209–216.

Whorf, B. L. *Language, thought and reality: selected writings.* Cambridge: Technology Press, 1956.

Wiener, N. *Cybernetics.* New York: John Wiley and Sons, 1948.

Wiener, M., & Schiller, P. H. Subliminal perception or perception of partial cues. *J. abnorm. soc. Psychol.*, 1960, 61, 124–137.

Williams, A. C., Jr. Perception of subliminal visual stimuli. *J. Psychol.*, 1938, 6, 187–199.

Witkin, H. A. The nature and importance of individual differences in perception. *J. Pers.*, 1949, 18, 145–170.

Witkin, H. A., & Asch, S. E. Studies in space orientation: III. Perception of the upright in the absence of a visual field. *J. exp. Psychol.*, 1948, 38, 603–614. (a)

Witkin, H. A., & Asch, S. E. Studies in space orientation: IV. Further experiments on perception of the upright with displaced visual fields. *J. exp. Psychol.*, 1948, 38, 762–782. (b)

Witkin, H. A., Lewis, Helen B., Hertzman, M., Machover, Karen, Meissner, Pearl B., & Wapner, S. *Personality through perception: an experimental and clinical study.* New York: Harper and Brothers, 1954.

Wohlwill, J. F. Developmental studies of perception. *Psychol. Bull.*, 1960, 57, 249–288.

Zener, K., & Gaffron, Mercedes. Perceptual experience: an analysis of its relations to the external world through internal processings. In S. Koch (Ed.) *Psychology: a study of science*, Vol. IV. New York: McGraw-Hill, 1962, 515–618.

Zubin, J. Objective evaluation of personality tests. *Amer. J. Psychiat.*, 1951, 107, 569–576.

Zubin, J., & Katz, M. Psychopharmacology and personality. In P. Worchel and D. Byrne (Eds.) *Personality change*. New York: John Wiley and Sons, 1964.

# 4 THE RORSCHACH TECHNIQUE:

*some historical perspectives; current status; methodological problems*

The next two chapters consider in some detail the status of the Rorschach technique as an instrument of measurement.

## BRIEF HISTORY

Like all human inventions, the Rorschach technique did not spring full-grown from the brow of its creator. The utilization of amorphous or ambiguous stimuli for divination, or reaching decisions, probably had a long prehistoric development. With the beginning of recorded history, such techniques as the shape and color assumed by clouds, flying birds, and the entrails of sacrificed animals were used as omens and for predictions of things to come. Perhaps the best known use of ambiguous stimuli is provided by the oracles of the ancient Greeks. But these methods are not direct precursors of the Rorschach, although they used the general principle of presenting ambiguous stimuli for eliciting personal responses. For the forerunners of the Rorschach, we must look to the history of inkblots.

*Pre-Rorschach: Early References to Inkblots.* One of the earliest recorded uses of inkblots and other vague, formless stimuli was to stimulate the imagination. Leonardo da Vinci left two notes bearing on the uses of such stimuli. In his *Introduction for the Painter*, written in the fifteenth century, he said:

166

He is not well rounded who does not have the same love for all things that are included under art: as is the case for example when one does not like landscapes and decides to give it only brief and ordinary study. In this connection our Botticelli said that such study is idle, for when nothing more than a sponge full of various colors is thrown against the wall, it leaves a blot on the wall in which one can perceive a beautiful landscape. It is quite true that various experiences can be seen in such a blot, provided one wants to find them in it—human heads, various animals, battles, cliffs, seas, clouds or forests and other things—and it is just as when a bell is ringing in which you can read in words if you want to. But if such blots already give you ideas, then they teach you not to completely finish any specific part of them. For the painter who does that, paints very sad landscapes (da Vinci, 1882, p. 117).

The second note deals with the manner and means of increasing and stimulating the mind for receiving varied experiences:

I will not refrain from setting among these precepts a new device for consideration which, although it may appear trivial and almost ludicrous, is nevertheless of great utility in arousing the mind to various inventions. And this is that if you look at any walls spotted with various stains or with a mixture of different kinds of stones, if you are about to invent some scene you will be able to see in it a resemblance to various different landscapes adorned with mountains, rivers, rocks, trees, plains, wide valleys and various groups of hills. You will also be able to see diverse combats and figures in quick movement, and strange expressions of faces, and outlandish costumes, and an infinite number of things which you can then reduce into separate and well-conceived forms. With such walls and blends of different stones it comes about as it does with the sound of bells, in whose clanging you may discover every name and word that you can imagine (MacCurdy, 1958, pp. 873–874).

Da Vinci also said:

Don't take my advice lightly when I advise you, even though it may appear boring to stop and gaze at wall spots, or at the ashes in the fire, in the clouds, or in the mud and at similar things; you will, if you consider it carefully, discover in it many wonderful things. For the painter's spirit is aroused to new things by it, be it in composition of battles, of animals and men, or in the various compositions of landscapes and of unusual things such as devils, and their like, which are calculated to bring you honor. Through the indescribable and indefinite things, the spirit becomes awakened to new discoveries (da Vinci, Ibid., p. 125).

Thus, both Botticelli and da Vinci in the fifteenth century had already grasped the significance of ambiguous or unclear figures and learned to apply them to some practical end. Binet stated that he was stimulated by Leonardo's observation to carry on his experiments with inkblots. Binet's work is no doubt related to subsequent American work and to that of Rybakow (Baumgarten-Tramer [1942], and Olga Rorschach [1944]).

According to Baumgarten-Tramer (*Ibid.*), Kerner (1786–1862) published *Die Klecksographie*. As a youth, he had pressed colored berries between the two folds of a piece of paper to obtain figures upon spreading open the sheet. In his old age, as he began to lose his sight, drops of ink would fall unnoticed from his pen; after he folded the paper they would form blots. He noted that they made symmetrical as well as asymmetrical figures—arabesque, human, and animal. These figures stimulated him to poetry. His friends liked the poetry and the blots under which they appeared and valued them for their "albums." They were also used for lotteries and social welfare purposes. Finally an admirer had them printed in 1857. The symmetrical blots were preferred. Fifty were printed, 39 with rhymed text—in which with a few strokes of the pen Kerner had completed the faces. The three groups in which they were placed were called: *Momento Mori; Hadesbilder;* and *Höllenbilder*. Kerner's explanation for these titles was, "*Diese Bilder aus dem Hades, Alle schwarz und schauerlich (Geister sind sehr niedern Grades), Haben selbst gebildet sich, Ohn' mein Zutun, mir zum Schrecken, Einzignur—aus Tintenflecken*" [1] (Baumgarten-Tramer, 1942, p. 10).

In his preface, Kerner noted that the pictures "bore the character of long past days out of the childhood of nations, such as idols—pictures —urns—memories and so forth. Pictures of man as well as animals appeared in the most different forms—and especially often human skeletons." Kerner also noted the fact that we cannot produce what we would like in these blots, and that very often an unexpected outcome or the very opposite of what is expected results. His attitude toward these blots was mystical, for he regarded them as messages from the other world; in fact, it became a fad in his day to make parlor games out of these inkblots in which each person tried to interpret the blot he had made as a message which foretold the future.

*Inkblots, "Mental Content," and Individual Differences.* Inkblots had an impressive history before the Rorschach appeared on the scene. One example of a nonmystical, test-oriented, pre-Rorschach approach, is the work of Binet and Henri in the last decade of the nineteenth century. These men followed up da Vinci's suggestion about inkblots, using them as a means of tapping imagination, as part of a general search for good test items to measure intelligence. Lacking a theory of intelligence, they utilized as many different types of performance situations

---

[1] These pictures out of Hades, all black and frightening (spirits are of very low order), have reared themselves alone, without my help, to frighten me, one by one—out of inkblots.

as possible, in the hope that they could thus accumulate test items which would distinguish intelligent from nonintelligent children—an approach, incidentally, not unlike that used by many sophisticated test builders today.

Thus, these authors wrote (1895):

It is necessary to recognize the state of these different forms of imagination in the individual by means of several rapid tests. After having asked him about his tastes, and his tendencies, about the number of novels which he is in the habit of reading, the kind of pleasure he finds in them, his taste for the theatre, music, games, etc., one may proceed to do some direct experiments: let there be a spot of ink with an irregular contour on a white paper; to some, this will mean nothing, to others who have a lively visual imagination (Leonardo da Vinci for example) the small inkblot will appear full of figures, whose number and type can be noted, without, of course pushing the experiment to the kind of hypnosis which the English like to evoke with their crystal gazing (pp. 443–444).

Later, inkblots were used in America for much the same purpose, as well as for the study of "mental content." Although such studies were concerned primarily with the traditional subject matter of psychology at that time (isolated "mental" variables such as memory, imagination, imagery, and contents of consciousness) rather than with the use of inkblot stimuli to describe or test the individual so as to know more about him, they yielded data bearing an unmistakable resemblance to later studies which were concerned primarily with individual differences. Some of these earlier studies, for example, while at the same time reflecting contemporary influences from German psychology, foreshadowed the typological orientation of Hermann Rorschach and his followers. Thus, early studies which were concerned with the typology of visual perception (matter-of-fact vs. scientific, analytic vs. synthetic, etc.) undoubtedly influenced Rorschach interpretation, which is essentially typological. It is possible that these influences in the early part of the twentieth century helped to steer future Rorschach work away from the testing movement and psychometrics. For the quantitative test movement, although based on a "trait" approach, seemed to grow out of a belief that all individuals could be identified with respect to any given trait as a point on a continuum or curve, usually regarded as implicitly normal in nature, and that there were no discrete types.

In a review of pre-Rorschach research on the use of inkblots, Tulchin (1940) traced them to Dearborn at Harvard (1897, 1898). Dearborn was primarily concerned with the use of inkblots in the study of the contents of consciousness—dividing these contents into memory, imagination (with both its quantitative and qualitative aspects), afterimages, and associative processes. He was also interested in the use of inkblots for testing discrimination of minute, formal differences in reaction time of his subjects.

Kirkpatrick (1900) explored developmental aspects of imagination through the use of inkblots in a study which anticipated recent attempts to explore attitude toward and acceptance of the Rorschach task as a dimension for personality study. He found that a curvilinear relationship existed between age and criticalness of attitudes toward the task. Ss in the earlier grades (I to III) as well as the older grades (VII to VIII) were less tentative (more positive) than Ss in the middle grades. Pyle (1913; 1915a) confirmed these results, and also found that dull children responded more like the younger children, that is, were less critical and gave more responses than the bright children. Pyle (1915b) also reported that Negro children were less responsive than white children.

Thus, in these early studies, the forerunners of approaches to Rorschach research, interpretation and "claims" which attempted to relate Rorschach performance to intelligence, developmental factors, and ethnic variables can be found. The need to take R (number of responses) into consideration was noted in these early studies, as well as the importance of other determinants such as location, approach, and various content categories. This is shown in some of the following studies.

Whipple (1910), who described various tests of imagination in his manual, classified inkblots as a task involving active rather than passive imagination, foreshadowing later distinctions which Rorschach workers have made between M and C responses. Sharp (1899) also differentiated between active and passive imagination and found two types in her seven subjects: (a) the constructive or imaginative type characterized by the capacity of putting together concrete details to form a significant whole and (b) the matter-of-fact, scientific type, characterized by a purely analytic approach. Bartlett (1916), using colored and achromatic blots, divided his Ss' responses into two groups on the basis of a content analysis: specific responses and general responses. Specific responses, according to Bartlett, contained personal reminiscences, whereas the general responses did not. Parsons (1917), studying children who were seven and one-half years of age, classified their responses into the following categories: (a) animal associations; (b) both wholes and parts; (c) human beings; (d) mythological creatures; (e) wearing apparel; (f) architecture; (g) landscapes; and (h) reminiscences. She also found descriptions of the blot (e.g., "This part is round") in many of her Ss' responses and a marked preponderance of the nonconstructive, matter-of-fact category, as defined by Sharp.

Although it has become increasingly popular in some quarters to regard the Rorschach technique as an opportunity to study the perceptual process, most Rorschach research is still personality-, rather than perception-oriented. A few early inkblot workers, however, felt that their research was significantly related to the study of perception. Some of this research was based on an assumption (more recent counterparts can be found in the work of Vernon [1937], [1952]; and Zubin [1941]) that with the more amorphous stimuli, the perceptual process is slowed up, making the process more accessible to closer scrutiny. When simple, meaningful objects are presented, the perceptual process is so rapid that it is difficult to recognize the four stages which were assumed to characterize visual perception: (a) stage of vague awareness of something present in the visual field; (b) generic object stage; (c) specific object; and (d) understanding of meaning. It was thought that when a relatively unstructured field such as an inkblot is presented, the stages of perception could be more readily identified, that is, the use of essentially "impoverished" stimuli such as inkblots would permit the emergence of a microgenetic process. Rogers (1917) found that some secondary phenomena occur in addition to the four primary stages. These phenomena are: (a) visual imagery which arises whenever thought is baffled and the perceptual object is unfamiliar or difficult to recognize; and (b) kinaesthetic and organic sensations which are of a diffused type or localized either in the eye muscles or in the muscular processes connected with vocalization. These seemed to be related to the affective attitudes of the observer to the perceptual situation. It might be noted that this approach is related to perceptual studies based on an actualgenetic or microgenetic approach to perception, which assumes that perception is a temporal event whose sequences are capable of analysis by stages—usually through the use of tachistoscopic procedures, from less than optimal to optimal (unambiguous) conditions (see Chapter 3).

*Hermann Rorschach and his Test.*[2] Although a considerable body of knowledge about inkblots was already in existence in 1911 when Rorschach began his studies, he was probably unaware of or unfamiliar with the content and scope of this previous work. According to his

---

[2] This material is drawn largely from Baumgarten-Tramer (1942), Kuhn (1944), and Olga Rorschach (1944).

widow, Olga Rorschach (1944), he worked with some material similar to that of Lippmann (she was not sure of this name) utilizing many colored, small geometric forms which had been cut out of paper. Lippmann had apparently also made a collection of American studies using inkblots such as Whipple's, and had Rybakow's album (see later).

Rorschach at first regarded these forms as "fantasy tests." In his subsequent work, however, he repudiated this point of view and claimed that such tests had more to do with sensation and perception than with fantasy. Rorschach soon found that his work with these geometric colored pieces of paper was too restricting and began to search for less rigid stimulus material. He was very good at drawing and had an appreciation of the problem of portraying movement in painting. He had played with inkblots in his school days, a pastime in vogue with school children at that time. He decided to substitute the less structured blots for the geometric colored pieces of paper, working with these rather casually. Soon after his marriage, he went with his wife to Russia—staying near Moscow where Rybakow worked with inkblots; but whether the two had ever met or heard of each other's work is not certain. Rybakow had regarded his inkblots as a test of fantasy and imagination. He found that people without fantasy or imagination saw nothing but formless inkblots. The gifted saw such things as human heads with beards; hands; a dwarf with a long beard; an eagle floating in the clouds; some monstrous figure similar to a wolf or dragon with a large horn; a row of human figures sitting on the back of a fantastic animal; head of a witch with a large horn; head of some ancient German warrior, etc.

In 1914, Rorschach returned to Switzerland and by this time had become somewhat interested in psychoanalysis. He began to experiment with inkblots with his patients and found such encouraging results that he decided to write a book about his technique. Immediately preceding Rorschach's work, there appeared a report by Hens (1917) on the use of inkblots with children, normal adults, and the mentally ill, based on research conducted in Bleuler's clinic. Rorschach criticized Hens' approach because of his limited analysis of the results (content, relevant to previous experience) and because of his classification of all responses against the framework of vocational, social, and personal interests, as well as current events. As a result of Hens' work, Rorschach decided to deal with the perceptual aspects of inkblot responses rather than with their content.

Rorschach died in 1922 at the age of 38. David M. Levy, who studied with Oberholzer in Europe, is generally credited with introducing the

Rorschach technique to America, and with introducing Samuel Beck to this technique. Levy organized the first Rorschach seminar in Chicago in 1925; by 1926, the first American Rorschach publication had appeared.

## CURRENT STATUS

The Rorschach literature is so voluminous that it is impossible to review it within the scope of this book. We hope, however, to capture the flavor and the essence of contemporary thinking and problems concerning the Rorschach technique by sampling the literature and discussing representative studies to illustrate particular points. Thus, although we intend to present an "overview" of the Rorschach field, the stress is on a critical discussion of problems. Perhaps the reader may even take delight in the fact that he is not being offered still another manual of skills, casebook, or list of "sure-fire" rules-of-thumb and "signs" to help guide the way.

Note might be made, however, of a few volumes and publications which *do* contain systematic reviews and/or instructions and guidance in the clinical use of the instrument, as well as material relevant to its administration, scoring, and interpretation: Anderson and Anderson ([1951], especially Chapters 4 and 5); Beck (1944, 1945, 1952, 1961); Klopfer *et al.* (1954, 1956); Klopfer and Kelley (1942); Piotrowski (1956); Rickers-Ovsiankina (1960); Rorschach (1942); and Sherman (1960). The work by Klopfer (1956) contains a 1500-item classified reference list from 1945–1955, it might be noted, covering general interpretation (manuals, scoring systems, etc.); problems of validity and reliability; genetic psychology; medical psychology (including differential diagnosis and prognosis, organic lesions, psychosomatic medicine and therapy); and social psychology (including personnel selection, vocational counseling, anthropology, and assessment). It is essentially a clinical book, and as such, is a good indication of the nature of the field, offering to the student and skilled clinician alike a wide sampling of the observational, intuitive, descriptive, and case-history approaches.

What is the status of the instrument today?

The extent of the Rorschach "territory" is indeed broad and commanding—in the eyes of many of its users. So ambitious are many Rorschach workers for their instrument, that one outstanding Rorschach worker (Kelley, 1951) made the following surmise about Rorschach's own reaction to the current status of his technique, if he were to return for a survey:

Rorschach today would still recognize the cards. Brilliant though he was, I doubt if he could find time to read the voluminous literature which is well enroute to the thousand mark. I am certain that, if he could, he would be startled that . . . 'following the scoring of the responses, there emerge invaluable facts relating specifically to the way in which the patient sees his world, approaches and handles it, and of what this world consists. His anxieties and insecurities, his hurts and wishes, his fictions, his needs, his assets and liabilities, his likes and dislikes—all of these and more emerge to be viewed by the examiner. Moreover, the pattern reveals also the meaning of these things to him, the configuration of his personality which thus results, and the motivations of his behavior. It, furthermore, aids in differential diagnosis, particularly between the organic and functional types of illness, and among the affect and content disorders. The expert examiner can also obtain from the response record a practical estimation of such important personality features as intellectual efficiency, emotional maturity and balance, and degree and depth of reality acceptance. Finally, the procedure serves as a guide to therapy and an index of its success or failure' (Lindner & Seliger, 1945, p. 356) (Kelley, p. 753).

Rorschach, in contrast, noted, "The conclusions drawn, therefore, are to be regarded more as observations than as theoretical deductions. The theoretical foundation for the experiment is, for the most part, still incomplete" (1942, p. 13). He even went as far as hoping that controlled research, in which each symptom would be taken up individually, would be instituted.

At the beginning of the 1950's there seemed to be an increased stress on relating the Rorschach technique to the rest of psychology, especially to perceptual theory and the field of personality. In addition, problems of set, instructional variables, background and cultural factors, E-S relationship, and factors within the test situation itself were considered to affect the Rorschach response. In interpretation of Rorschach records, there also seemed to be concern at this time with the use of content, often from a psychoanalytic viewpoint, as a major scoring variable.

Yet, despite provocative findings, and many research innovations, the status of the instrument has remained essentially unchanged. Experienced Rorschach workers, for example, Hertz (1951, 1952, 1959), were continuing to raise the same problems again and again, as they reviewed the massive literature which was accumulating. There is a lack of theory in the Rorschach field to explain why it seems to "work." There are variations in methods of administration, scoring, and interpretation (lack of standardization) which could account for the innumerable variations in results, and which prevent the accumulation of normative evidence which could be applicable within specific clinical situations. There are difficulties in demonstrating the reliability of the Rorschach, despite what might appear to be high objectivity and reliability in the hands of experienced and skilled clinicians. And, above all, evidence for validity of the instrument is inadequate.

With this introduction, then, let us examine more closely the current status of the Rorschach technique.

*Rorschach "Theory."* [3] Chapter 3 has already made reference to a group of studies designed to link Rorschach responses to perceptual theory. This approach, in general, was quite attractive to many workers outside the clinical fold. Thus, the Rorschach response becomes an expression of a perceptual event. By understanding perceptual processes, and especially individual differences in these processes, considerable light could be shed on the Rorschach response. The New Look position, on the one hand, had encouraged the viewing of Rorschach responses as if they were reflections of perceptual defense, sensitization, etc.; typologies such as those of Klein and Frenkel-Brunswik suggested that people perceive and view the Rorschach stimuli with characteristic styles and modes. The gestaltists, on the other hand, have stressed the configurational and organizational aspects of the response —pointing out the underlying isomorphism between the "experience" and the cortical processes giving rise to the experience. Characteristics of the Rorschach stimuli have been stressed by gestaltists not in terms of piecemeal qualities, nor even in terms of the associations to which they give rise, but rather in terms of their "wholistic," configurational, and patterned qualities.

With the exception of the few theorists already mentioned, the rest of psychology failed to tackle the problems which are involved when S produces a verbal response to a series of inkblots. Part of the difficulty arises from the fact that personality theory did not prove helpful in the endeavor to integrate the Rorschach movement. Holt (1954) attempted such an effort without too much success.

Although general psychological theory did not have too much to offer, Rorschach workers did not seem overconcerned about this state of affairs, for they were too busy, too much in demand, and too empirically oriented in terms of pragmatic results, to seek "explanations" for their technique in theoretical psychology. In addition, because of their early training and essentially "clinical" orientation, many Rorschach workers were not too concerned with technical and statistical problems —or did not accept the fact that these existed.

---

[3] Chapter 1 discusses some general assumptions of projective techniques which will not be discussed here.

Explanations, "theories," viewpoints, and hypotheses developed in abundance, along with rules-of-thumb, guide-books and manuals for clinical use. But these theories tended to be "inbred," insular, and rather divorced from the rest of psychology, understood, appreciated, or contentiously handled in the main, by Rorschachers themselves, who tended to speak a common language of symbols, scores, and ratios. The special Rorschach language (note essential contrast to the development of the TAT) was probably itself a major factor in creating a Rorschach fraternity; moreover, the Founding Member, Hermann Rorschach himself, although modest in his claims for his instrument, had already paved the way for those who were inspired to continue his tradition. What then, were Rorschach's views? What traditions had he established?

As already noted, in his monograph (1942), Rorschach cautioned that his interpretations were based on observations only, and were derived empirically, rather than from theory. He suggested that constant checking of results against those found with respect to normals was necessary —a legacy "more honoured in the breach than the observance." He believed firmly that his test was not a measure of imagination, but of perception or apperception. Although he recognized the interpretative aspects of an S's response, he felt that this was accompanied by *conscious* effort. Since many Ss did not manifest or display conscious effort, and since the differences between apperception and perception were differences in degree rather than kind, these feelings of his could not be validated or invalidated, and he could feel reasonably confident that his test was a measure of *perception*. He utilized Bleuler's definition of perception, which contained three interwoven elements: sensation, memory, and association. When S interprets an inkblot, there is a certain discrepancy between the sensations stemming from the stimulus and the memory trace aroused by it, a condition which does not necessarily obtain in direct, immediate perception. Rorschach, however, did not stress this discrepancy, as such. Instead, he gave the problem a more far-reaching application in the psychology of consciousness. As noted, he differentiated perception from interpretation by the fact that in perception the fusion process is unconscious, whereas in interpretation it is a conscious process. This distinction between perception and interpretation is often noted in Rorschach responses when the interpreter or subject regards his responses not as interpretations but as immediate perceptions and the interpretive attitude is completely absent. Following these definitions, Rorschach proceeded to analyze the responses in accordance with their location, determinants, and content. His chief contribution inheres in the central place which the movement (M) response occupies in his typology, and in its counterposition to the color response.

Rorschach's scoring system and list of symbols remain fairly intact in terms of methods used today. Rough norms for various groups (normals—educated and uneducated, psychopathic personality, alcoholics, morons, schizophrenics, manic-depressives, epileptics, etc.) were provided in terms of number of responses, reaction time, failures to answer, form, movement, color, etc.; and a general, vague, almost "common-sense" rationale was provided for some of the empirical findings, as well as to explain what the various scores and determinants are probably reflecting. The running assumption in much of Rorschach's approach is that the way we interpret the inkblot stimuli represents the way we behave in general. Moreover, people have characteristic "modes" or "styles" of responding which are fairly consistent and which fall into several major categories. Thus, an implicitly typological approach to Rorschach interpretation was born. On the basis of his system, Rorschach found it possible to make diagnoses of mental patients without actually seeing the patients themselves, by merely examining their responses to the inkblots (blind diagnosis).

Since the Rorschach technique is used so frequently by psychoanalysts, it is interesting to note that Rorschach himself was very much interested in psychoanalysis early in his career. He made an attempt to integrate Freud's theory of dreams with that of Mourly Vold, who had previously suggested that a dream involving the feeling of kinaesthesia will arouse a kinaesthetic impulse in the narrator when the dream is reported later. Rorschach attempted to relate this phenomenon to Freud's theory of dream censorship, and this laid the foundation for Rorschach's interpretation of M, as dependent on inhibited movement. Although much of Rorschach's interpretation was apparently based on psychoanalytic concepts, Freud is not mentioned even once in his monograph; and although Vold, W. Stern, C. G. Jung, and Schopenhauer are mentioned, there are references to few others.

In his later work, Rorschach tended to lean away from analysis of content as well as from psychoanalysis, stressing more strongly the formal aspects of his test, on the assumption, as noted, that S's performance is to be interpreted not as a reflection of his imagination, but as an indication of the way in which his visual perception takes place. In his posthumous article with Oberholzer, however, psychoanalysis was taken up again (1942, pp. 184–216). (At this time, popular responses and chiaroscuro were introduced.) It should be noted, of course, that content is not neglected altogether; Rorschach classified it under rather broad headings, however, such as human, animal, and inanimate content, objects, and nature. It is Rorschach's stress on the *formal* aspects of the performance, rather than the content, which distinguished his work with inkblots from that of others.

Rorschach had also paved the way for a series of interpretative assumptions ("Rorschach rationale") by presenting in his monograph a number of statements based both on brilliant empirical observation and intuitive hunches. For example:

From this summary it can be deduced *that the primary C answers are the representatives of impulsiveness.* The more C's, the greater the tendency to impulsive actions. Most of the deductions of this section are based on statistical methods. As many protocols as possible from as widely diversified clinical material as available were obtained and the results analysed according to the individual factors (C, M, FC, etc.). Thus it was discovered that those subjects giving the most primary color answers were exclusively epileptics, manics, imbeciles, paretics, scattered schizophrenics, or notoriously hotheaded and hyper-aggressive and irresponsible "normals." From this it was concluded that C answers have a "symptom value," that is they represent the common trait of all these cases, namely, the tendency to impulsive emotional discharge (*Ibid.,* pp. 31–33).

Or:

Several spheres of psychic function must combine in the form-color answers which take up the form first and then the color. In the interpretation of form, associative factors come into play; in the interpretation of color, emotional factors are influential. The form-color answer is, therefore, an associative as well as an emotional response; it is an assimilation of external stimuli. It also proves to be an expression of the capacity for getting into rapport, of the ability to adapt, and this can be shown by either the statistical or the etiological method of study. A better way of saying this is that the FC answer is the expression of the *desire* to adapt, for the FC may be poorly visualized. This would mean that only the emotional adaption (*sic*) was effective, the associative being insufficient. The poorer the visualization of form in the FC answer, the nearer it approaches the CF group, and, thereby, the appearance of egocentric emotional responsiveness. Egocentric affectivity may show a definite "will to emotional adaptability," but the associative component is insufficient, so that the affectivity usually, perhaps always, becomes egocentric (*Ibid.,* pp. 33–34).

Most of the current contributions to "rationale," procedural, and research approaches, and even interpretative phrases and customs found in contemporary Rorschach workers' clinical reports may all be found in Rorschach's monograph, pretty much intact!

Following in the pattern laid down by the master, Rorschach theory today still tends to be concerned with specific rationales for interpreting the meaning of various Rorschach factors and is primarily geared to clinical practice. With a few major exceptions, this theory has little implication beyond the clinic or Rorschach interpretation, and fails to interact or mesh with non-Rorschach research or theory. Not all the specific rationales can be tested empirically, and of those that are testable, only considerable reformulation and specification can render them amenable to verification.

In the section on *Validity*, many studies are noted which have direct bearing on a particular "rationale" or theory as to a determinant's meaning. Thus, Schumer (1949), in an investigation of some of the behavioral correlates of Rorschach M, canvassed the Rorschach literature at that time and constructed fifteen purported correlates of M from this survey. Similarly Janoff, in another behavioral investigation (1951), listed eighteen purported correlates of Rorschach F, form level, and form quality. Other theorizing and hypothesizing are illustrated by Ansbacher (1956) and Piotrowski (1960) with respect to M; the work of Singer and his associates, also concerned with M, is described in a subsequent section, as are some studies specifically concerned with "color theory." The book by Rickers-Ovsiankina (1960) contains detailed presentations of Rorschach theory in connection with "organization activity," white space response, form perception, movement, color and shading scores, experience-type, etc.

Good examples of the interpretive significance assigned to various scoring categories and their interrelationships are given in Klopfer, *et al.* (1954, pp. 254–316). Here can be found not only a general discussion of the "meaning" of each determinant and scoring category, such as M, FM, m, K, KF, FK, F, c and Fc, etc., and the various color responses, but also a discussion of different types of interrelationships among the foregoing, reaction times, location percentages ( % W, % D, etc.), types of succession, and percentage of popular and original responses. Moreover, these pages offer an extensive presentation of more specific "hypotheses"—many of them testable—for perusal and exploration by the research-oriented clinician. Here are some examples, with respect to human movement responses (M). These are only a few selected from a remarkably vast array, which have been presented for each determinant and scoring category:

Intelligence:     The appearance of M's of good form level is a counter-indication of a low intellectual level of capacity, while good quality M's in high number are signs of high intellectual capacity (p. 256).

Imagination:     To the extent to which M's appear in the psychogram, the individual is free to use his imaginal processes to enrich his perception of the world (p. 256).

A System of Values: M responses indicate an inner system of conscious values of one kind or other, in terms of which the person
tends to control his behavior, to guide his satisfactions,
and to postpone his gratifications (p. 262).

Similar hypotheses are presented for all variables and ratios. To be
found also (*Ibid.*, pp. 317–402) are "hypotheses" and discussions concerning card-by-card and response-by-response analysis (sequence
analysis), specific rules-of-thumb for the assessment of intellectual
level, control, creative potential, and the introversive-extratensive relationship, and a discussion of the significance of various types of content. Interestingly, the discussion here is built around a framework
which takes into significant account "card-pull" or "difficulty level"—
the types of areas and content "typically" brought into play for each of
the cards is presented, so that the clinician is made aware of the sorts of
responses facilitated by the various cards before he attaches any special significance to particular responses. Unfortunately, however, precise and detailed quantitative norms and listings are not presented.

It might be noted that the authors of this volume are careful to
present their ideas as hypotheses which "are based on the whole back-
log of dynamic personality theory as well as the clinical experiences of
many people. . . . They are presented not as facts, but as working hypotheses, hunches, or guesses which become available for experimental
investigation with their appearance in print" (*Ibid.*, p. 376). Nevertheless, the authoritative, discursive, "expert" discussion of interpretive
principles, will yield the impression (and especially to clinical trainees
and initiates to the Rorschach) that the principles are accepted
"dogma," rather than still-to-be confirmed hypotheses.

The number of purported relationships and interpretations in the
Rorschach field is sizable indeed. Some of these include the following:
a high frequency of color responses (C) indicates a tendency to emotionality or impulsiveness and a high degree of responsiveness to stimuli coming from without rather than from within the organism; a high
frequency of movement (M) responses represents a highly developed
inner life, creativity, and a high degree of responsiveness to stimuli
coming from within the organism including wishes, needs, and desires;
a high frequency of shading (Fc or c) responses represents sensitivity
or susceptibility to depressive moods; and good form responses (F+)
indicate "control" of mental functioning.

In addition, general assertions are made such as: popular responses
indicate conformity; unusual content or repetition of the same content
in various responses indicates some deep anxiety or conflict about the
material in the response; irregularity in the sequence of wholes, details,

and rare details indicates lack of orderliness; and a high frequency of poor form responses indicates lack of contact with reality.

Although these claims are generally accepted, it is usually pointed out that the significance of a given factor depends not only on its own frequency but on the pattern it forms with the other factors. As a result of some empirical as well as "clinical" studies, the following claims have also been made: feebleminded differ from normals in having fewer W, M, C, and F responses but more A (animal) responses; schizophrenics tend to have responses characterized by a high frequency of rare details, thought disturbances (confabulations and contaminations), positional characteristics, loose and confused succession, color naming, and abstractly diffuse responses; organic and brain-injured cases tend to have fewer responses in general and less M, F, and P, longer reaction time, more repetition, color naming, and perplexity and impotence in their responses (impotence referring to the inability to inhibit the response, that is, to give it despite full knowledge of its inadequacy); and psychoneurotics are alleged to suffer from color shock and tend to suppress W's and C's.

These are only a few of the salient claims that have been made for the Rorschach. They represent the extent of Rorschach theory—a series of unrelated, discrete statements of relationship between inkblot response characteristics and various classification systems. A cataloguing of all the claims would require much more space than is available in this chapter. Suffice it to say, however, that many individuals who work with the Rorschach method accept these claims as proven fact.

*Reliability*

*The Rorschach Score—Some Problems.* The nature of the Rorschach score presents many difficulties—and this fact must be considered in evaluating research connected with the instrument. Holtzman (1959) aptly summarized some of these problems when he wrote of the wide claims made by Rorschach workers as to the utility of their instrument: ". . . curiously enough, the same ten inkblots are used throughout!" (p. 130). He continued,

Providing the subject with only ten inkblots and then permitting him to give as many or as few responses to each card as he wishes characteristically results in a set of unreliable scores with sharply skewed distributions, the majority of which fail to possess the properties of even rank-order measurements. One record with an R of 20 may be comprised of single responses to the first nine cards and 11 responses to Card X, while another may consist of two responses per card. Any of the usual scores with the possible exception of form level will have quite different meanings in the two contrasting protocols even though the total number of responses is constant. Add to this the difficulties arising when R varies from less than ten to over 100, and it is easy to see why most quantitative studies involving the standard Rorschach yield confusing or negative results (p. 133).

How many responses must be secured to justify confidence in the record? Adequacy of response sampling is the question involved here, and little information in this area is available. For example, is "adequacy" a variable factor from S to S? (See Symonds [1954], and MacFarlane & Tuddenham [1951].)

Cronbach (1949) reviewed the ways in which R's effects on raw scores can be reduced. Some of these methods include: converting the absolute frequencies to percentages based on R; using partial regression techniques; dividing the sample into a number of subgroups that are homogeneous with respect to R, before attempting further analysis. The lack of a linear relationship between R and other Rorschach variables makes most of these procedures ineffective in accounting for R, however. The clinician will be dissatisfied with the homogeneous subgroup suggestion, primarily because the subgroups would obfuscate important differences among Ss due to the interrelationships of variables. It might also be noted that the relationship between R and various scoring categories is not consistent. Fiske and Baughman (1953), in their study of 790 protocols, found that for most scores the relationship of R to scoring categories is not only complex and nonlinear, but the form of the relationship varies from variable to variable. They concluded that scores based on frequency of responses are unsatisfactory, and those based on the percentage of R are only a partially adequate solution.

The problems raised with respect to Rorschach scores noted above are not the only problems to be faced when the question of reliability is raised. Some clinicians are of the opinion that the usual psychometric criteria and methods cannot be effectively applied to an instrument such as the Rorschach. When such an opinion stems from "tradition," bias, convenience, or from a belief that rigorous methodology is automatically anticlinical, further discussion is no longer possible because these objections are largely based on emotions and deeply rooted attitudes not amenable to the scientific process. If assessment of reliability is not regarded as a relevant task, there is little concern for developing adequate techniques by which Rorschach reliability can be estimated. Yet even workers with such attitudes report research findings and make generalizations which *imply* or take for granted a certain level of reliability!

Another group of clinicians do indeed recognize the need for a psychometric appraisal of the Rorschach, but they apply the ordinary techniques of such appraisal without a proper understanding of their assumptions and without appreciation of the difficulties involved. Fortunately there has been an increased tendency among research-oriented clinicians not only to accept the need for adequate appraisal of the reliability of the scores, interpretations, and the instrument with which they are working, but to wonder, in the light of the special problems inherent in the Rorschach technique, about the appropriateness of the usual techniques when applied to the Rorschach.

Those who stress "global," "patterned," "wholistic," or nonquantitative aspects of the Rorschach record will remind us again and again that a test which does not produce scores but interpretations cannot be subjected to reliability tests. The application of a test of reliability to Rorschach findings, we are told, negates the very nature of how the test is used in the clinic. But let us suggest that Rorschach workers *do* use scores; as a matter of fact, much of their training is devoted to a detailed and strenuous program of learning how to score. Not only are scores used—but ratios, relationships, and comparisons between and among scores are also utilized in making an interpretation. As global, qualitative or descriptive as these final interpretations may be, they are based, nevertheless, on some type of translation or abstraction from S's response, and involve a judgment, rating, or decision which could be subjected to a reliability test. Such reliability tests may require special modification, or may not even exist, for the time being, in appropriate form; perhaps the nature of the Rorschach scores may itself have to be changed. But if the Rorschach has any merit, and if it can be used for the adequate and valid description of people and for making certain types of predictions, it is essential to have further knowledge of its parameters.

Physicians, too, base a diagnosis of the physical problems of the patient on a "patterned" or global overview of many specific findings. Would anyone claim that tests of the validity and reliability of the specific components of the physician's diagnostic work-up are irrelevant, even though no one test could predict the final diagnosis? Do we not expect our measures of body temperature, blood pressure, blood count, etc., to possess a certain amount of objectivity and reliability? Furthermore, recent developments in computers have made it possible to obtain this patterned, globally based diagnosis by feeding the elements of the global diagnosis into a computer program. Naturally, if these elements are themselves unreliable, the result can hardly be worth much.

What component(s) of the Rorschach should be subjected to tests of reliability? [4] Most techniques for determining reliability have been developed for tests of a more quantitative nature than the Rorschach. The usual methods for tapping the nonquantitative aspects of a projective protocol involve discriminations of judges in categorizing, rating, or matching procedures. Matching procedures, in particular, are regarded as truly "getting at" wholistic and global aspects of the record, but involve enormous difficulties (see subsequent section). For this reason, many workers (e.g., MacFarlane & Tuddenham, 1951) are of the opinion that "qualitative" reliability can be best determined by utilizing some category or rating that is at a level midway between actual protocol and interpretation. Some workers (e.g., Anastasi [1954]; Fiske [1959]) feel that reliability of *interpretations* rather than of scores, is the crucial question for Rorschach research. Anastasi (*Ibid.*) has noted,

For projective techniques, a proper measure of scorer reliability should include not only the more objective preliminary scoring, but also the final integrative and interpretative stages. It is not enough, for example, to demonstrate that examiners agree closely in their tallying of such characteristics as whole, unusual detail, or color responses. On a projective test like the Rorschach, these raw quantitative measures cannot be interpreted directly from a table of norms, as in the usual type of psychological test (pp. 624–625).

In any event, there is some agreement that estimating reliability of raw scores alone is not sufficient for the Rorschach technique. Any type of reliability procedure which considers qualitative features of the record (except with respect to direct matching methods) does involve analysis of the material into component parts and some sort of scoring or rating principles, a task which itself raises formidable problems. In considering some of these problems, MacFarlane and Tuddenham have noted, ". . . it requires laborious trial and error to choose from among the enormous array of possibilities those formalistic categories that are not only reliably scorable but psychologically relevant" (1951, p. 38).

*Reliability of Scoring; Examiner Effects.* Although it may be generally taken for granted that scoring has a high degree of reliability, a survey of relevant research indicates that this is an unwarranted assumption. As a matter of fact, the picture has not changed much in this connection for over a quarter of a century (Hertz, 1935).

---

[4] The same question can be asked with respect to tests of validity. In the section on validity, another, somewhat longer discussion revolving around this general question is presented.

Reliability of scoring is generally based on some indication of agreement among or between scorers. An illustrative study is that of Ramzy and Pickard (1949), who found that only after considerable discussion and arbitrary acceptance of certain conventions were the authors able to obtain consistency in their scoring. It is noteworthy that appeal to textbooks only increased their confusion. Even after this collusion, the degree of agreement was only 90% for the location category. Since Beck's location tabulations were used, it is surprising that the degree of agreement was not 100%. For determinants of the F and M variety, the agreement dropped to 83%, and for color and shading, to 75%. As far as content was concerned, following Beck's classifications, they obtained an agreement of 99%, an indication that content categories are more "objective" than the other categories.

That the reliability of scoring of the major determinants is not as high as should be expected from a predictive and psychometric point of view is indicated by other studies, too. For example, Baughman (1951) reported a study which found that fifteen Veterans' Administration examiners disagreed significantly with respect to sixteen out of twenty-two scoring categories on a random selection of cases culled from their files.

But it might be noted that a fairly high degree of reliability can be achieved when there is pretraining and supervised practice with respect to a *specific scoring system*. Thus, a high degree of scorer reliability is commonly reported in many Rorschach validation studies, but this is likely to be a result of the design of the study and pre-experimental preparations which often involve specific "rules" and procedures for obtaining the relevant scores. Scorer reliability estimates based on the collection of scored records from clinicians with *differing* backgrounds and scoring habits, would be consistently lower, of course. Norms, generalizations of research findings, and comparisons between and among various research reports are subject to misinterpretation and distortion in the light of the fluctuations and differences in scoring procedures among clinicians in various "schools" of training and background. It goes without saying that research reports are often limited in their generalizations by the failure to make public the specific rules, practices, procedures, and norms on which the scoring for the specific study was based. Moreover, some of the frequent failures to confirm findings in replication studies might be explained on this basis.

What are some of the factors which possibly serve to lower scorer reliability? We might pause here to go back once again to the question of objectivity, a term which is often interpreted to mean agreement among many *E*s (independence from examiner effects) using some quantitative method. Concern with objectivity is probably even more relevant to projective techniques than to various paper-and-pencil, "group" tests. The latter, after all, with either-or, "yes"-"no," or multiple-choice items, can be scored by machine, and even by untrained clerks who can read or at least sort, with little or no error or variability in scoring. Test developers in the nonprojective field often do not even report this type of reliability, for it is taken for granted; they stress, instead, temporal aspects of reliability, item analysis, and equivalence of forms. But it is precisely with respect to projective instruments that questions of examiner or scorer reliability become especially crucial. If there is uncontrolled interaction between the test and the examiner, as there undoubtedly is in the Rorschach situation, objectivity is reduced. If the examiner guesses certain aspects of *S*'s response in order to arrive at a score, or elicits or fails to elicit scorable components (as in the Inquiry) by asking or not asking certain questions, or if *S*'s responses are inhibited as a result of the test situation and the *E-S* interaction, objectivity is thereby lowered. With respect to the Rorschach, then, scoring systems not only differ, but the practice of restricting scoring to verbalized responses is not uniform. Moreover, *S*'s initial verbalizations may not and frequently do not reveal all the determinants involved in his reactions. An Inquiry seems called for. But, in addition, variations in weights assigned to verbalizations in the Inquiry, and lack of uniformity in procedures for evaluating the primacy of form, color, shading, and movement in a response, also tend to lower scorer reliability.

An aspect of scoring reliability not yet mentioned is the consistency of the same scorer over a period of time in scoring the same records. Although memory factors play a role in estimates of this type of scorer reliability, if a large number of records, from which identifying data were removed, is presented to the same scorer for re-scoring, reasonably adequate estimates of such reliability can be obtained.

*Reliability of Interpretations.*[5] Although we can sometimes point with pride to the high degree of scorer reliability it is possible to obtain within the confines of a specific study, a more crucial question concerns

---

[5] The reliability of interpretations raises questions such as: Would clinicians agree on this diagnosis? Would the same set of predictions be made on the basis of Rorschach records by two or *x* number of experts? It should be obvious that these questions can also be regarded as validity questions. Indeed, as long as it is decided that one of the "experts" is the criterion (and often this is an arbitrary decision), then such research could be regarded as validity research. Needless to say, the problems raised in this section apply to this type of validity study as well as to the type of reliability study under consideration.

a type of reliability considerably less easy to demonstrate. After all, as already noted, it is E's *interpretation* which is the crux of the matter— his diagnosis, personality summary, and predictive statements. Can we talk of a high degree of scorer reliability if, in the last analysis, judges and clinicians differ widely in their interpretations of records, even if their scoring of the records more or less agree? And how can such reliability be estimated, since interpretative statements are generally nonquantitative and descriptively and "globally" oriented?

One of the typical means of studying agreement among interpreters is that of matching procedures. Matching procedures which allow the clinicians to choose their own categories, framework, language, and concepts for interpretative statements and summaries are doomed to failure, since Rorschach "experts" are notoriously unlike each other in terms of these characteristics (e.g., the study by Carr, *et al.* [1960] which is described in a later section). Moreover, a search for "communality" may, in fact, yield similarity and overlap when various interpretative comments are compared, but these may be artifacts of language, and actually the semantic referents involved may differ. In addition, some statements about personality dynamics are so vague and universally applicable that a false impression of high reliability may be obtained.

Another factor to be considered is illustrated by an extensive study of reliability of interpretations through use of matching procedures conducted by Krugman (1942), who reported some very encouraging findings. Three judges were able to match with perfect accuracy two independent interpretations of twenty Rorschach records, from which were removed all identifying data. It is not clear, however, whether or not a singular aspect of an interpretation (such as an extremely sparse record or particularly vivid original responses) contributed to the correct matching, rather than the overall interpretation.

When agreement in global interpretations is explored, a number of difficulties and problems must be faced. Elements such as vocabulary level, unusual characteristics of certain protocols, and "tell-tale" items, all of which may influence matching operations, can actually be explored by means of a parametric study, thus providing some information concerning the basis on which the matching was performed. Note should be made of the fact, also, that the heterogeneity or homogeneity of the protocols to be matched influence the degree of success obtained in the matching operation. The "expertness" of the judge and the length of time spent with the protocol may be factors accounting for variations in results when different judges are used in matching studies; the influence of the judge and test become confounded, therefore, in estimates of this type of reliability.

A question can be raised as to the stability or consistency of an interpretation of a single record by the same clinician over a period of time. Confounded into the picture is the following problem: Is the inconsistency of an interpretation of the same record by the same $E$ an indication of changes in $E$ himself? Or of the vagueness and unreliability of the instrument? Of these questions, Holzberg (1960) had this to say:

Here, of course, we are dealing again with problems of memory which would mean that the interpretations would have to occur at significant intervals of time. With the recognition of the importance of the background and psychological sophistication of the psychologist as a factor in the interpretive process with the Rorschach, it is quite likely that self-consistency or reliability of interpretation may yield low correlations principally because of the maturing process of the psychologist as a function of his experience. This by no means is a reflection on the instrument, but merely is a recognition that the deepening of one's understanding of personality, dynamics and psychopathology will be reflected in more penetrating interpretations of techniques such as the Rorschach (p. 374).

We may add, however, that this would assume that the second set of interpretive statements is more *valid*. Actually, the error involved in each set of interpretations is unknown, and Holzberg's suggestion that the "maturing" process in $E$ himself might contribute to inconsistency, begs the question.

*Temporal Reliability (Test-Retest)*. The administration of a test to the same group of Ss again after a predetermined period of time, in order to ascertain the consistency of results from test to retest, is a usual procedure for assessing reliability of psychometric instruments. Most clinicians and users of projective techniques, however, are of the belief that basic personality and emotional needs change over a period of time, and that temporary and situational factors within the S, will also result in changes of response to the Rorschach stimuli. On the other hand, should not enduring and stable characteristics of the personality be in some way reflected by a relatively stable projective performance, if the instrument is reliable? How can these stable characteristics be differentiated from transient, fleeting, and permanent changes; and how can the latter be differentiated from unreliability? Memory factors play a role in test-retest reliability of projective instruments as in other psychometric devices, contributing to the generally unsatisfactory status of temporal consistency as an indication of instrument reliability.[6] But if the intervening time between test and retest is

---

[6] It is not even clear as to exactly *how* memory affects reliability findings. Does it increase consistency of response? Although commonsense tells us "yes," this might not be true for all Ss at all times. That is, responses to the second test are colored

so long as to prevent memory factors from entering into the situation, will there be any guarantee that personality changes have not taken place?

The following study may well be explained by the operation of memory factors, but to what extent, is not clear. Holzberg and Wexler (1950), after reviewing the literature and finding the evidence for test-retest reliability to be very contradictory, attempted to determine the reliability of the Rorschach technique for chronic schizophrenics by repeating the test after an interval of three weeks. They tested twenty chronic schizophrenic patients whose illness was at least of one year's duration. The correlations for the various factors ranged from —.17 to .95, with the reliabilities for the content categories and the determinants of the form and movement variety clustering around .70, and the reliabilities for the color and shading categories around .30. The *mean* performance three weeks after the initial test, however, did not differ significantly from the first performance.

Although test-retest reliability findings with adults, based on a short interval (days or hours) between tests, have been quite good when memory factors have been "controlled" (such as by use of patients with severe memory impairment or with complete amnesia as a result of electroshock therapy—Griffith [1951]; and Kelley, Margulies, & Barrera [1941]), those based on the testing of children have been strikingly less successful. Some of these poor findings have been explained by the lowered attention span and uneven interest and motivation found in young Ss; when test-retest interval is several months or a year, lowered reliability can be explained by changes in personality and by developmental considerations. With so many variables to "explain," it is easy to see that test-retest reliability procedures have been regarded as generally unsatisfactory.

Fiske (1959) has suggested that since there is a wide distribution of responses to unstructured stimuli, and that at any point in time a projective stimulus has several potential responses, each with different response strengths, it would be useful to have answers to the following question: would interpretations of successive Rorschachs of a single individual be less divergent than of different individuals? We must distinguish, he said, between *stable* components of behavior and temporary dispositions.

---

not only by the current stimuli, but by memory of former responses, which may arouse impulses to repeat former responses, but also, in some instances, to modify, distort or withhold some responses in accordance with many unknown factors, which may include S's interpretation of the new test situation.

This comment raises a question concerning the long-term stability of Rorschach responses. Kagan (1960) reported a study in which he obtained three standard Rorschach protocols from 37 males and 38 females at the median ages of $10\frac{1}{2}$, $13\frac{1}{2}$, and $16\frac{1}{2}$. For 52 Ss, 32 modified Rorschach stimuli were also administered at age 35. He reported findings for number of responses, different types of movement, human detail, and various content factors. He concluded that human percepts, and aggressive responses in which there was no movement showed no evidence of stability, whereas number of responses, human movement, and some of the content factors showed low, but statistically significant, stability. Yet, as others have also noted (e.g., Little, 1959), all aspects of projective responses may not be entirely a reflection of enduring personality characteristics, but of many other factors including the nature of the stimulus, rather than the nature of the S. The stability of certain responses as reported by Kagan may similarly be a reflection of certain qualities of the stimulus and certain individual (temporary) factors, as well as of enduring characteristics of the behavior, and personality of the S. Furthermore, stability or lack of stability of certain responses or scores may or may not reflect the validity or lack of validity of the measure in question. For example, measurements of height of a child over a period of years disclose change, but such changes do not indicate lack of validity. Normative evidence as to what can or cannot be expected to remain relatively stable may serve as a useful yardstick. Deviations from, or concurrences with, the norm may then serve as good clinical predictors.

*Split-Half Reliability.* Some of the disadvantages of temporal tests of reliability are overcome when a test is "split" into equivalent halves. The odd-even split favored in psychometric circles would not, of course, apply to the Rorschach cards. The Rorschach cards are not "items" whose difficulty level can be easily established. The cards are heterogeneous in terms of "pull," both qualitatively and quantitatively, so that the task of creating equal or equivalent halves becomes difficult indeed. Furthermore, the uneven number of responses elicited by the cards, as well as the narrow sampling of responses involved when halves are created, contribute to the general difficulties facing us. Odd-even splits in terms of *responses,* rather than cards, offer more promising possibilities for estimating Rorschach reliability. Reliability of the scales to be described in Chapters 6 and 7 was explored by the latter method.

Suffice it to say, at this point, that there is a contradictory picture of reliability based on split-half techniques, with some authors reporting high and some low reliability. Vernon (1933), for example, reported high split-half reliability for R, but not for other scores, while Hertz (1934) reported high split-half reliability findings for all scores and ratios she used. Many workers are agreed that the greater the number of responses in a group's records, the greater is the reliability when determined by split-half methods; this must be the case perforce, since when R is increased, a better sampling of R, as well as location categories and other responses, becomes available.

In general, split-half methods have a number of serious limitations which often go unrecognized in reports of findings.

*Alternate Form Reliability.* Still another traditional method of establishing reliability involves the correlation of scores on two forms of the same test—a procedure which is relatively straightforward for most psychometric instruments. But establishing an equivalent form for the Rorschach series of inkblots involves knowledge and information of a complex and detailed nature, because questions of picture-pull, number of responses elicited, differential capacity of the cards to elicit certain types of content and interpretations, uneven organization of the stimuli, etc., must be considered when creating an alternate series. If the findings on the two equivalent forms are inconsistent, how is this fact to be interpreted? Is the instrument unreliable, or has the attempt to produce an *exactly* equivalent form not been successful? Although memory factors and personality changes need not be considered in this type of assessment, and although some of the other difficulties involved in measuring reliability can be bypassed, the use of alternate form reliability has not been very common because of the enormous amount of work involved in establishing an equivalent series.

A number of studies have appeared utilizing the series of blots developed by Behn-Eschenberg (Behn-Rorschach)—introduced as a "parallel" series (Zulliger, 1941). Holzberg has summarized some of these findings (1960, pp. 369-370). These studies (e.g., Buckle & Holt [1951]; Eichler [1951a]; and Swift [1944]) seem to indicate (not consistently, however) that although the Rorschach and the Behn-Rorschach are similar, they are not parallel. The utility of this particular "equivalent" series for testing reliability is therefore open to question, although it does seem that this general method is probably very useful for measuring the reliability of the Rorschach method.

Other inkblot series have been introduced, but often in the context of offering an additional rather than an equivalent series. Such tests, of course, fall or stand on their own, on the basis of usual psychometric criteria, including questions concerning their *own* reliability. The *Howard Ink Blot Test* (1953) is a good example of such an instrument. This test was not designed as an alternate form to the Rorschach, nor does it question or "test" traditional Rorschach assumptions. It is an additional inkblot test which does not seem to represent an advance over the Rorschach in terms of more refined scoring, administration procedures, or interpretation principles. The Howard Ink Blot Test is comprised of a twelve-card series. There are two achromatic cards, followed by three colored cards; the fifth card is entirely colored, as are two of the last three cards. The scoring is conventional, and there is no explanation as to the advantages of this instrument over the Rorschach. The disadvantages of the traditional scores and the problems of assessing reliability apply to this instrument as much as they do to the Rorschach. There is detailed normative evidence based on 229 adult Ss, ages 19–44. These data consist of norms for popular responses; average time per response and R for each card; frequency distributions and percentages for location, color, and movement responses, organization scores, etc.

Despite the foregoing comments, there are possible research avenues using this instrument which should be explored. If responses to inkblots reflect basic personality processes, would judges agree in their interpretations or in their pairing of protocols from the two instruments (Rorschach and Howard) obtained from the same individual? Research possibilities are manifold, but the instrument itself does require further refinement as a measuring device per se.

Another attempt to construct a *parallel* series is that of Drey-Fuchs (1958). Although in her manual the author described her ten blots as a parallel series, offering details of the scoring of her cards together with illustrations, the question of how parallel this series is to the Rorschach blots is still open to question, pending future studies with many different types of samples.

In subsequent chapters, we shall describe in some detail how two workers, Baughman and Holtzman, have each met some of the problems in the Rorschach situation, and how special attention to difficulties in the Inquiry and to the fact that there is an uneven number of responses to each card and from S to S resulted in modifications which may offer important solutions to the problems we have raised in connection with assessing reliability. Our own scales, described in Chapters 6 and 7, were also designed to meet some of these problems. In Chapter 5, some attention will be given to "extra-Rorschach" influences on test responses, such as set, E-S interaction and the test situation itself. It will be seen that such factors have strong influence on S's responses, contributing to the variance among test scores which reduces the reliability of the instrument. Meanwhile, it is only necessary to note that the problems attached to assessing the reliability of the Rorschach technique are still not completely solved, despite the fact that there is an increased awareness and understanding of their nature.

## Validity

*General Considerations.* Before discussing Rorschach validity studies, a statement might be made about acceptance of the Rorschach on faith. Subjective evaluation as a basis for Rorschach validity is more prevalent than many Rorschach workers would be willing to admit! Not only the "expert's" declaration of faith, but the examinee's also, should be critically examined, for corroboration or confirmation of a Rorschach interpretation by the patient is frequently accepted as an example of the success of the instrument.

Subjective validation of the testimonial variety in which he who comes to scoff remains to pray, although constituting a basis for subjective personal faith in this instrument on the part of many individuals, is, of course, not admissible as scientific evidence. There are several studies which indicate the fallacy involved in such declarations of faith. Thus, in a rather large study of handwriting specimens, each of the participants was given the identical character description regardless of the actual indicators in his handwriting. Very few of the subjects protested the interpretation and most of them accepted the character description as quite suitable to themselves (Dunlap [1922]; Krüger & Zietz [1933]; and Morgenthaler [1930]). An interesting literary adventure in this vein is offered by George Jean Nathan (1941). He gives the following personality description based on crystal gazing:

You are intelligent, sympathetic, and kind, and an originator to a considerable degree. You are a strong thinker and reasoner, somewhat opinionated, and not apt to believe everything that people tell you. You are fond of good living, rather nervous at times, and may gain the reputation—undeserved, of course—of being something of a crank. You would make a wonderful designer of beautiful dresses, but would need some capable assistant to do the real dressmaking work. Not that you are really lazy—far from it—but your grasp is too large for trivial details . . . (pp. 193–194).

You have great confidence in your own judgment, in spite of periodic doubts. You have, at bottom, an artistic nature. Beautiful colors and music delight you . . . (p. 194).

You are passionate, but anything debasing or low will promptly awaken your disgust and turn you against the offender. Whatever becomes a conviction to you will first have to appeal to your heart. Though intelligent, you feel rather than think. This is not always advantageous to you. You can hide the truth if you desire and now and then, if it suits your purpose, you can tell fibs . . . (p. 195).

You have great self-control—when and if you care to exercise it. You sometimes misplace confidence, and regret it. You are impatient of interference

in your affairs and of anyone who tries to dictate to you. Although you sometimes affect an air of indifference, you are deeply sensitive. You have a strong
will and do not like to confess to a mistake when you have made one. You
are not revengeful or vindictive, but let someone, in your own estimation,
wrong you in some way and you are through with him. You are inclined to
lay a little too much stress on outward appearances. You cannot tolerate
narrow-minded people. You can be taken in, but not often twice by the same
person. You are out of necessity at times materialistic, to a certain extent.
Generally honest and sincere, you can still be very inexact and unreliable
in things you say (pp. 197–198).

Would not many of our readers, despite their sophistication, nod in
the affirmative if asked whether some of the above description could
apply to them?

Having ruled out "faith" and testimonials as methods for appraising
validity, let us turn to a consideration of the validity studies which
have appeared with respect to the Rorschach technique. Before we do
so, however, attention is drawn to a consideration previously raised
under *Reliability*, when problems in connection with the Rorschach
score were considered. At that time, a question was raised concerning
which components of the Rorschach should be subjected to tests of
reliability. The discussion is also relevant to validity research.

There are those who believe that traditional, empirical validation
procedures, employing the use of a criterion and single Rorschach
scores, should be followed. Earlier sections have already noted some of
the difficulties attached to the Rorschach score itself. But, as noted in
connection with problems of assessing reliability, patterns or configurations of these scores, unreliable as they may or may not be, form the
basis of an interpretation—not single scores.

It has been suggested, therefore, that instead of validating single
scores against a simple quantitative criterion, scores can be combined
and weighted in various ways and then validated against a quantitative
criterion. The second approach does not "violate" the global, wholistic
and gestalt aspects of interpretation deemed so important by clinicians,
whereas the first one does. (But as attractive as this second possibility
is, a technique such as the Rorschach does not guarantee or insure a
sufficient or stable number of responses in various scoring categories.)
Meehl (1950) has discussed this "patterned" approach (configural
scoring) to scores, mostly with respect to the MMPI; but there are
many implications for Rorschach validity procedures. After all, this is
the way most clinicians do predict! Configural scoring, according to
Meehl, is nothing more than the use of validity coefficients based on
an item analysis using two or more items at the same time. Items with
little or no validity in themselves may be quite discriminating when

the pattern of other items is considered at the same time. Unfortunately, there has been only a minimum of research to date, using configural scoring principles applied to the Rorschach as well as to other instruments. Loevinger (1959), in a review of theory and techniques of assessment, has noted that pattern analysis and configural scoring has failed, or at least, its superiority to linear methods has not been demonstrated. What the future will disclose in terms of the rich (and logical, from a clinician's point of view) potential of configural validation, is hard to say.

But the picture is even more complicated. Clinicians do not utilize, in the process of writing a Rorschach report, a "set" series of interpretations for a particular pattern or configuration. Were this so, validity coefficients could be based on the relationship of a *pattern* of scores to a particular criterion. The situation, simplified, perhaps, amounts to this: most clinicians base their interpretations on a series of implicit and sometimes explicit "hypotheses" (differing ones, of course, are used by different clinicians) as to the meaning of a particular response, score, group of scores, configuration of scores, or the "quality" of a particular record—sometimes weighting one or the other of these in accordance with the "flavor" of the whole record, or the intensity or "vividness" of the ratio, response, score, etc., involved. Not only does this interpretative process vary from clinician to clinician, but clinicians may also vary in this procedure from record to record.

A third approach to Rorschach validation noted by MacFarlane and Tuddenham (1951) involves discarding quantitative scoring categories altogether, in favor of interpretative statements based on subjectively combined scores. Of this latter approach, they have said:

If it should turn out that the interpretation of certain skilled clinicians has greater predictive significance than that of the other methods, then the research attack would have to be shifted to the interpreter of the test. Experiments would have to be designed to find the relative weights he gives to the various cues (his subjective categories) by some such procedure as having him predict at each step of an additive exposure to the protocols (p. 46).

Others have suggested that the *interpretative hypotheses* extant in the field should be validated. Does the M-C ratio relate to certain personality types? Do movement responses reflect "inner, stable aspects of the S's fantasy?" Is the color response a reflection of the manner with which S handles the outer world in terms of his emotionality?

We shall soon see that Rorschach validation procedures have taken many paths, following one or another of the many possible avenues. Sometimes it appears that the form the research takes is not dictated by conviction as to the most appropriate validation procedure, but rather by convenience, availability of records, and the like. We agree that single score validity research does not necessarily reflect clinical usage, nor the manner in which results, predictions, and personality descriptions are constructed. On the other hand, validating on the basis of interpretations and traditional clinical usage introduces a host of other problems: clinical usage based on which clinicians? What are the implicit hypotheses? Not the least of these problems is the fact that validating or substantiating a particular hypothesis tells us little about *other* hypotheses or the test as a whole.

*Rorschach Validity Studies.* In the last analysis, a test cannot be valid unless it is reliable. We have already cast doubt on the reliability of the Rorschach. Thus, an examination of the present status of the Rorschach with regard to validity is most important. In 1954, Zubin discussed this problem and came to the following conclusions: (*a*) global interpretations of Rorschach protocols seem to work, that is, are positively correlated with independent evaluations of personality; (*b*) global as well as atomistic evaluations based on Rorschach content scales seem to work; (*c*) atomistic evaluations based on Rorschach perceptual variables alone are not successful; and (*d*) factor analysis of scores based on content scales as well as perceptual scores seems successful. Zubin explained these conclusions by hypothesizing that the Rorschach is essentially an interview. As such, the most appropriate analysis of Rorschach variables, as in any interview, should be based on an evaluation of content.

What is the status of the technique today, some time later? Before answering this question, let us examine the variety of ways in which the validity of the Rorschach technique has been investigated. First we will describe the global methods consisting of such procedures as blind analysis, matching techniques, and overall correspondence between the Rorschach and clinical evaluations. Then come the more specific approaches: evaluation of individual scores or signs in differentiating groups; evaluation of patterns or specific syndromes of signs; testing the alleged significance of a sign or syndrome against clinical evaluations or other criteria.

Cutting across the global vs. specific procedures are laboratory approaches to the evaluation of specific signs, as exemplified by correlation between Rorschach performance and physiological indicators or as exemplified by manipulation of the human organism by such techniques as hypnosis and surgical and other somatic intervention (e.g., lobotomy, shock therapy, etc.). Then come developmental studies in which the changes in performance are related to developmental changes that occur with maturation and learning. Prognostic and predictive studies in personnel selection and training or in therapeutic outcomes, and methodological approaches such as factor analytic investigations are discussed; illustrations of the validation of specific intrepretative hypotheses, studies with normals and several content analysis approaches, constitute the final considerations in the area of validity.

It is interesting to note that validity studies are relatively new to the Rorschach scene, the first one of any importance appearing as recently as 1938 (Benjamin & Ebaugh). It should be remembered that the Rorschach technique appeared in protest against the alleged lack of validity which characterized personality inventories. The specific predictions made possible by these instruments proved their own undoing when it was discovered that despite their standardization, objectivity, and reliability, they produced validity coefficients ranging from zero to the .30's and .40's only. Projective techniques arose to remedy this failure. How well has the Rorschach met this challenge?

*Blind Analysis.* An early method of demonstrating validity of the Rorschach was "blind analysis" in which the Rorschach expert analyzes the S's personality from the Rorschach record without seeing him. The correctness of the diagnosis, interpretation, or personality description is judged either by the expert himself or by other judges or the patient himself. In this method, the looseness of the terms and labels used, the generality of many of the statements made, as well as the implicit familiarity with the base rates for diagnostic groupings in the sample with which he is working, may yield what appears to be E, "evidence" that his test is valid.

Blind analysis is one of the spectacular aspects of the Rorschach technique and has probably been the most important factor in the acceptance of the Rorschach by psychiatrists. These techniques have been popularly used in the context of diagnostic studies. Benjamin and Ebaugh (1938), for example, using diagnoses arrived at in clinical conferences as the criterion, were able to show surprisingly good agreement between most of their "blind," independent analyses of Rorschach protocols and ultimate diagnoses.[7] Blind analysis has also been purported to be quite successful in anthropological research—see for example, DuBois and Oberholzer, (1942), who worked with the Alorese, in the Dutch East Indies. The method commonly used was to search for congruencies between the expert's blind interpretations of Rorschach protocols (at times, only a meager handful of records was

---

[7] Many subsequent studies presumably getting at validity, turned out to be what could more appropriately be labeled as reliability studies, for these involved the matching of "blind" analyses (with each other) or the search for congruencies between and among independent analyses of protocols.

used) and a description of personality "type" derived from other (non-test) sources such as observations, interviews, records, etc. Hallowell (1956, pp. 512–516) has summarized some of these "pioneer" anthropological studies. The successful studies reported were presumably not only a confirmation of Rorschach validity, but evidence that ideal "cultural types" exist.

One would wish that the method of blind analysis could be made more explicit and more public, and that the enthusiastic proponents of this method were as ready to report their failures as their successes. (One exception is a blind diagnosis study reported by Dawson [1949] which had disappointing results.) Successful "blind diagnosis" cannot be accepted as scientific evidence, even though it is impressive at first glance. Until this method becomes more open to public scrutiny, it has to be placed in the doubtful category, as far as validity is concerned.

*Signs: Clinical and Statistical Uses.* Some clinicians arrive at a belief in the trustworthiness of the results of a Rorschach analysis from their own experience with clinical cases. Often, this consists of administering and scoring the test, collecting data on S's subsequent behavior—sometimes randomly and subjectively—and then going back to the protocol, in which are "found" signs which "unmistakably" foretell such behavior. Unless cross-validation of these post-dicted signs is undertaken in another study with many cases and in different types of sampling situations, it is fruitless to accept them as indicative of future behavior, because with sufficient imagination and exertion of effort through trial-and-error, pseudosignificant signs can be found in any test. Unfortunately, such cross-validation is rarely encountered in the context of this type of "clinical sign construction." Even among more research-minded clinical psychologists, the use of signs and cutting points for frequency of a given score (determinant or locale, etc.) for predictive purposes has long held some fascination. Here too, the failure to cross-validate, the problem of base rates, and the lack of appraisal of situational, chance, and sampling problems, have introduced much confusion and contradictory evidence.

A number of sign studies are designed to establish useful criteria for differentiating groups. Even when such studies have essentially a practical and utilitarian orientation, such as developing a cutoff point for separating part of the sample for purposes of employee or student selection, etc., this particular use of signs should also be cross-validated.

Some sign studies make use of this approach as an aid in diagnostic classification, often comparing and contrasting various groups, and sometimes examining one group alone, in order to compile a group of signs, presumably not only to aid in the subsequent diagnoses of individual cases, but as a means for assessing and attesting to the validity of the instrument.

Weiner (1961) reported the results of a "sign" study which consisted of (a) an exploratory phase, during which three Rorschach signs (tendency to give 1 or 2 CF, have a Sum C between 1.5 and 3.0, and give at least 1 CF or C response with no C' response) emerged—the signs showing a relationship to degree of pathology; and (b) two successful attempts to cross-validate these signs—these three indicators being associated significantly more frequently with the schizophrenic groups than with the others (neurosis and character disorder).

The influence of response totals, as well as of age and sex were determined to be negligible, and several other possible sources of error were controlled. Despite the seeming success of this research, however, a number of additional features might be noted. Contamination of original diagnosis and Rorschach protocols was present. The Rorschachs themselves apparently made some contribution to the diagnosis with which the patient was labeled. This motivated the investigator to explore whether or not the psychologists felt that they had actually utilized the indicators under consideration in diagnosing the S. Although the psychologists indicated that the three signs did *not* influence them in making a diagnosis of schizophrenia—and we are not informed as to whether or not they knew about the nature of the study—we do not know the statistical relationship between these signs and those that they *did* indicate as influential. Furthermore, the author himself states that ". . . it would seem in many cases that the psychologists, sometimes of necessity and sometimes of choice, had based their diagnostic impressions on indicators other than those they endorsed in the checklist" (p. 438). Another consideration is that the cultural, educational, social, etc., characteristics of the samples are unspecified; cross-validation, however, was based on an almost identical population to that used in the exploratory phase, all being drawn from the files of a general hospital. Would the signs "hold up" with other samples of schizophrenics? The author's conclusion that ". . . it is felt that the data recommend these signs for inclusion among Rorschach criteria for the presence of schizophrenia" (p. 439) overlooks the essential point that the particular clinic population with which he was working may not be at all representative of schizophrenia as defined elsewhere, and may, in fact, represent a biased sample, with unknown characteristics. These signs, perhaps potentially quite utilitarian, are for the time being meaningless, without knowledge of their efficacy with other populations. Auld and Eron (1953), for example, reported a dramatic shrinkage of correlation when a Rorschach scoring formula, worked out and cross-validated on samples of Boston patients, was applied to a fresh sample in New Haven.

One type of criticism leveled at the "sign approach" stems from clinicians who are opposed to the mechanical, analytic, formalistic procedures involved in constructing signs (e.g., Klopfer & Spiegelman 1956a). The Rorschach technique, such workers claim, is a global, wholistic technique, and validity approaches should be firmly rooted in such a context. They point out the fact that even "proven" signs are useless when the clinician is confronted with the individual case.

There is some research support, as a matter of fact, to indicate that "global" approaches are more adequate than "sign" approaches. Zamansky and Goldman (1960), for example, have shown that global Rorschach evaluations were much better indicators of actual changes in social adjustment in the ward than were eleven quantitative Rorschach indices. Crumpton (1956), in a study of signs of "color shock," has reported that although statistical use of the usual signs failed to discriminate records based on an achromatic and a chromatic (standard) Rorschach series (judges did not know whether or not the records were based on the chromatic or achromatic series), the use of clinical, global ratings of the protocols did result in a statistically significant, valid, differentiation of the records. But the record of success of global evaluations is not encouraging. Furthermore, unless we find out the basis of the global evaluation, we are no further ahead, scientifically.

Subsequent sections of this chapter consider the utility of signs when their use in prognosis is discussed. Signs come up for discussion also in the section, *Differential Diagnosis*. Suffice it to say that the general picture concerning the use of signs is not hopeful.

*Matching.*[8] Early clinical attempts to validate the Rorschach technique were based on matching operations—often with the use of "independent blind analysis" (see previously). In general, the technique involves matching the Rorschach expert's findings with those of a psychiatrist or other expert. Specifically, methods used may involve the matching of sketches or descriptions from Rorschach protocols with those based on other sources such as case histories, and interviews. Matching might be based on specific interpretative statements, or more wholistic personality descriptions, or diagnoses. In any event, independent judgments must be obtained with respect to both Rorschach judgments and criterion judgments—that is, the Rorschach expert must

---

[8] Difficulties in matching procedures were also discussed previously under *Reliability*. The problems are of course the same, whether the focus of the study is reliability, or validity.

base his description on the Rorschach protocol, and on that alone, uncontaminated by knowledge of S, the population from which S was drawn, or various biographical factors. The criterion judge, similarly, must have no prior knowledge of S's test responses. There are too many possibilities, however, for unconscious collusion.[9] Furthermore, in the case of matching of diagnostic statements, the degree of correspondence between Rorschach interpretation and diagnosis is hardly a suitable measure, since diagnosis itself is not too stable or objective a criterion, and when the Rorschach worker "learns" to know his psychiatrist or criterion judge, the diagnosis could have really been based on the same type of "non-Rorschach" evidence that the criterion judge might have used. It is also quite apparent that the choice of patients or subjects within a given research setting (clinic, institution, hospital, university, school, etc.) is often very restricted, and the mere presence of the S in the particular research setting is often self-diagnostic. (In many research hospitals, for example, only patients of a certain type are admitted.) Moreover, "styles" and preferences in diagnostic choices and labels vary, often significantly, with the particular clinical setting —a factor which might well contribute to a spuriously high congruency in matches. The Rorschach expert, under such conditions, need consciously or unconsciously pay little, if any, attention to basic and intrinsic Rorschach factors in the protocols themselves. This discussion, it might be noted, again raises the problem of base rates and population differences.

Matching techniques in which Rorschach protocols or scores are matched against personality sketches or case histories in groups of five or more have also been used, not always with findings favorable to the instrument. There are certain basic objections to the procedures involved, an important one of which is that the determination of the precise grounds on which successful pairing is made is virtually impossible. Psychiatrists' or other experts' criterion judgments are not always infallible, and there is little knowledge as to the correctness or incorrectness of even perfectly matched statements. There are many inadvertent and tangential characteristics of this method, not germane to validity, which may influence the outcome. Successful matching is frequently effected on the basis of minor details or coincidences rather than essential equivalance. Heterogeneity of matchees also makes the

---

[9] Many of the earlier successful studies reported, it seems, did not make explicit the means by which collusion between clinician and diagnostic expert (usually psychiatrist) was prevented. Benjamin and Ebaugh (1938) were outstanding exceptions. In their report they indicated the care they took to avoid foreknowledge or collusion.

task too easy; similarly, complete failure in matching may be due to homogeneity of the sample. Another point is that the words, phrases, and content of the responses are often diagnostic in themselves. Some of the successful inferences made by the Rorschach expert depend not on the Rorschach technique *per se*, but on the interview-like material which the protocols provide. Thus, intellectual level can be estimated from the vocabulary level of the responses, bizarre thinking from the outlandish responses given by S, and perseverative tendencies from the actual repetition of responses. These are not basically Rorschach factors in the same sense as are W, M, and FC. Moreover, the generality, stereotypes, and "jargon" of clinical statements used in the matching study may create a picture which is specious. Terms such as sexual problems, anxiety, conflict, etc., are found both in Rorschach interpretations as well as in statements based on non-Rorschach material and can be applied with equal "validity" to many individuals in our culture! Another difficulty in matching studies involves the nature of the descriptive categories used. Anastasi (1954) had this to say about the latter point:

If the personality descriptions given in the case history and in the test protocol are couched in the terminology of different personality theories, behavioral similarities may be concealed by semantic discrepancies. On the other hand, if the same descriptive concepts are utilized in both, observed correspondences may be an artifact resulting from the broadness and looseness of the concepts. Such pseudo-congruencies would of course be detected in the control data from randomly paired records. But the use of control data is no real solution, since it might only mean that the results would have to be discarded as inconclusive (p. 627).

There has been much criticism of matching techniques (Cronbach [1948]; Meehl [1959]) with the overall conclusion that matching techniques are not adequate as validation methods. Meehl, stressing the necessity for construct validity, stated that blind-matching, globally, is not justified. What are the components? How do we know what contributed to what? Meehl prefers the Q-sort technique, which he feels is both quantifiable and global. Cronbach has proposed a trenchant methodology for freeing the matching methods from its many defects, but it is quite intricate and has not proved to be very popular.

Although successful matches have often been obtained, most of the results indicate that the matching is only better than chance, an insufficient criterion for validity (see Newton [1954] for an illustration of an unsuccessful matching study, and Krugman [1942], for an illustration of a successful study). The only general conclusion that may be drawn from some of the successful matching studies described in the

Rorschach literature, is that there is some connection between Rorschach technique results and personality description from other sources. But the all-important problem of the nature of this connection cannot be investigated through matching techniques of the type now used.

*Differential Diagnosis; Contrasted Groups.* Studies of differential diagnosis have been based not only on a wide variety of diagnostic entities, but on almost any available institutional group such as the feebleminded, delinquents, epileptics, or elderly patients, as well as on various groups of Ss seen and classified in clinics, such as behavior problems, stutterers, and the physically handicapped. More recently, studies of contrasted groups have been utilized in vocational and military settings as well as with various types of trainees, candidates, and students in different educational settings.

The need for cross-validation of all findings from such studies, is of course essential. But there are more serious limitations which should be noted. Sampling problems are enormous. Frequently, groups are not matched in terms of relevant variables, such as intelligence, educational background, and sociocultural indices, although age and sex are frequently controlled. Secondly, the question of base rates, already discussed, has been rarely considered. The nature of the criterion itself, and its reliability and validity, is of crucial importance, together with the fact that styles and preferences in diagnostic labeling in various clinical settings might well be easily "known" by the Rorschach worker. Moreover, the common practice of utilizing "institutional" Ss creates important sampling problems. Aged Ss in old age homes, for example, are certainly different from aged Ss who are not. Can we generalize about Rorschachs of the aged from institutional samples? An additional point bears on the fact that in many studies a large number of signs and scores are examined to discover those which discriminate. A number of significant signs can be expected to emerge on a chance basis alone.

The studies reported are by and large not all successful. For example, in three successive samples of about fifty neurotic patients each, who were given the Rorschach in orthodox fashion, Guilford (1948) found that no significant differences could be detected between their performance and that of a large normative group of cadets. Wittenborn and Holzberg (1951) found zero correlations between over three dozen separate Rorschach factors and diagnosis in 199 successive admissions. And Cox (1951) found that only five out of a total of forty-three scores differentiated normal and neurotic children; and of these five scores, three were in the content category, and only two in the determinant categories. Waxenberg (1955) used several projective techniques including the Rorschach to compare psychosomatic and other physically ill people, and he found no differences between patients with asthma or ulcerative colitis and those with tumors, for any of the many comparisons he made. He interpreted his findings to signify that certain "theories" of psychosomatic involvements were incorrect—a conclusion, incidentally, which presumes a high level of reliability and validity of the projective techniques he used, as well as the representativeness, in terms of psychosomatic disorders, of asthma and ulcerative colitis. In an apparently successful study, Stotsky and Lawrence (1955) explored the validity of several Rorschach indices of conceptual disorganization, utilizing two groups of schizophrenic Ss, one with considerable impairment of conceptual functioning and the other with very little as determined by an independent measure derived from the Multidimensional Scale for Rating Psychiatric Patients (Lorr, 1953). Predictions that the Ss could be distinguished on the basis of four Rorschach indices (form, location, number of popular responses, and quantity of determinant shifts from test to Inquiry) were confirmed at a high level of significance. This study has apparently not been replicated.

Corsini, Severson, Tunney, and Uehling (1955) explored the relative validity of a Rorschach checklist and judgments of clinicians in separating "normal" and "abnormal" Rorschach protocols. The normal records were obtained from fifty prison guards, and the abnormal records were obtained from fifty prisoners who had not only committed serious felonies, but had been referred for testing because of a possibility of having "serious personality deviations." All identifying data had been removed from the Rorschach protocols, and prisoners and guards were matched, as far as possible, for age. Inmates of average intelligence and of lower middle class status only were used. Ss were all white. Four psychologists were asked to rank all protocols, from 1 to 100, in terms of adjustment of the S. Reliability of rankings (interjudge comparisons) was of a relatively low order. But comparison of number of normal protocols placed in the top half of the rankings by the Davidson Rorschach Adjustment Scale and by each of the judges yielded the finding that global judgments were more accurate. Time spent in the judging process was shown to be positively related to the accuracy of the ranking. The findings do indeed suggest that global, clinical methods are more differential than mechanical checklists, but a question should be raised as to whether or not either of these methods could have effectively separated a more meaningful, better matched group—prisoners with and without "serious personality deviations." Language, content, and general approach to the Rorschach situation might well differ sufficiently between guards and prisoners to yield definite clues, independent of Rorschach scoring itself, as to which S is likely to come from which group.

Evidence stemming from studies of nonpsychiatric or noninstitutional groups has often served to cast doubt on some of the many assumptions underlying the interpretative meaning of various determinants and ratios; that is, expected differences between groups often do not emerge. Roe (1946a, b, and c), for example, in her studies of eminent artists, did not find a greater preponderance of M responses, despite the fact that this determinant is usually interpretatively linked to creativity, and Schachtel (1951) found no evidence that juvenile delinquent Ss gave more white space responses than a matched group of nondelinquents (1000 Ss in all), despite the fact that white space responses have usually been linked with oppositional tendencies.

The discouraging findings concerning diagnostic and contrasted group validity do not seem to prevent many clinicians from approaching their Rorschach work as if there were an accepted body of signs, rules, and indices concerning particular diagnostic groups. One particular area which has yielded innumerable research reports and many claims of success will be briefly discussed—the diagnosis of "organicity" from Rorschach records. The differentiation of organic from functional conditions has had a history of conspicuous success as well as marked failure and conflicting evidence. Generally, the pattern has been one of immediate, retrospective, empirical success, with several signs significantly differentiating the diagnostic groups, but of ultimate failure, when the results of such retrospective analysis are applied to a new sample. For example, Dörken and Kral (1952), after demolishing the signs of previous workers, proposed a new set of their own. A few years later, Fisher, Gonda, and Little (1955) explored the efficacy of the signs formulated by Dörken and Kral, as well as those of Piotrowski, Hughes, and Ross and Ross. They worked with 118 Ss from a Veterans' Administration hospital, who had been admitted to the neurology wards and had received complete neurological examinations. The criterion for organicity was comprised of ratings by two neurologists who had evaluated CNS involvement, as well as provided a rating as to degree of certainty of their decision. All systems except Piotrowski's showed a drop in validity when applied to this new sample. The indices of Piotrowski and of Ross and Ross held up quite well in identifying the organics (few false positives), but all the systems failed in terms of identifying cases as nonorganic (many false negatives). Thus, although these signs were sensitive to brain injury, they were not specific to it.

Some studies have had more success. These isolated achievements distort the picture because they generate more encouragement and acceptance of the Rorschach's validity than is warranted by the large group of failures. Schreiber and White (1954), for example, submitted the Rorschach to what they called a "true test." The question they raised is this: can the Rorschach be used as an independent device ("lab" test) for the diagnosis of organicity in a varied hospital population? These authors have made wide claims on the basis of their work —that is, the Rorschach is capable of specifying tissue changes (insofar as these have affected personality) and whether or not these are partial or widespread—but they have made no claims for the Rorschach's capacity to detect the nature, location, permanence, or severity of damage. Their amazing success was based on a subjective technique which varied from record to record. But they specified the methods they used, and if a factor influenced them 75% of the time, it was presented as a "sign." Content factors and S's attitude toward the test were among some of the qualitative features used. (Would knowledge of the latter, independently of the Rorschach, be successful as a sign? If so, is the Rorschach truly efficient?). Despite the authors' claims for success, as well as some indication of success in a small cross-validation study, the general questions remain: can the authors repeat their success with other samples? Would other workers do as well? The authors have presented a cookbook, or at least a recipe, but the subjectivity and lack of detail in their method may result in not enough proof in the eating! Once again we see, however, the relative success of global and clinical methods when compared to a more atomistic approach.

Baker (1956), in a summary of the problems and techniques involved in the diagnosis of organic brain damage, has repeatedly stated the importance of estimating the emotional responses and defenses of the individual to his particular brain injury. After a survey of some of the neurological as well as psychological findings concerning the behavior of brain damaged patients (independently of the Rorschach), she offered a set of twenty-six predictions (based on her survey as well as her rationale of response to injury), as to how an S might respond to the Rorschach, as well as to other tests. Although she had stated more than once that these are not signs, and that mechanical application of signs to individual cases without regard to the individual's personal and emotional needs and status will result in failure, her predictions, unfortunately, will undoubtedly be used by clinicians and trainees as "rules-of-thumb" for the diagnosis of brain damage—this despite the fact that one of Baker's "predictions" is, "We will be prepared for heterogeneity of test signs; we will not expect all patients having brain damage to show the same signs or any one patient to show all of the signs that can be regarded as useful for general diagnostic purposes" (p. 344).

On the other hand, in contrast to Baker's approach, Klopfer and Spiegelman's (1956b) paper on differential diagnosis does not offer a list of statements aimed at ultimate empirical verification, and which was derived from earlier research summaries and reports. Without any empirical substantiation, these authors have described certain characteristics of Rorschach responses, stating that this or that type of S will manifest such a response, occasionally presenting an example. There is no evidence to show whether or not none, several, or many cases have manifested such responses, whether or not these are predictions based on "rationale" and "theoretical" expectation, or whether or not these are hunches and expectations based on the clinical experience of the authors. Norms, contrasted groups, and questions of social, situational, and stimulus variables are not considered. And the validity of the Rorschach, as well as of the diagnostic groupings themselves are assumed.

Another type of validity approach which is also based on comparing or contrasting groups, involves the use of specially developed scores or scales. One such system has been developed as an outgrowth of Werner's developmental theories (1948, 1957), which suggests that development and the maturing process progress from a lack of differentiation to greater differentiation and integration. Although Werner's theories are relevant to perceptual development in general, there are many implications for psychopathological perceptual processes, for example, the process and structure of perceptual regression in abnormal states. Briefly stated, this approach suggests that regression of perceptual processes appears in pathology, and that this can be readily identified as possessing the characteristics of earlier forms through which the patient has already progressed. The structure of regressive responses is only similar, rather than identical to childhood perceptual processes, however, for aspects or vestiges of the more mature perceptual level through which S has presumably passed cannot be altogether erased and have "left their mark." Clark University research reported by Friedman (1953), Hemmendinger (1953), and Siegel (1953), attempted to utilize this approach to describe and differentiate various groups of schizophrenics, schizophrenics as contrasted to children, and children of various ages. The measures used were derived from assessing the pattern of location of Rorschach responses, and the results in general were highly successful, not only in terms of confirming Werner's hypotheses but in distinguishing groups in terms of "genetic level" at good levels of significance. A report by Levine (1960), who found that genetic-level scores did not successfully distinguish patterns of symptoms *within* a psychotic population, suggests that generalizations of some of the principles involved in the genetic-level approach are not yet completely warranted. A review of research in this area as well as of related researches has been presented by Hemmendinger (1960).

In another attempt to discriminate diagnostic groups (thirty Ss in each of the following groups comprised the sample: obsessive-compulsive neurosis; personality trait disturbance; depressive psychosis; schizophrenia, catatonic type; and schizophrenia, paranoid type), Bower, Testin, and Roberts (1960) developed an extensive series of scales which tapped content, thought processes, and determinants, as reflected by the Rorschach protocols. These scales were empirically weighted to result in maximum discriminatory power. Although some promising trends were found, further refinement of the scales and cross-validation on new populations must be awaited before any overall evaluation of this research can be made.

A global approach to comparing groups, or at least one which attempted to utilize the *pattern* of many of the traditional scoring categories is illustrated by a study reported by Wirt (1956). Wirt's general hypothesis is that the pattern of *determinants* of normal, neurotic, and schizophrenic groups would differ significantly from each other, whereas a pattern analysis of responsiveness to the cards themselves would not. Using a technique for pattern analysis developed by Block, Levine, and McNemar (1951), Wirt found that significant differences appeared with respect to configurations based on the determinants, but not the cards, although the patterns which did emerge were not entirely expected on the basis of a priori judgments.

An earlier study utilizing a patterned approach to Rorschach scores was reported by Thiesen (1952), who was interested in discovering whether or not a specific pattern of responses could identify a schizophrenic population. Ss were 60 schizophrenic adults; there was a control group of 157 adults. His first step was to designate as high, medium, or low, 17 of the 20 Rorschach variables which had been selected for study (three of the variables showed such a small range that only two categories, high and low were used for these). Designations of high, medium, or low were made on the basis of the variability of scores in the control group (e.g., one sigma above and one below the mean in the control group set the limits of the medium category).

Through systematic scrutiny of the categories for each variable for each S, certain outstanding combinations emerged which "could reasonably be identified as patterns associated with schizophrenia" (p. 367). Two criteria were used for the selection of a pattern—at least 10% of the patient population showed the pattern, and statistical significance at the .01 level of confidence. Five patterns met these criteria (e. g., Pattern A—high anatomy, high sex; and Pattern B—F+ % low, Z score low). Although Thiesen was well aware of the need to cross-validate his findings on other populations, it might be noted that the testing for significance was done on the same population from which the patterns were derived. Moreover, although a large group of normal controls (96.8%) showed no patterns at all, about half (51.6%) of the patient population also failed to do so (false negatives). The presence of *more* than one pattern occurred in 8 out of the 60 patient records, but not once in the control group—a pathognomic sign perhaps, but with a rather low incidence. Cross-validation of all of these findings seems essential.

Our survey of Rorschach research involving a contrasted group approach has disclosed that the methods used vary considerably. The familiar "sign" approach is giving way to a more patterned or configurational approach [10]; moreover, there is a trend to develop "custom made" scales and scores to tap a priori constructs, or "theories" concerning the relevant variables which might be at work. Global, overall judgments have also been used. If there is any trend at all, it might be that the sign methods seem to be less successful than the configurational, "special scale," or global approaches, in reflecting differences between the various groups explored.

*"Laboratory" Validation: Physiological Correlates; Specially Induced States.* Certain specific techniques and procedures borrowed from, or under the auspices of, the physiologist, surgeon, or psychiatrist have been utilized in conjunction with the Rorschach. Studies utilizing such procedures are not always directly concerned with assessing the validity of the Rorschach; instead, Rorschach validity is often assumed, and the purpose of the study is to shed light on a personality process, a surgical procedure, etc. Sometimes specific predictions are made as to changes in Rorschach responses; at other times the concern has been

---

[10] Note might be made of Beck's massive research on reaction patterns of various types of schizophrenics (1954), which attempted, through use of the Q-technique, to discover ideal "types" or "patterns" for various schizophrenic subgroups. That aspect of the research concerned with the Rorschach, however, can be regarded not so much as a "validity approach" as an attempt to shed light on schizophrenic behavior, typology, and process, and as such, will not be described here.

with discrimination of prognostic groups for purposes of preselection and prediction; the testing of specific non-Rorschach assumptions or hypotheses may also be involved. Rabin (1951) has reviewed many early studies, covering a wide range of physiological, pharmacological, psychosurgical, and convulsive shock techniques. Klopfer's volume (1956) contains, in its extensive bibliography, many recent references to researches employing these techniques.

Thus, the Rorschach technique has been used in conjunction with pre- and/or postoperative procedures (psychosurgery)—Allison and Allison (1954), Helman (1953), and Zubin (1949); electroencephalography—Bennett (1952) and Brudo (1954); galvanic skin responses—Steinberg (1949); electric shock therapy—Holzberg and Cahen (1952), and Rees and Jones (1951); and drugs and chemicals of various types such as alcohol, sodium amytal, hormones, cortisone, insulin, glutamic acid, etc.—Brozek, Guetzkow, and Keys (1946), vitamin B restriction; Caldwell (1954), hormone therapy; Dörken and Tunis (1949), narcosis; Kitzinger, Arnold, Cartwright, and Shapiro (1949), glutamic acid; Lipton, Tamarin, and Lotesta (1951), insulin; Lotsof and Chance (1954), cortisone; and Rabin, Papania, and McMichael (1954), alcohol.

Such studies are often excellently executed in terms of design and statistical treatment. The findings unfortunately often lack coordination with an overall theoretical framework which can integrate them with physiology, psychiatry, etc., despite the fact that interesting, provocative results are sometimes reported.

An extensive study of psychometric and psychological changes accompanying psychosurgical procedures, was reported by the Columbia Greystone Associates (Mettler, 1949). The operative procedure—topectomy (partial ablation of the frontal cortex)—offered an opportunity for testing what effect the lowering of anxiety induced by the operation might have on Rorschach performance. Neither orthodox scoring, anxiety indicators (with the single exception of reaction time), nor other types of scoring succeeded in demonstrating any changes in the Rorschach performance of the patients, although other psychological tests showed such changes. Psychometric scaling (see Chapters 6 and 7) however, did provide a prognostic indicator. Three pairs of patients were selected, each pair consisting of one individual who decreased in anxiety and one who increased in anxiety after operation. The judgment of loss and gain in anxiety was based on psychological interviewing by means of anchored scaling devices and on the judgment of the psychiatrist. Only patients in whom the two criteria concurred were selected. The results indicated that movement responses of

THE RORSCHACH TECHNIQUE 211

whatever variety correlated positively with anxiety, rising when the anxiety level rose and dropping when the anxiety level fell. The degree of tentativeness or insecurity in giving responses also correlated positively with anxiety. The following variables showed only a unilateral relationship to anxiety levels, declining with a decline in anxiety but showing no corresponding rise with rise in anxiety level: sensitivity to chiaroscuro, anatomical responses, number of animate objects and objects with texture, and degree of self-reference. The following variables also showed a unilateral but negative relationship with anxiety, showing increases as anxiety fell: accuracy of form perception and degree of congruity of the response. The statistical significance of these differences could be readily established since each patient could be analyzed as a separate sample and the significance of the difference for each patient determined. Only the variables that showed consistent changes from patient to patient were reported in this study (Garrison, 1948).

Another popular approach to establishing the validity of the Rorschach, or to testing certain assumptions concerning its interpretation, has been through the use of hypnosis. Many such studies seemed to be motivated by a desire to place the Rorschach technique on a level with the rest of psychology; however, frequent lack of attention to statistical problems of the Rorschach itself, plus lack of systematic testing of many implicit Rorschach hypotheses, has resulted in dozens of isolated studies and findings, often baffling in nature.

Levitt and Grosz (1960), for example, studied the effect of hypnotically induced anxiety on Rorschach performance. Using an extremely small, normal, unrepresentative sample (N of 12) with no control group, three Rorschach records from each S were obtained, without randomizing the order of presentation. One record was obtained in the waking state; another, during hypnosis, and a third, under conditions of hypnotically induced anxiety. On the basis of an analysis of 25 Rorschach variables, the authors concluded that several of the variables reflected the anxiety state. In their study, failure to cross-validate findings, the small number of cases, lack of information about the effects of repeated Rorschachs per se, or of the hypnotic state per se, lack of controls, lack of information concerning effect of knowledge that Ss would be hypnotized, special nature of sample (above average, socioeconomically, as well as capacity to be amnesic for performance in hypnosis)—all make the results of the study difficult, if not impossible, to interpret.

Other studies using hypnotically induced states make frequent use of a one-subject sample, usually with a "before" and "after" Rorschach under standard conditions, with several intervening administrations during an hypnotically induced mood, state, or age regression. Findings have been rather striking in that various predictions and expectations (such as an increase in M, O, and R when a "creative" role was induced) have been confirmed. Although such studies do suggest positive validity evidence for certain interpretative hypotheses concerning various determinants, the role of E and the kind of reinforcement he provides is not clear; these studies also highlight the significance of temporary moods, sets, and suggestion in the responses produced by S.

*Predicting Behavior.* Many clinicians have noted the failures of the Rorschach in predicting behavior. These failures have served at least one important purpose; they have brought about constant examination and re-examination of methodology, considerations concerning reliability, and the nature of the scores themselves, as well as the development of new ways of handling and treating Rorschach data statistically. Despite much evidence to the contrary, there is something about the Rorschach technique so fascinating, perhaps so *clinically* helpful, that over a generation of psychologists has been convinced that prediction of behavior is possible, and that only refinements in methodology are needed for a direct relationship to be established between performance on the Rorschach and behavior.

Some attention has been given to the whys and wherefores of these failures (e.g., Little [1959], Symonds [1954]); a brief discussion of some of the points raised might be in order. We have already discussed a host of problems concerning the scores, the sample, criterion problems, and questions of reliability; we have also questioned whether the ten plates provide a representative and large enough sampling of responses. Additional questions might be raised: are *all* responses to unstructured stimuli related to basic, enduring personality? Is personality itself so extremely complex and manifold in its behavioral expression, that chance factors, situational factors, as well as incidental daily occurrences also affect the response? Moreover, in terms of the criterion, do we know enough about the behavioral or personality correlates of successful pilots, say, or salesmen, in order to say that a test of *personality* can make predictions in these areas? Symonds wondered: are we predicting manifest or latent trends? In addition, he noted that the Rorschach is probably too coarse an instrument for purposes of specific behavioral prediction. He used Rorschach anxiety indicators, as an example. In terms of the individual subject, the prediction becomes complex: anxiety to what? and how does the person express his anxiety? His conclusion is that the capacity of the Rorschach to predict is still unknown. Little's suggestion is that we construct more accurate scales for specific areas, and that we devote much energy to the empirical correlates of such scales; or, he suggested, we might construct new instruments to measure specific personality variables, within a specific, theoretical frame.

When "behavior" is defined globally, and is judged, rated, or observed outside a controlled experimental situation, attempts to predict from the Rorschach generally fail. But what happens when more specific predictions are made in controlled situations? Such studies involve procedures in which Rorschach variables (or specially developed scores) are examined in the light of various behavioral or experimentally manipulated criteria, or correlated with data (perceptual, motor, etc.) obtained under various "laboratory" conditions.[11]

Remarking on the few studies in this area, Williams (1952) has noted that they fall essentially into three groups: (a) comparison of Rorschach variables with independent, behavioral criteria (his own study [1947] falls into this category); (b) correlation of changes in response with variations during administration of the Rorschach (drugs, hypnosis, experimental anxiety production); he questioned the status of these studies of special states as validity evidence—since so little is known about them, they can hardly be used as criteria for validation; and (c) relationship of the Rorschach to intervening or prior experimentally controlled experiences—this type of study, he noted was quite rare.

Williams (1947), in an early study, attempted to "validate" a specific determinant against behavioral criteria. In his experiment he found that decrement on the Wechsler-Bellevue Digit-Symbol test during stress (electric shock, frustration accompanying "failure," and the presence of an audience) was associated with several Rorschach factors—measures presumably reflecting emotional and intellectual control (such as F+ and color scores). This experiment stimulated much subsequent research. Unfortunately, replication of the study failed to confirm the original findings. Because of the small number of cases involved, as well as questions concerning the ability of the Rorschach to reflect such stress, Carlson and Lazarus (1953), for example, repeated the study but failed to find any relationship between various Rorschach measures and decrement under stress producing loads.

In a study also concerned with the influence of experimentally in-

---

[11] Studies include those of Carlson and Lazarus (1953); Gibby (1951); Goldberger (1961); Klein and Schlesinger (1951); Linton (1954); Lord (1950a); Meltzoff, Singer, and Korchin (1953); Schumer (1949); Singer, Meltzoff, and Goldman (1952); Steisel (1952); and Williams (1947). On the whole, findings have been positive.

duced stress on so-called Rorschach indicators of anxiety, Eichler (1951b), who utilized intermittent shock and threat of shock as the anxiety-provoking stimulus, also found some significant differences between his experimental and control groups in various scoring categories, such as shading, traditionally felt to be anxiety indicators. No replication of this study is available.

Schumer (1949) isolated 15 (not mutually exclusive) broad generalizations and statements concerning the alleged interpretative significance of the human movement response (M). She found, for example, that M has been purportedly related to creativeness and imagination, ability to empathize, fantasies and wish-fulfillments, introversive functioning, (inversely related to) suggestibility, etc. After refining, rewording, and collapsing these generalizations so that their behavioral implications could be tested, 13 predictions were constructed, each of which was testable in one of several behavioral and perceptual situations. Her Ss were 95 Yale University undergraduates, who were administered individual, standard Rorschachs, and, in two sessions, various other behavioral and perceptual tasks.

Each of the 13 predictions were generally "derived" from four general assumptions about which the discussion of her findings revolved. These assumptions were: (a) movement responses reflect inner, personal, and subjective factors; (b) they reflect a tendency to approach a problem-solving situation conceptually rather than concretely; (c) they reflect a tendency to be a "thinker" rather than a "doer"; and (d) if the perceiving of many human movement responses represents a distinctive way of responding, then those who are movement oriented would be expected to respond distinctively to other perceptual situations.

The 13 behavioral predictions were tested in one of the following: a word-association task; an autokinetic situation; a modification of the Vigotsky task (a test of concept-formation); and a phi phenomenon situation. Some of these predictions were that movement-oriented Ss when contrasted with nonmovement-oriented Ss: tend to have lower thresholds for the perception of apparent motion—(unverified); spend a smaller proportion of total time in actual manipulation and sorting of the Vigotsky blocks—(unverified); produce more unique responses and fewer "outward" responses (repetitions and rhymes) in the word-association test—(verified); have lower suggestibility scores in the autokinetic situation (in the presence of a confederate with "planned" responses)—(verified); have smaller time-error scores in the Vigotsky situation (i.e., do better on this task)—(verified); and tend to differ in the kinds of motion seen in the phi phenomenon situation (movement-oriented Ss tended to see three-dimensional motion less frequently than the other Ss)—(verified).[12]

An integrated series of researches exploring a specific hypothesis concerning M have been reported by Levine and Meltzoff (1956), Meltzoff and Levine (1954), Meltzoff and Litwin (1956), Meltzoff, Singer, and Korchin (1953), Singer and Herman (1954), Singer, Meltzoff, and Goldman (1952), Singer and Spohn (1954), et al. These authors were interested in exploring an hypothesis based on Werner's sensori-tonic theory as well as on some of Hermann Rorschach's notions, that in the affective, motor, and cognitive spheres there is a direct relationship between the production of human movement responses and an inhibitory function. On the basis of experimental findings, which have suggested an antagonism between the M response and motor activity (prior or concurrent), the authors have claimed support for both Werner's and Rorschach's statements.

Since a recent summary of these and other related researches and a theoretical integration have been presented by Singer (1960a), only a few brief illustrations of the experimental approach utilized in some of these studies will be provided. For example, the purported relationship between cognitive, affective, and motor inhibition and Rorschach movement has been demonstrated by Herman (1956), who found a significant difference in the predicted direction, in number of bodily movements displayed by extratensive and introversive Ss while orally defining a list of verbs. In a study which explored differences in the Ss' ability to suppress laughter (conscious inhibition of affect) while listening to the "Laughing Record" of Spike Jones under instructions to listen without laughing, Meltzoff and Litwin (1956) demonstrated again a difference in the predicted direction between the high and low M groups.

In a recent test of the movement-inhibition theory, Neel (1960) failed to find supporting evidence. Changes in some of the experimental procedures, however, might explain the lack of duplication of results. Fager (1960) also failed to confirm the work of Levine, Glass, and Meltzoff (1957), who found that Ss with low Rorschach human movement productivity tended to write in the overlearned symbol N ("failure to delay") instead of the mirror image of N as required by the

---

[12] Sarason's book (1954, pp. 203–216) contains a detailed presentation of Schumer's findings; other behavioral Rorschach studies including that of Janoff (1951), who tested various predictions which followed from a survey of the clinical and research literature concerning the significance of Rorschach form-quality, are also discussed.

digit-symbol subtest of the Wechsler-Bellevue Intelligence Scale. Fager's replication of this study did not produce evidence which confirmed the proposed relationship. Finding no explanation after exploration of several possible influential variables for this discrepancy in findings (such as sampling differences, interaction between intelligence and inhibition), he concluded that the relationship of M and various color responses to "cognitive inhibition" is still not clear. Thus, even this experimentally controlled situation failed to yield positive confirmation.

More global or broader behavioral criteria than those just noted have also been used in Rorschach validation studies. Vernier, Whiting, and Meltzer (1955), for example, attempted to predict the behavior of a group of tuberculous patients in terms of whether or not they would leave the hospital against medical advice, from an examination of various scores, ratios, and indices derived from the Rorschach, TAT, and House-Tree-Person techniques. The two groups of patients with whom they worked were matched for age, race, education, degree of disease, as well as several other variables. They differed only in terms of the crucial variables: length of hospital stay and whether or not they left the hospital against medical advice. Both the TAT and the Rorschach failed to yield differences useful for clinical prediction.[13]

As already noted, hazards of attempting to predict a broad behavioral criterion are manifold, and few studies have been reported which are successful in this attempt. Usually, the broader, or more generally defined the criterion is, the less successful are the results. Rader (1957) set out to see if he could predict overt aggressive verbal behavior from Rorschach content. His Ss were 38 state prison inmates, and his criterion was behavior in therapeutic discussion groups. The results were equivocal, and although his study was conceptually and methodologically interesting, his prediction level was not too high. In another report[14] Rader summarized a study of 45 prison inmates, and concluded, "The present study failed to find any relationships between three measures of Rorschach productivity and productivity in group psychotherapy. These results raise grave doubts about the common assumption that the Rorschach test is simply a standardized means of

---

[13] Results on the basis of the House-Tree-Person test were considerably more promising. The authors concluded, "The differential accuracy in prediction for the three projective tests studied would support the authors' basic hypothesis that accurate prediction of specific overt behavior from projective techniques is dependent upon the extent to which the test provides a measure of the interaction between the needs of the individual and a symbolization of the external factors of the situation in which the behavior occurs" (*Ibid.*, p. 182).

[14] Mimeographed summary sent to one of the authors.

sampling behavior and that such behavior is likely to be representative of behavior in analogous ordinary life situations" (p. 3).

Carr, Forer, Henry, Hooker, Hutt, and Piotrowski (1960) reported the results of an ambitious project of independent prediction of overt behavior on the basis of various projective techniques. The techniques employed included a sentence completion test, the TAT, Bender-Gestalt test and the Rorschach. Each expert had been asked to submit independent evaluations based on a particular technique as to the overt behavior which could be expected from the two subjects who were being studied. These Ss were identical adult male twins, one of whom was an overt homosexual. The latter information was made available to these experts prior to their evaluations.

The reported results, despite a display of considerable clinical brilliance, failed to predict overt behavior. As a matter of fact, there were few concrete references to overt behavior in the interpretations, which tended, instead, to be quite global. In addition, each expert used his own language and frame of reference; he even chose freely the area in which to make predictions. Moreover, the experts were allowed to decide for themselves whether or not predictions would be made as to overt or covert behavior. The test interpretations were impressive, but in terms of an actual study of predictive validity, the overall presentation and methodology left much to be desired. The variability in the use of concepts, language, and nature of predictions from expert to expert did not allow for any test of validity against the criterion (intensive case-history), nor was it possible to make inter-expert comparisons. As it turned out, even the question as to which could be regarded as the most effective instrument could not be answered, since the experts' opinions were not compared, and since there was no way of validating each of their evaluations. So much more the pity, since the time and energy involved, as well as the availability of the experts, could certainly have been put to more productive use. For example, an a priori established list of predictions and statements (presented in understandable language) could have been given to the experts for acceptance or rejection on the basis of their intensive study of their particular projective protocol.

In general, then, the further we get from specific, clearly defined and delineated behaviors, elicited under laboratory conditions, the more difficult it becomes to demonstrate meaningful relationships between various aspects of the Rorschach and those behaviors.

*Screening Studies; Large-Scale Correlational Studies.* The many failures of the Rorschach technique in large-scale screening programs in the armed forces, and in selection studies for clinical psychologists, psychoanalytic trainees, and industrial personnel are too well known to warrant extensive discussion. For illustrative puposes, three studies are described. All stem from armed forces research programs.

Guilford (1948), in reviewing lessons learned from aviation psychology, reported on a large-scale validity study of the Rorschach test in a personnel-selection setting, based on 500 students. Both the individual method of administration and two group versions were used. Validity evidence (based on a pass-fail criterion at the end of pilot training) was almost entirely negative, both for 25 indicators, taken separately or collectively, as well as for a prediction by the examiner based on an intuitive, global evaluation. The Harrower group administration procedure fared as badly as the individual Rorschach in terms of predicting pilot selection; the AAF version of the group Rorschach, when scored for the number of most popular responses, did show a correlation coefficient of .24 with the criterion, however.

Eschenbach and Borgatta (1953) published an extensive listing of major Rorschach scoring categories and their purported personality correlates. The correlates included intelligence, adaptability, abstractness, self-control, aggressiveness, empathy, inferiority, anxiety, compulsiveness, attitude, sex, and organic, neurotic, and psychotic disorders. These variables had been quite explicitly related to various Rorschach factors such as R, location, determinants, and content in a large number of research and clinical reports. The authors' purpose was to make possible systematic, empirical exploration of these purported relationships.

And so, indeed, the same authors made use of their systematic review a few years later (1955). They were not particularly interested in global, intuitive use of the Rorschach; they were concerned, instead, with whether or not specific scores, arbitrarily defined, "held up." Working with 125 normal male airforce enlisted personnel, whose average age was 27 years, they systematically tested through use of a massive correlational design, a large number of the "hypotheses" they had previously gleaned from research and clinical reports. Criterion indices were derived from measures of S's performance in a social interaction situation, ratings by superiors, primary mental abilities scores, sociometric status indices, and background information, such as age, educational level, and military grade. Their extensive results were reported in the form of a lengthy list of statements of the purported relationship of each Rorschach variable to the criterion (hypothesis), at least one reference from which such a "claim" was derived, the criterion used, expected sign, and sign actually found. They found that most of the relationships—except those concerning intelligence—were not dissimilar from chance expectations. They noted, further, that the intellectual factor could be evaluated more efficiently and more adequately by instruments other than the Rorschach.

Another large-scale study, using the group Rorschach technique, and testing the degree of success in making an overall prediction on the part of experts, was reported by Holtzman (1952). Holtzman also wondered whether or not the Rorschach could predict success in an aviation cadet program. From a total of 1504 men, of whom 798 had completed the flight training program successfully, a sample of 100 was drawn, consisting of 50 successful and 50 unsuccessful cadets. Their pretraining tests were sent to 19 outstanding clinical psychologists (many of whom had served as military psychologists during World War II) for evaluation as to probable success or failure in training. Each psychologist was sent 20 records, so that by chance alone he was expected to make 10 correct and 10 incorrect predictions. On the basis of a frequency distribution of the number of correct predictions (out of 20) each of the experts had made (12 experts based their predictions on the Rorschach), Holtzman concluded that predictions from the Rorschach were no better than could be expected from a chance relationship. The mean number of correct predictions was 10.5 (S.D., 4.7), and the mode was exactly at 10, the number expected by chance. For the successful candidates, the proportion of correct and incorrect predictions was 19:15 whereas for the failures it was 17:15, yielding a ratio of correct to incorrect predictions for the total group, of 36:30. When estimates of the certainty with which the predictions were made were taken into consideration, no improvement in the efficiency of the prediction was noted.

Large-scale correlational studies relating scores to personality variables, as well as studies utilizing both global judgments or specific scores to predict success in training programs, have generally failed to produce positive results, as illustrated by the foregoing studies.

*Prognostic Studies.* There is a long history of research concerning the use of the Rorschach for predicting therapeutic change, acceptance of the therapeutic situation, etc. For example, Muench (1947), in an evaluation of nondirective therapy, claimed positive findings. Lord (1950b) and Carr (1949) claimed negative findings (brief-term therapy and psychotherapy, respectively). Hamlin and Albee (1948) found that Muench's indicators of improvement did not hold up when groups exhibiting different levels of adjustment were compared. Similarly, Roberts (1954) failed to find predictive significance for eleven Rorschach factors purported to be effective predictors of psychotherapeutic change. Barry, Blyth, and Albrecht (1952) compared test and retest data from the Rorschach with pooled judgments of patients at a Veterans' Administration Mental Hygiene Clinic. Changes in ratings of adjustment level failed to correlate with changes on the Rorschach.

Evidence of the failure of the Rorschach in the prognostic sphere also can be found in the following studies. Barron (1950) reported on a study in which the Rorschach, together with several other tests including the MMPI, were given to both patients and therapists before the beginning of therapy. Whereas the MMPI predicted outcome significantly, the Rorschach, despite all attempts ranging from the global to the atomistic, failed to do so. Rogers, Knauss, and Hammond (1951) reported a similar experience. As long as other tests failed to predict outcome, the failure might have been attributed to the heterogeneous nature of the patient group—to an admixture of early and chronic cases, for example. When other tests succeed where the Rorschach fails, we can conclude either that the Rorschach is unsuited to prediction, or that basic personality factors, as evaluated by the Rorschach, are unrelated to the type of therapy involved. Neither alternative conclusion seems satisfactory.

Some evidence of the success of a score based on an evaluation of the psychological maturity of the response (Rorschach genetic-level score—see previous section) was reported by Levine (1959). This Rorschach score significantly differentiated two hospital groups (functional psychotics) one year after hospital admission, one group having been hospitalized continuously during this period, and the other group having been discharged.

Another positive viewpoint was expressed by Harrower (1958), who attempted to determine whether projective techniques reflect personality changes which come about as a result of therapy. She devoted most of her discussion and analysis to the extensive pre- and post-test data of slightly more than thirty subjects. In the main, Harrower answered her question in the affirmative, but the failure to be concerned with questions of reliability of her methods, the inadequate statistical approaches employed, and similar methodological considerations, raise serious questions when her conclusions are evaluated. Although she worked with several projective methods, specific Rorschach findings were that higher intelligence level, increased Rorschach productivity, and more controlled use of color accompanied successful therapy. A more detailed (generally critical) evaluation of this book, with attention to some cogent methodological issues, has been made by Singer (1960b).

Zamansky and Goldman (1960) have reviewed the literature with respect to the use of the Rorschach to assess the correlation with therapeutic changes, and have concluded, along with most of the reviewers in this area, that there is much contradictory, and difficult-to-interpret evidence as to the Rorschach's effectiveness. Findings based on their own research (*Ibid.*), however, have suggested some support for the notion that global Rorschach evaluations, rather than specific quantitative indices, were more highly correlated with the criterion (ratings of social adjustment in the ward after various "ancillary" therapies, in a group of male and female hospitalized psychotics).

Windle (1952), after reviewing the relationship of psychological tests (including projective techniques) to prognosis in psychopathology, concluded that there was no demonstrable correlation between the two. Fulkerson and Barry (1961), in an extensive review of methodology and research on prognostic uses of psychological tests, picked up where Windle had left off, covering the relevant literature from 1952 to 1959. Specifically with respect to the Rorschach, some success was reported for the Prognostic Rating Scale (Klopfer, Kirkner, Wisham, & Baker, 1951), which yields a configurational score; various signs as reported by some authors also successfully discriminated groups of patients. These signs, however, did not show any clear pattern, and the authors (Fulkerson and Barry) felt that further cross-validation with respect to many of these purportedly successful findings seemed necessary.

A successful "sign" study is reported by Stotsky (1952), who cross-validated significantly 5 out of 19 Rorschach signs in predicting discharge from a hospital of a group of schizophrenics. But in general, Fulkerson and Barry noted that research on the prediction of termination using projective techniques shows a fairly consistent pattern: positive findings in the first phase of the research, but negative or inconclusive findings when initial results are cross-validated.[15] In general, the Rorschach variable R (number of responses) retains its predictive powers more consistently than other indicators. But the authors pointed out that this is an unnecessarily cumbersome way of measuring a variable which is more easily available elsewhere. For example, Gallagher (1954) found that a more efficient way of predicting the S's problems than Rorschach R was the number of words used by S on the Mooney Problem Check List.

The reasons for the failure of the Rorschach in prognosis are many. Some of these include: unreliable psychiatric diagnosis, the uncontrolled variance due to the heterogeneity of the samples, the problem

---

[15] The authors cited as an example the research connected with the Kotkov and Meadows formula (1952, 1953) which, in replication and cross-validation studies did not "hold up" (Rogers, Knauss, and Hammond [1951]; Auld and Eron [1953]). Number of responses, however, did show some positive relationships to the criterion.

of base rates, and lack of specification and unreliability of the criteria which are used to evaluate outcome (such as duration of treatment, course of illness, ratings of improvement by patient and/or therapist and/or others). The general failures of studies in the prediction of outcome of therapy as well as general inadequacy of the Rorschach to reflect changes induced by various therapies might be interpreted as fitting in with the notion that the Rorschach technique reflects only basic personality structure. If basic personality structure is unalterable, disease processes may not be able to affect it. All that therapy can accomplish in that case is to halt the progressive nature of the illness, transform it to a static defect, and then teach the patient to accept the defect. If therapy consists in nothing more than the acceptance of one's disabilities, no change in fundamental personality is to be expected. But then, the Rorschach becomes an irrelevant technique in predicting and/or evaluating outcome and prognosis and should be replaced by simpler, less time-consuming indices which would make for more efficient, economical, and more reliable indicators.

*Developmental Studies; Norms.* No attempt will be made to describe the clinical use of the Rorschach technique with children. There is a considerable reservoir of largely descriptive material which is adequately covered elsewhere.[16] Attention will be turned instead, to the use of developmental data and the collection of norms as methods, presumably, of establishing Rorschach validity.[17]

W. Klopfer (1956) has offered some material pertinent to problems concerning the application of the Rorschach in the geriatric field. Our comments concerning norm collecting and standardization in the Rorschach field apply generally to the children's area as well as the geriatric area.

It might be noted at the outset, that a review of recent material in this area, whether oriented from a clinical viewpoint, or from a theoretical or research viewpoint, indicates a curious state of affairs. There seems to be an interweaving (vacillation, perhaps) of two points of view in much of the material covered. Norms are collected, analyzed, and discussed, presumably to help the clinician by providing him with a yardstick by which he can judge, evaluate, or interpret the record before him; at the same time, these data are collected, analyzed, and

---

[16] For example, Halpern (1953); Klopfer, Fox, and Troup (1956); and Klopfer, Spiegelman, and Fox (1956).
[17] Dworetzki's developmental research (1939) is briefly described in Chapter 8. Through a series of related explorations utilizing Rorschach as well as non-Rorschach data, she attempted to describe certain developmental aspects of perception.

discussed to shed light on what is going on, psychologically and developmentally, in Ss of various ages. It goes without saying that when the Rorschach is used as a developmental measure, the validity of the Rorschach is taken for granted—so much so, as a matter of fact, that various authors have attempted to describe in great and vivid detail, the precise machinations of the psyches of, say, 8-year olds as compared to 10-year olds, on the basis of respective Rorschach data. Thus, norm collecting in the Rorschach field has taken on a quality quite different from that found in other psychometric endeavors. Research initiated as validation research somewhere in the process becomes *criterion* research, hopefully shedding light on a variety of developmental, perceptual, and theoretical problems.

Some workers in developmental psychology recognize these problems, but cautiously utilize what they can from the vast number of Rorschach studies as evidence to confirm or shed light on their developmental theories or generalizations. Wohlwill (1960), for example, has reviewed a large number of developmental studies of perception, occasionally drawing on Rorschach findings to support generalizations found elsewhere. Yet there is no doubt that this author is aware of the limitations in such a procedure, even to the extent of expressing surprise that there is some agreement between Rorschach and various laboratory findings. Wohlwill was especially aware of the significance of interpretive and cognitive processes in the S's Rorschach response, and has implied that the use of the Rorschach for purposes of making generalizations about developmental aspects of perception involves thorny problems, an implication with which, of course, we are in agreement.

Ricciuti's discussion (1956) of the important value the Rorschach has in longitudinal studies reveals the same underlying problem. Do we get norms from longitudinal studies for Rorschach scoring and interpretation? Or do we shed light on age factors and developmental growth patterns? Obviously, one "criterion" cannot be used as a "criterion" for the other. If two complex criteria are used to validate each other, what have we learned about either? Although the author feels that developmental studies having two criteria can make important contributions to both the Rorschach technique *and* developmental theory, particularly if the processes involved in the Rorschach performance are stressed, he is not unaware of the fact that problems can and do arise with this procedure:

. . . we commonly find ourselves in a position where our theory of developmental changes may be reasonably convincing but in need of a great deal of elaboration and verification, while much the same thing can be said

about the rationale and validity of our projective techniques. In such instances, we look for some congruence between projective test results and the
changes postulated by developmental theory, or between projective test results and observed developmental changes. When we find such congruence,
the validity and rationale of the projective technique, as well as the developmental theory are given added support. When such congruence is not
found, then one has to decide in each case whether to question the validity
of the projective test or the developmental theory, or both (p. 257).

Of course, we are left with the uncomfortable feeling that making such
a decision is quite a responsibility! On what basis is the decision made?
The dilemma remains, and speculation concerning two complex criteria
with many unknown parameters brings us full circle around to where
we began.

Stein (1956) reported on a study which made no claims to shed
light on developmental theory, in general. Rather, he was concerned
only with testing Piotrowski's hypothesis that M responses increase in a
situation requiring compliance under conditions of frustration, and
when adjustment to more powerful persons is required. He examined
the Rorschach protocols of three groups of 8-, 12-, and 16-year-old children, finding no evidence to support Piotrowski's notions that childhood M's are assertive and that these change, through development, to
more compliant M's in adulthood.

As for normative studies *qua* norms, many references can be found
in any extensive bibliography, such as that in the volume by Klopfer *et
al.* (1956). Hertz (1960) has summarized in great detail normative
material with respect to adolescents. An extensive recent normative
study of 291 children, ages 6–11, which utilized both a longitudinal as
well as a cross-sectional approach, has been described by Ledwith
(1959). Data were presented for R, S, W, D, F, M, FM, FK, FC, etc.

One large scale normative study of children, illustrative of several
that the same group of authors has conducted, is that of Ames, Learned,
Métraux, and Walker (1952). Extensive Rorschach material was
gathered and presented, based on 50 records at each half-yearly
interval from 2 to 5½ years of age, and yearly intervals from ages 6 to 10.
The detailed Rorschach material for each age level formed the basis for
the accompanying description of the psychological characteristics of
children at different ages (validity of the Rorschach was taken for
granted, of course). Thus, each age group was described in terms of
rather stereotyped Rorschach "dynamics," which, in turn, were based
on the presumed "meaning" of the determinants found. Comparisons of
different age levels resulted in generalizations such as the following:

Probably the most conspicuous finding of the present study is that the total
Rorschach picture at each age level—that is the individuality of the generic

subject of any given age as revealed by the Rorschach—has a unique and distinctive characteristic which sets it apart from every other age level. . . . The child does not simply grow "better" as he grows older. Behavior does not necessarily become better integrated and better organized. On the contrary, ages of equilibrium to some extent alternate with ages of disequilibrium, ages of expansiveness with ages of inwardizing. Ages when behavior appears to be well organized may be followed by ages which show marked inner disturbance. Ages at which subjects respond favorably to persons and things in the environment may be followed by ages of marked rejection of and rebellion against the environment (p. 289).

It can be seen that lack of cross-validation and failure to question the validity of the traditional meanings assigned to determinants and to consider the role of fluctuations and error from age sample to age sample, may well pose serious questions as to the correctness of the generalizations made with respect to behavior. Few linear developmental trends were found. Each age level is described in terms of a typical "profile" of distributions of determinants, and the Rorschach is then used as a criterion for describing what is going on at each age level. This procedure, in a sense, represents one opposite from that used in the Binet validation, where changes in difficulty level of various items showed a relationship to age. Items were regarded as invalid which did not show this relationship with age, and discarded. Changes in "profiles" of the age levels in this (Rorschach) procedure, however, are utilized as important, distinctive, descriptive characteristics of children from age to age. Consider, for example, some of the following statements:

Thus, in summary FOUR shows himself to be exact, unmodulated, expansive, out of bounds, imaginative, violent, curious, resistant, predictable, and stereotyped. . . .

. . . Thus FIVE appears as focal, factual, matter of fact, "here and now," calm, well-equilibrated, self-controlled, compliant, self-critical and thoughtful. . . .

. . . FIVE-AND-A-HALF thus shows himself to be sensitive, vulnerable, insecure, unpredictable and in considerable disequilibrium. He is outgoing, excitable, impetuous, subject to uncontrolled attacks of temper. He is also rigid and unmodulated and poor at interpersonal relations (Ibid., pp. 291–292).

Despite these specific generalizations to behavior, behavioral validation and prediction were not attempted. Moreover, the impression is gained that deviations from "typical" Rorschach profiles at various age levels indicate pathology. (One important contribution, however, is the finding that many things regarded as pathological in adults, are, in fact, found in children's records.) It is here that the failure to cross-validate is particularly conspicuous. It might be noted that Elkins (1958), in a cross-validational study of the Ames "danger signals" in children's Rorschach responses, found little or no corroborating evidence that these distinguish maladjusted from nondisturbed samples, 8–10 years of age. She found, as a matter of fact, that certain "danger signs" were found frequently in normal records, and that some were never found in the maladjusted records. (This tendency to accept the basic Rorschach "mythology" as proven, and then labeling as deviant or even abnormal an individual who violates the expected Rorschach canons and the subsequent discovery that the violators are as normal as the nonviolators, has occurred too often to pass unnoticed.)

The general features of the Ames' normative study of children are found in their work with other age populations, it might be noted (Ames, Métraux, & Walker [1959]—adolescents; and Ames, Learned, Métraux, & Walker [1954]—old age).

*Factor Analysis.* Exploration of the factorial validity of the Rorschach technique has not been one of the "traditional" approaches to Rorschach validation. There has been increased attention to factorial methods, however, paralleling the popular use of factor analysis in the psychometric field. Early factorial research was reported by Wittenborn (1949a, 1950), who factor analyzed various Rorschach scoring categories. His work has stimulated much subsequent research.

A detailed historical review of the use of factor analysis in Rorschach research will not be presented here. Murstein (1960) has presented an excellent critique and survey of studies in this area. This author noted, as we do, the need for external validation of factors by behavior and outside ratings, so that the meaning of factorial dimensions can be related to reality. He did not express faith in the Rorschach as a psychometric instrument, and suggested that the factor analysis of Rorschach responses is a shaky procedure. As the instrument now stands, the Rorschach does not lend itself to psychometric treatment. For example, the interrelationship of determinants such as M, H, and Hd, as well as the fact that the limitation of one score per response forces certain determinants to take precedence over others (for example, M over C, which takes precedence over Fc), create statistical and research problems; these factors yield an inaccurate quantitative summary of S's percepts.

The utility of factor analysis of Rorschach scores is lessened not only by these considerations, but by the small number of cards, the quasi-quantitative scoring system, the lack of uniformity in scoring and Inquiry procedures, and the importance of E's skills in asking the right kinds of questions during the Inquiry. The verbal nature of the Rorschach, and the susceptibility of the response to class and educational influences is also of some significance. A few words might completely alter the scoring of a particular response. With these comments in mind, let us review some illustrative studies.

Sandler and Ackner (1951), in England, working with Rorschach's content categories, made a factor analysis of the content scores of fifty psychiatric patients at the Maudsley Hospital, ranging over eight types of mental disorder. They emerged with four factors and determined the psychological meaning of each factor by its correlation with the personality evaluation made by psychiatric interview and case history methods. Personality evaluations were drawn from three sources—previous personality, general background data, and present symptoms. The Productivity factor was highly related to previous productivity in life, to chronicity of symptoms and to a schizo-affective picture at the time of hospitalization. The Anatomy factor—internal anatomical objects vs. external objects—was related to an insecure, withdrawn, "previous" personality picture, bad physical health, and an emotional, deluded state for the present symptoms. The remaining factors were analyzed in similar fashion.

Sen (1950), also in England, applied the Rorschach to 100 Indian students who had lived together for at least two years. When scored by means of Beck's scoring system, the correlations with personality evaluations by their colleagues were nonsignificant. But when scored for content (à la Burt), the correlations rose as high as .57 to .66. When matching was resorted to—a global method—both scoring methods yielded a high degree of success, .85 for Beck's system, and 1.00 for Burt's system! Interestingly enough, however, when a factor analysis was performed on the Beck Scores and on the Burt Scores, the results of both analyses were equally high in their relationship between the derived factor scores and personality.

Podell and Phillips (1959), in a factorial study of cognition and the Rorschach, investigated the relationship between the Rorschach and other tests. Despite the methodological sophistication of this as well as other factorial studies, however, little light is shed on the psychological processes involved in S's responses, nor is the clinician helped, in terms of prediction, diagnosis, and interpretation of the record before him. "Names" assigned to factorial dimensions are *ex post facto* and unfortunately suggest greater theoretical knowledge of inherent processes than is warranted, as well as imply a type of clinical approach to the instrument which has little behavioral or practical significance. An example of one conclusion stated by these authors is, "Since W— and D— fell into different dimensions it was concluded that minus responses, as an indicator of primitive function should be interpreted with respect to location choice" (*Ibid.*, p. 461). This is probably sound advice, but how would it be followed? How would interpretation differ in a record of many minus W responses, as opposed to one containing many minus D responses?

A factorial study with disappointing results was reported by Bendig and Hamlin (1955). These authors, using an inverted factor analytic technique (Q technique), and working with Rorschach scores of four Ss in each of four distinct clinical groups, found that the three orthogonal original or rotated factors were not significantly related to diagnostic category. They explained the greater success of "blind" categorizations of clinical records by experts on the basis of "several sources of information in the complete Rorschach protocol which are ignored by the usual scoring method" (pp. 187–188). This information, they felt, is specifically drawn by most clinicians from knowledge of where and on what card a particular response was seen, and the intracard and intercard sequence of responses—factors usually ignored in typical scoring procedures. Borgatta and Eschenbach (1955) also reported disappointing results on the basis of an extensive factorial study of a large number of Rorschach variables as well as those based on external (behavioral) criteria. They concluded, "Since Rorschach scores had little or no common variation with a number of significant external variables, extreme caution should be exercised in using these scores in studies of personality and culture, and in the prediction of interaction behavior" (p. 136).

But in general, factorial studies have shown some striking correlations with behavior, provided broad and "meaningful" external categories are used. Factorial techniques are useful not only in testing many of the implicit assumptions about the *meaning* of Rorschach determinants and their relationships, but in helping to shed light on the instrument itself, as well. It might be noted that some support for a few traditional hypotheses has been found (such as the relationship of intelligence to certain formal factors).[18] But, depending on the sam-

---

[18] Note should be made, however, of the generally negative results of attempts to demonstrate a relationship between intelligence and various Rorschach factors in nonfactorial studies. Wittenborn, for example, compared extreme groups selected on the basis of college entrance examinations on 18 scores of the Rorschach and failed to find any significant relationship (1949b). The relationship of M to intelligence has been investigated by Tucker (1950), who found a very low correlation: .26. Wilson (1952) made a more extensive study of a large college population, using M, form level, W, Z, diversity of content, and a specially designed variable called "specification," and found zero correlations. Working with the Levy Movement Blots, a test designed specifically to elicit M, Levy, Schumer, and Zubin (1964), found no relationship between movement and intelligence among groups

ple as well as on the factorial techniques used, findings have varied. Difficulties already noted concerning the nature of the scores themselves, add to the general picture of inconsistency and ambiguity of findings. It is of some interest to note that although single Rorschach scores often do not yield significant relationships to criterion measures, a factor analysis of these same scores sometimes does yield significant relationships to criteria. A suggestion for explaining this paradox has already been made, that is, content factors may be contributing to positive results.

Finally, some notion of the large number and range of factors which have emerged from factorial studies might be suggested from the following (incomplete) list of factors reported by various researchers: fluency, productivity, intelligence, generalizing ability, emotionality, imagination, extraversion-introversion, neurotic tendencies, empathy, various types of verbal facility, bizarre originality, reproductive association, initiative-passivity, maturity-adjustment, ego strength, expressive-repressive, etc.

*Validation of Specific Interpretative Hypotheses: Color and White Space.* Although many believe that the Rorschach "works" clinically, it fails when specific interpretative hypotheses are put to a test. Globally oriented clinicians might well say that experimental investigations concerning isolated interpretative hypotheses are doomed to failure. But we suggest that although this may well be the case, we cannot "get at" the factors involved in interpretations to test their validity without testing them one by one or in combination with each other. Global evaluations, even when successful, will not tell us why we are correct and why we are incorrect. Many Rorschach investigators seem to share this opinion, for a large body of reports have accumulated summarizing research on a wide variety of interpretative hypotheses. Only two illustrative areas of such research will be presented. Mention has already been made of some of the work done with respect to validating interpretations of M.

*1. Color shock.* Stated simply, one of the striking claims of Rorschach experts is that Ss who show long reaction time on the color cards are

---

of children, as well as adults, nor did Rust (1948), working with the same instrument, with children. Wishner (1948), on the other hand, did find some evidence that a few Rorschach indicators were related to various subtest scores on the Wechsler-Bellevue test, in a group of 42 neurotic patients; but Davis (1961) found that judgments based on vocabulary alone were superior to judgments based on the profile of Rorschach scores in terms of correlation with IQ scores, suggesting that content rather than formal factors is of significance in this kind of prediction.

230 AN EXPERIMENTAL APPROACH TO PROJECTIVE TECHNIQUES

prone to be "neurotic," whereas those who show long reaction time on the shading cards (cards in which shading is prominent) are prone to be depressed. The data collected by Baughman (1954), in which reaction time was available for the same card when color was eliminated and when shading was eliminated, were submitted to experienced Rorschach workers to see whether the shock pattern occurred only in the appropriate series. As a result of this investigation, it was reported that the time and response patterns supposedly typical of color shock occurred with the same frequency whether color was present or not. The same was found to hold for shading and shading shock. A very substantial question is thus raised as to the wisdom of continued use of the shock indicators. Further evidence against the concept of "color shock" was provided by Siipola, Kuhns, and Taylor (1950). In an ingenious experiment, they concluded that the affinity that color bears to emotion is based on a misunderstanding. Color shock, for example, is not due to color itself, but to the incongruity between the color and contour of a given blot area. The conflict engendered in the observer will take different paths, depending on the personality of the subject. Siipola and Basseches (1959) subjected the color-form incongruity hypothesis to a direct experimental test, with positive results. Meyer (1951), on the basis of experimental evidence, also questioned the validity of color shock as an indicator of neuroticism.

Another study pointing in this same direction is that of Siipola (1950). She prepared copies of the well-known details of the Rorschach blots and presented each of these details separately in two versions—with color and without color. She compared the first conceptual reaction to these matched chromatic and achromatic stimuli in two equivalent groups of college students, one of whom was given the chromatic test and the other the achromatic test. No switchback experiment was conducted because the investigator was primarily interested in the first conceptual response to the cards. She found that when color is present in the stimuli, (a) an increase in reaction time occurs; (b) there is an increase in the likelihood that emotional attitudes, both pleasant and unpleasant will be aroused; and (c) there are two kinds of influences on the character of the conceptual response, a weak, selective influence among form dominated concepts, and a strong, disruptive influence, involving symptoms suggestive of conceptual conflict and behavioral disorganization. The author proposed the following hypothesis to explain her findings:

Colored blots, in comparison to achromatic blots, present a fundamentally different conceptual problem for the subject. The form-aspect of any blot exerts the primary influence upon conceptualization. The black-gray color of an achromatic blot places no constraint upon the freedom of this primary process; the form-forces can operate freely without the restriction imposed by any particular color. In the case of a colored blot, the presence of a particular color always imposes a definite restriction upon the freedom of the primary process; the form-forces cannot operate with complete freedom since the hue must be taken into account. The conceptual problem remains a relatively simple one when the hue of the blot happens to be appropriate to the form-suggested concept, but the problem becomes greatly complicated when the stimulus-hue happens to be inappropriate. Such hue-form incongruity is usually resolved in an integrated fashion by substituting for an incongruent concept another concept more appropriate to the hue but still consistent with the form-properties. But a further complication may enter. The incongruity may arouse severe stress and conflict, resulting in primitivation of the conceptual process accompanied by the usual behavioral symptoms of conflict. . . . Our primary evidence in support of this hypothesis consists of the finding that only certain colored blots, namely those characterized by hue-form incongruity, show striking effects upon the content and reaction times. Apparently, the mere presence of color in a blot does not endow it automatically with magic affect-arousing properties (pp. 380–381).

Lazarus (1949) studied one hundred high school seniors by means of two sets of Rorschach slides, one, the standard set and the other, a modified version from which only the color had been removed, everything else remaining untouched. The group of Ss was divided into two halves, one of which received the hue test first and the other, the black-white test first. Six weeks intervened between the giving of the first set of slides and the second set. The results indicated that the assumption that color influences performance is not valid. The only possible exception to this conclusion is that the "popular" and the "space" categories of responses seemed to increase when color was absent. No evidence was found for the concept of "shock" since there is no valid basis for comparing the performance on different slides because of the variation in their difficulty.

In an extensive review of the experimental literature on color shock, Keehn (1953) examined this single indicator, and its purported relationship to affectivity, overt and covert. He listed 28 indices of color shock which had been put forth by various workers—all presumably displayed by neurotics. He showed that not only do these workers disagree as to what constitutes color shock, but also, as to what constitutes a neurotic.

So-called indices of color shock, according to Keehn, could be explained by factors other than neuroticism, such as resistance to shift and differential difficulties of the cards (achromatic series of Rorschach cards also have shown color shock indices). He concluded his review by stating, "The experimental evidence, then, seems to offer little or no support either for the continued use of colour shock in the diagnosis of neuroticism, or for the supposition that the signs of such shock are due to the presence of colour" (p. 230).

Benton (1952) also examined certain assumptions concerning color shock, but was especially interested in experimental investigations of one of Rorschach's specific hypotheses concerning color—that is, that the color response is related to impulsive affectivity, and color shock to neurotic repression of affectivity. In reviewing some of the literature about color, he found some contradictory evidence, but concluded that the bulk of the evidence was against this color theory. He blamed the scoring of color responses as well as the Inquiry concerning them, for some of the positive findings. This author felt that a vast revision of ideas concerning the significance of color responses is necessary.

Perhaps the most incisive review of research in this area has been presented by Baughman (1958), who, because of his interest in the stimulus, focused a great deal of attention on experimental work with the color stimulus. His review of studies using both group and individual administrations in which, for the most part, chromatic and achromatic series were compared, has caused him to conclude, with little reservation, that color seems to have little effect on such Rorschach variables as total productivity, productivity on the last three cards, color shock signs, popular responses, figure-ground reversals, location scores, latency of response, form accuracy, movement and shading responses, and the usual content categories. There is some suggestion, however, that both preferences for the cards, as well as certain content considerations are affected by the presence of color. He also reviewed studies concerned with physiological correlates of response to the cards, since, if they (the cards) elicit an affective response, there should also be some correlated autonomic response. Continuous records of the psychogalvanic response, as well as of blood pressure, heart rate, respiration, and eye blinks have been made, while S takes the Rorschach. By and large, Baughman has concluded that such indicators do not suggest broad and significant differences between the colored and noncolored cards—although position of the card in the administration order is important, since there seem to be adaptation effects.

Despite accumulated evidence pointing to the invalidity of the color shock hypothesis, and to the significance of factors such as difficulty level of the cards (which could account for increased reaction time), as well as certain difficulties in integrating form and color, many clinicians have continued to utilize some variation of the color shock sign, in the interpretation of their records. Reports indicating that many color shock signs are equally frequent in chromatic and nonchromatic series of Rorschach plates are apparently not convincing enough to cause any wavering in faith.

2. *White space response* (S). Some authors have attempted to validate a particular interpretation of a scoring category by using "perceptual" response indicators. Bandura (1954), for example, was interested in whether or not a relationship could be found between the Rorschach white space response and performance on a conventional figure-ground reversal task. He hypothesized that the number of Rorschach white space responses would be positively related to ease of Necker Cube test figure reversals, and with duration of exposure of the inkblots. There was moderate support for both of these hypotheses, according to the author. Since the exposure time of the Rorschach card (a variable not controlled in the standard procedure) was positively associated with figure-ground reversals, the author cautioned that the significance of white space responses should be evaluated only in the context of knowledge about duration of exposure. Questions can be raised, of course, as to whether simple analogies can be made between Rorschach performance and perceptual, noncognitive tasks.

Traditional interpretations assigned to white space responses have implied that they are related to outwardly directed, oppositional tendencies. A fairly detailed clinical, interpretative discussion and research review by Fonda (1960), it might be noted, suggests that there is considerable evidence that the white space response is a meaningful, valid, and important Rorschach scoring category. Fonda's discussion revolves around a need for clarifying and explaining some additional fine points of interpretation, specifically linking the production of primary S to a "psychoanalytic concept of the drive to achieve active mastery." Reviewers themselves, however, are in disagreement when experimental and research evidence is considered. Murray (1957*a*, 1957*b*) for example, has also reviewed the research in this area to date, but found generally *negative* evidence as to the validity of the purported correlates. He concluded that a survey of the different interpretations of S, of various types of S, of the relationship of S to various diagnostic groups and to other Rorschach scores, yielded very little which could be termed definitive, ". . . and that while no studies to date suggest that any of the interpretations are sufficiently valid insofar as the individual Rorschach record is concerned, the weakness in present studies prevent this judgment from being final. Very few of the many suggested interpretations have yet been tested" (1957*b*, pp. 51–52).

*Studies with Normals.* Despite the popular use of the Rorschach in a wide range of settings, such as executive selection, industrial placement, vocational counseling, professional screening programs, college screening, and prediction of occupational success, there is little evidence of a conclusive or definitive nature, to justify the time, expense, and conviction that accompanies the application of this technique in these diverse fields.[19] Claims of success have been many but not convincing, and are most often couched in terms of how potentially marvelous the Rorschach *could* be, or how it *should* be used in say, an industrial or executive setting (e.g., Snowden [1956]; and Williams & Kellman [1956]).

Specific studies designed to show correlations between Rorschach evaluations and case-history evaluations of *adjustment* have generally failed (e.g., Grant, Ives, & Ranzoni, 1952). The evidence showing a relationship to *intelligence* is not definitive, although some success here has been reported, especially with factorial studies. Studies of *creativity*, generally, have been discouraging. For example, research conducted under the supervision of the senior author on creative vs. noncreative writers, mathematical statisticians, and high school students have failed to reveal any differences on Rorschach performance; even tests especially designed to elicit M (a category often interpreted as linked with creativity), such as the Levy Movement Blots (LMB), have failed. Griffin (1958), for example, working with the LMB, failed to find a relationship between creativity and movement (among college females) nor did Rust (1948), using this instrument with children. Their results generally support those of Roe (1946*a*, 1946*b*, and 1946*c*) in her studies of the Rorschachs of eminent artists.

In general, then, validity evidence supporting the use of the Rorschach technique in various settings primarily with normals, is essentially now lacking, despite enthusiastic support from many circles, including other disciplines.

*Content Approaches.*[20] The content category as used by Hermann

---

[19] Eron (1954) found, for example, that no score or combination of scores differentiated third year medical students from third year divinity students. Furthermore, three experts were unable to sort the unidentified protocols considered globally into the appropriate group. Whatever success they had was due to the chance presence of unique content in an occasional record. They were also unable to distinguish the most from the least successful students.

[20] Additional material pertaining to content approaches to the Rorschach can be found in Chapter 5. Note might also be made of a work by Levy (1963), which is concerned with the principles of psychological interpretation in psychodiagnostic and psychotherapeutic settings. The author's interest was chiefly in constructing a set of general, theoretical principles useful to the "clinician-scientist" covering the interpretative process; he was of the belief that these principles apply not only to the content analysis of Rorschach responses, but to other projective material (e.g., TAT responses) as well.

Rorschach was one of three types of classifications of responses—location and determinants are the other two. These last two categories were traditionally regarded as the formal categories. The content categories involved a simple classification of the response into one of several groups—human, animal, anatomical, object, etc.

In the past several years there has been increased attention to content considerations, but with considerable extension of Rorschach's simple classification. Included are not only many additional considerations as to the content of S's responses, but there has also been some focus on more "dynamic" or psychoanalytic aspects of the response and its symbolic referent. The point is that contemporary content analysis has gone beyond a simple designation as to whether or not a response is "animal," "vegetable," or "mineral"!

Our own content scales, described in Chapter 7, cover many aspects of the response not regarded as "perceptual" or formal, and touch, as do other content-analysis systems, on the quality and nature of S's verbalizations and interpretative attitudes. The inclusive quality of our scales, plus the fact that their reliability and validity, for various purposes, are open to public inspection and use, contrast this approach to those preferred by some clinicians who are concerned with what they claim to be more clinically meaningful and provocative schemes.

Some history of success with content analysis has been found, a consideration which bears keeping in mind, when an overall evaluation of the Rorschach method is made. For example, note has already been made of successful factorial studies utilizing content (Sandler & Ackner [1951], and Sen [1950]). Elizur (1949) found that an analysis of content in relation to hostility yielded significant correlations with ratings of hostility. Using the Harrower Group Rorschach slides, Rychlak and Guinouard (1960) reported confirmation of their hypothesis that certain measures of content would be related to independent measures of personality and popularity. Watkins and Stauffacher (1952) constructed a series of indices for "deviant verbalizations" based on content considerations, and found that these indicators had a high reliability (.774) between two raters, and that they distinguished normals from neurotics and the latter from psychotics. McCall (1951) found that certain psychometrically weighted nonperceptual categories related significantly to outcome in psychosurgery, either pre- or postoperatively, or both. Chief among these were ascendance-submission, plant importance, dehumanization, reaction time, and popularity. Of these, the ascendance-submission scale was the most "sensitive," although no rationale was provided for the fact that those destined for eventual improvement showed a consistent tendency to see more submissive human figures in the Rorschach cards.

But it should be borne in mind that while psychometrically oriented researchers were turning to developing objective methods for scoring and evaluating various types of content scales, some clinicians, especially those with experience and background in psychoanalysis, or psychoanalytic therapy, were also fascinated by the possibilities that content offered for interpretative purposes. Among these men was Lindner (1946, 1947, 1950), who was convinced that *what* S perceived is as important as *how* he perceived it. He felt that if Rorschach had lived, he would most certainly have explored this avenue. On the basis of his own clinical experience, Lindner "isolated" certain responses as reflections of basic personality, and as characterizing different types of diagnostic groupings. Confirmation of these significant responses, he believed, could be found by "pragmatic" means based on his own experience, as well as that of other clinicians. A few examples of such significant responses are:

*Card I.* Lower central D: normal males—"female torso"; homosexuals—"male torso" or "mannish female."

*Card X.* Reverse position, middle blue dd: "Extracted tooth" seen by chronic masturbators and those with severe conflicts in this area.

Experienced clinicians and Rorschach workers will be familiar, no doubt, with some of the foregoing. What is more, frequent use of such interpretations is common practice. But despite his strong feelings with respect to the validity (based on his own clinical experiences) of the interpretations of his "significant" responses, Lindner has cautioned:

It cannot be too often stressed nevertheless that the conclusions from content analysis have to be treated cautiously and with scientific circumspection. An attitude of objective skepticism is the one best suited to the content analyst. The forty-three responses thus far isolated should be subjected to the severest tests—statistical and empirical—before they are accepted fully and integrated wholly into the compendium of Rorschach knowledge (1950, p. 90).

Finally, note should be made of Schafer's volume (1954) which was devoted mostly to an examination of the total Rorschach situation, from a psychoanalytic point of view. The principles, "rules-of-thumb," and skills presented here are based largely on insightful, undoubtedly wise, but not necessarily "public" procedures, in that they are derived almost entirely from the author's own clinical background and experience. In the chapter on thematic analyses, the author illustrates his psychoanalytic method of thematic (content) analysis. He does caution, however, that it is important not to be too "wild" in psychoanalytic interpretations; the clinician is urged to corroborate interpretations by turning to other tests to see if the same themes recur. The general methods for content analyses Schafer proposes may be extremely helpful, clinically, but they await validation through more advanced methodological and theoretical developments than are now available, in addition to more precise knowledge as to the validity of psychoanalytic theory and methods.

In general then, content approaches offer some promise, and the validity picture is not dim. Two main streams have been delineated in manner of approach to problems and procedures, research and clinical uses: (a) psychometric and objective, and (b) generally psychoanalytic and clinical. We can only wait hopefully for some welding of ideas, and for continued research efforts.

## SUMMARY AND CONCLUSIONS

The use of inkblots as a device for finding out indirectly something about individuals had a long history before Rorschach began his work. The first recorded instance available is the use of inkblots by Justinus Kerner. His semi-artistic use of inkblots finally grew into a respectable medium for distinguishing between individuals.

At first inkblots were used for studying mental content and imagination, and much of the early work may be regarded as an attempt at making a content analysis of the responses in order to classify the type of imagery or imagination present.

Then they were used for studying the mechanism of visual perception, since the apparent formlessness of the inkblots provided a nonsense figure similar to the nonsense syllables in the study of memory. It was soon discovered that even in the same inkblot, different individuals tended to see different things. This lack of constancy in the response of individuals was regarded as a stumbling block in the path of experimental psychology since no generalizations could be made from such inconstant results. But just as discrepancies in the astronomical observatories led to the establishment of the "personal equation" in the act of sighting stars, discrepancies in the reports of the subjects to inkblots led to the discovery of the existence of personality types. At first it was noted that some individuals tended to be analytic in their approach, starting with the whole inkblot and dissecting it into its parts. Others began at the other end and built up the wholes from the details. In this way, the subjects were divided into two contrasting groups, the analyzers and the synthesizers. Other bipolar typologies were also developed on the basis of habitual patterns that characterized the subjects.

It soon became apparent that the objective stimulus to visual perception was only partly responsible in the determination of a given response. Some of the responsibility could be laid at the door of the attitudinal factors that characterized a given individual.

It is difficult to trace the influences which led Rorschach to his investigation, but early in his career he was influenced by Bleuler's psychiatric approaches and by Külpe's psychology. He seemed to have been influenced less by psychoanalysis. Rorschach differed in his approach to the work with inkblots from his predecessors by stressing the importance of *how* the person perceives rather than *what* he perceives. By discarding the content, he opened the road to an analysis of the relationship between perception and personality.

The current status of the Rorschach technique was evaluated by exploring various considerations. It was noted that Rorschach "theory" as such, consisted of a large series of interpretative assumptions and rationales as to the meaning of various determinants, following in the traditions established by Hermann Rorschach. Such "theories" have little implication outside the clinical fold. Problems in connection with assessing the reliability of the instrument were discussed, including difficulties revolving around the nature of the Rorschach *score*, itself. The usual psychometric criteria for assessing reliability were evaluated in terms of applicability to the Rorschach, and it was concluded that although a high degree of scorer reliability can be obtained when there is pretraining and supervised practice with respect to a specific system, most other estimates of reliability have yielded unsatisfactory results. Moreover, the usual techniques when applied to the Rorschach have enormous difficulties, whereas attempts to make such techniques more appropriate, through matching procedures or global judgments, are not satisfactory.

The general problem of the validity of the Rorschach was raised. After ruling out "subjective testimonials" as scientific evidence for validity, attention was turned to some problems in connection with choosing the most appropriate units or components of the Rorschach which should be subjected to validity tests. These introductory sections were followed by a presentation of various types of validity approaches, including at the outset, the use of "blind analysis," signs, and matching procedures. (A recent survey [Gleser, 1963] indicates that there is a general decrease of validity studies using these methods.)

Establishing validity through the use of differential diagnosis and contrasted groups was discussed; special attention was given to the diagnosis of "organicity." It was concluded that the many methodological difficulties and generally contradictory evidence yielded a rather unfavorable picture of this method. "Laboratory" validation procedures were also discussed, with special attention to studies using hypnosis. These studies lack integration with the rest of psychology, and the studies using hypnotic procedures, especially, are often methodologically unsound. Studies attempting to predict behavior were reviewed. It was concluded that the further we get from specific, clearly defined behaviors, the more difficult it becomes to demonstrate meaningful relationships. Large-scale correlational studies using either global judgments or specific scores to predict success in various training programs, have been rather unsuccessful, and, in addition, only limited success has been reported in the use of the Rorschach for prognostic purposes. Various difficulties with respect to normative and developmental research were presented. Factorial studies have achieved generally more success than some of the other validity approaches, it was noted, as is true for various validity approaches using content analysis. Lack of positive findings seems to be the case when work with normals has been the goal of the validity research. Finally, validity approaches based on the exploration of specific Rorschach hypotheses seem to yield contradictory results, as was illustrated in two areas: "color theory," and hypotheses in connection with the white space response.

The current survey, which has also suggested that global methods as well as content approaches have had somewhat more success than atomistic methods, lends support to Zubin's (1954) earlier conclusion that the Rorschach is essentially an interview, and as such, the most appropriate analysis of Rorschach variables, as in any interview, should be based on an evaluation of content. Regardless of whether or not this conclusion is correct, the possibilities offered by this avenue of approach should be further explored.

It can be concluded from this review that the clinical status of the Rorschach technique, based on an evaluation of research evidence, is not wholly satisfactory, despite claims to the contrary. In Chapter 5, a different approach to evaluating the status of the Rorschach is adopted —that of viewing it as an experimental situation.

## REFERENCES

Allison, H. W., & Allison, Sarah G. Personality changes following transorbital lobotomy. *J. abnorm. soc. Psychol.*, 1954, 49, 219–223.

Ames, Louise B., Learned, Janet, Métraux, Ruth W., & Walker, R. N. *Child Rorschach responses*. New York: Paul B. Hoeber, 1952.

Ames, Louise B., Learned, Janet, Métraux, Ruth W., & Walker, R. N. *Rorschach responses in old age*. New York: Harper and Brothers, 1954.

Ames, Louise B., Métraux, Ruth W., & Walker, R. N. *Adolescent Rorschach responses*. New York: Paul B. Hoeber, 1959.

Anastasi, Anne. *Psychological testing.* New York: Macmillan, 1954.

Anderson, H. H., & Anderson, Gladys L. *An introduction to projective techniques.* Englewood Cliffs, N.J.: Prentice-Hall, 1951.

Ansbacher, H. L. Social interest, an Adlerian rationale for the Rorschach human movement response. *J. proj. Tech.,* 1956, **20,** 363–365.

Auld, F., Jr., & Eron, L. The use of Rorschach scores to predict whether patients will continue psychotherapy. *J. consult. Psychol.,* 1953, **17,** 104–109.

Baker, Gertrude. Diagnosis of organic brain damage in the adult. In B. Klopfer, *et al. Developments in the Rorschach technique. Vol. II. Fields of application.* Yonkers-on-Hudson, N.Y.: World Book Co., 1956, 318–375.

Bandura, A. The Rorschach white space response and perceptual reversal. *J. exp. Psychol.,* 1954, **48,** 113–118.

Barron, F. Psychotherapy as a special case of personal interaction: prediction of its course. Unpublished doctoral dissertation, University of California, Berkeley, 1950.

Barry, J. R., Blyth, D. D., & Albrecht, R. Relationships between Rorschach scores and adjustment level. *J. consult. Psychol.,* 1952, **16,** 30–36.

Bartlett, F. C. An experimental study of some problems of perceiving and imaging. *Brit. J. Psychol.,* 1916, **8,** 222–267.

Baughman, E. E. Rorschach scores as a function of examiner difference. *J. proj. Tech.,* 1951, **15,** 243–249.

Baughman, E. E. A comparative analysis of Rorschach forms with altered stimulus characteristics. *J. proj. Tech.,* 1954, **18,** 151–164.

Baughman, E. E. The role of the stimulus in Rorschach responses. *Psychol. Bull.,* 1958, **55,** 121–147.

Baumgarten-Tramer, Franziska. Zur Geschichte des Rorschachtests. *Schweiz. Arch. Neur. Psychiat.,* 1942, **50,** 1–13.

Beck, S. J. *Rorschach's test: I. Basic processes.* New York: Grune and Stratton, 1944.

Beck, S. J. *Rorschach's test: II. A variety of personality pictures.* New York: Grune and Stratton, 1945.

Beck, S. J. *Rorschach's test: III. Advances in interpretation.* New York: Grune and Stratton, 1952.

Beck, S. J. The six schizophrenias: reaction patterns in children and adults. *Amer. Orthopsychiat. Assoc. Res. Monogr.,* 1954, No. 6.

Beck, S. J., Beck, Anne G., Levitt, E. E., & Molish, H. B. *Rorschach's test: I. Basic processes.* New York: Grune and Stratton, 1961.

Bendig, A. W., & Hamlin, R. M. The psychiatric validity of an inverted factor analysis of Rorschach scoring categories. *J. consult. Psychol.,* 1955, **19,** 183–188.

Benjamin, J. D., & Ebaugh, F. G. The diagnostic validity of the Rorschach test. *Amer. J. Psychiat.,* 1938, **94,** 1163–1178.

Bennett, C. L. An experimental study of relationships between human electro-encephalograms and certain Rorschach scoring categories. *Speech Monogr.,* 1952, **19,** 112–113.

Benton, A. L. The experimental validation of the Rorschach test. II. The significance of Rorschach color responses. *Amer. J. Orthopsychiat.,* 1952, **22,** 755–763.

Binet, A., & Henri, V. La psychologie individuelle. *L'Année psychologique,* 1895, **2,** 411–465.

Block, J., Levine, L. S., & McNemar, Q. Testing for the existence of psychometric patterns. *J. abnorm. soc. Psychol.*, 1951, **46**, 356–359.

Borgatta, E. F., & Eschenbach, A. E. Factor analysis of Rorschach variables and behavioral observation. *Psychol. Reports*, 1955, **1**, 129–136.

Bower, P. A., Testin, R., & Roberts, A. Rorschach diagnosis by a systematic combining of content, thought process and determinant scales. *Genet. Psychol. Monogr.*, 1960, **62**, 105–183.

Brozek, J., Guetzkow, H., & Keys, A. A study of personality of normal young men maintained on restricted intakes of vitamins of the B complex. *Psychosom. Med.*, 1946, **8**, 98–109.

Brudo, C. The alpha index in the electro-encephalogram and movement responses on the Rorschach and PMS tests. Unpublished doctoral dissertation, Northwestern University, 1954.

Buckle, D. F., & Holt, N. F. Comparison of Rorschach and Behn inkblots. *J. proj. Tech.*, 1951, **15**, 486–493.

Caldwell, Bettye McD. An evaluation of psychological effects of sex hormone administration in aged women. II. Results of therapy after 18 months. *J. Geront.*, 1954, **9**, 168–174.

Carlson, V., & Lazarus, R. S. A repetition of Meyer Williams' study of intellectual control under stress and associated Rorschach factors. *J. consult. Psychol.*, 1953, **17**, 247–253.

Carr, A. C. An evaluation of nine non-directive psychotherapy cases by means of the Rorschach. *J. consult. Psychol.*, 1949, **13**, 196–205.

Carr, A. C., Forer, B. R., Henry, W. E., Hooker, Evelyn, Hutt, M. L., & Piotrowski, Z. A. *The prediction of overt behavior through the use of projective techniques.* Springfield, Ill.: Charles C Thomas, 1960.

Corsini, R. J., Severson, W. E., Tunney, T. E., & Uehling, H. F. The separation capacity of the Rorschach. *J. consult. Psychol.*, 1955, **19**, 194–196.

Cox, Shelagh M. A factorial study of the Rorschach responses of normal and maladjusted boys. *J. genet. Psychol.*, 1951, **79**, 95–115.

Cronbach, L. J. A validation design for qualitative studies of personality. *J. consult. Psychol.*, 1948, **12**, 365–374.

Cronbach, L. J. Statistical methods applied to Rorschach scores: a review. *Psychol. Bull.*, 1949, **46**, 393–429.

Crumpton, Evelyn. The influence of color on the Rorschach test. *J. proj. Tech.*, 1956, **20**, 150–158.

da Vinci, Leonardo. *Das Buch von der Malerie.* Nach dem Codex Vaticanus, 1270. In *Quellenschriften f. Kunstgeschichte*, Vol. 15. Vienna: W. Braumuller, 1882.

Davis, Hannah S. Judgments of intellectual level from various features of the Rorschach including vocabulary. *J. proj. Tech.*, 1961, **25**, 155–157.

Dawson, J. G., Jr. A comparative investigation of three diagnostic indicators of brain damage. Unpublished doctoral dissertation, University of Chicago, 1949.

Dearborn, G. Blots of ink in experimental psychology. *Psychol. Rev.*, 1897, **4**, 390–391.

Dearborn, G. A study of imaginations. *Amer. J. Psychol.*, 1898, **9**, 183–190.

Dörken, H., Jr., & Kral, V. A. The psychological differentiation of organic brain lesions and their localization by means of Rorschach test. *Amer. J. Psychiat.*, 1952, **108**, 764–770.

Dörken, H., Jr., & Tunis, M. M. Projective technique with narcosis. *Amer. J. Psychiat.*, 1949, **106**, 216–221.

Drey-Fuchs, Christel. *Der Fuchs–Rorschach Test: Einführung in die Technik des Versuches.* (The Fuchs–Rorschach test: introduction to test technique.) Göttingen, Germany: Verlag für Psychologie, 1958.

DuBois, Cora, & Oberholzer, E. Rorschach tests and native personality in Alor, Dutch East Indies. *Trans. New York Acad. Sci.,* 1942, **4,** 168–170.

Dunlap, K. The reading of character from external signs. *Scientif. Monthly,* 1922, **15,** 153–165.

Dworetzki, Gertrude. Le test de Rorschach et l'évolution de la perception. *Arch. Psychol., Genève,* 1939, **27,** 233–396.

Eichler, R. A comparison of the Rorschach and Behn-Rorschach inkblot tests. *J. consult. Psychol.,* 1951, **15,** 185–189. (*a*)

Eichler, R. Experimental stress and alleged Rorschach indices of anxiety. *J. abnorm. soc. Psychol.,* 1951, **46,** 344–355. (*b*)

Elizur, A. Content analysis of the Rorschach with regard to anxiety and hostility. *Rorschach Res. Exch.,* 1949, **13,** 247–284.

Elkins, Elise. The diagnostic validity of the Ames "danger signals." *J. consult. Psychol.,* 1958, **22,** 281–287.

Eron, L. D. Use of the Rorschach method in medical student selection. *J. med. Educ.,* 1954, **29,** 35–39.

Eschenbach, A. E., & Borgatta, E. F. A review of some major Rorschach scoring categories and hypothesized personality correlates. *USAF Hum. Resour. Res. Inst. Res. Memo.,* 1953, No. 19.

Eschenbach, A. E., & Borgatta, E. F. Testing behavior hypotheses with the Rorschach: an exploration in validation. *J. consult. Psychol.,* 1955, **19,** 267–273.

Fager, R. E. Relation of Rorschach movement and color responses to cognitive inhibition. *J. consult. Psychol.,* 1960, **24,** 276.

Fisher, J., Gonda, T. A., & Little, K. B. The Rorschach and central nervous system pathology: a cross-validation study. *Amer. J. Psychiat.,* 1955, **111,** 487–492.

Fiske, D. W. Variability of responses and the stability of scores and interpretations of projective protocols. *J. proj. Tech.,* 1959, **23,** 263–267.

Fiske, D. W., & Baughman, E. E. Relationships between Rorschach scoring categories and the total number of responses. *J. abnorm. soc. Psychol.,* 1953, **48,** 25–32.

Fonda, C. P. The white space response. In Maria A. Rickers-Ovsiankina (Ed.) *Rorschach psychology.* New York: John Wiley and Sons, 1960, 80–105.

Friedman, H. Perceptual regression in schizophrenia: an hypothesis suggested by the use of the Rorschach test. *J. proj. Tech.,* 1953, **17,** 171–185.

Fulkerson, S. C., & Barry, J. R. Methodology and research on the prognostic use of psychological tests. *Psychol. Bull.,* 1961, **58,** 177–204.

Gallagher, J. J. Test indicators for therapy prognosis. *J. consult. Psychol.,* 1954, **18,** 409–413.

Garrison, M., Jr. Relationships between Rorschach scores and clinical changes in mental patients. *J. Pers.,* 1948, **17,** 146–152.

Gibby, R. G. The stability of certain Rorschach variables under conditions of experimentally induced sets. 1. The intellectual variables. *J. proj. Tech.,* 1951, **15,** 3–25.

Gleser, Goldine C. Projective methodologies. *Annu. Rev. Psychol.,* 1963, **14,** 391–422.

Goldberger, L. Reactions to perceptual isolation and Rorschach manifestations of the primary process. *J. proj. Tech.,* 1961, **25,** 287–302.

Grant, Marguerite Q., Ives, Virginia, & Ranzoni, Jane H. Reliability and validity of judges' ratings of adjustment on the Rorschach. *Psychol. Monogr.*, 1952, **66** (Whole No. 334).

Griffin, Dorothy P. Movement responses and creativity. *J. consult. Psychol.*, 1958, **22**, 134–136.

Griffith, R. M. Test-retest similarities of the Rorschachs of patients without retention, Korsakoff. *J. proj. Tech.*, 1951, **15**, 516–525.

Guilford, J. P. Some lessons from aviation psychology. *Amer. Psychologist*, 1948, 3, 3–11.

Hallowell, A. I. The Rorschach technique in personality and culture studies. In B. Klopfer, *et al. Developments in the Rorschach technique. Vol. II. Fields of application*. Yonkers-on-Hudson, N.Y.: World Book Co., 1956, 458–544.

Halpern, Florence. *A clinical guide to children's Rorschachs*. New York: Grune and Stratton, 1953.

Hamlin, R. M., & Albee, G. W. Muench's tests before and after nondirective therapy: a control group for his subjects. *J. consult. Psychol.*, 1948, **12**, 412–416.

Harrower, Molly. *Personality change and development: as measured by the projective techniques*. New York: Grune and Stratton, 1958.

Helman, Z. Rorschach et dessins dans un cas de lobotomie. *Bull. Group. Franc. Rorschach.*, 1953, 3, 9–15.

Hemmendinger, L. Perceptual organization and development as reflected in the structure of Rorschach test responses. *J. proj. Tech.*, 1953, **17**, 162–170.

Hemmendinger, L. Developmental theory and the Rorschach method. In Maria A. Rickers-Ovsiankina (Ed.) *Rorschach psychology*. New York: John Wiley and Sons, 1960, 58–79.

Hens, Szymon. *Phantasieprufung mit formlosen Klecksen bei Schulkindern, normalen Erwachsenen und Geisteskranken*. (Diss. Zurich, 1917.)

Herman, J. A study of some behavioral and test correlates of the Rorschach experience type. Unpublished doctoral dissertation, New York University, 1956.

Hertz, Marguerite R. Reliability of the Rorschach inkblot test. *J. appl. Psychol.*, 1934, **18**, 461–477.

Hertz, Marguerite R. The Rorschach inkblot test: historical summary. *Psychol. Bull.*, 1935, **32**, 33–66.

Hertz, Marguerite R. Current problems in Rorschach theory and technique. *J. proj. Tech.*, 1951, **15**, 307–338.

Hertz, Marguerite R. The Rorschach: thirty years after. In D. Brower and L. E. Abt (Eds.) *Progress in clinical psychology*. Vol. I. New York: Grune and Stratton, 1952, 108–148.

Hertz, Marguerite R. The use and misuse of the Rorschach method. I. Variations in Rorschach procedure. *J. proj. Tech.*, 1959, **23**, 33–48.

Hertz, Marguerite R. The Rorschach in adolescence. In A. I. Rabin and M. R. Haworth (Eds.) *Projective techniques with children*. New York: Grune and Stratton, 1960, 29–60.

Holt, R. R. Implications of some contemporary personality theories for Rorschach rationale. In B. Klopfer *et al. Developments in the Rorschach technique. Vol. I. Technique and theory*. Yonkers-on-Hudson, N.Y.: World Book Co., 1954, 501–560.

Holtzman, W. H. Prediction of adjustment in the USAF flight training program: clinical assessment of selected test protocols. March 5, 1952 (dittoed).

Holtzman, W. H. Objective scoring of projective techniques. In B. M. Bass and I. A. Berg (Eds.) *Objective approaches to personality assessment.* Princeton, N.J.: D. Van Nostrand, 1959, 119–145.

Holzberg, J. D. Reliability re-examined. In Maria A. Rickers-Ovsiankina (Ed.) *Rorschach psychology.* New York: John Wiley and Sons, 1960, 361–379.

Holzberg, J. D., & Cahen, Eleanor R. The relationship between psychiatric improvement and certain pathologic changes in the Rorschach during electroconvulsive therapy. *J. clin. exper. Psychopathol.,* 1952, **13**, 237–246.

Holzberg, J. D., & Wexler, M. The predictability of schizophrenic performance on the Rorschach test. *J. consult. Psychol.,* 1950, **14**, 395–399.

Howard, J. W. The Howard Ink Blot Test: a descriptive manual. *J. clin. Psychol. Monogr. Suppl.,* 1953, **9**, 209–254.

Janoff, Irma Z. The relation between Rorschach form quality measures and children's behavior. Unpublished doctoral dissertation, Yale University, 1951.

Kagan, J. The long term stability of selected Rorschach responses. *J. consult. Psychol.,* 1960, **24**, 67–73.

Keehn, J. D. Rorschach validation II: the validity of colour shock in the diagnosis of neuroticism. *J. ment. Sci.,* 1953, **99**, 224–234.

Kelley, D. M. Clinical reality and projective technique. *Amer. J. Psychiat.,* 1951, **107**, 753–757.

Kelley, D. M., Margulies, H., & Barrera, S. E. The stability of the Rorschach method as demonstrated in electric convulsive therapy cases. *Rorschach Res. Exch.,* 1941, **5**, 35–43.

Kirkpatrick, E. A. Individual tests of school children. *Psychol. Rev.,* 1900, **7**, 274–280.

Kitzinger, Helen, Arnold, D. G., Cartwright, R. W., & Shapiro, D. A preliminary study of the effects of glutamic acid on catatonic schizophrenics. *J. proj. Tech.,* 1949, **13**, 210–218.

Klein, G. S., & Schlesinger, H. J. Perceptual attitudes toward instability: I. Prediction of apparent movement experiences from Rorschach responses. *J. Pers.,* 1951, **19**, 289–302.

Klopfer, B., et al. *Developments in the Rorschach technique. Vol. I. Technique and theory.* Yonkers-on-Hudson, N.Y.: World Book Co., 1954.

Klopfer, B., et al. *Developments in the Rorschach technique. Vol. II. Fields of application.* Yonkers-on-Hudson, N.Y.: World Book Co., 1956.

Klopfer, B., Fox, J., & Troup, Evelyn. Problems in the use of the Rorschach technique with children. In B. Klopfer, et al. *Developments in the Rorschach technique. Vol. II. Fields of application.* Yonkers-on-Hudson, N.Y.: World Book Co., 1956, 3–21.

Klopfer, B., & Kelley, D. *The Rorschach technique.* Yonkers-on-Hudson, N.Y.: World Book Co., 1942.

Klopfer, B., Kirkner, F. J., Wisham, W., & Baker, Gertrude. Rorschach Prognostic Rating Scale. *J. proj. Tech.,* 1951, **15**, 425–428.

Klopfer, B., & Spiegelman, M. Methodological research problems. In B. Klopfer, et al. *Developments in the Rorschach technique. Vol. II. Fields of application.* Yonkers-on-Hudson, N.Y.: World Book Co., 1956, 267–280. (a)

Klopfer, B., & Spiegelman, M. Differential diagnosis. In B. Klopfer, et al. *Developments in the Rorschach technique. Vol. II. Fields of application.* Yonkers-on-Hudson, N.Y.: World Book Co., 1956, 281–317. (b)

Klopfer, B., Spiegelman, M., & Fox, J. The interpretation of children's records. In B. Klopfer, et al. Developments in the Rorschach technique. Vol. II. Fields of application. Yonkers-on-Hudson, N.Y.: World Book Co., 1956, 22–44.

Klopfer, W. The application of the Rorschach technique to geriatrics. In B. Klopfer, et al. Developments in the Rorschach technique. Vol. II. Fields of application. Yonkers-on-Hudson, N.Y.: World Book Co., 1956, 195–212.

Kotkov, B., & Meadow, A. Rorschach criteria for continuing group psychotherapy. Int. J. Group Psychother., 1952, 2, 324–333.

Kotkov, B., & Meadow, A. Rorschach criteria for predicting continuation in individual psychotherapy. J. consult. Psychol., 1953, 17, 16–20.

Krüger, H., & Zietz, K. Das Verifikationsproblem. Zeitschr. f. Angew. Psychol., 1933, 45, 140–171.

Krugman, Judith. A clinical validation of the Rorschach with problem children. Rorschach Res. Exch., 1942, 6, 61–70.

Kuhn, R. Ueber Rorschach's Psychologie und die psychologischen Grundlagen des Formdeutversuches. Schweiz. Arch. Neurol. Psychiat., 1944, 53, 29–47.

Lazarus, R. S. The influence of color on the protocol of the Rorschach test. J. abnorm. soc. Psychol., 1949, 44, 506–516.

Ledwith, Nettie H. Rorschach responses of elementary school children. Pittsburgh: University of Pittsburgh Press, 1959.

Levine, D. Rorschach genetic level and mental disorder. J. proj. Tech., 1959, 23, 436–439.

Levine, D. Rorschach genetic level and psychotic symptomatology. J. clin. Psychol., 1960, 16, 164–167.

Levine, M., Glass, H., & Meltzoff, J. The inhibition process, Rorschach human movement responses, and intelligence. J. consult. Psychol., 1957, 21, 41–45.

Levine, M., & Meltzoff, J. Cognitive inhibition and Rorschach human movement responses. J. consult. Psychol., 1956, 20, 119–122.

Levitt, E. E., & Grosz, H. J. A comparison of quantifiable Rorschach anxiety indicators in hypnotically induced anxiety and normal states. J. consult. Psychol., 1960, 24, 31–34.

Levy, D. M., Schumer, Florence C., & Zubin, J. The Levy Movement Blots: a study of correlates and validity. In preparation, 1964.

Levy, L. H. Psychological interpretation. New York: Holt, Rinehart, and Winston, 1963.

Lindner, R. M. Content analysis in Rorschach work. Rorschach Res. Exch., 1946, 10, 121–129.

Lindner, R. M. Analysis of the Rorschach test by content. J. clin. Psychopath., 1947, 8, 707–719.

Lindner, R. M. The content analysis of the Rorschach protocol. In L. E. Abt & L. Bellak (Eds.) Projective psychology. New York: Knopf, 1950, 75–90.

Lindner, R. M., & Seliger, R. V. Projective techniques and the medical psychologist. South. Gen. Pract. Med. Surg., 1945, 107, 355–356.

Linton, Harriet B. Rorschach correlates of response to suggestion. J. abnorm. soc. Psychol., 1954, 49, 75–83.

Lipton, M. B., Tamarin, S., & Lotesta, P. Test evidence of personality change and prognosis by means of the Rorschach and Wechsler-Bellevue tests on 17 insulin-treated paranoid schizophrenics. Psychiat. Quart., 1951, 25, 434–444.

Little, K. B. Problems in the validation of projective techniques. J. proj. Tech., 1959, 23, 287–290.

Loevinger, Jane. Theory and techniques of assessment. *Annu. Rev. Psychol.*, 1959, **10**, 287–316.

Lord, Edith. Experimentally induced variations in Rorschach performance. *Psychol. Monogr.*, 1950, **64** (Whole No. 316). (*a*)

Lord, Edith. Two sets of Rorschach records obtained before and after brief psychotherapy. *J. consult. Psychol.*, 1950, **14**, 134–139. (*b*)

Lorr, M. Multidimensional scales for rating psychiatric patients. Hospital form. *Vet. Adm. tech. Bull.*, 10–507, November 16, 1953.

Lotsof, E. J., & Chance, June. Effects of cortisone on Rorschach performance. *J. proj. Tech.*, 1954, **18**, 470–474.

MacCurdy, E. *The notebooks of Leonardi da Vinci.* New York: George Braziller, 1958.

MacFarlane, Jean W., & Tuddenham, R. D. Problems in the validation of projective techniques. In H. H. Anderson & G. L. Anderson (Eds.) *An introduction to projective technique.* Englewood Cliffs, N.J.: Prentice-Hall, 1951, 26–54.

McCall, R. J. Psychometric evaluation of Rorschach records in brain-operated patients. Unpublished doctoral dissertation, Columbia University, 1951.

Meehl, P. E. Configural scoring. *J. consult. Psychol.*, 1950, **14**, 165–171.

Meehl, P. E. Some ruminations on the validation of clinical procedures. *Canad. J. Psychol.*, 1959, **13**, 102–128.

Meltzoff, J., & Levine, M. The relationship between motor and cognitive inhibition. *J. consult. Psychol.*, 1954, **18**, 355–358.

Meltzoff, J., & Litwin, Dorothy. Affective control and Rorschach human movement responses. *J. consult. Psychol.*, 1956, **20**, 463–465.

Meltzoff, J., Singer, J. L., & Korchin, S. Motor inhibition and Rorschach movement responses: a test of sensory-tonic theory. *J. Pers.*, 1953, **21**, 400–410.

Mettler, F. A. (Ed.) *Columbia Greystone Associates: Selective partial ablations of the frontal cortex.* New York: Paul Hoeber, 1949.

Meyer, B. T. An investigation of color shock in the Rorschach test. *J. clin. Psychol.*, 1951, **7**, 367–370.

Morgenthaler, W. Ueber Populaere Charakter Diagnostik. *Schweiz. Med. Wochenschr.*, 1930, **60**, 912–914.

Muench, G. A. An evaluation of non-directive psychotherapy by means of the Rorschach and other indices. *Appl. Psychol. Monogr.*, 1947, No. 13.

Murray, D. C. An investigation of the Rorschach white space response in an extratensive experience balance as a measure of outwardly directed opposition. *J. proj. Tech.*, 1957, **21**, 40–46. (*a*)

Murray, D. C. White space on the Rorschach: interpretation and validity. *J. proj. Tech.*, 1957, **21**, 47–53. (*b*)

Murstein, B. I. Factor analyses of the Rorschach. *J. consult. Psychol.*, 1960, **24**, 262–275.

Nathan, G. J. *The bachelor life.* New York: Reynal and Hitchcock, 1941.

Neel, Ann F. Inhibition and perception of movement on the Rorschach. *J. consult. Psychol.*, 1960, **24**, 224–230.

Newton, R. L. The clinician as judge: total Rorschachs and clinical case material. *J. consult. Psychol.*, 1954, **18**, 248–250.

Parsons, C. J. Children's interpretation of inkblots. *Brit. J. Psychol.*, 1917, **9**, 74–92.

Piotrowski, Z. A. Rorschach method in review. In D. Brower & L. E. Abt (Eds.) *Progress in clinical psychology, II.* New York: Grune and Stratton, 1956, 16–31.

Piotrowski, Z. A. The movement score. In M. A. Rickers-Ovsiankina (Ed.) *Rorschach psychology*. New York: John Wiley and Sons, 1960, 130–153.

Podell, J. E., & Phillips, L. A developmental analysis of cognition as observed in dimensions of Rorschach and objective test performance. *J. Pers.*, 1959, 27, 439–463.

Pyle, W. H. *Examination of school children*. New York: Macmillan, 1913.

Pyle, W. H. A psychological study of bright and dull pupils. *J. educ. Psychol.*, 1915, 6, 151–156. (a)

Pyle, W. H. The mind of the Negro child. *School and Society*, 1915, 1, 357–360. (b)

Rabin, A. I. Validating and experimental studies with the Rorschach method. In H. H. Anderson and G. L. Anderson (Eds.) *An introduction to projective techniques*. Englewood Cliffs, N.J.: Prentice-Hall, 1951.

Rabin, A. I., Papania, N., & McMichael, A. Some effects of alcohol on Rorschach performance. *J. clin. Psychol.*, 1954, 10, 252–255.

Rader, G. E. The prediction of overt aggressive verbal behavior from Rorschach content. *J. proj. Tech.*, 1957, 21, 294–306.

Ramzy, I., & Pickard, P. M. A study in the reliability of scoring the Rorschach ink-blot test. *J. gen. Psychol.*, 1949, 40, 3–10.

Rees, W. L., & Jones, A. M. An evaluation of the Rorschach test as a prognostic aid in the treatment of schizophrenia by insulin coma therapy, electronarcosis, electroconvulsive therapy, and leucotomy. *J. ment. Sci.*, 1951, 97, 681–689.

Ricciuti, H. N. Use of the Rorschach test in longitudinal studies of personality development. *J. proj. Tech.*, 1956, 20, 256–260.

Rickers-Ovsiankina, Maria A. (Ed.) *Rorschach psychology*. New York: John Wiley and Sons, 1960.

Roberts, L. K. The failure of some Rorschach indices to predict the outcome of psychotherapy. *J. consult. Psychol.*, 1954, 18, 96–98.

Roe, Anne. Alcohol and creative work. I. Painters. *Quart. J. Stud. Alcohol*, 1946, 6, 415–467. (a)

Roe, Anne. Artists and their work. *J. Pers.*, 1946, 15, 1–40. (b)

Roe, Anne. Painting and personality. *Rorschach Res. Exch.*, 1946, 10, 86–100. (c)

Rogers, A. S. An analytic study of visual perceptions. *Amer. J. Psychol.*, 1917, 28, 519–577.

Rogers, L. S., Knauss, Joanne, & Hammond, K. R. Predicting continuation in therapy by means of the Rorschach test. *J. consult. Psychol.*, 1951, 15, 368–371.

Rorschach, H. *Psychodiagnostics*. Berne: Verlag Hans Huber, 1942.

Rorschach, Olga. Ueber das Leben und die Wesenart von Hermann Rorschach. *Schweiz. Arch. Neurol. Psychiat.*, 1944, 53, 1–11.

Rust, R. Some correlates of the movement response. *J. Pers.*, 1948, 16, 369–401.

Rychlak, J. F., & Guinouard, D. Rorschach content, personality and popularity. *J. proj. Tech.*, 1960, 24, 322–332.

Sandler, J., & Ackner, B. Rorschach content analysis: an experimental investigation. *Brit. J. med. Psychol.*, 1951, 24, 180–201.

Sarason, S. B. *The clinical interaction*. New York: Harper and Brothers, 1954.

Schachtel, E. G. Notes on Rorschach tests of 500 juvenile delinquents and a control group of 500 non-delinquent adolescents. *J. proj. Tech.*, 1951, 15, 144–172.

Schafer, R. *Psychoanalytic interpretation in Rorschach testing.* New York: Grune and Stratton, 1954.

Schreiber, Hanna, & White, Mary Alice. Diagnosing organicity on the Rorschach. *Psychiat. Quart. Suppl.,* 1954, **28**, 255–277.

Schumer, Florence C. Some behavioral correlates of the Rorschach human movement response. Unpublished doctoral dissertation, Yale University, 1949.

Sen, Amya. A statistical study of the Rorschach test. *Brit. J. Psychol. statist. Sect.,* 1950, **3**, 21–39.

Sharp, S. E. Individual psychology: a study in psychological method. *Amer. J. Psychol.,* 1899, **10**, 329–391.

Sherman, M. H. (Ed.) *A Rorschach reader.* New York: International Universities Press, 1960.

Siegel, E. L. Genetic parallels of perceptual structuralization in paranoid schizophrenia: an analysis by means of the Rorschach technique. *J. proj. Tech.,* 1953, **17**, 151–161.

Siipola, Elsa M. The influence of color on reactions to inkblots. *J. Pers.,* 1950, **18**, 358–382.

Siipola, Elsa M., & Basseches, Harriet. The relation of color-form incongruity and maladjustment to reaction time. *J. Pers.,* 1959, **27**, 324–345.

Siipola, Elsa M., Kuhns, Florence, & Taylor, Vivian. Measurement of the individual's reactions to color in inkblots. *J. Pers.,* 1950, **19**, 153–171.

Singer, J. L. The experience type: some behavioral correlates and theoretical implications. In M. A. Rickers-Ovsiankina (Ed.) *Rorschach psychology.* New York: John Wiley and Sons, 1960, 223–259. (*a*)

Singer, J. L. What do we know of projective techniques? A review of Harrower's *Personality change and development: as measured by projective techniques.* *Contemp. Psychol.,* 1960, **5**, No. 3, 76–77. (*b*)

Singer, J. L., & Herman, J. Motor and fantasy correlates of Rorschach human movement responses. *J. consult. Psychol.,* 1954, **18**, 325–331.

Singer, J. L., Meltzoff, J., & Goldman, G. D. Rorschach movement responses following motor inhibition and hyperactivity. *J. consult. Psychol.,* 1952, **16**, 359–364.

Singer, J. L., & Spohn, H. Some behavioral correlates of Rorschach's experience-type. *J. consult. Psychol.,* 1954, **18**, 1–9.

Snowden, R. F. Top management and the Rorschach technique. In B. Klopfer *et al. Developments in the Rorschach technique. Vol. II. Fields of application.* Yonkers-on-Hudson, N.Y.: World Book Co., 1956, 582–592.

Stein, H. Developmental changes in content of movement responses. *J. proj. Tech.,* 1956, **20**, 216–223.

Steinberg, A. An experimental investigation of the relation of galvanic skin response to Rorschach shock. Unpublished doctoral dissertation, Boston University, 1949.

Steisel, I. The Rorschach test and suggestibility. *J. abnorm. soc. Psychol.,* 1952, **47**, 607–614.

Stotsky, B. A. A comparison of remitting and non-remitting schizophrenics on psychological tests. *J. abnorm. soc. Psychol.,* 1952, **47**, 489–496.

Stotsky, B. A., & Lawrence, J. F. Various Rorschach indices as discriminators of marked and little conceptual disorganization among schizophrenics. *J. consult. Psychol.,* 1955, **19**, 189–193.

Swift, Joan W. Reliability of Rorschach scoring categories with preschool children. *Child Developm.,* 1944, **15**, 207–216.

Symonds, P. M. Are projective test data valid bases for prediction? *J. proj. Tech.*, 1954, **18**, 515–519.

Thiesen, J. W. A pattern analysis of structural characteristics of the Rorschach test in schizophrenia. *J. consult. Psychol.*, 1952, **16**, 365–370.

Tucker, J. E. Rorschach human and other movement responses in relation to intelligence. *J. consult. Psychol.*, 1950, **14**, 283–286.

Tulchin, S. H. The pre-Rorschach use of inkblot tests. *Rorschach Res. Exch.*, 1940, **4**, 1–7.

Vernier, Claire M., Whiting, J. F., & Meltzer, M. L. Differential prediction of a specific behavior from three projective techniques. *J. consult. Psychol.*, 1955, **19**, 175–182.

Vernon, Magdalen D. *Visual perception.* Cambridge: Cambridge University Press, 1937.

Vernon, Magdalen D. *A further study of visual perception.* Cambridge: Cambridge University Press, 1952.

Vernon, P. E. The Rorschach inkblot test, II. *Brit. J. med. Psychol.*, 1933, **13**, 179–205.

Watkins, J. G., & Stauffacher, J. C. An index of pathological thinking in the Rorschach. *J. proj. Tech.*, 1952, **16**, 276–286.

Waxenberg, S. E. Psychosomatic patients and other physically ill persons: a comparative study. *J. consult. Psychol.*, 1955, **19**, 163–169.

Weiner, I. B. Three Rorschach scores indicative of schizophrenia. *J. consult. Psychol.*, 1961, **25**, 436–439.

Werner, H. *Comparative psychology of mental development* (rev. ed.). Chicago: Follet, 1948.

Werner, H. The concept of development from a comparative and organismic point of view. In D. B. Harris (Ed.) *The concept of development: an issue in the study of human behavior.* Minneapolis: University of Minnesota Press, 1957, 125–148.

Whipple, G. M. *Manual of mental and physical tests.* Baltimore: Warwick and York, 1910. Chapter XI, tests of imagination and invention: Test 45, Ink Blots, 430–435.

Williams, Gertha, & Kellman, S. The Rorschach technique in industrial psychology. In B. Klopfer, *et al. Developments in the Rorschach technique. Vol. II. Fields of application.* Yonkers-on-Hudson, N.Y.: World Book Co., 1956, 545–581.

Williams, M. An experimental study of intellectual control under stress and associated Rorschach factors. *J. consult. Psychol.*, 1947, **11**, 21–29.

Williams, M. The experimental validation of the Rorschach test. I. Experimental correlations. *Amer. J. Orthopsychiat.*, 1952, **22**, 749–754.

Wilson, G. P. Intellectual indicators in the Rorschach test. Unpublished doctoral dissertation, University of Texas, 1952.

Windle, C. Psychological tests in psychopathological prognosis. *Psychol. Bull.*, 1952, **49**, 451–482.

Wirt, R. D. Pattern analysis of the Rorschach. *J. clin. Psychol.*, 1956, **12**, 382–384.

Wishner, J. Rorschach intellectual indicators in neurotics. *Amer. J. Orthopsychiat.*, 1948, **18**, 265–279.

Wittenborn, J. R. A factor analysis of discrete responses to the Rorschach inkblots. *J. consult. Psychol.*, 1949, **13**, 335–340. (*a*)

Wittenborn, J. R. Certain Rorschach response categories and mental abilities. *J. appl. Psychol.*, 1949, **33**, 330–338. (*b*)

Wittenborn, J. R. A factor analysis of Rorschach scoring categories. *J. consult. Psychol.*, 1950, 14, 261–267.

Wittenborn, J. R., & Holzberg, J. D. The Rorschach and descriptive diagnosis. *J. consult. Psychol.*, 1951, 15, 460–463.

Wohlwill, J. F. Developmental studies of perception. *Psychol. Bull.*, 1960, 57, 249–288.

Zamansky, H. S., & Goldman, A. E. A comparison of two methods of analyzing Rorschach data in assessing therapeutic change. *J. proj. Tech.*, 1960, 24, 75–82.

Zubin, J. A psychometric approach to the evaluation of the Rorschach test. *Psychiat.*, 1941, 4, 547–566.

Zubin, J. Rorschach test. In F. A. Mettler (Ed.) *Columbia Greystone Associates: Selective partial ablations of the frontal cortex.* New York: Paul Hoeber, 1949, 283–295.

Zubin, J. Failures of the Rorschach technique. *J. proj. Tech.*, 1954, 18, 303–315.

Zulliger, H. *Einführung in den Behn-Rorschach-Test.* Berne: Verlag Hans Huber, 1941.

# 5 THE RORSCHACH TECHNIQUE AS A PSYCHOLOGICAL EXPERIMENT

The current popularity of the Rorschach technique has focused attention on the paradox it presents. No other technique has captured the attention of so many on such little evidence. This in itself warrants sociological investigation into the problem of social acceptance of unestablished measuring devices, but it also presents the scientific psychologist with a dilemma. On the one hand, many intuitively gifted clinicians claim that it is impossible to verify clinical evaluations experimentally and that the deeper understanding of personality can be achieved only on an idiographic basis, since each case is a law unto itself. On the other hand, some of these same clinicians indicate that many of the claims of the Rorschach workers have already been tried and found true in the crucible of daily experience with patients. Despite these difficulties, many experimental psychologists are interested in determining the scientific value of the Rorschach technique. Unfortunately, the test and its method have never been thoroughly examined experimentally.

Rorschach himself had regarded the test as an experiment, empirically founded and in need of much further investigation (1942). It is in keeping with this empirical tendency in Rorschach's work that the present analysis of the experimental roots of the Rorschach technique is offered. An attempt will be made to analyze the Rorschach response

251

into its underlying components, beginning with the task set before the subject and ending with his final interpretation of the blot. It is at least possible that when such an analysis is completed some of the mystery in the evaluation of Rorschach responses will be dissipated.

Psychological experiments usually begin with an hypothesis and end with an evaluation of the tenability of the hypothesis in the light of the obtained data. The essential elements in any experiment may be catalogued as follows:

1. Hypothesis
2. Experimenter
3. Subject
4. Apparatus and stimulus
5. Task
6. Administration of task by examiner
7. Acceptance of task by subject
8. Carrying out of task by subject
9. Recording of result by experimenter
10. Analysis and evaluation of responses
11. Weighing of original hypothesis

In analyzing the Rorschach experiment we shall examine these essential elements and attempt to point out their importance to the experiment as a whole.

*Hypothesis.* In Chapter 1 we discuss the several assumptions underlying the use of projective techniques. Chapter 4 presents in some detail not only Hermann Rorschach's orientation to his "experiment," but some explicit illustrations of the unbelievably large number of hypotheses (actually, "rules" for interpretation) which abound in the Rorschach field. The general "projective" hypotheses, as well as the more detailed, specific Rorschach hypotheses, do not concern us at the moment. We are faced with a general question: are there broad hypotheses which can serve as a general framework for the analysis of this technique as an experimental situation, that is, is there a scientific model for the Rorschach technique?

A careful perusal of Rorschach's work fails to reveal a formal statement of hypothesis underlying his experiment. In a sense, his work may be regarded as pre-experimental—a search for an hypothesis. Nevertheless, the implicit hypothesis which seems to have motivated his work consists of several parts:

1. The Rorschach technique elicits perceptual responses.

2. Perception is not simply a stimulus-response affair, but depends also on the perceiver.

3. Perceivers (subjects) have characteristic "modes" or "styles" of responding which fall into several major categories (typologies).

4. Perception in Rorschach space obeys the same laws as perception in real space.

5. Since perception in real space depends on the characteristics of the perceiver (his personality), perception in Rorschach space is also dependent on personality.

Stated more generally, the hypothesis which underlies the Rorschach experiment is that the perception of inkblots parallels perception in the everyday world and that the unstructured character of the inkblots themselves permits us to observe those features of the perceptual process which are due to the observer's own habitual modes and ingrained patterns of subjective organization. The Rorschach technique reveals the subject's own way of looking at the world, only more so! For what he sees is not imposed from without—as is largely the case in everyday perception—but projected from within. The laws of color, form, and size constancy which modify and formalize the sensory data do not apply, at least not to the same extent, to the "amorphous" stimuli provided by the Rorschach cards. It would follow, then, that the character of the Rorschach responses is, to the greatest possible extent (short of free association or hallucination), a reflection of the subjective propensities, qualities, and needs of the observer.[1]

Thus, perceiving the inkblots as a whole is not only a reflection of the tendency to see wholes in everyday life but an indication of an integrative or wholistic approach to life situations, whereas seeing details in the blots is expressive of an analytic approach to life. So at least we are told! In similar fashion, it is maintained that perceiving definite contours in the amorphous stimuli of the Rorschach plates is related to intellectual control, whereas the capacity to integrate color and contour into a single response is reputedly indicative of emotional control. A whole series—one might indeed say "system" —of such hypotheses has been forwarded by Rorschach adherents, and although their merely hypothetical character is not customarily advertised to the layman, it would probably be admitted under

---

[1] To the ordinary Rorschach adherent the blots themselves are a kind of Kantian *Ding-an-sich* which is transmuted into "experience" only through the agency of "forms" resident within the perceiving subject.

questioning by even the most sanguine "Rorschacher." When, however, we turn to the attempted experimental verification of these hypotheses, we are greeted with strenuous objection if we dare to isolate,
for purposes of experimental testing, one hypothesis from the system.
The interpretation of the responses must, it is said, take into consideration the entire complex of hypotheses now employed, for it is only as
an imbrication or patterning of evidence that the interpretation is
meaningful, as the individual tested is not the sum, but the product or
interaction of his traits. The various aspects of the interpretation, like
the various facets of a personality, can be distinguished but they cannot be separated without doing violence to the original unity of the
object studied. It follows that in the attempt to validate these methods
of interpretation, the integrity of the system must not be disrupted.

Although this "organismic" approach may strike many experimentalists as evasive, if not "mystical," and although, as we shall see later, it is
indefensible to insist so strongly on a "wholistic" approach as to preclude any analysis of elements, it should nevertheless be possible to set
up an experimental situation in which the various interpretive indicators may be tested together and the validity of the system of hypotheses
examined systematically rather than atomistically. If the adherent
of the Rorschach method is unwilling to submit to the discipline
of experimental validation even on these terms, he implicitly confesses
that the method is scientifically sterile, whatever its alleged intuitive
value may be.

*Experimenter and Subject.* The ideal experimenter should have a
sound background in experimental psychology—especially in visual
perception—and in clinical application of tests, personality theory, and
psychopathology. At present there are few individuals sufficiently
equipped in each of these areas to carry out the experimental validation in a satisfactory fashion. Perhaps this is the one reason that so little
scientific progress has been made in this area.

Recent research has demonstrated that the experimenter is an important variable in Rorschach administration. The quantity and quality of
responses elicited by the cards are affected to a measurable degree by
the individual characteristics of the administrator (Zax, Stricker, &
Weiss, 1960). Furthermore, *E*'s behavior during the test can have
a direct effect on *S*'s responses.

Gibby, Miller, and Walker (1953) compared the Rorschach protocols
obtained by different examiners from comparable groups of patients.
The variation in the frequency of the various determinants elicited by
each of the examiners was eight times greater than would be expected
by chance. Baughman (1951), after examining 633 records, found differ-

ences among 15 examiners in 12 out of a total of 22 scoring categories which were significant at the .001 level of confidence. Similar results were reported by Meyer and Partipilo (1961). In a study not immediately addressed to the problem of examiner differences (Phares, Stewart, & Foster, 1960), the variation between examiners in the total number of responses that they elicited from their S's was statistically significant. Although the major interest of this study was to examine the effect of variations in instructions on test performance, it serves to highlight the fact that examiner differences can confound an experimental situation, making interpretation of results equivocal.

The kind of subtle or direct reinforcement that E may give to S's responses, by nodding or by verbally suggesting approval, has been shown to influence S's behavior in the interview, as well as in test situations. A subsequent section will deal with these matters in greater detail, when the administration of the task is discussed.

The S should come to the testing situation of his own free will, should know the general use that will be made of the results, and should be willing to undertake the task. When tests are taken under external coercion or other types of duress or exceptional circumstances, the results are likely to be unrepresentative and invalid. (Needless to say, a good many testing situations, both clinical and experimental, do not satisfy these criteria.)

The S parameters can be analyzed in order to determine what variables besides those we call "personality" contribute to the Rorschach response. In general, the behavior of an individual in response to a given stimulus can be grossly classified as determined by (a) biological factors; (b) sociocultural factors; (c) chance or erratic factors; and/or (d) personality factors. Although (a) and (b) may yield highly consistent and characteristic responses for a given individual, if these responses can be predicted from a knowledge of his membership in some sociocultural and/or biological subgroup, they are not useful as personality measures. (Chapter 2 contains a more complete discussion of the concept of personality.) To give some specific examples, S's verbal fluency, intelligence, and particularly education affect the quality and style of his responses. Such variables can be measured independently of personality. Before Rorschach productivity and content are given interpretive significance, the influences of these variables should be considered. An effective instrument for personality measurement should not correlate highly with variables which are not specific to personality (one of the attributes of construct validity); the nature and extent of correlations between test scores and those S variables which are not immediately relevant to the test should be made explicit in a systematic fashion.

Lesser (1959) dealt with this problem in considering sociocultural factors in cross-validational studies. He regarded *population differences* as an important contributor to discrepancies between the results of different groups. The measuring instrument is not always at fault in failures of cross-validation. To explore this problem he designed a study which permitted population differences to emerge, and which allowed for prediction of the nature and the direction of these differences. His variable was anxiety arousal in the expression of aggression: "The hypothesis tested is that, under conditions of high anxiety over the expression of aggression, the intercorrelation among various measures of aggression are significantly lower than under conditions of low anxiety over the expression of aggression" (p. 61). Lesser's index of the "conditions" he explored was based on an assessment of maternal attitudes and practices supporting or prohibiting aggression. Scores from three techniques (Rosenzweig's Picture-Frustration Study, a modified version of the TAT, and a sociometric measure) were used to indicate the degree of aggression. He worked with a group of 10- to 13-year-old boys and their mothers. The intercorrelations among the aggression measures, he found, were greater for the boys with low anxiety about aggression than for the boys with high anxiety. Lesser's research highlights the importance of considering population differences (in terms of social and cultural factors) before an adequate appraisal of the validity of certain measures can be made. More specifically, we would suggest that although the frequency and quality of certain responses to projective techniques may vary from group to group, this fact, of itself, should not be interpreted to indicate the invalidity of the particular index. Variability might, in fact, attest to the *validity* of an index, depending on knowledge of the populations involved.

There has been some exploration of social-class variables as related to projective test behavior, in terms of the interaction of various social and cultural differences between *E* and *S*. Riessman and Miller (1958), in an excellent review of some of these problems, especially with regard to lower and working-class subjects, indicated that such factors as language difficulties, educational differences between *E* and *S*, cross-class rapport problems, and lack of interest and involvement, all may have serious and important influences on test responses. Such variables as the sex, age, and status of both *E* and *S*, and especially the manner in which *S* perceives *E*, seem to have decided impact on productivity and the quality of *S*'s responses. Failure to recognize these factors and their interaction may lead to spurious and artificial interpretation of results. Sarason's volume (1954) contains an excellent and detailed review of the problems and issues of *E-S* interaction, the awareness and understanding of the purpose of the test situation by $E$ and $S$, and other situational and instructional variables. The review by Zax, Stricker, and Weiss (1960) also contains material relevant to this problem.

*Apparatus and Stimulus.* The apparatus for the Rorschach experiment consists of ten cards with inkblots which provide the stimuli for eliciting responses. In the usual psychological experiment, the task of describing the apparatus and stimuli presents a complex but relatively straightforward problem, although this task is probably not as simple as we have become accustomed to believe (see discussion of the stimulus in Chapter 2). The stimuli in the Rorschach experiment are extremely complex, but this may be because we have not chosen the appropriate variables, not developed the appropriate language, nor possibly even found the techniques for measuring and describing them. We continue to be baffled by the question of the nature of the stimuli for the movement response, and we have shown fleeting concern that our Inquiry methods are not adequate and consistent indicators of "what in the blots" made $S$ say what he did.

Some methodologists have stressed the "psychodynamic" (response-response) approach to understanding the Rorschach responses, as opposed to the "psychophysical" (stimulus-response) method. The former methodology involves the exploration of relationships between Rorschach behavior and *other* responses, whereas the latter is designed to explore the correspondence between physical attributes of the Rorschach stimuli and responses to them. Try as we may, however, we cannot avoid the issue of defining the stimulus in attempting to make some sense of our interpretations. Although there are many weaknesses in the present-day Rorschach scoring system, the most important weakness becomes apparent when we ask, "what is the *stimulus* for the given response?" This, of course, is the primary question in all psychology. The *response* in contrast with the *stimulus* can either be observed directly, or can be inferred from techniques designed to "indicate" it indirectly. A good many of our efforts in psychology, as a matter of fact, are concerned with the development of techniques for measuring responses. We have not lavished as much attention on the stimulus (Gibson, 1960*a*), however.

As we shall soon see, methods for determining the nature of the stimuli in the Rorschach cards are still being developed, and many different techniques are being explored. The need for specifying the stimulus properties of the Rorschach blots becomes especially great when we realize that present-day scoring systems attribute determinants (stimulus correlates of responses) to responses by fiat, rather than by experimentally verifiable evidence. Certain conventions have grown up regarding the scoring of specific responses such as "bat" to Card I (W, F+, A, P: whole, form, animal, popular) without regard to any experimental evidence. As a matter of fact, Baughman (1954) has demonstrated that F is not a sufficient determinant for this response. Since the Rorschach technique rests upon the assumption that Ss perceive or select the various attributes of the stimuli on the basis of their "personality," it becomes most important to make certain that the alleged determinants of the response did indeed elicit it. Otherwise, the entire structure of the Rorschach interpretation system topples.

Before proceeding with the attempt to isolate the specific stimulus properties of the Rorschach blots, let us examine the relationship between the stimulus and the response with special reference to the Rorschach experiment. It must be admitted to begin with that the stimulus to which the S responds is not limited to the blot. The whole testing situation including especially the directions for responding must be included in a consideration of the stimulus. Since the directions require the subject to tell not what the stimulus blot *is*, but what it *might* be (what it reminds him of), the conceptual aspects of the response (dependent on stored memory) become an important part in the pattern of physiological, sensory, perceptual, and psychomotor responses which the stimulus evokes. But it is also clear that the conceptual component by itself (except in an hallucination) is not sufficient to elicit the response. The interaction between the physiological, sensory, perceptual, psychomotor, and conceptual responses following upon the presentation of the stimulus situation (the card plus the entire testing situation) constitutes the response. By proper manipulation of variables, any one of these five levels of response could become prominent.

Thus far, the primary elements that have been examined are the stimulus properties of the blot and the overall stimulus situation, since these are the only elements amenable to direct manipulation. Attempts have been made to manipulate the psychomotor aspects by inhibiting motor movements prior to the presentation of the Rorschach stimulus and by manipulating the physiological, autonomic level through the introduction of stress-producing loads. But the primary parameters subjected to manipulation so far have been the stimulus properties of the blot and the conceptual component which is manipulated through changes in instructions or indirect alteration of mental set. The relative importance and usefulness of these two types of manipulation will be examined in subsequent sections.

We shall first turn our attention to the general problem of the stimulus correlates in pictorial space, visual space, and in the specific situation of inkblot space. Next, we will consider the question: what aspects of the stimulus are cogent for the response? There are several ways of answering this question. First, is the phenomenological approach, in which trained subjects are requested to examine the visual stimulus and describe its properties. Second, is the experimental approach in which specific parts of the stimulus are removed and the results on the responses noted. Third, is the statistical approach which searches first for similar responses to the various cards and then tries to determine the common element in these cards which may have produced the similarity in response. Finally, we can inquire into the kinds of conceptual dimensions or symbolic values which the Rorschach cards have, to investigate the connection between the stimulus properties and the stored memories of a cultural or personal origin which they may elicit.

*Stimulus Correlates of Visual Phenomena*

1. *Pictorial Perception.* Let us for a moment imagine ourselves in Hermann Rorschach's study when he examined his first group of protocols. He is confronted with a mass of material, and has to devise some method for classifying and categorizing them. Some responses are more animated, others are static descriptions, and the notion of movement (M) perhaps comes to the fore. Some patients find difficulty in dealing with the colored stimuli, others find no trouble, and the notion of color as a category is born. And so on. Finally, the idea that the perceptual aspects of the response may be related to the personality of the patient emerges.

Rorschach probably noted that not only do the ten Rorschach cards differ from each other in their potential stimulus qualities, but each card itself is made up of a variety of stimulus areas. Furthermore, the examinee selects only those areas in which he is interested and, within the chosen area, he usually limits himself to the stimulus properties which he can utilize in his percept. The approach Rorschach followed in the classification of responses was concerned primarily with contours (F) formed by abrupt gradients; color (C); and movement (M), an elaboration by the subject of the perceived determinants. In his posthumous paper with Oberholzer he added chiaroscuro (Ch) formed by irregular and gradual gradients.

In analyzing the so-called perceptual response in the Rorschach situation, we need to determine the different levels of influence which bring about the final "percept." It is difficult enough to attempt this task in "real" perception, that is, perception of objects in space. It is all the more difficult to accomplish this analysis in pictures (pictorial space), and virtually impossible in "Rorschach space." Furthermore, as already noted in preceding chapters and especially at the end of Chapter 3, the verbal response produced by S is determined by a variety of variables—many of a nonperceptual nature. For the moment, however, we are concerned with assessing the importance of the visual stimulus. More specifically, we are concerned with *stimulus-response relationships*. As suggested several times in preceding sections, analysis of stimulus structure for its own sake has little utility, except as a methodological exercise, but if it permits predictions or interpretation and assessment of S's responses, it becomes highly useful. How shall we proceed? One approach is to examine pictorial perception—how we perceive pictures.

Pictorial perception may indeed serve as an analogue to perception in the Rorschach situation, but the scientific study of pictorial perception itself is still very undeveloped. Furthermore, in pictorial perception, except when the picture is ambiguous or unclear, the stimulus value of the picture (though perhaps not its esthetic effect) is generally the same from subject to subject. This is not the case in Rorschach perception. As Gibson has stated, the Rorschach presents pictures of low fidelity (1954, 1956).

There has been little exploration of a theoretical or practical nature of the principles of pictorial perception. Gibson (1954), in an analysis of pictorial perception, presented a series of hypotheses flowing from his general theoretical position. He noted that pictorial perception involves "obtaining experience at second hand . . ." (p. 4). In his discussion, he introduced the concept, *surrogate,* which is a "stimulus produced by another individual which is relatively specific to some object, place or event not at present affecting the sense organs of the perceiving individual" (pp. 5–6). Gibson has noted that surrogates are artificial stimuli, do not specify how S will behave in their presence, and are relatively specific "to an absent object, place, or event" (p. 6). Moreover, he stressed the fact that surrogates are specifically created by individuals to mediate a specific perception; the implication being that accidental forms like inkblots would not necessarily qualify for inclusion in his definition. Yet his analysis of surrogates and surrogate making does offer some interesting suggestions for our purposes. For example, his concept of *fidelity* can be applied to the Rorschach stimuli. Pictorial fidelity is best illustrated by Gibson's description of a faithful picture: "A faithful picture is a delimited physical surface processed in such a way that it reflects (or transmits) a sheaf of light rays to a given point which is the same as would be the sheaf of rays from the original to that point" (p. 14).

Scope and background characteristics of surrogates, of course, differ from the original stimulus in pictorial representations. We would suggest, in the case of Rorschach stimuli, that not only do scope and background features of the surrogate differ from "the real thing," but the *fidelity* of these stimuli is so low (except with respect to popular responses) as to require a series of cognitive, selective, and interpretive acts, rather than perceptual (nonmediated), on the part of S. On the other hand, Gibson's analysis of pictorial perception further suggests that the Rorschach stimuli, even though they are pictures of low fidelity, do contain many elements which predispose normal Ss to perceive depth and vista. How is this accomplished? Gibson asks how one can, in a picture, see both a flat surface and a three-dimensional scene. He proceeds to answer this question as follows:

The misunderstanding about pictures arises because it is only half of the fact to say that a picture is a two-dimensional surface. It is a surface *and it is also a peculiar sheaf of rays.* The sheaf of rays is an essential part of the total fact of a picture. The fact of physical optics (the sheaf) and the fact of physical chemistry (the processed surface) must be combined. The surface as such is flat, but the surface as the source of a sheaf of rays may be equivalent to that of the original scene, and the latter is not flat. The hypothesis to be proposed is that a picture can ordinarily be perceived in two different ways, as a surface and as a three-dimensional scene, and that this is so because the sheaf of rays ordinarily contains within it elements which are specific to a flat surface and also elements which are specific to a three-dimensional scene (pp. 16–17).

In a later report, Gibson (1960b) clarified and refined some of his earlier formulations about pictorial perception but again did not specifically discuss the Rorschach technique.[2] One of his statements about perception, however, is of particular interest to us, for it highlights the factor of set and attention, variables which are probably of crucial importance in explaining how the same "physical" stimuli can produce such markedly different responses in different Ss:

The essence of perception is selective attention to something important. The receptive system "tunes itself" by adjusting the apparatus for clear reception. The lens-retina-nerve-muscle system is not passive but active. It continually creates new stimuli for itself, searching out in an optic array the relations, ratios, grades, and invariants of pattern which specify facts of the world. The amount of potential information in the light reaching the eyes is unlimited.

As a consequence of the unlimited possibilities for informative stimulation, and of the exploring and selecting activity, two conclusions follow with regard to perception: first, it depends on stimulation; and second, it depends on the interests of the individual observer. These conclusions have appeared

---

[2] In a personal communication (1962), Gibson has suggested that the "essence of the Rorschach is multiple ambiguous stimulus meanings."

contradictory in the past, and the horns of a dilemma seemed inescapable: the perceiver can only mirror the world, or else he creates the world for himself. But this is a false issue (p. 220).

Elements in Rorschach stimuli which give the impression of depth and distance, for example, may be overlooked by some Ss, because of set, attention, or even inability to verbalize their impressions. But these elements, we suggest, do indeed exist, and are open to inspection, measurement, and description, pending further refinements in methodology for this type of analysis. Failure to respond to such objective stimulation will have to be examined further to find significant correlates, once knowledge of the nature of the stimulation has accumulated.

Although, as noted, little research effort has been expended in the direction of understanding just what goes on in pictorial perception—much less in the Rorschach—artists for years have amassed a series of rules and principles for "translating" the perception of a real scene onto a surface.[3] Recently there has been some increased research interest in pictorial perception.

In a detailed discussion of the psychophysics of pictorial perception, Hochberg (1962) presented some pertinent findings and hypotheses concerning the variables which are involved in the perception of pictorial space. He has suggested that the empiricist view, which holds that we *learn* to associate depth cues with various spatial arrangements in the real world, is untenable. Similarly, Hochberg developed the thesis that our response to outline pictures or drawings of objects is not determined by our learning to associate them (as if they were symbols) with the real objects they are supposed to represent. He reported a study by Hochberg and Brooks (1962), for example, with a 19-month-old child, who had no experience or training with respect to pictures, but was successful in recognizing objects represented by two-dimensional outline drawings and photographs. Hochberg's general notion is that the conditions which determine our seeing the edges of objects in the real world are the same as those which are involved when we see a line on a piece of paper. "In short, outline-drawings are surrogates for edges, as are silhouettes" (p. 37). The "optic arrays" in edges in the real world and in an outline drawing involving such edges are similar, and an analysis of these arrays, in terms of

---

[3] Leonardo da Vinci, in the 1480's, was one of the first to analyze the rules by which pictures could be made. "Surrogates" for a scene can be obtained, according to da Vinci, by having the observer place a sheet of glass directly in front of him. If he fixates the eye on the real scene and traces the outline of objects in the scene before him on the sheet of glass, he will obtain a "surrogate" of the real scene. Da Vinci felt that such picture-plane tracings serve as aids to the painter.

concepts suggested by various research findings, forms the basis of his discussion.

Hochberg also turned his attention to pictures of solid forms, and again suggested that pictorial qualities produce optic arrays which are similar to those presented by real objects. But primarily, Hochberg ends his discussion of pictorial perception by raising the crucial factor of selective attention—where people will look—as the all-important determinant of their response to a pictorial display. This brings us smack into the old familiar problems of set and attention faced when the Rorschach is examined.

Hochberg and Brooks (1963) have investigated some of the "rules" for compressing pictorial space so that what previously had "depth" is made to look "flatter," that is, restricted to the vicinity of the picture plane. Such "rules" are probably relevant to Rorschach stimuli, and might appropriately be applied to an examination of attributes of various cards to understand further certain "depth" or vista responses and/or "flat" and two-dimensional responses.

There is considerable attention paid to pictorial *depth* perception, whereas other aspects of pictorial perception (the impression of movement, for example) are given less attention. In a specific investigation of differences in pictorial depth perception, Hudson (1960) presented a series of line drawings and a photograph (a hunting scene and a flying bird scene) which utilized three cues of pictorial depth (object size, superimposition, and linear perspective) to eleven samples (*N* of 562). These Ss, all tested in the Union of South Africa, had various territorial origins, and ethnic and educational backgrounds. Children as well as adults were included in the sample; 315 Ss from this group were "Blacks," and the rest were "Whites." The Ss were individually asked a few simple questions about these pictures in the tongue best understood by *E* and *S*; if communication was difficult, an interpreter was used. The questions (and possible answers to them) were so constructed as to indicate whether or not the *S* perceived the contents of the picture in a flat, two-dimensional manner, or in a three-dimensional manner. The author examined his data from four points of view: "inter-sample differences in depth perception for outline drawings; inter-sample differences in depth perception for photographs; object identification as a factor in dimensional perception; intelligence and educational levels as factors affecting dimensional perception" (p. 190).

There were many significant differences among the different educational and cultural samples tested. The author interpreted his findings to suggest that cultural and educational factors are extremely influential in determining three-dimensional perceptions, and that three-dimensional perceiving can be "taught." He concluded that:

With illiterate and isolated sub-cultures in Africa, it would be fairly safe to conclude at present that 2D perception was characteristic. Educated African groups would require more detailed sampling. These general rules have equal force in the field of pictorial advertisement, safety and health propaganda, and in the illustrated press, whether political, religious, or academic. It is pointless to use the conventions of object size, superimposition, and perspective, and to structure manifest content on these cues, if the sub-culture to be exposed to them perceives pictorial material two-dimensionally. . . . The hypothesis that their dimensional perception was an artifact of test construction was rejected. Formal schooling and informal training combined to supply an exposure threshold necessary for the development of the process. Cultural isolation was effective in preventing or retarding the process, even in candidates possessing formal education of an advanced level. An intelligence threshold existed also for the process, but its development with candidates of average or higher intellectual endowment depended upon exposure to the specific experience and probably upon cultural characteristics which in Africa might have genetic perceptual determinants (pp. 207–208).

Hudson's interpretation of his findings is decidedly "cultural" and rests on a general "learning" approach (in contrast to Hochberg's approach). Yet, judging from some of his discussion, he has implied some genetic and racial differences in pictorial three-dimensional perception —an interpretation which does not seem to flow from his data and which receives little support from other research sources.

In a recent communication relevant to our discussion, but again not necessarily oriented to Rorschach space, Hochberg (1961) elaborated on the distinction between the visual world and the visual field, following the general suggestions proposed by Gibson (1952) in a rebuttal to a paper by Boring (1952). Since, we have already described these terms in Chapter 2, we will simply note here that the visual field refers to the perception of space with little or no depth; the constancies more or less do not hold; railroad tracks converge; distant objects seem smaller, rather than farther away, and the visual scene shifts with changes in the observer's position. The visual world, on the other hand, is the world of constancies, of parallel railroad tracks which recede into the distance, of depth, distance, and scope; it is comprised of stable objects which do not shift and become distorted with the observer's positional changes. In short, the visual world is in correspondence with physical reality, and it is the world in which we move about, encounter objects, and make continual judgments of size, distance, and shape. Why can we make shifts from the visual world to the visual field under the same conditions of stimulation (e. g., all of us *do* see railroad tracks converge in the distance)? What is visual field perception?

As in the case of Hudson's interpretation of his data (see above) which suggested that the inability of many of his Ss to respond to pictorial depth cues came about as a result of cultural and learned factors (e.g., lack of training and familiarity with pictorial presenta-tion), so, in the case of seeing the visual field, we can do so because of factors of training, too—we have an "attitude" which we have all been trained to adopt. Gibson, in connection with this line of reasoning, has noted, "The visual field . . . is simply the pictorial mode of visual perception, and it depends . . . not on conditions of stimulation but on conditions of attitude. The visual field is a product of the chronic habit of civilized men of seeing the world as a picture. In the case of the railroad tracks, it is what the scene looks like when O attends not to depth but to the clues to depth" (1952, p. 149). (An interesting question emerges: can Hudson's Ss, untrained in pictorial perception, shift from visual world to visual field perception as readily as "civi-lized" observers?)

Visual field perception, then, would be picture-plane perception. Hochberg's discussion (1961) was designed to offer some principles and hypotheses in connection with why viewing and "seeing" in terms of the visual field approximates the retinal image (actually, according to Hochberg, Gibson believes that the visual field corresponds to lower order geometric variables in the optic array entering the eye, whereas the visual world corresponds to higher order geometric variables in this array). Hochberg supported Gibson's notion that the ability to see the visual field (as we would in viewing a frontal picture-plane projec-tion) is due to civilized man's attitude toward, and habituation with pictorial perception. But Hochberg suggested that *all* of us have the picture-plane attitude (seeing of the visual field) "indicated to us in daily usage" (p. 8). He has described what he has called a manual-visual field—the manual work-surface:

As the hand moves across the optic array, the same-sized thumb, the same-sized palm, the same-sized cigarette at essentially the same distance from the eye, occlude different parts of the world, and in so doing *traces out the visual field over and over again.* . . . We do not have to be told that a 4 foot wide railroad track is 24 thumbs wide at 30° below the horizon, and only one thumb wide at 2° below the horizon: we have seen this to be the case innumerable times. And this, I suggest, is *the visual field as it exists in the world of normal behavior,* for all but the artist, photographer and struc-turalist psychologist: the potentially-present work-surface with its occlusion relationships which, since they are centered near the eye, *resemble* the size and shape relationships within the retinal image and optic array . . . (p. 9).

Hochberg has further suggested that the "cues" for depth perception which artists have utilized through the ages (e.g., Leonardo da Vinci) are simply rules and procedures for projecting the world onto a two-dimensional, pictorial plane, rather than the psychological cues for the perception of depth in the real world around us, as we have all been taught. (This would suggest, it might be noted, that Hudson's study—see earlier—investigates the response to *picture-plane* depth cues, rather than depth perception *per se*. Obviously, Hudson's Ss hunt, fish, locomote, and generally get about without too much personal injury in their real worlds!)

Although Hochberg did not extend his reasoning to the Rorschach, we might add that the picture-plane (visual field) attitude may be just the perceptual attitude we bring to Rorschach stimuli—the perceptual shift from visual world to visual field perception. As we view the two-dimensional frontal plane of the blots, we interpret (rather than perceive) the tracks which converge and the figures which obscure or are larger than other figures, as indications of distance and depth. That is, we may have learned to shift back to a visual world attitude (we ask ourselves, what could these two-dimensional attributes mean or represent, in the real visual world), the kind of shift in interpretation which Hudson's subjects obviously did not make. Hudson's subjects, rather than failing to perceive pictorial three-dimensional space, may, in fact, have actually responded to pictorial depth cues (visual field attitude), displaying an attitude, according to Hochberg, which would actually prevent them from seeing depth. Such Ss are viewing the 2-dimensional picture-plane *qua* picture, rather than assuming an interpretive, representational, cognitive intent, as we all are accustomed to do, and they may have precisely a *pictorial* rather than an *interpretive* attitude to the stimuli presented to them.

Another approach to two-dimensional perception, this time a developmental one, was described by Nelson and Bartley (1962) who based their research on the known finding that with age, there is a differential ability to copy a triangle, circle, square, etc. By asking Ss of various ages which ones, among several carefully constructed comparison "targets," looked most like the standard, the authors were able to determine whether or not contour (edge, form—caused by abrupt gradients) or shape (area contained within a contour) or a combination of both, was influential in how S perceived the standard. In one of their procedures, the authors used a penned diamond (similar to the one used in the Stanford-Binet test) and five comparison targets, each stressing, or consisting entirely of one or another or both, of shape or contour properties (for example, a black wire outline identical to the penned outline was used to stress the contour aspects of the diamond).

The authors found that, in general, shape rather than contour was the more significant cue at the earliest ages (Ss ranged from ages three to eleven) while contour determinants increased in significance with age. Both shape and contour seemed to be significant at older ages, however.

A similar experimental procedure was used in another section of this study, but this time Ss were also asked to trace the figures. Squares and circles, as well as diamonds were used for the standard and target figures (Ss were four- and nine-year-olds). In this part of the study also, responses to area (shape) were more numerous than to contour at the youngest age levels.

That edges become "salient" with age is a feature of the general findings which—although the authors were not necessarily concerned with the implications of their findings for the Rorschach—do, indeed, interest us. For Rorschach plates themselves contain, among other attributes, shapes and contours; and if the perception of shape or contour attributes is a prerequisite before a reasonable "interpretation" is arrived at, the importance of age in such perception becomes quite clear.

The studies described in this section add to a growing body of knowledge of plane (two-dimensional) pictorial perception, but we still do not have full definitive answers to our basic questions concerning Rorschach space.

In the Rorschach situation, the final percept emerges either as a dynamic or a static figure, with or without a characteristic structure such as a two-dimensional or three-dimensional aspect or perspective containing scenes or objects, and with definite surface qualities such as colored and fleecy. What converts the basic stimuli of the blot into lines, contour, shapes, etc., and again into objects possessing the above mentioned qualities? This is still a moot question. Is pictorial perception mediated by the same stimulus correlates as "real" perception? This, too, is unanswered. An additional problem plagues us. Is perception of amorphous inkblots referable to the same stimulus correlates as real perception or pictorial perception? These questions cannot be answered now, but we will continue our efforts by turning to the problem of visual perception in general.

2. *Perception in the Visual Field as a Basis for Perception in the Visual World.* Let us assume with Rorschach that visual perception with respect to his cards is essentially the same as visual perception in the natural world. What is known of the characteristics of visual perception? We perceive objects that may vary from simple lines to continuous contours, possessing shape, surface quality, solidity, distance, size, slant, color, and movement. These are the basic types of visual perception.

*Contour* applies to that aspect of the perceived visual field which divides space into parts possessing an inside and an outside, and which acts to enclose space inwardly so as to produce *shapes,* making the shaped figure emerge from the unshaped background. The stimulus correlate for the perception of an outline or a contour is presumably an abrupt change in the gradient of stimulation between adjacent retinal areas. This was demonstrated by Mach in the last century (Mach, 1914).

The abrupt change in gradient of stimulation may be studied tachistoscopically by brief intervals of exposure and by the psychophysical method of just noticeable intensity or color differences. This method provides a procedure for comparing thresholds of different Ss in contour perception. Cranston and Zubin (1949) have repeated Mach's experiment in contour formation by adapting the color wheel for this purpose. By introducing a variable arc drawn in India ink concentric with the circumference of the circular disc, the amount of arc required to produce a just noticeable contour is determined. Under these circumstances, the contour appears as an indentation in the surface rather than as a drawing on the surface. It now becomes possible to compare the perceptual sensitivity to contours in normals and abnormals as well as in various personality types. It should be noted that the perception of contours can arise from at least three different sources: (*a*) abrupt changes in intensity; (*b*) abrupt changes in color; or (*c*) mixtures of the previous two (which might be called abrupt changes in saturation). It is possible that sensitivity to these three different types of contour may reflect personality differences.

With the Rorschach blots, abrupt changes of retinal stimulation are probably most often produced by abrupt gradients in brightness in the blot. These abrupt gradients may be produced by the juxtaposition of black and white which occurs in the margin of the cards, or inside of the blot when white spaces border the black, or by a sudden decrease in the intensity gradient within the black area, that is, by what are seen as sudden changes from darker grays to lighter (or brighter) grays. Another possible source of gradient formation arises from the juxtaposition of two different colors. The intensity gradient, of course, may apply to chromatic as well as to achromatic stimuli.

Let us now turn to the perception of *surface,* or the surface quality of objects. Our knowledge of this property of visual objects amounts to no more than the opinion that it probably depends on the sensing of the microstructure, or texture of the object. According to Metzger (1930), whenever a surface is seen, it is seen because the area in question is characterized by grains or spots, or other irregularities of intensity. Visual texture is evident in introspection and its stimulus correlate probably varies with the homogeneity of retinal stimulation.

When an area of perfectly homogeneous light stimulation is presented to the retina, as when one looks at a clear sky or certain artificial "fields," no surface is seen and the area appears at an indeterminate distance. The area is then said to possess film color instead of surface color.

What in the Rorschach blot corresponds to this graining or texture in the real surface of an object? We might suggest the visual texture of the blot probably arises from small, sudden, globular gradients in intensity which are too slight to give rise to continuous shape-producing contours. Hence, we may venture the opinion that it is the heterogeneity either in color or intensity which gives rise to surface quality in Rorschach percepts. If the stimulus area is perfectly homogeneous, perception of surface is improbable. Instead, perception of a film color is likely.

With regard to the perception of *solidity*, one of the established stimulus correlates is a difference in the visual images on the two retinas. This is technically known as parallax, that is, the fact that the two eyes get their images from slightly different positions in space. The basis for this phenomenon was laid down by Wheatstone more than a hundred years ago through the invention of the stereoscope, which enabled him to reproduce and experimentally manipulate varying degrees of artificially induced retinal disparity. Thus, the term "stereoscopic vision" is usually employed in describing the perception of solidity as a result of binocular disparities.

This binocular stimulus correlate accounts in part for the appearances of solidity, for emergence of figure from ground and for *depth*, but it cannot wholly account for it because one-eyed persons also perceive depth and distance. There must be some monocular cues for these three-dimensional properties as well as the binocular cues. These monocular cues are, however, only imperfectly identified. Some workers believe that they are secondary cues for the perception of space which have been learned in the course of experience. It is a possibility that the monocular cues for distance, depth, and solidity, when considered as stimulus correlates, will be definable in terms of gradients of retinal stimulation. A gradient is a continuous transitional change of stimulation over a retinal area and is to be contrasted with the abrupt change of stimulation between two adjacent retinal areas, which is related to contour. According to Gibson (1950), the gradient of intensity (brightness), suitably situated, seems to give the effect of solidity, whereas the gradient of texture seems to give the effect of distance. Thus, when the light and dark variation is interpreted as representing highlights and shadows, the attribute of solidity is given to the object; that is, instead of being interpreted as a two-dimensional figure, it is interpreted as three-dimensional. However, when the heterogeneity is interpreted as texture, it gives rise to the perception of surface or distance.

There are other cues for perception of *distance* such as the one described by Leonardo, that buildings of the same color appear bluer with distance, etc., and these may also have some application to Rorschach interpretation. Some of the principles of linear perspective with which artists are familiar are probably involved, too. The impression of depth, solidity, and distance can be achieved by perspective effects used on a picture plane; diminishing size of objects or people yield distance effects; and objects or figures obscuring parts of others produce similar effects.

What gives rise to the perception of *hue?* Here, it is generally accepted that wavelength is the primary measurable stimulus correlate.

What about *movement?* We must remember that we are dealing here with a completely stationary field, so that "apparent movement" phenomena which depend on some change in the stimulus field, do not apply. The stimulus for perception of movement in the inkblots is still unknown. From some preliminary work, it appears that the presence of certain types of gradual intensity gradients perceived as fuzzy outlines facilitates interpretation of movement. The actual nature of the intensity gradient required for the interpretation of movement is still unknown. Meantime, Baughman (1954) reported that the silhouette form of the Rorschach stimulus with all gradients eliminated and with strong figure-ground contrast shows the greatest potential for eliciting movement.

A recapitulation of the foregoing analysis of types of visual perception and their possible blot-correlates is presented in Table A.

Let us now examine Card I to determine the actual stimuli present in it. It will be seen that gradients in intensity (including the entire range from black to white) which are sufficiently abrupt to produce contours have already been noted as the boundaries of D's and Dd's in Beck's system of location and in those of other Rorschach analysts. The location of these contours can be seen in Part II of the *Supplement* (see footnote on p. 318 in the next chapter) by noting the boundaries of the D's and Dd's.

The abrupt gradients which are too small in extent to give rise to contours but are sufficient to give rise to surfaces or surface qualities are found in almost every part of the blot, since it is essentially an ahomogeneous blot. Hence, surface and surface qualities are likely to play an important role in the percepts arising from the blot. The only homogeneous areas are the white enclosed spaces and the white inlets at the edges of the blot. There are several gradual gradients that may give rise to depth or solidity perception—the edge of Dd24 bordering on white space Dds 30, the upper part of the wing in D8, etc. Gradual gradients from coarse to fine texture are not very apparent in this card. But there is a sprinkling of alternating coarse and fine texture which may give the impression of aerial perspective.

*Table A. Visual Modes and their Possible Stimulus Correlates*

| *Phenomenological Mode* | *Correlate* |
| --- | --- |
| Contour enclosing shape | An abrupt gradient with a lateral continuity |
| Surface and surface properties | Several abrupt gradients in close juxtaposition so that they are not visually separable (?) |
| Solidity or depth | Gradual gradient with a lateral continuity |
| Distance | Abrupt gradient in transition (discontinuous) to gradual gradient |
| Film color—without surface quality | Homogeneous area with regard to intensity (achromatic or chromatic) |
| Movement | ? |
| Hue | Colored areas (reflecting specific wave lengths of light) |

Let us take Card II. Here again the abrupt gradients are already noted in the boundaries of the D's and Dd's. Ahomogeneous areas of the type producing surface characteristics are evident in D1, D4, etc. Homogeneous areas are found in the white enclosed spaces, parts of Dd26, etc.; gradual fine gradients in the sides of D1; and gradual gradients from coarse to fine texture in D4. Color and intensity gradients appear in D2 and D3, and a combination of these as well in D2.

These are the blot properties and some of the more likely interpretations to which they may give rise. But subjects differ in their attentiveness to the different aspects of the blot. Thus, one subject may ignore completely the color in a given area and pay attention only to the contours which the gradient in color produces. Another person may ignore contour-producing abrupt gradients and limit himself to the color only. Another will react to gradual gradients as though they were abrupt and vice versa. It would be well to study the stimulus characteristics of each subdivision of the blot so as to determine their values, but this is a Herculean task which will have to wait. Meantime, it might be well to utilize these seven types of properties (contour, surface, solidity, distance or depth, movement, film color, hue) in evaluating responses and to judge each response according to the degree of importance placed on each of these seven characteristics. Scales for this procedure are presented in Chapter 6.

Even if we knew in general the stimulus correlates of contour perception or of surface perception, we would still have to determine for each response the particular combination of stimulus correlates which gave rise to it. Indeed, as Dewey has emphasized (see Boring [1952, p. 144]), one of our chief problems is the discovery of the stimulus. For the effective stimulus is not an object (portion of an inkblot, in our case), but a *property* of the stimulus object. It is some crucial property of the inkblot and probably of some of the elements in the stimulating situation (including stimulation within the organism). The only way of determining these stimulus correlates is to alter the stimulus properties in some way and note the effect on the response. If the response remains invariant, despite the alteration of the stimulus property, it may be concluded that the stimulus property in question was not a determinant of the response.

How to find the invariant properties of the inkblot and of the general stimulating situation necessary for the response is indeed the basic problem in scoring and evaluating Rorschach responses. It is such a formidable question that it has served to deter experimental psychologists from examining this technique. The present practice of some Rorschach workers of attributing a given determinant—say, color—to a response simply because it happened to be present in the stimulus area in which the response was located, is a type of categorization which hardly merits scientific interest.

For the purpose of bringing the analysis of Rorschach responses into some degree of harmony with the accepted terminology of experimental psychology, it would be desirable to speak of the following six levels of analysis.

1. *Location:* The stimulus area of the response or the primary location in the inkblot in which the response was perceived.

The location may be the entire card, large prominent details of the card or small details. The topography of the Rorschach cards has been mapped by many Rorschach workers; the system of locations developed by Beck (1949) has been adapted for the purpose of this book, and will be found in the *Supplement*, Part II. The first category, then, that of the location of the response, can be looked up in a chart.

2. *Stimulus properties:* The stimulus properties of the selected location.

These are the objective attributes of the stimulus area which the subject may utilize in the formation of his response. They are: (*a*) color; (*b*) intensity; and (*c*) heterogeneity (or variations in brightness and/or intensity). Color as a stimulus is so well known that it need not be discussed further except to point out that it includes the entire range of chromatic and achromatic stimuli and gray. Intensity (brightness) refers to the luminous flux reflected from a given area (amount of white). Heterogeneity refers to the presence or absence of variations in color and/or intensity. These variations (or gradients) in color and intensity can be abrupt, irregular, or gradual. Since each of these variables gives rise to differentiated visual phenomena, it is important to bear them in mind in the analysis of the response.

The second category—stimulus properties—is relatively independent of the observer, and once a catalogue is made of these stimulus properties for each area, this category would present little or no difficulty in the scoring. It would represent the characteristics of the area to which the subject is attracted in making his response.

3. *Objective determinants of percept:* The stimulus correlates of the response.

Not all the stimulus properties of the selected location are perceived or reacted to by the subject. From the final response, an inference can often be made regarding the subject's utilization of stimulus properties such as color or intensity gradients. Sometimes the Inquiry which follows the administration gives information as to whether a given stimulus property was utilized or whether it was completely overlooked or ignored.

This third category, that of the selected properties—those to which the subject chose to respond—presents a greater difficulty for analysis, since the selected properties have to be inferred from the response given.

4. *Phenomenal determinants:* Phenomenal interpretation of the stimulus properties that served as stimulus correlates of the response.

The phenomenal interpretation of the objective stimulus correlates refers to the way the subject interprets the stimulus properties to which he reacts. Thus, the brightness gradients, regardless of their "real" nature, may be perceived as changing abruptly and thus give rise to the percept of a contour, or the same gradients may be interpreted by others as gradual and give rise to depth or solidity, or they may give rise to the percept of a surface.

The fourth category, that of the phenomenal determinants, includes such factors as contours, hue, and shading effects, and these, although relatively objective, are probably not as invariant in perception as the stimuli themselves.

The distinction between stimulus correlates or objective determinants of the percept and the phenomenal interpretations of these determinants may be viewed statistically as based on the degree of agreement of competent observers. Thus the majority of observers will agree when questioned as to whether a certain stimulus area has color, and intensity gradients. It is true that some observers may overlook these stimuli, but they can readily be made to acknowledge their presence. These factors may then be regarded as the basic framework upon which the response is built. Or, independent of statistical considerations, they may be regarded as more objective in the sense that they may be detected by purely mechanical means, and do not necessarily depend on the testimony of observers. These stimuli show less variation from observer to observer than some of the other categories to be discussed. The fourth category of phenomenal determinants is subject to much more variation from subject to subject. Thus some may interpret the gradients as changing abruptly (contours) and others, as changing gradually (distance).

5. *Characteristics of the perceived object:* The phenomenal characteristics of the perceived object.

The perception of color and intensity gradients may be elaborated into such phenomenal percepts as objects possessing hue, surface qualities, shape, solidity, distance, movement, size, and luminosity.

The fifth category, that of characteristics of the perceived object, includes such factors as perception of varying degrees of movement, structure, distance, and surface appearance. These are not as palpable as the first category of stimuli, and they are designated as elaborations because they indicate the manner in which the determinants are integrated into the completed percept. There is no one-to-one correspondence between the two categories. Thus, heterogeneity, which is usually the basis for the interpretation of dimensional structure (abrupt or irregular gradients), may also serve as the basis for the interpretation of movement and of surface appearance.

6. *Formal content:* The recognition of the genus or species of the perceived object (content of percept).

This level describes the type of object perceived and may vary from human, animal, plant, object to a variety of other types of possible perceived objects.

Utilizing these six levels of analysis, the response, "Two clowns playing patty cakes" to Card II, may be described as follows.

1. *Location of stimulus area:* The entire card, with but little exclusion. The black, red, and shaded portion are all included in the figure, and the white margin serves as a background.

2. *Stimulus properties:* Color (red), gradual and abrupt gradients of intensity, black, white, homogeneous areas of white and of black.

3. *Objective determinants of percept:* Red (area in which the face is seen); gradients of brightness producing contours which enclose the figures and juxtaposition of black and white to form contours, and variation in brightness producing shading effects which may give rise to interpretation of "clothes."

4. *Phenomenal determinants:* Contours of figures, hue of face, and shading of clothing.

5. *Characteristics of perceived object:* Shapes of figures, movement, solid three dimensional figures, surface texture of clothing.

6. *Formal content:* Human figures in motion.

These six levels of analysis form the framework for the scales for evaluating Rorschach responses which are presented in Chapters 6 and 7.

It should be noted that all that is usually obtained from the subject is his final response. Information regarding the manner of elaborating determinants, the determinants themselves, or the stimulus correlates of these determinants is obtained only by inference or by inquiry. That is why the scientific evaluation of Rorschach responses is so difficult—and why it requires a far more searching inquiry than that usually required in administering the test for clinical purposes.

Objective, detailed analyses of the structure of inkblots may lead to the establishment of norms and expectations of phenomenological experience, as expressed in verbal responses, as well as a knowledge of what constitutes significant deviations from these expectations. If, under standardized instructions, most Ss should be able to "perceive" the blots in accordance with the structure of the stimulus, deviant individuals can be recognized. However, deviations from expected patterns may be a question of such S variables as set, attention, verbal and intellectual factors, cultural background, or perhaps even organic, perceptual, or sensory deficiency, as well as personality. Only experimental manipulation can determine which are the crucial factors and how they interact.

It is quite easy to understand why the stimulus in the Rorschach has been neglected. Even in the perception of the real world and its objects, the identity of the stimulus correlates which lead to the perception of the determinants (contour, hue, and shading) or to the interpretation categories of objects with surface quality, solidity, distance, movement, etc., are only vaguely identified. The factors producing these perceptions in viewing a two-dimensional picture are even less known, although artists have devoted much time and energy to the question. As far as the amorphous inkblots of the Rorschach are concerned, little progress has been made in the direction of isolating the stimulus correlates of determinants and their elaborations.

*Isolating the Stimuli in the Rorschach Cards.* It is a well-known fact that the Rorschach cards differ from each other not only in their stimulus properties but each card represents a heterogeneous collection of stimulus properties. As a result, the frequency with which the various cards elicit responses and the frequency with which given locales elicit specific types of responses show a good deal of variability from card to card and from locale to locale. The determination of the pulling power ("card-pull") of each locale with regard to the different types of responses that it can elicit, corresponds to the determination of the difficulty of items in psychometric analysis—*viz.,* the relative frequency with which a specific response is given.

To determine potential card-pull, a phenomenological analysis of the cards might be undertaken, since this kind of analysis can be done without utilizing the usual approach of dealing with Rorschach protocols, but can be done by an examination of the cards themselves.

1. *Phenomenological Analysis.* One technique for analyzing the stimulus components of the cards without recourse to the Rorschach protocol involves, following Katz (1935), the application of a reduction screen which exposes, say, only a square millimeter of area at a time. In this way the entire area of a given card could be studied for its stimulus properties. In making such a study, it would be well to have sophisticated observers who would not allow themselves to perceive objects, but would devote themselves to the bare stimulus values of the card.

What are the categories that might emerge from such an analysis? That is, what questions about the properties of the cards are likely to give rise to uniform answers? Generally, the following questions would give rise to more or less uniform answers. What is the color of the given area (hues, ranging through the entire color series and including white, the grays, and blacks)? Are there any variations in shading or intensity in the given area (the entire range from the perfect homogeneity of intensity in the white space to the variations observed in the grays and some of the colored portions)? Are there any contours in the observed area (lines which separate two adjacent areas)? The last question is not likely to give rise to complete unanimity since some contours may be missed by some persons but perceived by others. Perhaps the same lack of unanimity may be found in the color and intensity properties if they are not very pronounced, but the perception of contour is perhaps even more subject to variation in observers. When we come to such phenomenologically conceived questions as distance, solidity, or surface appearance in the given area, the answers would vary more widely. When we raise the question regarding the interpretation of lifelike movement in the area, we shall probably get even less unanimity. If we now go a step further and uncover the entire card and inquire whether the subject sees two waiters bowing in Card III, we shall probably get the least unanimity. In this way, we can arrange the variables into which a Rorschach response can be classified into three levels: (a) generally perceived or recognizable elements; (b) less frequently perceived elements; and (c) uniquely perceived elements.

We can tentatively define the stimuli in the Rorschach cards as consisting of the elements that appear under the reduction screen conditions to nearly everyone possessed of normal vision and that can be measured by some mechanical device in terms of: (a) the various colors present in the blots ranging from the bright hues to black, gray, and white; (b) the intensity (or brightness) depending on the amount of reflection of the luminous flux from the stimulus area; and (c) gradients in brightness and color which vary either abruptly, irregularly, or gradually. These are the stimulus correlates which give rise to the various perceptions and interpretations in the more complex levels of the response.

In addition to the basic elements which make up the stimuli, the *organization* of these elements may also serve as stimuli. For example, the symmetry of the blot may be regarded as a second-level stimulus for eliciting certain types of responses (Arnheim, 1951). Klein and Arnheim (1953) have illustrated this point of view with an extensive analysis of Card I, utilizing various gestalt principles of perceptual organization such as grouping, shape, similarity, and proximity. (Other contributions of gestalt-oriented researchers concerned with the Rorschach are discussed in Chapter 3.)

2. *Experimental Manipulation of the Stimulus Properties of the Cards.* Another method for isolating the stimulus properties of the Rorschach blots is to physically alter a given stimulus property and note what effect, if any, it has on the subsequent response. If the response remains unaltered, the stimulus property in question was not a determinant of the response. If the response is altered, the stimulus itself, or its interaction with the remaining properties, constitute the stimulus correlates of the response.

Baughman, who has done perhaps the most extensive work in this area (see Baughman [1958a] for an excellent review of the role of the stimulus in Rorschach responses), systematically altered various stimulus properties of the Rorschach blots to determine the stimulus correlates of the response (1954). Baughman's aim was to differentiate as far as possible the responses that inhere in the stimulus (occur in almost all subjects who select a given stimulus area) and those that inhere in the responder himself. Stated more specifically, he wished to differentiate the responses attributable to the stimulus cards from those whose stimulus is still unknown or whose stimulus value resides in some aspects of the responding organism rather than in the stimulus cards. Having found, for example, that "bat" is a response to Card I, how much can the stimulus be changed before the response disappears, or, what is the potential strength of each of the altered stimuli in eliciting the same response? (It will be noted that this is Klüver's method of equivalent stimuli which was used so effectively in testing the limits of tolerance for change in a given stimulus eliciting a given response in the animal laboratory.)

Baughman devised a series of modifications of the Rorschach plates so as to reveal the potency of a given part of the stimulus for evoking characteristic responses. In his first modified series, he began with the standard card and eliminated the color factor, through photographing the standard series in black and white on panchromatic film; the nuances of the shading, differences in intensity, and all the other characteristics of the blot were retained. Then in the second modified series, he removed the heterogeneity of the shading by making line drawings of the more striking contours within the blot and the periphery. The third modification consisted of blotting out the inside details by making the entire inside of the blot black, but leaving the islands of pure white that occur—yielding a silhouette effect. The final modification consisted simply of the periphery or outline of the blot.

Baughman's subjects were 100 veterans, hospitalized for neuroses and character disorders. Each of the five series of blots was given to a randomly selected group of 20 patients, equated with the other groups for IQ and educational level. Beck's scoring system was employed.

Although it is difficult to draw a correspondence between the altered form of the card and the Rorschach determinant which is most prominently present or absent, some of the findings were: the cards in which only the periphery was present tended to accentuate whole responses and form responses; the cards with the inside details tended to accentuate detail responses and perhaps organization (Beck's Z); the silhouette cards tended to accentuate form responses and perhaps to suppress white space responses. When he compared the protocols of the various groups, Baughman found a remarkable constancy in categories theoretically influenced by certain of the varied stimulus properties. The importance of color and shading as determinants was strongly challenged. Virtually all of the significant differences were attributable to differences in stimuli which were simply objectively necessary to the category. For example, D responses were found uniformly in all the variant stimulus cards, but dropped in the series in which the stimulus for D had been eliminated. This finding indicates that color and shading are not important for the D response, even though they are often regarded as such.

Surprisingly, the M response occurred with the significantly highest frequency in the silhouette version, indicating that it, too, is independent of color and shading. Some of the categories showing but slight differences from series to series were: number of responses; number of whole and popular responses; animal and animal movement responses; total time; form level; diversity of content; and percentage of responses to Cards VIII, IX, and X. Baughman aptly summarized these findings: "The data are clear and impressive in their demonstration that the major dimensions of perceptual behavior in the Rorschach task remain remarkably constant even though marked alterations are made in the stimulus attributes"(1954, p. 161).

On the basis of his findings, Baughman questioned the validity of the interpretive significance of many of the stimulus attributes (determinants); he stressed geometrical form and figure-ground dimensions (productivity increased as a positive function of figure-ground articulation and structure of the stimulus).

In subsequent research (e.g., 1959b), Baughman continued his investigations along the same lines, confirming his conclusions that in addition to variables such as situational conditions, set, subjective definitions, and examiner influences (his personality, etc.), stimulus structure also accounts for changes in response. As a matter of fact, most responses seem "form determined," with color and shading less influential than might be suspected. One major conclusion was that many responses are completely dependent on the attributes of the particular stimulus, and that this is quite independent of what S says or does not say during the Inquiry.

The effect of stimulus characteristics on productivity was explored in a study by Grayson (1956). He administered ten sets of Rorschach cards to a group of nurses. These sets were: the original series, three achromatic sets of varying blackness-intensities, and six monochromatic sets, each of varying colors. Productivity, he found, was not related to color, shading, or card preference, but was influenced by card design and design-color interaction.

In a study concerned specifically with Cards IV and VI and their modifications, Exner (1961) found no significant differences in the scores (location, determinants, content, number of responses) although average reaction time for first responses was significantly longer to the standard series when the standard cards and a blue monochromatic version were compared, using two matched groups of Ss. The author concluded, "This research seems to support earlier findings that shading and form, rather than achromatic color, are more influential in precipitating the popular 'skin' responses to these cards" (p. 39).

An entirely different approach to an analysis of the Rorschach situation, but one which also involves experimental manipulation of stimulus variables, is found in the work of investigators with a microgenetic orientation. Chapter 3 has summarized in some detail the nature of this approach as well as the work of Kragh (1960a, 1960b, 1960c), who utilized TAT-type of stimuli. Application of microgenetic principles to the projective field generally involves the exposure of projective stimuli tachistoscopically, at increasingly greater exposure durations; this procedure presumably provides an opportunity to study perceptual and cognitive processes from early "preconscious" and primitive forms to the fullblown perceptual response that is accompanied by conscious recognition and cognitive content. This approach does not stress stimulus structure so much as it does the perceptual response to a projective stimulus, attempting to analyze its various stages *through time* in order to understand the nature of the response as well as its personal significance. Some studies utilizing this approach have an "ontogenetic" orientation, that is, the response, in going through its various temporal phases, recaptures earlier organizations and cognitive and emotional aspects of S. Some of the proponents of this approach, therefore, get caught in a web of essentially nonverifiable, often vague and loose psychoanalytic assumptions about early traumas and experiences, which are "corroborated" by case-history and dream material, as well as the therapist's insights.

Studies that utilized variations in Rorschach stimulus duration were reported by Stein (1949) and more recently by Horiuchi (1961). In neither of these studies is there a stress on the "ontogenetic" aspects of perception just described. Horiuchi worked with 240 Ss (80 normals, 80 schizophrenics, and 80 neurotics, with sex evenly distributed in each group) to whom she exposed Cards III and VI. Ss were allocated to one of the following experimental conditions (tachistoscopic exposure time): 10 millisec., 30 millisec., 1 sec., and free untimed exposure. Not only were there marked differences in responses (the author was specifically interested in movement and shading responses) at various exposure levels, but consistent differences appeared among the groups with whom she worked.

Eckhardt (1955) expanded and tested some of the thinking of Klein and Arnheim (1953) in an experimental situation designed to test their notion that perception of movement occurs to stimulus variables in the inkblots themselves, that is, perceptual gradients. According to Klein and Arnheim, the stimuli conducive to movement are figures in the blots which are pointed and/or at an oblique angle to the perceived framework: ". . . gradients of size, which lead from a broad base to a narrow peak are frequent in the Rorschach and produce outward-bound movement" (p. 68). Card position, therefore, would be important in whether or not movement responses are produced.

Accordingly, Eckhardt drew geometrical figures, some with axes at an angle to the paper they were on, others not. His hypothesis that movement responses would be made to shape gradients, rather than to regular shapes, was in general confirmed. He found that vista responses also were elicited by shape gradients. In addition, movement responses were produced by angular figures and *asymmetry* whereas vista was produced by angularity and *symmetry*. On the basis of his findings, the author felt that vista and movement responses could be placed on an equal footing with form and color responses, and that the Rorschach may be viewed as a test of perception.

We might add, however, that even if a stimulus elicits or "favors" certain types of responses, the individual differences in response, as well as what S attends to, and the fact that S is asked to assign *cognitive* content to what he sees (rather than describe shapes, forms, and the quality of what he is seeing) places the Rorschach in another context. For the instructions are such as to capture past experience, vocabulary, cultural and intellectual factors *rather than* strictly perceptual factors. S's interpretations and cognitive responses must certainly in part, however, reflect the stimulation, or that aspect of stimulation to which he is attending.

3. *Statistical Analysis of Stimulus Attributes.* Another way of determining the stimulus properties of a locale is to examine all the locales that give rise to a high frequency of identical or similar responses, or responses having a common element. The property or properties which form the common denominator for all of these locales could then be regarded as the stimulus correlate for the given response. This is essentially the method used by Kendall (1962). His research procedure involved three general hypotheses:

(a) . . . if highly similar responses are elicited by two ambiguous inkblots, then these inkblots probably share some common stimulus dimensions;  (b) inkblots which are grouped according to similarity in the responses they elicit will also be highly similar in physical dimensions; and (c) if personality variables influence preferences to respond to certain variables in an ambiguous stimulus array, then the same inkblot will elicit similar responses from subjects having similar personalities, and different responses from subjects having different personalities" (pp. 6–7).

We might add that his study was not designed to shed light (nor does it) on the last of these hypotheses. He worked with 170 undergraduates, divided into three groups of 28, 26, and 116 Ss. The first two groups were shown the Rorschach cards presented in the usual order; Ss in the third group were presented with Rorschach and Behn-Rorschach slides, shown in a specified random order.

Ss were given a check list of the following 14 response categories: person(s) doing something; fur; clouds, smoke; animal(s) doing something; explosion, blood, paint; person(s) just there; face; part of body, insides; flowers; animal(s) just there; X-ray, chart, map, etc.; something squashed; physical object; nothing at all. The responses in this list could be given reasonably to many of the cards. The subject's task was to look at the blots and check one response category which he felt best described what he saw. The percentage of individuals giving each of the 14 responses to each of the cards was computed and an index of similarity was obtained utilizing Rosner's index (1956).

Indices of similarity were obtained for all the 45 pairs of cards and the matrix of indices was analyzed into clusters by a method suggested by McQuitty (1957), which is similar to a method described earlier by Zubin (1938). The same type of analysis was made for each of the three groups and the reliability of the indices was obtained by getting the agreement for the same card between two groups. These reliabilities were high, averaging around .88.

The cluster analysis of the matrix of similarity indices showed a first cluster consisting of Cards II, III, and VII, a second cluster consisting of I and V, a third cluster of IV and VI, and a fourth cluster of VIII, IX, and X.

A similar analysis of results for the third sample yielded five clusters —four were related to those obtained with the earlier analysis, and one contained two cards from the Behn-Rorschach series. Finally, the author proceeded with what he regarded as the "most difficult part of the study"—the construction of hypotheses concerning the stimulus determinants in each cluster by noting the common denominators in the stimulus properties of the cards in each cluster. His analysis of the various clusters can be illustrated by his hypotheses concerning Cluster A (third group of 116 Ss—Behn-Rorschach Cards I and II):

Cluster A elicited predominantly animal movement responses . . . these cards are relatively unambiguous, showing appreciable correlations only with Cluster C. In line with Eckhardt's (1955) results with geometric forms, it seems that angularity of the figure, and asymmetry of orientation of half of the blot are the stimulus determinants of movement responses. The stimulus determinant for the animal content is very likely the relative proportions of the area of the two major parts of the figure in each half of the blots (p. 10).

The author proceeded to indicate how these hunches derived from the statistical analysis could possibly be verified by experimental manipulation of the stimulus properties. It would seem that Kendall is suggesting, on the basis of Eckhardt's findings (see previous discussion) as well as his own analysis, that the preponderance of animal movement responses in this cluster can be accounted for by: (a) movement—the angularity of the figures as well as the fact that the figures in each half of the blot have axes at an angle to the paper they are on; and (b) animal content—the relative distribution of area of each half of the blot (apparently, a smaller top portion and a larger bottom portion). His "explanations" of animal movement responses in terms of two separate attributes—animal content and movement—may not be entirely warranted. This separation itself can be tested by experimental procedures utilizing modified stimuli. (Is it possible to elicit movement alone, or animal content alone by various stimulus manipulations?) Moreover, the hypotheses he has suggested (relative distribution of two major areas in each half of the blot; angularity and orientation of figures) can be tested not only by modifying the blots, but in a variety of other experimental situations.

Kendall presented hypotheses for each of the other clusters, but these will not be summarized in detail. Cluster B elicited mostly human movement and some animal movement responses. The stimulus determinants for movement and for animal content have already been described (see description of Cluster A, above). The stimulus determinant for human content would be the relative proportions of area of the three major parts of the figure in each half of the blot. Experimental verification could be based on procedures which introduce variations of the relevant forms.

Cluster C elicited mostly animal responses, as well as some animal movement responses. One stimulus determinant might be the bilateral symmetry of the blot, an hypothesis which could be verified by presenting the same blots in different positions, as well as by only utilizing half of each blot.

Many responses in Cluster D had indefinite form, with all cards in this cluster eliciting responses such as "something squashed' and "physical object." The author suggested that cards in this cluster might prove "difficult for normal subjects to respond to" because normal subjects utilize form as a major determinant, and since these cards are characterized by indefinite form, normals would not be stimulated to give responses. A subcluster contained many "fur" responses. The author felt that the stimulus determinant could be shading and/or a ragged outline, and once more suggested that experimental variations could be introduced to verify this hypothesis.

Cluster E, the fifth cluster, contained a wide variety of responses, and all cards elicited flower responses, anatomy responses, as well as some "nothing at all" responses. The author offered the same interpretation as he did with respect to Cluster D—the difficulty that normal subjects might have in the light of absence of clear-cut "form" in the cards within this cluster. Once more the author suggested that introducing variations of the cards in this cluster (achromatic variants, since most of the cards in this cluster were chromatic) might be one way of verifying his hypothesis.

Kendall concluded that his findings supported the general notion that inkblots clustered in terms of similarity of distributions of response also are similar in physical (stimulus) attributes, and that these are probably "determinants" of the responses elicited, but wondered whether or not his procedure, which was designed to ferret out the stimulus determinants of responses, was worth the effort: "A simpler approach for testing the diagnostic efficacy of inkblots would be to compare the clustering of inkblots based on responses elicited by different diagnostic groups. If personality is reflected in responses to different determinants available in ambiguous stimuli, then different clustering should result for different diagnostic groups" (p. 12a). This method is, of course, not new, since it has been already tried in many studies. It is postulated on the assumption that different diagnostic groups differ in "personality." It is at least a tenable hypothesis that a variety of personalities may be found in the same diagnostic cluster and, furthermore, that these personalities may transcend diagnostic boundaries. With regard to Kendall's original method, however, his ingenious technique is worthy of further application. Whether it should be done within or across diagnostic categories is immaterial, as long as behavioral criteria are available for personality assessment.

As already noted, some of the work on "card-pull" involves an assessment of "difficulty-level" as in item analysis procedures with psychometric instruments. Meer (1955), for example, noted that the Rorschach cards vary in difficulty and that this affects reactions to, and interpretations of, the material produced by S. His research was relatively unsophisticated, however. To assess difficulty level, he used reaction times of first response, form-level of first response, and a subjective judgment of how easy or difficult it is to respond to each card—measures which may or may not be reliable, or have validity with respect to the variables in which he was interested.

In a later report, Richards (1958) pulled together previous research findings relevant to this problem and presented this material in one table consisting of rank-orders for each card on variables such as "card-pull," reaction time, number of rejections, and subjective preference. From these reports, as well as others, the general conclusion can be drawn that the cards differ widely from each other in terms of response potential—a factor often overlooked by the clinician.

*Stimulus Correlates of Symbolic or Conceptual Responses.* One of the components of the Rorschach response is the conceptual component induced by the directions to tell what the blot might represent. A direct measure of the conceptual component evoked by the stimulus situation is difficult to obtain, but some indirect methods have proved to be useful. One is Osgood's Semantic Differential, and a second depends on other types of rating scales for the type of content provided by the response, or on a content analysis of the responses.

The Semantic Differential (Osgood [1952]; Osgood, Suci, & Tannenbaum [1957]) has been used with increasing frequency to describe properties of Rorschach inkblots, particularly with respect to connotative meanings ascribed to the cards. Many clinicians have long been assigning certain "properties" to the cards, such as "femaleness" to Card VII ("mother card"); Card IV is often referred to as the "authority" or "father card." Presumably, knowledge of such properties is important because patients, it is claimed, unconsciously respond to these card qualities with deep-rooted wishes, conflicts and anxieties—reactions important for the clinician to elicit in his psychodiagnostic appraisal. Osgood's semantic scales involve pairs of antipodal words, for example, feminine-masculine or dull-exciting, and S is required to rate the "meaning" of the cards along a continuum between each of the words of such pairs.

Many Rorschach studies using the Semantic Differential technique (e.g., Rosen, 1960) have yielded findings which have supported usual clinical hunches and statements, and have suggested that each of the blots differs widely in connotative meaning. Some relevant studies are described below, but first a word of caution must be mentioned. Most of these studies fail to take account of the fact that *both* clinician and S alike are subject to the same cultural stereotypes, mass media, cultural symbols, etc.; the fact that uniformity in attributed "meaning" is found, and that this "meaning" fits in with the clinician's "hunches" should be interpreted in terms of this context. Furthermore, we have not answered the question as to whether or not the S's responses in the actual Rorschach situation are related to the meanings he ascribes to the cards in a semantic differential test, nor whether these, in turn, are indicative of unconscious personality processes.[4]

Zax, Loiselle, and Karras (1960) studied the stimulus characteristics of the inkblots as perceived by a group of schizophrenics and a control group, the latter consisting of 40 veterans hospitalized for medical purposes. The Rorschach cards were rated by the Ss on each of 21 scales of Osgood's Semantic Differential series, for example, beautiful-ugly and active-passive. The authors noted, "The connotative meaning of the blots were deduced from those scales found to be rated in a given direction consistently enough to yield significant chi-squares. On this basis it was found that Plates I and IV yield the strongest impressions as negative and potent stimuli with V being consistently seen as low in potency and suggesting activity"[5] (p. 443). Zax and Loiselle (1960) further noted that preferences and values for various Rorschach cards, as elicited by the Semantic Differential, might be a function of the *order* of the cards. (Earlier indications were that no matter *what* the order of the card, later appearing cards elicited more responses. The authors were not concerned with R, however, at this time.) In the study to investigate the hypothesis concerning order, two groups of 40 female Ss rated the Rorschach cards on each of 21 of the Semantic Differential scales. One group was presented the cards in the standard order; from the second group, 10 groups of 4 Ss were selected at random; each of these groups was presented with one of 10 possible orders,

---

[4] Studies based on the semantic differential scales (e.g., Rosen, 1960) have generally supported previous findings and clinical statements that Cards IV and VII are associated with masculinity and femininity. As a matter of fact, in her recent review, Gleser (1963) has stated, "The evidence is now quite convincing that masculinity is associated with Card IV . . ." (p. 402).

[5] Osgood has employed the use of "semantic dimensions" in the development of his scales, such as *evaluation* (very bad, bad . . . good, very good), and *potency* (very weak, weak . . . strong, very strong). Such "dimensions" have been applied to self-ratings of various types, and to different stimuli such as words (Allison, 1963) and Rorschach cards. Zax, Loiselle, and Karras have utilized "dimensions" such as these in their study.

following a Latin square design. The authors found, in general, that order of presentation *does* affect stimulus value (as determined by S's ratings), noting that on three of the cards there were statistically significant differences in the distributions of ratings on several of the scales.

Schleifer and Hire (1960) used a checklist technique in exploring certain assumptions about the "impact" of each card on S. After constructing a list of adjectival descriptions (based on S's descriptions, and including additional adjectives added by the authors), the adjectives were classified by the authors on the basis of similarity of meanings and the list was "tried" on a group of Ss. On the basis of percentages (frequency counts), adjectival "attributes" of each card were designated as "unique," "common," or "specific" characteristics. In their summary and discussion, the authors implied that such attributes are related to affective experience, that is, the authors generalized from choice of words (and all the cultural and stereotyped variables in such verbal expression) to the emotional experiences and reactions of each subject—a hazardous leap which presupposes many intervening variables. From their findings (for example, Card I elicits reactions related to punitiveness; Card III evokes feminine reactions), they concluded that many clinical formulations concerning the "significance" of each card, are correct: "It seems evident that there is differential responding to the various cards in terms of the affective experience which they initiate, and, further, that the differential responses are closely related to the types of formulations offered for the individual cards" (p. 169). Such a study, it might be noted once more, is limited by its failure to account for culturally induced stereotypes and by sampling difficulties. The case illustration at the end, of a *single* response to Card I, and its corresponding relationship to psychotherapy, illustrates *par excellence* the overgeneralized use to which the authors put their findings. What the logical relationship is between this illustration and the research summary which preceded it, is difficult to infer.

Marsh (1961) also applied a rating technique in his investigation of the "meaning" and significance of Cards IV and VII. After citing a number of studies which have related Cards IV and VII to masculinity and femininity respectively, he set out to investigate the nature of these purported relationships. He wanted to know whether these cards are categorized as "father" and "mother" cards on the basis of "card-pull" or on the basis of some personality variables and parent-child relationships. In other words, is there something in the structure of the stimuli, perhaps certain textural qualities (Klopfer, 1954), which provide parental associations by themselves in all Ss or do they elicit such associations only according to the degree of conflict the S suffers over parent-child relations?

Marsh hypothesized that certain personality measures derived from two personality instruments would be significantly related to S's ratings of Cards IV and VII as representing the father and mother respectively. Ss were 334 college students, 185 males, and 149 females, who were asked to rank all ten blots, on a scale of 1–10, as representing the mother and father concepts. He concluded,

The overall results indicate that if there are measurable parent-child conflicts these disturbances are likely to be projected onto cards IV and VII. Even though such inferences have importance, extreme caution should be exercised in making interpretations related to parents, especially in individual cases. In conclusion it appears that the unqualified designation of Rorschach cards IV and VII as the "father" and "mother" cards respectively appears to be unjustified (p. 73).

An attempt to eliminate the influence of the stimulus *per se,* and to tease out the conceptual trends in the S was undertaken by McFarland (1956). He worked with four projective situations, each differing in materials and/or method of presentation: (*a*) modified Rorschach; (*b*) modified Behn-Rorschach—one response per card [time limit and slides were used for (*a*) and (*b*)]; (*c*) Picture-Title test; and (*d*) Object Recognition test. His quantitative approach was designed to yield scores for each S which would presumably be useful as personality measures, independently of the stimulus. His two basic scores for assessing test structure were frequency of response to discrete stimuli and range of concepts contained in such responses. The Ss were 48 female V.A. employees, and the order of tests was randomized for all Ss.

For each response, the *basic percept* was determined: "The central percept *verbalized* by S which indicated the nature, meaning, order, and/or the class of object or objects seen by him" (p. 399). Each stimulus or stimulus area (such as D1 or D7, on the Rorschach) was assigned a "selection variable value" (SV) based on percentage responding, independent of content. A "percept variation value" (PV) was also determined (number of *different* concepts) for each stimulus. SV and PV values were correlated and an analysis was made of SV and PV values for each instrument. The author has suggested that knowledge of these parameters could be useful in assessing the structure of various tests, and has noted that other variables, such as number of words, level of certainty, number of modifiers a stimulus elicits, could be treated in the same way. As a matter of fact, he has utilized information derived from the analysis of his findings to offer a few notions about "ideal" tests; for example, "It would appear desirable to have the normal subject respond to a large majority of the stimuli in the 'ideal' test, but not to all" (p. 403). The author concluded,

The primary advantage in this approach lies in the fact that these dimensions lend themselves to the study of both different tests and different individuals. This approach may possibly lead to the construction of new projective tests based on *known* test parameters. The goal of this research is the reduction of the mystery in projective techniques without removing their projective characteristics (p. 404).

Attempts such as this to understand further the structure of the test stimuli are useful in classifying and isolating projective stimuli, and provide an opportunity for accumulating norms of a different sort than has traditionally been collected. Yet, we would still not know the relevance of findings to personality variables (of the sort we tend to expect projective techniques to illuminate). Validity research, especially with respect to constructs, would be a desirable extension of these research lines.

Lawton (1956) was also concerned with the parameters of the stimulus—specifically, degree of ambiguity. By means of a non-Rorschach perceptual task, he explored the hypothesis that stimulus ambiguity as well as maladjustment is an important determinant of "perceptual adequacy," and that both increased maladjustment and ambiguity would have the net effect of decreasing "perceptual adequacy." Lawton utilized black, randomly cut figures on a white background, rated by a group of psychologists on degree of structuredness, or ease with which the figures suggested a percept. Fifteen figures (five each for similar degrees of structure) were presented to 30 Ss (in a neurotic, latent schizophrenic, and hospitalized schizophrenic group) who were asked to say what the cards looked like. "Perceptual adequacy" was determined by: (a) the author's judgment of how well the percept fit the stimulus properties (form level—rated on a four-point scale); (b) structural peculiarities, such as incongruity of the parts of the percept, or fabulation; and (c) sexual content. The author concluded that his hypothesis was confirmed; greater stimulus ambiguity and greater personality maladjustment were associated with lesser "perceptual adequacy," and "stimulus characteristics are often important determinants of projective responses, and that consideration of form ambiguity is necessary to the best interpretation of projective records" (p. 355).

In this section, the stimulus in the Rorschach experiment has been considered. This has proved to be no simple task. To understand better the nature of the stimulus in the Rorschach, attention was first turned to studies concerned with pictorial perception. Although such work does have relevance to the problems before us, definitive answers to questions concerning Rorschach space were not provided. Next, visual perception in the natural world was considered. Although it is still a moot question as to whether or not perception in the Rorschach situation is the same as perception in the natural world, some basic characteristics of the perception of objects in the real world were reviewed, such as contour, surface, solidity, etc. An attempt was made to find correlates in the amorphous blots of the "phenomenological" characteristics which were isolated. This resulted in some suggestions for analysis of Rorschach responses in terms of six levels.[6]

Procedures for isolating and identifying Rorschach stimuli were reviewed which included phenomenological approaches, experimental manipulation of stimulus variables, and statistical analyses of stimulus attributes. In addition, various methods for discovering the stimulus correlates of symbolic or conceptual responses were surveyed.

Our consideration of the problems of the stimulus in the Rorschach task yields a striking conclusion: the Rorschach stimuli not only are extremely complex, but attempts to relate them, in one-to-one fashion, to responses which Ss produce when asked to interpret these stimuli, are fraught with difficulties. Other aspects of the Rorschach situation, besides those already discussed, such as E and S, and the stimulus, contribute to the response. Some of these are considered in the next sections of this chapter.

*The Task and Its Administration.* The task in the Rorschach situation is some variant, or a paraphrased version of: "Tell me what this (the inkblot) might be." Usually S is told that there are no correct or incorrect responses, and that people see different things—no two people see the same things. S is given the cards (or E attempts to hand S the cards or the cards are placed before S) one at a time, and S is encouraged to see more than one thing. He is asked to place the card on the table when he is through, this becoming the cue for the next card. E usually starts his stopwatch upon exposing the card and this is often interpreted as a cue that rapidity of response is probably important; frequently, however, S is told that "speed of response is not a factor in this test." In this procedure, E sits opposite, diagonally opposite or behind S, recording, hopefully, all of S's responses, verbalizations, in-

---

[6] The six levels of analysis, discussed previously, are: (a) location of stimulus area; (b) stimulus properties; (c) objective determinants of percept; (d) phenomenal determinants; (e) characteristics of perceived object; and (f) formal content.

terjections, and mannerisms as carefully as possible. $E$ encourages $S$ to feel as free and as spontaneous as he can. If he is too verbose, however (thresholds for different $E$s vary), he is encouraged to produce less on the next card. After the entire procedure is completed, $E$ reviews each of the responses with $S$ to determine its exact location. At this time, also, certain nonleading questions are asked in order to determine the elements in the stimulus area that underlie the response (the Inquiry). (Some psychologists recommend a procedure whereby the Inquiry is conducted immediately after the free association on each card.)

This procedure, simple enough, is replete with pitfalls for the psychometrician and experimentalist alike. It should be clear that in addition to the fact that no two $S$s respond exactly alike, no two $E$s respond or behave exactly alike either—the general point being that standardization of administration procedures is not one of the strong points of the Rorschach technique. In each of the elements in the administration of the task, there are a host of variations, preferences, and procedural habits deliberately introduced by $E$ because he has found them "workable." There are, in addition, variations and modifications in administration which arise because of exigencies of the circumstances—resulting from a kind of freedom and desire on $E$'s part to respond to and handle $S$'s needs in the situation as they arise. But, in addition, there are innumerable unplanned procedural variations of which $E$ is unaware—reflections of his own behavior, personality, and characteristic modes of response. Some of these, such as those related to $E$'s social status, ethnic background, sex, and personality have been touched on in a preceding section of this chapter. Others are less "sociological" and more individual. Whatever their sources or origins, variations in procedure, planned or unplanned, introduce variations in response— error, as it were. Only recently has there been increased attention to variables in the administration of the task as important determinants of $S$'s response.[7] Thus, position of the Rorschach in the test battery and the nature of the tests preceding it, the exact nature of the situation itself (prison, employment office, judge's chambers, executive personnel laboratory, school, clinic, research office), the manner and method of the Inquiry, $E$'s mannerisms, or reinforcing behavior, whether or not group or individual procedures are used—these all have significant effects on productivity and quality of responses. It would be expected,

---

[7] There is evidence to suggest that card order itself is an important determinant in the quality and quantity of responses produced—a variable which should be understood and carefully examined in light of its important implications for interpretation of responses.

therefore, that norms, research comparisons, generalizations, cross-validation attempts, search for confirmation of "signs," etc., based on so many diverse and unstandardized procedures, would involve many hazards.

Gross (1959), in an exploration of verbal and nonverbal reinforcement in the Rorschach situation, found that cues given by the E affected Rorschach responses. Ss were 30 psychiatric patients, randomly selected, who were given modified Rorschachs, so that only three responses per card were elicited. Whenever a human content response was given, E either said "good," nodded, or did nothing. The author reported that both reinforcement groups produced significantly more human content than the nonreinforcement group. He cautioned against interpreting Rorschach responses *in vacuo*, and suggested that test response and behavior must always be interpreted in the light of the total situation. Magnussen (1960), in a virtual replication of Gross' study, using 33 males randomly selected from a group of industrial job applicants, and employing popular responses as the dependent variable, found that both reinforcement groups (verbal and nonverbal reinforcement) produced significantly more popular responses than the control group, and that there were no significant differences between the two reinforcement groups.

Some variations in administration procedures have been deliberately introduced, for example, group methods. During and following World War II, increased stress was placed on group procedures; for reasons of economy and efficiency, large-scale methods were quickly adopted for college selection and industrial use, and a considerable number of research reports followed, based on modifications and special adaptations of large-scale methods for specific purposes. In general, group methods involve the use of a slide or opaque projector for projecting the Rorschach stimuli on a screen to groups of Ss; each stimulus has a specific duration of exposure, and Ss are given a few minutes to indicate their responses, either by writing them down, or by choosing them from a predetermined list of responses. Sometimes a checklist of determinants is used, as well as location charts, so that Ss can supply the sort of information obtained in the Inquiry. The multiple-choice technique, in which certain predetermined responses for each card are presented to S for checking, is credited largely to Harrower. Harrower and Steiner's volume (1945), as well as Harrower's review of group techniques (1950), serve as excellent introductions to group procedures. Munroe (1945, 1950) has described a group "inspection" technique, by which, using tallies and "signs," the standing of an S in a large group, in terms of adjustment criteria, can be easily detected. Williams and Kellman (1956) have reviewed the use of some of these methods in industrial settings.

Another procedure used for rapid diagnostic screening, which is a variation of standard Rorschach procedure, was introduced by O'Reilly (1956), but does not involve group methods. The author called his technique the "Objective Rorschach." He analyzed 100 neurotic and 100 psychotic records as well as those produced by a large group of normals, from which he selected four typically "neurotic" responses, four typically "psychotic" responses and four typically "normal" responses, for each card. The test is administered individually, and each S is asked to pick two (out of twelve) responses for each card which best describe the card. A numerical score is obtained for the total Rorschach, based on a score of three—for psychotic choices or rejection; two—for neurotic choices; and one—for normal choices. The author has reported a test-retest reliability coefficient of .91 (student nurses). Examples of "typical" responses for Card I are: neurotic—X-ray, silhouetted figure of a woman, a dark cloud; psychotic—triangles (white space), dancing toad; normal—bat, pelvis.

O'Reilly's single basic score differentiated new groups of normals, neurotics, and psychotics quite strikingly. The cutoffs involved few false positives and the mean scores for each group are statistically significant from each other. His norms are inadequate, however, and there is a need for a large number of additional cross-validation studies. Variables such as sex, intelligence, and socioeconomic background were not considered in the standardization procedures.

It should be noted in passing that despite their ease of administration, scoring, etc., these modifications of Rorschach procedures involve many of the same problems of test construction and psychometrics as are found in the standard procedure. Although some multiple-choice techniques may be quite reliable and objective their essential economy should not obscure the larger issue of their validity.

The *Inquiry* procedure in the Rorschach method is so intrinsic a part of traditional Rorschach orientation and interpretation, and so essential for scoring, that it is quite surprising that until fairly recently Rorschach research has not stressed this aspect of administration procedure. The lack of standardization and variability in Inquiry methods is so well known as not to merit a detailed presentation. Moreover, some clinicians are so "convinced' 'that an adequate and well-conducted Inquiry yields "valid" information as to determinants (with a parallel assumption that the determinants yield valid information about personality) that considerable stress is placed on rules for conducting an adequate Inquiry, so as to insure validity of results. Blatt, Engel, and

Mirmow (1961), for example, have thoroughly examined some of the "failures" in the Inquiry procedure with children, and have suggested not only possible explanations for the failures, but methods for handling them. Despite the undoubted effectiveness of these aids in the face-to-face clinical situation (e.g., interrupting the Inquiry to "try to work through the feelings of the child about the Inquiry" [p. 36]; or having the child make drawings of the cards; or "embedding the Rorschach responses in a word association procedure" [p. 35], this report indirectly underscores the variability, lack of objectivity, and lack of standardization in the Inquiry procedure itself. The training, perceptiveness and intuition involved seem relevant in a clinical, nonstandardized interview situation. However, no matter how rich, fruitful and provocative a procedure it may be, this would not qualify as a *test* procedure *per se*, unless rigorously and systematically controlled.

Zax and Stricker (1960) were interested in exploring the effect of certain types of Inquiry procedures on the determinants elicited. Their procedure involved varying the degree of structure of their Inquiry. Specifically, they administered the Rorschach to 75 Ss, followed by a relatively unstructured Inquiry, which in turn was followed by a structured Inquiry, which contained a description of the determinants. Determinants were scored separately for the free association, free association plus first Inquiry, and free association plus both Inquiries. Some important changes in scoring were found. This study tends to support the notion that depending on type of Inquiry, many shifts and changes in scoring can be produced—a discouraging feature of the Rorschach Inquiry.

In addition to the lack of uniformity of Inquiry procedures and the consequent difficulty in interpreting scores obtained, as well as what would seem to be a significant influence of such variability on certain types of scores, the introspection involved in this general procedure has contributed to a general dissatisfaction, in some circles, with the standard procedure of asking the S, virtually, to do his own scoring without knowing the scoring system! The S's educational level, verbal ability, general articulateness, and general motivational level might well determine the "ease" with which he *says* he saw movement, shading, and the like. Similarly, social-cultural background, E–S interaction, and even E's reinforcing behavior may influence S's verbalizations as well as E's evaluation of it.

Perhaps some of the most extensive work on Inquiry procedures was initiated by Baughman (1958b, 1959a) based on researches on the effect of stimulus structure and stimulus variations on the Rorschach response (1954, 1958a, 1959b), as described earlier. To achieve more precision in the Inquiry, Baughman used several versions of each Rorschach card in a paired comparison technique, referring to the various modified blots when necessary. He claims that his technique simplifies and objectifies the Inquiry by making the procedure more repeatable and objective, freed from the dependence on introspection.

Baughman's method involves the use of six types of modified Rorschach cards, an extension of his original series of four modifications, and a standard set of questions during the Inquiry. The cards, identical in form to those of the standard Rorschach, varied color, shading, figure-ground contrast, and complexity of form in a systematic manner. Each set (a set for each card) consists of: (a) A—achromatic—color is eliminated, but everything else is retained; (b) CS—complex silhouette—shading variation is removed, but major detail areas are retained by utilizing differing contrast values; (c) S—silhouette—shading variations and differentiations between major detail areas are eliminated, making a uniform gray; (d) W—white—a white figure is placed on a uniformly gray background; (e) CF—complex form—figure-ground contrast due to brightness contrast is removed, but forms of major detail areas are retained; and (f) F—form—comparable to S and W, but figure-ground contrast due to brightness difference is removed.

During the Inquiry, S is asked to contrast the standard card with the modified card by responding to a series of standardized questions. By these questions E can determine precisely the influence and relevance of color, shading, etc., in the S's response. The same questions are asked with respect to each of the modified cards in a set, in order to evaluate each of the determinants, although it is not necessary for all comparisons to be made for all cards. Baughman feels that his technique permits S to produce directly relevant material during the Inquiry; this is not always assured in the less structured, "standard" procedure. Moreover, the procedure is easily taught, entirely standardized, and allows other clinicians and researchers to "know" exactly what was said during a particular Rorschach Inquiry. Not only is scoring facilitated, but since S's responses involve a simple "yes" or "no," inarticulate Ss, children, and "difficult" Ss are more easily handled with this procedure.

Baughman has indicated that the paired comparison technique has produced significantly more shading responses when the standard and modified Inquiries were compared, suggesting that his technique affords greater opportunity for more valid as well as more reliable indicators of determinants to emerge. Although his technique has been criticized for being unwieldy and time consuming, the modifications Baughman has introduced seem to represent considerable improvement over standard Inquiry procedure, and yet are readily absorbed and understood by most clinicians since the standard cards and scoring are utilized. The question of validity of the scores themselves, however, as well as the numerous problems pertaining to the scores from a methodological and statistical point of view (discussed in the preceding chapter) still remain as pertinent questions, with or without the use of Baughman's method.

The instructions and directions E states at the beginning of the task, as well as implicit expectations he communicates to S through more subtle and indirect cues, create a "set" in S as to the significance of the test situation, as well as what might be expected of him. These aspects of administration and of the test situation itself are discussed in the following section.

*Acceptance of the Task.* Psychological experiments usually involve the assumption that the subject has willingly undertaken the specific task set before him and cooperates to the fullest extent in carrying it out. As a matter of fact, experimentalists go to considerable lengths to control various motivational factors in the design of their studies. The "acceptance factor" is particularly crucial with children and with certain clinical groups. The use of trained subjects in some experiments stemmed especially from the fact that they could be "counted on" to accept the task before them and to cooperate with the instructions presented to them.

With psychological *testing*, especially when projective techniques are involved, the picture changes somewhat. Projective testing grew up in the clinic—and the Rorschach technique, in particular, has been associated by many people with "mental testing" and clinical diagnosis. As a matter of fact, the evaluative nature of many psychological and projective tests, especially in certain contexts (in industry, school, clinic, placement offices, prisons, courts, hospitals, etc.), often lends an anxiety-producing, threatening aura to the test situation. Many Ss do not fully "accept" the instructions because of fear of revealing themselves, and because of general resistance to the situation before them.

Another factor to be considered is the cultural and social orientation of the S. In addition to fear, suspicion, or resistance, we have learned from the cross-cultural worker about the wide range of behaviors which may be exhibited among various groups undergoing psychological and projective testing. It may be that lack of task-acceptance (underproduction; failure to name objects and things; blot-description-orientation; marked lack of verbalization) has deep-rooted origins in the culture of the individual, and as such does not reflect resistance or lack of cooperation, or even personality. In fact, changes in the task presented to S, the examiner, the language used, etc., may produce startlingly contrasting results in terms of personality findings for any given S. (See Chapter 1 for a general discussion of cross-cultural problems in projective testing.)

But task-acceptance, or lack of it, may indeed reflect the "style" and characteristic mode of response of S. Ss may bring to all situations certain attitudes and habitual behaviours, which, if "captured" by the Rorschach, would be a valid instance of Rorschach usefulness in appropriate diagnosis and personality interpretation.

The overlap and unavoidable similarity in response accompanying these different types of task-acceptance or rejection might well result in considerable confusion and misinterpretation for the unwary clinician. The need for further research and understanding of these types of task-acceptance is obvious. In addition, some method other than an overall "hunch" or inference on the part of the clinician is necessary for the recording and scaling of such behaviors when they occur.

What is the range of task-acceptance behavior? The task placed before S is not unlike the task given by Langfeld (1910, 1911) to his Ss, in which he asked them to say the first thing that came to mind upon presentation of an object, but directed them not to name the object or any part of it. He found that while normal Ss could adopt and maintain the negative set of not responding with the name of the object, the mental patients failed to do so. In the Rorschach experiment, S is similarly discouraged from naming the object—"inkblot"—and is asked to give any other response that comes to mind. The following results may occur: (a) S refuses to tell what he sees, or says that he sees nothing— this is technically known as "rejection of the card" and plays an important part in the interpretation; (b) S may accept the task, but the injunction to say anything else but inkblot may be broken, and he responds with either "inkblot" or with a description of the component parts of the inkblot such as color enumeration, description of contours, shadings, etc.; (c) S may accept the task of seeing something in the blot literally rather than in the interpretive sense, and set out to find real objects or scenes; (d) S does not give his response until after considerable hesitation; and (e) S simply accepts the task and gives his response accordingly.

It should be noted that each of these five categories of compliance is not limited to the Rorschach task itself and could occur in a word association test, TAT, Incomplete Sentences Test, a psychophysical experiment, or during an interview. As already noted, the basis for the behavior may be the nature of the material itself, the examiner, the temporary or stable emotional state of the subject, attitude toward *E*, or some other cause not mentioned among the usual Rorschach factors.

Of crucial relevance to our discussion is the question of "set"—the attitudes and expectations S brings with him as he faces the task before him. Experimental studies of set have frequently involved manipulation of S's attitudes by instructional variations (induced set) in order to measure the degree to which responses are thus changed or altered. Although many of the studies reported leave much to be desired in terms of methodology, the general trend in their findings is that responses are frequently modified and altered in accordance with experimentally induced sets.

Abramson (1951) explored the influence of an instructional set to see wholes or details. Not only were location categories (W, D, Dd) affected, but the determinants and content were also influenced by the experimental set. On the basis of his findings, the author stressed the importance of standardized instructions, and suggested also that knowledge of S's preconceptions and set prior to taking the test is important. Gibby (1951) was particularly interested in the problem of set with respect to "intellectual" Rorschach variables. By introducing various sets—of a conscious and volitional nature—he found that the different measures with which he worked were changed in varying degrees (F+ %, R, and content factors were the relatively more stable variables). Gibby's conclusions also stressed the importance of having complete knowledge of conditions of administration as well as of the population from which an S comes, before a Rorschach record can be interpreted adequately.

Henry and Rotter (1956) were concerned with the exploration of the assumption that many factors other than basic personality influence test behavior, and have summarized some of the relevant literature (see also, Ainsworth [1954, pp. 452–458] for a review of some pertinent studies). In Henry and Rotter's study, S's definition of the Rorschach situation was explored. Specifically, the authors hypothesized that Ss who viewed the Rorschach as a test of "sanity" implicitly or explicitly (induced through verbal instructions) would show more caution (e.g., fewer R, more F+, fewer W) than a group of controls who were given straightforward information. Their Ss were 60 female college students. Except for location of responses, their expectations were generally confirmed at a significant level, that is, there were fewer responses, more F+, P, A, and F responses, and fewer aggressive responses in the experimental group than in the control. They concluded,

The results tend to support the general hypotheses that: (*a*) a knowledge of the S's beliefs regarding the purpose of the test should be an important aspect of the interpretation of the test, (b) a "common-sense" analysis of the S's approach to the whole testing situation would be a fruitful part of the test interpretation, and (c) situational determinants significantly influence test responses (p. 461).

In general, the foregoing studies do suggest that extra-test factors, set, instructions, examiner behavior, etc., can and do influence test performance, and that without proper understanding of the nature of these factors, interpretation of any individual record, as well as overall research findings, cannot proceed with a good degree of certainty. And finally, the reader is referred to a report by Zax, Stricker, and Weiss (1960), which contains a review of many pertinent studies with respect to examiner differences, consciously induced sets, manipulation of situational factors, etc. Although stressing the important influence of such factors on Rorschach performance, the authors have indicated that the nature of such influences, as well as degree of influence, are still not clear.

**Carrying Out of the Task by the Subject.** Needless to say, the influence of the variables noted in the two preceding sections is not the same for each subject. Each individual will not only have internal goals, expectations and sets toward the test situation, the examiner, and the test itself, but, in addition to essential and basic differences in personality structure, there seem to be differences in "styles" and response habits while the subject is carrying out the task before him. The exact relationship between stable and enduring personality characteristics and these response "styles" is not clear; certainly we can hardly talk of one without the other, nor are we sure of the distinction between response-tendencies such as those soon to be described, and personality aspects the clinician is trying to "get at" with the Rorschach technique. Still another question relates to the generality of such response-tendencies. Do they carry over into other testing situations? Into nontest situations?

In the Rorschach experiment, there are several experimentally recognizable factors which may influence the performance. These include: (a) completion tendency; (b) free association capacity; (c) capacity to shift a mental set or transfer from one stimulus to another; (d) perceptual "type" to which the S may belong; (e) his response to incongruous elements in the stimulus; and (f) his capacity for structuring of figure and ground. Before appealing to personality variables per se as an explanation for a given performance, the influence of these experimentally recognizable factors must be taken into account.

The Rorschach experiment involves the completion tendency, since the response is only initiated by the inkblot and the subject must depend on his own resources for the final structuring of the cues into a completed percept. This completion tendency has long been regarded as an intellectual capacity. Hence, it is to be expected that some intellectual component will emerge in Rorschach responses.

A second factor in the production of responses is the stimulation of free association which the Rorschach technique has in common with the word asociation technique. The well-founded generalizations based on several decades of experimental work with the word association technique ought to prove useful in an understanding of Rorschach responses. The breakdown and the telescoping of associations which give rise to neologisms, perseveration, and clang associations are well-known phenomena, and their counterparts in the Rorschach (contaminated responses, confabulated responses, repeated responses, etc.) are easy to recognize.

A third capacity closely connected with association is the ability to shift from one response to another. Perseveration of a previous response is a well-known psychological phenomenon characteristic of certain types of individuals. Furthermore, some individuals can shift readily from one task to another whereas others find difficulty in such shifting. There is evidence to suggest that the ease of shifting depends to a great extent on the modality from which the shift is being made and the modality to which attention is transferred. Thus Hess has shown, by means of Ach's sorting test procedure (Suchsmethode) using the variables of weight, size, form, and color, that we cannot speak in the abstract of good and poor shifters (see Ach, 1935). The ease with which shifts are made depends on the properties of the objects between which the shift takes place. It is quite likely that lengthened reaction time may depend more on this shift ability than on neurotic tendency. This is perhaps the basis for the negative results sometimes obtained in experimentation with color and shading shock indicators (Lazarus [1949]; Meyer [1951]). Whether the variation in ability to shift is itself dependent on more basic personality traits is, of course, still an open question.

A fourth factor to be taken into consideration is the possibility of the existence of perceptual types. Many individuals will give responses which would tend to classify them as synthetic rather than analytic perceivers. Some may be more prone to be subjective rather than objective in their perceptions, whereas others may be more capable of dealing with form than with color; but all may be otherwise apparently equivalent in their degree, if not type, of adjustment to life. Consequently, before such typological considerations are made

THE RORSCHACH TECHNIQUE AS A PSYCHOLOGICAL EXPERIMENT      301

the basis for classifying personality, it is necessary to study them further in the laboratory (see description of the researches of Klein, Witkin, and Frenkel-Brunswik in Chapter 3).

A fifth factor, the role of incongruity between the color and form of a stimulus as a possible cause of interference with perception, has already been noted in Chapter 3, in connection with some of the directive-state studies of perception. Other incongruities may play a similar role.

A sixth factor is the capacity to structure figure and ground relationships. It is quite likely that some individuals have a better and more facile capacity than the average for structuring figure and ground relationships. A consideration of many of the responses based on heterogeneity (chiaroscuro) may reveal a weakness in figure-ground differentiation. Whether or not this is a reflection of personality remains to be demonstrated.

All these factors are important in the classification of a percept but may or may not be related to personality. There are some factors which supposedly have a bearing on personality which may still operate in the formation of a given response, even after the above-mentioned factors are eliminated from consideration. Among such factors is the stimulation of the cortex by impulses which enter simultaneously with the impulses from the retinal image, for example, anxiety and fear. But these factors need be invoked only after the more experimentally established factors have been duly controlled. From the point of view of an objective approach, it becomes necessary to evaluate a given response in terms of all of the foregoing general factors as well as in terms of still unvalidated clinical claims.

What are some of the clinical characteristics of patients that may serve to produce deviant behavior in the Rorschach situation? Clinical observation of schizophrenic patients, for example, has yielded the following descriptive categories, which, in isolation or in combination, presumably characterize this particular disease process: (a) poverty of ideas; (b) perseveration; (c) confused and bizarre thinking; (d) confabulation (filling in of a gap by imagined episodes of events); (e) contamination (telescoping of two ideas into one, thus producing a bizarre result); (f) preoccupation with the irrelevant or rare; (g) obsessive thinking; (h) delusions; (i) vague ideas; (j) feelings of disintegration or of cosmic calamity; and (k) ideas of reference, etc.

Each of these psychopathological trends has long been known as an earmark of mental illness, and its appearance in a Rorschach record is taken into consideration in making a diagnosis as it would be if it had occurred during the usual clinical examination. Poverty of ideas is usually reflected in a small number of responses. Perseveration is recognized by the repetition of a response previously given which has no apparent basis in the new stimulus area to which the repeated response is made. Confused and bizarre thinking appear in the incongruent elements of the content of the response. Confabulations appear when one striking item in the stimulus area determines the character of the rest of the blot (e.g., calling the entire blot or part of it a crab because of claw-like elements in the center). Contamination appears in such responses as "grass bear" in which the greenness of the stimulus area is perceived as grass and the contours are perceived as belonging to a bear—the two concepts being telescoped into one. Poorly perceived concepts are reflected in the usual F— (poorly perceived percepts) in contrast with the F+ (clearly perceived percepts). The remaining psychopathological factors reveal themselves directly in the content of the response.

It should be borne in mind, however, that the Rorschach technique is not the only one suitable for revealing the above-mentioned psychopathological trends. They usually reveal themselves under more direct clinical examination. The virtue that the Rorschach technique possesses in this connection is that it provides a systematic framework for eliciting these psychopathological trends, and, furthermore, it may elicit them in patients who are otherwise not communicative.

Already noted in connection with the problems before us is the verbal ability of S, and the degree to which he can articulate and express his thoughts. The verbal factor is related to intelligence and educational and cultural background, but there may certainly be emotional components here, too. The problem of assessing the importance of S's ability to verbalize (and to "introspect") arises especially in the Inquiry. Does our scoring reflect S's percepts or his language style and verbal ability or some (unknown) combination of both?

**Recording of Results.** The responses of the subject are usually recorded verbatim, and the times at which the card is exposed and the first response elicited are also recorded. The time for subsequent responses may be recorded but this is sometimes difficult to estimate. It has been found feasible in research studies to tape-record the responses. The responses are then played back to the subject for the Inquiry, and the comments of both the examiner and the subject are recorded. The introduction of recording devices, although desirable for research purposes and for completeness of data is regarded by some clinicians as producing differential influences on various Ss in terms of restriction of verbal output, anxiety, etc. For this reason, they prefer to record S's responses in longhand, with the risk, of course, of not recording the entire verbal output of both E and S during the performance proper and the Inquiry. It might be noted that E's reinforcing comments as well as questions during the Inquiry have frequently been overlooked, or at least their importance has been minimized in the usual longhand Rorschach recording procedures.

Whether E assumes responsibility for the manner of recording responses (in longhand, or through mechanical devices) or S (in group administration), these procedures do seem to bear some relationship to the responses produced in a test situation. This is suggested by studies with other projective techniques, such as the TAT, as well as by comparative studies involving group and individual Rorschach procedures. Needless to say, the researcher should be aware of this confounding variable in the presentation and interpretation of his results, as well as when he generalizes his findings; similarly, the clinician is cautioned not to overlook the significance of the type of recording procedure used, when projective findings are interpreted.[8]

**Analysis and Evaluation of the Responses.** As contrasted with the TAT, there are essentially only a few "standard" systems used for analyzing S's Rorschach responses—and these are fairly similar to each other, stemming in general from Rorschach's own description of and orientation to his instrument.

Rorschach himself stressed the perceptual process involved in the test rather than the content of the response, to which he paid little attention. Usually, however, the determinants or characteristics of the stimulus such as color and contours are not observed directly by the S, and the final percept emerges without any awareness of the elements that went into its formation. We can get at the determinants of the percepts only when conscious attention is paid to the characteristics of the blot rather than to the percept. We might ask at this point, "Why bother with the determinants at all—why not classify the final responses?" Such a procedure would change the test into a content test, and the alleged significance of the basic Rorschach determinants of form, color, and movement would be lost.

What are the available methods of Rorschach scoring? Since this volume was not designed to be used as a "skills book," brief reference is

---

[8] The danger of interfering with productivity through the introduction of taperecording has been greatly exaggerated. Most research investigations utilizing tape recordings have found no significant differences in the results when control studies were made.

made to excellent descriptions of scoring systems presented elsewhere. Beck (1949) and Klopfer (1954) have presented their own systems which, between them, probably account for the scoring procedures used by the vast majority of clinicians. Toomey and Rickers-Ovsiankina (1960) have compared and presented in tabular fashion the scoring systems of Rorschach, Binder, Rapaport and Schafer, Beck, Piotrowski, Hertz, and Klopfer. Holt has developed a scoring method (based on classical psychoanalytic theory) for analyzing Rorschach responses from the point of view of primary and secondary process (Holt [1956]; Holt & Havel [1960]). This is essentially a system based on content analysis as well as analysis of certain formal characteristics of the response and represents a considerable departure from the usual Rorschach scoring methods. Fisher and Cleveland (1958) have similarly developed a content scoring system based on constructs relating to body image. Responses may have vulnerable boundaries (scored P—penetration) or nonvulnerable boundaries (scored B—barrier), and this dichotomy, these authors believe, is related to the more basic and thoroughgoing attitudes and feelings S has about his own body—attitudes which in turn reflect various personality and diagnostic groupings. Various authors (e.g., Bühler, Bühler, & LeFever [1959]; Munroe, [1945], and O'Reilly [1956]) have developed a "basic score" or "basic scale"—a single, overall quantitative score which attempts to discriminate between various groups. Of course the many methodological difficulties already discussed in connection with the Rorschach instrument would also reflect on the validity and reliability of such a single, overall score, suggesting that this procedure should be used with caution. Some of these scores, it should be noted, have been developed in connection with group procedures or with some modification of standard procedure.

Are the available, standard methods for evaluating Rorschach responses suitable from a scientific point of view?

An examination of Rorschach's own scoring (1942), as well as those of his followers, indicates that the clinical scoring system cannot qualify as a scientific method for measuring the tendencies which these scores are reputed to represent (see Chapter 4 for a fuller discussion of this problem). The scoring system is arbitrary and yields scores that are very crude and rudimentary. (In fact, most Rorschach workers regard their scoring system as simply a mnemonic device for remembering each individual response.) An arbitrary hierarchy has been developed in which certain factors such as M take precedence implicitly over others. Usually, only the major factor in the response is scored, whereas all other factors are either relegated to secondary status and not counted, or are completely eliminated. Furthermore, scoring is always done with an eye to the final interpretation, so that the independence of different scores is violated and forced into a preconceived mold. Such procedures may have their virtues, but they do not fit into the usual scientific definitions of scores. It therefore becomes necessary to provide a more rigorous framework for the evaluation of Rorschach responses. Chapters 6 and 7 present a series of specially developed scales, designed to eliminate some of the deficiencies in traditional Rorschach scoring.

It should be noted that some of the moot questions in scoring could be answered by Baughman's research (see earlier sections). Thus, "bat" to Card I practically disappears as a response when shading and black are removed, whereas "butterfly" occurs equally frequently in all the modified presentations. Similarly, "map" occurs only when shading is present. Colored areas which yield anatomy responses practically cease to do so when color is eliminated. Color is of little importance in the response "bat" to Card II—D3; "monkeys" in Card III—D2; and "bow-tie" and "ribbon"—D3, in the same card. Rejection is more prominent when color and shading are absent, indicating that form rather than shading or color is the primary source of rejection. "Color shock" and "shading shock" occur equally frequently in all the series, indicating that color is not needed for "color shock" or shading for "shading shock."

Are there other possible ways of evaluating Rorschach performance? Another approach might be based on an heuristic model borrowed from communication theory.[9] In the usual model for communication theory, we have three elements: the input or signal, the filter, and the output or message. The general purpose of such a system is to reduce the noise as much as possible by a suitably selected filter, so as to obtain as clear a message as possible. Corresponding to this system, the input in the Rorschach experiment is the stimulus card, the filter is the subject, and the output is the response. In contrast with the usual communication model, we cannot select our filter at will; instead we wish to study the filter properties and infer from the relationship between the input and output, the kind of properties the filter possesses, what frequencies are selected, which ones are absorbed, which ones reflected, what frequencies arise from the filter itself regardless of the stimulating frequencies, etc.

An outstanding characteristic of the filter is its selective properties. It may receive certain frequencies, reject others, distort still others, and vibrate sympathetically with a selected few. For the subject, the "perceptual type" to which he may belong, his personal values, his kin-

---

[9] This approach has been suggested by Dr. Eugene I. Burdock.

aesthetic cues, etc., may play an important part in the selection of the properties of the stimulus to which he attends. The special capacities of the subject with regard to free association, shift ability, completion tendency, and other features may be important in the reception and elaboration of the stimulus properties. The response may occur, but be inhibited or suppressed by the filter. His readiness to respond is an important determinant in such outcomes. Organismic factors such as tonus or presence of contradictory visual and kinaesthetic cues may slant the direction of the response. Then there are a whole host of personality and psychopathological factors which may influence the response.

It becomes debatable whether we need to analyze the input message at all to exploit the information in the response, since we must not only study the stimulus properties of the input messages but must also study independently the properties of the filter before we can understand the output response. What about studying the filter directly? This would require a shift of emphasis from the perceptual to the thought process and content aspects of the Rorschach. It is true that Rorschach veered away from the content analysis of inkblots which was so popular with the psychologists of his day, and espoused the perceptual aspects. He stated that the content of the responses yielded little insight into the content of the "psyche." But he may have been wrong, or may have defined content too narrowly. If we define content as an essential element of the protocol, and regard it as we would regard any other interview material, the mystery surrounding the Rorschach expert's interpretation may yield to scientific scrutiny.

Let us examine this problem from the point of view of the interaction that exists between the conceptual components (stored memory) and the sensory and perceptual components when a response occurs to any stimulus, be it in inkblot space or in other types of visual space. It has been pointed out earlier that there are no pure physiological, sensory, perceptual, psychomotor, or conceptual responses; these are only heuristic terms. Such responses never occur in a vacuum; there is always a patterning of responses on all five levels whenever stimulation occurs. When we deny the usefulness of examining and evaluating the stimulus properties of the blot to which the response occurs, we are not casting it out into limbo. It is still important in eliciting the response. All we have done is demonstrate that the conceptual component in the Rorschach response is at the present time more amenable to categorization and more useful in prediction of behavior than the other levels of responses (physiological, sensory, perceptual, and psychomotor). When the latter levels become more detectable and more amenable to scrutiny, we may find that Rorschach was right after all, and that the *way* a person perceives rather than *what* he perceives is a better index of personality. Unfortunately these other aspects of the response are not yet amenable to classification.

An investigation by Zubin, Eron, and Sultan (1956) lends considerable support to the view that it is the content of the responses in a protocol rather than the perceptual scores that reveals factors which can be said to characterize individuals consistently. Similarly, Bower, Testin, and Roberts (1960) found that content rather than determinants were effective in discriminating various types of schizophrenics. In rating the records of 43 superior individuals according to scales which are described in subsequent chapters, Zubin, Eron, and Sultan found that the scales that measured so-called perceptual tendencies, for example, use of color, form, and texture, produced reliabilities so low as to indicate that they revealed little that is consistently characteristic of individuals. Those scales which measured content factors and ways of thinking had such high reliabilities, however, that it was obvious they were reflecting consistent trends in the Ss. It would be expected that if an individual perceives in Rorschach space as he perceives in real life space, these characteristic habits of perception would mark his performance, and we therefore could make inferences about his personality from inkblot perception. Since perceptual scoring reveals nothing that is consistently characteristic of the individual while the content scoring reveals considerable consistency, it was concluded that the content of the protocols and not the perceptual factors are the basis for whatever success the Rorschach has achieved. At present, it is a moot question whether Rorschach experts do not derive most of their insights into personality from a direct or indirect analysis of content.

In this connection, it should be noted that there has been an increased stress on language and verbal factors in Rorschach interpretation in recent years. One approach stems from a conviction that language factors may be indicative of what is going on perceptually, and that a formal, detailed analysis of S's language may be a clue to the perception-personality bond. Lorenz (1959), for example, illustrated for several features of the Rorschach, how the recorded language could yield relevant information explaining the "significance" of the variables she isolated. The features she was concerned with were: (*a*) the perceiver; (*b*) the perceptual stimulus and the percept; (*c*) the "psychic representation" or the "image" derived; and (*d*) the mental context or associative and memory background. Despite the creativity and ingenuity of the author's approach, it is based on an assumption of full knowledge and understanding of how these four features are related to personality—and on an acceptance of the validity of the Rorschach as a whole as a "clue" to personality. The author's analysis was not implemented by suggestions for either validating her ideas and constructs, or for determining the reliability of her procedures. Moreover, despite her apparent sophistication about language, Lorenz did not handle the complex of problems relating to the cultural, educational, and intellectual factors which any language analysis would raise. The basic question still unanswered is: would a language analysis of interview material or of everyday speech be equally productive? If so, why bother with the Rorschach? Must language be used as a clue to perception in order to "get at" personality, or can language and content be used as a direct indicator of personality? Perhaps the Rorschach does not yield direct information about the perceptual response, but this may not be necessary for personality analysis, since *verbal* behavior may be a sufficient indicator for our purposes.

Once the perceptual scoring is eliminated, the verbal productions of the subject can be placed into such categories as: compulsive thinking, disorganized thinking, or creative thinking; poverty of ideas or fluency; confabulation or clarity, rigidity or flexibility; contamination or its opposite; perplexity or straightforwardness; rejection or compliance. It may be discovered that such characteristics reveal themselves in the Rorschach the way they reveal themselves in the interview. To be sure, the Rorschach interview is a standard interview and may lead to results which less controlled interviews cannot lead to. Nevertheless it is, perhaps, an interview—an interview under the veil of inkblots.

The foregoing discussion may explain why the content of the protocols has been successfully related to personality, whether evaluated globally or by isolated scales, whereas perceptual factors have more or less failed to relate to personality. It may also explain why factor analysis of both perceptual and content factors has had some success. During the factor analysis, the content factors affecting the perceptual scores are teased out, *viz.*, the kind of mental content which serves to reduce R, disorganize F, disembody C, or prevent good M from arising in the mental patient and, *mutatis mutandis*, the kind of mental content which increases productivity and good responses in the normal, reveal themselves in the rotated factors. If this hypothesis is true, we should turn away from the indirect expression of mental content through determinants and location and begin building scales for analyzing the content of the verbal productions directly. Such a beginning has been made by several workers, and if we spend but 10% of the harnessed energy behind the spinning Rorschach wheel in studying the interview basis of the Rorschach, we may bring nearer the day when the contradictions that now exist within the Rorschach field are resolved. New developments in the interview itself are fast turning it into a scientific tool, and since the interview in the last analysis is still the basis for personality evaluation, no test today can rise above it. If we obtain objective criteria via the interview for the classification and evaluation of personality, perhaps such criteria may serve as a basis for the validation of tests. But without an anchored interview, we float aimlessly in the sea of personality without compass or rudder.

In view of the complexity of the Rorschach, a multiplicity of variables becomes available for scoring. To preserve the integrity of this technique, it is necessary to score every response on each of these variables, giving rise to a rather formidable scoring task. Another procedure may also be utilized. The Rorschach may be resolved into its components and separate tests provided for measuring each of these components in isolation or in pairs. The reduction of the Rorschach into its components can be done either tachistoscopically or by actual separation of the physical determinants in each of the blots.

The following procedures have been devised for studying the Rorschach components experimentally (see Chapter 8). First, the Levy Movement Blots which consist primarily of chiaroscuro elements and in which the specific task is given to see people in movement. Second, the Color-Cut-Outs which consist of two contrasted determinants, color vs. chiaroscuro, and in which the subject is given the freedom to tell what it might be. Third are the Contour Blots which consist primarily of solid black and white without chiaroscuro, and the task again is to see people in movement. Dworetzki (1939) has also suggested a procedure for studying the capacity for seeing wholes vs. details by providing figures composed of parts so that the S can describe a given picture, for example, either as several monkeys, or as a chair, which the general composition of the component parts may also suggest. She also experimented with linear figures to induce movement responses.

By such combinations of the analytic and synthetic methods, the final solution of the problems of projective techniques may be attained. It might be argued, however, that the approaches just outlined are atomistic and unsuitable for the molar evaluation of personality. The battle between the wholistic and the atomistic approach is exceptionally acute in the field of personality. Gordon Allport (1937) has perhaps drawn the most rigid line between these two approaches by finding suitable labels for them, calling the former idiographic and the latter nomothetic and indicating that the two approaches are in essence antithetical. But this is an extreme position which may serve didactic purposes excellently, but need not deter the research worker. The confusion which the chaotic state of personality research presents today may very well be the basis for Allport's contention. Hughlings Jackson has noted that we all dislike the complex; we may mistake the subjective confusion in us to be attributes of the objective thing we are observing, which is really only very complex. It is only too easy to hide behind such concepts as total personality or wholism when the "subjective confusion" that Hughlings Jackson describes assails our thinking. Only by careful thinking and experimentation will the confusion yield to understanding. In the last analysis, as Lashley has indicated, our desire to understand the unity of the organism necessarily results in analysis of units and the interrelationships of "partial functions." The differences, he felt, between atomistic and global approaches, are purely verbal. Students of behavior must be concerned with units of behavior and the causal interaction among them.

## SUMMARY AND CONCLUSIONS

Weighing the hypothesis in the Rorschach experiment—the final element in the task we have set before us—is not yet possible. We have outlined the essential elements in the experimental procedure and have proceeded to examine these in some detail, in order to evaluate their importance in terms of the Rorschach performance of S. These elements consisted of: (a) hypotheses; (b) experimenter and subject; (c) apparatus and stimulus; (d) the task and its administration; (f) acceptance of the task; (g) carrying out of the task by the subject; (h) recording of results; and (i) analysis and evaluation of the responses. We have learned, at each hazardous step along the way, that there are an alarmingly large number of variables which can play a significant role in producing this or that type of response; moreover, the exact nature of such influences, as well as their interaction, are still unspecified. The proper evaluation of the hypotheses implicit in the Rorschach technique must await the detailed, exhaustive study of a host of oft-neglected variables. Unfortunately, even the precise and objective measurement of the Rorschach response itself has been handled relatively crudely—sometimes even naively. It is to this need for greater objectivity in measurement that the next two chapters are devoted.

Our discussion has indicated that there has been an increased understanding of the important effects of extratest variables on Rorschach responses. The general findings of a large number of relevant studies are such as to cast some doubt on the high level of confidence assigned to the Rorschach response, interpreted *qua* response, as an indication of stable and enduring personality characteristics. Yet, clinicians and researchers alike do not seem to have been influenced by the results of such findings. Standardization and uniformity of procedures of administration are explicit requisites in psychometrics. The Rorschach technique, however, because of intuitive, global uses and traditions, often has not been viewed with the same rigor and demands which most clinicians bring to other (generally nonprojective) test situations.

Special focus and attention was given to the question of the stimulus in the Rorschach experiment. Stimulus correlates of visual phenomena were discussed, and an attempt was made to see if there were any lessons to be learned from studies of pictorial perception. Some of the principles of natural visual perception (based on what is undoubtedly an oversimplification of some Gibsonian principles—see Chapter 2) were utilized in an examination of Rorschach perception, and an attempt was made to outline some of the physical characteristics of the Rorschach stimuli which might yield certain types of responses. This review of the stimulus properties resulted in suggestions for analysis of the Rorschach response involving six levels: (a) location; (b) stimulus properties; (c) objective determinants of percept; (d) phenomenal determinants; (e) characteristics of the perceived object; and (f) formal content. These levels form the framework for the scales for evaluating Rorschach responses presented in the next two chapters.

Attention was next turned to procedures concerned with isolating the stimuli in the Rorschach cards. Methods reviewed included: (a) phenomenological approaches which do not utilize the usual procedure of dealing with Rorschach protocols, but can be carried out directly, by an examination of the cards themselves; (b) experimental manipulation of the stimulus properties of the cards; and (c) statistical analyses of stimulus attributes.

Finally, attention was turned to stimulus correlates of symbolic or conceptual responses. In this connection several procedures were discussed for measuring conceptual components evoked by the stimulus situation.

The final section of this chapter was concerned with the analysis and evaluation of the response. Several "systems" of scoring as well as a general discussion of some problems in scoring were presented.

Other frameworks for evaluating the response were described, including a scientific model borrowed from communication theory, in which the Rorschach stimuli are matched with the signal or input, the subject with the filter, and the response with message or output. The characteristics of the signal (Rorschach cards) need to be further ana-

AN EXPERIMENTAL APPROACH TO PROJECTIVE TECHNIQUES

lyzed in order to establish their nature; the characteristics of the filter (subject) need to be studied so that the distortions or noise in the message can be attributed to its proper source. Because of our present lack of knowledge of the characteristics of the stimulus, it becomes difficult to separate the contribution of the stimuli from the contribution of the subject to the response. Are there means for assessing the contribution of the subject (the filter) more directly?

One suggestion is that the Rorschach is an interview, and that its correct evaluation, like the correct evaluation of any interview, depends on its content and the characteristic ways of thinking which it reveals. If we provide scales for analyzing this content, we shall be well on the way toward clarifying many of the present-day contradictions, and obtain a better perspective on personality.

## REFERENCES

Abramson, L. S. The influence of set for area on the Rorschach test results. *J. consult. Psychol.*, 1951, **15**, 337–341.

Ach, N. *Analyse des Willens. Handbuch der Biologischen Arbeitsmethoden, Abt. VI. Teil.* Berlin: Urban and Schwarzenberg, 1935.

Ainsworth, Mary D. Problems of validation. In B. Klopfer, *et al. Developments in the Rorschach technique. Technique and theory. Vol. I.* Yonkers-on-Hudson, N.Y.: World Book Co., 1954, 405–500.

Allison, R. B., Jr. A two-dimensional semantic differential. *J. consult. Psychol.*, 1963, **27**, 18–23.

Allport, G. W. *Personality: a psychological interpretation.* New York: Holt, 1937.

Arnheim, R. Perceptual and aesthetic aspects of the movement response. *J. Pers.*, 1951, **19**, 265–281.

Baughman, E. E. Rorschach scores as a function of examiner difference. *J. proj. Tech.*, 1951, **15**, 243–249.

Baughman, E. E. A comparative analysis of Rorschach forms with altered stimulus characteristics. *J. proj. Tech.*, 1954, **18**, 151–164.

Baughman, E. E. The role of the stimulus in Rorschach responses. *Psychol. Bull.*, 1958, **55**, 121–147. (*a*)

Baughman, E. E. A new method of Rorschach inquiry. *J. proj. Tech.*, 1958, **23**, 381–389. (*b*)

Baughman, E. E. The effect of inquiry method on Rorschach color and shading scores. *J. proj. Tech.*, 1959, **23**, 3–7. (*a*)

Baughman, E. E. An experimental analysis of the relationship between stimulus structure and behavior on the Rorschach. *J. proj. Tech.*, 1959, **23**, 134–183. (*b*)

Beck, S. J. *Rorschach's test. I. Basic processes.* New York: Grune and Stratton, 1949.

Blatt, S. J., Engel, Mary, & Mirmow, Esther L. When inquiry fails. *J. proj. Tech.*, 1961, **25**, 32–37.

Boring, E. G. Visual perception as invariance. *Psychol. Rev.*, 1952, **59**, 141–148.

Bower, P. A., Testin, R., & Roberts, A. Rorschach diagnosis by a systematic combining of content, thought process and determinant scales. *Genet. Psychol. Monogr.*, 1960, **62**, 105–183.

Bühler, Charlotte, Bühler, K., & LeFever, W. D. *Development of the Basic Rorschach Score with manual of directions.* University of Southern California, 1959.

Cranston, R., & Zubin, J. Unpublished Study, 1949.

Dworetzki, Gertrude. Le test de Rorschach et l'évolution de la perception. *Arch. Psychol., Genève*, 1939, **27**, 233–396.

Eckhardt, W. An experimental and theoretical analysis of movement and vista responses. *J. proj. Tech.*, 1955, **19**, 301–305.

Exner, J. E., Jr. Achromatic color in cards IV and VI of the Rorschach. *J. proj. Tech.*, 1961, **25**, 38–40.

Fisher, S., & Cleveland, S. E. *Body image and personality.* Princeton, N.J.: D. Van Nostrand, 1958.

Gibby, R. G. The stability of certain Rorschach variables under conditions of experimentally induced sets: 1. The intellectual variables. *J. proj. Tech.*, 1951, **15**, 3–25.

Gibby, R. G., Miller, D.R., & Walker, E. L. The examiner's influence in the Rorschach protocol. *J. consult. Psychol.*, 1953, **17**, 425–428.

Gibson, J. J. The perception of visual surfaces. *Amer. J. Psychol.*, 1950, **63**, 367–384.

Gibson, J. J. The visual field and the visual world: a reply to Professor Boring. *Psychol. Rev.*, 1952, **59**, 149–151.

Gibson, J. J. A theory of pictorial perception. *Audiovisual communic. Rev.*, 1954, **1**, 4–23.

Gibson, J. J. The non-projective aspects of the Rorschach experiment: IV. The Rorschach blots considered as pictures. *J. soc. Psychol.*, 1956, **44**, 203–206.

Gibson, J. J. The concept of the stimulus in psychology. *Amer. Psychologist*, 1960, **15**, 694–703. (*a*)

Gibson, J. J. Pictures, perspective and perception. *Daedalus*, 1960, **89**, 216–227. (*b*)

Gleser, Goldine C. Projective methodologies. *Annu. Rev. Psychol.*, 1963, **14**, 391–422.

Grayson, H. M. Rorschach productivity and card preferences as influenced by experimental variation of color and shading. *J. proj. Tech.*, 1956, **20**, 288–296.

Gross, L. R. Effects of verbal and nonverbal reinforcement in the Rorschach. *J. consult. Psychol.*, 1959, **23**, 66–68.

Harrower, Molly R. Group techniques for the Rorschach test. In L. E. Abt and L. Bellak (Eds.) *Projective psychology.* New York: Knopf, 1950, 146–184.

Harrower, Molly R., & Steiner, Matilda E. *Large-scale Rorschach techniques.* Springfield, Illinois: Charles C Thomas, 1945.

Henry, Edith, & Rotter, J. B. Situational influences on Rorschach responses. *J. consult. Psychol.*, 1956, **20**, 457–462.

Hochberg, J. Visual world and visual field: perception, sensation and pictorial observation. Personal communication. Mimeographed paper, Department of Psychology, Cornell University, 1961.

Hochberg, J. The psychophysics of pictorial perception. *Audiovisual communic. Rev.*, 1962, **10**, 22–54.

Hochberg, J., & Brooks, Virginia. Pictorial recognition as an unlearned ability: a study of one child's performance. *Amer. J. Psychol.*, 1962, **75**, 624–628.

Hochberg, J., & Brooks, Virginia. Compression of pictorial space through perspective reversal. *Percept. mot. Skills*, 1963, **16**, 262.

Holt, R. R. Gauging primary and secondary processes in Rorschach responses. *J. proj. Tech.*, 1956, **20**, 14–25.

Holt, R. R., & Havel, Joan. A method for assessing primary and secondary process in the Rorschach. In M. A. Rickers-Ovsiankina (Ed.) *Rorschach psychology.* New York: John Wiley and Sons, 1960, 263–315.

Horiuchi, Haruyo. A study of perceptual process of Rorschach cards by tachistoscopic method on movement and shading responses. *J. proj. Tech.*, 1961, **25**, 44–53.

Hudson, W. Pictorial depth perception in subcultural groups in Africa. *J. soc. Psychol.*, 1960, **52**, 183–208.

Katz, D. *The world of colour.* London: Kegan Paul, Trench, Trubner, 1935.

Kendall, L. M. The Rorschach, psychodynamics and psychophysics. Longer mimeographed version of a paper read at Canadian Psychological Association Meeting, May, 1962.

Klein, A., & Arnheim, R. Perceptual analysis of a Rorschach card. *J. Pers.*, 1953, **22**, 60–70.

Klopfer, B., *et al. Developments in the Rorschach technique. Technique and theory. Vol. I.* Yonkers-on-Hudson, N.Y.: World Book Co., 1954.

Kragh, U. Pathogenesis in dipsomania. An illustration of the actual-genetic model of perception-personality. Part One. Theoretical frame. Anamnesis. *Acta Psychiat. Neurol. Scand.*, 1960, **35**, 207–222. (*a*)

Kragh, U. Pathogenesis in dipsomania. An illustration of the actual-genetic model of perception-personality. Part Two. Presentation and analysis of the actual-genetic series. *Acta Psychiat. Neurol. Scand.* 1960, **35**, 261–288. (*b*)

Kragh, U. Pathogenesis in dipsomania. An illustration of the actual-genetic model of perception-personality. Part Three. The retest series. The pathogenic transformations. Repression and regression. *Acta Psychiat. Neurol. Scand.*, 1960, **35**, 480–497. (*c*)

Langfeld, H. S. Suppression with negative instruction. *Psychol. Bull.*, 1910, **7**, 200–208.

Langfeld, H. S. Suppression with negative instruction. *Psychol. Rev.*, 1911, **18**, 411–424.

Lawton, M. P. Stimulus structure as a determinant of the perceptual response. *J. consult. Psychol.*, 1956, **20**, 351–355.

Lazarus, R. S. The influence of color on the protocol of the Rorschach Test. *J. abnorm. soc. Psychol.*, 1949, **44**, 505–516.

Lesser, G. S. Population differences in construct validity. *J. consult. Psychol.*, 1959, **23**, 60–65.

Lorenz, Maria. Language as an index to perceptual modes. *J. proj. Tech.*, 1959, **23**, 440–452.

McFarland, R. L. Two dimensions of test structure in Rorschach-like projective tests. *J. proj. Tech.*, 1956, **20**, 398–404.

McQuitty, L. L. Elementary linkage analysis for isolating orthogonal and oblique types and typal relevancies. *Educ. psychol. measmt.*, 1957, **17**, 207–229.

Mach, E. *The analysis of sensations and the relation of the physical to the psychical.* Chicago: Open Court Publishing Co., 1914.

Magnussen, M. G. Verbal and nonverbal reinforcers in the Rorschach situation. *J. clin. Psychol.*, 1960, **16**, 167–169.

Marsh, L. F. Parental attitudes as the basis for attributing meaning to Rorschach cards IV and VII. *J. proj. Tech.*, 1961, **25**, 69–74.

Meer, B. The relative difficulty of the Rorschach cards. *J. proj. Tech.*, 1955, **19**, 43–53.

Metzger, W. Optische Untersuchungen am Gansfeld, II. Zur Phaenomenologie des homogenen Ganzfelds. *Psychol. Forsch.*, 1930, **13**, 6–29.

Meyer, B. T. An investigation of color shock in the Rorschach Test. *J. clin. Psychol.*, 1951, **7**, 367–370.

Meyer, M. L., & Partipilo, M. A. Examiner personality as an influence on the Rorschach test. *Psychol. Reports*, 1961, **9**, 221–222.

Munroe, Ruth L. Prediction of the adjustment and academic performance of college students by a modification of the Rorschach method. *Appl. Psychol. Monogr.*, 1945, No. 7.

Munroe, Ruth L. The inspection technique for the Rorschach protocol. In L. E. Abt and L. Bellak (Eds.) *Projective psychology.* New York: Knopf, 1950, 91–145.

Nelson, T. M., & Bartley, S. H. Various factors playing a role in children's responses to flat copy. *J. genet. Psychol.*, 1962, **100**, 289–308.

O'Reilly, P. O. The objective Rorschach: a suggested modification of Rorschach technique. *J. clin. Psychol.*, 1956, **12**, 27–31.

Osgood, C. E. The nature and measurement of meaning. *Psychol. Bull.*, 1952, **49**, 197–237.

Osgood, C. E., Suci, G. J., & Tannenbaum, P. H. *The measurement of meaning.* Urbana: University of Illinois Press, 1957.

Phares, E. J., Stewart, L. M., & Foster, J. M. Instruction variation and Rorschach performance. *J. proj. Tech.*, 1960, **24**, 28–31.

Richards, T. W. Personal significance of Rorschach figures. *J. proj. Tech.*, 1958, **22**, 97–101.

Riessman, F., Jr., & Miller, S. M. Social class and projective tests. *J. proj. Tech.*, 1958, **22**, 432–439.

Rorschach, H. *Psychodiagnostics.* Berne: Verlag Hans Huber, 1942.

Rosen, E. Connotative meanings of Rorschach inkblots, responses and determinants. *J. Pers.*, 1960, **28**, 413–426.

Rosner, B. S. A new scaling technique for absolute judgments. *Psychometrika*, 1956, **21**, 377–381.

Sarason, S. B. *The clinical interaction.* New York: Harper, 1954.

Schleifer, M. J., & Hire, A. W. Stimulus value of Rorschach inkblots expressed as trait and affective characteristics. *J. proj. Tech.*, 1960, **24**, 164–170.

Stein, M. I. Personality factors involved in the temporal development of Rorschach responses. *J. proj. Tech.*, 1949, **13**, 355–414.

Toomey, Laura C., & Rickers-Ovsiankina, Maria A. Tabular comparison of Rorschach scoring systems (Appendix). In M. A. Rickers-Ovsiankina (Ed.) *Rorschach psychology.* New York: John Wiley and Sons, 1960, 441–465.

Williams, Gertha, & Kellman, S. The Rorschach technique in industrial psychology. In B. Klopfer, et al. *Developments in the Rorschach technique. Fields of application. Vol. II.* Yonkers-on-Hudson: World Book Co., 1956, 545–581.

Zax, M., & Loiselle, R. H. Stimulus value of the Rorschach inkblots as measured by the Semantic Differential. *J. clin. Psychol.*, 1960, **16**, 160–163.

Zax, M., Loiselle, R. H., & Karras, A. Stimulus characteristics of Rorschach inkblots as perceived by a schizophrenic sample. *J. proj. Tech.*, 1960, **24**, 439–443.

Zax, M., & Stricker, G. The effect of a structured inquiry on Rorschach scores. *J. consult. Psychol.*, 1960, **24**, 328–332.

Zax, M., Stricker, G., & Weiss, J. H. Some effects of non-personality factors on Rorschach performance. *J. proj. Tech.*, 1960, **24**, 83–93.

Zubin, J. A technique for measuring like-mindedness. *J. abnorm. soc. Psychol.*, 1938, **33**, 508–516.

Zubin, J., Eron, L., & Sultan, Florence. A psychometric evaluation of the Rorschach experiment. *Amer. J. Orthopsychiat.*, 1956, **26**, 773–782.

# 6 A PSYCHOMETRIC APPROACH TO THE RORSCHACH TECHNIQUE:
## formal factors

The traditional scoring system provided by Hermann Rorschach and elaborated by his followers has proved to be of practical value in the clinic and of some theoretical value in clinical research, despite its psychometric shortcomings. Although psychometricians have always been somewhat skeptical of the primitive type of scoring that has been associated with the Rorschach, they have nevertheless tried to deal with it in a statistical fashion. When one attempts to utilize Rorschach scores psychometrically for the purpose of studying reliability, validity, and intercorrelation with other tests and traits, many difficulties arise.

Such efforts have generally failed, not necessarily because of the invalidity of the Rorschach technique, but because the face value of the scores does not always serve as the *basis* for the interpretation, but merely as the *jumping-off-point* for the interpretation. Consequently, before we can hope for a significant relationship between the psychometric and the traditional Rorschach approach, we must find a way of recording the additional factors which the Rorschach expert uses in preparing his interpretation. The scales described in this chapter represent an attempt in that direction.[1]

---

[1] The psychometric approach to the evaluation of the Rorschach technique was initiated by Zubin in 1941. Since then it has undergone several revisions. The present version has enjoyed the collaboration of Dr. R. J. McCall, who helped in the

317

The traditional scoring system contains three classifications: location, determinants, and content, and each of these is subdivided into categories, for example, the location into wholes (W), details (D), and uncommon or small details (Dd); the determinants into color (C), form (F), movement (M), and shading (Sh); and the content into human (H), animal (A), objects (Obj), etc. Traditional scoring consists in pigeonholing a response into one of the subcategories of each of the three classifications. Thus, a response is either a W or a D or Dd; and an M, F, Sh, or C.[2] The traditional scorer is, in reality, not wholly satisfied with simply recording the major location, determinant, or content. In practice, he notes the secondary locations or determinants also, but in many instances keeps them in mind without formally recording them. In the final interpretation, these unrecorded data and impressions are brought to the fore and integrated with the more formal material. In fact, it is this practice, which goes under the general name of "considering the total record" (rather than any isolated element in it), that makes it so difficult for the psychometrically trained psychologist to follow the presentations of Rorschach experts. It is hardly necessary to point out the danger of "forgetting" the factors that do not fit the apparent general trend in the emerging personality interpretation. By providing a method for recording the secondary as well as the primary scores, as is done in this chapter, the danger of remembering only the "congruent" material will be lessened. The interpreter may still be free to sift his material, but he can then do it by outright selection rather than by unconscious forgetting. Furthermore, when the number of responses is small, the secondary scores often help to provide sufficient data to make the results reliable.

---

revision of earlier scales and provided several new scales, and Mrs. Florence Sultan, who helped in further refinement of the scales by applying them to 45 records. A complete list of the scales described in Chapters 6 and 7 can be found at the end of Chapter 7. Illustrations of psychometric scoring utilizing these scales are presented in Parts VI and VII of the *Supplement*.

The *Supplement*, an appendix to this book, has been deposited as Document number 7955 with the ADI Auxiliary Publications Project, Photoduplication Service, Library of Congress, Washington 25, D.C. A copy may be secured by citing the Document number and by remitting $21.25 for photoprints, or $6.25 for 35 mm. microfilm. Advance payment is required. Make checks or money orders payable to: Chief, Photoduplication Service, Library of Congress. Separate parts of the material may also be ordered. Fees must be determined through written inquiries in advance, however.

[2] It should be noted, of course, that the various subcategories are themselves subdivided into additional categories, such as those for inanimate or animal movement, achromatic color, controlled or uncontrolled use of color, etc., and that different "systems" for scoring these are available.

Another problem with which the psychometrician is concerned is the precise definition of each variable and the provision of scales for rating the importance of each variable in determining the response. Unless the variables are specified and the scales for measuring each variable anchored, the results of the scoring procedure can be unreliable and very misleading.

To develop a system of scales for evaluating the Rorschach responses, a survey was made of all the various types of evaluations which Rorschach experts have utilized in developing personality interpretations from the raw material provided by the protocol. The source material for this survey was the recorded literature on traditional Rorschach scoring and interpretation, the growing literature on "signs," and the writers' experience in arriving at a personality picture from a combination of both objective and subjective estimates as well as from intuitive hunches. This analysis led to the development of some 75 different scales and classification categories. Not all these factors are of equal importance for the analysis of a given record, nor do these factors exhaust all the possible trends or tendencies which Rorschach workers have distinguished. They reflect, however, the trends which have appeared to be significant in the several hundred selected records which have been carefully examined.

In approaching the problem of classifying Rorschach responses, it should be noted, first of all, that the stimulus areas in which the different responses are located are not uniform in their attributes. The ten inkblots forming the Rorschach series differ radically from each other in the distribution of these attributes, and considerable variation exists between the constituent areas of the same blot. It is therefore important to note the objective characteristics of each area in which a response is located (see the *Supplement*, Part III).

A second point to be noted is that the responses that arise within the same stimulus area often differ considerably in their content and general characteristics. An area such as the upper colored portion in Card III which contains all the three possible attributes of color, brightness, and variations in color and brightness (heterogeneity), may yield responses that ignore color completely, depending only on the abrupt, irregular, or gradual gradients of brightness (which give rise to shading and/or contour). We must, therefore, study on the one hand the objective characteristics of the stimulus area that gave rise to the response, and on the other hand, the particular type of stimulus selection which the subject made within the stimulus area. An example will make this clear.

Let us select an area of one of the cards to which many people respond—the red area at the bottom of Card II. The basic attributes of this area are color, brightness, and heterogeneity. The presence of these three attributes can be established by a consensus of observers or by some physical measures appropriate to each of them. We can then proceed to analyze each response to this area in accordance with the relative contribution of each of the area's attributes to the formation of the response. Some responses, like "butterfly," are found to be primarily influenced by the abrupt gradient of the area and to a much lesser extent by color and irregular or gradual gradients. Since abrupt brightness gradients (or in some cases abrupt juxtaposition of different colors) produce contours, we can infer that heterogeneity was the primary attribute of the area to which S responded, whereas the area attributes of color and brightness were secondary or even ignored. Other responses, like "belching red flames," depend more on hue and shading than on definite contours. It may be concluded that for this response, color and brightness variations of a diffuse or gradual sort are the primary attributes of the stimulus area on which the response is based. Still other responses, like "splash of water," depend primarily on shading alone. It may be concluded that such responses are based on the attribute of gradual brightness gradients alone, the other attributes contributing little, if anything, to the formation of the response. The relative influence of each attribute can thus vary from zero to a maximum.

But the individual differences in response to the same stimulus area do not end in the differential selection of attributes. Even when the relative importance of the three attributes is the same for two responses, Ss' interpretations, expressed verbally, are not always the same. Thus, "a belching flame" and "sunset in back of the mountains" may represent similar constellations so far as the basic attributes go, but the first has a dynamic quality, the second a three-dimensional quality which the other lacks. Consequently, there are several levels on which the Rorschach responses may be classified. They may be classified first according to the portion of the blot selected for the response; second, according to the objective attributes of the stimulus area in which the response is located; third, according to the relative importance of each of the objective attributes in the formation of the response, that is, according to the manner in which the attributes are elaborated into units like hue, contours, and shading; fourth, in accordance with the characteristics of the perceived object emanating from the basic visual stimulus; and fifth, according to the conceptual characteristics with which the perceived object is endowed.

Unfortunately, studies of the objective characteristics of the blots have been initiated only recently. Scales attempting to gauge the importance of these attributes in the formation of the percept can only be tentative and only of temporary usefulness until the basic studies are completed. Meantime, however, gross failures to utilize very obvious features of the blot, or the introduction of elements patently not present in the stimulus area can be readily noted.

The five classifications into which the response may be classified can be regarded as answering the following major questions regarding the selective processes which the presentation of the blot arouses:

1. What part of the blot did S select as the stimulus area for his response?
2. What attributes are found in this stimulus area?
3. Which of these attributes were selected for utilization in the emerging percept?
4. What elaboration or organization was made of the determinants in producing the visual characteristics of the perceived object?
5. What was the nature of the actual object perceived?

These are the five basic questions which the Rorschach examiner should try to answer when he attempts to score and interpret a given protocol. This holds equally true for the traditional Rorschach approach as well as the psychometric approach. Once these questions are answered, disposing of the remaining classification categories is relatively simple.

The ways in which these five questions may be answered will now be presented:

1. *Portion of blot selected as stimulus area (location)*. This can vary from the totality of the blot (whole response), through a large portion (detail), to a small or infrequently selected portion (rare detail).

2. *Objective attributes of stimulus area (area attributes)*. These are the potential stimulus correlates of the response. They are: (*a*) color; (*b*) brightness; and (*c*) heterogeneity (the spatial distribution of color and brightness). The color attributes range from chromatic to achromatic black and white and the various shades of gray. Intensity (or brightness) refers to the amount of luminous flux reflected by the stimulus area. Heterogeneity refers to variations in color and brightness giving rise to gradual, irregular, or abrupt gradients; or there may be a total absence of gradients when the area is completely homogeneous. The impression of vista and distance is achieved by gradual gradients; the impression of surface quality and shading, by irregular gradients; and the impression of contour, by abrupt gradients of brightness or juxtaposition of colors.

3. *Selected attributes of stimulus area* (*stimulus correlates or determinants*). The mere presence of a given attribute in the stimulus area is no guarantee that it will make itself felt in the percept. For this reason it is important to note which of the attributes present in the stimulus area influence the response.

Consequently, the attributes of the stimulus area can be divided into two parts: (*a*) those utilized in the formation of the response; and (*b*) those which were ignored. The attributes that are utilized in the response are the stimulus correlates of the response or its determinants. The influence of the stimulus correlate or determinant on the formation of the response can only be inferred from the contents of the response in the usual Rorschach setting, although experimentally, the alleged stimulus correlate can be varied, eliminated or increased to determine its importance in eliciting a given response. If the abrupt gradients (heterogeneity) in a given stimulus area are perceived as contours of some object, these abrupt gradients are rated high as determinants, whereas if they are not perceived at all, insofar as they are not reflected in the response, they are rated low. If hue is perceived and constitutes an important element in the perceived object ( e.g., painted clown's face), this determinant or stimulus correlate is given a high rating and an inference is made regarding the importance of color as a determinant in the stimulus area. If the heterogeneity of the stimulus area constitutes an important part of the perceived object ( e.g., fur rug with texture), this determinant or stimulus correlate is rated high, and an inference is made regarding the importance of this factor as a determinant. Sometimes the response stops at this interpretive level and goes no further. This happens when S says he sees contours or shading or color, but does not perceive any specific object. In that event, no further consideration of this response for classification purposes is required, except insofar as it represents a special type of interpretation of the directions and a special type of content.

4. *Elaboration of determinants into the characteristics of the perceived object* (*interpretation of determinants*). The determinants (color, intensity, and heterogeneity) may be interpreted in isolation or elaborated in a variety of ways. A classification of these modes of interpretation follows:

(*a*) *Hue*, ranging from disembodied hue or film hue, in which the other determinants of intensity and heterogeneity play no role, to surface hue or object hue in which the other two determinants also enter.

(*b*) *Surface quality*, ranging from a response whose essence is a pure surface quality ( e.g., the top surface of a marble slab) to one in which both contours and hues enter to determine the surface.

(c) *Shape,* ranging from pure contours (profiles of faces) to shapes involving both color and heterogeneity.

(d) *Solidity* or *dimensionality,* in which the three determinants vary in their contributions to the final percept. The dimensionality may be unidimensional, bidimensional, or tridimensional, and may depend primarily on contours, shading, or even hue.

(e) *Distance,* ranging from proximity to vista effects and dependent on a combination of two or more of the determinants.

(f) *Movement,* ranging from static percepts without any movement to percepts imbued with movement.

(g) Other possible interpretations not explicitly used by Rorschach workers, such as *size* and *luminosity.*

5. *Classification of the perceived object according to conceptual categories (content).* This classification involves such generic and specific concepts as human, animal, plant, nature, etc. In addition, the *dynamic* qualities of the content are also rated (see Chapter 7).

We may summarize the five variables into which responses may be classified as follows:

1. *Location* (W—whole; D—large detail; Dd—very small or uncommon detail).

2. *Stimulus Area Attributes* (Color—A-C; Intensity—A-I; Heterogeneity—A-Ht).

3. *Stimulus Correlates in the Response, or Determinants* (Color—D-C; Intensity—D-I; Heterogeneity—D-Ht).

4. *Elaboration of Determinants*
   (a) *Hue*
   (b) *Surface quality* (Su)
   (c) *Shape* (Shp)
   (d) *Dimensionality* (Dim)
   (e) *Distance* (Dis)
   (f) *Movement* (Dy)
   (g) *Position* (Po)

5. *Content* (Human—H; Animal—A; etc.)

In addition to these variables that emerge from the survey of the analysis of factors underlying the response, a group of factors may be distinguished which indicate certain organizing tendencies and certain psychological characteristics and attitudes exhibited by S. We shall later provide rating scales for some of these variables. Now we will proceed to give the rating scales for the five major classifications.

The reliability of these scales was determined in a study by Zubin,

Eron, and Sultan (1956) in which the responses of 45 superior adults were analyzed. Two kinds of reliability were evaluated: (a) interscorer reliability, and (b) intra-individual consistency. The first type estimates the degree to which two scorers can agree on the ratings assigned to the responses. The agreement was excellent, ranging from perfect agreement on 70% of the response ratings on one scale to perfect agreement on all the responses on ten scales; the median perfect agreement on all the responses to all the scales was 94%. Table 1, in the *Supplement*, Part I, shows the median per cent of perfect agreement for the various scales grouped according to type. It is obvious that two independent analysts can rate the same responses with a considerable degree of agreement; thus, interscorer reliability of the scales is unquestioned.

The second type of reliability is not so much concerned with the system of scoring as it is with the consistency of performance of the individual. Split-half reliability, calculated by correlating average scores of two series composed of successive alternate responses, was not equally high for all the scales. Table 2, in the *Supplement*, Part I, presents the split-half correlations for all the scales together with the Spearman-Brown corrections. In general, the content scales have higher reliabilities than the formal scales.

## THE RORSCHACH RATING SCALES

*I. Location of Stimulus Area.* The stimulus area in which the response is located may be either the entire blot, a large or well-defined portion of it, or some small or rarely used portion of it. Rorschach workers have already studied the topography of the blots and their natural boundaries and have published tables for classifying responses occurring in each portion of the blot as either (W) whole, (D) large detail, or (Dd) small or uncommon detail response. Of the various classifications now available, we have selected that of Beck (1949) because of the rather large number of scored responses presented by him. This should be referred to when using Scales 1–3 (see the *Supplement*, Part II).

### A. Importance Scales

An examination of Rorschach responses indicates that only a small percentage of D and Dd responses are confined to that portion of the blot ordinarily scored as their locale. Other portions of the card often contribute a background quality which is indispensable for the emergence of the response. On the other hand, W responses differ in the degree to which they utilize the enclosed D's and Dd's. Thus, although a response may be primarily a W response, D's and Dd's may be important to a varying degree in its formation. Similarly, responses that are primarily D's may owe their existence, in part, to the presence of Dd's as well as to the totality of the blot (W).

In rating a response for the degree of importance of W, D, and Dd in its formation, a rating of 1 is used when a given locale serves merely as a background. When it is more than mere background, but not of major importance, it is rated 2; when it is of major assistance in the formation of the response, it is rated 3; and when it is the primary locale, it is rated 4. If two or more comparable areas (e.g., two D's) are employed in the same response but with varying degrees of importance, the rating representing the highest of these should be used. If two different locales (e.g., a D and a Dd) are of equal importance, the same rating may be used for both. At least one of the three (W, D, Dd) should be adjudged the primary locale and receive a rating of 4. Frequently, a negative criterion is of assistance in determining the importance of a locale. This criterion consists of determining whether the response in question would have occurred had the given area been omitted.

It is worth noting that even though a response takes in the entire card, W may not be the primary locale. For example, in Card I the central large detail may be seen as the figure of a woman with the rest of the card serving as a backdrop or curtain against which the figure of the woman is outlined. In the traditional method of Rorschach scoring this would be labeled simply W, but on our rating scale the higher value (4) would be given to the D. We may note also that responses located in whole or in part in the white spaces of the cards may be rated on the W, D, Dd continuum. If a response is entirely in the white space it will be rated as primarily a D or a Dd on the importance scale, in accordance with Beck's listing of the given white space as D or Dd.

The scales for evaluating the relative importance of W, D, and Dd are presented below:

## 1–3. *Importance* (*W, D, Dd*)

0. Of no importance whatsoever; totally ignored
1. Of some minor importance; merely background
2. Of secondary importance; helped in the determination
3. Of marked assistance
4. The most important locale

Sometimes it is possible to determine importance by noting whether verbal evidence of its importance is given in the Inquiry or in the original response, but this is not always a safe criterion. Whenever two figures are perceived as included in a W response (e.g., two men in front of an altar—Card I), the rating for D is at least 2. If the location of a response occupies up to 60% or more of the area of a W or D, it is customary to give a 4 rating for the type of location it approximates most and to give a 2 rating for the smaller detail. Whenever an incomplete response is made, such as a human or animal detail, the background is scored at least 1. Thus, if such a response is primarily a Dd, then D is rated 1; if the response is D, then W is rated 1.

### B. Type Scales

#### 4. Inclusiveness of Primary Locale (Inc)

After rating the relative importance of W, D, and Dd in a given response and determining the primary locale, we may turn our attention to the completeness with which this primary locale is utilized. Some responses include nearly all the subdivisions of the primary locale. Other responses fail to take into consideration either major or minor portions of the primary locale. Sometimes even rare detail responses do not include the entire area in which they are located. Since edge details, such as profiles, represent a complete cutting off of the inside of the stimulus area and a use of the contour only, they are given the lowest rating on inclusiveness. Next in rank is the omission of inside detail, where an island within a large or small detail is omitted. The highest rating for inclusiveness is given to responses that utilize the entire area in which the primary response is located.

0. Only edge detail used (rest cut off or background)
1. An inside large detail (D) or edge detail omitted from stimulus area
2. An inside rare detail (Dd) omitted from stimulus area
3. Minute portion of stimulus area omitted
4. Entire stimulus area used (nothing within its boundaries cut off)

#### 5. Frequency of Locale (FL)

This scale applies only to the primary locale of the response, the one for which the Importance rating is 4.

Rorschach workers have found, through studying large numbers of records, that certain locales tend to be utilized more frequently than others. Such frequency data were actually used by Beck as the criterion for distinguishing D's from Dd's. We have found it convenient, however, to treat size of area and frequency of use as two independent aspects of the response. Thus, Scales 1–3 refer to importance in terms of size alone. Until such time as D's and Dd's are catalogued on this basis, we may use Beck's classification.

Scale 5 thus refers to the frequency with which the primary locale tends to be used as such. Here again we do not have adequate data on which to base our subdivisions, but we can utilize the frequency data (provided by Brown) quoted in Beck (1949) and set up a tentative scale calibrated on the basis of the normal distribution curve. By taking the maximum frequency in each card as a fixed quantity which will probably never be exceeded in popularity, the range between this maximum frequency and 3.6 SD's below the mean is divided into four equal steps. The area below 3.6 SD's (0 on the scale) is reserved for idiosyncratic locales not yet reported. The distribution of scale values based on this technique is given in Table B.

*Table B. Ratings for Frequency of Locale*

Locale                                   Cards

| Locale | I | II | III | IV | V | VI | VII | VIII | IX | X |
|---|---|---|---|---|---|---|---|---|---|---|
| W | 4 | 4 | 3 | 4 | 4 | 4 | 4 | 3 | 3 | 3 |
| D1 | 3 | 4 | 4 | 3 | 3 | 4 | 4 | 4 | 4 | 4 |
| 2 | 2 | 4 | 4 | 3 | 3 | 3 | 4 | 4 | 4 | 4 |
| 3 | 2 | 4 | 4 | 3 | 3 | 3 | 4 | 4 | 4 | 4 |
| 4 | 2 | 3 | 4 | 3 | 3 | 3 | 4 | 3 | 4 | 4 |
| 5 | 2 | 3 | 4 | 3 | 2 | 3 | 3 | 3 | 4 | 4 |
| 6 | 2 | 0 | 3 | 2 | 2 | 3 | 3 | 3 | 4 | 4 |
| 7 |  |  | 3 | 2 | 2 | 3 | 3 | 3 | 4 | 4 |
| 8 |  |  | 3 | 2 | 0 | 3 | 3 |  | 4 | 4 |
| 9 |  |  | 3 |  | 0 |  | 0 |  | 4 | 4 |
| 10 |  |  | 3 |  | 0 |  |  |  | 4 | 4 |
| 11 |  |  | 3 |  |  |  |  |  | 0 | 3 |
| 12 |  |  | 0 |  |  |  |  |  | 0 | 3 |
| Dd21 | 2 | 3 | 2 | 2 | 2 | 3 | 3 | 2 | 4 | 3 |
| 22 | 2 | 3 | 2 | 1 | 2 | 3 | 3 | 2 | 3 | 3 |
| 23 | 2 | 3 | 2 | 1 | 2 | 3 | 0 | 2 | 3 | 3 |
| 24 | 2 | 2 | 2 | 1 | 0 | 2 | 0 | 2 | 3 | 3 |
| 25 | 2 | 2 | 2 | 1 | 0 | 2 | 0 | 2 | 3 | 2 |
| 26 | 2 | 2 | 0 | 0 | 0 | 2 | 0 | 2 | 3 | 2 |
| 27 | 2 | 2 | 0 | 1 | 0 | 1 | 0 | 2 | 3 | 2 |
| 28 | 2 | 0 | 0 | 0 | 0 | 1 | 0 | 2 | 3 | 2 |
| 29 | 1 | 0 | 0 | 0 | 0 | 0 |  | 0 | 3 | 2 |
| 30 | 1 | 0 | 0 |  | 0 | 0 |  | 0 | 2 | 2 |
| 31 | 0 | 0 |  |  |  | 0 |  | 0 | 0 | 1 |
| 32 | 0 |  |  |  |  |  |  |  | 0 | 0 |
| 33 |  |  |  |  |  |  |  |  |  | 0 |
| 34 |  |  |  |  |  |  |  |  |  | 0 |
| 35 |  |  |  |  |  |  |  |  |  | 0 |

Table B is read as follows: The left-hand margin gives the symbol used by Beck (1949) to designate the various portions of the blot. To find the frequency rating for the locale of a given response, find the symbol for the locale in question in the catalogue of locales given in Beck, or in the *Supplement*, Part II. Then enter the left-hand margin of Table B with the locale in question and find the rating in the column for the card on which the response was seen. Thus, if the response is located in D8 in Card III as its primary locale, look in Row D8 and under Card III to find the rating of 3.

It may be noted that when a white space is rated as the most important locale, a frequency rating may also be given, since white space responses are included in Beck's classification of locales.

*Note on abbreviation of locales.* It is sometimes difficult to determine whether some area, not listed by Beck, is more properly rated as an abbreviated D or as an idiosyncratic Dd. To aid in objectivity of scoring, the following criterion has been adopted. If the area in question constitutes at least 90% of a D (Beck), it should be rated as D, with the corresponding *FL* rating (Scale 5), and the appropriate *Inc* rating (Scale 4). If it is less than two-thirds of a D, it should be rated as Dd, with an *FL* rating of 0, and an *Inc* rating of 4. When several D's are combined, the rating for the most frequent D is used.

*II. Stimulus Area Attributes (C, I, Ht).* After locating the stimulus area to which the response was made, the objective attributes of this locale can be noted. The purpose of determining the stimulus attributes of the selected area is to have an inventory of the potential types of responses which the stimulus might elicit. In this way, the particular stimulus preferences of a given S, as well as his stimulus rejections or indifferences, can be inferred. Furthermore, the pattern of stimulus areas which attracts him can also be inferred from the areas which he selects. Thus, individuals who seek out the portions of the blot in which color is present to a great degree, regardless of whether they make use of this color or not, will reveal their proclivities by the choice of stimulus area.

The primary qualities of a given stimulus area which have thus far been selected for psychometric rating are: (*a*) color, dependent physically on wavelength; (*b*) intensity or brightness, dependent physically on the luminous flux reflected from a given area (amount of white); and (*c*) degree of heterogeneity, dependent on whether the area is uniform with reference to color and brightness, or whether there are variations in these attributes. The factor of saturation is not dealt with because of the difficulty in evaluating its extent, although if psychophysical measures are eventually developed for measuring its degree, it can be included in the scaling system. We do not yet have any psychophysical measures of the color, brightness, or heterogeneity of the Rorschach cards, but it is not too difficult to rate these qualities relative to each other. Until each of the areas is scanned for its properties by psychophysical methods, however, ratings of the stimulus attributes will have to remain on a subjective level. Once this psychophysical mapping is accomplished, the characteristics of each W, D, and Dd can be tabulated with the Importance ratings for each dimension. (It should be noted that a given portion of the blot which is a Dd may have ratings which differ from those of the larger D of which it is a component.) From then on, rating of the stimulus properties would become a simple matter of looking up the tabulated norms. A beginning step in this direction has been made. In conjunction with another study, Zubin, Eron, and Sultan (1956) have mapped out the attributes of certain selected areas of each of the Rorschach cards. They comprise every location used by any or all of 45 superior Ss, and appear in the *Supplement,* Part III.

The scales for gauging the relative importance of Color (C), Intensity (I), and Heterogeneity (Ht) are given under *Importance Scales of Attributes.* For each area a rating of 4 should be given on one scale.

### A. Importance Scales

**6–8. Importance of Attributes (A-C, A-I, A-Ht)**

0. Attribute not present
1. Attribute present but insignificant
2. Attribute of little importance
3. Attribute of moderate importance
4. Most important attribute present

Thus, for Card VI, the most important attribute is the heterogeneity of the stimulus card; whereas for Card IX, color is the most important attribute; and for Card II, area Ds5, brightness would be the most important attribute.

### B. Type Scales

After determining the relative importance of color, intensity, and heterogeneity of the stimulus area, the type of color, intensity, and heterogeneity is evaluated on the Type Scales.

If the original Importance scale value falls below 3, no Type scale rating need be given for this dimension.

The color stimulus can be either chromatic or achromatic or a mixture of both, and rating scales are provided below for rating the relative importance of each type of stimulus in the given area. In rating for achromatic color, the white spaces included within the outline of the blot should be evaluated, but not the marginal white surrounding the outer borders of the blot.

### 9a. Chromatic Colors (Chr)

### 9b. Achromatic Colors (Ach)

X. Not applicable because no 3 ratings given under Importance scales
0. Not present at all
1. Present to a slight degree
2. Present to a moderate degree
3. Present to a considerable degree
4. Most important type present

The intensity stimulus can be either very bright or very dull or be any degree of variation between these two extremes, and should be rated according to Scale 10.

### 10. Degree of Intensity (Deg I)

X. Not applicable because no 3 ratings given under Importance scales
0. Complete lack of reflection of luminous flux (e.g., black)
1. Small degree of intensity present (e.g., dark gray, brown)
2. Moderate degree of intensity (e.g., medium gray, tan)
3. Considerable degree of intensity (e.g., light gray, beige)
4. Complete reflection of luminous flux (e.g., white)

The heterogeneity attributes can be classified as very high, moderately high, or as absent (when the stimulus area is entirely homogeneous).
Scale 11 evaluates the degree of heterogeneity.

### 11. Degree of Heterogeneity (Deg Ht)

X. Not applicable because no 3 ratings given under Importance scales
0. Homogeneous
1. Slightly heterogeneous
2. Moderately heterogeneous
3. Considerably heterogeneous
4. Very heterogeneous

Since this attribute can vary from complete homogeneity, giving rise to film color effects, to heterogeneity, which may give rise to such varied phenomenological percepts as contour, surface effects, depth, and distance, it has been found useful to classify the heterogeneity variable (usually called chiaroscuro in orthodox Rorschach terminology) into type of gradient present: (a) abrupt gradient, which gives rise to contour; (b) irregular gradient, not continuous enough to give rise to an abrupt gradient but sufficient to give the impression of surface (shading or texture); and (c) continuous gradual gradients, giving rise to the impression of distance or depth.

It should be borne in mind that the boundaries of the selected area usually consist of contours produced by either abrupt brightness gradients or juxtaposed colors. Consequently, every area will contain this attribute at least in its boundary. In order not to weight the abrupt gradient attribute too heavily, the boundary gradients are not to be considered in rating the relative importance of the attributes, and only the internal abrupt gradients will be rated.

The types of abrupt, irregular, and gradual gradients should be classified on the following scales:

*12a. Abrupt Gradients (Ab Grad)*

*12b. Irregular Gradients (Ir Grad)*

*12c. Gradual Gradients (Gr Grad)*

X. Not applicable because no 3 ratings given under Importance scales
0. Not present at all
1. Present to a slight degree
2. Present to a moderate degree
3. Present to a considerable degree
4. Most important type present

Since the *stimulus* areas of course remain constant and only the *responses* to each area vary from S to S, it is possible, as already noted, to map out the attributes of each area in advance. Thus, the selected attributes which influence the response can be easily compared to the total potential stimulus correlates in the selected area.

*III. Determinants (D-C, D-I, D-Ht).* The determinant scales are identical with the scales for stimulus attributes, since a stimulus attribute becomes a determinant if the test interpreter infers that it was selected by S as a basis for the response.[3] Thus, a response such as fur rug, in which the surface quality is important, represents a sensitivity to the irregular gradient attribute of the blot, and a response such as snow, in which the brightness is important, represents a sensitivity to the inten-

---

[3] This dependence on inference rather than on direct experimental evidence is perhaps the greatest weakness of the orthodox Rorschach method. If many observations on different materials whose attribute qualities are well defined were available, a statistical basis for this inference could be provided.

sity attribute. It is important to note whether the attributes of the area selected for response are actually utilized in the determination of the response. For example, one of the most interesting comparisons consists of comparing the A-C scale with D-C scale for a given response, since such comparisons reveal the degree to which physical color influences the response. The stimulus color may be present but not utilized or utilized to the same degree or a greater degree than its presence warrants. Furthermore, the response may contain a color reference even when there is no color in the stimulus area.

### A. Importance Scales

The determinants of the response refer to the elementary constructs of color, intensity, and heterogeneity, which form the perceptual scaffold of the response. If abrupt gradients were not perceived in the blot, no contour could emerge. Similarly, if color were not perceived, "the painted faces of the clowns" in Card II could not be reported; and if heterogeneity were not perceived, the hazes, vistas, textures, or depths of scenes and objects could not be reported by S. Thus, the determinants are closely connected on the one hand, with the characteristics of the final object perceived, and on the other hand, with the attributes present in the stimulus area. This middle position which the determinant occupies, between the attributes of the percept and the attributes of the stimulus area, makes it a most important element in scoring and classifying the response. It must be remembered that the mere presence of an attribute is no guarantee that it will influence the response. The only way to judge the importance of a determinant (color, intensity, and heterogeneity) in the formation of a response is to inquire whether the response would have been possible if the stimulus correlate of the determinant in question were not present in the stimulus area, or were present to a lesser degree than actually was the case. Furthermore, an attribute can be said to influence the response to the extent that there is congruity between the attribute in question and the final percept. Thus, if the gradients in the stimulus area bear no relationship to the resulting contours which shape the perceived object, the importance of the attribute is minimal. If there is perfect correspondence, the importance of the attribute as a stimulus correlate is maximal. The degree of congruence is rated later. The scales for rating the determinants are given in scales 13–15. A rating of 4 must always be given on one of these scales. The scale steps are as follows:

### 13–15. Importance of Determinants (D-C, D-I, D-Ht)

0. Of no importance whatsoever; totally ignored, if present
1. Of some minor importance

2. Of secondary importance
3. Assisted in the formation of the response
4. The most important determinant

As an aid in judging the importance of each determinant, the following special considerations for each determinant may be kept in mind.

### 13. Importance of the Color Determinant (D-C)

This includes the importance of both chromatic and achromatic color in the formation of the response. The chromatic determinant depends on the utilization in the response of chromatic color in the stimulus area. Reactions to variation in the brightness of the color would be rated under heterogeneity, but the color and heterogeneity determinants are not necessarily mutually exclusive. The achromatic determinant depends on the presence of relatively homogeneous black, white, and gray in the stimulus area. Thus, the designation of the white space in Card II as a "white beet," or the whole of Card V as a "black bat," is at least, in part, an achromatically determined response. Responses to homogeneous gray are possible, in principle, but seem seldom to occur in Rorschach records. In such rare responses as "gray bearded Chinese idol" to D4 in Card II, the achromatic determinant should probably be given some weight. Later, in the quality scales, the relative importance of achromatic and chromatic elements is weighed. Here we are concerned with the relative importance of color, intensity, and heterogeneity and are therefore neglecting type differences within each determinant. Sometimes color serves merely as a background for determining an area, or as a conventional means for separating two countries on a map. In such cases, the importance of color is not as high as when it is a germane part of the percept—for example, "painted clowns' faces," or "red of blood," or "blackness of pitch."

### 14. Importance of the Intensity Determinant (D-I)

The intensity attribute of the stimulus area has not been dealt with directly by orthodox Rorschach workers. When a stimulus area is interpreted as brilliant, or as saturated or unsaturated, an inference may be made that brightness (amount of luminous flux reflected) was an important determinant.

### 15. Importance of the Heterogeneity Determinant (D-Ht)

This determinant depends on variations in the brightness and/or color of the stimulus area which may tend to produce definite shapes or contours, and which are sufficient to prevent the impression of *uniform* black, white, or chromatic color. Most surface appearance (texture) and distance (vista) responses depend on this determinant. There are two types of variation in brightness: regular and irregular. The regular variation shows gradual gradients which are sometimes interpreted as depth or solidity, while the irregular variation has no gradients and gives rise, sometimes, to interpretations of diffusion or surface quality. These types of brightness variation are scaled in the Type scales below. The contour determinant depends on the abrupt variations in brightness gradients as well as on the abrupt juxtaposition of chromatic or achromatic colors.

### B. Type Scales—Congruence

The mere presence of a given stimulus attribute will not insure the emergence of its corresponding determinant, nor will its absence invariably prevent its appearance. Sometimes areas that have definite abrupt gradients will not be perceived as possessing contours. On the other hand, contours will sometimes be perceived where no brightness gradients are apparent to the normal person, or shading will be attributed to a perfectly homogeneous area. Sometimes, even hue will be attributed to the perceived object where no color is present in the stimulus area. Because of this possibility, the determinants must always be contrasted with the stimulus correlates for the degree of correspondence or congruence that exists between the two. This is, in a sense, a test of whether S is stimulus-centered, perceiving only those elements which have a stimulus correlate in the blot, or concept-dominated, utilizing elements which are dictated by the concept regardless of the properties of the blot. The degree of congruence that exists between the determinants and their potential stimulus correlates is rated in these scales. Thus, if the abrupt brightness or color gradients of the stimulus area give rise to contours which bear no relationship to the contours that shape the reported perceived object, the rating for congruence is low or zero. If the contours ordinarily produced by the stimulus area show good correspondence with the contours that shape the perceived object, the rating for congruence is high. If the contours show greater congruence than color, the ratings are distributed accordingly. These congruence scales correspond to the F plus and F minus ratings in the traditional Rorschach scoring, and are extended in addition to the color, intensity, and heterogeneity determinants. The scale steps are as follows:

### 16–18. Congruence Scales

X. Not applicable, since response does not use the determinant, or the area containing the attribute

Y. Determinant not explicitly used but compatible with stimulus attribute of the area
0. No correspondence betweeen attribute of area and determinant
1. Slight correspondence
2. Some correspondence
3. Considerable correspondence
4. Perfect correspondence

### 16. Color

#### 16a. Chromatic Hue (Co-Chr)

#### 16b. Achromatic Color (Co-Ach)

If the natural color of the perceived object is suitably matched by the hue of the stimulus area (e.g., green caterpillar in Card X), the rating for Co-Chr is 4. If, on the other hand, there is no correspondence whatsoever between the color of the perceived object and the color of the stimulus area, the rating is 0. If the color of the perceived object is fortuitous or arbitrary (e.g., "green area is map of Russia because that is the way they usually designate it"), the rating would be 1. In similar fashion, the degree of appropriateness of the achromatic color can also be gauged.

### 17. Intensity (Co-I)

If the brightness of the perceived object is suitably matched by the amount of luminous flux reflected by the stimulus area (the brilliance of driven snow in Ds5, Card II, or the bright blue of the Mediterranean in D1, Card X), the rating for Co-I is high. Although the brightness attribute is present in the blots, it is rarely used as a determinant, at least in the sense of orthodox Rorschach terminology. A rating for Co-I, therefore, will not often be made.

### 18. Heterogeneity

#### 18a. Irregular Gradients (Co-Ir Grad)

#### 18b. Regular Gradients (Co-Gr Grad)

The congruence for Ht is high if irregular gradients are interpreted as surface quality. But if an area with irregular gradients is interpreted as black, the congruence is not as high. Similarly, if the gradual gradients are interpreted as a dimensionality determinant, the congruence is high, but if they are interpreted as surface quality, the congruence is low.

#### 18c. Abrupt Brightness Gradients (Co-Ab Grad B)

### 18d. Abrupt Color Gradients (Co-Ab Grad C)

The congruence of the contours of the perceived object with the abrupt gradients of the stimulus area can be gauged with the help of Beck's Tables for F+ and F— scores. Generally speaking, F+ corresponds to a rating of 4, and F— to a rating of zero. A simple F score corresponds to a rating of 2. Steps 1 and 3 can be used for intermediate judgments. The contours formed by brightness gradients are more distinct than the contours formed by color gradients and will ordinarily get higher ratings.

**IV. Elaboration Categories.** The various determinants interact to give rise to a variety of elaborations.[4] In some cases it is easy to find the line of relationship between the attributes of the stimulus area, the determinants to which they gave rise, and the resulting organization of these determinants into a final percept with specific elaborated visual characteristics like shape, depth, distance, etc. Sometimes, however, the line of relationship among the three types of visual variables is not so clear. In any event, the characteristics of the perceived object have been described in terms of the following: hue (Hue), surface appearance (Su), shape (Shp), dimensional structure (Dim), distance (Dis), movement (Dy), and position (Po). The steps for rating the relative importance of these variables are given in scales 19–25. In classifying responses in accordance with these scales, it is well to bear in mind that their purpose is to determine what particular characteristic is most important in the perceived object. Remembering that the response is based on a high degree of selectivity and that this selectivity presumably is characteristic of the S, we wish to know what are the characteristics of objects which the individual is more interested in, or more prone to see.

### A. Importance Scales

**19–25. Importance of Elaboration Categories (Hue, Su, Shp, Dim, Dis, Dy, Po)**

0. Of no importance
1. Of some minor importance
2. Of secondary importance
3. Important interpretation factor
4. Most important interpretation factor

---

[4] These elaborations are ordinarily regarded as determinants by orthodox Rorschach workers. However, from our logical analysis of the area attributes and response determinants, it is apparent, for example, that M is not a determinant in the same sense as C, I, and Ht.

Since the purpose of these scales is to determine the relative importance of the seven elaboration categories, it is desirable to rate at least one of them a 4, and give the others corresponding values.

### 19. Hue Elaboration (Hue)

In determining the relative importance of hue as a characteristic of the perceived object, the question to be answered is: would the response have been the same if hue were not included? For example, in the response "clowns" to Card II, would S have said "clowns" if he were not including the painted faces? The chances are that without the painted faces, the response would have been some other type of person. Hue is therefore given a high rating in this response. Had the response been monks with black cowls, the black of the cowls would be rated high, although not as high as hue was rated in the previous example. Both chromatic and achromatic colors are rated on this scale. The distinction between chromatic and achromatic has already been recorded in the determinant scale.

### 20. Surface Appearance (Su)

The surface appearance of the perceived object deals with such qualities as fleeciness, furriness, texture, hardness, softness, and other tactual qualities perceived through the visual modality. The perception of objects whose outstanding characteristic is surface appearance (clouds, fur rugs, etc.) and in which the other visual dimensions are of secondary or no importance are rated high on this scale. A profile, for example, would have a zero rating for surface appearance.

### 21. Shape (Shp)

Whenever the characteristics of the perceived object depend on its shape alone and on no other visual qualities, the shape rating is high. For example, silhouettes, profiles, etc., are primarily based on shape and on little else.

### 22. Dimensional Structure (Dim)

Percepts whose chief visual characteristic is dimensional structure, either one-dimensional, two-dimensional, or three-dimensional, are rated high on this scale. For example, a statue, a pictorial two-dimensional figure, an X-ray etc., would be rated high on this scale, whereas percepts in which dimensionality is of lesser import—a picture of something, a cloud, a drop of blood, a vista (scaled under distance)—receive a low rating on this scale, even though they might receive a high rating on the shape scale.

### 23. Distance (Dis)

Vista scenes, views from airplanes, and scenes in perspective receive high ratings on this scale, whereas nearby objects lacking in distance or perspective receive low ratings. One way of determining the spatial distance between the perceiver and the object perceived is to ask *S*, "From where do you see this? Where would you be if you saw this? How do you see it?" These questions sometimes help in determining the nature of the response. Thus, an airplane may be seen as above, flying, or on the ground, or at a long distance, and the determination of where the airplane is seen from can give information regarding movement and other modes of interpretation.

### 24. Dynamic-Static Continuum (Dy)

The movement aspects of the perceived objects are rated on this scale. Objects perceived in motion, regardless of the nature of the object (human, animal, or inanimate) and regardless of whether *S* feels the perceived movements, are rated high on this scale, whereas static percepts are rated low.

### 25. Position (Po)

Some Ss will sometimes utilize the symmetry of two parts of the blot or their sheer location, as a determinant. They interpret a given location to signify a heart if it is in the center of the blot, regardless of the contours it presents. The position elaboration category is said to be important only when the topographical location of a certain area is a factor in eliciting the response. Responses determined completely by the positional elaboration are not common among normal Ss. The question to be answered in rating this variable is: how important is the position of the perceived stimulus area with reference to the rest of the blot (or of part of the stimulus area with reference to the rest) in determining the response? Since this scale is somewhat of an innovation as a continuum, the detailed steps for evaluating its importance will be given.

0. Of no importance—position has nothing to do with the character of the response
1. Of some minor importance—position plays some slight role in determining the response
2. Of secondary importance—position plays a definite role in determining the response, but other factors (shape, etc.) outweigh it
3. Important interpretive factor—position outweighs other interpretations in determining the response
4. Most important interpretive factor—the only congruent element in

determining the response is position (e.g., "Kidneys because they are on the side") when neither the shape nor the color nor the surface appearance support this interpretation

## B. Type Scales

Each of the elaboration categories may give rise to a variety of types of elaboration. In the previous set of scales for Importance, a judgment was made regarding the importance of each elaboration category. Now we shall proceed to determine *within* the most important category, the particular type selected. Only elaboration categories which have a rating of 4 or 3 need to be rated on the Type scales. In general, an X rating indicates that the scale is not applicable because a 3 or 4 rating was not given on the appropriate Importance scale. A rating of 0 indicates that although the scale is applicable, since a 3 or 4 rating was given on the appropriate Importance scale, the Type scale cannot be applied to the particular concept given.

### 26. Types of Hue Categories

There is a wide variety of color phenomena which could be distinguished as types of color interpretations. Among these are: (*a*) film color; (*b*) surface color; (*c*) volume color; (*d*) transparent color; (*e*) lustrous color; and (*f*) luminous color. The film and surface color phenomena can be included in a continuum which parallels Rorschach's C, CF, and FC continuum and Beck's Y, YF, and FY continuum. A transparency–opaqueness continuum can also be established. Lustrous, luminous, and volume colors are so rarely found that they will not be considered in the scales.

### 26a. Surface as Film Color (Su-C)

This scale applies both to chromatic and achromatic color and attempts to gauge the continuum extending from object colors, which adhere to the surface of objects, to film colors, which are more or less disembodied from objects (cf. Katz's phenomenological analysis of these two types of color [1935]).

X. Scale does not apply
0. Surface as film color element does not appear in percept
1. Film color
2. Blue of the sky; red of fire and blood; gray of dawn; blackness of night; white of sunshine
3. Surface color, but attached to rather amorphous objects (Rorschach's CF, Beck's YF): gray rocks or clouds; yellow amoeba

4. Definite surface or object color (Rorschach's FC, Beck's FY): painted clown's face; white porcelain sink

### 26b. Transparency–Opaqueness (Tr-Op)

X. Scale does not apply
0. Transparent–opaque elements do not appear in percept
1. Completely transparent
2. Diffused transparency: veiled figures, silhouettes, underwater scene
3. Mirror image, reflection in water
4. Completely opaque

### 27. Types of Surface Appearance Categories

Sometimes the visual characteristics of the surface of an object are interpreted in terms of tactual phenomena, or thermal or kinaesthetic phenomena. Probably the most important aspect of the surface appearance of objects on the Rorschach plates is texture, the visual correlate of tactual experience. But thermal responses, as well as kinaesthetic, in terms of hardness–softness, are also obtained.

### 27a. Surface Texture (Su-T)

X. Scale does not apply
0. Textural or tactual qualities do not appear in the percept
1. Slight evidence of textural quality: object identified as bones, cloth, etc., but no further elaboration; shape or particular hues predominate rather than texture
2. Definite evidence of texture: response still primarily governed by other interpretations, but response would probably not have occurred without the perception of texture
3. Texture predominates over the other types of surface appearance: "This has consistency of rough stone" or "fur" where shape is not very definite
4. Purely textural response: shape and color have little or nothing to do with formation of response

Note: If S fingers card as if trying to touch texture, a rating of at least 2 on this scale should be given.

### 27b. Softness–Hardness (S-H)

X. Scale does not apply
0. Softness–hardness elements do not appear in percept
1. Extremely soft surface, offers no resistance, for example, smoke, fog, mist; or very soft surface, offers mild resistance, for example, soft snow, water, cotton, fleecy wool

2. Soft surface, offers some resistance, for example, fur, leaves, soft material; cloth—neither hard nor soft
3. Hard, considerable resistance, for example, tree, bark, wood, elephant skin
4. Very hard, for example, rocks, metals, diamonds, ice

### 27c. Smoothness–Roughness (S-R)

X. Scale does not apply
0. Smoothness–roughness elements do not appear in percept
1. Very smooth, for example, satin, silver, wire, bones, coal, water, ice, liver
2. Moderately smooth, for example, grass, material, ocean, clouds, cement road
3. Rough, for example, bark of tree, lava, scratchy, hairy
4. Very rough, for example, barbed wire, rocky surface, stucco

### 28. Types of Shape Categories

No particular types of shape categories seem to be important in Rorschach evaluations. There is a possibility that the symbolic value of shape might be analyzed, for example, continuous vs. discontinuous, or pointed, angular vs. curved shapes, but no such scales have yet been developed.

### 29. Types of Dimensional Structure Categories

The percept reported by S may vary in its dimensionality from linear objects possessing essentially only one dimension, for example, lines, or spire of church, to solid objects possessing three dimensions. Since there is no psychological continuum that corresponds to these types of space perception, an Importance scale is provided for each of the three dimensions. Each percept is rated on the degree to which each of these factors—unidimensionality, bidimensionality, and tridimensionality—contributes to the final percept. In addition, Rorschach workers have included another type of perception—seeing three-dimensional objects telescoped or flattened into two dimensions, for example, X-rays, silhouettes, and profiles. The following scales are to be used:

### 29a. Unidimensionality (I)

X. Scale does not apply
0. No linear or unidimensional characteristics in percept
1. Unidimensionality as a background factor, for example, horizon seen
2. Of some importance

3. Of considerable importance—a spire on a church helping in interpretation of building as church
4. The most important determinant, for example, spire, pencil, string, stick, or other essentially linear object, where the linear dimension is the most important

### 29b. Bidimensionality (II)

X. Scale does not apply
0. No area characteristics in percept (completely unidimensional)
1. Background factor, for example, range of mountains in the distance
2. Some importance
3. Considerable importance, for example, objects presenting areas such as buildings with walls, profiles, silhouettes, architect's plans, flat pictures
4. Most important—primarily flat bidimensional objects; geometrical figures, shadows, clouds, leaves, rugs, skins, etc.

### 29c. Tridimensionality (III)

X. Scale does not apply
0. No tridimensional characteristics, for example, string, clouds
1. Background factor, for example, silhouettes, profiles
2. Of some importance
3. Of considerable importance, for example, column of smoke
4. Three-dimensional objects perceived as solid, or the perception of volume, for example, human figure, statue, mushrooming atomic cloud (Card IX)

### 29d. Tridimensionality Projected into Two Dimensions (IV)

X. Scale does not apply
0. No projection characteristics
1. Background factor—figures seen against a flat background
2. Of some importance
3. Of considerable importance, for example, flattened animals or crushed animals
4. Most important, for example, X-rays, silhouettes, profiles, bas-relief, topographical maps

### 30. Types of Distance Categories

The only specific modes of distance perception with which Rorschach workers deal are those attributable to perspective and to haze and atmospheric diffusion (vista), with the latter predominating.

Other monocular cues for distance, such as interposition and comparative size, have not been discussed. Only two Type scales for vista and perspective will be presented.

The vista scale refers to scenic views of mountain ranges, castles in the distance, valleys, views from airplanes, etc. By perspective views is meant the viewing of scenes or objects without awareness of distance (as in vista) but in which certain distortions or illusions are perceived, for example, the railroad track illusion, or the giant in Card IV, seen with large boots and a small head because of perspective distortion.

### 30a. Vista (V)

X. Does not apply
0. No vista present
1. Slight degree of vista
2. Some degree of vista
3. Considerable degree of vista
4. Vista is the most important interpretation

### 30b. Perspective (Pv)

X. Scale does not apply
0. No perspective present
1. Of background value, for example, range of mountains seen in distance with figure in front
2. Of some importance
3. Of considerable importance
4. Most important—vista scenes, valleys, mountain ranges

### 31. Types of Dynamic–Static Categories

The Levy Movement Blots provide some seventeen scales for the evaluation of movement, and a selection of these can be made for the evaluation of the types of movement perceived (Supplement, Part IV). One generally useful Type scale is that which ranges from static or frozen movement to active movement.

### 31a. Strength of Movement (M)

X. Scale does not apply
0. Total absence of movement characteristics
1. Forced movement (being moved by external force, being dropped, revolved, restrained, etc.)
2. Static or frozen movement (standing, sitting, lying, spreading, as wings of animals without any apparent movement); not caught in midst of action

3. Tension (bending, rising, actively outstretched, poised, smiling, or showing some other expression); caught in midst of action
4. Active movement (shaking hands, playing patty cake, talking, stirring something, engaged in sexual intercourse, dancing, whirling, or other dynamic activities)

Another Type scale could be one that gauges the presence of empathy in the movement—to what degree was the movement felt. Since it is difficult to rate this elaboration of a determinant, no scale is provided. However, if the examiner wishes to inquire about the presence of empathy he might use five steps such as not felt at all, slightly felt, moderately felt, definitely felt, and strongly felt.

### 32. Types of Positional Categories

These are the following types of positional elements that could be scaled for importance: symmetry, slant, and central as opposed to peripheral position. The following scales can be provided:

### 32a. Symmetry (Sy)

X. Does not apply
0. No symmetry elements in response
1. Slight indication of use of symmetry
2. Some indication of use of symmetry in formation of response
3. Considerable indication of use of symmetry in formation of response
4. Symmetry is the most important element in the interpretation

It should be noted that symmetry is present in all the blots and hence serves as background in many responses. The absence of any symmetry element in a given record may be indicative of some personality distortion. On the other hand, the overworking of this element may also be an important indicator. Responses in which the midline and its symmetry are referred to, enter in this category.

Since slant and central vs. peripheral position are not utilized at the present time in Rorschach interpretation, no scales will be provided for them. Perhaps the topographic location of the response—whether it is in the center, at the edge, below, or above—can be rated in a topographical relation scale.

### 32b. Topographical Relation (Top)

X. Does not apply
0. Of no significance
1. Of minor significance

2. Of some significance
3. Of considerable significance
4. The most significant element in determining the response

*V. Organization.* Organization activity refers to S's structuring of the vague material presented in the inkblot so as to form a meaningful configuration. We have distinguished three aspects of organization: mode, type, and figure–ground relationships.

### 33. Mode of Organization (Mz)

This scale estimates S's ability in organization in terms of the type of blot material used and relative difficulty for the individual cards. The scale uses a modification of Beck's Z score. Beck's presentation (1949) is a helpful reference. His more recent book (1961) also contains a detailed description of the Z score.

As a result of a study of the modes of organization, Beck formulated four pure and two mixed modes, as follows:

w   whole
j   adjacent details
t   distant details, that is, separated either by filled material or by white space
s   filled material and white spaces
wj  simultaneous organization involving both w and j
wt  simultaneous organization involving both w and t

Beck has made a statistical study of the difficulty of each type of organization, to which he applied the symbol Z. This scale is weighted for the relative organizational difficulties that each card presents and ranges in value from 1.0 to 6.5. For the purposes of our scale we have reduced Beck's values to scores running from 0 to 4, in order to make them conform to the scales used for scoring the other factors in the responses. Zero is reserved for those responses using only individual details. Beck lists the Z value for each of his 4000 scored responses, and this reservoir of scores can be used to obtain our transformed values. The transformed values are shown in Table C.

### 34. Type of Organization (Tz)

In this scale we attempt to judge the manner in which the organized response has been built up. Sometimes the response appears full-blown without yielding any evidence as to how it was organized, while at other times the successive stages in the formation of the response are quite evident. Sometimes, a response is considered to be a whole just because a

*Table C. Ratings for Mode of Organization Corresponding to Beck's Score*

| Cards | Whole | Adjacent | Distant | Black with White | Mixed | |
|---|---|---|---|---|---|---|
| | w | j | t | s | z | |
| I | 1 | 3 | 4 | 2 | wj | 3 |
| II | 3 | 2 | 4 | 3 | wj | 3 |
| III | 4 | 2 | 3 | 3 | D1 | 3 |
| | | | | | D9 | 2 |
| IV | 1 | 3 | 2 | 3 | | |
| V | 1 | 2 | 3 | 3 | | |
| VI | 2 | 2 | 4 | 4 | wj | 2 |
| VII | 2 | 1 | 2 | 3 | wt | 2 |
| | | | | | wj | 2 |
| VIII | 3 | 2 | 2 | 3 | | |
| IX | 4 | 2 | 3 | 3 | | |
| X | 4 | 3 | 3 | 4 | | |

D1 and D9 refer to certain specified areas in Card III.

single detail suggests this whole, with little or no attention paid to the appropriateness of the rest of the blot to this response. For example, the whole of Card VI may be labeled "a cat" merely because the upper protuberances of D2 suggest "cat's whiskers." This is the confabulated whole (DW or DdW), and is regarded as confined to abnormal Ss. Although the DW is considered the classic example of confabulation, this type of response may proceed (as in the example cited) from a Dd rather than a D, or it may occur with regard to a smaller division of the card than W. To call one of the figures in Card III a horse because the "foot" suggests a "horse's hoof" is confabulation of the DdD type.

Thus, it is important to distinguish at least three types of organization: (a) confabulatory or pseudo-organization as in DW, DdW, and DdD; (b) combinatory organization, corresponding largely to Rorschach's *sukzessiv* W; and (c) immediate or instant organization which, at least as far as whole responses are concerned, corresponds to Rorschach's obvious *Ganzantwort*. As Beck noted (1949), Rorschach himself did not distinguish the first two adequately, although clinical experience indicates an enormous difference between the purely specious organization of confabulatory DW, for example, which is probably pathognomic, and the combinatory response, which involves the more or less laborious structuring of parts into an acceptable whole; for the latter may occur in normal and even in superior Ss. The DW, DdW, and DdD will always receive a rating of 0 on the Tz scale, and the presence of confabulation will usually be indicated further by the low rating which the given response receives on the Congruence scales (16–18). The Tz scale might then be arranged as follows:

X. Response confined to one undifferentiated area of the blot; Mz score is 0, but no confabulation present

0. Confabulation: DW, DdW, or DdD

1. Response laboriously built up by successive association to different parts of the blot

2. Response quite apparently built up by successive association to different parts of the blot

3. Some slight evidence of elaboration of the response by successive association

4. Sudden emergence of the completed response, exclusive of responses scored as X

### 35. Figure-Ground (White Spaces) (S)

The white spaces in the Rorschach cards may be of varying or no importance in the production of a response. Even when the white spaces are alluded to, they are customarily regarded as background and the figure is located in the filled-in areas. Such is not always the case, however, and with some individuals we note a marked tendency to see figures in the white spaces and to regard the filled-in areas as ground. This tendency to make greater or lesser use of the white spaces is gauged on the following scale:

X. Response area contains no white space

0. White space is seen neither as figure nor ground (not a recognized part of the stimulus area used in the response)

1. White space is seen as ground, for example, when black surrounded by white is interpreted as island

2. White space serves as a minor part of the figure

3. White space serves as a major part of the figure

4. White space alone is figure

## REFERENCES

Beck, S. J. *Rorschach's test: I. Basic processes.* New York: Grune and Stratton, 1949.

Beck, S. J., Beck, Anne G., Levitt, E. E., & Molish, H. B. *Rorschach's test: I. Basic processes.* New York: Grune and Stratton, 1961.

Katz, D. *The world of colour.* London: Kegan Paul, Trench, Trubner, 1935.

Zubin, J. A psychometric approach to the evaluation of the Rorschach test. *Psychiat.,* 1941, 4, 547–566.

Zubin, J., Eron, L. D., & Sultan, Florence. A psychometric evaluation of the Rorschach experiment. *Amer. J. Orthopsychiat.,* 1956, 26, 773–782.

# 7 A PSYCHOMETRIC APPROACH TO THE RORSCHACH TECHNIQUE: *content factors* [1]

The formal factors in the evaluation of Rorschach responses have been described in the preceding chapter. We shall now turn our attention to the analysis of the content of Rorschach responses.

## THE RORSCHACH RATING SCALES (CONTINUED)

*VI. Content.* The content of the Rorschach responses may be divided into two major subdivisions: "dynamic" content and "objective" content.

*Dynamic Aspects of Content.* In addition to the ordinary categories of content utilized by Rorschach workers, to be discussed later, there has been some attempt to evaluate the content in terms of self-referred "dynamic" concepts. Schachtel (1941) drew a distinction between "detached" and "dynamic" percepts. "Detached" percepts are objective and impersonal. In this category belong certain very popular responses like "bat" to Card I, which so approach the character of picture recognition that they need not depend on personal factors for their perception. Such responses probably represent the lowest level of self-involvement. Diametrically opposed to these are the "dynamic," self-referred, nonpopular responses, which are more dependent on internal factors in S and represent some degree of self-involvement. It is possible that these

---

[1] See Footnote 1, Chapter 6.

348

"dynamic" aspects of content reflect more the interests and self-evaluative characteristics of Ss than do such factors as form, color, and movement. While the particular content of responses, according to generally accepted opinion, is largely subject to the accidental influence of experience, this may not be true of the "dynamic" content. It is also possible that when S does not exhibit sufficient involvement in the task, his record may not be representative. This factor of involvement may explain why some records are revealing of personality and others are not.

In discussing such determinants as color, intensity, and heterogeneity, we are referring to stimuli present in the inkblots to which S is (by a selective process) responsive. But this is not entirely true of the movement determinants, since these are largely projected by S into the inkblots. It should be possible, indeed, to make out a good case for including movement among the "dynamic" aspects of *content* rather than among the determinants, since movement is a response rather than a stimulus. The further specification of movement as human movement (M), animal movement (FM), or inanimate movement (Fm), certainly pertains to the content of the response rather than to the stimuli which provoke it, and if Rorschach is right in maintaining that the movement response involves an empathic kinaesthesis on the part of S, that is a further reason for regarding movement as a "dynamic" aspect of content. For the present, however, we waive this point and proceed to the construction of certain other "dynamic" content scales.

## 36. Evaluative Scale (Ev)

0. No indication of any evaluative attitude: matter-of-fact responses and responses of the popular variety; bat, butterfly, two people, phallic symbol, ribs, etc.
1. Evaluative attitude in background; mentioning size, weight or appearance of objects in a somewhat detached, objective manner: hard rocks, soft fur, tall trees, old women, etc.
2. Some evaluative attitude: quite large or tiny objects, faces grimacing or sad, "cute" dogs, powerful rats, people engaged in everyday activity such as women talking, cooks stirring broth, etc.
3. Marked evaluative attitude: a very lofty mountain, a very unpleasant face, people struggling, falling to their death, enjoying themselves hugely, etc.
4. Extreme evaluative attitude: a terrifying gorilla, a very beautiful and enticing woman, gruesome and horrible men, leering and threatening faces, a gorgeous underwater tropical scene, etc.

When rating a response on this scale, only the free association should be considered and material elicited in the Inquiry disregarded. It should be noted that the direction of the evaluation is omitted, since it is difficult to know whether the individual who under- or overevaluates is identifying or compensating. In certain cases, the direction of the evaluation may be very significant, as in the human-like (H) responses, which some Rorschach workers have regarded as indicative of S's attitude toward his fellows. The traditional scoring system designates all such responses simply as (H), while the rating-scale method permits us to estimate whether the human-like response is in a flattering or disparaging direction. In general, an evaluative attitude can be detected by the frequency of adjectives in the responses.

### 37. Human-like Scale [2] (H-L)

X. Scale does not apply
0. Ennobled or divinized humans: angels, gods, Jesus Christ, the Blessed Virgin, clerics
1. Ordinary human beings in modern dress
2. Slightly caricatured human beings: clowns, cartoon characters, Donald Duck, manikins, oriental faces, theatrical masks, primitives, medieval men, women in 1890 garb, humans in costume
3. Fabulous and somewhat ominous creatures of human-like character: witches, goblins, devils, ghosts, skull-like humans, etc.
4. Human-like monsters: ape-men, prehistoric humans, vampire-men, aborted fetuses, decaying corpses, etc.

Akin to the human-like responses are those responses in which human beings are seen in more or less unflattering aspects or situations. The following scale endeavors to assess this tendency:

### 38. Human Debasement Scale [3] (H-D)

X. Scale does not apply
0. Human beings who are pleasing in appearance or engaged in ennobling situations: a very beautiful or happy woman, a man praying, etc.
1. Ordinary human beings or humans engaged in ordinary activities
2. Human beings who are somewhat ugly in appearance or engaged in somewhat unflattering activities: an old woman with shrunken jaws, a man arguing or fighting, primitive tribal fights, etc.

---

[2] This scale is bipolar. In obtaining means for ratings on this scale, special procedures must be taken (see end of this chapter).
[3] See Footnote 2.

3. Human beings who are markedly ugly or engaged in highly un-flattering situations: misshapen, disintegrating, defecating, etc.
4. Humans who are thoroughly repulsive or engaged in disgusting or morally evil situations: a man pushing a woman off a cliff, a human being having sexual relations with an animal, etc.

A widely studied aspect of human behavior is ascendance-submission. An immediate interpretation of Rorschach responses in terms of this continuum would probably be unwise in view of the difficulty in distinguishing between representation (direct expression of this trait) and compensation, but it should be worthwhile at least to attempt to estimate the dominant or submissive character of the *human figures* seen in the Rorschach plates.

### 39. Ascendance-Submission Scale (A-S)

X. Scale does not apply
0. Human figures are extremely weak, submissive, helpless: a new-born baby, a decrepit old man, human beings at the complete mercy of external forces, etc.
1. Human figures in a general attitude of passivity, submission, or dependence: children, a woman with arms raised in supplication, etc.
2. Human figures neither markedly ascendant nor submissive
3. Rather aggressive or dominating human beings: a man carrying a bundle up a steep hill, or overcoming an obstacle, fighting, etc.
4. Markedly dominating or aggressive human beings: a king, a prize-fighter, etc.

There remain many "dynamic" aspects of content which may require qualitative interpretation, or for which scales covering each response cannot be conveniently constructed. Some of these, such as the tendency to see aggressive weapons and sharp-pointed objects, may be highly significant. Others, like the tendency to pick out U- or V-shaped objects, trees, caves, and the like, are regarded by many as unimportant. In any case, however, when such an aspect of the Rorschach record is deemed worthy of note, a scale may be constructed to estimate its importance throughout the record rather than for each individual response. Scales of this type might run from a zero value for one or two such responses to a four value for a record which is fairly surcharged, for example, with aggressive symbols like knives or other weapons. In this fashion, even some of the so-called "purely qualitative indicators" need not escape psychometric evaluation. If we are going to employ such factors, it is prudent to have them scaled in some fashion, however imperfect, so that the temptation to overestimate their significance in accordance with subjective conceptions may be somewhat reduced.

### 40. Personal Distance Scale (PD)

The degree of social, spatial, or temporal distance that S experiences with regard to the people, animals, and objects he perceives in the blot may be rated on the following scale:

X. Does not apply (the only animals scored on this scale are four legged mammals)
0. Caricatures, drawings, statues
1. Mythological creatures and specific story book characters: witches, elves, angels, dragons, unicorns, Snow White, Alice in Wonderland, gingerbread castle
2. People, animals, or objects of different geological ages: Neanderthal man, prehistoric arrow heads
3. People of different historical periods, chronological age, race, or social status (with respect to S): toga-clad Roman, baby, octogenarian, African aborigine; all animals and objects appropriate to this scale but not included in preceding categories
4. Contemporary persons

Some Ss find it impossible to put any distance at all between themselves and the persons, animals, and objects seen in the cards, referring every response to themselves personally, and stating that what is seen reminds them of a situation, object, or person in childhood or later life. Responses of other Ss give no overt indication of any personal reference. The degree of personal reference may be estimated on the following scale:

### 40a. Degree of Self-Reference (Se)

The personal reference must be stated specifically in order to receive more than a 0 rating.

0. Impersonal response
1. Slight degree of self-reference, for example, objects seen which are in some way connected with the trade or occupation of S
2. Some degree of self-reference: object recognized as similar to one experienced by S
3. Marked self-reference: members of S's family, objects involved in important or traumatic experiences of S

4. Completely self-referred: S sees himself as a child, some part of himself, eyes looking at him, gorilla coming at him

*Objective Aspects of Content.* Although some Rorschach workers have minimized the importance of formal content as a reflection of personality, they have admitted that certain categories of content are probably significant. The chief of these are human (H); animal (A); inanimate object (In); natural phenomenon (Nat); anatomy (At); sexual response (Sex); and abstract concept (Ab). In addition, some stress has been placed on the contrary tendencies to see primarily whole objects, or simply details, or parts of objects. To bring these aspects of the record within the compass of the psychometric method proposed here, a series of Importance scales and Type scales is suggested. In classifying a response on the Importance scales, we must ask to what class of objects does the response primarily belong. Is it primarily human (H), animal (A), plant (Pl), inanimate (In), anatomical (At), or is it primarily abstract (Ab)? Some responses are simply human figures and would be rated 4 for (H), and 0 for all other factors. Other responses are entirely animal, plant, or inanimate. When a response includes, however, both human and animal elements, the relative importance of each must be gauged; and similarly for other combinations of content categories. The Importance scales for each of the categories will thus be the same.

A. *Importance Scales* [4]

*41. Human (H); 42. Animal (A); 43. Plant (Pl);*

*44. Inanimate (In); 45. Abstract (Ab); 46. Anatomy (At)*

0. Not important
1. In the background but not definitely seen either in the original responses or during the Inquiry, for example, "a man's coat" would receive a rating of H1, In4
2. Of secondary importance as evidenced by the Inquiry or inferred directly from the original response
3. A most important element as evidenced by mention in the original response
4. The most important category

If the object is a symbol of some kind, for example, crown, mitre, or crest, a rating of at least 1 should be given on the Abstract scale.

---

[4] Every response is rated 4 once and only once on one of the Importance scales.

"Clothes on a human figure" is given at least a rating of 2 on the Inanimate scale.

Some of the traditional Rorschach categories for classifying content overlap several of the psychometric scales. Thus, animal objects, like skins of animals (AObj), are scored 4 on scale 42 (A), and 3 on scale 44 (In). Human anatomy *in vitro* is scored 3 on scale 41 (H), 3 on scale 44 (In), and 4 on scale 46 (At). Sex responses in which sex organs are seen in isolation (penis, vagina, etc.) are scored 2 on scale 41 (H), 4 on scale 46 (At), and 4 on scale 48 (Sex).

### B. Type Scales

The tendencies to see whole objects or merely parts of objects and to see sexual organs or activities are rated on the following Type scales:

### 47. Whole-Part Scale (W-P)

X. Scale does not apply: maps, qualities, color, blood, landscapes, clouds, rock formation and other percepts that lack either integral or partial quality

0. Relatively small part of an object seen, not sufficient for individual identification: hand, leg, labia, phallus, nose, internal anatomy and other objects that do not ordinarily exist in isolation

1. Large part of an object seen but significant part is missing: human head, head and shoulders of bear, headless torso

2. Only small part of perceived object missing (complement of what is present in step 0)

3. Whole not seen entirely but suggested as present, for example, two entire female figures in Card VII, but lower portions hidden behind couch or draperies or merging into ground

4. Entire object seen: no parts missing

### 48. Sex Reference Scale (Sex)

0. No apparent sex reference

1. Sexual symbolism: snakes, caves, tunnels, etc.

2. Possible sex reference: an attractive woman, two young people dancing, 2 bears rubbing noses, pelvic anatomy

3. Secondary sex characteristics (breasts, buttocks, thighs, etc.), or secondary sex activity (kissing, embracing, etc.)

4. Primary sex organs or primary sex activity

Such tendencies as those revealed by a great number of artistic responses, or the morbid penchant for seeing corpses and dead animals, as well as the putative homosexual tendency to see only or principally persons of the same sex should be rated for the entire record, as suggested in treating symbolically aggressive responses (knives, weapons, etc.) rather than for each individual response. These and related responses are rare in "normal" records, so that it would be imprudent to complicate further an already complicated scoring system for the sake of covering a relatively small number of cases.

### 49. Definiteness of Content Scale [5] (Def)

The definiteness or specificity of content may vary from vague, amorphous objects like "shapes in the clouds" or "things you might see in a kaleidoscope" to such specific responses as: "Michelangelo's Moses" or a "gossiping old woman wearing a ridiculous hair-do."

0. Vague, formless, lacking in specific content: reflection of something with nothing else specified; mist, splotches, clouds of no particular shape
1. Highly generic and indefinite: a spread eagle effect, an animal or something like that
2. Less generic: a fish-like animal, an insect, some sort of pumping instrument, a tree, responses in which two possibilities are mentioned, for example, a dog or a lion
3. Specifically designated objects: a praying mantis, an old man, huge pink rats, etc.
4. Specifically designated and definite objects: Mark Twain, a Spanish dancer with mantilla and flowing cape, Arc de Triomphe

### 50. Gender of the Observed Figure (Ge)

We have already suggested a scale for determining the importance of sex reference (symbolism or representation) in a given response. The present scale attempts to gauge the gender preference for the animal or human figures reported by S. The same figure may be interpreted by one individual as a male and by another as a female. Moreover, the gender indicated may be the same as that of S (e.g., reference to a male figure by a male S) or may be the opposite of that of S. In the following scale, opposite and same refer to the sex of S.

0. Response bears no reference to gender
1. Doubtful reference
2. Reference to either male or female figure or part of anatomy without specifying gender, unsure of gender

---

[5] In the orthodox Rorschach scoring, the lower categories in the scale are noted as F—, C—, etc. A minus can arise from two sources, lack of correspondence between determinants and interpretation, or vagueness of content. Scale 49 has been introduced to differentiate between these two sources of minus scores.

3. Reference to the opposite sex [6]—either figure or part of anatomy
4. Reference to the same sex—either figure or part of anatomy

*VII. Psychological Characteristics of the Response.* In addition to the categories of location, determinants, and content, there are certain psychological features that characterize the responses of a given S. The majority of these are more closely related to content than to location or determinants, so that their treatment may be fittingly appended to the content scales just discussed. Perhaps the most significant of these is the tendency toward perseveration.

### 51. Perseverative Tendency (Pe)

Perseveration may make itself manifest in exact repetitions of previous responses, or in responses of generically or specifically similar form or content.

0. Response completely unrelated to previous responses
1. Slight similarity, but more than that implied by two H, or two A responses: a repetition of such responses as old women, bats
2. Moderate similarity: two-X-rays, two animal skins
3. Marked similarity, content almost identical: pointing fingers, eyes lurking in shadows, pelvis, sex organs, same portions of anatomy
4. Exact or almost exact repetition of previous response: form as well as content almost identical, area comparable, action the same, etc.

### 52. Elaborative Tendency (El)

Some Ss tend to elaborate their responses markedly. They weave a story about what they see or use the blots as stimuli for extensive free association. In its extreme form, this tendency may make it difficult for the examiner to discover much correspondence between the Rorschach figures and the content of the response, and may develop in confabulations and incongruencies. When rating on this scale, primary weight should be given to the initial response rather than the Inquiry.

0. No tendency toward elaboration: matter-of-fact responses closely tied to the general characteristics of the blot
1. Some tendency toward elaboration
2. Marked tendency toward elaboration
3. Richly elaborated but still related to observed features of the card
4. Highly elaborated responses without effort to locate appropriate referents in the blot itself: free association and "apperception"

---

[6] Opposite to sex of S. The value of 4 attached to "same sex" and of 3 attached to "opposite sex" is only tentative, and will have to await further validation.

## 53. Tendency toward Blot Description (Des)

0. No blot description irrelevant to the response
1. Slight tendency toward blot description
2. Moderate tendency toward blot description but more or less connected with the response
3. Marked tendency toward blot description: scorable response incidental to description
4. Extreme tendency: blot description only, no scorable response

It should be noted that the tendency toward blot description, reportedly well marked in schizophrenics, need not preclude the giving of scorable responses. It may result, rather, in the situation wherein the scorable response is thickly interlarded with irrelevant descriptions of color, shading, lines, symmetry, and the like. In the marked tendency, as noted, the content of the response becomes quite incidental to the description of the blot, and in the extreme tendency there is no response whatsoever. In rating on this scale, the amount of description given in the Inquiry should generally not be considered.

## 54. Mood of the Response (Mo)

The situation perceived on the card often has a highly pleasant or unpleasant quality, and since this is a projection, in some sense, of S's own emotional state, it is certainly worthy of note. We designate this characteristic the mood of the response.

0. Very unpleasant
1. Unpleasant
2. Indifferent
3. Pleasant
4. Extremely pleasant

## 55. Affect of the Subject (Aff)

More subjective than the mood of the response is S's emotional reaction to his own projection. At times there may be marked incongruity between the mood of the response and S's reaction thereto, for example, S laughing uproariously while describing two men being burned alive. This response would be rated as Mo0, Aff4. When the rating is done by someone other than the test administrator, it may be impossible to rate on this scale if careful notes have not been made. In such cases a 2 rating should be given.

0. Very unpleasant
1. Unpleasant

2. No indication of affect
3. Pleasant
4. Extremely pleasant

### 56. Congruousness of Response (Cg)

By congruousness is meant the degree to which various elements in a given response hang together. It may be reasonable to assume that this in turn is a measure of S's clarity of association. Most simple responses are apriori congruent, so that it is only in fairly complex responses that the question of incongruency arises. For example, "black bear" or "white bear" are congruent responses, whereas "grass bear" is completely incongruent. Rorschach had obtained such a response from a schizophrenic patient who had fused two percepts, green grass and the shape of a bear, into one. Contaminated responses of this type may be expected from certain schizophrenics, but there are *degrees* of incongruency and not all responses are as thoroughly "contaminated" as "grass bear."

0. Completely incongruous response: two different concepts, completely unrelated to each other and arising in the same area of the blot, are telescoped or fused into one, for example, grass bear
1. Intrinsically incongruous but some associative connection present: a lamb-camel, a Madonna-candelabra, a penis-vagina
2. Incongruousness between distinct elements in the response: two men shaking hands and a drop of blood falling between (inability to detach distinct concepts)
3. Whimsical or fanciful responses: a bull with a sense of humor, characters of the Alice-in-Wonderland type, monsters, centaurs, freaks, sports, when object can be either animal or human
4. Completely congruent response

### 57. Communality Scale [7] (Com)

This scale attempts to gauge the degree of communality exhibited by S in his Rorschach responses, that is, the degree to which S's responses are those frequently given by others. The scorer should refer to the listings of "popular responses" given by Beck (1949, 1961), Klopfer and Kelley (1942), and by Hertz (1946). These listings were compiled on different statistical bases.

Until inclusive statistical data on frequency of responses are available, ratings at the lower end of this scale can only be tentative, dependent on the scorer's judgment and experience with the test.

---

[7] This scale was revised by Dr. Dorothy Park Griffin.

0. Original; not appearing in any of the published frequency counts: Beck (B), Hertz (H), or Klopfer (K)
1. Tending toward originality; listed by H as original either + or —; occurs only one time in 100 records
2. Common but not popular; listed in only one of the published frequency lists; includes H's popular responses exclusive of those listed under 3 and 4 below, two of B's and ten alternative responses listed by K
3. Quite popular; listed in two of the published frequency lists
4. Very popular; listed in all three published frequency lists

It should be noted that the distinction usually made between good and poor original responses is not made in this scale. The quality of the response is gauged elsewhere under quality scales.

All the responses falling in categories 1 to 4 inclusive are given in the *Supplement*, Part V, which contains material pertinent to children as well as to adults.

*VIII. Rating of Subject's Attitude Toward Responses.* The attitudes exhibited by S toward his own responses may be important in Rorschach interpretations. These attitudes may be divided into the attitude toward the general task of interpreting inkblots, and the attitude toward the response already given. The attitude toward the response given *post rem* is measured in the following scale.

*58. Self-Estimate of the Adequacy of the Response (Adq)*
0. Self-condemnatory; aware of general inadequacy of the response, but helpless to improve it (impotent)
1. Insecure: anxious about the response; wants to know if it is acceptable
2. Autocritical: points out deficiencies or discrepancies but feels that on the whole it is good enough
3. Some slight evidence of dissatisfaction with the given response
4. Simple acceptance of the response as adequate

By comparing the ratings on this scale with those on the quality and congruency scales, the examiner will be able to judge how well the S's estimate of the adequacy of his responses compares with less subjective estimates.

*59. Interpretive Attitude*

The attitude of S toward the task in hand is evidenced in several ways. According to Rorschach, the difference between a routine perception and an interpretation derives from the fact that in interpretations there is a conscious awareness of the incomplete identity of the sensory complex and the memory-trace which it arouses. The effort involved in adjusting the complex sensory impression to the memory-trace is the basis for the differentiation. Whether or not it is necessary to adhere to such concepts of associationist psychology to understand the phenomenon is debatable. It is nevertheless clear that Ss differ in their interpretive attitude toward the blots. Some, especially those less endowed intellectually, take a very concrete attitude, supposing that the task is to find the likenesses of specific objects. Others, more gifted intellectually, soon immerse themselves in the task and "forget" that they are interpreting. There are some individuals, however, and these are not necessarily deficient in intelligence, who are continually aware of the discrepancy between stimulus and response. They repeatedly remind themselves and E that their responses do not correspond exactly to the blots, and express doubt of their validity in advance.

When the interpretive process proceeds smoothly from the moment of the acceptance of the task to the final giving of the response, it may very well be said, following Rorschach, that the interpretation is immediate and there is no consciousness of the interpretive process at all. When, however, the integration of perception and interpretation is absent or disrupted, the performance of the task requires the exercise of continued effort.

To obtain unidimensional continua, the scale has been divided into two parts: type of interpretive attitude (T-A) and awareness of interpretive attitude (A-A).

### 59a. Type of Interpretive Attitude (Without Reference to Awareness) (T-A)

0. Crude acceptance of figures as real: "recognizing" or "guessing" what it is
1. Figures in blot considered almost, but not quite, real
2. Ordinary interpretive distance
3. Tendency to regard figures as a picture or representation: art response, X-ray; "This looks like the picture of an old woman"
4. Extreme of 3; emphasis is on the representation, rather than on what is represented

Note: This scale is bipolar and should be evaluated separately for statistical purposes (see end of this chapter).

### 59b. Awareness of Interpretive Attitude (A-A)

X. If 0 on 56

0. Painfully conscious that the percept does not correspond to the

blot: "It might possibly look like . . .", "If you use your imagination . . .", etc.

2. Moderately conscious of interpretive attitude: "It might be . . .", "You get the impression of . . .", "Could be . . .", "Looks a little like . . ."

4. Fully assimilated interpretive attitude: matter-of-fact responses without mention of interpretive distance

If on this scale E feels that the rating belongs between 0 and 2 or 2 and 4, he is free to employ the 1 or 3 values.

## 60. Reaction Time (RT)

0. First (shortest) quarter in reaction time
1. Second quarter
2. Third quarter
3. Fourth (longest) quarter

The distribution of reaction times is divided into four quarters at the quartile points, and the rating for responses in each quarter is shown in this scale. This scale can be used only for interresponse comparisons, for example, for comparing reaction times of chromatic and achromatic cards, or for similar purposes. Until such time as some accurate method of measuring reaction time for each response is devised, this scale can be used only for the initial response to a card.

It has been claimed that the variation in reaction time results from attempts to repress responses or from confusion resulting when several responses occur simultaneously. Usually, only the reaction time for the first response to each card is noted. The time required for producing the successive responses to the same card is rather difficult to gauge because we can never be sure of the beginning and end points for each response. Despite this difficulty, it is well to gauge approximately the beginning of each new response and to consider the time intervening between the beginning of one response and its successor as the reaction time for the succeeding response. Extremely long pauses in the course of the response should also be noted and the frequency of these tabulated. Since the reaction time scale is rough, the errors introduced by this method should not obscure the results unduly.

*IX. General Data.*[8] This section includes certain overall scales used in recording some of the general facts regarding the total record which

---

[8] Some of these scales are not intended to represent continua. Hence, the data collected by means of these scales can be tabulated by categories, but not added.

may be of importance in interpretation. The ratings are made for the total performance or for each card, but not for each response.

### 61. Turning of the Card (TC)

Each card is handed to S in turn, and no instructions restricting turning are given. The way in which S handles and turns the card, therefore, may be indicative of such qualities as inhibition, assurance, and spontaneity. The situation is perfectly free. Any restraint exhibited by S must, in consequence, be self-imposed. This, too, may be taken as an indication of S's general attitude toward the task at hand.

X. No information available
0. Does not retain card in hands, but leaves it on the table while responding
1. Handles card tentatively on table without turning
2. Holds card off table but does little or no turning
3. Asks permission to turn card
4. Turns card freely

In most cases it will probably be sufficient to score this type of behavior for each card rather than for each response. When S handles and turns the cards freely, the position of the card for each response should be noted on the score sheet.

### 62. Succession (Suc)

Succession is usually measured roughly by noting the order of appearance of W, D, and Dd responses on each card. Several types of succession have been enumerated by Rorschach, Skalweit, Beck, and Klopfer. Without exception, however, their methods of analysis are qualitative rather than quantitative in nature. Since succession as defined by Rorschach assumes the normality of the order: W to D to Dd, it lends itself directly to measurement. For this purpose, a quantitative scale has been devised which is explained in detail elsewhere (Zubin, 1941). Here it is sufficient to indicate that a coefficient can be obtained from the scores which indicates in a rather precise quantitative fashion the degree of regularity of the succession.

### 63. Observational Data (Handling of Cards) (O-D)

Record number of times each is observed.

X. No information available
a. Squints at card, often holding at arm's length
b. Looks at back of card

c. Very rapid turning of card

d. "Edging": holds card flat, looks across surface from one edge

e. Moves card through air to represent movement of object seen

**64. Subject's Readiness to Respond (RR)**

0. Complete refusal

1. Card descriptions merely: inkblots, color naming, shading, lines and contours

2. Much hesitation, only one or two responses per card

3. Restrained flow of responses (three to five responses per card)

4. Easy flow of responses (more than five responses per card)

**65. Type of Responses (TR)**

Record the frequency of each type.

a. Number of primary responses—those given in the free association period (R)

b. Number of additional responses—new responses given for the first time during the Inquiry (AR)

c. Number of cards rejected—cards to which no response was given (Rej)

**66. Temporal Data (TD)**

Record frequency of each of the following:

a. Time for original record—sum of times consumed in responding to each of the ten cards (TT)

b. Average reaction time for all cards—mean of times elapsed between presentation of each card and beginning of first response to it (MRT)

c. Average reaction time for achromatic cards—mean as in (b), for cards I, IV, V, VI, VII only (MRT-A)

d. Average reaction time for chromatic cards—mean as in (b), for cards II, III, VIII, IX, X only (MRT-C)

**X. Rating Scales for Drawing of Percepts.** S's drawing of his responses are of value not only as an aid in clarifying the objective scoring of the responses, but also in revealing further qualitative features of his interpretation of the inkblots. The purpose of these scales is to determine to what extent and in what manner S utilized the specific physical elements of the blot in drawing his responses. Grassi and Levine (1943) have developed a complete series of rating scales for evaluating the drawings. The following scales constitute an adaptation of these.

Each of S's *percepts* (i.e., the thing perceived, object described) may be regarded as the result of "interaction" between the *blot* (i.e., the physical attributes of the visual stimulus) and a *concept* (i.e., the generalized class to which the specific object belongs). A drawing which represents the percept in a recognizable manner, with due regard for both blot and concept, may be said to show optimum balance between the tendencies to reproduce the stimulus and to represent the general concept. On either side of this balanced midpoint, deviations of varying degrees may be found. We thus have a scale ranging from extreme "blot-dominance" or slavish, mechanical copying of the stimulus, through optimum balance, to extreme "concept-dominance" or generalized representation of the object-type. The following scales attempt to rate three aspects of the drawings on this continuum: inclusion and relevance of (*a*) contours, (*b*) colors, and (*c*) modifications and ornamentations. Relevance is always judged in relation to the percept, the specific thing seen.

In comparing results with those based on Grassi and Levine's Graphic Rorschach, note that the rating scales herein used (range 0–4) involve a one-point translation throughout, of those employed by Grassi and Levine (range 1–5).

### 67. Blot Contours (B-C)

0. Irrelevant blot contour details included to such an extent that the thing perceived is no longer recognizable: relevance to the percept plays no part in determining which details are included; spatial disorientation may be a by-product, since relevance to the whole is not seen

1. Some irrelevant blot contour details included, but the thing perceived is recognizable: component parts all included, part-whole relationships adequate, but still some stress on minor details

2. Only the relevant blot contours included, irrelevant ones omitted: both blot contour and percept contour are recognizable

3. Some relevant blot contour details omitted, but the percept is still recognizable: part-whole relationships present in schematized form, representing only the essential contours

4. Many relevant blot contour details omitted, therefore percept is no longer recognizable: stimulus parts hardly recognizable, representative of the concept rather than percept; may include alterations, replacement by S's own creations, etc.

### 68. Blot Colors (B-Co)

This scale refers also to achromatic colors.

0. All blot colors within the stimulus area included, emphasis on exact

matching; colors are irrelevant to the percept, therefore thing perceived not recognizable with respect to color; S may express concern over precise matching of blot colors, ask for pencils of exact shades, etc.

1. Some blot colors not directly relevant to percept are included, but percept recognizable; includes also use of color when Chr or Ach not used as a determinant of the response; S may say, for example, "It needn't be this color, but it might be"

2. Relevant colors included, irrelevant colors disregarded; relevance here means the use of appropriate colors when Chr or Ach was used as a determinant in the response or use of the black lead pencil when Chr or Ach not used

3. Some relevant blot-color omitted (or no color used at all) when there was evidence of use of Chr or Ach as a determinant of response

4. Blot-color relevant to percept omitted and other color (Chr or Ach), relevant only to concept, substituted

### 69. Modification and Ornamentation (Mod)

In this scale, modification refers to changes in blot shape, whereas ornamentation refers to addition of details not represented in the stimulus.

0. Precise reproduction of blot-form without relevant modifications or additions, therefore percept not recognizable; verbal report or manner of drawing may stress importance of exact copying; drawing may appear incomplete

1. Reproduction of general blot-form without relevant modifications or additions, but percept recognizable; selection of relevant blot portions, drawn in proper relationship, may make percept recognizable; no deliberate alteration or addition, but no evidence of careful attempt at precise reproduction

2. Relevant alterations of blot-form and additions, percept easily recognizable; alterations are usually minor adaptations of given blot-form: additions usually supplement features at least partly present in the blot

3. Some irrelevant modifications and additions but percept still recognizable; drawing adapted more to concept than percept; additions only remotely derived from the blot; some prominent contours and given elements of blot may be obscured

4. Modifications and additions so irrelevant that percept no longer recognizable: drawing bears little or no resemblance to blot, may seem "impressionistic"; representation of concept rather than percept

# SUMMARY

## SCALES FOR PSYCHOMETRIC SCORING OF RORSCHACH RESPONSES

| Scale | Symbol |
| --- | --- |
| I. Location of Stimulus Area | |
| A. Importance | |
| 1. Whole | W |
| 2. Detail | D |
| 3. Small Detail | Dd |
| B. Type | |
| 4. Inclusiveness | Inc |
| 5. Frequency of Locale | FL |
| II. Stimulus Area Attributes | |
| A. Importance | |
| 6. Color | A-C |
| 7. Intensity | A-I |
| 8. Heterogeneity | A-Ht |
| B. Type | |
| 9. Type of Color | |
| 9a. Chromatic Color | Chr |
| 9b. Achromatic Color | Ach |
| 10. Degree of Intensity | Deg I |
| 11. Degree of Heterogeneity | Deg Ht |
| 12. Type of Gradient | |
| 12a. Abrupt Gradient | Ab Grad |
| 12b. Irregular Gradient | Ir Grad |
| 12c. Gradual Gradient | Gr Grad |
| III. Determinants | |
| A. Importance | |
| 13. Color | D-C |
| 14. Intensity | D-I |
| 15. Heterogeneity | D-Ht |
| B. Type-Congruence | |
| 16a. Color | Co-Chr |
| 16b. Achromatic Color | Co-Ach |
| 17. Intensity | Co-I |
| 18. Heterogeneity | |
| 18a. Irregular Gradients | Co-Ir Grad |
| 18b. Regular Gradients | Co-Gr Grad |
| 18c. Abrupt Brightness Gradients | Co-Ab Grad B |

| Scale | Symbol |
|---|---|
| 18d. Abrupt Color Gradients | Co-Ab Grad C |
| IV. Elaboration Categories | |
| A. Importance | |
| 19. Hue Elaboration | Hue |
| 20. Surface Appearance | Su |
| 21. Shape | Shp |
| 22. Dimensional Structure | Dim |
| 23. Distance | Dis |
| 24. Dynamic-Static Continuum | Dy |
| 25. Position | Po |
| B. Type | |
| 26. Types of Hue Categories | |
| 26a. Surface as Film Color | Su-C |
| 26b. Transparency-Opaqueness | Tr-Op |
| 27. Types of Surface Categories | |
| 27a. Surface Texture | Su-T |
| 27b. Softness–Hardness | S-H |
| 27c. Smoothness–Roughness | S-R |
| 28. Types of Shape Categories | |
| 29. Types of Dimensional Structure | |
| 29a. Unidimensionality | I |
| 29b. Bidimensionality | II |
| 29c. Tridimensionality | III |
| 29d. Tridimensionality Projected into Two Dimensions | IV |
| 30. Types of Distance Categories | |
| 30a. Vista | V |
| 30b. Perspective | Pv |
| 31. Types of Dynamic-Static Categories | |
| 31a. Strength of Movement | M |
| 32. Types of Positional Categories | |
| 32a. Symmetry | Sy |
| 32b. Topographical Relation | Top |
| V. Organization | |
| 33. Mode of Organization | Mz |
| 34. Type of Organization | Tz |
| 35. Figure-Ground (White Spaces) | S |
| VI. Content | |
| Dynamic Aspects | |
| 36. Evaluative | Ev |
| 37. Human-like | H-L |
| 38. Human Debasement | H-D |
| 39. Ascendance-Submission | A-S |

## SCALES FOR PSYCHOMETRIC SCORING
## OF RORSCHACH RESPONSES (continued)

| Scale | Symbol |
|---|---|
| 40. Personal Distance | PD |
| 40a. Degree of Self-Reference | Se |
| Objective Aspects | |
| A. Importance | |
| 41. Human | H |
| 42. Animal | A |
| 43. Plant | Pl |
| 44. Inanimate | In |
| 45. Abstract | Ab |
| 46. Anatomy | At |
| B. Type | |
| 47. Whole-Part | W-P |
| 48. Sex Reference | Sex |
| 49. Definiteness of Content | Def |
| 50. Gender of the Observed Figure | Ge |
| VII. Psychological Characteristics of the Response | |
| 51. Perseverative Tendency | Pe |
| 52. Elaborative Tendency | El |
| 53. Tendency toward Blot Description | Des |
| 54. Mood of the Response | Mo |
| 55. Affect of the Subject | Aff |
| 56. Congruousness of Response | Cg |
| 57. Communality Scale | Com |
| VIII. Rating of Subject's Attitude toward Responses | |
| 58. Self-Estimate of the Adequacy of Response | Adq |
| 59. Interpretive Attitude | |
| 59a. Type of Interpretive Attitude | T-A |
| 59b. Awareness of Interpretive Attitude | A-A |
| 60. Reaction Time | RT |
| IX. General Data | |
| 61. Turning of the Card | TC |
| 62. Succession | Suc |
| 63. Observational Data | O-D |
| 64. Subject's Readiness to Respond | RR |
| 65. Type of Response | TR |
| 66. Temporal Data | TD |
| X. Rating Scales for Drawing of Percepts | |
| 67. Blot Contours | B-C |
| 68. Blot Colors | B-Co |
| 69. Modification and Ornamentation | Mod |

*Guide for Tabulation of Scores.* In most of the scales, the number of 4's, 3's, 2's, 1's, 0's, and X's can be readily tabulated and the frequency of each noted. If the scale is continuous, a mean may be computed (excluding X's), and this mean may be regarded as representing the strength of the tendency measured by the scale. Attempts to utilize medians or modes for this purpose have not been very successful. If there is reason to believe that a binomial distribution might fit the data of a given scale, the value of $p$ for the binomial may be computed and this used as a measure of the strength of the tendency represented by the scale (see Zubin, 1943). If the scale is bipolar, the binomial may be used to fit it if it is suitable. If not, a per cent distribution of the categories or a mode might be utilized to summarize the data.

The final integration of all the scales into overall measures cannot be accomplished until factor analysis methods or pattern analysis methods are worked out (see Zubin, 1938).

## REFERENCES

Beck, S. J. *Rorschach's test: I. Basic processes.* New York: Grune and Stratton, 1949.

Beck, S. J., Beck, Anne G., Levitt, E. E., & Molish, H. B. *Rorschach's test: I. Basic processes.* New York: Grune and Stratton, 1961.

Grassi, J. R., & Levine, K. N. The Graphic Rorschach manual. *Psychiat. Quart.,* 1943, 17, 258–281.

Hertz, Marguerite. *Frequency tables to be used in scoring responses to the Rorschach ink-blot test.* Western Reserve University, 1946.

Klopfer, B., & Kelley, D. *The Rorschach technique.* Yonkers-on-Hudson, N.Y.: World Book Co., 1942.

Schachtel, E. G. The dynamic perception and the symbolism of form with special reference to the Rorschach test. *Psychiat.,* 1941, 4, 79–96.

Zubin, J. A technique for measuring like-mindedness. *J. abnorm. soc. Psychol.,* 1938, 33, 508–516.

Zubin, J. A quantitative approach to measuring regularity of succession in the Rorschach experiment. *Charact. & Pers.,* 1941, 10, 67–68.

Zubin, J. A proposed measure of social conformity. *Sociometry,* 1943, 6, 72–93.

# 8 DERIVATIVES OF
# THE RORSCHACH TECHNIQUE

Because of the global nature of the Rorschach technique and the wide range of personality it tries to deal with, attempts have been made to narrow its focus and prepare more limited approaches to the evaluation of personality. By utilizing smaller sectors of the wide Rorschach spectrum, intensive exploration of various specific, interpretative hypotheses is possible. Such attempts have been made through the development of special tests derived from the traditional Rorschach procedure.

This chapter presents a discussion of several of these approaches in some detail to illustrate the directions which such research can follow. The research efforts to be described are not merely administrative modifications (e.g., new group procedures) of the Rorschach; they are, instead, attempts to establish new instruments, motivated by a need to test some of the old assumptions, or by dissatisfaction with the old technique. As such, the usual standards of validity, reliability, objectivity, normative evidence, cross-validation, etc., must be applied with equal rigor to these new instruments as to the old.

It is well to recall that Rorschach himself set the stage for such experimentation by calling his technique experimental in nature and suggesting methods for experimenting with the M response. Although his wife, Olga, never released his original experimental material, there is evidence (presented by Roemer at the 1957 International Congress of

370

Psychiatry) that Rorschach was experimenting with several new cards at the time of his death.

Note might be made of several early researches, all seemingly motivated by a desire to explore further through related techniques some basic Rorschach tenets and principles, or developmental aspects of perception: Stern's Cloud Pictures (Stern & MacDonald, 1937); Roemer's Symbol Test (Roemer was one of Rorschach's assistants)—which consisted of eliciting free associations to Rorschach responses (1938); and Roemer's Projection Test, described by van Lennep (1951) as consisting "of a complex picture, put together as a photograph montage containing a number of cuttings from photographs, stuck pell-mell onto a piece of cardboard" (p. 158).

Dworetzki's extensive researches (1939) into developmental aspects of perception should also be noted. This author was interested in tracing perceptual development from early childhood to adulthood and in examining developmental Rorschach norms in order to shed light on certain of her hypotheses, as well as in evaluating specific aspects of Rorschach theory. She worked with 210 Ss ranging in age from 2 years 4 months to adult. The adult Ss were drawn from "educated," "uneducated," and schizophrenic samples. Her method consisted chiefly in a detailed analysis of results obtained from the standard Rorschach, and from specially constructed tests designed to examine a variety of Rorschach factors, such as the differentiation of "globale vs. analytique" (whole-part) perception. This (latter) procedure consisted of six ambiguous drawings (e.g., a figure whose parts are made up of fruits; or a face whose parts are made up of a pair of scissors and a spool of thread). Ss were presented with the drawings and asked, "What is this? Tell me all that you see." Responses were classified as G (global) or D (analytic), depending on the spontaneous verbalizations of the Ss. When the results were tabulated, definite trends were found. In the younger age groups, global perception predominated. There was a gradual increase of analytic responses with age and the vast majority of adults produced both G and D responses.

One of Dworetzki's chief conclusions relates not to the decrease of global responses with age, but rather to a more general statement concerning "perceptual structure": plasticity (flexibility—ability to see both global and analytic aspects of the drawings) increases with age. An example of her conclusions concerning the Rorschach material is that form–quality (precision, accuracy) is not the chief distinguishing factor between responses of children and those of adults, but rather the complexity of forms and the quality of their integration (primitive vs. synthetic forms). She also investigated the development of the M response. Her research findings, not summarized here in any detail, are of interest because they were based on the utilization of a specially constructed device designed to "test" certain Rorschach tenets; yet the scope of her research and the conclusions stemming from it are broader than that subsumed under Rorschach theory, since they have implication for a wide number of problems in developmental theory.

The developmental scoring system which grew out of several researches at Clark University as a result of some of Heinz Werner's work deals with similar dimensions, but since no new techniques were developed, it is not discussed here (see Chapter 4). Similarly, the various modifications of the Rorschach blots produced by Baughman and others are not new techniques and thus are also not discussed (see Chapter 5). Other parallel or nonparallel inkblot tests (such as the Howard Ink Blot Test) have been discussed in Chapter 4, in the section on *Reliability*.

*Levy Movement Blots* (*LMB*). [1] One of the most important determinants in the Rorschach technique is the M or human movement response. The clinical evaluation of M is fraught with many hazards, but it nevertheless deals with a fundamental psychological problem, namely the interpretation ("perception") of movement in a stationary field. This is a central problem in art, as well as in the psychological laboratory and clinic, and its solution may bring the three disciplines of art, science, and clinical practice into greater rapport with each other. In Chapter 4, numerous hypotheses and researches concerning Rorschach M were discussed. It should be obvious that although there is little agreement as to the clinical and behavioral correlates of M, a respectable collection of empirical observations has been accumulated.

How does the onlooker perceive motion in a static field? Does he actually perceive motion in the case of the Rorschach blots, or does he say the figures *look* as if they are in motion? How does the artist contrive to induce such perception in the onlooker?

Turning first to the last problem, we find that Nicolaides (1941), suggested that in order to portray movement, the artist must himself "feel" what he is drawing. Other artists utilize certain stylized ways which they believe the onlooker has previously associated with movement. Cartoonists, of course, indicate direction of movement and movement itself by lines of force emanating from their figures. As to the theories of movement perception, several artists have proposed the

---

[1] The Levy Movement Blots were devised by Dr. David M. Levy to whom the authors are greatly indebted both for his stimulating influence as well as permission to experiment with his blots.

sympathy theory, according to which the observer "imitates" (carries out unconsciously) in imperceptible ways the tendencies toward movement in the perceived figure, and this "imitation" gives rise to the perception of movement. The imbalance theory tries to explain this phenomenon on the basis of some imbalance in the presented figure, indicative of an unfinished movement, which prompts the onlooker to supply the missing part by perceiving within himself the uncompleted motion. Rodin utilized this principle by sculpturing different parts of the same figure (legs of a horse) in successive stages of movement—positions which are impossible or never seen in actual life—and in this way induced the perception of movement by the onlooker (1912). Hollingworth contended, however, that to portray movement, the figure to be thus perceived must be caught at an actual point of rest (1913).

The first two questions previously posed suggest that there may be a distinction between the perception of movement in a stationary field and the kind of movement reported in the Rorschach situation. Moreover, reporting or perceiving movement in a stationary visual field should be distinguished from the phi phenomenon and related apparent movement phenomena which involve some type of alteration in the visual stimulus. The psychological events which occur during these experiences and their neurophysiological substrates are still vague, and their clinical correlates and relationships to personality (if any) even more vague, despite the fact that perception of movement in a stationary visual field has been studied rather extensively (see Graham, 1951).

There are, as a matter of fact, several different types of apparent movement which have been distinguished in addition to Wertheimer's "phi phenomenon" (1912), which refers to the perception of pure movement without object reference. Kenkel, in his early investigations (1913), differentiated three types of apparent movement: alpha movement—the apparent change in the size of an object under successive presentations; beta movement—the apparent movement of an object from one position to another when it is viewed through a tachistoscope at intervals near 60 milliseconds; and gamma movement—the apparent expansion or contraction of an object upon an increase or decrease of illumination. Korte (1915) has also noted an additional type, delta movement—the apparent retrograde motion when a second stimulus is brighter than the first.

Being an artist, as well as the son of an artist, Rorschach borrowed the artistic concept of empathy as a basis for explaining and identifying the movement response. He limited the true M response to only those responses in which kinaesthesia accompanied the "perception" of the movement. It is not surprising that in the literature following Rorschach, much confusion resulted from the attempt to apply this vague criterion, and several different types of M responses have been described.

One of the alleged advantages of the Rorschach technique is the complete freedom given the subject in dealing with the unstructured material presented in the inkblots. The task given the subject is to tell what the inkblot might be, and his interpretation of this loosely formulated task becomes the basis for the personality evaluation. The generality of the *Aufgabe* brings with it, however, certain disadvantages. Since the task is so undirected, it is not always possible to fathom the causes leading to such behavior as the rejection of the task. Some rejections may be caused by lack of capacity to integrate the vague forms of the blot, others by inhibition, still others by preoccupation. To be sure, the skilled clinician can sometimes discover the probable basis of the rejection, but such situations usually do not increase the validity or reliability of the procedure. Even in cases when the task is not rejected, certain types of rather popular responses may be entirely absent from the record. If such omissions were not stressed, no great loss would occur. But very often the mere absence of a given type of response involving movement, or contour in combination with color, may change the entire interpretation of a record. On the other hand, the presence of such responses, even if only one or two occur, may also alter the personality interpretation. An absence of movement responses may be due to attention to some other aspects of the interpretation, to an inhibition of the perceived movement because of an emotional factor such as embarrassment, or to some other causes or groups of causes which may best be described at the present time as fortuitous circumstances or chance. A test in which the presence or absence of even one instance of a given type of response becomes crucial in the interpretation of results, invites many false conclusions.

Some recognition of the fortuitous nature of omitted responses was given by Klopfer and Kelley (1942) when they introduced the method of "testing the limits" at the end of the Inquiry, a procedure introduced to unproductive subjects or to those who show a conspicuous lack of responses falling into one or more scoring categories. But usually the results obtained in "testing the limits" do not enter directly into the evaluation of the test. Consequently, it became highly desirable to prepare certain variants of the Rorschach in which chance elements in inclusion or omission for certain types of interpretations are reduced to a minimum.

One method for preparing such tests is to reduce the number of possible determinants or types of interpretations in an inkblot and then give S specific directions for seeing the type of interpretation for which the blot had been prepared. An acceptance or rejection of the task under such circumstances is more safely interpreted as corresponding to the presence or absence of the capacity in question.

The LMB was specifically designed to elicit human movement. The blots contain only one traditional determinant, chiaroscuro. The contours perceived in these blots are directly attributable only to the abrupt gradients of light and shade, and not to the juxtaposition of different hues or black and white. S is given the specific task of seeing people in movement, and his acceptance or rejection of this task, as well as his capacity to perceive movement, will determine his degree of success in the experiment.

The LMB consists of finger paintings prepared by spreading the paint on suitable paper, folding the sheet inwardly, and then running the thumb nail over the outside in a studied manner. When the sheet is opened, two symmetrical figures appear on each side of the middle crease. In this manner, symmetrical figures of various sorts can be produced. After experimenting with this method, seven designs were found which elicited variegated responses, and these constitute the present set of cards. Since one of these designs is used in three positions, and the first design is repeated at the end, there is a total of ten cards.

Instead of utilizing the rather free directions of the Rorschach technique, "What might this be?", S is given specific directions for seeing people in action. Consequently, the Levy Movement Blots may be regarded as a variant of the Rorschach procedure in which the physical determinants have been reduced to one, and the mental set of the subject has been directed toward finding one type of response.

In some of the work with this procedure, S had been requested to tell a story about the figures he had seen in action—indicating what happened previously, what is happening now, and what the outcome will be. This use of the test, therefore, utilized aspects of both the Rorschach and the TAT. There has been little research concerning this additional procedure with the LMB, and no attempt will be made here to describe the scoring techniques which have been developed to assess story content.

(A) *Early research* with the Levy Movement Blots was concerned with the development and testing of several scales utilized in the scoring; at this time, a number of studies were conducted in an attempt to test the diagnostic power of the movement response, its relationship to certain developmental considerations, as well as relationship to creativity. The original scoring for these responses was developed by Levy. Additional scales for evaluating these responses were devised by Zubin, and were elaborated and refined by Rust (1948a, 1948b). These scales are presented in the *Supplement*, Part IV (see Footnote 1, Chapter 6). A brief summary of some of these early findings follows.

Rust (1948a) reported a study based on children, ages 8 to 12, who had been rated for creativity. There was a small but significant negative relationship between "creativity" and the movement response. "Creativity" was measured by ratings of color and pencil drawings by art supervisors, and was said to be characterized by "sensitivity of line, use of color, amount of detail, spatial arrangement, and interest value of subject matter." Those rated as "less creative" tended to produce more movement responses than those rated as "more creative." This result indicates that the production of movement responses on the Levy Movement Blots does not have the same relationship to "creativity" as is claimed for the M response on the Rorschach.

O'Neill (1949)[2] found little relationship between ratings of creativity and movement responses in a group of graduate students working toward their Ph.D. degree at Columbia University in mathematical statistics and in English. This held true for movement responses elicited by the Rorschach as well as those elicited by the LMB. O'Neill also studied the LMB protocols of a group of high school students who excelled in mathematics, and found no relationship between their movement blot scores and teacher ratings on their capabilities in mathematics. Similarly, Griffin (1958) found little relationship between ratings of creativity and movement responses in a group of college females. These findings tend to confirm those reported by Roe (1946) with respect to Rorschach M: artists did not differ significantly from the general adult population in M responses. It would seem, then, that Rorschach's suggestion that capacity for creativity is related to the number of movement responses on the Rorschach technique is not verified by findings with respect to movement on the LMB, nor is there any evidence for this claim in various published Rorshach studies.

With respect to developmental aspects of the movement response, Rust (1948a) had reported that no relationship with age existed in a group of 88 public school children, 9–13 years of age, and with mental ages ranging from 7½–16. Nor were significant differences in movement responses found with respect to mental age, intelligence quotient, or sex. Carp and Kawlicke found that movement responses *did* increase

---

[2] Personal communication.

with age, however, when a wider age spectrum (6–13) was examined.[3]

Rust (*Ibid.*, 1948*a*, 1948*b*) explored the differences in LMB movement responses among 51 schizophrenics, 49 psychopaths, 50 neurotics, and 30 normals. Movement responses occurred less frequently in schizophrenic, psychopathic, and neurotic patients than in normal adults. After the rejection tendency was accounted for, he found that seven of the eighteen scales which were utilized differentiated significantly among these patients, with the schizophrenics giving the lowest scores and the normals the highest scores. The psychopathic and neurotic groups showed considerable overlap. The differences found are similar in direction to those reported by Rorschach workers regarding the incidence of the M response in schizophrenics and neurotics.

Pre- and postoperative LMB responses were also studied in a group of 27 mental hospital patients, in conjunction with a large-scale study of topectomized patients (Rust [1948*a*]; Mettler [1949]). Of this group, 17 patients had ablations of areas of the frontal lobes; 10 patients were controls. There was an increase in the number of Levy Movement responses following the removal of Brodmann's Area 9 in the operated patients. Although differences in gain or loss following ablations of areas of the frontal lobe revealed no significant differences between the control and operated groups taken as a whole, a comparison of those patients having Area 9 removed and those patients who had other areas removed, indicated significantly greater gain in scores on the movement scales following operation for Area 9. The cause of this increase is not clear. In general, however, the effect of induced organic brain damage by means of prefrontal brain operations as performed in this experiment, does not lower the tendency to give movement responses to the LMB.

A few additional early studies have been reported. For example, studies of handicaps of various types disclosed that the severity and age of onset of handicaps were related to the movement responses insofar as the greater the severity and the earlier the age of onset, the fewer the movement responses. Fitzgerald (1949), in a study of handicapped children, found that the *Control of Movement* (Scale 5) rating was related to some of the TAT variables. Handicapped males differed from the controls, but female handicapped patients did not differ from their controls.

Research concerning the relationship between LMB responses and Rorschach M has been disappointing in that little or no evidence of

---

[3] Personal communication.

relationship has been reported (Allen, Ray, & Poole [1953]; King [1955]; and Okarski [1958]). However, these studies contain gross methodological difficulties and/or irrelevant scoring procedures, including failure to suggest seeing movement on the LMB; scoring for Klopfer's M, FM, and m instead of special movement measures; or using rejection and reaction time as scores. As will be seen, more extensive, refined, and recent research has not confirmed these authors' findings.

(B) *Recent research* with the LMB was undertaken by Schumer under the sponsorship of David M. Levy in the light of promising findings of the earlier studies. The purpose of this research was a varied and comprehensive examination of LMB responses, and when the several aspects of the coordinated research plan are viewed as a whole, a considerable amount of evidence for reliability and construct validity is provided. The goals of the research included the following: (*a*) re-evaluation, revision and refinement, and exploration of the efficacy, objectivity, and reliability of various scoring procedures, as well as the introduction of additional scales which, because of clinical evidence, seemed crucial and significant; (*b*) exploration of relationships between LMB scores and a number of sociopsychological variables, as well as other test scores, including Rorschach M; (*c*) an extensive validity program based on contrasting diagnostic groups and normals, children as well as adults, and involving cross-validation of earlier findings; (*d*) specific exploration of an hypothesis concerning the relationship of empathy to movement scores, based on several samples and more than one criterion of empathy; (*e*) an assessment of various aspects of reliability; (*f*) exploration of developmental considerations; and (*g*) the accumulation of norms for content, as well as other considerations, for normal children as well as adults. The detailed findings of this extensive program are reported elsewhere (Levy, Schumer, & Zubin, 1964). A summary of some of the chief findings follows.

1. Several of the Zubin scales found to be effective by Rust were utilized in this research, but additional scores were developed, based on certain modifications also found to be useful. The additional scales tap repetitious content, failures on the first and last cards, unusual behavior, tendency to respond to various aspects of the *ground* rather than the *figure,* and common and rare content. Illustrations are provided for all scores and scales, and extensive norms are provided for the content scales for normal children and adults, separately. Split-half reliability methods, scorer reliability, and agreement of ratings be-

tween judges based on entire protocols, all yielded high reliability estimates.

2. LMB scores were found to be correlated with Rorschach human movement scores. Differences between this finding and findings described earlier were attributed to differences in scoring as well as in administration and instructions.

3. LMB scores were not found to be related to estimates of intelligence level. This held true for a large group of normal adults, normal children, psychoanalytic trainees, and a smaller group of ambulatory patients.

4. On the basis of a variety of diagnostic and normal groupings of various age and educational levels, a suggestion for the existence of a sex difference emerged: as age increased, there seemed to be an increase in the differences between males and females, in terms of various movement scores, with females gradually showing the higher "movement productivity" (as defined by various movement measures).

5. Findings based on LMB data of large groups of children and adults, and comparisons of these groups to each other, have indicated that gradual increases in movement productivity were found with age in children, but that a plateau is reached in early adolescence, beyond which, age does not seem to be a significant factor. Although there were striking differences in movement productivity between children and adults, age was not a significant factor *within* each group.

6. Achievement and occupation (such as whether or not S is a "white-collar" employee, psychoanalytic trainee, or college student) seem to be related to the movement response, but intelligence was ruled out as a significant factor in these findings.

7. In a study of 155 ambulatory psychiatric patients with a wide range in age and diagnostic and prognostic features, the general hypothesis was explored that lowered thresholds for the human movement response on the LMB would be positively related to the empathic process and some of its correlates. Independent ratings of these Ss were made, based on extensive case and interview material. The ratings were for empathic capacity, spontaneity of fantasy, emotional control, and for the presence of an oppositional pattern. It was predicted that movement productivity, as defined by the different measures, would be positively related to the first three ratings, but negatively related to ratings of oppositional behavior. By and large, the findings confirmed the predictions, although the predictions concerning the relationship of movement productivity to the control over impulsive behavior and to the absence of an oppositional pattern were confirmed primarily in the younger group of Ss (N of 80).

8. It was hypothesized that if the assumptions concerning the relationship between movement orientation and empathy and its correlates were correct, then in a group of 63 psychoanalytic trainees, those who were rated by their faculty as more skillful as therapists should show greater movement productivity than those who were rated as less skillful. Indeed, productivity in the LMB was significantly related to ratings of therapeutic skill, and it was concluded that the hypothesis was confirmed, especially in the light of the fact that intellectual factors did not account for the differences found among the LMB measures in the various groups.

9. Data made available by D. M. Levy, a sample of 205 protocols obtained from groups of schizophrenics, psychoneurotics, depressives (psychotic and nonpsychotic), psychopaths, and normals, were re-examined. These classifications were based entirely on independent diagnoses. Significant differences among these diagnostic groups for most of the movement measures were found. Predictions concerning which groups would show higher and which groups lower productivity were confirmed.

10. Two samples of psychotic and normal children, equivalent in age, ethnic, and socioeconomic background, were compared as to LMB productivity. There were 22 psychotics and 45 normals, and each group ranged in age from six to eleven. On all measures explored, psychotic children showed lower movement productivity than normal children. Most of these differences were significant. When children eight years of age and older were studied, the discriminatory power of the instrument was increased. Additional studies were conducted with respect to distinguishing those psychotic children with organic components from those without any organic features, on the basis of their LMB protocols. Finally, a third group of neither normal nor psychotic children ("mixed"—neurotic) were compared to the two groups of normal and psychotic children. In these latter studies, the groups could be distinguished from each other in terms of their "patterns" of scores.

11. Norms in terms of various movement measures as well as content of responses for (a) 133 Ss from a public school population (ages 6–1 to 13–11), (b) 205 normal adults in the Civil Service, and (c) 200 superior young adults (college females, psychoanalytic trainees, graduate students) have been made available.

12. Various adult groups, superior, average, and psychiatric, were compared (N > 500). Psychoanalytic students showed the highest movement orientation when compared to all adult groups, including each of the superior groups. There was a consistent decrease of productivity from group to group in the following order: superior adult; average

adult; ambulatory neurotic adult; hospitalized neurotic and schizo-phrenic. On the basis of the variables explored, differences among contrasted groups in the expected direction were found, and all groups designated as normal were more productive than all other groups.

In short, the LMB appears promising as a clinical instrument that is easy to administer, as well as a useful device for exploring and testing the validity of assumptions and hypotheses concerning Ror-schach M. Further exploration of the empathy-movement hypothesis seems desirable, with other groups, other measures of empathy, and with, perhaps, other techniques for eliciting movement.

*Color-Cut-Out Test.*[4] This section describes work in connection with studying color and chiaroscuro elements in the Rorschach stimuli. These types of stimuli are present in such varied quantity from area to area in the ten cards that it is sometimes impossible to determine what particular element or elements in the stimulus area induced the re-sponse.

In general practice, responses are usually classified with regard to their determinants into the following major categories: form, move-ment, color, and chiaroscuro. The form determinant is perhaps the easiest to understand. Whenever the subject utilizes the contours of the inkblot and very little else in the formation of the response, it is classi-fied as an F response. The contours of the blot may be produced by white-black contrasts, color contrasts, or chiaroscuro effects, but as long as only the contours are involved in the response, it remains an F

---

[4] The material described in connection with the Color-Cut-Out Test is based on a study made by L. O. Eldridge (1948) under the joint direction of D. M. Levy and J. Zubin. Preliminary work has also been done in connection with *contour* elements in Rorschach responses. To do so, contours were obtained by the juxta-position of black masses against white, and the brightness gradients (chiaroscuro) were completely eliminated. The cards were produced as follows: black poster ink was dropped on charcoal drawing paper, $9\frac{1}{2}'' \times 12\frac{1}{2}''$, in various ways, and the paper was folded to produce a symmetrical design. No special effort was made to produce human figures. The first use of these cards was to test the capacity to perceive movement in the same way as the Levy Movement Blots are used. The results of the preliminary experiment indicate that the contour cards do not give rise to as many movement responses and to as intensive movement responses as do the Levy Movement Blots. Whether the presence of chiaroscuro in the latter is the deter-mining factor, or whether some other factor brings about the differential in move-ment responses, has not yet been determined. More experimentation is necessary before the particular value of the chiaroscuro-free contour blots can be determined. These blots were prepared by M. Middlebrook, who, together with W. Fuchs, con-ducted the research just described under the supervision of J. Zubin.

response. The movement response has no definite physical correlate in the blot. It is first of all an F response, but involves, in addition to F, certain specifications with regard to the nature of the figure seen in movement (it must be human or human-like). Thus, both F as well as M responses depend on contours arising from color contrasts, black-white juxtaposition, or chiaroscuro. When the color or chiaroscuro of a given stimulus area does more than provide contours for the responses, and actually becomes an essential element in the formation of the responses, the emerging percept is called either a form-color (FC) response or a form-chiaroscuro (FY or Fc) response. Whenever the color of the stimulus area is the chief determiner of the response, and contours or other characteristics play little or no role, the response is regarded as a pure color response (C). Similarly, if the chiaroscuro aspects of the stimulus area are the most important, the response is classified as a pure chiaroscuro response.

Responses involving color may emerge from stimulus areas in which no color appears, and chiaroscuro effects are not limited to areas in which chiaroscuro is present. Other combinations of stimuli may produce such responses. On the other hand, the mere presence of color in the stimulus area, even in a predominant amount, does not insure the emergence of a color response, and the abundance of chiaroscuro does not insure the emergence of a shading response. It is clear then, that the nature of the stimulus area does not bear a one-to-one relationship to the kind of response that emerges.

It should be noted that we are dealing here not with a purely objective but a subjective framework. Even our classifications of stimulus characteristics are not absolute since they depend on judgments and ratings. But the degree of discrepancy in judging the presence or absence of color or chiaroscuro in a given stimulus is not of the same order of inconsistency as the variegated interpretations to which a given colored area gives rise on the Rorschach. The problem, thus, is one of trying to evaluate the more varied interpretations in terms of the more consistently judged stimulus characteristics. A separation should therefore be made between the two concepts, viz., characteristics of the stimulus area and the interpretation of the stimulus in the form of the final response. In this way, the stimulus area can be varied systematically to determine what particular combination of stimulus properties will give rise to given responses. To study the influence of the determinants, it would be well to obtain stimuli whose composition is known. In this way, it would become possible to determine experimentally what types of responses are evoked by each of these stimuli. The Color-Cut-Out Test represents such an attempt.

In Chapter 4, various studies specifically designed to test Rorschach "color theory" were discussed. Is there evidence *outside* the Rorschach field which can shed light on the influence of color and chiaroscuro on S's responses?

There is a group of studies concerned with color preference. It has been suggested that there are certain sex preferences in color (Nicolaides, 1941), and that warm colors (red, orange, yellow) affect psychophysical judgments differently than cold colors (green, blue and violet) (Rodin, 1912). In general, these studies have not received much attention or follow-up. Eysenck (1947) reported that there are typological differences with regard to saturated as opposed to unsaturated colors. Certain developmental studies also indicate that color preferences depend upon age (Garth & Porter, 1934). These studies indicate that before making personality interpretations on the basis of color preferences, a careful analysis should be made of the experimental work dealing with this topic.

Barrett and Eaton (1947) studied the preference for shade vs. tint in relation to personality characteristics. Shade refers to hues darker than median gray and tint refers to hues lighter than median gray. For each hue, a darker (shade) and a lighter (tint) version were presented simultaneously, and S was asked to express a preference. The expressed preferences were found to be highly reliable ($r = .83$ for tint and .79 for shade, on 63 subjects). Ss with "shade" preferences differed on several tests from Ss with tint preferences even though there were variations within each group. Some of these differences were: Ss with shade preferences had fewer associations to words, a lower morale score on the Minnesota Personality Scale, higher masculinity scores on the Terman and Miles Scale; they tended to overestimate the number of dots on cards, showed increased annoyance scores, and seemed to be more rigid on various other tests.

Another investigator, Warner (1949), studied the preferences of psychiatric patients for hues, brightness (lightness), and saturation. He tested groups of patients, in each of the following diagnostic categories, for their preferences: 60 manic Ss; 60 depressives; 60 anxiety neurotics; and 120 catatonic schizophrenics. He utilized a forced-choice procedure to determine the patients' relative preferences for four distinct hues, three levels of brightness for each hue, and three degrees of saturation for each hue. No differences were found between the psychiatric classification and saturation preferences. The anxiety neurotics preferred green to yellow more strongly than did the other groups. The anxiety neurotics also preferred the lighter colors more strongly than did the other groups.

Another area of research deals with attempts to correlate physiological effects with color. Thus, Schachtel (1943) reported a study by Féré, who demonstrated that dynamometer measurements and plethysmographic tracings of the forearm were increased by colored light in the following order: blue, green, yellow, orange, and red. Other studies have attempted to investigate the influence of color on patient behavior. Red threads seem to increase productivity on looms during occupational therapy periods when compared to black and white threads (reported by Schachtel [1943]).

Another consideration is the theoretical analysis of personality correlates of color. Schachtel (*Ibid.*) suggested that since color perception is more passive and more immediate than form or gestalt perception, it is more analogous to emotion, which is also more passive and more immediate than intellectual experience. The former seizes or overcomes the personality whereas the latter is a product of mental effort. Although this argument rests merely on an analogy, it is widely accepted by Rorschach workers, and much of Rorschach interpretation revolves around the identification of color with affect. Similarly, the attribution of extratensiveness to people with many color responses rests on the analogy that responsiveness to color indicates responsiveness to external stimulation.

To provide a test which might permit the validation of the claims of the Rorschach technique regarding color and chiaroscuro, the following materials were selected. A search was made of magazine color advertisements which contained samples of homogeneous color and brightness areas as well as of the two types of gradients in color and brightness, the sudden and gradual gradients. These specimens were rated for the degree of color and for sharpness of gradient. Several hundred cutouts were selected to be included in the test material. These were administered to mental patients, normal children, and adults. A final battery of ten cards was obtained which sampled the different varieties of color and chiaroscuro combinations and, at the same time, yielded differential responses.

The directions for giving this test are the same as those for the Rorschach. An Inquiry is made to determine what particular stimulus in the blot was more important in producing the response. Several scales have been drawn up to evaluate the results. Each of these scales can be related to the characteristics of the cards in which the given response was observed. The characteristics of the cutouts were rated by several competent judges on the following stimulus scales: color, brightness, and gradients of color and brightness (chiaroscuro). These scales ranged from 0 for no importance for the variable in question, to 2, for maximum importance. The presence of contours ranged from precise, to vague, to absent.

Only cards with complete agreement in rating on all three scales were chosen for administration. Table D presents the ratings of the ten cards which comprised the material finally selected.

*Table D. Ratings of Color-Cut-Out Cards*

| Card | Contour | Chiaroscuro | Color |
|------|---------|-------------|-------|
| 1 | 2 | 1 | 2 |
| 2 | 2 | 1 | 1 |
| 3 | 2 | 2 | 0 |
| 4 | 1 | 2 | 1 |
| 5 | 2 | 1 | 2 |
| 6 | 2 | 2 | 0 |
| 7 | 1 | 1 | 1 |
| 8 | 0 | 0 | 2 |
| 9 | 2 | 0 | 2 |
| 10 | 2 | 2 | 1 |

Although all possible variations of chiaroscuro and color ratings are not present in the cards, it will be seen that the ends and the middle of the continuum are adequately covered. The combinations of chiaroscuro and color ratings according to individual cards are shown in Table E.

*Table E. Combinations of Chiaroscuro-Color Ratings of Color-Cut-Out Cards*

| Chiaroscuro-Color Ratings | Card |
|---------------------------|------|
| 2 – 0 | 3, 6 |
| 2 – 1 | 4, 10 |
| 1 – 1 | 2, 7 |
| 1 – 2 | 1, 5 |
| 0 – 2 | 8, 9 |

When the cards are analyzed in accordance with the preciseness of contour, the distribution in Table F is obtained.

Table F. Ratings of Preciseness
of Contour of Color-Cut-
Out Cards

| Rating | Card |
|--------|------|
| 2 | 1, 2, 3, 5, 6, 9, 10 |
| 1 | 4, 7 |
| 0 | 8 |

To differentiate the use of color as a stimulus from the use of color in the response, the former will be designated as color and the latter as hue. Similarly, chiaroscuro will be used to designate the characteristics of the stimulus area, and shading will designate the use of chiaroscuro in the response.

Responses are scored on the following scales:

1. Compliance Scale:
   Rating
   3       Interpretation given
   2       Comment on characteristics of card: for example, painting, design, Rorschach card
   1       Enumeration of contents: for example, colors, inkblot, paints
   0       No comment on card: for example, don't know
2. Hue Response Scale:
   Rating
   2       Most important characteristic of response
   1       Of some importance in response
   0       Of no importance in response
3. Shading Response Scale:
   Rating
   2       Most important characteristic of response
   1       Of some importance in response
   0       Of no importance in response

Additional scales which can be used are presented in Chapters 6 and 7.

Although the color cards have been administered to some 500 individuals, only one systematic study has been reported (Eldridge, 1948). This was a developmental study which attempted to determine the variations in the types of responses to cards characterized by different amounts of chiaroscuro and color. The sample consisted of 233 students at a private school in New York City. Approximately twenty children, ten boys and ten girls, in grades one through twelve, were tested in each grade. The stimulus contents of the cards were determined by the ratings of four graduate students on the amount of chiaroscuro and color present in each card. Responses were rated on the importance of shading and/or color and were also rated on the following: Roughness-Smoothness scale, Hardness-Softness scale, Animate-Inanimate scale, and Compliance scale. A summary of the results follows:

1. Hue-dominant responses predominated in the younger ages regardless of the content of the stimulus.

2. Shading-dominant responses predominated in the older ages regardless of the content of the stimulus.

3. Males showed these trends quite clearly, whereas in the female records, shading-dominant responses were spread more evenly throughout the age groups. The females differed from the males, not in the distribution of hue-dominant responses but in the presence of shading responses in all age groups in the female records.

4. There was a general positive relationship between the amount of chiaroscuro present in the stimulus and the roughness of the response as rated on the Roughness-Smoothness scale.

5. For both males and females, it was found that roughness responses were more prevalent in the younger age groups and fell off steadily as age increased.

6. With an increase in age, soft responses increased regularly as rated on the Hardness-Softness scale.

7. Males followed this pattern of a decrease in hard responses very clearly, whereas the females showed a preponderance of soft responses in the *middle* age range.

8. Animate responses, as rated on the Animate-Inanimate scale, were much more prevalent in the younger age groups and fell off regularly in the older age groups.

9. It was suggested that chiaroscuro is one of the determinants of the animate type of response.

10. Compliance scores, in general, were quite high, although an exceedingly low compliance score was obtained from all age groups for one card. It was not possible to ascertain the reasons for this, but it was believed that the card might have had some sexual connotations.

A more thorough investigation of the sensitivity of females to chiaroscuro stimuli at young ages is needed. Subtle sex differences seemed to be present in the response to color stimuli. A statistical analysis of the data should bring these differences out more clearly. Perhaps cross-cultural studies might cast light on whether the observed sex differences are culturally determined.

*Holtzman Inkblot Technique.* Holtzman (1958, 1959, 1961) has described a new inkblot technique which has received considerable interest and attention. This Rorschach "derivative" is unlike those described previously in that Holtzman was not interested in contriving an instrument to test assumptions concerning certain determinants; rather, his goal was to construct an entirely new inkblot technique which would avoid some of the pitfalls of the parent instrument. His dissatisfaction with the Rorschach technique stemmed from some of the same considerations we have already noted in preceding chapters. A crude ordinal scale for Rorschach scores is erroneously assumed when interpreting a protocol; stimulus attributes for a given response are difficult to determine; and most scoring systems are rather arbitrary. Holtzman was particularly concerned about the troublesome question of R, number of responses, and has indicated that attempts to meet this problem in the past have not been satisfactory. Moreover, other factors contribute to confusion concerning the meaning of scores such as the "subjectivity of the method, the influence of factors extraneous to the blots such as examiner-subject interaction, and variation in style of inquiry . . ." (1959, p. 131).

As noted, Holtzman's solution to some of these problems was the construction of a new instrument. After extensive preliminary testing and trials with various populations, and on the basis of such criteria as "pulling power," split-half reliability, and discriminatory power between normals and patients, two sets of inkblots of 45 cards each were prepared. The cards were randomly assigned to each set after matching was done on the basis of known parameters. Subsequent research showed that these sets have high split-half reliability and high inter-scorer agreement. Responses are limited to one per card, and instructions are similar to those of the standard Rorschach. Every response is scored for six major variables, each logically independent of the other; the variables were selected as being pertinent and relevant, and as permitting high scoring agreement. These variables are: (*a*) location; (*b*) form appropriateness; (*c*) form definiteness; (*d*) color; (*e*) shading; and (*f*) movement energy level. These variables are scored on the basis of three to five point scales which had been shown to have high reliability. Additional variables are noted such as the number of rejections, enumeration of space responses (reversal of figure-ground), remarks about symmetry-asymmetry, and pathognomic verbalizations.[5] Content *per se* is not handled in a detailed manner, but any of the Rorschach content scales described in Chapter 7 could easily be applied.

The advantages of this instrument are many, according to the author: (*a*) R is constant; (*b*) each response is given to a separate stimulus-card eliminating an important complicating factor (i.e., all responses in the traditional Rorschach are lumped together, regardless of whether or not they are given mostly to one card, evenly distributed among several cards, etc.); (*c*) it provides a richer and lengthier variety of stimulus cards with good "pull," designed with the explicit intention of varying and controlling the stimulation in terms of color, shading, etc.; (*d*) a parallel form of the test is now available, thus permitting studies of reliability, and (*e*) the test lends itself easily to multiple choice versions for explorations of a specific nature (work on group procedures has already begun—Herron [1963]; Holtzman, Moseley, Reinehr, & Abbott [1963]; Moseley, Gorham, & Hill [1963]; and Swartz and Holtzman [1963]).

It should be noted that in some respects, Holtzman has succeeded in preparing a technique which, on the one hand, utilizes many of the scales which were prepared and advocated by Zubin (1948), and on the other hand, avoids the pitfalls of the traditional Rorschach technique. His utilization of sophisticated factorial methods over sixteen populations, and his demonstration that a suitable rotation of the vectors can be found which will yield some congruity of factors across various populations, are indeed achievements. It is only regrettable that he stopped short of answering the question as to whether the Rorschach is an "interview" or a "test." To establish the test nature of the instrument, its stimulus properties would have to be more clearly evaluated. Holtzman has pointed out that in the selection of test material he was guided by the pulling power of a given stimulus card, by its capacity to elicit interesting, variegated responses, and not by its particular stimulus properties. He stated (1961), "In the last analysis, however, initial selection and rejection of techniques and inkblots remained largely intuitive, with more objective criteria emerging slowly on an empirical basis after much trial and error" (p. 13).

It should also be noted that the scoring categories he selected are

---

[5] There are 22 standardized scoring variables. These are: Reaction Time; Rejection; Location; Space; Form Definiteness; Form Appropriateness; Color; Shading; Movement; Pathognomic Verbalization; Integration; Human; Animal; Anatomy; Sex; Abstract; Anxiety; Hostility; Barrier; Penetration; Balance; and Popular.

heavily weighted with content: form appropriateness, form definiteness, and movement energy. Only location, color, and shading reflect the perceptual aspects of the blot. This comes out even more clearly in his factor analysis, where only one factor—Factor II—is perceptual in character, and even this contains a heavy loading of content—form definiteness. The other factors, Factor I—integration, movement, human, popular, and form definiteness, and Factor III—pathognomic verbalization, anxiety, hostility, and movement, are entirely content factors, whereas Factor IV—location and form appropriateness—is at least partially content in character. As Zubin has suggested (1954), factor analysis of the traditional Rorschach determinants has been found to be related to personality, because the factorial technique could squeeze out the content-connected elements in the perceptual scores.

The fact that the Holtzman Inkblot Technique is superior to the traditional Rorschach for experimental purposes cannot be denied. Whether it can serve as a better tool for clinical practice, or whether it will also eventually cast light on the basic problem of the relationship between perception and personality, remain open questions. Perhaps some such technique as developed by Baughman or Kendall (see Chapter 5) can be used for teasing out the stimulus properties of the Holtzman blots, and then we might be in a better position to test Rorschach's hypothesis.

## SUMMARY

Several derivatives of the Rorschach technique were described in this chapter. These are essentially attempts to establish new instruments to test some of the old assumptions or to eliminate some of the problems in the parent technique. It was noted that the usual psychometric standards must be applied to these instruments if they are to possess any merit. The instruments chiefly discussed were the *Levy Movement Blots* (LMB), *Color-Cut-Out Test,* and the *Holtzman Inkblot Technique.*

The series of related researches concerning the LMB, viewed as a whole, seems to suggest that this may prove to be a fruitful technique for testing some assumptions and hypotheses concerning Rorschach M. The promising relationships found between ratings of empathy and various LMB scores should certainly be explored further with other groups and with other means for assessing empathy. The instrument itself offers some promise as a clinical tool that is easy to administer; perhaps its greatest strength may lie in its use as a quick, screening device. Additional research findings as well as cumulative clinical experience with this instrument seem most desirable.

The *Color-Cut-Out Test* was designed to study color and chiaroscuro elements of the Rorschach stimuli. Although only one major study has been reported utilizing this instrument, some interesting findings have emerged, with implications not only for the relevant Rorschach variables, but also for developmental theory. Sex differences in responsiveness to chiaroscuro stimuli were reported, a finding which might be further explored through use of other techniques.

The *Holtzman Inkblot Technique* was described in some detail; its advantages over the traditional Rorschach were discussed as well as the fact that some important solutions to several problems in the parent instrument were effected. This instrument, unlike the two described earlier, was not designed to "test" certain assumptions about isolated Rorschach variables. Rather, Holtzman has offered his technique as a *substitute* for, or at least as a more rigorously designed instrument than the Rorschach, capable of doing what the Rorschach claims to do, only "better."

Unfortunately, Holtzman's use of an Inquiry still presents problems, relying, as it does, on S's verbal ability and other extraneous factors. Moreover, he has not solved the difficulties involved in determining the primacy of color or shading in a response, a problem inherited from the old Rorschach. This is, of course, one of the problems that arises from neglecting to specify the stimulus. It was noted, too, that Holtzman's factors, derived from an extensive factorial study, seemed to be, at least in part, content-connected. Again, the question was raised as to how much the "interview" or content aspects of S's responses are of significance, as opposed to the so-called perceptual factors. There is, nevertheless, much to be admired in Holtzman's extensive research, and further developments and refinements in research and clinical use of his instrument are awaited.

## REFERENCES

Allen, R. M., Ray, C. D., & Poole, R. C. The Levy movement test: suggestions for scoring and relationship to Rorschach movement responses. *J. consult. Psychol.*, 1953, **17**, 195–198.

Barrett, Dorothy M., & Eaton, Elizabeth B. Preference for color or tint and some related personality data. *J. Pers.*, 1947, **15**, 222–232.

Dworetzki, Gertrude. Le test de Rorschach et l'évolution de la perception. *Arch. Psychol., Genève*, 1939, **27**, 233–296.

Eldridge, L. O. An investigation of responses to visual stimuli varying in color and chiaroscuro. Unpublished master's thesis, Columbia University, 1948.

Eysenck, H. J. *Dimensions of personality*. London: Routledge and Kegan Paul, 1947.

Fitzgerald, D. C. Projective techniques and success-failure reactions of orthopedically-crippled as compared with physically normal adolescents. Unpublished doctoral dissertation, State University of Iowa, 1949.

Garth, T., & Porter, Electa. The color preference of 1032 young children. *Amer. J. Psychol.*, 1934, **46**, 448–451.

Graham, C. Visual perception. In S. S. Stevens (Ed.) *Handbook of experimental psychology*. New York: John Wiley and Sons, 1951, 868–920.

Griffin, Dorothy P. Movement responses and creativity. *J. consult. Psychol.*, 1958, **22**, 134–136.

Herron, E. W. Psychometric characteristics of a thirty-item version of the group method of the Holtzman Inkblot Technique. *J. clin. Psychol.*, 1963, **19**, 450–453.

Hollingworth, H. L. A new experiment in the psychology of perception. *J. Phil. Psychol. sci. Meth.*, 1913, **10**, 505–510.

Holtzman, W. H. *The Inkblot Test—a provisional manual for research purposes only*. University of Texas, 1958.

Holtzman, W. H. Objective scoring of projective techniques. In B. M. Bass and I. A. Berg (Eds.) *Objective approaches to personality assessment*. Princeton, N.J.: D. Van Nostrand, 1959, 119–145.

Holtzman, W. H., Moseley, E. C., Reinehr, R. C., & Abbott, Elaine. Comparison of the group method and the standard individual version of the Holtzman Inkblot Technique. *J. clin. Psychol.*, 1963, **19**, 441–449.

Holtzman, W. H., Thorpe, J. S., Swartz, J. D., & Herron, E. W. *Inkblot perception and personality—Holtzman Inkblot Technique*. Austin: University of Texas Press, 1961.

Kenkel, F. Untersuchungen über den Zusammenhang zwischen Erscheinungsgrösse und Erscheinungsbewegung bei einingen sogenannten optischen Täuschungen. *Z. Psychol.*, 1913, **67**, 358–449.

King, G. F. Rorschach and Levy movement responses: a research note. *J. clin. Psychol.*, 1955, **11**, 193–195.

Klopfer, B., & Kelley, D. *The Rorschach technique*. Yonkers-on-Hudson, N.Y.: World Book Co., 1942.

Korte, A. Kinematoskopische Untersuchungen. *Z. Psychol.*, 1915, **72**, 193–296.

Lennep, D. J. van. The Four-Picture Test. In H. H. Anderson and G. L. Anderson (Eds.) *An introduction to projective techniques*. Englewood Cliffs, N.J.: Prentice-Hall, 1951, 149–180.

Levy, D. M., Schumer, Florence C., & Zubin, J. *The Levy Movement Blots: a study of correlates and validity*. In preparation, 1964.

Mettler, F. A. (Ed.) *Columbia Greystone Associates: Selective partial ablations of the frontal cortex*. New York: Paul Hoeber, 1949.

Moseley, E. C., Gorham, D. R., & Hill, Evelyn F. A computer method for evaluating inkblot perceptions. Mimeographed paper, 1963.

Nicolaides, K. *The natural way to draw*. Boston: Houghton Mifflin, 1941.

Okarski, J. F. Consistency of projective movement responses. *Psychol. Monogr.*, 1958, **72** (Whole No. 459).

Rodin, A. *Art*. Boston: Small, Maynard, 1912.

Roe, Anne. Painting and personality. *Rorschach Res. Exch.*, 1946, **10**, 86–100.

Roemer, G. A. Vom Rorschach zum Symboltest. *Zbl. Psychother.*, 1938, **10**, 310–370.

Rust, R. Some correlates of the movement response. *J. Pers.*, 1948, 16, 369–401. (*a*)

Rust, R. The Levy Movement Cards: EPA round table. *J. Pers.*, 1948, 17, 153–156. (*b*)

Schachtel, E. G. On color and affect. *Psychiatry*, 1943, 6, 393–409.

Stern, W., & MacDonald, J. Cloud pictures: a new method for testing imagination. *Charact. & Pers.*, 1937, 6, 132–146.

Swartz, J. D., & Holtzman, W. H. Group method of administration for the Holtzman Inkblot Technique. *J. clin. Psychol.*, 1963, 19, 433–441.

Warner, S. J. The color preferences of psychiatric groups. *Psychol. Monogr.*, 1949, 63 (Whole No. 301).

Wertheimer, M. Experimentelle Studien über das Sehen von Bewegung. *Z. Psychol.*, 1912, 61, 161–265.

Zubin, J., in collaboration with Kathleen M. Young. *Manual of projective and cognate techniques.* Madison, Wisc.: College Typing Co., 1948.

Zubin, J. Failures of the Rorschach technique. *J. proj. Tech.*, 1954, 18, 303–315.

# 9 THE THEMATIC
APPERCEPTION TEST:

*some historical perspectives;*
*current status; methodological problems*

## BRIEF HISTORY

Morgan and Murray, the authors of the Thematic Apperception Test (TAT), in introducing the technique over 25 years ago, had as their purpose the demonstration of a method for investigating the fantasy of normal individuals (1935). It was one of fifteen techniques devised to obtain data about normal people by means of which the authors attempted to build a theoretical framework of personality. It was subsequently indicated that the chief merits of the technique were to be found in the laboratory and that it is a research tool rather than a clinical instrument (Sanford, 1949). The implications of this technique for investigating the personality of patients were immediately obvious, however, and the clinical use of the test soon outstripped its research application. Only a little over a decade after the introduction of the test, a survey of forty-three representative institutions, including colleges and universities, psychiatric hospitals, public schools, juvenile research bureaus, child guidance clinics, children's homes, training schools, counseling and adjustment services, and public clinics, revealed that it was the third most frequently used test. Only the Stanford-Binet and the Wechsler-Bellevue received more mentions than did the TAT in response to a questionnaire about 130 different instruments (Louttit

& Browne, 1947). A more recent survey by Sundberg (1961) has indicated that the TAT is now tied for second place with the Machover Drawing Test, following the Rorschach, which is in first place.

The pre-TAT use of pictures for evoking verbal responses was primarily in developmental studies concerned with the growth of intelligence in children. Binet and Simon (1905) found that they could distinguish three successive stages in the verbal responses of children to pictures. At age three, there was a mere enumeration of objects. By age seven a child could describe the picture rather adequately in terms of its more obvious qualities. As he grew older he could describe the action, but not until age fifteen was the child really able to comprehend and interpret fully what was happening. Thus Binet was able to use these developmental differences in deriving his age scale of intelligence.[1] In this country at about the same time, Libby (1908), studying the imagination of adolescents, asked a class of forty-one fourth-year high school students to write a story about a "very sentimental" picture which he showed them. He then compared their responses with those of grade school children and found a very marked difference in that the stories of the younger children were more "objective" whereas those of the older children were more "subjective." The cleavage, he felt, came after the fourteenth year. He found a close interrelationship between imagination and feeling and believed that this "feeling factor" differentiated prosaic thinking from imagination. However, this was a developmental study investigating the relationship between imagination and maturation as defined in age differences, and the author ignored the psychological interpretation of the stories he collected.

Brittain (1907), however, who actually published a year earlier than Libby, was interested in the differences between stories told by boys and girls, and in his investigation utilized their productions in a manner which clearly anticipated present day clinical usage. The girls revealed more religious, moral, and social elements in their stories and more interest in clothes and the preparation of food. The boys seemed more interested in the consumption of food. The stories told by the girls were full of pity, sadness, and the fear of being left alone. Brittain considered this "almost a neurotic tendency" caused by the unnatural conditions of the social environment which prohibited "healthful activities." He concluded that the concomitance of a particular kind of physical activity, affective life, and imaginal activity suggested some causal

---

[1] Terman and Merrill (1937), in their revision of the earlier scales, used simpler pictures and expected an enumeration at three years-six months, description at year six, and interpretation at year twelve.

relationship. He hypothesized that these three aspects of life were mutually interactive.

Despite Brittain's provocative findings, the picture story method was not used other than in intelligence testing for 25 years until Schwartz (1932), a psychiatrist attached to the juvenile court in Chicago, found that he could use pictures as an adjunct to the psychiatric interviewing of delinquent boys. He reported that his technique, consisting of eight pictures representing situations most frequently found in the histories of delinquents, shortened the question-answer approach and increased rapport with the child. S was first asked to describe what he saw, then to tell what the boy in the picture was thinking. On the basis of S's responses, the examiner then questioned him further, following up leads suggested by the responses. The child was then asked to tell what he would think and do if he were the boy in the picture. Schwartz described some of the usual responses to the pictures, based on his experience with forty boys, age ten to twelve years, but no reports of further work on this test have been published. Although it attracted some attention at the time, it has not been widely used, probably because of its circumscribed area of application and the difficulty of standardizing the procedure due to the complex follow-up questions which had to be asked.

One additional early test should be noted, the Four-Picture Test (FPT) developed by van Lennep in 1930 (1948, 1951). Four vaguely drawn colored pictures of human figures are presented to S who is instructed to tell a story in which all four pictures appear. Analysis of results is based on both formal and content factors. This test has not gained wide popularity in the United States.

Thus, before the advent of the Murray procedure, the clinical application of the picture-story method had been largely ignored. Murray, however, saw the utility of the technique in uncovering the particular images, strivings, and sentiments which are formed in the course of an individual's development. As Murray explained:

The test is based upon the well recognized fact that when a person interprets an ambiguous social situation he is apt to expose his own personality as much as the phenomenon to which he is attending. Absorbed in his attempt to explain the objective occurrence, he becomes naively unconscious of himself and of the scrutiny of others and, therefore, defensively less vigilant. To one with double hearing, however, he is disclosing certain inner tendencies and cathexes: wishes, fears, and traces of past experience (1938, p. 52).

On the basis of their experience with fifty students at Harvard, Morgan and Murray concluded that of all the short procedures and tests which were tried, the TAT gave the best understanding of the "deeper layers of personality" (1935).

Because of Murray's initial reported successes with this procedure, and because he had assembled at the Harvard Psychological Clinic many researchers who were, or were later to become, leading figures in clinical psychology, the TAT took hold where previous attempts at using the picture-story method had attracted only momentary attention. The test has been revised a few times by the elimination of certain pictures and the addition of others. The third edition, published 8 years after the original, is the one most widely used (Murray, 1943). There were also some changes in administration. Originally the subjects had been told to interpret the action in each picture and to guess as to the preceding events and final outcome; experience showed, however, that much more of the personality was revealed by asking the subject to make up a dramatic story using the picture as a point of departure.

## CURRENT STATUS

The literature based on the TAT, like that of the Rorschach, is voluminous. No attempt will be made to summarize this literature, but the reader is referred to several reviews, manuals, and edited symposia, some early and some recent, which survey the field from a clinical as well as a research and methodological point of view or which describe specific scoring "systems." These include among several others: Aron (1949); Atkinson (1958a); Bell (1948); Bellak (1950, 1954); Eron (1950); Henry (1956); Holt (1951); Kagan and Lesser (1961); Lindzey, et al. (1960); Morgan and Murray (1935); Murray (1938); Murstein (1963); Shneidman, et al. (1951); Stein (1948); Stern (1952); Tomkins (1947); and Wyatt (1958). As in preceding chapters, instead of a detailed review, our discussion will focus on problems— sometimes in historical context and sometimes not.

The reader will note that recent work with the TAT stresses methodological problems. There is by and large a greater sophistication, a greater sensitivity to and understanding of experimental methods, and a greater attempt to work within the framework of general psychological theory in the TAT than in the Rorschach field. The specific causes of this decided difference in orientation are not clear. Perhaps the reason lies in the fact that the TAT is a newer instrument, and as such, students trained in its use also were being trained at the same time in experimental and statistical methods in the general field of psychology;

perhaps the early trial-and-error and intuitive activity which character-ized much of the early Rorschach work provided lessons to be learned, and these lessons were later put to use in TAT work; perhaps the now acceptable view that clinicians should be trained in regular depart-ments of psychology, along with their colleagues in more "traditional" fields, helped to shape the orientation of those clinical students subse-quently going into TAT research; or perhaps the very *language* of TAT interpretations—for example, drives, needs, motives, and goals—helped this instrument to gain a foothold, not only as a clinical tool, but as a measure useful in theoretical and experimental studies of anxiety, learning, aggression, achievement, and the like. Elusive as the causes are, the fact remains that the TAT, more than the Rorschach, is emerg-ing as a clinical instrument in the context of more sophisticated and perhaps more elegant research designs, often reflecting theory in general psychology.

Impressive as many of these studies are, this state of affairs is not without considerable danger. Basic attention to questions of validity and reliability is often not found; the theorizing, speculation, and stress on refined methodological problems have sometimes lessened attention to simpler standards and questions. Is the TAT effective as an instrument in measuring personality as a whole or for answering only certain specific questions? Can the material derived from analyses of TAT material be derived from simpler, more direct observations? Does the vast research material now accumulated fall into a clear-cut picture of the clinical usefulness of the TAT, and if so, are there rules of thumb for the analysis of an individual's record?

The trend in much of current TAT research, as noted, is to focus on methodological issues and on a detailed understanding of the vast complex of variables (social status, stimulus situation, $E$-$S$ interaction, etc.) which contribute to a response.

Although this trend is very fortunate for science, the clinician is easily lost here; he may lack both the time and interest necessary to keep up to date with the literature, which is too complex to yield straightforward and direct "rules" for interpretation. Thus, despite the sophistication of many research workers in the TAT area, the clinician, as might be expected, must fall back on his own intuition, clinical ex-perience, and judgment, a state of affairs which is quite characteristic of the Rorschach in clinical use. The picture is further complicated by the fact that it has become popular in TAT research to "tailor-make" the instrument to research needs. New stimulus pictures relevant to the problem being studied, novel scoring systems, and variations in admin-istration procedures have characterized much recent research. Each worker, whether he regards himself as a "test-developer" or not, has a routine responsibility for exploring the reliability and validity of his instrument. By the time he is through designing and executing his study, and then analyzing and publishing his results, he is too tired or too disinterested to wonder about the generalizability of his findings and to test his questions by replication and cross-validational studies.

As already noted, not even the old and trusted Rorschach enjoys the status of the TAT in terms of the company it keeps and its association with theoretical psychology. The TAT seems to be *the* instrument, without peer, which is regarded as sufficiently complex, sensitive and attractive in terms of its semantic flexibility, so that it can be used to "test" crucial hypotheses about drives, needs, and motivations. Moreover, the TAT has become more and more associated with work in the field of personality with normal Ss (as opposed to its use as a diagnostic instrument). It often is the measure of drive, need, or personality used in the context of studies typically considered outside the field of clinical psychology, for example, group adjustment or level of aspiration. Psychologists with backgrounds in social psychology, personality, or group dynamics will often turn to the TAT, rather than to some of the other projective instruments. Use of the TAT is facilitated since its language is not "exclusive" or special, nor even necessarily psychoanalytic, but seems to fit in with the language habits of many psychologists trained outside the usual clinical facilities. So well accepted is the TAT as a measure of various constructs, that it is often not even mentioned in the title of an article. Much in the way that the Stanford-Binet has been accepted as a measure of intelligence, in which it serves as the chief instrument, so it is frequently taken for granted that the TAT measures fantasy, drives, needs, or motivational states (e.g., McClelland, 1955). Some of the material appearing below will highlight the special status and theoretical significance, often unjustified, that the TAT enjoys in the mainstream of psychology.[2]

*Theory and the TAT.* Several illustrative approaches to "TAT theory" will be noted without attempting an actual survey. Following Rapaport and Gill (1958), five psychoanalytic points of view toward the organism's personality were discussed by Holt (1961). These were: (a) dyna-

---

[2] In a cleverly written, deceptively "naive" article, Astin (1961) highlighted the state of affairs with respect to psychotherapy, wherein nobody questions its efficacy or outcome, but concentrates on mechanics and methodology—a blissful state for which he appropriated the title "functional autonomy." Many of his comments are painfully appropriate to the TAT, Rorschach, and projective techniques in general.

mic; (*b*) economic; (*c*) structural; (*d*) genetic; and (*e*) adaptive. In his brief discussion of these, the author attempted to draw analogies to TAT products. Just what this accomplishes is not clear, for this non-quantitative model simply restates variables other workers have assumed to be significant features of TAT material. To bring in this material under an implicit assumption that the TAT is testing them, or as if a theory of projective behavior is being offered, begs the question. Holt, however, does highlight a significant question related to a problem already noted. Are TAT stories and private fantasies distinguishable? For a discussion of his viewpoint along these lines, see the section on *Assumptions and Hypotheses* which follows.

Feshbach (1961), in his exploration of conflict situations and of the subsequent effects on cognitive and motivational variables, as well as on their expression in fantasy, seems to accept TAT responses as a measure of motives. He was concerned, along with many of his predecessors, with certain findings concerning *n* Achievement (achievement motivation) as measured by the TAT, and in the somewhat confusing finding that high *n* Achievement on the TAT was not always associated with high achievement drive scores derived from other measures. Similarly, Ss with high *n* Achievement but with anxiety over failure did not necessarily produce *low n* Achievement scores on TAT variables, as was commonly expected. Feshbach's contention was that high *n* Achievement scores are not of uniform significance, and he described a dissertation by Glass (1957), which confirmed his suggestion that, "Though the TAT *may* more clearly reflect human motivation than any other instrument that we have available, it is not the x-ray that will lay bare the naked pattern of the organism's inner drives undisguised and uncomplicated by the transformations of fear and guilt" (Feshbach, 1961, p. 124). Thus, although Feshbach accepts the TAT as a measure of both need and "fantasy," by his awareness of the complexity of TAT responses and scores, he implies that such scores are not useful in predicting actual behavior without a good deal of other knowledge. This brings up the question of how expedient and economical is the TAT as an *instrument* for predicting behavior in real-life situations.

Feshbach orients his discussion toward the point of view of learning theory, especially those aspects concerned with conflict; but his language is essentially only descriptive of certain problems of measurement. On the other hand, his formulations do raise extremely interesting problems. For example, the terms response-strength and response-competition suggest that differing TAT scores for two Ss on *n* Achievement may not necessarily mean that one S possesses more drive toward achievement than the other. Achievement motivation may actually be *equal* for both Ss, but if strengths of competing drives differ, one S may actually produce fewer *n* Achievement responses as a result of a competing drive in another area.

Feshbach's solution lies in the appropriate selection of stimulus cards which have a high probability of eliciting only the relevant theme, but which vary with respect to the probability of eliciting *other* themes, so that response competition is minimized. Frequency counts of TAT themes in this instance can be uniformly interpreted to reflect drive strength. In the continuation of his discussion, Feshbach concerned himself with approach-avoidance conflicts and the concept of displacement. His theoretical notions have led him to suggest that only approach-avoidance conflicts lead to defensive or compromise "fantasy" (TAT) responses. His suggestion here is that inhibition of a drive through fear or guilt manifests itself in *greater* "fantasy" imagery and less overt manifestation, on an assumption of lack of awareness of one's motives and of "projective" processes.

Feshbach supports a representational hypothesis which implies direct attribution of one's drives and motives to TAT characters, but argues for a more sophisticated approach which differentiates between direct verbal expression and defensive and compensatory expression. Drive strengths may be high in two different groups, but their expression in verbal "fantasy" may differ as a result of the amount of inhibition.

In general, Feshbach's model serves to highlight the interesting methodological problem of differentiating weak motives and inhibited motives in TAT responses (or as he calls it, fantasy). He mentions briefly the relationship between these fantasy responses and overt behavior, but suggests that the question is complex and that the more appropriate question is not the nature of the relationship, "but rather under what conditions would we expect to find a positive, inverse or negligible correlation" (p. 137).

In an interesting paper, Auld (1954) applied some principles of Hullian behavior theory to an analysis of TAT material derived from the clinic. Auld's general point was that S's response to TAT material is derived from *emotional habits* learned in the past in *origin situations* (original learning situations). Ultimately, prediction to a real *criterion* situation must be based not only on knowledge of the criterion situation, but on knowledge as to how similar or dissimilar the stimuli in the test situation are to the origin situation; otherwise errors in interpretation can easily be made. Auld noted that the following concepts are crucial to a full understanding of the test situation: habit, generalization, test situation, origin situation, criterion situation, habit strength (measured by frequency, vigor, and speed or latency of response), and conflict ("whether the overt response will occur or not depends on the balance between approach and avoidance tendencies. If we can measure both the approach and the avoidance we can predict whether the overt response will occur, and to what degree the subject will act on his tendencies to approach" p. 425).

In terms of the application of such concepts to TAT material, it might be noted that despite the ease and logic of their translation to the TAT, there is no methodological attention to problems of the *test* as such, in terms of prediction. Thus, for example, Auld noted that habit strength could be measured by the frequency of certain TAT themes, or by the vigor of S's verbal description of the action, his tone, and his emotional responses while telling the story; and that speed or latency could be measured by how early in a story a particular theme appears. Useful as these notions are as clear and simple hypotheses, they remain essentially hypotheses and must be validated against other criteria. Does position of a theme in a story indicate habit latency, measurable by other means—say, overtly? Is increased frequency of a theme a measure of increased habit strength (or of card-pull or cultural and communal themes and stereotypes; or an indication of *low* drive accompanied by anxiety over having low drive because of cultural pressure—for example, low sex drive; or of expectations and subjective instructions on S's part as to the nature of the situation)? Psychometric and experimental standards for construct validity, as well as usual standards of reliability, validity, and objectivity must be applied here as well as in the laboratory if the TAT is to have any value as an *instrument* for predicting behavior.

In a general discussion and research report based on the early work on needs and perception, Eriksen (1951) offered some implications for TAT interpretation. His discussion was based on the early concept of perceptual defense and sensitization, that is, the notion that needs affect thresholds of perceptual recognition. Eriksen made a direct and unwarranted parallel between projective stimuli and stimuli used in the early experiments on which these concepts were based. Furthermore, his notion that perception *per se* is involved in response to projective stimuli is probably not a valid one.[3] (It should be noted, however, that Eriksen [1964] has modified these views considerably.)

Eriksen tested the following hypotheses: (*a*) needs which produce sensitization are expressed directly in TAT responses; (*b*) needs which do not produce marked changes in perceptual thresholds will seldom

---

[3] See Chapters 2 and 3 for a detailed discussion of some of these problems.

appear as an important theme in TAT stories; and (c) needs which produce perceptual defense are not openly expressed in TAT stories but there will be distortions, signs of emotional disturbance, less elaboration, etc., with respect to scenes relevant to this need. These hypotheses were generally confirmed in an experiment using twenty-eight Ss whose perceptual recognition thresholds to aggressive stimuli were predetermined. Ss with low recognition thresholds for aggressive stimuli (perceptual sensitization) gave more TAT stories (four weeks later) in which aggression was the main content than Ss with high recognition thresholds (perceptual defense). The latter group of Ss revealed aggressive needs, according to the author, by such signs as blocking, inaccurate interpretations, and incoherent and unelaborated stories when responding to pictures usually given aggressive interpretations. Whether or not perceptual sensitization and defense are valid concepts to begin with, and whether or not, as noted, generalizations from perceptual phenomena can be directly utilized in "explaining" TAT responses (essentially a cognitive task) is questionable.

Finally, this section can be concluded with a brief description of some of the notions of Atkinson (especially, 1958b). After describing motives as enduring characteristics of the individual, Atkinson faced the empirical finding that TAT themes may vary as a result of situational and stimulus conditions. He hypothesized that TAT themes are an expression of the momentary state of aroused motivation. (It should be noted that Atkinson never seems to handle adequately the question of why or how we can be so sure that TAT themes are reflections of motives.) Since for several TAT stimuli the *average* motivational content may be assumed to be the same for all Ss, each S has the same opportunity to reveal his motives. In other words, deviations from this *average* may be assumed to reflect the particular and specific individual's motivation.[4] Atkinson introduced the concept of *expectancy* which arouses certain motivational states. These states may change (although for each individual, strength of a particular motive remains the same). Moreover, his framework accounts for the important role of picture cues in influencing these momentary motivational states; he indicates the need for an explicit and detailed understanding of the instrument as such, and its ability to fulfill certain assumptions.

According to this point of view, the stimulus and general test situation (as well as instructions to S) must be carefully planned and methodically structured in terms of the motivational state (and enduring

---

[4] See Chapter 1 as well as other sections of the present chapter for concurring views as to the efficacy of such a "deviation" approach.

motive) in which $E$ is interested. An implication here is that picture cues must be quite relevant to the motive being tapped, similar to the face validity orientation of achievement testers in the educational field. Thus, should each clinician choose his pictures in terms of expected relevance to the area of his interest on the basis of similarity to expected situations in which a particular motive is likely to reveal itself? And what might be the procedure for eliciting information for several motives? Shall a TAT series contain, then, several "subtests," each relevant to a particular motive or group of motives?

Atkinson notes that his scheme is based on the many studies that he and his co-workers have conducted in the area of achievement motivation, and he indicates that other motives, especially those about which the individual may be in serious conflict, for example, sex and aggression, yield measurement problems which might not be so simple. The evidence suggests that inferences as to strength of such motives could not be based on frequency of themes in TAT material, since expression of such motives is often blocked, distorted, or modified in some way. Atkinson meets this stumbling block by suggesting that under conditions of arousal of motivational states or expectancies relating to such motives, *other* expectancies and motivational states are aroused, in this instance, avoidance, which conflict with the expression of the former. These motives might be called pain-avoidance motives or fears, such as fear of failure or fear of rejection.

The question emerges, then, whether or not it is possible to measure motives about which there is conflict through the manifest content of thematic material. Atkinson believes that the accurate measurement of motives such as aggression and sex is possible through the construction of test situations which arouse expectancies of satisfying approach tendencies without arousing expectancies concerning punishment for them. The use of alcohol or the manipulation of situational variables, e.g., an extremely informal and permissive $E$, as in studies by Clark (1952) and Mussen and Scodel (1955) respectively (see later sections for descriptions of these studies), would be relevant examples of this procedure. Moreover, Atkinson feels that it might be possible to develop valid and reliable indices for assessing competing tendencies through analysis of latent content, for example, by exploring symbolic expression of motivational states.

These theoretical models offer many possibilities for the construction of hypotheses, and illustrate the nature of TAT theorizing. The next section reviews some specific formal, informal, explicit, or implicit hypotheses and assumptions underlying TAT procedures of interpretation and the TAT as an instrument of assessment.

*Assumptions and Hypotheses.* Are *enduring* personality characteristics, goals, drives, and dispositions reflected in TAT responses? Situational factors, differential response to picture cues, temporary drives, etc., apparently influence TAT responses. Feshbach (1955), for example, found that experimentally induced aggressive drive was reflected in the TAT. How do we differentiate enduring dispositions from temporary ones? Veroff, Atkinson, Feld, and Gurin (1960) raised this problem in connection with a national survey. They analyzed *n* Achievement, *n* Power, and *n* Affiliation in terms of occupational level of 486 men employed full time and found that:

Achievement motivation scores are much more frequently high among persons in higher status occupations than among men in lower status occupations. . . . Should the difference here be considered a manifestation of differences in basic personality disposition which has led one group of men to positions of supervision and another not, or should the difference in motivation scores be considered a reflection of the difference in motivational influences contained in the day-to-day life situation of managers, as a group, versus those classified as professionals? Or should the result conceivably be attributed to some biasing in the content of the picture cues favoring one group and not another with respect to the suggestion of power-related imagery? (pp. 23–24)

Assumptions noted in Chapter 1 have direct bearing on specific TAT assumptions. If enduring personality characteristics are measured, are these measured in equal degree in each individual? Does the TAT minimize the role of cultural forces in determining S's response—that is, does it get at his real, *private* world? Is the TAT protocol a sufficiently extensive and representative sampling of this "inner world" to justify generalizations about S's needs and fantasies? Are all TAT responses reflections of S's psychological attributes, and if not, is it possible to differentiate fortuitous and "accidental" elements (error, as it were) from the relevant variables we are hoping to measure? These questions—inverted into premises—are only a few of those which need testing. Some additional questions pertaining to assumptions will be noted, with the understanding that the picture is not bleak, since, fortunately, assumptions often have the good grace to be open to investigation and empirical confirmation.

Even if these assumptions are substantiated, however, there is another group of questions which relates to the nature of the material elicited. Are the wishes, needs, and motivational components revealed in TAT material of such nature that S would be unwilling or unable to talk about them in the ordinary interview situation? To what extent are these productions a reflection of conscious effort and how much of unconscious processes? Is the TAT a short cut to material which is reportable but which S is not revealing? If so, in therapy or under optimal conditions *would* he reveal this material? [5]

Are there not individual differences in the "frankness" of individuals and the degree to which the material they present is repressed, shameworthy, etc.? Is the nature of TAT products different for different Ss? Does one S have more insight about his own motives, for example, than another S? How do we know this, and would this affect the meaningfulness and interpretation of the S's TAT material?

Some workers have assumed a direct relationship between perception and TAT products. However, Lebo (1960) and Lebo and Harrigan (1957) have reported that verbal descriptions of Murray's TAT pictures were equally as effective as the plates themselves in evoking various responses. This finding, although of general interest, is particularly relevant to the question of whether or not one must assume that perceptual processes should be explored as a key to the understanding and interpretation of TAT material. Ss are apparently responding to an internalized image of the stimuli, and their responses reflect cognitive and imaginative material, rather than the direct perception of the stimulus itself. Verbal descriptions and pictorial presentations have been shown to elicit such similar content that one may well wonder whether or not the pictures are essential in a psychological instrument of this sort. Interpretation of the situation at hand, rather than the sheer perception of it, seems to be the response variable involved, and it would follow, therefore, that a psychology of TAT responses should be "interpretation oriented" (with all due stress on and cognizance of intellectual, cultural, and situational variables) rather than "perception oriented."

The "hero" assumption is another example of a frequently accepted premise which actually is fairly testable. Lindzey (1958) and Lindzey and Kalnins (1958) were specifically interested in testing this assumption, which implies that the teller of a story identifies with one person rather than with several persons who figure in a particular narrative, and that to these *other* people the hero behaves as S would in real life. Lindzey was particularly interested in determining whether or not *all* figures in a particular story have some characteristics of the teller. After a group of experiments designed to test this assumption, Lindzey concluded that the hero assumption was borne out, that is, only the hero possesses the characteristics of the story teller. These experiments, incidentally, were cited by the author as examples of TAT research

---

[5] See section, *The Function of Projective Techniques* in Chapter 1, for a relevant framework in which to place some of these questions.

concerned with the testing of assumptions and the psychological processes underlying the TAT response—a procedure which he feels is
more reasonable and productive than the nontheoretical "blind grop-
ings" which characterize the "sign" approach.

Another important group of assumptions—perhaps the most important—which have not been touched on as yet, have to do with whether
or not TAT products are actual reflections of needs, motives, and
drives; whether or not TAT responses are reflections of fantasy processes; and the general question (rather than assumption) of the relationship of the TAT to behavior. So basic and important are these
considerations that they are discussed at length in the next section, and
relevant material will also be presented in the section on *Validity*.
Meanwhile, we continue with additional illustrations of hypotheses and
assumptions.

There are no formal hypotheses agreed on and accepted as such in
the large body of TAT literature. We will illustrate, however, with a
description of two published statements, the *types* of hypotheses, some
implicit and others explicit, which can be found. The first relates mainly
to "rules" for interpretation, in a general sense, and rests largely on the
clinical experience of the author. The other set of hypotheses derives
mainly from the literature and is much more specifically related to
empirical findings.

Piotrowski (1950) listed nine rules for interpretation of TAT material, presumably based on his vast clinical experience. These actually
are rules of thumb which, if restated as testable hypotheses (which
they were not in their present form), could easily serve as a good
jumping-off point for testing various aspects of construct validity and
many of the public and private assumptions made by a number of TAT
workers. Some of these rules, without Piotrowski's elaboration, are that
when interpreting TAT stories, proceed on the assumption that (pp.
106–118):

. . . every figure in the TAT stories expresses some aspect of the testee's
personality; . . .

the more acceptable is an intended action (drive) to the consciousness of the
testee, the greater the similarity between the testee and TAT figure to whom
the drive is attributed; . . .

the more varied and the more incompatible the drives in a subject's stories,
the greater the possibility of poor personality integration, of great inner tension, of fear that the unacceptable drives will undermine self-control and will
prompt the subject to act contrary to his self-interest. The greater the diversity of the TAT drives, the greater the testee's indecisiveness and anxiety; . . .

Finally, employ all formal rules which have been proven valuable in the
study of creative associative power. . . . These rules are not specific to the

TAT and refer to a variety of formal aspects of the TAT performance; uneven pace in the production of the stories, long and variable pauses, marked differences in the number and elaboration of ideas elicited by some pictures as compared with those prompted by other pictures, disregarding of picture details which usually produce comments, farfetched and bizarre notions, sudden or gradual increase or decrease of ideas, etc.

The foregoing quotation has been presented because it demonstrates the nature of assumptions made by many clinicians. A tendency to avoid reference to aspects and attributes of the stimulus situation is noted, as well as failure to note class and cultural variables, E–S relationships, and "picture-pull." There is an assumption that needs and motives are being measured, as opposed to other variables. Although formal aspects are mentioned, content, primarily, is the keynote, presumably because TAT stories for a long time were associated with fantasy content. In connection with the point just noted, the question again might be raised: why are needs and motives and fantasies so irrevocably the dominant aspects of TAT interpretation? Is this an inherent feature of the instrument, or an accident of history, or a development from Murray's original notions? Should not other dimensions be explored? Mood, self-concept, personal style, maturity, etc., might well be relevant also. Lazarus (1961), for example, has stated that ego-control processes, rather than needs directly, are measured by TAT responses.

A second group of hypotheses is illustrated by the work of Lindzey, Bradford, Tejessy, and Davids (1959). Here, hypotheses are stated in terms of specific, purported relationships between TAT responses and some other criterion. These authors summarized and systematized interpretive statements from the literature concerning the TAT—specifically, published statements which related TAT responses to characteristics of S. All generalizations prior to 1958 were included. No attempt to evaluate these was made. "It is quite literally a dictionary of interpretive generalizations" (p. 1). Such a comprehensive statement could well be used for hypotheses for future empirical tests, cross-validation studies, and replications. But, in addition, this work provides a bird's-eye view of what clinicians seem to glean from TAT material, what their expectations and generalizations are, and which areas and purported relationships seem to reflect a concensus. Thus, a "climate of opinion" is presented, with a rich potential for research work, as well as a crude map of those areas barren of research or generalization. The authors imply that some clinical usefulness lies in their lexicon, although it is difficult to see how a sheer accumulation from the literature can have utility of this sort. They have stated: "There has been no attempt to select only those interpretive statements that appear plausible, mutually consistent, or that are supported by convincing empirical evidence" (p. 3).

Essentially, the lexicon is comprised of correlational statements culled from the literature (with the reference cited), along with a code which represents the nature of the empirical evidence upon which the generalization rested. The code covers the following: empirical evidence, quantitatively expressed with results stated in terms of their statistical significance; empirical evidence without tests of significance; observational conclusions; and general "clinical experience" and logical derivations only, without empirical or observational data. The lexicon is divided into thirteen major sections, each with several major subsections, and consists primarily of descriptive phrases concerning a characteristic of S (such as "consistent with schizophrenia" or "disturbance over masturbation" or "often feels no guilt for his aggression") and purported TAT correlates. Some of the TAT correlates are vaguely stated, and little or no evidence for objectivity of scoring, nature of experimental design, or for validity or reliability, etc., is offered.

The work should prove interesting to future researchers in terms of what ultimately shape up to be the stereotypes, cultural myths, and common fallacies among the current crop of clinicians, as well as what turns out to be correct judgments. A glance through the lexicon suggests that there is an uncomfortably large number of classifications based on observational and clinical generalizations without empirical data.

*Assumptions (continued): the Validity of Some Important Constructs.* Of the numerous assumptions inherent in both TAT research and clinical use, the one almost universally accepted is that TAT responses are a measure of "fantasy." This assumption is so commonly made, often implicitly, but frequently explicitly, that examples are not even necessary. A glance at any TAT reference list over the past decade or two will show the frequency with which this assumption is made; it is quite common to find articles with titles which note that the study is investigating fantasy and some other variable; there is no mention of the TAT as the measure of fantasy (e.g., Fisher & Morton [1957], Henry [1956], and Wyatt [1958]). As already noted, this pattern was common in early studies of intelligence, wherein the *instrument* was accepted as *the* measure to such a degree that its mention in the title of the article was absent.

Tomkins (1949) offered a dissenting note. He noted that crucial fantasies and indications of behavior are often actually withheld from the TAT response, whereas "every variety of antisocial behavior is found in the stories of those who exhibit none of these tendencies in their overt behavior." Tomkins claimed that the TAT is particularly insensitive in eliciting representations of fantasy about antisocial behavior. In normals, he felt, there is "distance" between a person and his wishes, so that they are more easily represented in the TAT. Might this not suggest that usual themes, intensity of actions, etc., have little diagnostic value, and that perhaps some of the diagnostic failures of the TAT are based on a too naive, "isomorphic" parallelism which equates verbal responses with fantasies? Although later studies have stressed ego defenses and various mechanisms which could block, distort, or change the direction of a TAT verbal response as a result of anxiety or guilt, a TAT interpretation unfortunately is and must be based on responses *per se*. Although the clinician is theoretically cognizant of the fact that defenses play an important role in the nature and degree of expression of a theme, he often cannot easily evaluate whether or not they are operating.

As already noted, the equation of TAT products, responses, or stories with fantasies is routine for many TAT workers. It is not necessary to cite the scores of published reports, including Morgan and Murray's original publication (1935), which have made this assumption. More recent thinking, however, suggests that the relationship between dreams, daydreams, reveries, autistic thinking, and fantasies is not clear, and that each of these may vary along a variety of dimensions, including level of affect, reality-orientation, explicitness, nature of logic, degree of wish-fulfillment, etc. For a discussion of these variables and their interrelationships, see Holt (1961). Following Freud (1953), Holt listed some of the similarities between fantasies and TAT stories. Quoting directly from Holt's table these similarities are:

1. Both tend to follow the general narrative format, with a central figure or *hero* who has various adventures.
2. In both there tends to be little characterization of persons other than the hero; they are just auxiliary and supplementary figures.
3. The goals and activities portrayed in both reflect S's personal goals and needs; likewise, abilities, personal memories, defenses, information, sentiments and attitudes, patterns of interpersonal relations, personal style and many other aspects of personality are used in the construction of both.
4. Both exist in a variety of forms, using various mixtures of primary process and secondary process (p. 20).

Holt's extensive list of *differences*, however, is much more impressive and far reaching. He listed fifteen areas of significant differences including variables such as the quality of consciousness (the TAT response is elicited in a full waking state with reflective awareness, which is not the case for fantasies); spontaneity vs. effortfulness (the TAT response is an active, conscious, deliberate response to an externally imposed task); imagery vs. verbalization (the TAT response is always verbal, but the fantasy may be entirely nonverbal); implication vs. explicitness (continuity and transitions in fantasy are often implicit whereas these are often explicit in TAT responses); memorability (the fantasy is often unremembered whereas the TAT story is usually remembered); and involvement of affect (the TAT response only infrequently involves crude, strong affect). Other differences include: primary vs. secondary process; narrative structure; self-relevance; dynamic aspect: role of drives and defenses; role of external reality: stimulus; role of abilities; relation to action; role of communication; and range of subject-matter.

The lesson to be learned may not be positive, but cautionary. A question of construct validity is involved when fantasies and TAT responses are equated; there is considerable need for further study of the relationship between TAT verbal products and fantasies. Certainly, it seems premature to generalize from TAT responses as if they were fantasies, and as if further knowledge about the conditions and circumstances associated with certain types of TAT responses is a direct link to the further understanding of the fantasy process.

Holt, incidentally, suggested that differences between TAT stories and fantasies are so characteristic and stable that when there is a failure of a difference to occur, this is itself significant. Deviations from expected differences may serve a diagnostic purpose, as in the case of an excess of affect, or acting-out, or when a primary process has emerged in the context of a TAT story.

Feshbach (1951, 1955) attempted to answer the question as to whether or not fantasy behavior served a drive-reducing function. His measure of fantasy was the TAT. His questions—does fantasy behavior satisfy needs and would fantasy behavior partially reduce aggressive drive—were answered in the affirmative. He experimentally induced aggression by insulting various groups of Ss, introduced "fantasy" or "nonfantasy" activity, and then measured the strength of the aggressive drive. The insulted group which expressed aggression in "fantasy" displayed less toward E, that is, there was a negative relationship between the amount of aggression in "fantasy" and aggression expressed toward E. The insulted Ss expressed significantly more aggression in "fantasy" than did the noninsulted Ss. Despite the interesting experiment, however, and the fact that the findings suggest some relationship between a temporarily induced mood state and verbal responses on the TAT, as well as a relationship between verbal responses and behavior, the question still remains—does the TAT measure fantasy?

Another basic question of construct validity is this: do needs influence TAT products? If so, are TAT products a *direct* reflection of needs and drive states? Reference need only be made to Chapters 2 and 3 to demonstrate the complexity of this question as to needs and perception. The relation between needs and apperception, or cognitive products like TAT stories, may be even more complex. The naive assumption that TAT content directly reflects needs is currently tempered by evidence to the contrary. Level of anxiety, guilt, and nature of defenses are involved. But also, "structural" variables such as popular responses, card-pull, E-S variables, even the myths and taboos of a culture as well as the content of its mass media products are involved.[6] S's interpretation and expectations concerning the examiner and the situation may also influence his products. One of the authors, in her work with the Levy Movement Blots (Levy, Schumer, & Zubin, 1964), was impressed with the frequent open sexuality, sometimes even obscenities, found in the protocols of a group of psychiatrists seeking entrance into a well-known, metropolitan psychoanalytic training school. These candidates apparently "categorized" the situation they found themselves in (screening and evaluation) as one which placed a strong positive value on a frankly accepting, "free" and casual attitude toward sex and certain Anglo-Saxon words. The TAT may measure S's views of what he thinks E regards as important, or the TAT may measure *low* drive level (e.g., sex) in a situation in which possessing high or moderate drive is culturally stressed and S feels anxious about it.

In a discussion of some of these problems, Lazarus (1961) postulated a substitutive mechanism as well as a defensive mechanism, which may alter and modify a need, even into its direct opposite. Pittluck (1950) and others had introduced this notion earlier. Lazarus, although accepting the general notion of needs bearing on apperceptive material, indicated that the relationship is not simple. He noted that in food deprivation studies there was a positive association between need and imagery, but that with more extended periods of deprivation, the relationship was negative. Broverman, Jordan, and Phillips (1960), in a study of thirty-seven subjects, found no relationship between actual achievement, and either achievement fantasy or achievement striv-

---

[6] For further development of the effect of variables other than need on TAT stories, see Chapter 11.

ing. But achievement striving and an apperceptive measure of achievement were *inversely* related to each other. Referring also to the approach of Werner and Wapner (sensory-tonic field theory, see Chapter 2) as well as to the studies of Singer, Meltzoff, *et al.* (see Chapter 4), Lazarus suggested that when there is overt, reality-oriented, motoric behavior in the direction of need-gratification, there will be *less* evidence of the need in apperceptive products; the opposite is also true—individuals who are blocked from gratifying needs in real life may use the "test" situation as an opportunity to express such needs in substitute fashion. Clark (1952) found *reduced* erotic imagery on the TAT under conditions of sexual stimulation, presumably because of strong anxiety. Lazarus, in discussing this experiment, contended, however, that anxiety, guilt, and social taboos are not the only variables affecting the expression of needs on TAT material, but that ego-processes and adaptive mechanisms are also at work. In other words, as the intensity of needs is increased, various ego-controls will be brought into play as a result of the organism's stress, and it is *this* which is reflected in a variety of ways for different Ss in their TAT material.

An experiment by Pittluck (1950) may furnish an explanation for the lack of consistent relationship between total amount of aggressive content in stories and the overt behavior of an individual. Pittluck found that there was a positive relationship between the amount of aggressive behavior expressed overtly and in TAT stories, but that this relationship was modified by the amount of anxiety in the stories that was engendered by overt expression of aggression. She used as her behavioral measure reports by nurses and attendants of the spontaneous aggressive behavior of seventy-two neuropsychiatric patients on the hospital wards. She found that more aggressive responses on the TAT were associated with more behavioral expressions. But she had to consider the aggressive responses in relation to modifying mechanisms in the stories, such as rejection or denial of the aggression, excusing of the aggression by placement in a socially acceptable context, noncompletion of aggression planned by a story character, and displacement of the aggression to nonhuman objects. These mechanisms were considered to be motivated by anxiety and to be defensive in their purpose. By their use, the aggressive response becomes a compromise between aggressive impulses and the anxiety opposing their expression. She found that the tendency to use these mechanisms was negatively related to the tendency to act out. The patients who used more defense in proportion to their outgoing aggressive "fantasies" tended to act out less than the patients who used proportionately fewer such mechanisms. In addition, patients who used proportionally more unmodified primitive responses in fantasy tended to act out more than patients with proportionally fewer fantasies of this nature. She concluded, therefore, that measures of aggressive fantasy can provide direct clues to overt aggressive behavior if these measures stress not the absolute frequency of aggressive responses but the extent to which such responses are free from modifications which are presumably the result of anxiety.

Bellak (1950) also introduced the concept of defense to explain some of the known failures in predicting diagnostic groupings. Besides noting the paucity of responses in many records, he illustrated dramatically what others have also indicated—the insensitivity of the TAT, that is, its inability to reveal known pathology. Bellak also suggested that a shift was necessary from a consideration of drive to a consideration of ego processes so that defenses against anxiety would be considered. He made some interesting suggestions which followed from these notions. One is that pretest sedation might decrease anxiety, so that defenses would be less potent; and that the use of extremely short time limits might similarly decrease ego strength.

In their experiments concerning the effect of food deprivation on the content of TAT stories, Atkinson and McClelland (1948) [7] found that with increasing periods without food, the subjects tended to give less stories about food and eating, and more stories about deprivation in general and ways of solving the deprivation. If fantasy, as measured by TAT-type stories, was compensational in nature, it would be expected that with increasing hunger there would be more stories about food and consumption of food. Since this was not the case, the authors felt that, "the amount of need deprivation and instrumental activity present in stories is a better index of the strength of need than is the goal activity" (p. 657). They also stated that, ". . . it is to the obvious advantage of the organism to concern itself more and more with instrumental rather than goal activity as the need increases. It is also useful to emphasize the problem (deprivation) and ways of overcoming it. . . . mobilization at the imaginative level of the resources of the organism toward solving or handling the problem of food deprivation goes on apparently very largely without the S's knowledge or conscious intent" (p. 655).

McClelland, Clark, Roby, and Atkinson (1949) found the same proc-

---

[7] A previous section, *Theory and the TAT,* described some of Atkinson's more recent views. This worker feels that need is related to apperceptive products, although the conditions of expression are rather complex (Atkinson, 1961, pp. 72–79).

ess operating when they analyzed a more complex type of motivation
—need for achievement. They had their Ss write stories in response to
pictures after conditions of ego involvement (neutral, success, failure)
and similarly found that with increased motivation there was an increase in number of plots dealing primarily with deprivation of the
goal, an increase in number of times that characters in the stories were
said to want or wish for the goal, and an increase in the mention of
instrumental activities which are successful in dealing with the need-
related problem. There was no increase in the number of plots dealing
with the direct attainment of the goal or with substitute activity. Thus,
they saw the stories as reflecting the present state of the individual.
He is frustrated, the frustration appears in the "fantasy"; he is
exploring ways to overcome the frustration, this instrumental activity
also appears in the "fantasy." He is deprived of the goal, but attainment of the goal does not appear to a significant degree.

The authors overlooked one important consideration in the interpretation of their results, however. The fact that they found more mentions of instrumental activity than goal activity may be an artifact of
the instructions to make up a story. In making up a story, it is quite
natural that more attention will be paid to the body of the story and
that the conclusions will be just tacked on at the end. This is often the
case in individual administration when the examiner is right there to
encourage the subject. With the subject taking the test in a group situation, without an examiner to prompt him, and with a five minute time
limit, the probability is even greater that he will just add on the conclusion as the "stop" signal is given or forget it altogether. And it is in
the conclusion of the story that the goal activity is likely to appear, not
in the body of the story which is usually taken up with a description of
the tension, striving, etc. This is because a story has to have "a beginning, a middle, and an end." Eron's results (1948) would support this
explanation for McClelland's findings, since he found a preponderance
of disequilibrium themes over equilibrium themes in TAT stories. It is
perhaps in the nature of things that, in telling stories, the "instrumental"
rather than the "goal activity" is stressed. McClelland, *et al.* did not
control for this factor, and it is quite possible that the stress on instrumental rather than goal activity was the result of the instructions to
make up a story and not of the intrinsic relationship between TAT
stories and behavior.

Clark (1952), in extending the McClelland methodology to another
need, sex, obtained results which need not be interpreted as showing a
direct relationship between need as manifested in behavior and in TAT
productions. Sexual motivation in male college students was aroused

by presentation of slides of nude females. The TAT protocols were analyzed for manifest sex imagery and sex-involved guilt. The results showed that the experimental group (with slides) expressed significantly less sex and guilt in their TAT stories than did the control group (no slides). This might be interpreted as a compensational relationship. Assuming that sexual need was aroused by the slides, the Ss may have felt guilt because of the sexual arousal and thus inhibited the expression of sex, by which inhibition, consequently, they were able to reduce the guilt which generally accompanies expression of sex needs in such a situation. It is interesting that when this same experiment was done with the Ss under the influence of alcohol, the results were just the reverse, with the experimental group showing significantly more sex and guilt than did the control group. Thus, it seems that under alcohol the guilt over sexual arousal was sufficiently reduced initially to permit the expression of sex, with a resultant increase of the guilt. Although results of the first half of Clark's experiment fit in more with a compensational point of view, this second half is more in line with the representational nature of "fantasy"—increased sexual need, increased sexual imagery in the stories; increased guilt, more themes of guilt in the stories. By considering the conditions of the two parts of the experiment in Pittluck's terms, we can perhaps understand the seeming contradiction. Under normal conditions the usual defenses against anxiety were called into play, sexual imagery was repressed (at least it was not reported), and guilt was not engendered. With anxiety dispelled under the alcohol conditions, the usual defenses were not called into play and there was no repression of the expression of sexual imagery. Once the sexual imagery had been expressed, however, it was natural for the guilt engendered by this to seek expression also. Thus, Clark's results, despite what seems to be a contradiction, can be explained in the light of Pittluck's findings concerning the interaction of need expression and anxiety over its expression.

In a study concerned with strength of drive and TAT content, Murray (1959) explored a drive induced by sleep deprivation. His hypothesis was based on a previous indication that at low and moderate drive levels, "sensitization" occurred—that is, TAT responses would reflect the deprivation. But at high drive levels, a defensive process is brought into play. The author was interested in exploring the possibility that prolonged sleep deprivation produced a conflict, and that by a denial of sleep thema and a general avoidance of situations and self-descriptions which would increase sleep needs, S could maintain wakefulness. His Ss were forty-eight soldiers divided into an experimental and a control group. Six TAT cards were administered, carefully preselected to fit in with the design of the experiment (three cards presumably represented high, medium, or low sleep suggestion). Scores were computed reflecting sleep (goal as well as instrumental) and fatigue themes; also included were hostility and tension ratings, word counts and scores for some of Eron's categories (see Chapter 12).

One of the chief results was that sleep deprivation decreased the thematic expression of sleep needs, especially for high sleep cards, but did not affect other measures such as word counts, and tension and hostility ratings. The author concluded that,

The decrease may be viewed as an increase in the threshold for sleep themes in response to TAT stimuli since as the sleep suggestion of the cards increases, some sleep themes can be evoked although not as many as with the control group. . . . The decrease in sleep themes does not appear to be an artifact of a general inhibitory effect of sleep deprivation since fatigue themes, word counts, hostility ratings and tension ratings showed no decreases with sleep loss (p. 99).

These findings seem to coordinate fairly well with findings in other studies; however, a question must be raised as to the generalizability of these findings in terms of various drives, especially those of which S is not consciously aware. Presumably it is these latter drives and motivational states which would interest the clinician. The TAT is not frequently used as an instrument to assess or measure the strength of S's need for sleep! It could be argued, of course, that studies such as Murray's and some of the others serve a theoretical, rather than a clinical purpose. This cannot be denied, and is a cogent argument with which the current authors cannot disagree. On the other hand, the question still remains as to the role of conscious factors. S's awareness of sleep deprivation may have resulted in a conscious turning away from verbalizations in this area, especially because he was under some sort of social pressure to stay awake. These factors may have had an important influence on some of the results. In this sense, then, Murray's results may not be applicable to drive states about which S is unaware or about which S experiences no social pressure.

An approach-avoidance conflict analysis of TAT material growing out of Pittluck's work was made by Lesser (1958), who compared evidence of conflict about aggression which appeared in the stories to a modified TAT, with ratings (using a modified sociometric device) of overt aggression made by peers. His Ss were seventy-two fifth-grade boys, and his TAT measure was a ratio of the strength of aggressive need to the strength of anxiety about expressing aggression. He found that the relationship between TAT material and behavior was stronger when both approach and avoidance tendencies were considered simultaneously (as by this index), than when each of the tendencies was analyzed separately. Another finding was that the earlier the anxiety indications about expression of aggression appeared in the stories after the recognition of instigation to aggression, the greater was the relationship to control of overt aggression; also, that punishment by peers in the stories was associated with a low degree of overt aggression, whereas punishment by authority figures was associated with a high degree of such behavior.

A related study concerning TAT aggression and overt behavior was reported by Jensen (1957), who examined a variety of hypotheses concerning the relationship between TAT responses and overt behavior in seventy-four high school boys, rated by their teachers as "aggressive-bad," "aggressive-good," and "passive" (no overt aggressiveness). His findings confirmed earlier reports that no direct relationship was found between aggression on the TAT and overt behavior. *Absence,* however, of either punishment or defense over the expression of aggression was positively related to overt aggressive behavior (at the .01 level of significance). In addition, other aspects of the TAT material (the author called these "behavior samples") did differentiate the Ss at a high level of significance. The "aggressive-bad" group, for example, produced significantly more sex, tabooed sex, tabooed language, and tabooed violence in their responses than did the other groups.

The relationship between aggressive "fantasy" and overt behavior was related to learning conditions in another report by Lesser (1959b). He compared the relationship that obtained between these two variables among boys whose mothers encouraged expression of aggression as contrasted with boys whose mothers discouraged such behavior. Where aggressive behavior had maternal encouragement, there was a significant positive relationship between aggression scores obtained from stories and behavioral ratings obtained from peers, but where mothers were relatively discouraging of aggression, there was a negative relationship of about the same magnitude. If both groups had been pooled, the resulting correlation would have been no better than zero.

These findings seem to suggest that when defenses against the expression of aggression are considered, TAT measures of aggression can be related to various aspects of overt behavior or to ratings of behavior. A similar point with respect to anxiety was suggested by the results of a study by Phares (1961), who worked with two groups of female Ss who scored high or low on the Taylor Anxiety Scale (Taylor, 1953). These Ss had been matched for the tendency to evade or cope with threatening stimuli. He demonstrated significant differences between these groups in terms of the degree to which they saw accident, threat, or trauma in the TAT cards. He used a modified TAT administration procedure involving the presentation of several brief themes along with each of seven TAT cards which S was asked to rank in terms of "how well they fitted the card." On the basis of his findings, Phares suggested that a behavior (TAT response) "occurs not simply as a function of one variable but as a function of the relationship among several variables" (p. 258). He noted that one could not predict that high anxious Ss would necessarily respond to threatening material in the TAT unless the nature of their evasion-coping defenses were known.

What about the *general* question of whether or not the TAT is an adequate instrument for the measurement of needs or need-states? This of course raises a question of validity, and the reader is referred to the appropriate section in this chapter. Despite many encouraging results and findings, there is by no means agreement or even confirmation of the general notion that the TAT is an instrument which can validly measure needs. For example, whether a need or drive, as measured in overt performance, can be validly measured by relevant TAT measures is considered doubtful by Child, Frank, and Storm (1956), whose study is discussed in the section on *Validity*.

In addition, the desirability or even appropriateness of isolating needs and equating them with scores or responses might be questioned. Can we isolate a motive as such? Do the scores actually represent motives? In a paper only indirectly related to the TAT, Lesser (1961b) described some of the theoretical and methodological difficulties involved in delimiting and defining the concept of need, and discussed problems involved in the interactions of needs and their controls within the individual. So complex are the problems of assessment, that Lesser proposes a model-building procedure based on computer simulation of the many variables involved. This seems to him the proper solution for a research area which is so multivariate and complex that a verbal theory could not possibly handle the ramifications and extensions of the propositions contained therein. Viewed in such a context, the use of a single instrument such as the TAT, which itself has a number of unresolved questions of validity and reliability, to assess need strength becomes a questionable procedure, or at least a procedure about the efficacy of which we have little or perhaps even negative information. Of this problem, Lesser (*Ibid.*, 1961b) said:

Several broad issues remain in the construction of techniques to assess need strength. What is the best type of measure to be used in assessing needs? Many methods for measuring need variables exist, but we have not proceeded very far in systematically comparing the relative effectiveness and applicability of alternative measurement procedures. While fantasy or projective measures of needs have been extremely prominent in research as well as in clinical practice, impressive evidence is accumulating for the value of behavioral measures of need strength for certain research problems. Comprehensive methodological studies are needed to compare the gains and losses of fantasy procedures, behavioral measures, ratings, direct preference or assent methods, and other assessment strategies. Much valuable information would be derived from pitting alternative measurement strategies against each other in the solution of common substantive problems (pp. 3–4).

## VALIDITY AND RELIABILITY

Previous sections, especially the last, have already raised problems with respect to a few important considerations concerning validity of certain constructs. That discussion stemmed from a consideration of some of the assumptions made by clinicians and workers regarding the TAT. Outside of some introductory but important remarks, the next several sections will focus on specific validation studies, as well as on those which provide some information as to the reliability of the instrument. Some problems in connection with both validity and reliability studies will be raised.

We begin with the question, "How efficient is this instrument in predicting a diagnostic category, prognostic outcome, personality variable, or dynamics?" One of the questions we must face is whether or not we know the relevant parameters of the sample we are studying. Without knowledge of base rates (Meehl & Rosen, 1955), instruments may appear to possess spurious validity. Moreover, it is difficult to assess differences between various samples or to generalize from results of a specific study without this knowledge. Instruments achieving high success in one study may fail to achieve that level of success when applied to another sample. Meehl and Rosen (*Ibid.*) have said, "a psychometric device, to be efficient, must make possible a greater number of correct decisions than could be made in terms of the base rate alone" (p. 194). Research clinicians often overlook this important consideration.

Lesser (1959*b*) futhermore noted the importance of considering population differences in the validation of a particular measure. He demonstrated the fact that TAT measures of aggression were highly intercorrelated for groups of children with low anxiety about aggression, but that these intercorrelations were significantly lower in a group of children with high anxiety about aggression. In a validity study of aggression-anxiety "fantasy" scores, the same author (1959*a*), although finding no differences between fifth- and sixth-grade Catholic, Jewish, and Protestant boys in terms of measures of both overt and "fantasy" aggression, did find some significant differences when aggression-anxiety scores were considered.

Such studies are among a growing number which demonstrate the importance of considering the validity of a score in terms of cultural, social, and class variables. Base rates and other characteristics of the sample studied should most certainly enter the picture when the validity of a score or of an instrument is being considered. Furthermore, sampling errors and chance factors may not be errors at all, but a result of decided, definable, and specific population differences which can be predicted, and some cross-validational failures should undoubtedly be interpreted in such a context.

The next several pages are devoted to a description of various types of validity studies. The purpose is to survey some of the most typical procedures and methods found in TAT research. No mention is made of the so-called "content validity" or "face validity" approach—a non-empirical approach which might be used when one begins to collect and assemble items for certain types of tests or when one looks over test content to see if it makes sense in terms of the variables one is trying to assess. Nor, because of infrequency, will note be made of factorial studies, presumably designed to shed light on the validity of the instrument. This last procedure probably offers a wide variety of research possibilities for the interested worker.

*Validity Studies.* The early studies in the validity of the TAT have been summarized by Tomkins (1947) and Bell (1948). Tomkins felt that insofar as the experiments went, the validity of the technique had been indicated. Bell, however, said that, "to a marked extent clinicians have been willing to accept the procedure as valid and reliable without further scientific evidence than their own experience which, to be sure, is a form of measurement" (p. 226). The research which has appeared since 1948 does not clear up the situation. Those studies immediately following this period were not especially successful in demonstrating the ability of the TAT to differentiate diagnostic groups. However, the criterion of validity through contrasted diagnostic groups by use of descriptive diagnosis is itself of uncertain validity, and the fact that the TAT fails to make such discriminations is no proof of its *invalidity.*

Davenport (1952) submitted 207 typical interpretative statements and forty-three author-originated statements to six clinical psychologists, and asked them to decide whether each could apply to six TAT records. Twenty-six other psychologists rated these statements as to their ambiguity and universality. Discrimination was neither reliable nor successful, and statements rated as universal were applied by judges to any patient. The judges avoided using the more specific statements. The dangers of demonstrating validity through "blind" matching techniques were thus demonstrated. What is the overall validity picture, then, using various procedures and criteria?

*Diagnostic Validity—Concurrent Validity through Use of Contrasted Groups.* Many simple perceptual and motor tasks have been shown to discriminate various nosological groups (Eysenck, Granger, & Brengelmann [1957]; also, Rabin & King [1958]). What is the state of affairs with more complex cognitive tasks such as the TAT?

The first studies to appear after publication of the original work at the Harvard Psychological Clinic were concerned primarily with the utilization of the technique in classifying patients according to nosological entities. As mentioned earlier, this work has been summarized by Bell (1948), who grouped the various published studies under appropriate diagnostic headings. An examination of this exhaustive list reveals many contradictions. A number of authors listed different characteristics as representative of the same clinical group and the same characteristics as representative of different clinical groups. For the most part, the studies summarized in Bell's volume presented little or no data with which to support the conclusions of the authors, and, if they did, there were either no adequate control groups or appropriate statistical measures by which the significance of the results could be estimated. An additional factor which may account for the contradictory results, of course, is the poorly defined classification systems which were used as criteria. For example, an individual diagnosed as schizophrenic in Topeka might easily be pigeonholed otherwise in Chicago or New York. This, of course, is a perennial problem in clinical research.

Many of these early studies of validity were not, methodologically speaking, studies of validity at all, but rather "case" presentations or illustrations designed to demonstrate the effectiveness of the TAT with various diagnostic groups. Such studies were often couched in a framework which attempted to show how the instrument could shed light on personality dynamics of a given group, or, as in the case of the next study to be described, to show how the "dynamics" of a given population could be interpreted in the same light, and using the same language of the instrument as applied to other (normal) groups. Cross-validation was rarely attempted in many of these studies.

Sarason, for example (1943*a*; 1943*b*), described themes of high-grade mentally deficient youngsters. (An earlier study had attempted to demonstrate validity through the matching of TAT themes with case-history material, with little consideration for base rates and cross-validation of findings and without accounting for some of the pitfalls of matching procedures.) Without presenting validity evidence, Sarason's conclusions were: "The present study reveals that severely retarded children have the same feelings and desires as normal children and want affection and security as strongly as any other group" (1943b, p. 173). Beier, Gorlow, and Stacey (1951), in reporting that severe emotional disturbance is an essential aspect of mental deficiency, based their conclusions on TAT material of forty mentally defective girls, age fourteen to eighteen, but did not use adequate controls, nor did they cross-validate their findings. Another example of an early study is that of Sarason (1944), in which thematic material and dreams produced by twenty-five mentally deficient women were compared; the author reported that similar thema were found in dreams and in thematic material. The same material is also often found, it should be noted, in a wide variety of other groups. An additional early study is one reported by Klebanoff (1947), who explored TAT material of chronic alcholics. In this report, the validity of the TAT is accepted, and the study—only a small group of Ss was used—was done to shed light primarily on the personality dynamics of alcholics, rather than to shed light on the TAT or to demonstrate its efficacy. Although results were compared to a non-matched group of normals, tests of significance were not done. These studies of validity are similar to early Rorschach studies, which consisted of comparing and contrasting Rorschach scores of various groups in this and other cultures, not only to show that the Rorschach works, but also to describe the dynamics and modal characteristics of the groups in question. Validity, reliability, and objectivity of the instrument were taken for granted.

Kutash (1943), in a study similar to those already noted, worked with psychopathic defective criminals. In describing the responses of this group in terms of their conflicts and "fantasies," there was, of course, no cross-validation and no comparison to other groups; his overall conclusion was, "The results indicate that the psychopathic defective can be adequately studied by the use of the Thematic Apperception Test so as to reveal facets of his personality which cannot be reached by other non-projective responses" (p. 339). His study was unusual for its time because it foreshadowed some of the interest in and importance of considering the role of the stimulus itself and variations among the cards as determinants, in part, of the response. Kutash summarized each story for each card by breaking it down into "responses"—each response representing a "thought whole"—or a statement of dynamic significance, capable of interpretation. He listed the frequency of various types of responses for each picture, and discovered to his surprise that the pictures varied considerably (he was not sure whether or not Murray did this intentionally) in "bringing out certain qualitatively different types of fantasy material" (p. 331).

More recently, Kerner (1956), in a study concerned with the problem of adaptation to stress, offered the general hypothesis that schizophrenics and normals will react differentially to stress as reflected in their fantasies. Many additional subsidiary hypotheses concerning ego-integration, reaction to stress, and modes of adaptation and differences between the groups were also stated. Additional assumptions were made that TAT material reflects reactions to stress and that TAT material is fantasy material. He worked with twenty schizophrenics and twenty normals, matched as far as possible, and used as a "stressor agent" a target ball test which involved consistent failure on the part of the Ss. TAT responses were scored for modes and effectiveness of adaptation. Kerner devised a rather detailed and complicated scoring system. In the design he controlled the presence or absence of stress and the sequence of two matched TAT series. Eleven out of fifty-six comparisons ("hypotheses") distinguished the two groups. These eleven significant "signs," however, should have been cross-validated with a new group, but this was not done.

Foulds (1953), using a simple TAT scoring system which included reaction time, total number of words, time taken on test, and fluency as well as content of response, found significant differences among many of these measures when psychopaths, hysterics, anxiety states, depressives, and obsessionals were compared (N of 14 to 44 in each group). Unfortunately again, failure to cross-validate these findings, and failure to make explicit the nature of the principles and procedures upon which the diagnostic label was assigned, detract from the value of these findings.

More recently, Takahashi (1958) reported significant differences between college students and delinquent youths, roughly matched for age and IQ, in terms of plots, press, language style, emotional tone, etc. These findings were again not cross-validated, however. Waxenberg (1955) worked with 20 asthmatic women, 20 women who had histories of ulcerative colitis, and 20 women with malignant tumors, in order to explore hypotheses about psychosomatic disease. A large battery of tests were given, including the TAT (using Eron's rating scale of emotional tone). No differences between groups were found, not only on the TAT, but on other tests. Carlile (1952) similarly found that the TAT possessed little discriminatory power with respect to matched pairs of thirty normal and neurotic girls; in addition, little agreement was found between the TAT and teacher ratings.

Dana (1956c; 1957; 1959) however, has described a method for scoring TAT material based on three scoring categories: Perceptual Organization; Perceptual Range; and Perceptual Personalization. In various validity studies (with clinical diagnosis as a criterion) involving the use of this special scoring system, he found that the score based on Perceptual Organization (PO) was particularly discriminating among groups of normals, neurotics, and psychotics, and that at least 80% of the diagnostic groups were sucessfully identified by any of the three scores. He provided norms based on 390 Ss, normal, neurotic, and psychotic.

Serious doubts as to the validity of using the TAT in classificatory diagnosis have been raised by Eron (1950). He compared the productions of two groups of 25 college students each, 25 nonhospitalized psychoneurotics, 25 hospitalized psychoneurotics, 25 hospitalized schizophrenics, and a group of 25 patients representing a general neuropsychiatric hospital population. All groups were comparable in terms of age, education, and IQ. The variables analyzed were emotional tone of the stories, outcomes, identifications of characters and objects, themes, and levels of interpretation (see Chapter 12 for a more specific description). When the groups were compared using appropriate statistical methods, not many more differences emerged than would be expected by chance. Furthermore, many of the specific diagnostic cues which had been presented by previous investigators, when put to the statistical test, were found to be either non-differentiating or were even more frequent among normal individuals or other clinical groups. He warned that the "TAT should not be used as a diagnostic instrument in the sense of yielding signs or patterns characteristic of specific nosological entities." These results were largely confirmed in a later study by Davison (1950).

When, however, as in a research by Harlow (1951), two groups known to differ behaviorally were compared on specific TAT variables which had been selected because they seemed to fit in with a theoretical basis for differentiation between the two groups, results seemed to be a good deal better. Harlow was interested in the personality characteristics of weight lifters. On the basis of psychoanalytic theory, he derived certain hypotheses about the dynamics of such individuals and then selected 14 need-press variables which, it seemed, should bear directly on these hypotheses. He demonstrated that these variables could be rated reliably (interrater coefficients of .62 to .92 with a median coefficient of .85) and then, comparing 20 weight lifters with a carefully matched group of 20 non-weight lifting athletes, made predictions about the differences that would be found. Eleven out of his fourteen predictions were significant at the .05 level of confidence or better. Futhermore, there was a very close agreement with predictions made on the basis of a sentence-completion test. Although the TAT was used in this study for the purpose of validating certain psychoanalytic hypotheses, the consistency with which the predictions were made and fulfilled contribute evidence for the validity of the TAT variables and scores the author used.

A series of studies by Valentine and Robin (1950a, 1950b) seemed to indicate the appropriateness of using the TAT in differential diagnosis. The authors were able to list characteristics of stories representative of depressed and schizophrenic patients and then distinguish both of these groups from normal individuals. Various time factors seemed particularly discriminating. Findings were also correlated with certain relevant Rorschach scoring categories as well as other variables. There were several positive findings. For example, a particularly high correlation coefficient (.90) was found between Rorschach total time and TAT total time; TAT misperceptions and Rorschach poor original responses were correlated .63. Although the authors reported good normative data, their differentiation of the three groups is questionable because of the inappropriate statistical method used to calculate significance. When the appropriate statistical procedure is used, the significance of most of the differences disappears and the groups are no more different than would be expected by chance. For example, using the "t" test they found thirty-one differences significant at or beyond the .05 level of confidence; but, when chi square is applied appropriately to the difference in frequency, only five of these differences are significant at the .05 level.

In a test of the "hero assumption," Friedman (1957b) found differences between heroes of normals, neurotics, and psychotics. There has not been consistent confirmation of this assumption, however. Using a Q-sort method, Shneidman and Farberow (1958) attempted to sort on the basis of attributes of TAT heroes, for nonsuicidal Ss, suicidal Ss, and Ss who had attempted suicide. The results were disappointing. The judge, moreover, was unable to make an overall judgment better than chance as to suicidal status of S, but was more successful in his judgments as to the sex of S. The poor results with the "hero" variable were explained by the authors as a by-product of the methodological difficulty of sorting on the basis of one hero from several TAT stories from one protocol. Friedman (1958), in a critique of this study, offered additional methodological and statistical reasons for the failure of the Shneidman and Farberow study; but as well taken as these comments are, his presentation overlooked the more parsimonious suggestion that the TAT, perhaps, may just not be a good predictive instrument in this area.

Thus it is very unlikely that any differences can be found in the content of TAT stories between any two groups of patients or between patients and normals which will permit the use of the test in differential diagnosis or even in a descriptive characterization of the groups. The analysis of an individual story may permit valid inferences about the important strivings and needs of the narrator and some of his characteristic ways of handling problems in specific areas, but it apparently does not present a picture of him as a schizophrenic or a psychoneurotic or a manic-depressive. The TAT, however, from a content point of view, may be a diagnostic instrument perhaps in the sense that it gives an understanding of an individual in his own life setting rather than as a member of a Kraepelinian nosological entity.

One more point might be raised. With respect to failures to establish diagnostic validity for the TAT, might not the deviation approach, already mentioned in Chapter 1, be appropriately used? For example, a possible way to utilize the TAT diagnostically is to note the total number of deviations any individual has from the group norm. It is hypothesized that more individuals in abnormal classifications should have a larger number of deviations from the norm than individuals in a normal group. Such an hypothesis is supported by a re-examination of Eron's original data according to the number of deviations each individual in the subject population had from the norms of the criterion group (Ss in the two normal groups were thrown together to form a criterion group) (Ritter & Eron, 1952). It was found that with the use of appropriate cut-off points, the authors could reliably differentiate between the clinical and normal groups so that it was possible to state that an individual with a certain number of deviations was abnormal, although it could not be said that individuals with less than the critical number of deviations were not abnormal. Cross-validation of this suggestion was not attempted, however.

Although no overall generalization is possible, the findings noted previously seem to suggest that global judgments of TAT material are not particularly discriminating; specific and relevant variables chosen for a particular study, and in terms of a specific hypothesis, fare somewhat better; and formal and structural TAT factors have been shown to be more effective than content factors.

*Concurrent Validity through Use of Ratings, Judgments, and Test*

*Scores.* Cox and Sargent (1950) compared the responses of fifteen stable and fifteen disturbed boys, of normal or better IQ, to 10 neutral TAT pictures flashed on the screen. The only outstanding difference they found was the greater constriction of the disturbed group. The TAT protocols of the fifteen stable boys were then sent to eight clinical psychologists who had used the TAT clinically and had done research with it. Each psychologist received two records along with certain information about the cases. He was told that he might have received the records of two disturbed children, two stable children, or one of each. Eleven of the fifteen were judged to be disturbed by the clinical psychologists. Results such as this do not recommend the use of the test for diagnostic study, but also suggest that judges' ratings are likely to be biased in the direction of disturbance. The authors suggest that this result may well be due to the absence of normative material, and that disturbed children's protocols are not necessarily the obverse of those of normal children. The use of a group situation, with the TAT pictures flashed on the screen, also does not make this procedure readily comparable to the ordinary clinical use of the TAT.

In a carefully designed and executed study, Little and Shneidman (1959) explored both the validity and reliability of various psychological instruments. Their concern was with congruencies among judges from descriptions based on differing sources of information. They investigated congruencies for several kinds of Ss (psychotics, neurotics, psychosomatic reactions, and psychiatrically normal), using several instruments (Rorschach, TAT, MAPS, MMPI, and psychiatric anamnesis) and several interpretive tasks (true-false factual items, true-false inferential items, Q-sort items, diagnostic labels, and ratings). There were twelve Ss, all hospitalized, and forty-eight test judges, all skilled test interpreters. Twenty-three psychiatrists and one psychologist evaluated anamnestic materials. The validity picture for the various instruments was rather discouraging. Typical findings were that diagnostic labeling was largely inaccurate and varied, particularly with normals. Blind diagnosis was for the most part unsuccessful. The same judge, with different test data of the same S, used a variety of different labels. In general, ratings of maladjustment were more appropriate for psychotics, not because of the validity of the ratings, but because the psychologist-raters tended to rate Ss as more pathological.

Henry and Farley (1959), in another carefuly planned study, explored the validity of the TAT in the study of adolescent personality. Following a complex matching procedure outlined by Cronbach (1948), their design called for a group of expert clinicians to identify Ss from TAT analyses. Blind interpretations of TAT records from a homogeneous group of thirty-six Ss were compared with blind interpretations of various aspects of criterion data. They used several tests and data from various sources (Stanford-Binet, Standard Achievement Tests, questionnaires, observation and interview material, Rorschach, etc.); data from *all* instruments were summarized within the same conceptual framework. They were interested in seeking the level of agreement between the TAT and more direct instruments, or more subjective reports from observations, etc. Their results were highly encouraging, and the authors concluded that the TAT was a valid instrument which possessed great predictive and clinical value. Reference should be made to Chapter 4, which contains a brief summary of a collaborative effort (Carr, *et al.*, 1960), to examine the predictive powers of various clinical instruments, including the TAT, with very discouraging results. This study, however, did not involve the rigorous conceptual and methodological approach found in Henry and Farley's work.

Ossorio and Rigby (1957) attempted to predict from TAT conformity scores (deviation from norms) to superiors' ratings of effectiveness of junior marine officers. These ratings divided the men into five groups, and the cutting scores, determined on the basis of one sample, failed to be at all useful in differentiating a new sample. This study highlights some of the methodological and design problems in various attempts at TAT validation. Conformity scores, as such, could be related to effectiveness in being an officer on some cards and lack of effectiveness on others. Some deviations could be regarded as "good," and some not, depending on the criterion predicted. The remoteness of the criterion from the actual TAT scores presents another problem, as well as the relevance of the TAT in general, for predicting as complex a judgment as officer effectiveness. Despite careful selection of cutting scores and efficient items in the developmental sample, the small number of cases used to develop the scores to be examined in the cross-validation study was another limitation of this research. The authors further felt that because of failure to meet their standards, certain items, perhaps relevant to the criterion, had to be eliminated, and that the nature of the criterion measures may have been too complex for this study to produce significant results. On the other hand, Davids and Rosenblatt (1958) reported good agreement between judge's ratings and TAT measures of "alienation." The authors used a specially devised scoring system to tap this syndrome (negative attitudes which include pessimism, distrust, egocentricity, anxiety, and resentment).

One attempt to use the TAT diagnostically had more apparent success than some of the previously mentioned studies (Hartman, 1949). This investigator, however, did not use broad nosological categories. Rather, he correlated each of fifty-six specific TAT variables with forty-two personality variables on thirty-five subjects. Although he obtained more significant correlations than could be expected by chance, the low magnitude of these relationships makes them useless for individual prediction. Of the 2240 bi-serial r's, only five were of the magnitude of .70 or above, and the median r was .44 with a range from .38 to .82. Furthermore, the independence of the behavior ratings themselves, or of the TAT variables, was not ascertained, and thus it is not clear whether they were all measuring the same or different things. The most optimistic conclusion that can be drawn from the results of this study is that there is a very slight positive relationship between certain physical and personality traits and areas of disturbance, and certain TAT response categories as defined by the author.

In a study presumably exploring relationships between fantasy and self-report behavior, but which can be regarded as a TAT validation study, Calogeras (1958) compared intrafamily attitudes, as measured by a group-administered TAT, and various types of self-report behavior (direct and indirect attitude questionnaires and an individual interview). His subjects were fifty-seven tenth-grade boys of average to superior intelligence. Significant positive relationships were found between various TAT measures and relevant self-report measures, but, on the whole, the author felt that the significant correlations were too low for purposes of individual prediction.

Shatin (1953, 1955) reported encouraging results with respect to the relationship between various Rorschach and TAT variables. In a later study (1958), he found significant relationships between certain Rorschach measures of constriction-dilation and certain TAT measures (mostly formal, such as word count and number of popular stories).

Success in studies comparing various Rorschach and TAT variables is found elsewhere. Singer and Sugarman (1955), for example, divided sixty hospitalized adult male schizophrenics on the basis of high M and low M on the Rorschach. Parental figures, or parent-child relationships as depicted on several TAT cards were rated for positive and negative characteristics. The high M group depicted parental figures more positively than the low M group. Predictions from the TAT to personality ratings or other personality inventories and tests fare less well, however. Dilworth (1958), for example, reported no significant correlation between the fifteen Edwards Personal Preference Schedule variables and TAT material, in terms of relative strengths of various needs. In a study by Magnusson (1959), when ratings which sixty-four male students made of each other on twenty personality variables were used as criteria, the TAT, Rorschach, and Sentence Completion tests were shown to have little validity.

The relationship between TAT variables and material gained from psychotherapeutic interviews has also not been successfully established. Meyer and Tolman (1955a) found little correspondence between attitudes toward and images of parents as expressd in TAT stories and in psychotherapy. In a follow-up study (1955b), moreover, the Forer Sentence Completion Test was found to have little predictability as far as either the TAT or therapeutic interviews were concerned, in terms of these variables.

Saxe (1950) used psychotherapists' judgments as the criterion for his analyses of the TAT. He wrote a brief integrated summary about each patient, based entirely on his TAT responses. On the basis of these summaries, he formulated a list of eighty-three statements covering such topics as relationships with parents, socialization, reaction to anxiety, and ability to form affectional relationships. Each statement applied to one or more of the cases. The experimenter then checked the list, as did the therapist after he had seen the patients for at last four months. A total of twenty children ranging in age from nine to seventeen years were the subjects. For half of the patients there was significant agreement (2% level of confidence or beyond) among items checked by therapist and experimenter. But an item analysis disclosed that, of the total number of items in the questionnaire, twenty-one showed agreement at the 5% level or better, one showed disagreement beyond the 5% level, and there was neither significant agreement nor disagreement on 60 items. Thus "the evidence is not overwhelmingly strong" that diagnostic clues from the TAT are similar to those gained from therapeutic contact.

*Relationship to Behavior.* All studies reported in this section have in common an attempt to relate TAT responses to some aspect of behavior. Sometimes the crucial variables are experimentally manipulated; at other times, correlational procedures are used without attempt to manipulate the independent variable. A large number of such studies is concerned with exploring the dimensions of a drive or motivation such as achievement or aggression, and findings from such studies can be related to each other in order to create a body of data of relevance and interest to the worker who may not be solely interested in the TAT or in test development. At the outset, reference should be made to the work of McClelland, Atkinson, and associates, who, in their studies of various aspects of drive and motivation, have made an inestimable contribution to increasing knowledge of the validity of various aspects of the TAT. In this connection, to avoid the thankless task of listing a large number of studies conducted either under the aegis or as a result of the stimulation of these workers, reference is made to a compendium work edited by Atkinson (1958a), which contains reprints or adaptations of much of the relevant material which had appeared previously in the various journals.

The ideal way of demonstrating the validity of the TAT as a measure of a drive, need, or isolated personality variable is to define an independent variable which is meaningful for personality or motivation theory, and then to determine whether differences in the magnitude of this variable are correlated with differences in TAT stories. (Note, this procedure would not ascertain or speak for the validity of the instrument as a whole, nor for *other* criteria, such as diagnostic, prognostic, etc.)

The early work of McClelland and his associates was a beginning effort in this direction. In some of these studies (e.g., Atkinson & Mc-Clelland [1948]; McClelland & Atkinson [1948]), they worked with the hunger drive, which they found simple to define and manipulate, and were able to show that with increasing periods of food deprivation, there was consistent change in the way Ss responded to TAT-type pictures with stories of their own imagination. In further experiments, they were able to extend this type of procedure, in which the intensity of a particular motive was controlled experimentally and changes that occurred in the TAT were classified as the intensity of motivation increased, to more complex kinds of motivation which had meaning for personality description of individuals, for example, need for achievement (Atkinson, 1950), need for security (Roby, 1948), and need for affiliation (Shipley & Veroff, 1952). They manipulated the intensity of motivation for achievement, for example, in line with traditional experiments in the field, by reporting fake norms and thus inducing feelings of success or failure; they found that the need for achievement score was a valid measure.

A point might be noted with respect to the pioneer work of McClelland and Atkinson (1948). In dealing with the hunger drive through food deprivation, they failed to consider the fact that Ss were consciously aware of their hunger. This might well have affected their "guesses" as to what the faint or subliminally presented visual cues were. Their conclusion that the amount of instrumental activity appearing in S's responses is a more valid indication of the strength of a need than goal-related activities, was generalized to TAT-type responses and to projective techniques, as well as to the nature of perception and apperception under certain drive conditions—a step, however, as shown in Chapters 2 and 3, which is questionable. Moreover, the suggestion throughout their paper is that their work was applicable to *other* drive states. In later studies, however, the authors and their associates used considerably more caution, as well as more careful controls in their design and generalizations.

The question also arises as to whether TAT scores are so sensitive as measures that persistent personality traits cannot be measured by them, since immediately preceding conditions affect responses so noticeably (really a question of reliability). McClelland and Liberman (1949) demonstrated, however, that the need achievement scores obtained from the stories of individuals under neutral conditions were significantly related to the speed with which these same individuals recognized need related words three or four months later when they were presented tachistoscopically. This, the authors felt, provided confirmation of the hypothesis that the need achievement score did not reflect "simply a temporary motivational state" but rather "approximately, at least, the level of achievement motivation a subject maintains over a period of months."

The same scoring measures of achievement motivation used by McClelland and Liberman (1949) were found to be applicable to a younger population of high school boys, since the same consistent increases in mean need achievement score occurred when a similar experimental procedure for producing achievement motivation was used with this group as was used with the college group (Veroff, Wilcox, & Atkinson, 1953). A replication was not successful with college women, primarily because their initial scores were sufficiently high to suggest high achievement motivation in female subjects both before and after the introduction of the experimental variable.

A recent report by Lesser, Krawitz, and Packard (1963), however, suggests that the conflicting results with respect to females and achievement motivation may be due to failure to account for variables such as the academic achievement of these Ss, and the characteristics of the stimuli. For they found that,

. . . the achievement motivation scores of achievers increase significantly in response to Achievement Oriented conditions when they produce stories to pictures of females but do not increase in response to pictures of males; by contrast, the achievement motivation scores of underachievers increase significantly in response to Achievement Oriented conditions when they produce stories to pictures of males but do not increase in response to pictures of females (p. 63).

There is a wide body of literature on achievement motivation. Some of this material can be found in Atkinson (1958a), and in Lesser, *et al.*

(*Ibid.*, 1963). Possibly because of the early work of researchers with this particular "drive," much recent attention and effort have been devoted to TAT studies in this area—so much so, that one can almost speak of a "psychology of achievement." As a matter of fact, in a recent volume, McClelland (1961) advanced a novel approach to an understanding of the economic development of various societies, contemporary and ancient, based essentially on his extensive work with the achievement motive. His thesis is that achievement-orientation, an identifiable and measurable personality trait, has been associated with economic growth in all societies, through the ages.

Some illustrative studies will be noted, primarily to disclose the problems of behavioral validation in this area, even though many of the studies were oriented more from the point of view of exploring achievement motivation and motivational theory, as such, rather than test validation. Clark and McClelland (1956) have described the complexities of relating TAT *n* Achievement to actual performance. Veroff (1961) and Veroff, Atkinson, Feld, and Gurin (1960) have studied several motives, including achievement, in a nationwide sample, with considerable awareness of methodological problems. Some of their findings have related age (grouped into three levels) as well as occupational level to *n* Achievement. These reports suggest that despite the detail and thoroughness of work in this area, we are far from discovering the precise nature of the relationship between TAT measures of achievement and achievement as measured in actual behavior.

Further clarification of previously inconsistent results in studies using the interrupted task technique is provided by the work of Atkinson (1950) in his research with the need achievement score. He performed a standard type of experiment on the effect of interruption of task on recall with eighty subjects, obtaining immediately afterwards an estimate of individual differences in motivation for achievement from stories written in response to pictures and scored according to a previously discussed system (McClelland, Atkinson, & Clark, 1949). It was found that the individual differences in motivation for achievement accounted for differences in the way individuals perceived the tasks and goal, and it was suggested that the basic contradiction in earlier experiments using the interrupted task technique was due to differences in achievement motivation in the different samples.

McClelland (1956*a*) related high *n* Achievement scores to preferences for occupations with some financial risk; an unexpected finding was that high *n* Achievement was *not* related to preference for occupations with highest prestige value. Although this study is not a behavioral validation study, it is mentioned here because it is relevant to the general points under consideration. McClelland (1956b) found that children with high n Achievement took only moderate risks in a ring-tossing game, but children with low n Achievement took little or extreme risks.

French and Chadwick (1956), in exploring behavioral correlates of both n Achievement and n Affiliation, reported that in choice of a work partner, Ss high in n Achievement, and low in n Affiliation chose competent nonfriends, whereas Ss with the opposite set of scores tended to choose the less-competent friend. Karolchuck and Worell (1956) explored the relationship between n Achievement and learning and found no correlation; they did report, however, a positive relationship to incidental learning. Hurley (1957), on the other hand, reported a positive relationship between n Achievement and rate of learning under low-motivating rather than high-motivating conditions, indicating that this is an atypical finding since others have reported high n Achievement to be positively related to learning in achievement-oriented situations.

In a study concerned with both stability and validity of achievement fantasy (again, this word is substituted in the title for achievement themes or content in TAT material), Kagan and Moss (1959) studied findings based on three successive administrations of the TAT at ages 8–9, 11–6, and 14–6 to forty-four boys and forty-two girls. Achievement themes in these protocols were analyzed in relation to educational level of parents, ratings of maternal concern with achievement for the first three years of the child's life, and changes in IQ scores during the years six to ten. The findings suggested that there was an increase of achievement themes through the years, and that there was a better-than-chance stability of occurrence of these themes over the period studied. In girls, it was found that early maternal concern with achievement was positively related to achievement fantasy as well as to IQ gain. In both girls and boys a generally positive relationship was found between occurrence of achievement fantasy and IQ gain. There was also a suggestion that achievement fantasy and educational level of the parent of the same sex are related.

An additional study of achievement motivation might also be noted. Atkinson and Raphelson (1956) found that n Achievement was related to various behavioral indices (persistence in task performance and recall of interrupted tasks) only when Ss had been placed in situations they interpreted as involving personal accomplishment; when this interpretation was not present, there was no systematic relationship between n Achievment and behavior. When the situational context was changed so that Ss were oriented toward pleasing E, there was no relationship between n Achievement and the recall of interrupted tasks. But a positive relationship was found between $n$ Affiliation and recall.

Another variable which has received the interest and research attention of many workers in the TAT area is aggression. Relevant material has already been discussed, particularly early studies which recognized that direct indices of overt aggression in TAT material are probably not possible to obtain, and that a consideration of defenses as well as anxiety over the expression of aggression must be present before adequate predictions can be made. Meanwhile, some additional relevant studies will be cited. Gluck (1955) found that the amount of hostility in a TAT record was no reliable indication of whether or not an hostility-provoking situation would produce overt hostility. Kagan (1956) successfully demonstrated a significant positive relationship between frequency of fighting themes and teacher ratings of fighting behavior. The pictures used were nonambiguous, being specially devised, and moreover, the ratings were quite specific. In an additional validity study, Kagan (1958) demonstrated that extremely aggressive boys told more stories which depicted hostile parent-child interactions, as well as fewer stories with dependence on parents themes, than did nonaggressive boys. Kagan felt, therefore, that children's perception of parental attitudes influenced their behavior. But a good case can also be made out for the opposite state of affairs. Purcell (1956), exploring the TAT protocols of fifty-seven army trainees referred to a mental hygiene clinic, found that overtly antisocial Ss expressed TAT aggression more extensively, as well as more crudely and directly, than those Ss who were less antisocial. But Scodel and Lipetz (1957) did not find that acting-out psychotics (suicidal or assaultive) showed more TAT hostility than nonacting-out psychotics. As a matter of fact, neurotics showed more TAT hostility than did the psychotics.

Many other types of behavioral validation studies have been reported, utilizing a wide number of needs and motives. For example, Kagan and Mussen (1956) found that Ss who produced more dependency themes or themes in which the hero was disturbed as a result of losing love or support, manifested more conformity behavior in the Asch (1952) conformity situation (a group behavioral situation), than Ss who did not. Atkinson and Walker (1956), basing their hypothesis on a finding that those with high $n$ Achievement have lower recognition thresholds for achievement-related words, explored a similar possibility with respect to $n$ Affiliation. They found a positive relationship between $n$ Affiliation and threshold for recognition of pictures of faces presented tachistoscopically, under low illumination, below the level of awareness.

Epstein and Smith reported two studies concerned with hunger and sex drives (1956, 1957). In their first study, two groups of Ss were administered modified TATs—one group being tested after eating, and the other before eating (hungry group). Although the hungry and control groups were not differentiated on the basis of food imagery, when the stimuli were grouped according to "picture-pull," the findings indicated that the hungry group gave relatively more hunger-related responses to stimuli with low picture-pull than did the control group, but gave fewer such responses to stimuli with high picture-pull. The groups did not differ with respect to pictures of moderate picture-pull. These findings were explained in terms of the work of McClelland. In their study of the sex drive (not a direct behavioral validation study), the same authors administered three projective tests, including the TAT, to 59 college males, as well as a questionnaire (anonymously filled out) concerning average rate of sexual orgasm, present sexual responsiveness, and number of days since last orgasm. The findings indicated that projective measures were significantly and positively associated with rate, but not with satiation. It should be emphasized here that since both predictor and criterion were verbal reports, each may have been subject to similar types of bias.

Clark (1952, 1955), in a behavioral validation study, showed that defensive reactions to taboo fantasy are reflected in TAT responses and it is *these* that are measured, not just sheer drive state (see previous section under *Assumptions* for a more detailed description of this study). He induced the arousal of sexual drive under alcoholic and nonalcoholic conditions, concluding that "these results seem to indicate that under normal (nonalcohol) conditions, the sexual arousal causes sufficient anxiety to lead to the inhibition of manifest sexual imagery, whereas under the influence of alcohol this anxiety or guilt is sufficiently reduced to permit increased expression of manifest sexuality reflecting directly the heightened state of arousal" (1955, p. 48). In addition, Clark went into great detail with respect to symbolism, and on the basis of his findings, concluded, "classical symbolism serves as a disguised expression of sexuality"; or "symbolism as a mode of expression seems to be preferred only to the extent that anxiety is present," etc.

Mussen and Scodel (1955), using a modification of Clark's procedure, studied the influence of sexual stimulation under different types of conditions on TAT responses. Their hypothesis was: ". . . (sex) responses will be more inhibited following sex arousal in the presence of a stern father figure than following such arousal in the presence of a young permissive individual." Ss were shown nude female slides by a stern, formal man in his sixties; another group of Ss was shown the slides by an informal, permissive, youngish man. A group form of the TAT was given. Both manifest and implied sexual content were scored on a scale which tapped intensity of sexual activity. The authors indicated that their hypothesis was confirmed by their empirical results.

It should be noted that this study, as well as many of the others described earlier, seem to suggest that needs and drives are measurable by the TAT. Do these studies, however, rule out the possibility that conscious awareness of needs and attitudes, as well as control over verbal behavior, may be important variables in producing the relationships that have been found? Are needs of which S is completely unaware also measured by the TAT? If so, how can this be demonstrated?

Fisher and Morton (1957) suggest that TAT responses are subject to conscious control. They related two TAT measures to several behavioral measures in a group of Ss hospitalized for tuberculosis and hypothesized that TAT measures would be better predictors of those behaviors which are less subject to control or camouflage by the Ss. Their hypothesis was generally confirmed: "Apparently, if the individual is set to conceal certain aspects of his behavior, this decreases the correlation of such behavior with logically related fantasy" (p. 115).

A study by Goldman and Greenblatt (1955) is an illustration of a validation approach involving a behavioral rating. In this study, identification of degree of withdrawal on the basis of "blind" judgments made in regard to each pair of TAT stories given by acutely ill schizophrenics at hospital admission, and when discharged, was successful. In this instance the task required of the TAT is not very difficult; unfortunately, the clinician is rarely called on to make such black-and-white judgments. Moreover, sheer behavior in general would probably be a better indicator of the status of the patient than the test material itself.

Another attempt at behavioral validation, along slightly different lines, is the research of Calvin and Ward (1950). A group of 90 subjects had to rate on a five point scale the certainty of their prediction that a buzzer would follow a light. (The buzzer followed 50 per cent of the time, in random order.) The ten individuals with the highest degree of certainty and the ten with the least degree of certainty were then selected from the original group and their TAT productions compared. On the whole, the two groups of subjects revealed no striking differences in their TAT stories. The data suggest, however, that the high certainty group tells more stories in which the characters indicate need for harm-avoidance, autonomy, and dominance, that their language is not quite so filled with value terms and cautious terminology, and that their stories have unfavorable outcomes more frequently than the low certainty group. The lack of striking findings in this study may be the result of an unreliable scoring method since there is no indication in the report of any reliability estimates of the procedure. Also, it may be that "certainty" is a characteristic which is highly specific to the situation, and an individual cannot be described as generally "very certain" or "very hesitant" on the basis of the simple task that was used to differentiate the two groups of subjects.

In general, then, these behavioral validation studies seem to be much more productive in terms of positive findings than some of the other approaches to validation. Their design seems more efficient, and frequently both stimulus cards and scoring systems are quite specific to the particular study in question. The general point seems to be that vague, holistic, random scoring of content does not distinguish various diagnostic groups very effectively or relate particularly well to other ratings and measures. The behavioral validation studies do not attest to the validity of the instrument as a whole, of course, but only to the use of the particular measures for the particular purposes described in the specific reports. There seems to be a large body of evidence indicating that at least *some* measures are appropriate predictors of behavior. Whether these are useful to the clinician, or whether or not the original purpose of the instrument as a projective technique for eliciting material unobtainable elsewhere or through other means is being fulfilled is a good question. It does seem, however, that the psychologist working in motivation theory or in personality has put the TAT to good use.

There are dissenting opinions even with respect to this generalization, however. In a study concerned with various forms of social behavior and anxiety about it, Child, Frank, and Storm (1956), after an analysis of their data, suggested that there was little or no validity with respect to several TAT measures, including achievement, in relation to actual overt performance. TAT measures were not found by these authors to be related to self-ratings, anxiety with respect to relevant variables, or to retrospective reports of later childhood. Questionnaire measures fared somewhat better, having shown consistent but small correlations with retrospective reports of later childhood. The authors concluded, "Meanwhile, our results provide ample evidence that any general view of all TAT content as reliable and directly indicative of motive strength is not tenable" (p. 114).

*TAT and Prognosis.* TAT studies pertaining to prognosis are beset with difficulties. For a recent detailed review of research problems in this area for this, as well as other psychological instruments, see Fulkerson and Barry (1961); for an earlier review, see Windle (1952). Measures of prognosis (whether of duration, course, or outcome) are difficult to define and are associated with the usual problems of validity and reliability, as well as base rates. Amount of change is often confounded with absolute level of adjustment. Is terminal adjustment to be used as a criterion? This is often associated with adjustment at the outset of therapy. Who is to rate adjustment—the patient, therapist, family, co-workers? How is improvement defined and what sources are used to implement this definition? Should they be introspective reports, follow-up in school or in work situation, assessment of S's symptoms, ratings of overall behavior, or by judgment as to accessibility to therapy? How valid and reliable are the measures used to assess the criterion, once other problems have been solved? In a discussion which is quite relevant to some of these problems, Scott (1958) has reviewed some of the methodological difficulties in working with various concepts of mental health.

As for the studies themselves, few findings of any significance are reported. The TAT, as a test alone, or together with other instruments, does not seem to recommend itself as a promising indicator of prognosis. Ullmann (1957) did find that clinical judgments of TAT material correlated significantly with improvement criteria. Libo (1957), from material similar to that obtainable from the TAT, was able to predict the S's return to the therapist a week after the test administration. He did so on the basis of relevant scores based on content: an "attraction" score (based on allusions to moving toward a therapist) or on expectations of satisfaction as a result of therapy. On the other hand, although both the H-T-P and Rorschach were able to discriminate patients who left a tuberculosis hospital against medical advice from those who completed treatment, the TAT was unsuccessful in this respect, according to Vernier, Whiting, and Meltzer (1955).

Fulkerson and Barry (1961), after an extensive review of prognostic research, concluded that the strongest relationship to outcome has been found with respect to nontest variables, such as severity and duration of illness, or acuteness of onset. This statement does not speak well for the prognostic efficiency of psychological tests, either projective or nonprojective.

*The "Sign" Approach.* Lindzey and Newburg (1954) reported discouraging results with respect to eighteen signs (taken from the literature) as to the presence of anxiety, but did indicate that formal measures fared better than content measures, in terms of the criteria used. Mandler, Lindzey, and Crouch (1957), in another study which attempted to relate the TAT signs developed by Lindzey and Newburg with an independent measure of anxiety (Test Anxiety Scale—TAQ—

developed by Mandler and Sarason [1952]), also did not find promising results, although again, formal variables fared better than content variables.

An additional failure of the "sign" approach was reported by Lindzey and Tejessy (1956), with respect to predicting covert aspects of aggression. On the basis of relating ten signs from TAT protocols to various behavioral, test, and judgmental measures (including self- and observer ratings), the authors concluded that, "These findings suggest rather strongly that the scores we had derived painstakingly from the TAT protocols represent rather accurately the information we could have secured from the subjects themselves by simply asking them to appraise their own behavior" (p. 573). Lindzey, Tejessy, and Zamansky (1958), in further studies of the effectiveness of TAT signs—this time in the prediction of homosexual tendencies—once more reported discouraging findings. Not only did general clinical ratings prove to be more effective, but the nature of the signs themselves was such as to be easily susceptible to distortion or inhibition on the part of S, thus limiting their utility in a wide variety of settings. Although Davids, Joelson, and McArthur (1956) found that homosexual males gave significantly more Rorschach and TAT signs than the other male groups studied (neurotics and normal students), cross-validation of these signs was not attempted. The sign approach dramatically illustrates the lack of meaningfulness which characterizes studies that simply "generalize" from a sample those findings that seem to discriminate, without further empirical attempts to cross-validate.

*Reliability Studies.* Many TAT studies cited in the literature, especially the early ones, make no mention of having examined reliability, either scorer agreement, or any of the other types.[8] There is sufficient evidence which indicates, however, that scorer reliability is reasonably good when there is pretraining and supervision of the judges and scorers, and when the scoring system is specific with systematic rules.

In a review of several studies of interjudge reliability, using certain types of content analyses, Feld and Smith (1958) reported scoring reliabilities ranging from .66 to .96 with a median of .89. Rank-order correlations between scores of different scorers ranged from .72 to .91 in a study reported by Veroff, Atkinson, Feld, and Gurin (1960). These scores were based on a specific and clear-cut content analysis rel-

---

[8] Early studies which have reported detailed reliability data include: Coleman (1947); Eron, Terry, and Callahan (1950); Garfield and Eron (1948); McClelland, Clark, Roby, and Atkinson (1949); Mussen (1950); and Pittluck (1950).

evant to *n* Achievement, *n* Affiliation, and *n* Power. Sarason and Sarason (1958), using Eron's scales for emotional tone and outcome, found an average interrater reliability, for twelve cards, of .87 for emotional tone and .79 for outcome; this is of the same order as obtained in earlier studies using these scales (Eron, Terry, & Callahan [1950]; Liccione [1955]).

In general, specific scoring systems have yielded relatively high scorer reliability figures whereas more holistic procedures of interpretation have tended to yield, as would be expected, lower reliability figures. Friedman (1957a), for example, in exploring the scorer reliability of subjective and holistic interpretation of TAT material, found moderately lower intercorrelations (.74). Other workers reporting fairly high reliability of scores in terms of rather specific scoring systems have been: Auld, Eron, and Laffal (1955), using specific scales for sex and aggression; Fine (1955a, 1955b), using a specially designed scoring system which mainly covered feelings, outcomes, and interpersonal relationships; Davids and Rosenblatt (1958), using a special scoring system designed to measure the "alienation syndrome"; and Ossorio and Rigby (1957), who worked with conformity (deviation) scores.

Dana (1955, 1956a, 1956b, 1956c, 1957, 1959), in developing a TAT scoring which stressed what he calls Perceptual Organization (PO) (the degree to which standard test directions are followed in S's TAT story), reported high item reliability for a series of TAT cards, based on correlation of PO scores of the shortened series with the total. Correlations increased as number of cards in the series increased. His scoring system seems to possess good internal consistency. In studies of three female groups of normals, neurotics, and psychotics, as well as of several male groups, and using three scoring categories, Perceptual Organization, Perceptual Range (PR) and Perceptual Personalization (PP), high scorer reliability was found (89 to 91% agreement).

In a TAT study which yielded poor validity findings (see section on *Validity*), Child, Frank, and Storm (1956) found that although the reliability of TAT scores they used was quite low (based on a measure of internal consistency), *scorer* reliability was quite high. Kerner (1956), however, found a high percentage of unreliable items in a detailed scoring system he devised for his study of schizophrenic adaptation to stress. (By eliminating these items, Kerner suggested that he had increased the validity of his scale.)

Thus, researches which have appeared since 1948 have tended to use the method of interinterpreter agreement to get at reliability. It has been quite amply demonstrated that a number of observers can agree to a considerably significant extent on most variables for which stories are scored, especially if they are exposed to some training with the scoring scheme, and if properly defined and not too complicated scales are utilized.

Reliability at a different level than the scoring of specific variables and responses was demonstrated by a study in which fourteen experienced TAT analysts were sent copies of the same protocol for blind analysis (Shneidman, Joel, & Little, 1951). The only data given to the experts, in addition to the test responses, were the subject's sex, age, and marital status. Each interpreter submitted his impressions of the subject along with a demonstration of the analytic technique he used to arrive at the impressions. The authors of this volume did not present any statistical evaluation of the agreement, but qualitatively compared the findings of the various analysts. They concluded: "Our overall impression was that the reports show a high degree of correspondence with one another in their description of John Doe and that they correlate quite well with the behavioral data" (Ibid., p. 303). A more discouraging note was offered later, however, by the same authors (Little & Shneidman, 1959), who conducted an extensive study of both validity and reliability, utilizing forty-eight judges. (This study was described in greater detail in the section on Validity.) Agreement between judges was rather poor, in terms of the TAT, as well as other instruments and material (anamnestic data yielded more agreement than the tests). The authors felt, incidentally, that there was so much variability from judge to judge in amount of agreement, that "each individual clinical psychologist and psychiatrist should make it part of his own business to ascertain his own personal validity and reliability coefficient with various categories of patients, as measured against various criteria" (p. 27).

Needless to say, the same kind of scorer "reliability" and objectivity for which Rorschachers reach, wherein workers independently of one another use more or less the same type of scoring system, does not obtain with regard to the TAT. There are almost as many scoring systems as there are TAT studies; not only are stimulus materials custom made, but the system for quantifying the crucial variable or variables is also custom made in many TAT studies. In this sense, then, the TAT is not a test or an instrument. It is almost as if each worker, starting from scratch, were forced to devise his own instrument and to be concerned all over again with problems of objectivity, reliability, and validity, having to accumulate norms, train scorers, and develop standardized conditions for the administration of his instrument. The clinician, then, must emerge a little bewildered and perhaps weighed down with a sense of guilt (hopefully) and helplessness because of his inability to "keep up" with the literature.

TAT research workers themselves lack agreement as to what constitutes a measure of reliability of their instrument, nor, apart from scorer reliability, can they provide a succinct statement as to what the status of TAT reliability might be. Veroff (1961), and Veroff, et al. (1960), in an extensive TAT study of American "national character," using mass survey techniques, could not handle the problem of test reliability. Moreover, these workers were strikingly aware of the fact that motivational factors as well as "unwanted" situational factors were being measured at the same time—and that these could not all be eliminated in statistical analyses. Specifically, these were verbal fluency, picture differences, and interviewer differences.

In a detailed discussion of the problem of reliability with special reference to projective techniques and the TAT, Henry and Farley (1959) noted some of the problems in estimating reliability in projective testing. Projective instruments should be sensitive to changes of S over a period of time, and yet should reflect stable and enduring characteristics. Stability and sensitivity are both desirable, and are presumably being measured at the same time! In projective testing, "error" or variance from test to retest is really individuality, and is a natural reflection of variations in subject-test relationship as well as of his changes in varying contexts. These authors dismiss split-half, alternate form, and item consistency methods of obtaining estimates of reliability as inappropriate to projective testing, since patterning and *sequence* of responses, a crucial element in projective instrument interpretation, is thereby lost. Henry and Farley are convinced that stability across time is the crucial test of projective instrument reliability. But they have raised problems here, also, since too short an interval between successive administrations introduces the memory factor, and too long an interval introduces the possibility of actual changes taking place in S.

Schaefer (1962) found many important changes in manifest themes in a group of 135 Ss tested as adolescents and then again, up to eight years after the initial testing, as adults. She was unable to find confirmation for her hypothesis, however, that such changes will show a relationship to single, marital, or parental status at the time of the second administration. (Her first administration, it should be noted, employed a group procedure, whereas her second was an individual one.)

An additional problem concerning estimates of reliability is that not only are scores and scoring systems involved, but also interpretation of these scores. Thus some workers feel that interpreter agreement is the only reasonable and crucial test of reliability. Henry and Farley (1959) state that lack of agreement between scorers might not mean that the instrument is unreliable; lack of agreement might be a reflection of the complexity of evaluating the multitude of S's stimulus-response interactions. These workers contend that the stability of a prediction can be assessed in two ways. They solved the problem of reliability in their own study by assessing the accuracy of a future prediction from the test data. Another way would be the "matching" of interpretation to an S, S being identified at a point of time previous to or subsequent to the test administration. In their own study, judges made these predictions at a better than chance level, but the judges differed markedly from each other. Thus, although there was little judge agreement, the test as a whole was regarded as reliable (in the limited sense stated by the authors, on the basis of what might be regarded as essentially validity concepts) and valid. With regard to the difficult problem of reliability, the authors have stated:

. . . There was little item agreement between judges, but each judge made enough "correct" decisions to yield a highly significant agreement figure. Judges may arrive at essentially the same interpretive implications of the test report, by quite different routes; or judges may differ individually in their ability to utilize TAT predictions in different areas . . . or for different subjects. . . . But whatever the route used or the implications noted, all judges arrived at a substantially accurate understanding of each subject, despite great interjudge variation (p. 22).

It is not clear what this statement signifies. Using what might be a spurious analogy, what would be the significance of the following? A medical questionnaire containing several dozen "bits" of data as to blood pressure, EEG readings, and the like, elicited little or no agreement among several physicians as to the interpretations or significance of various items. Yet, each physician, on a better-than-chance basis, succeeded in aligning questionnaires with patients. Is the questionnaire valid? Is the questionnaire reliable?

As for a more conventional operation associated with estimates of reliability, test-retest reliability is generally regarded to be rather low. Some workers feel, however (e.g., Tomkins in Kagan & Lesser [1961, p. 279]), that test-retest reliability cannot be accurately measured for the TAT. Tomkins stated: "Assuming that we can accurately estimate the test-retest reliability of fantasy responses is like assuming we can measure the reliability of a response to a joke. If I tell it to you twice in a row, or even separated by two days, and you don't laugh as much the second time, I say this is no measure of the reliability of that first response." There is some disagreement, it might be noted, as to what constitutes an adequate interval for the measurement of test-retest reliability. Some workers have based statements about reliability on an interval of several months, others on a few days. In either case, as noted, reliability is low.

Some researchers have noted that since it is unlikely that S would repeat the same story to a picture shown to him on successive days, the measurement of test-retest reliability is a virtually impossible task. Is the subject required to repeat the same story for the instrument to be reliable? Some workers seem to forget that *scores* and *ratings* of an instrument are the bases for estimates of reliability rather than overall story similarity or dissimilarity. Presumably, a projective instrument's ability to measure a motive, drive, need, or mood should be a stable aspect of that instrument. What if S were asked to construct a different story to the same stimulus picture on a successive administration? Might it not be possible to demonstrate that intra-individual scores on various types of scales remain stable despite differences in story structure or content? This would be a fairly accurate estimate of test-retest reliability, but it does require a change from the traditional frame of reference of some TAT workers. If, for example, Ss' successive scores on a scale measuring aggressive outcome or mood are relatively stable, that is, vary together in terms of the group's scores despite instructions to change the story, we may have a good indication that the instrument (in terms of these scales) is fairly reliable.

As previously noted, the question of reliability is related to the question of stability. Kagan and Moss have been concerned with some problems in this area, and have been especially interested in the relationship of stability of a theme or press, over a period of years, to the ambiguity of the stimulus. Kagan (1959) reported on the basis of exploration of the stability of eight TAT scoring categories over almost a six-year period using eighty-six children tested at three intervals, ages 8–9, 11–6, and 14–6, that only physical aggression by the hero and achievement themes showed better-than-chance stability. His findings suggest that the more likely it is that a stimulus produces a given theme, the more likely would this remain stable.

Sen (1953), working with Burt's technique for rating traits, found that correlations between judgments made by the same judge at intervals nine months apart, based on TAT records of 100 British Civil Service candidates, was .59. Correlations between independent ratings made by two judges, although moderately high, were not extremely encouraging.

Haber and Alpert (1958), in an interesting series of studies, explored test-retest reliability of *n* Achievement scores using a carefully pre-tested equivalent set of pictures. College students (*N* of 26) were tested under controlled, relaxed conditions and then again, with an equivalent set of pictures, after a three-week interval. The correlation coefficient was .54. When six pictures which were strongly suggestive (highly structured and cued in terms of *n* Achievement) were used, the esti-mate of reliability was .74; when six weakly cued pictures were used, a substantial drop in reliability was found, the coefficient dropping to .54. When another group (*N* of 54) was tested first under relaxed, then under achievement conditions, the correlation of equivalent forms dropped to .45. Reliability estimates, once again, are demonstrated not only to be related to the specific stimulus situation and their ambiguity, cue-value, etc., but also to the specific motivating cues in the situation in general. This notion is also suggested indirectly by another study conducted by Birney (1959), who, using sets of weakly cued pictures, and scoring for four *n* Achievement measures, reported coefficients ranging from .03 to .56 on the basis of a test-retest study over a two-year period, considerably lower than those reported in other studies.

It should be noted that the evidence seems to suggest that test-retest reliability (or at least stability of scores) is probably increased as stim-ulus pictures decrease in ambiguity. This may seem a bit discouraging for some projectivists, especially those of the "old school," for whom stimulus ambiguity was almost the *raison d'être* for the projective movement!

Split-half reliability presents more difficult problems. The cards vary in picture-pull, cue-value, content ambiguity, etc., and it is difficult to construct two half-series equivalent to each other. More detailed knowledge of these stimulus variants which has been accumulating, however, might make it possible to construct such a division in order to assess this type of variability—a complex, but not an impossible task. Lindzey and Herman (1955), reporting the results of two reliability studies based on six TAT measures, noted that they found rather low split-half reliability and rather high test-retest reliability (two-month interval); the latter, they felt was surprising in the light of all of the expected inconsistencies owing to a wide variety of variables. How-ever, memory factors may have accounted for the relative stability found in this instance.

Establishing the reliability of the instrument thus presents many research and methodological problems for the interested worker. Although fairly good reliability of various scoring systems has been found, it is too early to make any overall statement about the reliability of the TAT as a psychometric device.

## INNOVATIONS AND MODIFICATIONS— ADMINISTRATION, STIMULI, AND SCORING

As already noted in Chapter 1, caution must be used when tailor-made instruments are introduced. The reader is referred to the appropriate section in that chapter for a review of some of the problems involved when departures from "standardized" procedures are contemplated. Meanwhile, it should be noted that the history of the TAT is notably associated with innovations and modifications. Variations in administration procedures are introduced sometimes to test the influence of such variations on test responses, at other times, in the context of a study unrelated to questions concerning the instrument.

Some of these variations consist of new stimulus pictures designed to be more relevant to specific clinical, cultural, or subcultural groups. Often these new series involve special scoring systems. Occasionally, the author of a particular study may orient his work from the point of view of establishing norms on the basis of his findings for a particular group. At other times, the orientation of a study is theoretical and of general psychological interest, the hypothesis concerning itself with nontest variables. And still again, specific questions concerning the TAT response and variations in ambiguity, structure, "card-pull," etc., of the stimuli are raised; attempts to answer these questions are placed in the framework of various modifications.

For a review of some of this literature, the reader is referred to Lesser (1961a) and Murstein (1959, 1961). In each of these references, summaries of numerous modifications of the TAT, essentially with respect to studies oriented toward discovering more about the TAT *qua* test (stimulus and response variations under differing conditions) can be found. Various generalizations can be made from these studies, and these are elaborated in appropriate sections in Chapter 11. New instruments, derivatives of the TAT and cognate techniques, are discussed in Chapter 10.

It has been shown in the discussion of the Rorschach, that it is possible to get at the psychological significance of that procedure by breaking the responses down into their component parts and then setting up experiments to test hypotheses about these components. Thus, by designing specific stimuli for eliciting movement, color, or chiaroscuro responses, the essential significance of these aspects of the response in the Rorschach experiment can be investigated. Studies of this sort are fairly infrequent, however; "theoretical" and test-oriented research in the Rorschach area, with a few notable exceptions, adheres to the traditional stimulus set, scoring systems (of which there are essentially only several major ones), and instructions. Deviations from these are often "errors" of design or careless, unplanned for happenings, not crucial to the design of the study.

The TAT, on the other hand, does not really have a set scoring procedure, nor are the stimulus cards, their number, order of presentation, and actual content fixed and acceptable for all clinicians and researchers. Historically, popular usage of TAT material has been in the direction of exploration of motivational systems (e.g., achievement, aggression, sex, etc.) and areas of behavior (e.g., interpersonal, parent-child, husband-wife). On the assumption that pictorial stimuli should be relevant to the area investigated, many researchers have devised new sets of pictures or modified the original set toward this end. Scoring systems, too, had to be devised to reflect such content. More recently, the stress on the effects of situational and stimulus influences on the response, as well as the importance of formal and stylistic variables in the response has caused many further departures, innovations, and modifications in the context of exploration and manipulation of such factors. Meanwhile, without attempting an elaborate review, reference will be made to "typical" studies which illustrate the innovations noted earlier.

*Variations in Administration.* Jones (1956) described what he called the Negation TAT, a modified form of TAT administration designed to elicit repressed content, by taking cognizance of the Freudian notion of negation. After the standard TAT is obtained, S is asked to make up the most unlikely story that comes to mind for each picture. The author suggests that there are other ways of obtaining "negation" material, such as by asking S, "What could *not* be going on here?" Jones reported that blind ratings of protocols administered with standard and negation instructions were made by S's therapist (with relevant references removed from the protocols so as not to cue the rater) as to which story of each pair more lucidly suggested the patient's repressed psychic content. In 46 of the 55 pairs of TAT stories, the negation story was rated as such ($p < .001$). Yet, it should be noted that the negation instruction is such as virtually to guarantee bizarre or farfetched content. Would not this be automatically rated as representing "repressed psychic content?" How "repressed" is content to a stimulus when S is asked deliberately to produce unlikely stories?

The use of short motion pictures, based on five TAT cards, was explored by McIntyre (1954, 1955) with somewhat discouraging results.

Variations in the length of series, modifications of verbal instructions to S, use of various timing procedures, variations in the conditions of lighting, use of only a *selected* group of standard TAT cards, and the like, have all been reported and described in the TAT literature. As already noted, various authors are sometimes specifically interested in studying the effect of such variations on the test response; at other times, however, modifications of this sort are introduced for reasons of efficiency, expediency, and economy, or because they seem particularly relevant and appropriate in the light of the nature and design of the study. The numerous studies illustrating these procedural changes will not be described here. However, the use of *group* procedures is so frequent, that mention of some relevant studies is felt to be essential. It might be noted, in passing, that so many authors have introduced group administration procedures that a listing of their studies is not possible (e.g., Calogeras [1958]; Child, Frank, & Storm [1956]; Eron & Ritter [1951]; and Kagan & Mussen [1956]). Reviews of relevant studies, as well as studies specifically designed to test the influence of group vs. standard procedures, have been rather encouraging. Lindzey and Heinemann (1955), for example, in a review of relevant research, noted that group and individual TAT's are moderately equivalent. In a more recent study, Lindzey and Silverman (1959) found that individual and group procedures as well as exposure time (20 seconds or 5 minutes and 20 seconds) did not materially affect results in terms of various themes, transcendence, verbal productivity as well as other variables. Sarason and Sarason (1958), however, did find that type of administration affected their results.

*Introduction of New Stimuli.* The variables to be considered when new pictures are devised for a particular research purpose are manifold. Attention is given to some of these variables in Chapter 11. Meanwhile, to provide the reader with some sort of framework by which he can note the complexity of the task before him when he embarks on a TAT modification project, some suggestions, offered by a few workers, will be noted.

Heppell and Raimy (1951) have outlined some criteria for selecting pictures for a particular problem, which they culled from the literature and adapted for their own use. They presented these criteria as follows:

1. The picture should relate to the particular problem under investigation. . . .
2. The pictures should represent situations familiar to the subjects. . . .
3. The picture should contain a central figure of the same sex and approximately the same age as the subjects. . .

4. The pictures should not contain characters or situations which are intrinsically humorous. . . .

5. The pictures should contain a minimum of detail. . . .

6. The picture should depict an event episodic in nature but should not tell a complete story (p. 406).

Note should be made of the fact that these comments are best viewed as hypotheses, open to investigation and clarification; as a matter of fact, some of them have been subjected to experimental investigation, with either nonsignificant or negative findings.

Crandall (1951) listed four criteria which are particularly pertinent for controlled types of investigations:

1. There should be a maximum number of pictures to insure reliability consistent with a minimum number to maintain high motivation in the subject.

2. The pictures should contain situations relevant to important needs and strivings of the subject. They should represent both situations entailing strivings similar to those frustrated in the experiment and ones eliciting strivings other than these.

3. Pictures representing situations eliciting a given need should call forth stories eliciting that need in a clear majority of the subjects.

4. Two roughly equivalent sets of pictures should be developed. This is necessary in order to match the experimental and control subjects on the dependent variable in a pretest before the introduction of the experimental variable (p. 401).

Most of the investigators do not cite any kind of evidence other than their own private experience to substantiate the efficacy of their criteria for selecting pictures designed to elicit information about specific motivational systems and/or areas of behavior. Although it is not explicitly stated, it can be assumed that the usual procedure has been to select or reject certain pictures by inspection and then, on the basis of trial runs, to eliminate those pictures which do not seem to yield the desired information. The criteria are then derived from the characteristics of these "successful" pictures with no further study of the efficiency of the selected cards. Heppell and Raimy (1951), however, although they did not test the efficacy of the individual criteria they listed, were able to rank according to "usefulness" fifteen pictures, originally selected on the basis of their six criteria, by rating the resulting stories on scales of emotional involvement and significance of conceptual relationships. They found a significant difference in "usefulness" between the first eight and last seven pictures of their sample, although no picture originally considered to meet the criteria very well or poorly was consistently ranked as high or low. Despite the ambiguous nature of the results, which may be due to the inadequacy of their scales which were subjectively and not empirically derived, this would seem to be an efficient method for selecting pictures maximally useful for eliciting information about various motivational systems and areas of behavior.

Some illustrations of studies which have introduced new pictures or modifications of the old ones follow. Veroff, et al. (1960) and Veroff (1961) used a set of specially developed cards and a set series of questions to elicit apperceptive content (spontaneous stories were not used); Kagan (1956) used a set of specially devised pictures in his study of the relationship of aggressive TAT content and teacher's ratings of fighting behavior; Lesser (1959a), who studied the relationship between religious affiliation and aggression-anxiety responses on the TAT, also utilized a specially developed set of stimulus cards.

Illustrations of specially developed sets in the context of anthropological studies are numerous, indeed. Only a few will be mentioned:

Shore (1954) used a special set with Mexican rural children, utilizing familiar cues, clothing, surroundings, etc. Ansari and Ghose (1957) used eleven different family situations to test assumptions about the relationship of socioeconomic status in India and familial attitudes. Test development criteria and norms were not utilized or presented. Chowdhury (1960), on the other hand, also working with an Indian (Asiatic) population, did attempt to provide norms with respect to their specially devised instrument which took into account important differences between Indian and Euro-American cultures.

Bachrach (1949) devised a special set of TAT materials showing or suggesting crippled children, for use with the handicapped. In an evaluation of the premise that handicapped persons would have greater ease of identification with pictures showing handicapped persons, Greenbaum, Qualtere, Carruth, and Cruickshank (1953) utilized two Bachrach cards for one group of handicapped children and two non-Bachrach cards for a second group, matched for age, sex, intelligence, and type of handicap. Greater spontaneity, as well as more clues concerning interpersonal relationships were found in the material elicited by the non-Bachrach cards, it might be noted. As a matter of fact, a review of the literature suggests, unfortunately, that pictorial representations and images of figures similar to the group being studied, ethnic, racial, chronological, or even clinical, are probably not more effective, and are perhaps even *less* effective than the standard pictures.

Another example of a specially developed set of stimuli is provided by Briggs (1954), who reported a special modification of the TAT for use with naval enlisted personnel (submarine), three of the ten pictures used being particularly appropriate to the Navy. A method of scoring the N-TAT was presented by Eron, Sultan, and Auld (1955), using an adaptation of the scoring system developed by Eron for use with the standard Murray (1943) set of cards. Murphree and Carnaghan (1955) developed a system for scoring the N-TAT, based on S's conformity to the group's reactions.

There have been many other adaptations of the TAT pictures in order to obtain data about various areas of behavior, defense mechanisms, and motivational systems. Some early studies which have not already been discussed will be mentioned briefly. Amen (1941) devised a series of fifteen pictures, some with colored backgrounds with movable parts, and others which were either colored, or black and white silhouettes. These pictures were administered to seventy-seven preschool children, age two to five years, and developmental tendencies in the "perceptual" reaction to pictures were noted. Temple and Amen (1944) devised a similar technique for a study of anxiety reactions in young children. They used a series of twelve pictures representing situations familiar to young children. The central figure in each scene was so drawn that it might be interpreted either as a boy or as a girl, and the face of the figure was left blank, the incomplete drawing suggesting the bare outlines of a head. Two separate heads, one with a happy, one with a sad expression, one of which the child selected in order to complete the central figure, were drawn for each picture. Two groups (normal and clinical) of twenty-five children, age three to ten years, were tested, and many different anxiety areas in the experience of little children, both normal and clinical, were revealed. A close relationship was also demonstrated between patterns of anxiety and type of behavioral adjustment. Balken and Vander Veer (1944) used pictures of their own selection in addition to some from the TAT to study the "fantasies" of neurotic children. Buchanan (1945) developed a picture interpretation test for use with children: two series of black and white pictures, one for each sex, were selected depicting a child in an everyday situation. In most of the pictures the facial expressions were indistinct, and the child was encouraged to interpret the expression in his own way.

*Scoring Systems.* A striking feature of the TAT literature is that there are almost as many scoring systems as there are studies, a fact which creates a burdensome task for the researcher who questions the validity and reliability of TAT scores. (See Shneidman, *et al.* [1951], for a presentation of the different systems of fifteen experts working with the same TAT record.) As with some of the modifications described earlier, some of the scoring systems are based on theoretical and general interest in a psychological problem; others are based on test-oriented problems. Intensive investigation of reliability, objectivity, and validity problems is not always present. Sometimes the main purpose of the study is to construct a special scoring system; frequently this is only incidental.

Chapter 11 contains a detailed review of Murray's scoring system. Many clinical workers use this system or their own approximation of some of the procedures outlined by Murray. Reference should also be made to the detailed descriptions and manuals of scoring for $n$ Achievement, $n$ Affiliation, and $n$ Power in Atkinson's book (1958a). This system has been used by numerous workers in the exploration of these motives. The large number of studies based on achievement, aggression, and sex motivation have also, in the main, utilized special scoring systems. These will not be described here.

Many other systems, in addition to those described by Aron (1949), Hartman (1949), Holt (1951), and Stein (1948, 1955), have been described in the literature. Brief examples of other scoring systems follow: Fine (1955a, 1955b) offered a scoring system based mainly on feelings, outcomes, and interpersonal relationships. With this system, some significant differences were found between asthmatic children and their siblings. Davids and Rosenblatt (1958) have devised a special scoring system to measure the syndrome of "alienation," for which validity and reliability evidence was presented. Stone (1956) has described a special TAT aggressive content scale. Dana (1955, 1956c, 1957, 1959) has provided a special scoring system, as well as norms, validity, and reliability evidence (see sections on *Validity* and *Reliability*). Shipley and Veroff (1952) have utilized a special measure of $n$ Affiliation. Other systems have been described by Foulds (1953), and Shorr (1948). Finally, one example of a recent scoring system growing out of an author's theoretical orientation will now be provided as an illustration of another "justification" for a new system.

Pine (1960) has described a scoring system based on an analysis of drive content. His interest was in impulse expression, ego control operations, and the coordination between the two. According to this author, his manual was specifically designed for "rating libidinal and aggressive drive material in manifest content of TAT stories" (p. 32). His interest was also in the ego control over the drive content, for he described a "procedure for rating the degree to which drive content is integrated into the theme of a TAT story, the effectiveness of such integration being considered as an index of ego control" (p. 32). In his scoring system, Pine differentiated between types of drive in terms of the story: thematic, incidental, and inappropriate. The level of drive expression is also rated, that is, direct-unsocialized drive expression;

direct-socialized expression; and disguised, indirect or weak drive expression. The relationship among these three variables have important implications. Pine claims that his scoring system is linked to psychoanalytic theory. He reported fairly good scorer agreement and stated that his system possesses good validity (concurrent) based on Q-sorts. These, in turn, were based on test material which included the TAT; hence contamination is present.

The foregoing material has been presented not as a systematic review, but as an indication of the bewildering array of innovations, modifications, and special systems available for the clinician and researcher. The clinician, facing so insurmountable a job as to untangle the evidence for or against a particular system or innovation, often proceeds on his own, using intuition, experience and, hopefully, some crude internal frame of reference—frequently without awareness.

One particular aspect of various approaches to the scoring of the protocol, has not yet been discussed. This approach is described in the section immediately following.

*Structural and Stylistic Aspects.* There has been an increased emphasis, of late, in both TAT research and in clinical application, on structural aspects of S's protocol, as opposed to the traditional analysis of content considerations. Actually, in his normative study (1950), Eron found that it was only such formal factors, and not content, which distinguished TAT productions of schizophrenic and other hospitalized psychiatric patients from each other and from those of normal subjects. These structural aspects would include the verbal, language, or logical "style" of S (e.g., Shneidman, 1961); those aspects of the stimulus and their sequence to which he tends to respond (similar to location and succession in Rorschach terminology); the tendency or lack of tendency to bring into the response attributes not present in the stimulus (transcendence, Weisskopf [1950]); and behavioral features of S which are not related to the stimulus situation, such as shifting foci of attention. Henry (1956), Holt (1958), Kagan (1961), Schafer (1958), and others have offered other classifications of such stylistic aspects of the response, and although there is some overlap in classes used, these systems stress different aspects of this type of analysis.

As noted, Holt (1958) has stressed the importance of formal aspects of the TAT. Although he has stated that generally low correlations are found between formal aspects of the TAT and various criteria, the current review of relevant literature did not yield such a discouraging point of view. As a matter of fact, we are left with the impression that "formal" aspects of TAT protocols tended to hold up better than the so-called "content" aspects. Interestingly, the opposite point of view seems to hold with respect to the Rorschach, judging by the swing to content analysis in recent years, and some of the validity evidence reported in the Rorschach literature.[9] Although Holt reported relatively low reliability and validity data concerning formal aspects, he did quote a study by Landsberger on the relationship between formal ratings and criterion ratings of eighteen labor mediators (Holt, 1958). The validities of many formal scales, such as stereotypy of story and genuineness vs. façade, were significantly high.

Kagan (1961) presented findings concerning research with one stylistic variable, the tendency to use affect words in describing or conceptualizing social stimuli. He worked with four types of "human-like" stimuli: TAT figures; tachistoscopically presented figures; a figure-sorting situation; and the Rorschach (occurrence of M). His assumptions and hypotheses are general, and are based on a set of notions which would suggest that the use of affect labels, sorting on the basis of affect, attribution of movement to inkblots, etc., all reflect a tendency to view the environment from the point of view of human motives. After intercorrelating scores from these four situations, Kagan concluded that, although the obtained coefficients were not high, "the tendency to infer affect states to social stimuli has a generality across a variety of conceptual tasks" (p. 206). Furthermore, additional exploration has indicated that the tendency to use affect labels is also associated with introspectiveness (as rated on the basis of interviews). In addition, he found that affect scores on the TAT and M on the Rorschach were moderately stable (tested in adolescence and then again in adulthood), and that the Rorschach and TAT scores obtained in adolescence predicted degree of introspectiveness in adulthood. Although there were other interesting findings, these will not be summarized here. Kagan's work does demonstrate some interesting relationships concerning the tendency to ascribe affect to figures in several situations. On the basis of additional findings, he speculated that Ss can be differentiated in terms of repression or nonrepression of conflictful thoughts, and that Ss who ascribe affect states to various figures are more aware of their motives and conflicts. This may be so, but it is suggested that there are more direct routes and avenues to testing the applicability of Kagan's notions. If Ss are differentiated on the basis of

---

[9] Actually, a good case can be made for the fact that there is no contradiction here at all. Indeed, the so-called formal and structural characteristics of TAT responses are similar to what has often been called Rorschach *content* factors. With respect to both of these instruments, such factors (no matter what they are called) seem to be quite promising in terms of validity.

one or more of these scores, can it be shown directly that they are related to some of the variables he noted, such as progress in therapy? Unfortunately, as with other workers, his provocative thinking ends at this point. The specific utilization of the TAT as an instrument will not be furthered until more specifically oriented test research is conducted.

Shneidman (1961) was specifically interested in the thought processes people use in the solution of problems, whether "correct" or "incorrect"—that is, in their logic (not in the philosophical sense). He did not assume a dichotomy between Aristotelian and non-Aristotelian logic (as, say, in conventional studies of schizophrenic thinking) but a continuum. Furthermore, he assumed that S's "logical processes" are idiosyncratic and related to his overall state. In his study of suicide notes (of Ss who have committed suicide, have attempted suicide, and who are nonsuicidal, as well as of suicidal and nonsuicidal TAT material), he developed three categories of suicidal "logic": (a) *logical suicides*—e.g., those who are in pain, and who wish surcease from this pain; (b) *paleological suicides*—these are psychotic suicides in which deductive fallacies are made; and (c) *catalogic suicides*—in which semantic errors are made, and the thinking is almost always dichotomous.

Shneidman accepts Whorf's notions as to how language and cultural usage determine our thinking, but suggests that individuals within this context may also deviate along idiosyncratic lines. Illustrating from several sources, Shneidman demonstrated how to go from the style of thought to the personality structure of S. Utilizing data from a previous study (Little & Shneidman, 1955), he demonstrated that thought processes and general personality characteristics are correlated. Although based on an ingenious use of Q-sort technique, his demonstration that "ways of thinking are a reflection of general ways of psychological being" is based on judgments and correlations derived from statements about a TAT protocol of a single case. Is there not a more direct way of demonstrating this approach? Perhaps a detailed presentation of a reliable method of scoring such stylistic variables would be helpful, together with data concerning validity, norms, and cross-validational findings. Lastly, it might be noted that Shneidman's approach is not so different, after all, from other workers who have posited a deviational approach to test responses (including the current authors). As a matter of fact, Rotter (1961), in his discussion of Shneidman's paper, indicated that assumptions were being made for which there still was not complete evidence. These included: (a) it is possible to identify deviations from commonly accepted logic, and this can be reliably done and the "reason" for the error reliably supplied by several experts—e.g., missing premises, mistaken identities; (b) the nature of such errors are "typical" of S, and this fact can be used for predictive purposes; and (c) that this characteristic mode of thinking is predictive of other personality characteristics. Not only should these assumptions be tested, but it might also be noted that Shneidman, although ostensibly discussing "logic" and thinking processes, extends his point of view to include various stylistic considerations and characteristics which seem to go beyond his original conception. If these variables are predictive, so much the better! But the overlap and generality of some of his suggestions should certainly be made explicit.

In a discussion of Kagan's (1961) paper by Sigel (1961) and others, several methodological and theoretical problems were raised, including whether or not "style" is actually separable from "need" or "motive." This problem is by no means solved, but it certainly offers a rich field for research. Atkinson (1961) highlighted the whole problem thus:

When you go at projectives the way some of us have, looking only at isolated motives, you lose contact with the whole person. It seems to me the cognitive style-motive issue might have in it the beginning of a way to integrate the total person, the type of person who has a dominant motive, and who develops a particular style that characterizes him in a wide variety of situations. That, of course, is arguing one hypothesis. The other one, and again I think equally plausible, is that cognitive styles are completely independent of motives. If that turns out to be true we will have to examine seriously the way we are measuring motives. If we have a complete confounding, then what I call high need for achievement may not be that at all, but a kind of cognitive style (pp. 227–228).

## SOCIAL PSYCHOLOGY AND THE TAT

Reference has already been made to the use of projective techniques in anthropological research. TAT studies in this area will not be summarized here, although several illustrations of such studies will be noted. But first, a general question might be raised. If the TAT is accepted as a valid means for revealing cultural images, especially when control groups and cross-validation procedures are not used, how, at the same time, can it be made to yield idiosyncratic elements, and how do we differentiate these elements in any given record? Other pertinent questions and problems are raised in Chapter 1. Some illustrative studies follow.

Alexander and Anderson (1957) worked with children of Northern Cheyenne Indians in a study which attempted to shed light on the relations between the "perceptions" of individuals and the disintegrating society in which they are developing. Ansari and Ghose (1957) studied Indian (Asiatic) children from different socioeconomic backgrounds in an attempt to discover whether or not family attitudes varied with group membership. Chowdhury (1960) also found differences in TAT content and productivity among Ss in South Bengal classified in terms of caste. Although findings in these studies were positive, cross-validation was not attempted. Another study, this time of our own culture by Neugarten and Gutman (1958), explored age and sex roles in responses to a set of specially designed pictures consisting of young and older adults. Subjects included a group of 131 male and female Ss, age 40–70, from either a middle or working-class group. Here, TAT responses were used to gain anthrosociological information in regard to collective images of various members of the family; the validity of the TAT was taken for granted.

Attention will now be turned to TAT studies in the context of social-psychological explorations, in order to illustrate a point already made —the wide adoption of this technique as a measure and as an instrument outside of clinical psychology. Such studies are numerous; only a few will be cited, and although they take the TAT for granted, some of them may indirectly add to the wide body of validity evidence rapidly accumulating.

The extensive studies of Frenkel-Brunswik utilized responses to TAT-type pictures to investigate the personality correlates of prejudice (Frenkel-Brunswik [1948]; Frenkel-Brunswik, Levinson, & Sanford [1947]; and Frenkel-Brunswik & Sanford [1945]). In her work on *The Authoritarian Personality,* Aron (1950) compared the responses to ten pictures (six of which were the Murray cards and four of which were specifically selected) of four groups of twenty subjects each, males and females, with high scores on their prejudice scale, and males and females with low prejudice scores. The stories were analyzed according to two separate techniques. First, they were scored according to Sanford's revised Murray need-press system which breaks each story down into discrete variables which are rated on a five-point scale for intensity. The second technique, which was developed by Aron, adapted the Murray scheme so that differences in patterns of combinations of need-press variables could be scored. The reliability of the first scoring method when applied to these stories is dubious. Twenty of the records were re-scored by a second scorer, and the rank order r's varied between .41 and .83, except for one which fell to .26. Only fifteen of the sixty variables had reliability ratings higher than .63. Furthermore, there is no evaluation of the significance of the difference in scores between the groups, and actually the means reported do not appear to be highly discrepant.

Although the differences among the groups appear to be greater when the variables are analyzed in combination, or thematically, as in the second scoring method, there is no indication of the significance of these differences either. A superficial examination of the data reveals that there are many less significant differences than could be accounted for by chance, and this method of analysis is not really superior to the first. Thus, although the differences that are reported fit in very nicely with the collaborators' conceptions of the authoritarian personality,[10] the TAT, as used here, cannot be accepted as a validation for this conceptualization, nor, on the other hand, can it be said with any certainty that the personality correlates of the authoritarian personality are revealed in the responses to these TAT-type pictures. An interesting incidental result of this study is that the six pictures taken from the Murray series proved more differentiating than the ones especially designed for the study.

Lindzey (1950) used four of the Murray TAT cards (3BM, 8BM, 16, and 20) in an effort to differentiate the high and low in prejudice and to relate the findings to a theory of prejudice.[11] The author counted the number of incidents in which "self-figures" carried out aggressive acts against "nonself-figures" as a measure of outwardly directed aggression and found that the high in prejudice did not show significantly more outwardly directed aggression than did the low in prejudice. He also subtracted the difference in scores before and after frustration for the high and low groups and found that the high in prejudice showed no more tendency toward displacement of aggression after frustration than the low in prejudice. Thus, in this experiment, the TAT was used as the dependent variable, whose change or lack of change was used to demonstrate a theoretical point. But Lindzey did not use scores similar to other workers who have explored aggression in making his analyses. Had he used a tally of instances of defense against expression of aggression, as did Pittluck (1950), it is questionable whether he might not have found a difference between the high and low in prejudice consistent with a theoretical viewpoint.

Mussen (1950), who administered twelve of the Murray cards plus one other and, in scoring, used a modification of the need-press system,

---

[10] The authors felt that the superiority of the second method of analysis lent support to one of the main conclusions of the project: that the prejudiced and unprejudiced differ less in the nature of their basic needs than in their ways of coping with them.

[11] In another study, Lindzey and Riecken (1951) had found that extrapunitive behavior on the part of the hero in TAT protocols increased significantly following failure in a social situation.

found in his investigation of the change in attitude of 106 white boys toward Negroes after intimate contact at an interracial camp, that those boys who were high in prejudice before intimate contact with Negroes had more aggressive and dominance needs, more hostility toward their parents, and more feelings of aggressive press from the environment than boys who were low in prejudice. There were also consistent differences in personality structure and content, which were reflected in this type of scoring of the TAT, between boys who increased and decreased in prejudice after the camp experience. One of the author's chief conclusions, incidentally, is that:

These findings make it clear that intimate contact with Negroes *per se* does not insure a decrease of prejudice. Whether a child increases or decreases in prejudice following such an experience seems to be related to his personality structure ("susceptibility to change") and whether or not the camp situation is felt to be a rewarding one (p. 441).

It would seem, therefore, that the kind of results obtained in these studies of prejudice and aggression is very much a function of the scoring system used.[12] Another reason for differences may be in the variable number and kind of stimulus cards used. These inconsistent results point up our lack of understanding of just what is happening when an individual tells a story about an ambiguous picture, since different pictures, different scoring schemes, and different subjects can yield such different results. This should not limit the usefulness of the Thematic Apperception Technique, however, in either the measurement of attitudes or in relating the measure to some theoretical framework. Only by empirical juggling will it be determined which are the stimuli maximally potential for eliciting information about a specific need or attitude in a certain kind of population, and by which method of ordering the data can the relationship of the data to the hypothesis best be shown. Once these conditions have been specified along with the parameters and base rates of the samples studied, it will then be possible to obtain consistent results from one experiment to another.

## SUMMARY AND CONCLUSIONS

This chapter has attempted to review the current status of the TAT in terms of various assumptions and hypotheses, both implicit and explicit, as well as to provide an overview of some of the chief methodological problems facing the clinical researcher who is interested in approaching the TAT as an *instrument* of personality assess-

---

[12] This is not a function of the reliability of the scales since the scales of both Lindzey and Mussen were demonstrated to be reliable.

ment. Although some historical perspective was presented, and a large number of studies noted, the material contained in this chapter was not offered as a complete review of the literature. On the other hand, the illustrative material can be regarded as sufficiently "representative" of the literature, and the problems raised as characteristically typical of the TAT field, so as to provide both clinician or researcher alike with a framework on which he may hang some of his own questions and expectations concerning the TAT.

Within this framework, the following points were developed:

1. A brief history of the TAT as both a research and clinical tool was presented; in addition, some indications of the prestige and "status" of the TAT outside of the clinical fold were noted.

2. The nature of TAT "theorizing" was illustrated through a discussion of several reports. More important, some basic assumptions and hypotheses which many workers implicitly and explicitly make were reviewed, with especial stress on three questions: (a) Do TAT protocols reflect needs, motives, and drives? (b) Are TAT responses and "fantasies" equated? (c) Does TAT material predict overt behavior? The emphasis in this discussion was placed on the need for clarifying and testing such assumptions.

3. Considerable attention was devoted to validity and reliability problems. Various types of validity approaches were illustrated and discussed. Some of the diagnostic failures of the TAT were noted, as well as some significant and positive findings. The research summary presented indicated that it is not possible to regard the TAT as a valid instrument of personality assessment, as such. Rather, the TAT seems useful and "valid" under certain conditions and for specific tasks and criteria. The material pertaining to reliability indicated that scoring reliability, under circumscribed and specific conditions, is relatively good. Methodological problems with respect to other questions and procedures of estimating reliability were noted.

4. Various innovations and modifications in TAT administration and scoring procedures, as well as stimuli used were noted, together with a brief discussion of the recent stress on formal and "stylistic" variables, as opposed to content of S's products. It was indicated that research with the former has been quite encouraging.

5. Finally, a brief overview of the use of the TAT in a field outside of clinical psychology was presented, specifically, social psychology. It was felt that studies of this sort contribute to general knowledge concerning the validity of the TAT.

The general status of the TAT as a psychometric device, it can be concluded, leaves something to be desired. Recent methodological advances and sophistication in the field, as well as the ever-growing numbers of trained, research-oriented workers who are interested in the TAT are extremely encouraging indications of the direction in which the TAT is going. On the other hand, the enormous number of systems of scoring, stimulus cards, techniques for interpretation, etc., create a bewildering array of alternatives which the clinician encounters when he is confronted with a single protocol to interpret. The TAT is not one, but *many* instruments. Are there generalizations which go beyond each specific study? Can the TAT be regarded as a psychological situation which can be analyzed for its component parts? Chapter 10 presents some material relating to popular derivatives of the TAT, in terms of new instruments. Chapter 11, however, returns to the questions just posed.

## REFERENCES

Alexander, T., & Anderson, R. Children in a society under stress. *Behav. Sci.*, 1957, 2, 46–55.

Amen, Elizabeth. Individual differences in apperceptive reaction: a study of the responses of pre-school children to pictures. *Genet. Psychol. Monogr.*, 1941, 23, 319–385.

Ansari, A., & Ghose, B. A study of family attitudes of children with contrasting socio-economic background. *Educ. Psychol.*, Delhi, 1957, 4(2), 90–102.

Aron, Betty. A *manual for analysis of the Thematic Apperception Test.* Berkeley, Calif.: Willis E. Berg, 1949.

Aron, Betty. The Thematic Apperception Test in the study of prejudiced and un-prejudiced individuals. In T. W. Adorno, E. Frenkel-Brunswik, D. Levinson, R. N. Sanford, *et al. The authoritarian personality.* New York: Harper and Brothers, 1950, 489–544.

Asch, S. E. *Social psychology.* New York: Prentice-Hall, 1952.

Astin, A. W. The functional autonomy of psychotherapy. *Amer. Psychologist*, 1961, 16, 75–78.

Atkinson, J. W. Studies in projective measurement of achievement motivation. Unpublished doctoral dissertation, University of Michigan, 1950.

Atkinson, J. W. (Ed.) *Motives in fantasy, action, and society.* Princeton, N.J.: D. Van Nostrand, 1958. (a)

Atkinson, J. W. Thematic apperceptive measurement of motives within the context of a theory of motivation. In J. W. Atkinson (Ed.) *Motives in fantasy, action, and society.* Princeton, N.J.: D. Van Nostrand, 1958, 596–616. (b)

Atkinson, J. W. Discussion of Dr. Kagan's paper. In J. Kagan and G. S. Lesser (Eds.) *Contemporary issues in thematic apperceptive methods.* Springfield, Ill.: Charles C Thomas, 1961, 221–228.

Atkinson, J. W., & McClelland, D. C. The projective expression of needs. II. The effect of different intensities of the hunger drive on thematic apperception. *J. exp. Psychol.*, 1948, 38, 643–658.

Atkinson, J. W., & Raphelson, A. C. Individual differences in motivation and behavior in particular situations. *J. Pers.*, 1956, 24, 349–363.

Atkinson, J. W., & Walker, E. L. The affiliation motive and perceptual sensitivity to faces. *J. abnorm. soc. Psychol.*, 1956, 53, 38–41.

Auld, F., Jr. Contributions of behavior theory to projective testing. *J. proj. Tech.*, 1954, **18**, 421–426.

Auld, F., Jr., Eron, L. D., & Laffal, J. Application of Guttman's scaling method to the TAT. *Educ. psychol. Measmt.*, 1955, **15**, 422–435.

Bachrach, A. J. Personality test for the handicapped. *Crippled Child*, 1949, **27**(4), 18–19.

Balken, Eva R., & Vander Veer, A. H. Clinical application of the Thematic Apperception Test to neurotic children. *Amer. J. Orthopsychiat.*, 1944, **14**, 421–440.

Beier, E. G., Gorlow, L., & Stacey, C. L. The fantasy life of the mental defective. *Amer. J. ment. Defic.*, 1951, **55**, 582–589.

Bell, J. E. *Projective techniques.* New York: Longmans, Green, 1948.

Bellak, L. Thematic apperception: failures and the defenses. *Trans. N.Y. Acad. Sci.*, 1950, Series II, **12**, 122–126.

Bellak, L. *The Thematic Apperception Test and the Children's Apperception Test in clinical use.* New York: Grune and Stratton, 1954.

Binet, A., & Simon, T. Application des méthodes nouvelles au diagnostic du niveau intellectuel chez des enfants normaux et anormaux d'hospice et d'école primaire. *Année psychol.*, 1905, **11**, 245–336.

Birney, R. C. The reliability of the achievement motive. *J. abnorm. soc. Psychol.*, 1959, **58**, 266–267.

Briggs, D. L. A modification of the Thematic Apperception Test for Naval enlisted personnel (N-TAT). *J. Psychol.*, 1954, **37**, 233–241.

Brittain, H. L. A study in imagination. *Pedag. Sem.*, 1907, **14**, 137–207.

Broverman, D. M., Jordan, E. J., Jr., & Phillips, L. Achievement motivation in fantasy and behavior. *J. abnorm. soc. Psychol.*, 1960, **60**, 374–378.

Buchanan, Margaret P. A picture-interpretation personality test. *Brit. J. educ. Psychol.*, 1945, **15**, 151–152. (Abstract)

Calogeraş, R. C. Some relationships between fantasy and self-report behavior. *Genet. Psychol. Monogr.*, 1958, **58**, 273–325.

Calvin, J. S., & Ward, L. C. An attempted experimental validation of the Thematic Apperception Test. *J. clin. Psychol.*, 1950, **6**, 377–381.

Carlile, June St. H. The Thematic Apperception Test applied to neurotic and normal adolescent girls. *Brit. J. med. Psychol.*, 1952, **25**, 244–248.

Carr, A. C., Forer, B. R., Henry, W. E., Hooker, Evelyn, Hutt, M. L., & Piotrowski, Z. A. *The prediction of overt behavior through the use of projective techniques.* Springfield, Ill.: Charles C Thomas, 1960.

Child, I. L., Frank, Kitty F., & Storm, T. Self-ratings and the TAT: their relations to each other and to childhood background. *J. Pers.*, 1956, **25**, 96–114.

Chowdhury, Uma. An Indian modification of the Thematic Apperception Test. *J. soc. Psychol.*, 1960, **51**, 245–263.

Clark, R. A. The projective measurement of experimentally induced levels of sexual motivation. *J. exper. Psychol.*, 1952, **44**, 391–399.

Clark, R. A. The effects of sexual motivation on phantasy. In D. C. McClelland (Ed.) *Studies in motivation.* New York: Appleton, 1955, 44–57.

Clark, R. A., & McClelland, D. C. A factor analytic integration of imaginative and performance measures of the need for achievement. *J. gen. Psychol.*, 1956, **55**, 73–83.

Coleman, W. The Thematic Apperception Test: I. Effect of recent experience. II. Some quantitative observations. *J. clin. Psychol.*, 1947, **3**, 257–264.

Cox, Beverly, & Sargent, Helen. TAT responses of emotionally disturbed and emotionally stable children: clinical judgment vs. normative data. *J. proj. Tech.*, 1950, **14**, 61–74.

Crandall, V. J. Induced frustration and punishment-reward expectancy in thematic apperception stories. *J. consult. Psychol.*, 1951, **15**, 400–404.

Cronbach, L. J. A validation design for qualitative studies of personality. *J. consult. Psychol.*, 1948, **12**, 365–374.

Dana, R. H. Clinical diagnosis and objective TAT scoring. *J. abnorm. soc. Psychol.*, 1955, **50**, 19–24.

Dana, R. H. Cross validation of objective TAT scoring. *J. consult. Psychol.*, 1956, **20**, 33–36. (*a*)

Dana, R. H. Selection of abbreviated TAT sets. *J. clin. Psychol.*, 1956, **12**, 36–40. (*b*)

Dana, R. H. An application of objective TAT scoring. *J. proj. Tech.*, 1956, **20**, 159–163. (*c*)

Dana, R. H. Norms for three aspects of TAT behavior. *J. gen. Psychol.*, 1957, **57**, 83–89.

Dana, R. H. Proposal for objective scoring of the TAT. *Percept. mot. Skills*, 1959, **9**, 27–43.

Davenport, Beverly F. The semantic validity of TAT interpretations. *J. consult. Psychol.*, 1952, **16**, 171–175.

Davids, A., Joelson, M., & McArthur, C. Rorschach and TAT indices of homosexuality in overt homosexuals, neurotics and normal males. *J. abnorm. soc. Psychol.*, 1956, **53**, 161–172.

Davids, A., & Rosenblatt, D. Use of the TAT in assessment of the personality syndrome of alienation. *J. proj. Tech.*, 1958, **22**, 145–152.

Davison, A. H. A comparison of the fantasy productions on the Thematic Apperception Test of sixty hospitalized psychoneurotic and psychotic patients. Unpublished doctoral dissertation, Purdue University, 1950.

Dilworth, T., IV. A comparison of the Edwards PPS variables with some aspects of the TAT. *J. consult. Psychol.*, 1958, **22**, 486.

Epstein, S., & Smith, R. Thematic apperception as a measure of the hunger drive. *J. proj. Tech.*, 1956, **20**, 372–384.

Epstein, S., & Smith, R. Thematic apperception, Rorschach content, and ratings of sexual attractiveness of women as measures of the sex drive. *J. consult. Psychol.*, 1957, **21**, 473–478.

Eriksen, C. W. Some implications for TAT interpretation arising from need and perception experiments. *J. Pers.*, 1951, **19**, 282–288.

Eriksen, C. W. Perceptual defense. In P. H. Hoch and J. Zubin (Eds.) *Psychopathology of perception.* New York: Grune and Stratton, 1964.

Eron, L. D. Frequencies of themes and identifications in the stories of schizophrenic patients and non-hospitalized college students. *J. consult. Psychol.*, 1948, **12**, 387–395.

Eron, L. D. A normative study of the Thematic Apperception Test. *Psychol. Monogr.*, 1950, **64** (Whole No. 315).

Eron, L. D., & Ritter, Anne M. A comparison of two methods of administration of the Thematic Apperception Test. *J. consult. Psychol.*, 1951, **15**, 55–61.

Eron, L. D., Terry, Dorothy, & Callahan, R. The use of rating scales for emotional tone of TAT stories. *J. consult. Psychol.*, 1950, **14**, 473–478.

Eron, L. D., Sultan, Florence, & Auld, F., Jr. The application of a psychometric scoring procedure to a group modification of the Thematic Apperception Test (N-TAT). *J. consult. Psychol.,* 1955, **19,** 83–89.

Eysenck, H. J., Granger, G. W., & Brengelmann, J. C. Perceptual processes and mental illness. *Maudsley Monogr. No. 2.* London: Chapman and Hall, 1957.

Feld, Sheila, & Smith, C. P. An evaluation of the objectivity of the method of content analysis. In J. W. Atkinson (Ed.) *Motives in fantasy, action, and society.* Princeton, N.J.: D. Van Nostrand, 1958, 234–241.

Feshbach, S. The drive-reducing function of fantasy behavior. Unpublished doctoral dissertation, Yale University, 1951.

Feshbach, S. The drive-reducing function of fantasy behavior. *J. abnorm. soc. Psychol.,* 1955, **50,** 3–11.

Feshbach, S. The influence of drive arousal and conflict upon fantasy behavior. In J. Kagan and G. S. Lesser (Eds.) *Contemporary issues in thematic apperceptive methods.* Springfield, Ill.: Charles C Thomas, 1961, 119–140.

Fine, R. A scoring scheme for the TAT and other verbal projective techniques. *J. proj. Tech.,* 1955, **19,** 306–309. (a)

Fine, R. Manual for a scoring scheme for verbal projective techniques (TAT, MAPS, stories and the like). *J. proj. Tech.,* 1955, **19,** 310–316. (b)

Fisher, S., & Morton, R. B. Levels of prediction from the TAT. *J. consult. Psychol.,* 1957, **21,** 115–120.

Foulds, G. A method of scoring the TAT applied to psychoneurotics. *J. ment. Sci.,* 1953, **99,** 235–246.

French, Elizabeth G., & Chadwick, Irene. Some characteristics of affiliation motivation. *J. abnorm. soc. Psychol.,* 1956, **52,** 296–300.

Frenkel-Brunswik, Else. Dynamic and cognitive categorization of qualitative material: I. General problems and the Thematic Apperception Test. *J. Psychol.,* 1948, **25,** 253–260.

Frenkel-Brunswik, Else, Levinson, D., & Sanford, R. N. The antidemocratic personality. In T. M. Newcomb, E. L. Hartley, *et al.* (Eds.) *Readings in social psychology.* New York: Holt, 1947.

Frenkel-Brunswik, Else, & Sanford, R. N. Some personality factors of antisemitism. *J. Psychol.,* 1945, **20,** 271–291.

Freud, S. The relation of the poet to day-dreaming. *Collected Papers.* Vol. II. London: Hogarth Press, 1953.

Friedman, I. Objectifying the subjective—a methodological approach to the TAT. *J. proj. Tech.,* 1957, **21,** 243–247. (a)

Friedman, I. Characteristics of the Thematic Apperception Test heroes of normal, psychoneurotic, and paranoid schizophrenic subjects. *J. proj. Tech.,* 1957, **21,** 372–376. (b)

Friedman, I. A critique of Shneidman and Farberow's "TAT heroes of suicidal and non-suicidal subjects." *J. proj. Tech.,* 1958, **22,** 281–283.

Fulkerson, S. C., & Barry, J. R. Methodology and research on the prognostic use of psychological tests. *Psychol. Bull.,* 1961, **58,** 177–204.

Garfield, S. L., & Eron, L. D. Interpreting mood and activity in TAT stories. *J. abnorm. soc. Psychol.,* 1948, **43,** 338–345.

Glass, H. L. The effects on fantasy of achievement motivation based on "fear of failure," and "hope of success." Unpublished doctoral dissertation, University of Pennsylvania, 1957.

Gluck, M. R. The relationship between hostility in the TAT and behavioral hostility. *J. proj. Tech.,* 1955, **19,** 21–26.

Goldman, Rosaline, & Greenblatt, M. Changes in Thematic Apperception Test stories paralleling changes in clinical status of schizophrenic patients. *J. nerv. ment. Dis.*, 1955, **121**, 243–249.

Greenbaum, M., Qualtere, T., Carruth, B., & Cruickshank, W. Evaluation of a modification of the TAT for use with physically handicapped children. *J. clin. Psychol.*, 1953, **9**, 40–44.

Haber, R. N., & Alpert, R. The role of situation and picture cues in projective measurement of the achievement motive. In J. W. Atkinson (Ed.) *Motives in fantasy, action, and society*. Princeton, N.J.: D. Van Nostrand, 1958, 644–663.

Harlow, R. G. Masculine inadequacy and compensatory development of physique. *J. Pers.*, 1951, **19**, 312–323.

Hartman, A. A. An experimental examination of the Thematic Apperception Technique in clinical diagnosis. *Psychol. Monogr.*, 1949, **63** (Whole No. 303).

Henry, W. E. *The analysis of fantasy: the Thematic Apperception Technique in the study of personality*. New York: John Wiley and Sons, 1956.

Henry, W. E., & Farley, Jane. The validity of the Thematic Apperception Test in the study of adolescent personality. *Psychol. Monogr.*, 1959, **73** (Whole No. 487).

Heppell, H. K., & Raimy, V. C. Projective pictures as interview devices. *J. consult. Psychol.*, 1951, **15**, 405–411.

Holt, R. R. The Thematic Apperception Test. In H. H. Anderson and G. L. Anderson (Eds.) *An introduction to projective techniques*. Englewood Cliffs, N.J.: Prentice-Hall, 1951, 181–229.

Holt, R. R. Formal aspects of the TAT: a neglected resource. *J. proj. Tech.*, 1958, **22**, 163–172.

Holt, R. R. The nature of TAT stories as cognitive products: a psychoanalytic approach. In J. Kagan and G. S. Lesser (Eds.) *Contemporary issues in thematic apperceptive methods*. Springfield, Ill.: Charles C Thomas, 1961, 3–43.

Hurley, J. R. Achievement imagery and motivational instructions as determinants of verbal learning. *J. Pers.*, 1957, **25**, 274–82.

Jensen, A. R. Aggression in fantasy and overt behavior. *Psychol. Monogr.*, 1957, **71** (Whole No. 445).

Jones, R. M. The negation TAT: a projective method for eliciting repressed thought content. *J. proj. Tech.*, 1956, **20**, 297–303.

Kagan, J. The measurement of overt aggression from fantasy. *J. abnorm. soc. Psychol.*, 1956, **52**, 390–393.

Kagan, J. Socialization of aggression and the perception of parents in fantasy. *Child Develpm.*, 1958, **29**, 311–320.

Kagan, J. The stability of TAT fantasy and stimulus ambiguity. *J. consult. Psychol.*, 1959, **23**, 266–271.

Kagan, J. Stylistic variables in fantasy behavior: the ascription of affect states to social stimuli. In J. Kagan and G. S. Lesser (Eds.) *Contemporary issues in thematic apperceptive methods*. Springfield, Ill.: Charles C Thomas, 1961, 196–220.

Kagan, J., & Lesser, G. S. (Eds.) *Contemporary issues in thematic apperceptive methods*. Springfield, Ill.: Charles C Thomas, 1961.

Kagan, J., & Mussen, P. H. Dependency themes on the TAT and group conformity. *J. consult. Psychol.*, 1956, **20**, 29–32.

Kagan, J., & Moss, H. A. Stability and validity of achievement fantasy. *J. abnorm. soc. Psychol.*, 1959, **58**, 357–364.

Karolchuck, Patricia A., & Worell, L. Achievement motivation and learning. *J. abnorm. soc. Psychol.*, 1956, **53**, 255–257.

Kerner, O. J. Stress, fantasy, and schizophrenia: a study of the adaptive processes. *Genet. psychol. Monogr.*, 1956, **53**, 189–281.

Klebanoff, S. Personality factors in symptomatic chronic alcoholism as indicated by the Thematic Apperception Test. *J. consult. Psychol.*, 1947, **11**, 111–119.

Kutash, S. B. Performance of psychopathic defective criminals on the Thematic Apperception Test. *J. crim. Psychopath.*, 1943, **5**, 319–340.

Lazarus, R. S. A substitutive-defensive conception of apperceptive fantasy. In J. Kagan and G. S. Lesser (Eds.) *Contemporary issues in thematic apperceptive methods.* Springfield, Ill.: Charles C Thomas, 1961, 51–82.

Lebo, D. The development and employment of VTAT's or pictureless TAT's. *J. Psychol.*, 1960, **50**, 197–204.

Lebo, D., & Harrigan, Margaret. Visual and verbal presentation of TAT stimuli. *J. consult. Psychol.*, 1957, **21**, 339–342.

Lennep, D. J. van. *Four-Picture Test.* The Hague: Martinus Nijhoff, 1948.

Lennep, D. J. van. The Four-Picture Test. In H. H. Anderson and G. L. Anderson (Eds.) *An introduction to projective techniques.* Englewood Cliffs, N.J.: Prentice-Hall, 1951, 149–180.

Lesser, G. S. Conflict analysis of fantasy aggression. *J. Pers.*, 1958, **26**, 29–41.

Lesser, G. S. Religion and the defensive responses in children's fantasy. *J. proj. Tech.*, 1959, **23**, 64–68. (a)

Lesser, G. S. Population differences in construct validity. *J. consult. Psychol.*, 1959, **23**, 60–65. (b)

Lesser, G. S. Custom-making projective tests for research. *J. proj. Tech.*, 1961, **25**, 21–31. (a)

Lesser, G. S. Studying needs in social contexts by means of computer simulation. Paper read at APA Symposium, 1961. (b)

Lesser, G. S., Krawitz, Rhoda, & Packard, Rita. Experimental arousal of achievement motivation in adolescent girls. *J. abnorm. soc. Psychol.*, 1963, **66**, 59–66.

Levy, D. M., Schumer, Florence C., & Zubin, J. *The Levy Movement Blots: a study of correlates and validity.* In preparation, 1964.

Libby, W. The imagination of adolescents. *Amer. J. Psychol.*, 1908, **19**, 249–252.

Libo, L. M. The projective expression of patient-therapist attraction. *J. clin. Psychol.*, 1957, **13**, 33–36.

Liccione, J. V. The changing family relationships of adolescent girls. *J. abnorm. soc. Psychol.*, 1955, **51**, 421–426.

Lindzey, G. Differences between the high and low in prejudice and their implications for a theory of prejudice. *J. Pers.*, 1950, **19**, 16–40.

Lindzey, G. Thematic Apperception Test: the strategy of research. *J. proj. Tech.*, 1958, **22**, 173–180.

Lindzey, G., Bradford, Jean, Tejessy, Charlotte, & Davids, A. The Thematic Apperception Test: an interpretive lexicon. *J. clin. Psychol. Monogr. Suppl.*, 1959, No. 12.

Lindzey, G., & Heinemann, Shirley H. Thematic Apperception Test: individual and group administration. *J. Pers.*, 1955, **24**, 34–55.

Lindzey, G., & Herman, P. S. Thematic Apperception Test: a note on reliability and situational validity. *J. proj. Tech.*, 1955, **19**, 36–42.

Lindzey, G., & Kalnins, D. Thematic Apperception Test: some evidence bearing on the "hero assumption." *J. abnorm. soc. Psychol.*, 1958, **57**, 76–83.

Lindzey, G., & Newburg, A. S. Thematic Apperception Test: a tentative appraisal of some "signs" of anxiety. *J. consult. Psychol.*, 1954, **18**, 389–395.

Lindzey, G., & Riecken, H. W. Inducing frustration in adult subjects. *J. consult. Psychol.*, 1951, **15**, 18–23.

Lindzey, G., & Silverman, M. Thematic Apperception Test: techniques of group administration, sex differences, and the role of verbal productivity. *J. Pers.*, 1959, **27**, 311–323.

Lindzey, G., & Tejessy, Charlotte. Thematic Apperception Test: indices of aggression in relation to measures of overt and covert behavior. *Amer. J. Orthopsychiat.*, 1956, **26**, 567–576.

Lindzey, G., Tejessy, Charlotte, & Zamansky, H. S. Thematic Apperception Test: an empirical examination of some indices of homosexuality. *J. abnorm. soc. Psychol.*, 1958, **57**, 67–75.

Little, K. B., & Shneidman, E. S. The validity of thematic projective technique interpretations. *J. Pers.*, 1955, **23**, 285–294.

Little, K. B., & Shneidman, E. S. Congruencies among interpretations of psychological test and anamnestic data. *Psychol. Monogr.*, 1959, **73** (Whole No. 476).

Louttit, C. M., & Browne, C. G. The use of psychometric instruments in psychological clinics. *J. consult. Psychol.*, 1947, **11**, 49–54.

Magnusson, D. A study of ratings based on TAT. Stockholm, Sweden: Grafikon, AB., 1959.

Mandler, G., Lindzey, G., & Crouch, R. G. Thematic Apperception Test: indices of anxiety in relation to test anxiety. *Educ. psychol. Measmt.*, 1957, **17**, 466–474.

Mandler, G., & Sarason, S. B. A study of anxiety and learning. *J. abnorm. soc. Psychol.*, 1952, **47**, 166–173.

McClelland, D. C. (Ed.) *Studies in motivation.* New York: Appleton, 1955.

McClelland, D. C. Interest in risky occupations among subjects with high achievement motivation. *Tech. Rept., Need Analysis Research Project NR 172–363* (Office of Naval Research, U.S. Navy, June, 1956). (*a*)

McClelland, D. C. Risk-taking in children with high and low need for achievement. *Tech. Rept. NR 172–363* (Office of Naval Research, U.S. Navy, July, 1956). (*b*)

McClelland, D. C. *The achieving society.* Princeton, N.J.: D. Van Nostrand, 1961.

McClelland, D. C., & Atkinson, J. W. The projective expression of needs: I. The effect of different intensities of the hunger drive on perception. *J. Psychol.*, 1948, **25**, 205–222.

McClelland, D. C., Atkinson, J. W., & Clark, R. A. The projective expression of needs: III. The effect of ego-involvement, success and failure on perception. *J. Psychol.*, 1949, **27**, 311–330.

McClelland, D. C., Clark, R. A., Roby, T. B., & Atkinson, J. W. The projective expression of needs: IV. The effect of the need for achievement on thematic apperception. *J. exp. Psychol.*, 1949, **39**, 242–255.

McClelland, D. C., & Liberman, A. M. The effect of need for achievement on recognition of need-related words. *J. Pers.*, 1949, **18**, 236–251.

McIntyre, C. J. Sex, age and iconicity as factors in projective film tests. *J. consult. Psychol.*, 1954, **18**, 337–343.

McIntyre, C. J. Evaluation of motion pictures to simulate reality in the Thematic Apperception Test. *USN Spec. Dev. Cent. Tech. Rep.*, 1955, No. SDC 269-7-47.

Meehl, P. E., & Rosen, A. Antecedent probability and the efficiency of psychometric signs, patterns, or cutting scores. *Psychol. Bull.*, 1955, **52**, 194–216.

Meyer, M. M., & Tolman, Ruth S. Correspondence between attitudes and images of parental figures in TAT stories and in therapeutic interviews. *J. consult. Psychol.*, 1955, **19**, 79–82. (*a*)

Meyer, M. M., & Tolman, Ruth S. Parental figures in sentence completion test, in TAT, and in therapeutic interviews. *J. consult. Psychol.*, 1955, **19**, 170. (*b*)

Morgan, Christiana D., & Murray, H. A. A method for investigating fantasies: the Thematic Apperception Test. *Arch. Neurol. Psychiat.*, 1935, **34**, 289–306.

Murphree, H. B., & Carnaghan, Jean G. A hypothetical basis for quantitative scoring of the Navy Thematic Apperception Test (N-TAT). *USN Submar. Med. Res. Lab. Rep.*, 1955, **14** (7) (No. 267).

Murray, E. J. Conflict and repression during sleep deprivation. *J. abnorm. soc. Psychol.*, 1959, **59**, 95–101.

Murray, H. A. (Ed.) *Explorations in personality.* New York: Oxford University Press, 1938.

Murray, H. A. *Thematic Apperception Test.* Cambridge: Harvard University Press, 1943.

Murstein, B. I. A conceptual model of projective techniques applied to stimulus variations with thematic techniques. *J. consult. Psychol.*, 1959, **23**, 3–14.

Murstein, B. I. The role of the stimulus in the manifestation of fantasy. In J. Kagan and G. S. Lesser (Eds.) *Contemporary issues in thematic apperceptive methods.* Springfield, Ill.: Charles C Thomas, 1961, 229–273.

Murstein, B. I. *Theory and research in projective techniques (emphasizing the TAT).* New York: John Wiley and Sons, 1963.

Mussen, P. H. Some personality and social factors related to changes in children's attitudes toward Negroes. *J. abnorm. soc. Psychol.*, 1950, **45**, 423–441.

Mussen, P. H., & Scodel, A. The effects of sexual stimulation under varying conditions on TAT sexual responsiveness. *J. consult. Psychol.*, 1955, **19**, 90.

Neugarten, Bernice L., & Gutman, D. L. Age-sex roles and personality in middle age: a thematic apperception study. *Psychol. Monogr.*, 1958, **72** (Whole No. 470).

Ossorio, Elizabeth D., & Rigby, Marilyn K. Thematic Apperception Test response patterns in the prediction of officer success. *ONR Research Contract N7 onr-40802 (NR 151–092), Technical Report No. 7*, March, 1957.

Phares, E. J. TAT performance as a function of anxiety and coping-avoiding behavior. *J. consult. Psychol.*, 1961, **25**, 257–259.

Pine, F. A manual for rating drive content in the Thematic Apperception Test. *J. proj. Tech.*, 1960, **24**, 32–45.

Piotrowski, Z. A. A new evaluation of the Thematic Apperception Test. *Psychoanal. Rev.*, 1950, **37**, 101–127.

Pittluck, Patricia. The relation between aggressive fantasy and overt behavior. Unpublished doctoral dissertation, Yale University, 1950.

Purcell, K. The TAT and antisocial behavior. *J. consult. Psychol.*, 1956, **20**, 449–456.

Rabin, A. I., & King, G. F. Psychological studies. In L. Bellak (Ed.) *Schizophrenia: a review of the syndrome.* New York: Logos Press, 1958, 216–278.

Rapaport, D., & Gill, M. M. On psychoanalytic metapsychology. Paper presented to the New York Psychoanalytic Society, March, 1958.

Ritter, Anne M., & Eron, L. D. The use of the Thematic Apperception Test to differentiate normal from abnormal groups. *J. abnorm. soc. Psychol.*, 1952, 47, 147–158.

Roby, T. B. Effect of need for security on thematic apperception. Unpublished master's thesis, Wesleyan University, 1948.

Rotter, J. B. Discussion of Dr. Shneidman's paper. In J. Kagan and G. S. Lesser (Eds.) *Contemporary issues in thematic apperceptive methods.* Springfield, Ill.: Charles C Thomas, 1961, 191–195.

Sanford, R. N. Foreword in Betty Aron, *A manual for the analysis of the Thematic Apperception Test.* Berkeley, Cal.: Willis E. Berg, 1949.

Sarason, Barbara R., & Sarason, I. G. The effect of type of administration and sex of subject on emotional tone and outcome ratings of TAT stories. *J. proj. Tech.*, 1958, 22, 333–337.

Sarason, S. B. The use of the Thematic Apperception Test with mentally deficient children. I. A study of high grade girls. *Amer. J. ment. Defic.*, 1943, 47, 414–421. (*a*)

Sarason, S. B. The use of the Thematic Apperception Test with mentally deficient children. II. A study of high grade boys. *Amer. J. ment. Defic.*, 1943, 48, 169–173. (*b*)

Sarason, S. B. Dreams and Thematic Apperception Test stories. *J. abnorm. soc. Psychol.*, 1944, 39, 486–492.

Saxe, C. H. A quantitative comparison of psychodiagnostic formulations from the TAT and therapeutic contacts. *J. consult. Psychol.*, 1950, 14, 116–127.

Schaefer, Judith B. Stability and change in Thematic Apperception Test response from adolescence to adulthood. Unpublished doctoral dissertation, University of Chicago, 1962.

Schafer, R. How was this story told? *J. proj. Tech.*, 1958, 22, 181–210.

Schwartz, L. A. Social-situation pictures in the psychiatric interview. *Amer. J. Orthopsychiat.*, 1932, 2, 124–133.

Scodel, A., & Lipetz, M. E. TAT hostility and psychopathology. *J. proj. Tech.*, 1957, 21, 161–165.

Scott, W. A. Research definitions of mental health and mental illness. *Psychol. Bull.*, 1958, 55, 29–45.

Sen, Amya. A preliminary study of the Thematic Apperception Test. *Brit. J. statis. Psychol.* 1953, 6, 91–100.

Shatin, L. Rorschach adjustment and the Thematic Apperception Test. *J. proj. Tech.*, 1953, 17, 92–101.

Shatin, L. Relationships between the Rorschach Test and the Thematic Apperception Test. *J. proj. Tech.* 1955, 19, 317–331.

Shatin, L. The constriction-dilation dimension in Rorschach and TAT. *J. clin. Psychol.*, 1958, 14, 150–154.

Shipley, T. E., & Veroff, J. A projective measure of need for affiliation. *J. exp. Psychol.*, 1952, 43, 349–356.

Shneidman, E. S. Psycho-logic: a personality approach to patterns of thinking. In J. Kagan and G. S. Lesser (Eds.) *Contemporary issues in thematic apperceptive methods.* Springfield, Ill.: Charles C Thomas, 1961, 153–190.

Shneidman, E. S., & Farberow, N. L. TAT heroes of suicidal and non-suicidal subjects. *J. proj. Tech.*, 1958, 22, 211–228.

Shneidman, E. S., Joel, W., & Little, K. B. *Thematic test analysis*. New York: Grune and Stratton, 1951.

Shore, A. Special developed TAT set for Mexican rural children. *Autoritarismo y agresion en una addea Mexicana*. Mexico, D. F., 1954.

Shorr, J. A proposed system for scoring the TAT. *J. clin. Psychol.*, 1948, 4, 189–194.

Sigel, I. E. Discussion of Dr. Kagan's paper. In J. Kagan and G. S. Lesser (Eds.) *Contemporary issues in thematic apperceptive methods*. Springfield, Ill.: Charles C Thomas, 1961, 221–228.

Singer, J. L., & Sugarman, D. A. A note on some projected familial attitudes associated with Rorschach movement responses. *J. consult. Psychol.*, 1955, 19, 117–119.

Stein, M. I. *The Thematic Apperception Test; an introductory manual for its clinical use with adult males*. Cambridge, Mass.: Addison-Wesley, 1948.

Stein, M. I. *The Thematic Apperception Test*. Cambridge, Mass.: Addison-Wesley, 1955.

Stern, E. *Experimentelle Persönlichkeitsanalyse nach dem Murray-Test (TAT)*. Zurich, Switzerland: Rascher Verlag, 1952.

Stone, H. The TAT aggressive content scale. *J. proj. Tech.*, 1956, 20, 445–452.

Sundberg, N. D. The practice of psychological testing in clinical services in the United States. *Amer. Psychologist*, 1961, 16, 79–83.

Takahashi, S. The comparative study of TAT results between college students and delinquent youths. *Memoirs fac. lib. arts*, Kagawa University, 1958, 11, 1–8.

Taylor, Janet, A. A personality scale of manifest anxiety. *J. abnorm. soc. Psychol.*, 1953, 48, 285–290.

Temple, R., & Amen, Elizabeth. A study of anxiety reactions in young children by means of a projective technique. *Genet. Psychol. Monogr.*, 1944, 30, 61–113.

Terman, L. M. and Merrill, M. A. *Measuring intelligence*. New York: Houghton Mifflin, 1937.

Tomkins, S. S. *The Thematic Apperception Test*. New York: Grune and Stratton, 1947.

Tomkins, S. S. The present status of the Thematic Apperception Test. *Amer. J. Orthopsychiat.*, 1949, 19, 358–362.

Ullmann, L. P. Selection of neuropsychiatric patients for group psychotherapy. *J. consult. Psychol.*, 1957, 21, 277–280.

Valentine, M., & Robin, A. A. Aspects of Thematic Apperception testing: depression. *J. ment. Sci.*, 1950, 96, 435–447. (*a*)

Valentine, M., & Robin, A. A. Aspects of Thematic Apperception testing: paranoid schizophrenia. *J. ment. Sci.*, 1950, 96, 869–888. (*b*)

Vernier, Claire M., Whiting, J. F., & Meltzer, M. L. Differential prediction of a specific behavior from three projective techniques. *J. consult. Psychol.*, 1955, 19, 175–182.

Veroff, J. Thematic apperception in a nationwide sample survey. In J. Kagan and G. S. Lesser (Eds.) *Contemporary issues in thematic apperceptive methods*. Springfield, Ill.: Charles C Thomas, 1961, 83–111.

Veroff, J., Atkinson, J. W., Feld, Sheila, & Gurin, G. The use of thematic apperception to assess motivation in a nationwide interview study. *Psychol. Monogr.*, 1960, 74 (Whole No. 499).

Veroff, J., Wilcox, Sue, & Atkinson, J. W. The achievement motive in high school and college age women. *J. abnorm. soc. Psychol.*, 1953, 48, 108–119.

Waxenberg, S. E. Psychosomatic patients and other physically ill persons: a comparative study. *J. consult. Psychol.*, 1955, 19, 163–169.

Weisskopf, Edith A. A transcendence index as a proposed measure in the TAT. *J. Psychol.*, 1950, 29, 379–390.

Windle, C. Psychological tests in psychopathological prognosis. *Psychol. Bull.*, 1952, 49, 451–482.

Wyatt, F. A principle for the interpretation of fantasy. *J. proj. Tech.*, 1958, 22, 229–245.

# 10 DERIVATIVES OF THE TAT
## AND COGNATE TECHNIQUES

This chapter will be devoted primarily to a discussion of modifications and derivatives of the TAT and pictorial techniques which have been popularly received, and for which there is at least some relevant literature concerning instrument-oriented questions such as reliability and validity. Such derivatives have been accepted as instruments or tests in their own right and, thus, their usefulness and rationale can be evaluated independently of the TAT.

In Chapter 9 mention was made of some of the problems involved in the selection of pictures for use in different studies. Experimenters who have investigated individual variables usually have started by selecting specific pictures which, it was felt, would point up the motivation, attitude, or defense in question. There are a few conditions, however, which may upset the expected relationships, and these should be considered.

In the selection of pictures, an assumption of greater identification with figures of the same physical type as S is frequently made; the researcher often introduces instruments which contain figures who are handicapped, Negro, etc. According to the accumulated evidence this assumption is not always valid. For example, Symonds (1939) pointed out that investigators who have used thematic apperception techniques to study children with special handicaps have found that the
474

stories contained no reference whatsoever to the specific handicap or item of behavior in which the experimenter was interested. He believed that the reason for this may be that if a child sought a solution for his problem in reality, "fantasy" solutions were no longer necessary. Thus, according to Symonds, a one-to-one relationship of TAT stories to overt physical, psychological, or behavioral manifestations should not be assumed. The inclusion of a number of neutral pictures which might help to determine the base line of an individual's reactivity to the thematic apperception situation itself should also be considered. Chapter 11 presents some material pertinent to these considerations, as well as material related to the overall question of the effect of the pictures themselves in determining the responses. That discussion points up the need for careful selection of stimuli when it is hoped to elicit information about a specific motivational system or area of interpersonal relations.

## DERIVATIVES NOT IN WIDESPREAD USE[1]

Although many illustrations of TAT adaptations and modifications have already been given, several additional examples are presented of early derivatives and modifications which have not received widespread attention. The first example comes from the field of attitude measurement. The use of pictures in attitude studies stemmed from the assumption that disguised techniques could be utilized to uncover opinions which individuals were unwilling or unable to reveal in more direct techniques.

The pioneer investigation in this field is that of Proshansky (1943), who was interested in the effect of attitudes toward labor on the perception of, and memory for ambiguous pictures of situations involving labor. He selected a series of pictures which, on the basis of judgments by three observers, were ambiguous with respect to outcome as far as labor was concerned. These pictures were exposed for five seconds each, and college Ss were asked to write for two and one-half minutes on what they thought each picture represented. Three judges rated these stories on a five-point scale, and it was found that their ratings of attitude toward labor on the basis of the stories correlated .87 and .67 in two groups (one anti-labor and one pro-labor) with scores obtained

---

[1] The next sections present only a partial listing. Note might be made of the IES Test (impulse, ego, and superego) developed by Dombrose and Slobin (1953, 1958), which utilizes 12 pictures for which S creates titles, and 13 incomplete cartoon series, which S completes by selecting a final cartoon, as well as two other subtests.

by the same subjects on the Newcomb (Verbal) Scale of Attitude toward Organized Labor. It would seem, then, that attitude toward labor, as measured by the Newcombe scale, is a factor in influencing the perception and elaboration of situations involving labor, and that we can get some measure of an individual's attitude toward labor by evaluating his responses to pictures such as those used in this study.

Wekstein (1945) was concerned with the limitations that he felt Murray had imposed on fantasy by using "concrete human forms" in his pictures. He developed a fantasy projection test of Disney-like figures surrounded by smoke and mist to give them a dream-like appearance. He also utilized color in his pictures; some were achromatic and without chiaroscuro elements; others contained one or more colored figures or objects. Murray and Stein (1943) devised a multiple-choice Rapid Projection Test in which pictures are shown on the screen and the S chooses from a list of possible alternatives the one he feels most adequately answers the questions: "What is he thinking? What is he feeling? What will he do? and How will it turn out?" Sentiments toward war, religion, parents, and sex were studied by Murray and Morgan (1945a, 1945b) through a variety of instruments which included the Picture Selection Test, made up of 225 pictures, depicting 45 foci of sentiments. The pictures were arranged in groups of five and the subjects selected those which they liked and disliked in each group. The choices that were made were found to reflect the sentiments of the eleven subjects in the study as revealed by other procedures. Henry (1947) made up a new set of cards, twelve line drawings, with characters and situations familiar to American Indian children and found that he was able to make a "blind analysis" of the Navaho and Hopi cultures which, in the opinion of independent experts, agreed with all the known facts available.

There are several additional modifications which have been offered as instruments in their own right. Although some relevant literature is already accumulating with respect to a number of them, in terms of either research or clinical usage, they have not as yet achieved widespread popularity. A listing of some of these instruments with brief descriptions and critical comment follows.

*Pictureless TAT.* Mention has already been made of a special type of TAT modification—a pictureless presentation of a verbal description of a scene which S either reads or which is read to S and to which he responds by constructing a story in traditional fashion. Lebo, who has done extensive work with this modification (Lebo [1958]; [1959]; [1960]; Lebo & Bruce [1960]; Lebo & Harrigan [1957]; and Lebo & Sherry [1959]), has suggested that such a presentation provides an opportunity for the S to construct his *own* mental pictures, thereby maximizing the "projective" process. Group administration procedures, intracultural investigations, and the testing of the blind are thus facilitated, according to this author.

In this procedure, S is presented with verbal descriptions of the standard TAT series based on Murray's original notations, or on those written by Rankin (see Lebo, 1960). For example, for Card 1: "A young boy is contemplating a violin which rests on a table in front of him" (Murray); "A boy is sitting at a table on which there is a violin and some papers which could be music" (Rankin).

Rankin, who is herself blind, has informally reported to Lebo that sighted and blind persons produce pretty much the same TAT content, even when the former are responding to pictorial stimuli. In general, other research with this modification has suggested that pictorial, printed, and vocal presentations are roughly equivalent in terms of a variety of measures.

*Puppet Film.* An interesting projective technique has been described by Haworth (1957, 1960, 1961), and Haworth and Woltmann (1959). This device consists of a puppet film, *Rock-A-Bye, Baby,* which can be shown to groups of 10 to 15 children. The story line is based on events concerning a young boy, Casper, who is jealous of his baby sister; he begs a witch to cast a spell on the baby's milk. After the baby is rushed to the hospital, the young hero is remorseful and kills the witch. There is a happy ending: the baby's health is restored and Casper is reassured of his parents' love. The test administration calls for stopping the film in the middle and having each S complete the story. At the end of the film presentation, S is individually asked a standard series of questions such as how Casper felt when the baby got sick, which part he liked best, etc.

A scoring system is available, as well as norms based on 244 children, from nursery school to fifth grade. Cross-validation of earlier empirical findings has been attempted (Haworth, 1961), with specific reference to some of the personality variables which are purportedly tapped by this instrument. These variables, which include identification; jealousy (sibling rivalry); aggression toward parents; guilt (masturbation); anxiety (castration); and obsessive trends, are reflected in the scoring scheme, but objectivity seems to differ from variable to variable. Average interscorer reliability coefficients for the four dimensions studied (Haworth, 1961) were: jealousy, .94; guilt, .83; anxiety, .92; and obsessive trends, .91. Reasons for the lowered coefficients for the guilt index have been explored and greater objectivity in scoring this index has been achieved.

The two samples studied, differing in socioeconomic status, yielded essentially the same results. There were also stable developmental progressions within and between samples which were felt to be evidence for the construct validity of the instrument.

*Thompson TAT (T-TAT)*. The initial presentation of a set of TAT cards designed especially for use with Negroes was described by Thompson (1949) (this set has been subsequently identified as the T-TAT). He assumed that if Negro figures were substituted for the white figures in the standard TAT (Murray, 1943 edition), the identification of Negro Ss would be increased. In this initial study, Thompson substituted figures in ten TAT cards: 1, 2, 4, 5, 6BM, 7BM, 8BM, 12M, 17BM, and 18BM. His subjects were 26 male Negro college students, tested first with either the T-TAT or the Murray TAT. There was an interval of one to seven days between tests. His basic measure of productivity was length of protocol. Thompson's null hypothesis, "there will be no difference in the productivity, as measured by the length of the protocols, between the data derived from the protocols obtained from the cards with Negroes pictured in them and the data from the protocols obtained from the cards with white people pictured in them" (p. 470), was rejected on the basis of his findings. He found that order of presentation and variation of time interval between test administrations did not influence the length of the protocols. He found, however, a difference, significant at the .01 level of confidence, between the T-TAT and the M-TAT, with the stories in response to the former being longer. Thompson concluded that identification with pictorial material of various cultural groups is increased when the pictorial material used reflects the culture of the individual.

Light (1955), in an investigation of the T-TAT, was interested in testing an extension of Thompson's identification assumption. Light worked with 26 white college students. To one matched half of this group he administered ten cards of the Murray TAT, and two weeks later the ten corresponding cards of the Thompson TAT. The second half of the group was given the sets of TAT cards in reverse order, at an interval of two weeks apart. Scoring included variables such as story length, theme content, and references and attitudes toward Negroes. The results, viewed in terms of Light's questions as to whether or not white Ss could identify as well with Negro as with white figures, and whether or not prejudicial attitudes would be evoked, indicated:

1. That there were no statistically significant differences in story length for the two TAT series.
2. That many white subjects were sensitive to differences in color on the two series of TAT cards.

3. That racial attitudes and prejudices were revealed in response to the T-TAT pictures, and where such attitudes existed, there seemed to be some impairment in projection.
4. That color did tend to make a difference in story content.
5. That a separate series of cards for Negroes may be warranted if Negroes possess similar racial attitudes and prejudices towards whites as whites possess toward Negroes (p. 150).

It should be noted that Light did not specify the characteristics of the subjects he worked with in regard to socioeconomic status and other pertinent variables. Cross-validation with another group seems quite appropriate. What *were* the specific attitudes of his Ss? Would these differ in a different college population? How can one generalize from a sample from West Virginia University, in 1955, to other colleges and universities?

Furthermore, some of Light's reasoning can be questioned. In a white-dominant culture, white Ss would surely learn to identify and be aware of Negro figures; in many settings, they would not be inhibited from expressing certain attitudes toward these figures. They have learned to do so in many subtle and not so subtle ways. Would a Negro respond the same way to *white* figures? Not necessarily. In a society in which the mass media—television, national magazines, and most of the literary and artistic output—are characteristically white, a Negro S confronted with *Negro* figures in a psychological test might not be *more* productive but less so. Might he not resent the special treatment, the implied "segregation" and "separatism" involved; or at least, depending on the Negro sample, would not some hostility as well as inhibition result when a Negro S is confronted with a test situation especially designed for Negro use? Riessman and Miller (1958) have made a similar point: The Thompson TAT may not be productive because the Negro is unfamiliar with having a "Negro Test." They have suggested that figures should be ambiguous as to race, rather than boldly Negro. Korchin, Mitchell, and Meltzoff (1950), in their evaluation of the T-TAT, have noted that the socioeconomic position of the Negro S is as important as his race in determining his response. It does seem, therefore, that the social milieu, ethnic background and attitudes, response sets, and the general social and cultural setting involved in a particular study are variables as important in a "clinical" study as they are in attitudinal studies.

*Iowa Picture Interpretation Test (IPIT)*. Hurley (1955) introduced the Iowa Picture Interpretation Test (IPIT), a multiple-choice variation of the TAT, as an attempt to integrate "the objective and quantitative advantages of traditional paper and pencil personality measures with the so-called 'depth' of projective techniques." Originally intended to objectify the scoring of $n$ Achievement as utilized by McClelland, Atkinson, and their associates, the scores were expanded to include other needs. For each of ten standard TAT cards, four brief alternative statements expressing achievement imagery, insecurity, blandness, and hostility were presented to Ss in groups, using slides exposed for 50 seconds. S was asked to rank the four choices from 1 to 4. Scores for each need consisted of the sum of ranks for all statements of that category. Means and S.D.'s for 455 young adults (undergraduates) were presented. Test-retest coefficients reported were moderately high as were measures of internal consistency. Limited validity evidence was provided, however. The tool seems to be promising, but much more normative evidence and validity data are needed. Since Hurley's original report, other forms of the test have appeared. Johnston (1957) has reported that one of the revisions (Form RK) is a more useful instrument for measuring achievement imagery than the other forms (O and RT).

*Cartoon Situations Test.* Shapiro, Biber, and Minuchin (1957) have described a technique developed out of their interest in predicting professional behavior—specifically, the teaching of young children. They were motivated by general dissatisfaction with techniques which had been used to predict teaching performance. Such techniques were either too directly concerned with concrete skills or specific opinions, or they attempted to assess global personality characteristics, and as such, were too general. Their technique, called the Cartoon Situations Test (CST), attempts to be neither too narrow nor too "global," according to the authors. On the basis of a careful job analysis of the particular teaching situation in which they were interested, they isolated what appeared to them to be relevant and important variables which should be tapped by any instrument purporting to predict teaching performance. The same job analysis suggested a framework for analyzing responses and pointed up the nature of the criterion measures which might be used.

The test itself contains seven cartoons of teachers, children, and parents in various situations. These cartoons were designed to tap variables such as S's "relation to authority," "depth of feeling for child experience," and "tendency toward hostile, punitive responses." The instrument is generally administered in group form with no set time limit. Ss are asked to write down what they see in each cartoon and to "develop some of the implications related to children, parents and teachers."

Some examples of these cartoons are: "I *Two young children playing:* One hands the other a doll saying, 'It's yours for keeps—until I want it.' IV *Family scene:* A mother looks at her young son who points to the baby elaborately tied to a chair with a ball of yarn; he says, 'Honest Mom, it was an accident.' VII *Block-building:* The children are building a structure of blocks which almost encases the teacher; only her head sticks out as she gaily says to a visitor at the door, 'For the first time this term they are really cooperating beautifully'" (pp. 174–175).

Analysis of records is based on a "systematic coding" method which, according to the authors, stresses personality attributes they thought to be relevant to their practical problem of prediction. Their validation sample consisted of 65 Ss (four of whom were males) ranging in age from 21 to 39, with a median age of 34. These Ss were students in a graduate teacher-training program. Intercoder reliability estimates were moderately low, at least not high enough to have practical usefulness for predictive purposes. There is no report of reliability of the instrument, based on split-half, equivalent form, or retest methods. The scorer reliability figures, it might be noted, are particularly low even for projective techniques where high scorer-reliability for many scoring systems is the rule rather than the exception. The authors have stated, however, that a revision of the scoring system should not only provide an opportunity to reassess reliability, but will probably result in increases in scorer reliability.

The validity criterion was based on ratings, made by members of the college staff, of student-teaching performance. These ratings were placed in the framework of an especially constructed "evaluation guide," which was oriented toward variables relevant to what the CST might be expected to predict.

Although the authors have reported some significant relationships to criterion measures, the number of such positive findings is not impressive in view of the large number of relationships tested. The poor scorer reliability, the lack of information concerning instrument reliability, lack of cross-validational evidence and normative data, and the small number of cases involved in the original validation study contribute to the lack of usefulness or objectivity of this instrument. But the authors have described some of their work-in-progress, which pays attention to the factors just noted. We will be interested in seeing whether or not more rigorous psychometric criteria have been applied. Although it is too early to evaluate the importance of the CST,[2] the

---

[2] A study (Zimiles, Biber, Rabinowitz, & Hay, 1964) which attempted to predict teacher performance from a group of personality tests, utilized the CST, among other measures. Findings based on the CST were rather discouraging, whereas those based on a sentence completion test and autobiographical data were

procedures used by the authors have been described in some detail because they highlight the problems involved in test development in the projective field.

## POPULAR DERIVATIVES AND OTHER PICTORIAL TECHNIQUES

*MAPS Test.* A variation of the TAT, whereby the subject constructs his own situation about which he then makes up a story, is the MAPS (Make-A-Picture Story) Test introduced by Shneidman (1948, 1949). In this procedure, S selects one or more cut-out figures from among 67 and places them in relation to 22 background pictures, presented one at a time. After arranging the characters with each scene, he tells a story about the situation he has created. Any figure can be placed with any background without violating realistic proportions. The figures include: adults and children, male and female, figures of indeterminate sex, animals, minority group figures such as Orientals, Negroes, and Jews, and legendary and fictitious figures. They are represented in various postures (mostly standing), with various facial expressions (including some blank faces), and in various stages of dress. The background drawings contain no figures, except in two cases (a head in a dream scene and an amorphous covered-up shape in a bed in the bedroom scene), portray a variety of settings (a forest, landscape, doorway, bathroom, closet, etc.), and vary in their degree of structuring from very ambiguous, for example, a stage, to completely structured, for example, a street scene. The examiner records S's placements and rejections by means of a figure location sheet and a figure identification card. The story is recorded in the same way as in TAT administration and, after it is told, the examiner may question S for more material ("Can you tell me more?") or for the title of the story. A more detailed description of this instrument, and its uses with children in particular, can be found in a report by Shneidman (1960).

Shneidman (1948) views his test as an attempt to add another "degree of freedom" to the TAT by giving S the opportunity to select the figures as well as to interpret and enliven the backgrounds. He reasons that if S is allowed to construct his own stimulus situation, he will be more apt to become engrossed in the procedure and give a more com-

---

more promising. The authors felt that subjectivity and complexity of CST scoring procedures, as well as the inadequate motivational level of the Ss, accounted, in part, for the failure of the CST to predict the criterion measures with any degree of success.

plete picture of his personal psychodynamics than would be obtained from the more stimulus bound type of projective test. Also, since he is required to use expressive activity in the test situation, S will reveal other facets of personality than are revealed in the projections of a mere story-telling procedure. Strongly influenced by psychodramatic techniques, Shneidman placed much emphasis on the formal aspects of his test. Thus the protocol content is less important than the more objective, scorable, and discernible part of the test—the choice, the placement, and interrelationships of the figures used in the constructions (e.g., see Burger, 1960).

In a validity study, Shneidman (1948) compared the responses of 50 normal and 50 schizophrenic veterans of World War II, equated for age and intelligence. He scored the productions according to ten test "signs": number of figures used, how often, where placed, which figure used, with whom interacting, kind of activity, meaning of figure, chronology, background, and total time used by the subject to select figures and tell the story. When treated statistically, this scoring led to the isolation of 64 significant (.10 level of confidence or beyond) signs for both groups. Using these significant signs, 42 of which characterized a greater proportion of normals and 22 a greater proportion of psychotics, Test Sign sheets were constructed for both normal and abnormal groups, and an attempt was made at "split-half" validation by developing a sign pattern based on the comparison of one half of the psychotics and normals and then applying this pattern without change as a "key" to the other half of the records, as though they were new cards. The author cautioned that the signs presented (which were the ones developed with the total population and hence not cross-validated) could not be used as general norms, and that to differentiate two other groups, a new sign pattern would have to be developed. It is well that the author was aware of this limitation since there are a number of statistical flaws in the design of this study which limit its generality, aside from the qualifications which the author made.

In devising the Test Sign list, the procedure was to list every possible sign and to test each one statistically. "The original list of signs was derived from a priori clinical judgment and logical deduction" (*Ibid.*, p. 179). Because of the selective character of these original signs, it is impossible to set a ceiling on the number of possible comparisons that could be made. In all, approximately 800 differences were evaluated, out of which 64 or eight per cent were found to be significant at or beyond the .10 level of confidence. This is less than would be expected to reach significance by chance.

Applicability of the MAPS Test to a different group was claimed by

Joel (1948), who investigated the productions of 50 disturbed adolescent boys and girls. He supplied frequency data for a number of formal characteristics, but there were no data from normal adolescents against which to evaluate the responses of the disturbed subjects. Goldenberg (1951) summarized a number of unpublished studies on samples which included aphasic, suicidal, neurotic, and hostile adults, and asthmatic children. Various qualitative characteristics were found which seemed representative of these groups, but no control groups were used against which the results could be evaluated.

In a study of homosexuality involving the use of several instruments, including the MAPS, Hooker (1957) has indirectly supplied some validity evidence, or lack of it, concerning the instrument. Rorschach, TAT, and MAPS protocols of 30 male homosexuals and 30 heterosexual males, matched for age, IQ, and education were given to three experts for ratings of adjustment. Pairs of protocols were also presented to the judges to see if they could correctly identify the sexual pattern of S from his projective material. Fairly good agreement between judges in adjustment ratings were found, but the two groups of Ss did not differ in terms of their adjustment ratings. As for distinguishing homosexual and heterosexual patterns from the protocols, the Rorschach experts could not do so on a better than chance basis. On the other hand, TAT and MAPS protocols were identified correctly far better than chance, but this was explained by the fact that almost all the homosexual Ss produced at least one homosexual story. These findings were used by Hooker in an attempt to shed further light on the nature of homosexuality. For example, she concluded, on the basis of her results, that homosexuality as a "clinical entity" does not exist, and that it may simply be a "deviation in sexual pattern" which is contained in the "normal range, psychologically." Such generalizations, it goes without saying, place great faith on the reliability and validity of these instruments. An equally plausible conclusion which Hooker does not seem to entertain would be that the instruments themselves are insensitive to differences in patterns of sexual adjustment; unless specific homosexual stories are produced, they fail to distinguish the groups. Moreover, Hooker's criterion—judge's ratings—may be invalid, or the instruments invalid, when ratings of adjustment are considered. In any event, this study does not help us to evaluate the instrument in terms of psychometric criteria. If anything, the evidence seems discouraging.

In another study, more specifically designed to explore validity and reliability of a particular scoring system applied to the MAPS, Spiegelman (1956) applied Fine's scoring system (see references, Chapter 9) for verbal projective techniques to MAPS protocols of 64 children, who had been referred to a child guidance clinic. These Ss were seen for a wide variety of psychological problems. There was excellent agreement among nine judges in the use of this system of scoring (coefficients for each of Fine's scores were .90 or higher), but the scores did not relate to age, sex, or referral problem. The author concluded that Fine's scoring system is reliable when applied to MAPS material, but that it probably is not sufficiently sensitive to have equal utility for all populations. We might add here, too, that this study fails to shed light on the instrument, as such. Would another scoring system distinguish the groups?

More encouraging results were reported by Bindon (1957) in her study of MAPS responses of deaf children. She worked with matched groups of rubella deaf, non-rubella deaf, and hearing 15-year-old children. The rubella deaf produced fewer "normal" signs and more "schizophrenic" signs than the nondeaf. The deaf and nondeaf were also distinguished by signs, but the rubella and matched non-rubella deaf Ss could not be so distinguished. The author concluded that the "social isolation and illogical unrealistic thinking" of the deaf are disclosed through their fantasy productions.

Some attempts have been made to control the wide range of background and figure combinations in order to assess the role of the stimulus in the MAPS. For example, Charen (1954) utilized two preselected backgrounds and five sets of characters; he presented the same sets of characters in each of the two backgrounds (ten sequences in all) to 25 male patients in a general hospital, and asked the Ss to tell stories to each stimulus presentation. His findings disclosed virtually no significant differences in the 24 scores he used when *background* was the independent variable. As the characters changed, however, many significant differences appeared. These findings suggest that the figures selected seem to influence responses more than the backgrounds—a suggestion which should be explored further with many other types of backgrounds, and combinations of figures and backgrounds.

Other studies involving the MAPS test have examined various details of administration and clinical use. Van Krevelen (1954), for example, concluded on the basis of a study with 20 normal adults, that stories told to E did not differ significantly from stories written in the absence of E, in terms of emotional tone, number of figures used, and particular figures selected. Studies such as some of those just noted provide only meager, vague evidence concerning the MAPS' validity.

Perhaps there are inherent difficulties in the MAPS technique from the point of view of test development. Although a study in which TAT and MAPS productions contributed by one patient were compared by fourteen experts showed that the area of agreement between the two techniques was large, and that scoring systems used with one are applicable to the other (Shneidman, Joel, & Little, 1951), a more careful scrutiny of differences in the *nature* of the two instruments suggests wherein the problems lie. The very advantage of stimulus flexibility, as compared to the TAT, may work as a disadvantage insofar as standardization of the MAPS might be concerned. Because the possible combinations of figures and backgrounds is so limitless, normative studies, which must be the forerunner of almost any kind of experimental treatment, are difficult to execute. For this reason, reliability and validity evidence for the MAPS have been rather slow in forthcoming. The methodological difficulties involved become even more evident when we view the problems in establishing such psychometric data when the stimulus is constant, as with the TAT. Since the MAPS test is so much less structured than the TAT, and the number of possibilities of response is so great, special experimental methods must be used to objectify and standardize the instrument. Charen's study (see earlier) would be an example of how certain controls over background-stimulus combinations could be introduced. Although a more or less rigid framework of scales and ratings would not be applicable in evaluating the MAPS because the number of possible combinations in test materials is great and, therefore, the number of possible situations and themes almost unlimited, some attempts could be made in the direction of assessing the types of backgrounds and figure arrangements chosen, and placing responses in the context of such settings. Simple checklists, ratings, and scaling procedures are difficult to apply in the MAPS situation, but they are not impossible.

As a clinical tool to be used "artistically," the MAPS may present similar problems to the clinician. Since the TAT pictures are more structured, depicting actual situations, S is forced to deal with the circumstance at hand; it is assumed, in an analysis of the protocol, that the way S interprets it is somehow related to the way in which he would react in real life to a similar situation (see discussion of assumptions underlying TAT in previous chapters). With the MAPS technique, however, he can arrange any kind of structure he wishes and in this way can easily avoid the implications of any situation with which he does not wish to deal. Thus, important material may be overlooked by allowing the subject to select the problems on which he will dwell. At the same time, however, there is the advantage of allowing the S greater freedom of response and permitting opportunities in which more aspects of his personality can be detected. As a matter of fact, the MAPS technique, despite its limitations as a *test* from a psychometric point of view, is said to be quite fruitful to the clinician, not only as a diagnostic aid, but in many aspects of psychotherapy, especially with children.

*Picture-Frustration Study (P-F Study).* An early pictorial method which tried to isolate and evaluate one particular aspect of personality was the Rosenzweig Picture-Frustration Study, or more properly, the Picture-Association Study for Assessing Reactions to Frustration (Rosenzweig, 1945). Rosenzweig has reviewed the historical background of his instrument as well as summarized research in connection with the children's form (1960). Pareek (1959) has also presented a review of studies concerning this instrument.

Although Rosenzweig was intimately connected with the Harvard personality studies out of which the TAT came into being (Murray, 1938), his theoretical and research interest in *frustration* was an outcome of his activities in experimentally validating certain psychoanalytic concepts and of his interest in psychoanalytic theory (see Rosenzweig [1960], especially pp. 149–150). Rosenzweig had not only classified types of reaction to frustration (1934), but had developed a behavioral test for measuring them (1935) before developing the F-Test, a four-part test of which one part (P, for Projective) was the "immediate forerunner" of the P-F Study. An outline of Rosenzweig's frustration theory as it was finally evolved (1944) was followed by a description of the picture-association method, and more specifically, his technique for measuring reactions to frustration (1945); the revised adult form was described by Rosenzweig, Fleming, and Clarke (1947) and the children's form by Rosenzweig, Fleming, and Rosenzweig (1948). According to Rosenzweig, "As a projective technique the P-F lies midway between the Word Association Test—historically the first of the projective methods—and the Thematic Apperception Test; it resembles the former in the association set induced by the instructions and the latter by virtue of the pictorial nature of the stimuli" (1960, p. 150).

The P-F Study consists of 24 cartoon-like pictures, each of which represents two characters involved in a mildly frustrating situation. The figure on the left is shown making a statement which either describes the frustration of the second figure or is itself actually frustrating to the latter. S is instructed to examine the situations one at a time and write in the blank "balloon" which is provided, the first reply that enters his mind as likely to be given by the anonymous figure. An Inquiry (nonleading) is conducted to help E score ambiguous responses. It is assumed that S identifies himself, consciously or unconsciously, with the frustrated individual in each situation, and that his responses thus are representative of his own characteristic ways of reacting to similar frustrations. The children's form also consists of 24 cartoon-like pictures; the frustrated character is always a child, and a majority of the pictures parallel the adult form. The children's form was developed for use with Ss ranging from four through thirteen years of age. Both forms of the P-F Study can be administered in groups.

Each response is scored according to Direction of Aggression and Type of Aggression (formerly called Type of Reaction). Direction refers to whether the response is: (a) extrapunitive, in which aggression is turned on to the environment; (b) intropunitive, whereby S turns the aggression upon himself; or (c) impunitive, in which aggression is evaded in an effort to gloss over the frustration in a conciliatory manner. The three Types of Aggression are: (a) obstacle-dominance, in which the barrier that causes the frustration is prominent in the response; (b) ego-defense, in which the response seems to refer to the ego-threatening qualities of the situation; and (c) need-persistence, in which the response emphasizes the solution of the frustrating problem. The nine factors thus represent a combination of Direction and Type of Aggression. A Group Conformity Rating (GCR)—a composite score —is derived from a comparison of each item score to the modal responses of the appropriate normative sample. Trends can also be determined—the tendency to shift from one mode of response in the first half of the record to another in the second half. Finally, various patterns of response to situations involving superego blocking are determined, based essentially on whether or not the character "assumes blame, absolves himself from blame, or attributes it to others."

The interpretation of the various scores, patterns, and trends, although based on a set of constructs and hypotheses, is firmly rooted in empirical data, for one of the unusual and advantageous aspects of the P-F Study is the early emphasis by its author on the construction of objective norms and the publication of numerous scoring samples and normative data (Rosenzweig [1950b]; Rosenzweig, Clarke, Garfield, & Lehndorff [1946]; and Rosenzweig, Fleming, & Clarke [1947]). For example, the GCR, described by Rosenzweig, as an "approximate index of social adjustment," tends to increase with age from four to nine years. This finding is based on an overall conclusion derived from a large number of normative studies of children, here and abroad, and is good evidence for the construct validity of the P-F, as pertains to the interpretation of the GCR. The wide normative evidence already accumulated similarly shows, as expected, that with age, extrapunitiveness decreases and intropunitiveness and impunitiveness increase.

Although early normative research tended to be based on large groups of normal Ss usually above average educationally (college and graduate student Ss tended to be "favored"), as is the case for studies reported by Rosenzweig (1950b), Bernard (1949a, 1949b) and Fry (1949)—the last study also included prison inmates—more recently, P-F research has been extended to a wide number of samples of all ages and groupings in this country and abroad. Much of such research has been focused on questions of validity, but provides, as an added benefit, considerable normative evidence.[3]

At this point, the wide popularity of this instrument should be noted, especially with respect to test-development research. The P-F has been particularly popular abroad, where various adaptations and normative studies (following Rosenzweig's initial example) have appeared. Perhaps the universality of the pictures and/or situations portrayed have been an appealing factor in the wide international distribution of the test, but, in addition, the instrument is easy to administer and is economical in terms of time and in being adaptable for group administration; scoring principles are easily taught, and, in contrast to a large number of other projective devices, interpretative aspects are concerned with a narrowly defined area with realistically testable constructs and hypotheses. Moreover, many workers are impressed with the psychometric status of the instrument. In France and Belgium, to cite one example, the P-F Study is widely used in the clinic to study juvenile delinquents and for vocational and educational guidance. In a review of P-F researches in these countries, Kramer (1958) noted that the popularity of the instrument is based on favorable reliability and validity findings.

Among the foreign adaptations there is a German children's form, complete with manual containing instructions for administration, scoring, and interpretation, as well as normative data (Duhm & Hansen, 1957); an adult German form, together with a manual containing similar material is also available (Hörmann & Moog, 1957). The P-F was also studied with a Finnish population. Finnish and American children, age 4–11, were compared in terms of P-F responses in a study by Takala and Takala (1957). This was a sociocultural rather than a normative study, however, in which P-F validity was assumed, and findings used to "explain" and "understand" ethnic and cultural varia-

---

[3] As is the case for the Rorschach, TAT, and other instruments discussed in this book, a review of researches in connection with the P-F Study is not possible. A complete bibliography (and the literature is extensive, indeed) has been compiled by Rosenzweig (Mimeographed Paper, 1955) and has been continuously updated (Mimeographed Supplements, 1957, 1959, and 1961).

bles. Standardization of the P-F (children's form) on 161 Sicilian children, age 6–13, was reported by Sacco (1955); adult male norms for Italian Ss, based on two groups of 100 each, ages 18–20 and 20–30, are also available (Banissoni, Misiti, & Nencini, 1955). Pichot, Freson, and Danjon (1956) have presented material pertaining to the standardization and scaling of a children's form of the P-F, based on a large group of French children, age 6–13. Even an African adaptation, standardized on 245 Congo children, is available, with norms compared to those of American children (Leblanc, 1956). Adaptations of the children's form in India and in Japan are available, and there are also adaptations of the adult form in France and Japan.

Problems of assessing the reliability of the P-F Study are similar to those already mentioned in connection with other projective techniques, especially with respect to split-half and test-retest methods. Scorer reliability seems quite good for both forms of the instrument. Clarke, Rosenzweig, and Fleming (1947) scored and rescored, at various time intervals, 343 different records. They reported 85% agreement between two scores on a sample of 100 normal records and 82% agreement on a sample of 25 clinical records. Rosenzweig (1960) reported over 80% initial agreement between two judges of scores of 300 Ss (children's form). In general, other authors have reported similar results (e.g., Pichot & Danjon [1955]; and Pareek [1958]).

Lowered estimates are obtained when other aspects of reliability are considered. Pichot and Danjon, in the study just noted, reported test-retest correlations ranging from .27 to .68; similarly, Pareek also reported lowered test-retest reliability. Bernard (1949a) reported a test-retest estimate of .45 for the GCR, and a range of .35 to .75 for Type and Direction of Agression scores; also, that consistency values for item reliability ranged from .51 to .79 with a modal value around .55. Clarke (1951), on the other hand, has stated that Rosenzweig had reported test-retest reliability coefficients of .60 to .80 on the adult form. More recently, Rosenzweig (1960) has described the results of odd-even item and test-retest correlation studies of the children's form. Results were encouraging (especially when viewed in the light of the discouraging nature of findings concerning other projective techniques), but again, as might be expected, not on the level of the high estimates reported for scorer reliability.

Before considering questions of validity, attention might be drawn to an extremely important problem concerning the "meaning" of P-F responses—a problem recognized and discussed by Rosenzweig at some length (1950c)—specifically the behavioral level being tapped by the instrument. We have already considered the ramifications of this problem as applied to other projective techniques, particularly the TAT. In this connection, Rosenzweig has noted:

Three possible levels of response must be considered in the evaluation of any protocol. There is, first, the *opinion* level, on which the subject gives self-critically censored answers such as he might make in the usual self-report questionnaire. A second and more naive level of response is the *overt*, which corresponds to what the person would actually say in a real life situation. . . . Finally, the subject's answers may reflect the *implicit*, covert or fantasy level of the personality. It is seldom possible in any projective method to differentiate these levels of response with certainty; the P-F Study shares this common fate (1960, p. 157).

The use of an Inquiry after the administration of the P-F can shed light on this general question, according to Rosenzweig. Especially in the children's form, if no information as to level is available, he has suggested that it is reasonable to assume that the second or overt level is being tapped. A study by Wechsberg (1951) has indicated, however, that there are important differences between groups of children (for example, normal and maladjusted) as to the level being tapped.

Some P-F validity research has been set into the framework of the "level" approach, for example, the study by Wechsberg just noted. Rosenzweig (1960) has described an early study which compared the degree to which the P-F responses and responses to a matched, open-ended questionnaire predicted S's everyday behavior (the P-F was found to be a better predictor of overt behavior than the questionnaire). According to Rosenzweig (1963), some of the contradictory and/or negative evidence reported concerning P-F response differences between physically assaultive and normal Ss is explainable by considerations concerning the level of response tapped by the instrument—a still unsolved problem for any given S at a given time.

The validity picture concerning the P-F Study is not consistent—a feature of projective techniques in general. Encouraging findings do exist, however; moreover, the constructs involved in the interpretation of responses are such as to permit, perhaps even encourage, specific, narrowly defined tests of validity—a desirable and rather infrequent state of affairs as far as most other projective techniques are concerned. Several P-F researches are described below—not as an attempt to review its extensive literature but to illustrate some of the various paths adopted by workers interested in exploring the validity of the instrument.

DuBois and Watson (1950) were unable to match Rosenzweig scores of police candidates with the criterion of success at the police academy. This study did not set up a "crucial" validation test, since the criterion, strictly speaking, is not relevant, a point which could be raised about a behavioral validation study reported by Boisbourdin, Michel, and Peltier (1956), who found that the French adaptation of the P-F Study did not differentiate successful student pilots from those who were eliminated in training, when the usual response categories were considered. Questions concerning the relevance of the criterion can also be raised with respect to a study by Wallon (1956), who compared the P-F responses of a group of cadets who had completed their flight training to those of a group of cadets who voluntarily withdrew from training. There were no significant differences between the groups. An examination of responses of Ss who withdrew, however, did yield some interesting findings. Ss who withdrew at the beginning of the flight training program were significantly more extrapunitive and significantly less impunitive than those who withdrew during advanced training.

Holzberg and Posner (1951) used an apparently more adequate criterion for testing the validity of the Picture-Frustration Study. A group of 47 student nurses who had been rated by their superiors and fellow students on "aggressiveness" were administered the Picture-Frustration Study and the Allport Ascendance-Submission Reaction Study; no reliable relationship was found between the Rosenzweig scores and any one of the criterion measures, even among those who made extreme scores. A slight, although not significant, correlation of the P-F scores with responses to four TAT cards suggested to the authors that although there was no relation between P-F responses and overt behavior, the former might be a measure of the presence of aggression in the fantasy life of the individual.

Even when such "outside" criteria are used, there are many difficulties. For example, Rosenzweig (1960) distinguishes aggression from hostility, the latter being only one form of aggression. Aggression is related to assertion, and if constructive or positive, can be conceptualized as need-persistence, whereas negative or destructive aggression can be conceptualized as ego-defense. A general question can thus be raised as to whether or not ratings on "aggressiveness" may be measures which are too crude to test the validity of various P-F scores.

It would seem that an instrument such as the P-F Study would lend itself easily to validation research involving certain "natural" samples, such as assaultive Ss or delinquent Ss whose aggression is "built in." This has actually been done; studies involving comparisons of normal and criminally aggressive groups, however, have failed to yield significant findings in most instances. A few studies (e.g., Pareek, 1960a) did yield expected differences, but some (e.g., Lindzey & Goldwyn, 1954) resulted in findings virtually opposite from what might be expected. Rosenzweig (1963) has briefly summarized some of these studies, and, as already noted, indicated that the contradictory results in this area are explainable by failure to account for the level—opinion, overt, or implicit—involved in the P-F response of the different Ss. Contradictory findings are perhaps less baffling when viewed in this light. Only one research in this area is described here, for general illustrative purposes.

Kaswan, Wasman, and Freedman (1960), in an extensive study of the validity of the P-F Study in a variety of different contexts, utilized not only a measure of P-F extrapunitiveness but also a measure of the intensity of this variable. These P-F scores (Ss were 121 male prison inmates) were related to 22 measures of aggression obtained from the Rorschach, an attitude scale, a psychiatric interview, and case material. Although many more significant relationships were found than could be attributed to chance, it was found that the P-F scores were not related to other, equally good criteria of aggression. The problem of evaluating construct validity was complicated by the fact that the authors, admittedly, could find no "rationale" or framework for explaining why or how and under what circumstances P-F scores could be expected to predict or not to predict aggressive behavior. Although they felt that with a large number of successive samples, P-F scores would relate more often to some criterion measures than others, with simple cross-validational procedures, such consistency would probably not be found. "Since even elaborate matching procedures are unlikely to yield identical samples of Ss, different samples can be expected to show different interrelationships between a particular measure, such as the P-F, and other measures designed to reflect a range of that attribute (e.g., Rorschach, attitude scale, other measures of aggression)" (p. 452). Although the authors felt that some validity evidence was provided by their study, they concluded that the P-F did not measure any particular level or aspect of aggression. It was suggested that "repeated cross-validation would be required before possible criteria validity could be established" (Ibid., p. 452).

Another group of validity studies is concerned with the degree and quality of shifts in P-F responses after frustration (usually artificially induced). The stress in design of some of these studies is not on exploring the sheer increase of so-called aggressive responses, but the kinds of shifts, if any, in direction of aggression elicited. Findings in this area have been, it would seem, somewhat encouraging, although not consistently so. Bennett and Rudoff (1960) found some support for a previously reported finding that prisoners tended to shift in P-F responses from extrapunitive to intropunitive, as a result of incarceration. Pareek (1960a) also found some significant shifts in Indian children's responses after artificially-induced frustration. Lindzey's Ss (1950) showed an increase in extrapunitiveness after frustration in an OSS (1948) situation under conditions of hunger, pain, need for bodily relief, and general discomfort; and the P-F study was more sensitive in this regard than four cards of the TAT scored in a specific way. Actually, extrapunitive and intropunitive scores, as measured by the two methods, were not correlated. Simos (1950) got less favorable results when he tested 24 neurotic and 24 psychotic patients before and after stress and frustration. He also found no relationship between scores on the test and psychiatric ratings of Rosenzweig's six categories, using all material available except the Picture-Frustration data.

No differences were found by Franklin and Brozek (1949) in their starvation studies among four caloric rehabilitation groups after 24 weeks of semistarvation, and then after 12 weeks of rehabilitation, although other physiological and psychological tests did differentiate the groups and their overt behavior changed markedly over this period. It should be mentioned that Rosenzweig (1950a) questioned the validity of this study since the nature of the criterion is uncertain—what significance the subjects attached to the experience in terms of frustration and just what the nature of the frustration was. Also, the investigators did not administer the Picture-Frustration Study before starvation, and they did not have a matched control group of subjects.

The accumulated extensive normative material concerning the P-F Study has been noted. Much of this material has considerable significance with respect to questions of validity. The impressive, detailed normative research of Pareek (Indian adaptation of the children's form) is perforce, and by design, of significance with respect to questions of validity (e.g., Pareek 1960a, 1960b), with rather encouraging results.

Rosenzweig (1960) has described various validity researches with the children's form which also appear to have rather promising results. Some of the methodologies employed represent interesting deviations from the more conventional attacks on the general problem. For example, in one study (Elementary School Project), on the basis of teachers' reports, Ss were classified into five social adjustment groups based on *pattern* of behavior, rather than on whether or not Ss were more or less aggressive; in another study (Mirmow, 1952), the "method of successive clinical predictions" was used. Briefly, this method consists of the following steps: (a) several judges attempt to predict an S's responses to a projective instrument on the basis of case history and relevant test data; (b) the success of these "composite" predictions is then determined, and the previous hypotheses concerning the "meaning" of the instrument are revised accordingly; and (c) the revised hypotheses are subjected to "testing" by repeating step (a) with another S, and so on, for successive Ss and hypotheses. The validity of the hypotheses concerning the instrument are presumed to increase at each step of this process —validity being measurable by the success as well as the improvement of the judges, as the composite, global prediction process continues.

Other researches in connection with the children's form have yielded differences between normals and Ss seen at a child guidance clinic (Rosenzweig & Rosenzweig, 1952). Various P-F scores have also been shown to distinguish the following groups of children: persistent enuretics, recurrent enuretics, and nonenuretics (Lord, 1952); diabetics and nondiabetics (Johannsen & Bennet, 1955); Ss divided into three categories according to sociometric status—high, middle, and low (Coons, 1957); Ss attending either a "traditional" or a "progressive" school (Mensh & Mason, 1951); and Ss with high or low suggestibility scores on a specially devised test (Kates, 1951). These studies are among a larger group which directly or indirectly add to a body of evidence concerning the construct validity of the P-F.

Evidence is also accumulating concerning the relationship of various P-F scores to those of other instruments. For example, in a comparison of P-F responses and experience–balance type on the Rorschach, Palmer (1957) reported some positive findings. Levitt and Lyle (1955) found that two groups of children, distinguished by having extremely high or low scores on the Problems Situations Test (an instrument devised by these authors which elicited responses scorable as punitive or nonpunitive), differed significantly from each other on several P-F variables.

Finally, in line with recent trends in both TAT and Rorschach research, there has been some attention to the effect of set and instructions on P-F responses. That these factors do influence P-F responses was indicated in a study by Wallon and Webb (1956). These workers administered the P-F test to two groups of naval aviation cadets. One group was given the standard instructions, and the other group was told to respond in the most socially acceptable manner. Significant differences in responses between the two groups were found for four of the six scales used. Silverstein (1957) reported a study in which the P-F test was administered to 42 Ss with three different sets of instructions —standard, "make the very best impression," and "make the very worst impression." Faking of scores was considerable in both directions, but greater changes were found under instructions calling for making the "worst impression." P-F scores, the author concluded, are susceptible to considerable faking. Mausner (1961) has reported differences in P-F scores between two comparable samples of engineers and accountants differing with respect to whether or not the instrument was administered anonymously or as part of an appraisal program.

In summary, then, it can be concluded that the P-F Study, in terms of objectivity and scoring procedures, simplicity of administration, and general psychometric characteristics, as well as the accumulation of norms, and reliability and validity evidence, stands up more favorably than many other projective instruments. Its adaptability for use with normals of all ages, as well as the specificity of its interpretative constructs, allows not only for widespread application inside and outside the clinic, but makes possible the kinds of tests of validity which are considerably more difficult to apply to other projective techniques. It is hoped that such research continues, especially in the direction of understanding further the role of the *individual* stimulus situations in eliciting certain types of responses. The "levels of behavior" problem about which Rosenzweig has so aptly written deserves (and will hopefully receive) considerable attention, not only with respect to the P-F Study, but also with respect to other projective techniques. Without further knowledge as to just what stratum of personality we are tapping when we elicit a projective response, our search for validity evidence will yield disappointing results, despite the reasonable levels of reliability we may achieve with our instruments.

*Blacky Pictures.* A TAT derivative which is even more closely wedded to theory than the Picture-Frustration Study is the Blacky Pictures, originally devised by Blum (1949). This technique attempts to evaluate the status of the subject's psychosexual development in terms of a number of specific psychoanalytic variables. Test findings are then used to validate the theory from which the technique grew. Some implications of this marriage of theory and test, and some criticisms of the design of the original experiment have been discussed by Seward (1950). Uses of this test with children have been described by Blum (1960).

The test itself consists of 11 cartoon drawings of a family of dog figures—Mama, Papa, and Blacky, presented as a young dog of the same sex as the subject, and Tippy, a sibling of unidentified age and sex. The cards are very highly structured to suggest specific problems of psychosexual development, including: oral eroticism, oral sadism, anal expulsiveness, anal retentiveness, Oedipal intensity, masturbation guilt, castration anxiety in males, penis envy in females, positive identification, sibling rivalry, guilt feelings, ego ideal, and narcissistic or anaclitic love object. The same cartoons are used for both sexes, but the sexes are tested separately. In the original experiment, the test was administered in group form with the Ss instructed to write a vivid story in two minutes. After each story a series of questions with multiple-choice answers was presented. In addition, each S was asked to select the pictures most liked and most disliked and to record what he thought was the purpose of the test and his general reactions to it. Also, data about the S's siblings were requested. On the basis of these five data sources, interpretations were made concerning the psychosexual history and status of the Ss. The original investigation included 119 male and 90 female students in elementary psychology.

Blum's basic assumption is that psychoanalytic dimensions are validly measured by his test, and thus that the psychosexual theory of development can be tested by it. He looked for concomitance between test results and psychoanalytic postulates in terms of sex differences in psychosexual development and through various interrelations which exist between the psychoanalytic dimensions. Only statistically significant differences were examined by Blum in this analysis, since he believed that insignificant differences would show that the test, not the theory, was ineffective. In going from test responses to theory, Blum outlined 13 dimensions assumed to be measured by the test (see foregoing list) and, on the basis of the five sources of data mentioned, rated S's strength of involvement in each of them, as strong, fairly strong, weak, or absent. Thus each individual's test responses could be expressed as a profile of scores along the dimensions. Although an attempt was made to set up scoring standards, Blum preferred a qualitative approach which searched for a psychosexual pattern lending congruence to data in all dimensions. He recommended that the experimenter scoring the test be well grounded in psychoanalytic theory and projective methods, since qualitative interpretation should proceed on the basis of looking for latent content rather than in terms of face-value acceptance of the S's statements.

In the area of sex differences, out of 121 comparisons between men's and women's responses (in regard to: (a) total scores on each dimension; (b) answers to items in the Inquiry; and (c) number ignoring introductory comments on two cards—anal sadism and masturbation guilt), 23 yielded chi squares significant at the .05 level of confidence or beyond. These significant differences were divided into fourteen areas, and on the basis of an examination of psychoanalytic theory as presented by Freud and Fenichel, it was found that explicit predictions could be made in seven areas; and in six of these, predictions from the test were in agreement with the theory. In two of the areas psychoanalytic predictions could be inferred, and both were in agreement with the Blacky data. Differences in the five remaining areas could not be explained by existing theory. In the intercorrelations of the psychoanalytic dimensions, in which total score on each dimension was correlated with total score on every other dimension, out of 225 tetrachoric correlations, 28 were significant at or beyond the .05 level of confidence. These correlations were arranged into seventeen theoretical relationships, eight of which were specifically covered in psychoanalytic writings. Six were inferred from the theory and three were not found in the literature. The experimental data upheld both the eight specific interrelationships and the six inferred ones, suggesting that the dimensions were related to each other in a nonrandom manner. Blum's conclusions, "these data strongly suggest that some aspects of psychoanalytic theory have demonstrable validity," were modest in the light of these rather tentative findings, and he suggested that more work be done to validate the test and its underlying assumptions.

As noted, Seward (1950) has pointed out some logical flaws in the design of the original experiment. His chief criticism was that Blum, after the administration and scoring, abandoned the deductive procedure in favor of an empirical one. Instead of selecting data relevant to the theory in question, he made all possible comparisons and then selected certain findings on the basis of statistical significance; he then returned to the theory to look for hypotheses to test. This order of procedure involves the twofold danger of taking into account neither all the relevant data nor all the theoretical implications involved. Consideration of only statistically significant data is fallacious, since statistically insignificant data are just as relevant in the proof or disproof of the theory involved. Seward also warned that in working from data to theory there is the danger of interpreting the data to fit the theory and that, inasmuch as psychosexual theory is not rigidly defined, logical flaws in the structure might easily escape detection in such a procedure. He therefore believed that before any experimental attempt could be made to test the theory, the postulates, theorems, and their logical articulations must first be exposed. Only then can we definitely say that a given finding confirms or refutes a theory. Despite these objections, however, Seward challenged only a few of Blum's specific findings and interpretations.

There are further flaws in this experiment which were not taken into account by Seward in his published critique of the Blacky Study. The most obvious one is the spurious nature of the "statistically significant" expected and obtained differences. Because 51 out of 346 differences were found to be significant at the .05 level of confidence when only 17 would be expected by chance, it does not mean that these are "real differences" nor does it reveal which are the "real" and which are the "chance" differences. Also, chance expectancy for agreement can hardly be established since, with such a "loose and sprawling" theory, there can be no estimation of the total number of theoretical predictions possible.

A shortcoming, insofar as the clinical utility of the scheme is concerned, as well as its experimental verification, has been the subjective nature of the scoring. Blum advised that the experimenter must be well grounded in psychoanalytic theory, individual interpretations of which, it may be added, are by no means consistent. Scoring decisions were left largely to clinical hunches concerning latent content rather than explicit demonstrations of what was manifest in the response. This affects interpretations of the data in ways which can be crucial.

Noting the a priori nature of the original scoring system, Blum (1962) has reported the results of an extensive research, designed to derive a new system. The sample consisted of 210 male college students. For each of the 11 cartoons, all Blacky themes were coded as well as data from the Inquiry; expressed preference (as well as judgments of "best" or "worst") and related comments made with respect to other cartoons were also noted. A large-scale factorial study of these data yielded 30 factors, each of which is utilized in the scoring system. A reservoir of supplementary information with respect to some of the subjects (44 Ss) was available, including scores for the Strong Vocational Interest Blank, Allport-Vernon-Lindzey Study of Values, and a test of perceptual accuracy; data from a biographical questionnaire as well as other test and nontest sources were also available for these Ss. For 155 Ss, number of siblings, their ordinal position, and sex were known, and for 71 Ss, also their college major.

Blum's report consisted primarily of a presentation of the 30 factors which comprise the scoring system, a listing of positive and negative relationships found to other factors, as well as to the data derived from the supplementary sources, and an interpretation of the "meaning" of the factors which "represent the author's own best syntheses of the currently available data." This comprehensive scoring system should of course be subjected to empirical tests of validity and reliability. But it seems to represent a refinement as well as an expansion of the earlier system. Blum rightfully reminds the reader that the new scoring system is based on a normal male college sample, that was administered the test in group sessions, and that similar studies with other groups (age, socioeconomic, psychiatric, female, etc.) should be initiated. Data relevant to construct validity are contained in this report, but reliability data with respect to this revised system are not presented.

What about earlier reliability studies? Charen (1956a), in a test-retest study of the reliability of the Blacky Test, reported generally low figures. A battery of tests had been given to tuberculosis patients at an early stage of illness, and again, four months later, at the end of the recovery period. He noted that the "measurement of reliability of the Blacky was possible in view of the test-retest situation and evidence from (the) other tests that no basic personality changes occurred during the four month period of recovery" (p. 16).

Blum (1956), in a brief reply to Charen, suggested that Charen's reasoning was faulty. He expressed disapproval not only of the scores Charen used in his estimates of reliability, but noted that the test had been administered incorrectly, that is, spontaneous stories were not elicited prior to the multiple-choice items Charen used. Furthermore, Blum noted, the use of other tests, especially the Rorschach as a "test" of the validity of the Blacky Test, is not justified; and the retest method, because it reflects unknown changes in variables such as set and familiarity with items as well as personality changes, is not an adequate measure of reliability.

Continuing the lively discussion, Charen (1956b) noted that since the multiple choice items from the Inquiry are one of the four sources which contribute to major Blacky scores, its low reliability is actually quite pertinent to the question of the reliability of the instrument as a whole. Charen also suggested that since Blum had not reported reliability studies for either the test as a whole or its four scoring sources, he had no way of knowing whether or not the omission of the spontaneous stories influenced the reliability. He once again indicated that since the Rorschach and fifteen paper-and-pencil tests suggested no evidence of personality changes, the changes indicated by the multiple-choice items of the Blacky Test could be attributed to low reliability. He also noted that some of Blum's objections to test-retest evaluation of the Blacky's reliability are not warranted, that is, according to Charen: "The question of set should not be involved in the Blacky Test as it might be in other personality tests since his (Blum's) scoring allows for evasiveness or attempts to use defenses. Familiarity with items is not likely to be a problem when a four-month or longer period elapses between the test and retest. Finally, since the Blacky Test purports to measure 'the deeper recesses of personality' (Blum & Hunt, 1952), namely the genetic psychosexual dimensions which should not change in the individual unless psychoanalysis or a marked life experience occurs, personality change is also not a factor which prevents use of the retest method" (p. 407). Charen here seems to take for granted the validity of the instrument (as a measure of genetic psychosexual dimensions) and uses this as an argument to state that the instrument is unreliable!

Although loth to add to these rebuttals, we cannot refrain from noting that Charen's reasoning and rationale do not appear to be convincing. On the other hand, since the "proof" of reliability lies not in contentious discussion but in demonstration, the question of reliability, unfortunately, is still not adequately handled by either worker.[4]

The Blacky Study suffers from the same limitations in its standarization population as do other projective devices, indeed as does the great bulk of psychological data which is based chiefly on responses of college Ss. The Blacky Study is even more vulnerable on this score, however, since a knowledge of psychoanalytic theory—even a smattering—could conceivably influence an S's responses to a significant degree. To assume that college sophomores are fairly naive because they have not yet covered the section of the introductory psychology course dealing with psychoanalytic concepts, seems in itself a little naive. Results based on a less selected population would be more convincing. The need for validation studies is especially important because the stimulus material itself has such obvious face validity—the pictures are so highly structured that it is unlikely that any material other than the desired psychoanalytic data would be forthcoming.

Studies in which various clinical groups of individuals with common dynamics are compared with each other and with normal groups are essential. Blum and Hunt (1952) made a preliminary report of some published and unpublished studies with the Blacky Pictures. These studies covered a wider variety of subjects and criteria and give cumulative evidence of some validity for the technique, although admittedly "one may find the seeds of ad hoc reasoning, capitalization on chance and kindred sins" (*Ibid.*, p. 249) in the studies which they summarized.

In a factor-analytic study of the validity of some of the assumptions underlying the Blacky Test, Neuman and Salvatore (1958) worked with Blum's original data. Although the factors found for a group of males corresponded roughly with the psychoanalytic oral, anal, phallic, Oedipal, latency, and genital areas, this was not true for a group of

---

[4] Moderately good reliability estimates were reported by Granick and Scheflen (1958) in their study of Blacky responses of children age 6–11.

females. The authors concluded that their results partially confirmed the validity of the test as well as of psychoanalytic theory as applied to males only. It is difficult to interpret these findings, however, in view of the results with the female Ss. Rossi and Solomon (1961) reported findings based on a semantic differential study, which indicated that college females rated the words "dog" and "Blacky" as significantly more masculine than the word "cat." It was suggested that the Blacky Pictures are probably more appropriate for males than females. In another type of validity study, Bernstein and Chase (1955) studied three hospitalized groups—an ulcer group, a nonulcer psychosomatic group, and a nonpsychosomatic group. Although a small number of significant differences were found with respect to various scoring dimensions, most comparisons yielded nonsignificant findings. Moreover, the dimension of "oral-eroticism," considered to be of considerable significance in a comparative study of this type, did not differentiate the groups. The authors concluded that the Blacky Pictures lacked discriminating ability with respect to the particular Ss with which they worked.

The foregoing findings suggest that the Blacky technique has not yet reached a stage of development where it can be used with confidence psychometrically, despite the clinical usefulness attributed to it.

*Children's Apperception Test (CAT)*. Another TAT derivative which uses animal figures is Bellak's Children's Apperception Test (1949). The need for such a derivative was apparent, since only three of the standard TAT cards were designed specifically for children, and, on the whole, the pictures are structured at an adult level of emotional experience. Although Leitch and Schafer (1947) had demonstrated that the standard set had applicability even for nursery school children, the material it provides is admittedly scanty, and this may be because the pictures are "traumatic" enough to result in blocking or resistance. Bellak, rather than design a series of cards representing young children with whom the subjects could easily identify, as did Symonds with his pictures for adolescents, used animals as the central characters. The rationale for this had been suggested by Ernst Kris, who assumed that animals might be the preferred identification figures for children aged three years to ten. This is also an hypothesis of certain Rorschach investigators (e.g., Klopfer & Kelley, 1942) but its validity had up until that time never been adequately tested. Another advantage which the author cited is the culture-free aspect of these stimuli since they are equally within the life experience of Negro children as well as many others in the western European cultural framework. However, just as no test can be absolutely culture free, neither can this one, since there are obvious socioeconomic and urban-rural variations which would differentially affect the ability of children to empathize with animals. Furthermore, the anthropomorphized animals in this series are outfitted with such culture tainted accessories as hats, pipes, tables and chairs, and bathrooms.

These ten test cards, like the Blacky Pictures, were designed to elicit material in certain areas of psychosexual development: feeding (oral) problems, sibling rivalry, attitudes toward parents and relation to parents as a couple ("the Oedipal complex and its culmination in the primal scene"), aggression, acceptance, loneliness (masturbation), and toilet behavior and the parents' response to it. Through the analysis of responses to these pictures, similar to Bellak's procedure with the standard TAT (Bellak, 1951), it was hoped that the dynamics of interpersonal relationships, drive constellations, and defenses could be obtained. It was recommended that the interpreter be thoroughly grounded in child psychology and psychoanalytic theory. Although the author provided typical responses to the cards based on a "sample population of 100 children of all ages between three and ten and of various ethnic and socioeconomic backgrounds," and although he did present some analyses of test results which are basically psychoanalytic, few quantitative data were given. There was no information as to reliability and validity since the author quite frankly admitted that he did not feel this type of test required it. He did state that norms for different age levels would be desirable, but realized that it is impossible for one team of investigators to assemble all that are needed.

More recently, norms for various groups of children have been reported, such as those presented by Boulanger-Balleyguier (1957), based on 105 French children age three to seven (approximately ten boys and ten girls at each age). In addition to listing various aspects of the S's response to the CAT, this author noted that "genetic evolution of responses" was found, since with increased age, the Ss gave more exact and elaborated responses which were increasingly coordinated with the stimulus. Another normative study was reported by Lehman (1959), based on 160 Canadian children of kindergarten age. There were twenty boys and twenty girls in four socioeconomic groups in the sample studied. The author reported very few differences based on socioeconomic groupings, it might be noted. Simon (1954) has also presented CAT norms based on 500 stories given by 49 Viennese children. These Ss were neurotic, physically handicapped, and control children age three to seven. The major themes of these children were presented in his report, and there was some attempt to demonstrate criteria by which the groups could be differentiated. No cross-

validation was attempted. Byrd and Witherspoon (1954) have reported norms based on eighty preschool children; major themes were
presented, as well as some indications of which themes did not appear
frequently at this age level. The authors also indicated that the presence or absence of certain themes depended somewhat on whether or
not the stimulus picture was specifically designed to elicit material in
this area. Although not specifically presented as a normative study,
one additional report will be noted. This is actually one of only a few
validation studies reported in the CAT literature. Gurevitz and Klapper (1951) studied the CAT responses of schizophrenic and cerebral
palsied children, evaluating the responses in terms of a number of formal and dynamic variables, and found the test permitted a differentiation and illumination of the problems in each group.

Earlier, it was noted that the rationale for the CAT is based on the
greater projection and identification children are supposed to feel with
animal figures as compared with human figures. This assumption has
fascinated many workers, partially because it is fairly easily tested.
What evidence has accumulated? Bills (1950) had been interested in
this general question, and constructed a series of ten colored pictures
containing animals in various situations in order to contrast material
obtained with these cards with that obtained by the standard TAT
cards. He used 48 Ss, age five to ten. Each S was given ten TAT cards
and ten animal cards, with half of the Ss getting the TAT first; their
responses were scored for word count, refusals, coherency, etc. On
most of these measures, the animal cards proved superior, for there
was a greater quantity of material, less blocking, more coherency, and
it seemed easier for Ss to make stories when the animal cards were
presented. However, the pictures were not matched for content, stimulus value, etc.

Other authors were more careful in the controls they used while
attempting to answer the general question, "Do children identify more
readily with animals than with human figures?" The matching of event
and background scene in animal and human cards, and/or the introduction of some control over which series comes first are found in
several studies attempting to answer this question. Furuya (1957),
working with first, fourth, and sixth graders, had his Ss tell stories in
response to six animal and to six human pictures, matched as far as
possible in background scene and event or situation pictured. His findings were that Ss were more productive with respect to the human
pictures at all age levels. Armstrong (1954), in a study based on 60
children in the first, second, and third grades, found that human figures
elicited more verbalizations which went beyond a descriptive level

than did the animal figures. Biersdorf and Marcuse (1953), working with 30 first graders with a mean age of seven, failed to find differences between the animal and human test series on various indices of productivity. Budoff (1963) reported that a group of mentally retarded children, contrary to expectation, were more productive with the human series than with the animal series, whereas no such distinction emerged in a control group of dull-low-average children. Light (1954), working with a group of 75 fourth and fifth graders, exposed five CAT cards and five TAT cards alternatively on a screen. Written stories were scored for length, feelings, conflicts, outcomes, themes, and figures introduced. The author suggested, on the basis of his findings, that there seemed to be better identification with the human series than the animal series.

Finally, Boyd and Mandler (1955) reported a study which attempted to test not only the assumption that children identify more with animal than human figures and that this tendency should decrease with age, but that human figures elicit more resistance than animal figures. In addition, they wondered if, because of the nature of children's stories, socially undesirable roles might continue to be identified with animal figures even when the story content shows increased human content. Ss were 96 third graders who were presented with stimulus stories and stimulus pictures in which the main characters were either human or animal. The stories were analyzed for various indices as to productivity as well as content aimed at determining "ego-involvement." The results tended to support the hypothesis that "animal pictures facilitate the expression of ego-involvement, particularly of negative affect; however, the overwhelming effect of human stimulus stories on the production of imaginative material fails to support a general theoretical assumption of children's primary identification with animals" (p. 371).

This brief summary suggests that there is little support for the notion that children identify more readily with animal figures. The paucity of validity and reliability studies in this area, the suggestion of poor construct validity, and the almost complete dependence on the experimenter's subjective evaluation of results, indicate that the CAT does not as yet qualify as an instrument of measurement. The stimulus cards are so constructed that almost any response the subject makes could be fitted by the experimenter into a psychoanalytic type of framework, or interpreted however the examiner wished. If this technique is to have any use as an experimental and clinical tool, a more rigorous quantification and standardization will have to be provided than has heretofore appeared.

*Michigan Picture Test (MPT)*. The dangers of proceeding without a basic fund of psychometric data are pointed up in a series of studies with the Michigan Picture Test (Andrew, Walton, Hartwell, & Hutt [1951]; Hartwell, Hutt, Andrew, & Walton [1951]; and Walton, Andrew, Hartwell, & Hutt [1951]). The originators of this technique (Michigan Department of Mental Health—Michigan Picture Test, 1953) gave a number of examples of how they could have been seriously misled by results with their clinic patients if they had not had a stabilizing anchor in their widespread study of the responses of normal children of various ages and adjustment groups. These investigations also provide an object lesson in how a TAT derivative could optimally be conceived, processed, and circulated.

Aware of the shortcomings of the standard TAT pictures for the investigation of children's "fantasies" and the reconstruction of personality content and structure from them, the researchers, Hartwell, Hutt, Andrew, and Walton (1951) set out "to develop a projective picture-story technique suitable for children which would offer quantified approaches that might be used by the clinician above and beyond his intuitive and interpretative skill" (*Ibid.,* p. 124). They went about the initial task of selecting appropriate pictures in a systematic manner. Nearly a thousand pictures of all kinds were pretested on varied groups of school children and clinic cases in the eight to fourteen year age range. It was decided beforehand, through conferences between a group of clinicians, including psychologists and psychiatrists, what crucial areas of personal-social adjustment in which conflicts are frequently present should be sampled. Then six criteria were established according to which the pictures should structure reality-like situations or figures. Using these criteria, fifteen pictures were selected from the original number. These plus a blank card were divided into two series of twelve cards each; some of the cards are common to both series, four of the cards are used only for boys, and four only for girls. Standardization of these cards was then attempted by administering the two final series to 303 children, ranging in age from eight to fourteen years, in three Michigan cities. A measure of adjustment was obtained for each child by use of a five-point Teacher Rating Scale, which evaluated the child along eleven dimensions in terms of objective behavior manifested in the classroom. A careful study was made of the picture-story variables that might be used to differentiate well-adjusted and poorly adjusted children as well as between types of maladjustment; and twelve variables, each based on specific hypotheses, were chosen for initial study.

In the first study, results were presented on four of the variables:

level of interpretation (rated on a 12-point scale), tense (a tally of the tense of each verb used), direction of forces impinging on the central character (divided into five categories: centrifugal, centripetal, ambivalent, neutral, and ambiguous), and popular objects (specific, tangible objects mentioned by 33% of the cases). In the summary of results on this school population, the investigators noted that not only did the pictures elicit different types of responses within each area, but that no overall trends were found for the variables used. For example, there were age differences with respect to some variables but not others, and several variables distinguished the well from the poorly adjusted children, whereas other variables did not.

The test was also given to more than sixty clinic children ranging in age from seven to fourteen years. No quantitative results were published in the original article, but the investigators pointed out that without the normative and developmental data previously established, it would have been very easy to make significantly erroneous interpretations of the data.

In a second paper (Andrew, et al., 1951), the authors attempted to appraise the stimulus value of ten of the pictures, to evaluate the effect of developmental differences, and to analyze the relationship between the manifest content of a picture and scores on test variables. To do this, the responses of twenty-four third grade and twenty-four fifth grade children were rated for level of response and scored for verb tense as described previously. The cards were found to differ among themselves on these variables; developmental differences were apparent, and it seemed that the manifest content of the pictures had little effect on the scoring of these two variables. These findings further reinforce the belief that specific normative data are essential for accurate interpretation of TAT-like projective tests.

In their third study, this group of researchers (Walton, et al., 1951) developed a tension index based on the expression of certain psychological needs in the story material (weighted in proportion as they appeared in well-adjusted and poorly adjusted groups) which successfully differentiated fifteen well-adjusted and fifteen poorly adjusted fifth-grade children with a negligible amount of overlapping. The tension index was then subjected to three cross-validations whereby: (a) two new groups of fifteen poorly adjusted and fifteen well-adjusted children were compared; (b) the poorly adjusted group of the new population was compared with the well-adjusted group of the criterion population; and (c) this criterion group was compared to a group of fifteen clinic cases of similar age. In all three comparisons the differences were significant with a minimum of overlap. The interscorer reliability for this tension index was .77. These findings also suggest that serious errors may be made in interpretation if normative data are not used as a reference point. For example, some variables were significant only for certain age ranges on which the test was standardized.

## SUMMARY

This chapter was devoted to a consideration of TAT derivatives and cognate techniques—those in widespread use, as well as some of those which are not. Popularity of these instruments unfortunately does not go hand in hand with their merits. Some comments were made concerning the problem of choosing the stimuli for such modifications; it was noted that there are many difficulties in establishing criteria for selection of pictures to elicit information about specific motivations or attitudes and in prior determination of what pictures are most suitable.

Some TAT adaptations have been aimed at obtaining data about various areas of behavior, defense mechanisms, and motivational systems, but very few of them have had the benefit of sustained programs of investigation, cross-validation, etc. Among the techniques discussed, with some indication of validity, reliability, and standardization, if this information is available, were: Pictureless TAT; Puppet Film, *Rock-A-Bye, Baby;* Thompson TAT; Iowa Picture Interpretation Test; and the Cartoon Situations Test. A few of the TAT derivatives and pictorial methods which have had wider applicability, specifically the MAPS test, the Blacky Pictures, the Picture-Frustration Study, the Children's Apperception Test, and the Michigan Picture Test were discussed in greater detail.

The Michigan Picture Test has had the advantage of careful preliminary thought and design, good standardization, adequate normative study, and careful cross-validation. If this projective test is a model of the proper construction and evaluation of a thematic apperceptive technique, it is apparent that the other TAT derivatives fall far short of the standard.

The Rosenzweig Picture-Frustration Study has had considerable quantitative adaptation and development with a demonstration of good interscorer reliability and the accumulation of substantial normative data. The Rosenzweig procedure has some advantage over most TAT-like procedures in that it is limited to a single variable, aggression, and is thus easier to validate than other, more global, procedures.

It would seem that the method of resolving the complex global tests into their components is the most profitable way of getting at their real psychological meaning and establishing the primary evidence for their utility.

## REFERENCES

Andrew, Gwen, Walton, R. E., Hartwell, S. W., & Hutt, M. L. The Michigan Picture Test: the stimulus values of the cards. *J. consult. Psychol.*, 1951, 15, 51–54.

Armstrong, Mary Ann S. Children's responses to animal and human figures in thematic pictures. *J. consult. Psychol.*, 1954, 18, 67–70.

Banissoni, P., Misiti, R., & Nencini, R. Taratura italiana del P. F. test di Rosenzweig. *Boll. Psicol. Sociol. appl.*, 1955, Nos. 9, 10, 11, 22–57.

Bellak, L. *The Children's Apperception Test.* New York: C. P. S. Co., 1949.

Bellak, L. *A guide to the interpretation of the Thematic Apperception Test.* (Revised) New York: Psychological Corp., 1951.

Bennett, L. A., & Rudoff, A. Changes in direction of hostility related to incarceration and treatment. *J. clin. Psychol.*, 1960, 16, 408–410.

Bernard, J. The Rosenzweig Picture-Frustration Study: I. Norms, reliability, and statistical evaluation. *J. Psychol.*, 1949, 28, 325–332. (*a*)

Bernard, J. The Rosenzweig Picture-Frustration Study: II. Interpretation. *J. Psychol.*, 1949, 28, 333–343. (*b*)

Bernstein, L., & Chase, P. H. The discriminative ability of the Blacky Pictures with ulcer patients. *J. consult. Psychol.*, 1955, 19, 377–380.

Biersdorf, Kathryn R., & Marcuse, F. L. Responses of children to human and to animal pictures. *J. proj. Tech.*, 1953, 17, 455–459.

Bills, R. E. Animal pictures for obtaining children's projections. *J. clin. Psychol.*, 1950, 6, 291–293.

Bindon, D. Marjorie. Make-A-Picture Story Test findings for rubella deaf children. *J. abnorm. soc. Psychol.*, 1957, 55, 38–42.

Blum, G. S. A study of the psychoanalytic theory of psychosexual development. *Genet. Psychol. Monogr.*, 1949, 39, 3–99.

Blum, G. S. "Reliability of the Blacky Test": a reply to Charen. *J. consult. Psychol.*, 1956, 20, 406.

Blum, G. S. The Blacky Pictures with children. In A. I. Rabin and M. R. Haworth (Eds.) *Projective techniques with children.* New York: Grune and Stratton, 1960, 95–104.

Blum, G. S. A guide for the research use of the Blacky Pictures. *J. proj. Tech.*, 1962, 26, 3–29.

Blum, G. S., & Hunt, H. F. The validity of the Blacky Pictures. *Psychol. Bull.*, 1952, 49, 238–250.

Boisbourdin, A., Michel, A., & Peltier, J. R. Expérimentation du Test P. F. de Rosenzweig sur un groupe d'élèves pilotes de L'Armée de l'Air. *Rev. Psychol. appl.*, 1956, 6, 15–27.

Boulanger-Balleyguier, G. Etude sur le CAT: influence du stimulus sur les récits d'enfants de 3 à 8 ans. *Rev. Psychol. appl.*, 1957, 7, 1–28.

Boyd, Nancy A., & Mandler, G. Children's responses to human and animal stories and pictures. *J. consult. Psychol.*, 1955, 19, 367–371.

Budoff, M. Animal vs. human figures in a picture story test for young, mentally backward children. *Amer. J. ment. Defic.*, 1963, 68, 245–250.

Burger, A. W. Over de "bizarre" plaatsing in de MAPS-test. *Ned. Tijdschr. Psychol.*, 1960, **15**, 340–358.

Byrd, E., & Witherspoon, R. L. Responses of preschool children to the Children's Apperception Test. *Child Develpm.*, 1954, **25**, 35–44.

Charen, S. The interaction of background and characters in picture test story telling. *J. clin. Psychol.*, 1954, **10**, 290–292.

Charen, S. Reliability of the Blacky Test. *J. consult. Psychol.*, 1956, **20**, 16. (*a*)

Charen, S. A reply to Blum. *J. consult. Psychol.*, 1956, **20**, 407. (*b*)

Clarke, Helen J. The Rosenzweig Picture-Frustration Study. In H. H. Anderson and G. L. Anderson (Eds.) *An introduction to projective techniques.* Englewood Cliffs, N.J.: Prentice-Hall, 1951, 312–323.

Clarke, Helen J., Rosenzweig, S., & Fleming, Edith E. The reliability of the scoring of the Rosenzweig Picture-Frustration Study. *J. clin. Psychol.*, 1947, **3**, 364–370.

Coons, Margery O. Rosenzweig differences in reaction to frustration in children of high, low and middle sociometric status. *Group Psychother.*, 1957, **10**, 60–63.

Dombrose, L., & Slobin, M. An approach to the measurement of the relative strengths of impulses, ego, and superego and the determination of the effects of impulses and superego upon ego functions. Unpublished doctoral dissertation, Western Reserve University, 1953.

Dombrose L., & Slobin, M. The IES test. *Percept. mot. Skills*, 1958, **8**, 347–389 (Monogr. Suppl. 3).

DuBois, P. H., & Watson, R. I. The selection of patrolmen. *J. appl. Psychol.*, 1950, **34**, 90–95.

Duhm, Erna, & Hansen, Jutta. *Der Rosenzweig P-F Test; Form für Kinder; Handanweisung.* Göttingen, Germany: Hogrefe Verlag für Psychologie, 1957.

Franklin, J. C., & Brozek, J. The Rosenzweig Picture-Frustration test as a measure of frustration response in semistarvation. *J. consult. Psychol.*, 1949, **13**, 293–301.

Fry, F. D. A study of reactions to frustration in 236 college students and in 207 inmates of state prisons. *J. Psychol.*, 1949, **28**, 427–438.

Furuya, K. Responses of school children to human and animal pictures. *J. proj. Tech.*, 1957, **21**, 248–252.

Goldenberg, H. C. A resume of some Make-A-Picture-Story (MAPS) test results. *J. proj. Tech.*, 1951, **15**, 79–86.

Granick, S., & Scheflen, Norma. Approaches to reliability of projective tests with special reference to the Blacky Pictures test. *J. consult. Psychol.*, 1958, **22**, 137–141.

Gurevitz, S., & Klapper, Zelda S. Techniques for and evaluation of the responses of schizophrenic and cerebral palsied children to the Children's Apperception Test (CAT). *Quart. J. Child. Behav.*, 1951, **3**, 38–65.

Hartwell, S. W., Hutt, M., Andrew, Gwen, & Walton, R. E. The Michigan Picture Test: diagnostic and therapeutic possibilities of a new projective test in child guidance. *Amer. J. Orthopsychiat.*, 1951, **21**, 124–137.

Haworth, Mary R. The use of a filmed puppet show as a group projective technique for children. *Genet. Psychol. Monogr.*, 1957, **56**, 257–296.

Haworth, Mary R. Films as a group technique. In A. I. Rabin and M. R. Haworth (Eds.) *Projective techniques with children.* New York: Grune and Stratton, 1960, 177–190.

Haworth, Mary R. Repeat study with a projective film for children. *J. consult. Psychol.*, 1961, **25**, 78–83.

Haworth, Mary R., & Woltmann, A. G. *Rock-A-Bye, Baby: a group projective test for children.* (Manual and film) University Park, Penna.: Psychological Cinema Register, 1959.

Henry, W. E. The TAT in the study of culture-personality relations. *Genet. Psychol. Monogr.*, 1947, **35**, 3–135.

Holzberg, J. D., & Posner, Rita. The relationship of extrapunitiveness on the Rosenzweig Picture-Frustration Study to aggression in overt behavior and fantasy. *Amer. J. Orthopsychiat.*, 1951, **21**, 767–779.

Hooker, Evelyn. The adjustment of the male overt homosexual. *J. proj. Tech.*, 1957, **21**, 18–31.

Hörmann, H., & Moog W. *Der Rosenzweig P-F Test; Form für Erwachsene; Handanweisung.* Göttingen, Germany: Hogrefe Verlag für Psychologie, 1957.

Hurley, J. R. The Iowa Picture Interpretation Test: a multiple-choice variation of the TAT. *J. consult. Psychol.*, 1955, **19**, 372–376.

Joel, W. The use of the Make-A-Picture Story (MAPS) test with disturbed adolescents. *Rorschach Res. Exch.*, 1948, **12**, 155–164.

Johannsen, Dorothea E., & Bennett, E. M. The personality of diabetic children. *J. genet. Psychol.*, 1955, **87**, 175–185.

Johnston, R. A. A methodological analysis of several revised forms of the Iowa Picture Interpretation Test. *J. Pers.*, 1957, **25**, 283–293.

Kaswan, J., Wasman, M., & Freedman, L. Z. Aggression and the Picture-Frustration Study. *J. consult. Psychol.*, 1960, **24**, 446–452.

Kates, S. L. Suggestibility, submission to parents and peers, and extrapunitiveness, intropunitiveness, and impunitiveness in children. *J. Psychol.*, 1951, **31**, 233–241.

Klopfer, B., & Kelley, D. M. *The Rorschach technique.* Yonkers-on-Hudson, N.Y.: World Book Co., 1942.

Korchin, S. J., Mitchell, H. E., & Meltzoff, J. A critical evaluation of the Thompson Thematic Apperception Test. *J. proj. Tech.*, 1950, **14**, 445–452.

Kramer, C. Expérimentation du Test de Frustration de Rosenzweig: travaux recents. *Rev. Psychol. appl.*, 1958, **8**, 153–158.

Leblanc, Maria. Adaptation africaine et comparaison interculturelle d'une épreuve projective: Test de Rosenzweig. *Rev. Psychol. appl.*, 1956, **6**, 91–109.

Lebo, D. Scoring the verbal TAT with illustrative protocols. Dittoed: Author, 1958.

Lebo, D. An empirical approach to problems concerning the diagnostic value of a pictureless TAT. *J. proj. Tech.*, 1959, **23**, 107.

Lebo, D. The development and employment of VTAT's or pictureless TAT's. *J. Psychol.*, 1960, **50**, 197–204.

Lebo, D., & Bruce, Roselyn S. Projective methods recommended for use with the blind. *J. Psychol.*, 1960, **50**, 15–38.

Lebo, D., & Harrigan, Margaret. Visual and verbal presentation of TAT stimuli. *J. consult. Psychol.*, 1957, **21**, 339–342.

Lebo, D., & Sherry, P. J. Visual and vocal presentation of TAT descriptions. *J. proj. Tech.*, 1959, **23**, 59–63.

Lehman, I. J. Responses of kindergarten children to the Children's Apperception Test. *J. clin. Psychol.*, 1959, **15**, 60–63.

Leitch, Mary, & Schafer, Sarah. A study of the Thematic Apperception Tests of psychotic children. *Amer. J. Orthopsychiat.*, 1947, **17**, 337–342.

Levitt, E. E., & Lyle, W. H., Jr. Evidence for the validity of the children's form of the Picture-Frustration Study. *J. consult. Psychol.*, 1955, **19**, 381–386.

Light, B. H. Comparative study of a series of TAT and CAT cards. *J. clin. Psychol.*, 1954, **10**, 179–181.

Light, B. H. A further test of the Thompson TAT rationale. *J. abnorm. soc. Psychol.*, 1955, **51**, 148–150.

Lindzey, G. An experimental test of the validity of the Rosenzweig Picture-Frustration Study. *J. Pers.*, 1950, **18**, 315–320.

Lindzey, G., & Goldwyn, R. M. Validity of the Rosenzweig Picture-Frustration Study. *J. Pers.*, 1954, **22**, 519–547.

Lord, J. P. Psychological correlates of nocturnal enuresis in male children. Unpublished doctoral dissertation, Harvard University, 1952.

Mausner, B. Situational effects on a projective test. *J. appl. Psychol.*, 1961, **45**, 186–192.

Mensh, I. N., and Mason, Evelyn P. Relationship of school atmosphere to reactions in frustrating situations. *J. educ. Res.*, 1951, **45**, 275–286.

Michigan Department of Mental Health. *Michigan Picture Test; the evaluation of emotional reactions of children eight to fourteen years of age:* Set of 16 pictures, manual, analysis sheet rating scale for pupil adjustment with manual. Chicago: Science Research Associates, Inc., 1953.

Mirmow, Esther L. The method of successive clinical predictions in the validation of projective techniques with special reference to the Rosenzweig Picture-Frustration Study. Unpublished doctoral dissertation, Washington University, 1952.

Murray, H. A. (Ed.) *Explorations in personality.* New York: Oxford University Press, 1938.

Murray, H. A. *Thematic Apperception Test.* Cambridge: Harvard University Press, 1943.

Murray, H. A., and Morgan, Christiana D. A clinical study of sentiments: I. *Genet. Psychol. Monogr.*, 1945, **32**, 3–149. (*a*)

Murray, H. A., and Morgan, Christiana D. A clinical study of sentiments: II. *Genet. Psychol. Monogr.*, 1945, **32**, 153–311. (*b*)

Murray, H. A., and Stein, M. Note on the selection of combat officers. *Psychosom. Med.*, 1943, **5**, 386–391.

Neuman, G., & Salvatore, J. The Blacky Test and psychoanalytic theory: a factor-analytic approach to validity. *J. proj. Tech.*, 1958, **22**, 427–431.

Office of Strategic Services. *Assessment of men: selection of personnel.* New York: Rinehart, 1948.

Palmer, J. O. Some relationships between Rorschach's experience balance and Rosenzweig's frustration-aggression patterns. *J. proj. Tech.*, 1957, **21**, 137–141.

Pareek, U. Reliability of the Indian adaptation of Rosenzweig P-F Study (Children's Form). *J. psychol. Res.*, 1958, **2**, 18–23.

Pareek, U. Rosenzweig Picture-Frustration Study: a review. *Psychol. Newsltr.*, 1959, **10**, 98–114.

Pareek, U. An investigation of the validity of the Indian adaptation of the Rosenzweig Picture-Frustration Study (Children's Form). *Indian J. Psychol.*, 1960, **35**, 71–88. (*a*)

Pareek, U. Developmental patterns of Rosenzweig P-F Study variables in Indian children. *MANAS*, 1960, 7, 19–35. (*b*)

Pichot, P., Freson, V., & Danjon, S. Le test de frustration de Rosenzweig (forme pour enfants): standardisation et étalonnage de la version française. *Rev. Psychol. appl.*, 1956, 6, 111–138.

Pichot, P., & Danjon, S. La fidélité du test de frustration de Rosenzweig. *Rev. Psychol. appl.*, 1955, 5, 1–11.

Proshansky, H. A projective method for the study of attitudes. *J. abnorm. soc. Psychol.*, 1943, 38, 393–395.

Riessman, F., Jr., & Miller, S. M. Social class and projective tests. *J. proj. Tech.*, 1958, 22, 432–439.

Rosenzweig, S. Types of reaction to frustration: an heuristic classification. *J. abnorm. soc. Psychol.*, 1934, 29, 298–300.

Rosenzweig, S. A test for types of reaction to frustration. *Amer. J. Orthopsychiat.*, 1935, 5, 395–403.

Rosenzweig, S. An outline of frustration theory. In J. McV. Hunt (Ed.) *Personality and the behavior disorders*. Vol. I. New York: Ronald Press, 1944, 379–388.

Rosenzweig, S. The picture-association method and its application in a study of reactions to frustration. *J. Pers.*, 1945, 14, 3–23.

Rosenzweig, S. Some problems relating to research on the Rosenzweig Picture-Frustration Study. *J. Pers.*, 1950, 18, 303–305. (*a*)

Rosenzweig, S. Revised norms for the adult form of the Rosenzweig Picture-Frustration Study. *J. Pers.*, 1950, 18, 344–346. (*b*)

Rosenzweig, S. Levels of behavior in psychodiagnosis with special reference to the Picture-Frustration Study. *Amer. J. Orthopsychiat.*, 1950, 20, 63–72. (*c*)

Rosenzweig, S. The Rosenzweig Picture-Frustration Study, Children's Form. In A. I. Rabin and M. R. Haworth (Eds.) *Projective techniques with children*. New York: Grune and Stratton, 1960, 149–176.

Rosenzweig, S. Validity of the Rosenzweig Picture-Frustration Study with felons and delinquents. *J. consult. Psychol.*, 1963, 27, 535–536.

Rosenzweig, S., Clarke, Helen J., Garfield, M. S., & Lehndorff, A. Scoring samples for the Rosenzweig Picture-Frustration Study. *J. Psychol.*, 1946, 21, 45–72.

Rosenzweig, S., Fleming, Edith E., & Clarke, Helen J. Revised scoring manual for the Rosenzweig Picture-Frustration Study. *J. Psychol.*, 1947, 24, 165–208.

Rosenzweig, S., Fleming, Edith E., & Rosenzweig, Louise. The children's form of the Rosenzweig Picture-Frustration Study. *J. Psychol.*, 1948, 26, 141–191.

Rosenzweig, S., & Rosenzweig, Louise. Aggression in problem children and normals as evaluated by the Rosenzweig P-F Study. *J. abnorm. soc. Psychol.*, 1952, 47, 683–687.

Rossi, A. M., & Solomon, P. A further note on female Blacky protocols. *J. proj. Tech.*, 1961, 25, 339–340.

Sacco, F. Studio della frustrazione col P. F. Test di Rosenzweig nei siciliani in èta evolutiva. *Infanz. abnorm.*, 1955, 11, 146–166.

Seward, J. P. Psychoanalysis, deductive method, and the Blacky Test. *J. abnorm. soc. Psychol.*, 1950, 45, 529–535.

Shapiro, Edna, Biber, Barbara, & Minuchin, Patricia. The Cartoon Situations Test: a semi-structured technique for assessing aspects of personality pertinent to the teaching process. *J. proj. Tech.*, 1957, 21, 172–184.

Shneidman, E. S. Schizophrenia and the MAPS Test. A study of certain formal psycho-social aspects of fantasy production in schizophrenia as revealed by performance on the Make-A-Picture-Story (MAPS) test. *Genet. Psychol. Monogr.*, 1948, **38**, 145–223.

Shneidman, E. S. *The Make-A-Picture-Story-Test.* New York: Psychological Corporation, 1949.

Shneidman, E. S. The MAPS test with children. In A. I. Rabin and M. R. Haworth (Eds.) *Projective techniques with children.* New York: Grune and Stratton, 1960, 130–148.

Shneidman, E. S., Joel, W., & Little, K. B. *Thematic test analysis.* New York: Grune and Stratton, 1951.

Silverstein, A. B. Faking on the Rosenzweig Picture-Frustration Study. *J. appl. Psychol.*, 1957, **41**, 192–194.

Simon, Maria D. Der Children's Apperception Test bei gesunden und gestörten Kindern. *Z. diagnost. Psychol.*, 1954, **2**, 195–219.

Simos, I. The Picture-Frustration Study in the psychiatric situation—preliminary findings. *J. Pers.*, 1950, **18**, 327–330.

Spiegelman, M. A note on the use of Fine's scoring system with the MAPS tests of children. *J. proj. Tech.*, 1956, **20**, 442–444.

Symonds, P. M. Criteria for the selection of pictures for the investigation of adolescent phantasies. *J. abnorm. soc. Psychol.*, 1939, **34**, 271–274.

Takala, Annika, & Takala, M. Finnish children's reactions to frustration in the Rosenzweig test: an ethnic and cultural comparison. *Acta psychol.*, 1957, **13**, 43–50.

Thompson, C. E. The Thompson modification of the Thematic Apperception Test. *Rorschach Res. Exch.*, 1949, **13**, 469–478.

Van Krevelen, Alice. A study of examiner influence on responses to MAPS test materials. *J. clin. Psychol.*, 1954, **10**, 292–293.

Wallon, E. J. A study of Rosenzweig scoring patterns among naval aviation cadets. *USN Sch. Aviat. Med. Res. Notes*, 1956, Proj. No. NM 001 109 100, Rep. No. 9.

Wallon, E. J., & Webb, W. B. A note on the effect of test set on the Rosenzweig Picture-Frustration Test. *USN Sch. Aviat. Med. Res. Rep.*, 1956, No. NM 001 108 100, Rep. No. 19.

Walton, R. E., Andrew, Gwen, Hartwell, S. W., & Hutt, M. L. A tension index of adjustment based on picture stories elicited by the Michigan Picture Test. *J. abnorm. soc. Psychol.*, 1951, **46**, 438–441.

Wechsberg, Florence O. An experimental investigation of levels of behavior with special reference to the Rosenzweig Picture-Frustration Study. Unpublished doctoral dissertation, Washington University, 1951.

Wekstein, L. A preliminary outline for a fantasy projective technique as a clinical instrument. *J. Psychol.*, 1945, **19**, 341–346.

Zimiles, H., Biber, Barbara, Rabinowitz, W., & Hay, L. Personalty aspects of teaching: a predictive study. *Genet. Psychol. Monogr.*, 1964, **69**, 101–149.

# 11 THE TAT AS A PSYCHOLOGICAL EXPERIMENT

With so little understanding of the psychological processes underlying TAT performance, it is felt that a profitable way to explore the efficacy of this technique as an instrument of personality assessment is to analyze it as an experimental situation by isolating relevant variables which can be explored and handled appropriately as they would be in a laboratory experiment.

*Hypothesis.* The many hypotheses underlying the use of the TAT as a psychological tool for prying open the covert personality characteristics of individuals are no different from those underlying other projective techniques. The major hypothesis (or assumption) is that when confronted with an ambiguous social situation, S will interpret it according to his own preconceived ideas, habits of perception, needs, and attitudes. It is further assumed that we can predict, from the way he interprets the situations depicted on the test cards, the way he will react to similar situations in real life. By increasing the number and variety of such depicted situations, it is expected that we can cover the range of important relationships in an individual's life—relationship to mate, like-sexed peers, parent or authority figures, children or dependent figures, siblings, etc., and thus can make specific predictions about extratest behavior in a wide variety of situations.

As noted, some clinicians assume, when predictions are made, that

515

there is a one-to-one relationship between the way S reacts to the situation depicted on the card and the way he will react to a similar situation in real life. It is recognized that there can be distortions, displacements, denials, etc. when the pictorial situations are interpreted. In fact, in the clinical situation, this often affords the interpreter an opportunity to infer characteristic defense mechanisms that S uses in handling conflictful material. The uncertain nature of the relationship, however, between the content of responses in the test situation and actuality poses some real problems in interpretation—is what S says about the characters in the stories representational of the way he feels and actually would *act* in real life, is it somehow compensational for the way he feels and knows he would react, or is there no relationship at all?

Lindzey (1952), who has evaluated the status of ten interpretative assumptions underlying the TAT in the light of empirical evidence and attempted to relate them to the main body of psychological knowledge, has stated, "in the light of evidence, the assumption that motivational factors are revealed in completing unstructured situations seems clearly warranted" (p. 5). One hypothesis, then, is that there is a relationship between needs as manifested in TAT stories and needs as manifested in behavior. However, how motives are revealed, which motives, the assessment of their strength, and the distinction between temporary states and enduring characteristics are not completely clear. Furthermore, the determination of just what is "motivational content" and what is not, is an important problem. Error variance, in this instance, may not be error variance at all, but material which is unexpected or whose correlates we do not clearly understand.

Chapter 9 contains a detailed description and discussion of a group of related studies concerning the relationship of needs (inferred, judged, or rated on the basis of overt behavior) and TAT material (see sections on *Assumptions*). Although the evidence suggests that some relationship may in fact exist, there is by no means agreement as to the nature of this relationship, nor are there positive findings for all needs and motives. There is some evidence to suggest that as the strength of some needs or as the amount of anxiety concerning their expression increases, a concomitant *decrease* of direct expression in the TAT material will result. Thus, even if the assumption concerning the relationship between needs and TAT material is borne out, the picture is not complete unless the conditions are defined under which this relationship is compensational, representational, or neither in nature. Murray (1943) has suggested that these considerations can be understood in terms of the social sanctions which result from the expression of certain needs; those tendencies *not* inhibited by cultural sanctions are apt to be highly correlated when their expression in TAT material and in overt behavior is considered. He reported a positive correlation (over .40) between the TAT and overt behavior for a group of college men on the following needs: abasement, creation, dominance, exposition, nurturance, passivity, rejection, and dejection. On the other hand, sexual expression on the TAT and in overt behavior correlated negatively, between —.33 and —.74, depending on the type of activity. He found no relationship between expression of aggression and achievement on the TAT and in overt behavior. Symonds (1949), after analyzing the stories of forty adolescents in response to a specially designed series of cards, came to the conclusion that we cannot make any generalizations about the relationship. He found that themes derived from the stories, in some instances, corresponded with personality trends in the narrator, but also sometimes the themes from the stories and the personality of the narrator were of a complementary or opposite nature. Even if a subject included an unusually large number of themes of aggression in the stories he told, Symonds felt that the only conclusion that could be drawn is that aggression occupies a prominent place in his "fantasy" life. We cannot make any gratuitous assumptions about whether this subject is aggressive in his social relations or lacking in aggressiveness, without comparing the stories to actual case material.

A second group of hypotheses states that TAT products are a reflection of the "fantasies," or are *themselves* "fantasies" of the individuals. Once again, the reader is referred to Chapter 9 for a discussion of this frequently made assumption. As noted, some doubt has been cast on the equation of TAT verbal products and fantasies.

A final group of hypotheses has to do with the relationship between TAT material and actual behavior. This particular group of hypotheses is in some respects antithetical to the one just noted; that is, if TAT products *are* fantasies or reflections of them, they (the TAT responses) are probably less valid indices of actual behavior than if they are not fantasies. Many studies summarized in Chapter 9, in the section on *Validity*, are relevant to the question of how efficiently the TAT predicts to behavioral situations. These studies suggest that there is probably no direct, simple relationship of TAT protocols and behavior. Moreover, the wide range of behavior tapped, the different scoring systems used, the varying scopes of different studies, and the number of behavioral indices used do not permit any broad generalizations. Some measures are apparently good predictors of behavior. The appropriateness of these segments of behavior, however, from the point of view of the clinical purposes of projective techniques, is another question.

More specific propositions, already discussed, will be briefly noted: (a) Perceptual "habits," modes, or thresholds are determined by need and personality; TAT responses, therefore, since they are perceptual in nature, also follow the same laws of "perception-personality." The two aspects of this assumption are by no means proven. (See Chapters 2 and 3 for a discussion of some relevant problems.) (b) TAT themes are an expression of the momentary state of aroused motivation. (c) Wishes, needs, and motivational components which S is unwilling or unable to talk about in the ordinary interview situation are revealed in TAT material. (d) S identifies with the "hero" of his story, and the hero behaves to *other* people in the story as S would in real life. (e) Frequency of and emotional intensity accompanying certain themes are a good index as to whether or not these themes will be manifested in overt behavior.

The hypotheses just mentioned are only a few which are implied in the TAT experiment, as judged by the studies and reports of many TAT workers. Not only are the *general* "projective" assumptions not necessarily valid, but the more specific TAT assumptions should all be subjected to rigorous scrutiny and examination. Fortunately, some notable progress along these lines is being made through the efforts of many interested researchers. Finally, it might be noted that the testing of such hypotheses and assumptions adds to an ever increasing body of evidence concerning the construct validity of the TAT—a body of evidence which is crucial and significant if the TAT continues to occupy the prestigeful position it holds in the clinician's (and researcher's) vast array of techniques.

*Experimenter and Subject.* The interaction between E and S is crucial in an experiment of this type. Results are assumed to be a representation of an individual's "private world." It is very unlikely, however, that S will communicate his "private world" readily. The more S is made to feel he is in a permissive, accepting, noncritical, nonevaluative situation, the more likely he is to produce material which might be a clue to his unshared ideation and imagery. E can no doubt control some of this atmosphere by the instructions he gives and the manner in which he gives them, by the extratest comments he makes, and by his general behavior. McClelland, Clark, Roby, and Atkinson (1949) concluded on the basis of their experiment that,

. . . the conditions of administration of the TAT are of considerable importance in determining the dynamic content of the stories. The clinician should be careful to investigate such matters as how the subject conceives of the test, his reason for taking it, his relation to the tester who may or may not have given him other tests that have involved success or failure, etc. (p.253).

That $E$ plays an important role in the frequency or content of thematic material was also suggested by Veroff (1961), who in an extensive national survey employing the TAT, discovered variance in TAT scores because of the different interviewers he used. A similar effect with respect to $n$ Achievement scores was reported by Birney (1956), who worked with a group of college students. Bernstein (1956) found that the presence of an examiner acted as an inhibitory influence with respect to strongly emotional material. This was explained on the basis of an expectancy in $S$ that $E$ planned to *evaluate* the material rather than on the basis of the sheer presence of $E$.

A later section of this chapter, *The Task and Its Administration*, gives attention to the work of Salzinger and his associates on the conditioning of verbal affect responses in interview situations. This work has highlighted the importance of $E$'s own response (in a clinical situation, often spontaneous and unplanned) to what $S$ is saying, in determining the number of affect responses $S$ produces. Needless to say, in the TAT situation the quality and number of such responses are often crucial factors in the interpretation assigned to the material $S$ produces.

There are other factors which cannot be changed or controlled by $E$ in a specific clinical face-to-face situation, for example, age, sex, and status. It is essential that the effect of these factors on TAT productions be assessed so that variance contributed by them can be controlled in an experimental setting, as well as further understood in the evaluation of the single, clinical case. Some of these variables are discussed below in terms of both $E$ and $S$, as well as in terms of their interaction.

*Sex.* Murray (1951) stated that the thematic content of stories will differ according to the sex of $E$. To check such a statement empirically, Garfield, Blek, and Melker (1952) used an experimental design in which equal groups of males and females (total $N$ of 110) were tested by male and female $Es$. They found there were no differences in terms of level of plot, mood and outcome of story, and activity of central character when males and females were tested by members of the same or opposite sex. So it would seem that for this sample of college students these characteristics of TAT responses were not affected by the sex of $E$. There might be differences when other aspects of the stories are evaluated, however. Bijou and Kenny (1951), for example, in comparing TAT protocols obtained by three examiners, two male and one female, found consistent differences indicating that one of the male examiners obtained reliably longer stories than either of the other two examiners. Also, one of the male examiner's subjects related stories which seemed to be more personally significant than the stories obtained by the female examiner, although not more so than those obtained by the other male examiner.

In considering sex of S, Rosenzweig and Fleming (1949) found statistically significant differences between males and females in their interpretation of specific figures in cards 2, 4, and 13MF, although, for the most part, the sexes agreed in their apperceptive responses to the other cards which they viewed in common. It has been demonstrated by Sanford (1943) that boys write longer stories and include more content than girls. He found that boys give more aggressive, self-assertive, and materialistic stories and include more themes of blame, remorse, and fear of punishment. On the other hand, he found that girls concern themselves more in their stories with social relations and esthetic feelings. This study did not control for differences in the sex of the examiner; however, Symonds (1949) found that among adolescents, when the examiner is of the same sex as the subject, much the same sex differences were noted.

In a more recent TAT study, Lindzey and Silverman (1959) found many significant sex differences among the variables they studied, corroborating findings of Lindzey and Goldberg (1953) that significant differences existed between responses of college males and females, with the former showing greater sex and the latter greater abasement and nurturance needs. Moreover, the females were more verbally responsive than males when the measure was number of words used. Thus, when both male and female Ss are used in an experiment, this difference should be taken into account in selecting the sample. There might very easily be a consistent bias favoring high scores on the part of the female Ss, especially if the protocols are scored in terms of the total number of elements of a response, for example, words, sentences, acts, etc.

Bijou and Kenny (1951) found no significant differences between male and female college students in their ranking of the twenty-one male cards according to ambiguity value. Weisskopf (1950a), however, found that women made significantly more comments beyond pure description about pictures in both the male and female series; and Eron, Terry, and Callahan (1950) also found differences in the emotional tone of stories told by college men and women. Stories told by male Ss tended to be less sad than those told by female Ss (differences significant beyond the .05 level of confidence on five out of the twelve cards which are the same for both sexes). The sex differences, however, were not as marked as the differences among the cards. The fact that they used a more refined and precise scale than Garfield et al. may account for lack of similarity of results, although both studies agree that the stimuli themselves are the most important factor in determining emotional tone of the stories. Sarason and Sarason (1958) also found that sex of S was significantly related to scores on Eron's scale for emotional tone, whereas Abel (1945), in a study of Negro and white morons, found that girls gave more themes of loneliness than boys, a finding which Sarason (1943a, 1943b) also obtained in his work with mentally deficient children. Newbigging (1955) reported that in response to instructions to "make up as happy a story as you can to each picture," men produced generally happier stories, used more words per story, and had longer response times than women. Webster (1953) reported a similar finding (the outcome of women's stories to card 12M tended to be more indifferent or unhappy than that of men to the same card) among other significant differences in TAT content variables between men and women.

In a presentation of some methodological problems involved in a national survey using the TAT, Veroff, Atkinson, Feld, and Gurin (1960) reviewed some studies, confirming the findings noted previously. Because of striking and important differences in TAT responses due to sex, these workers created a male form and a female form for the TAT type series they used to assess their population: "Indeed, the sex difference is so important a factor (Angelini [1955]; Davenport [1953]; Field [1951]; Morrison [1954]; Veroff, Wilcox, & Atkinson [1953]; Vogel [1954]) that it was necessary from the very beginning to plan a different set of pictures for men and women" (p. 2).

*Cultural and Ethnic Variables: Race, Class, and Nationality.* Chapter 10 presented some material pertaining to the rationale of the Thompson TAT, and it was noted then that the use of Negro figures in the pictorial stimuli did not necessarily insure greater identification with the test characters on the part of Negro Ss. Riessman and Miller (1958) have noted that the Thompson TAT is not productive because the Negro is unfamiliar with taking a "Negro Test." They have suggested that figures should be ambiguous as to race, rather than boldly Negro. On the other hand, racial differences between E and S might affect rapport and the kinds of stories produced. Schwartz, Riess, and Cottingham (1951), in cross-validating the Thompson version of the TAT for Negroes, had northern Negro and white Ss take both versions of the test with Es of both races, in a design where all S and E factors were orthogonal. They found that the examiner differences were more important than the stimulus card differences when number of words or number of ideas were evaluated. Yet, it is still not clear whether or not there is a real advantage in using Negro interviewers with Negro subjects. These same authors, for example, noted an opposite effect!

Negroes with *white* interviewers seemed more productive. Moreover, the use of an isolated variable such as race as the crucial determinant in the TAT response is not justified, since Korchin, Mitchell, and Meltzoff (1950), in their evaluation of the Thompson TAT, have noted that the socioeconomic position of the Negro is at least as important as race in determining his response.

As for differences in productivity attributable to ethnic and racial backgrounds, Abel (1945) disclosed that in a sample of retarded children, white girls and boys and Negro girls were more productive than Negro boys, but noted that there were no differences between Negro and white morons in number of words and number of ideas or themes expressed in response to the standard TAT. On the other hand, Mussen (1953) reported several important content differences between the protocols of normal Negro and white boys.

Some difference in responses produced to TAT stimuli due to nationality and other subcultural factors has been suggested. McClelland, Sturr, Knapp, and Wendt (1958) reported higher $n$ Achievement scores for American as compared to German students who were going on for higher education. And Lesser (1959) found differences in aggression-anxiety responses between Catholic, Jewish, and Protestant boys. Greater "transcendence"[1] scores for Irish as compared to Italian schizophrenics was reported by Singer and Opler (1956). In addition, McArthur (1955), Rosen (1958), and Singer (1954) have all reported various content differences among groups selected to represent differing class, social, and socioeconomic strata. Mason and Ammons (1956), in an additional study of social class and the TAT, noted striking class differences in stories told and emphasized that such differences should be considered when using the TAT for diagnostic purposes. They found differences among social classes in interest and willingness to participate; in subject matter and content; and in language usage. For a review of the literature on social class differences, not only for the TAT, but also for the Rorschach, see Riessman and Miller (1958).

Some of the socioeconomic differences are so striking that a brief pause to consider one of them seems in order. Verbal fluency, which is related to intelligence, education, and cultural background as well as to personality, may well be a contaminating factor in TAT interpretation. And here is precisely the nub of the problem. Are educational-cultural

---

[1] This term is defined later in the discussion. It is a purely quantitative term and thus cannot really be equated with "projection" since the latter may imply qualitative degrees of intensity.

variables or motivational variables being tapped by a TAT response, or is some complex, nonlinear combination of several variables being measured at the same time? Does a sparse record represent a defensive reaction, an impoverished cultural background, intellectual limitation, or habitual style of response? Veroff (1961), in an excellent discussion of some of these problems (also, see Veroff, Atkinson, Feld, & Gurin [1960]), has suggested that the TAT for people from lower educational levels is probably inappropriate for this very reason. There are some indications that length of a protocol varies with scores (Child, Storm, & Veroff [1958]; Walker & Atkinson [1958]; Ricciuti & Sadacca [1955]) and that some statistical correction is probably necessary in the light of this relationship. In addition to length, there should probably be corrections for refusals, rejections, and generally inadequate responses before we can generalize from results of a group study. Unless this is done, sheer educational and cultural factors may influence quite directly, and artifactually, the scores being studied. Lindzey and Silverman (1959), it should be noted, found that verbal productivity in a group of 80 male and female college students was correlated at the .05 level of significance or below with all of the variables they studied, including achievement, affiliation, dominance, sex, number of figures, ideas, thema, transcendence, compliance with instructions, involvement, and quality.

*Intelligence.* As noted, then, intelligence of S is probably a factor which strongly influences TAT responses, although Sarason (1943a) believed that even mentally defective individuals could respond to the pictures with stories revealing of personality conflicts. Abel (1945) also arrived at the same conclusion. Jacques (1945), on the basis of experience with 100 cases, stated that stories with satisfactory content for analysis have been obtained from Ss with IQ's as low as 80, and consistently satisfactory stories were obtained from Ss with IQ's of 90 and above, although the more intelligent S is, the more elaborate and skillfully worded are the stories. None of these studies, however, had adequate control groups of normal children and adults with which to compare the responses of the defectives.

Beier, Gorlow, and Stacey (1951) did compare the responses of forty defective adolescent girls, not to a specially selected control group, but to Symonds' population of adolescents. This comparison is of highly questionable validity since they used the standard Murray TAT cards whereas Symonds used a specially devised set of cards. Also, they had their subjects pick the five cards they liked most and the five cards they liked least and then make up stories only about these (assuming this would give more assurance of involvement in the stories). All differences in themes exceeding 3% between total of the two groups were considered as differentiating them, and on the basis of this differentiation, they described how the "fantasy" of the two groups differed. They gave no reason for selecting this arbitrary figure, and in addition, they utilized the questionable statistical practice of totalling scores on all stories for all children in making the comparisons. What is important for this discussion, however, is that they characterized the defectives' stories as being of surprisingly good quality, well organized, with a sensitivity to other people's feelings, good vocabulary, and showing evidence of rather extensive "fantasy" life.

Differences between bright and dull Ss have been noted by Masserman and Balken (1938). Ss with high intelligence told stories rich in novelty and creative invention. Ss of low intelligence told flat, sterile, stereotyped, and naive stories. However, Rotter (1946) reported that there was no correlation with mounting intelligence above normal, although estimates which one of his co-workers, Harrison (1940), made as to intelligence levels of their subjects from the TAT protocols correlated .78 with Stanford-Binet scores. Webb and Hilden (1953) reported a correlation of .40 between word count on four TAT cards and obtained IQ. Thus, there seems to be some relationship between intelligence and productivity as well as content. Formal aspects of the stories, however, may even be more highly correlated with intelligence than content factors. In a comparison of normal and retarded Ss, Ruess (1958) reported differences in formal variables such as coherence and logic. Henry (1956) has suggested that intelligence could actually be estimated from TAT stories. He outlined in considerable detail how such estimates could be obtained, basing his scheme on essentially formal factors. These included, among others, organization and balance of stories; integration of stimuli into a coherent plot; language, vocabulary and grammatical structure; number of original concepts; internal consistency; and number of elaborations of relevant concepts.

*Age.* Many investigators have found that the age of Ss influences the stories told. We have seen how Binet used this variable in his construction of an age scale of intelligence. Amen (1941) was able to spell out the individual differences in the apperceptive reactions of children to pictures according to developmental changes both in perceptual reactions (e.g., sequence of development in part-whole interpretation) and in motivation and interest (e.g., progressive changes in identification process toward self-identification and projection).

Balken and Vander Veer (1944) were able to divide their Ss into two age groups on the basis of whether the stories were mere enumeration of details or partial description. The dividing age was ten. They felt this was not so much a matter of intelligence but a result of the adequacy of verbal awareness of emotions, which is more directly related to the stage of ego development than to the factor of intelligence. Older children have more intense needs, and they employ a greater variety of defenses, including restitution, atonement, renunciation, reaction formation, displacement, and achievement. Sanford (1943) found the same types of differences with age and demonstrated that these changes were both consistent and independent of the sex of the child. Coleman (1947), using a five-point scale for level of response, found that he could separate his Ss into two groups, so that the critical ratio between the ages of the groups and the scores they obtained was significant beyond the 1% level of confidence. He found no differences in level of response between boys and girls. Developmental norms available for an instrument like the Children's Apperception Test also indicate the degree to which stories told to pictorial stimuli change with increased age. For example, preschool children's responses tend to be extremely brief and often lack a narrative thread (Byrd & Witherspoon, 1954).

Thus, it would seem that there are certain E and S variables which influence the type of stories elicited. The sex of the S seems to be important for the kinds of content obtained, emotional tone of story, extra comments, and total number of words and ideas used. Whether or not E is of the same sex as S does not seem to affect the emotional tone of the story, the level of plot, outcome, etc. Cultural and ethnic variables seem to be important determinants of the response, although similarity of the pictorial figures to S, in terms of racial or ethnic variables, does not seem to be a significant factor as far as productivity is concerned. Educational and cultural variables, reflected in verbal fluency and productivity of TAT material, may contribute to unwarranted interpretations and generalizations based on TAT records. Intelligence level as well as age also contribute to the responses obtained, probably especially in terms of various formal factors. E's personality, the rapport he establishes, and the general interaction between E and S have been shown to affect the TAT response, too.

*Experimenter's Interpretation.* Quite apart from the kinds of stories elicited by different Es is the effect of E on the interpretations of the stories which are made. No systematic studies of this kind of confounding have been reported, although many have warned of the danger of E injecting his own theoretical bias, personality shortcomings, and predilections into the interpretations (Eron [1950]; Rotter [1946]; and Department of the Army and Air Force Training Manual [1951]). Sarason (1948) had pointed out that the operations by which TAT analysts make deductions about an individual's personality from his productions are not an unanalyzable process which has to be explained by words like "intuition" or "clinical hunches." And very courageously, he reproduced the complete protocol contributed by a patient, showed how he interpreted and reacted to each story, and then gave the case history abstract. If more TAT analysts exposed their thinking processes to this kind of public scrutiny, perhaps some generalizations about interpreter bias could be made and then tested.

Davenport (1952) utilized another approach to the problem of the effect of $E$ on TAT interpretation. She studied the "semantic behavior" of six clinical psychologists in the evaluation of six TAT records contributed by a heterogeneous group of Ss. Each expert judged whether or not each of 207 typical interpreter statements, whose ambiguity had been previously determined by the ratings of 26 other clinical psychologists, applied to each record. She found that there was little agreement among the judges in the differential use of the statements for the six TAT records and that the judges tended to apply statements rated as universal and loaded with psychoanalytic terminology to almost any S while avoiding the use of more specific statements. Also, the judges rarely selected statements about positive assets or traits of personality even though some of the TAT records were obtained from normal individuals. A similar finding was reported by Little and Shneidman (1959), who, on the basis of their study of congruencies among judges utilizing several instruments including the TAT, and several subject groups including normals, neurotics, psychotics, etc., reported that ratings of maladjustment were more appropriate for the psychotic than for the other groups, not because of the validity of the ratings, but because the psychologist-raters tended to rate S as more pathological.

*Apparatus and Stimulus.* The standard stimuli [2] consist of a series of thirty-one cards divided into four groups considered appropriate for (a) males over 14 years; (b) females over 14 years; (c) young boys; and (d) young girls. Thirty of the cards have pictures of one or more individuals engaged in some activity; one of the cards is blank. Since these are more or less objective pictures, it is not as difficult to describe the stimuli in terms of their component content as it is in the case of the Rorschach. The authors of the TAT deliberately selected pictures, however, which are somewhat ambiguous and open to different interpretations. If the pictures were too well-structured, they thought, the

---

[2] See Chapter 9 for a review of modifications, changes, and departures from these standard stimuli.

opportunity for projections would be lost. The effect of the degree of structuring is discussed later in this section, as well as the notion that structure and ambiguity are differing concepts.

*Criteria for Selection.* On the basis of empirical and experimental findings, criteria have been defined for the best selection of pictures. Symonds (1939) felt that the most serviceable pictures were those which (a) had a minimum of detail; (b) were vague in theme; (c) incomplete in content; and (d) suggestive of characters with whom those telling the stories could identify. It was also suggested that the pictures should represent situations familiar to the subject, that is, everyday situations, and should depict an event episodic in nature rather than suggest a complete story. Rotter (1946) noted among his criteria that pictures with large figures are better than landscapes. Heppell and Raimy (1951) added one more criterion, that the pictures should not contain characters or situations which are intrinsically humorous.

Empirical findings have cast doubt on the validity of some of these criteria. The suggestion that the characters be similar to the narrator in order to facilitate identification is not supported by the studies of Schwartz, Riess, and Cottingham (1951), Riess, Schwartz, and Cottingham (1950), and Korchin, Mitchell, and Meltzoff (1950) with the Thompson version of the TAT for Negroes. They found no difference in length of story or number of ideas, whether or not the characters resembled the racial characteristics of the Ss. Murstein (1961), in reviewing these studies, stated: ". . . The degree of similarity between stimulus and S is of itself insufficient as an explanation of the type of response elicited because it does not take cognizance of the background characteristics . . . The influence of the stimulus is not a simple function of its similarity to subject. The culture plays a crucial role in the interpretation of perception" (pp. 250–251).

Weisskopf and Dunlevy (1952) showed that increasing bodily similarity between the storyteller and the pictorial central figure did not increase the amount of projection, as defined by the transcendence index, when obese, crippled, and normal subjects were compared in responses to modified TAT cards containing either obese, crippled, or normal central characters. Similarly, when the stimulus pictures were altered so that S's own face appeared, the increase in similarity between the subject and the central character did not result in statistically significant changes either in the amount of projection elicited by the pictures or in their diagnostic value as estimated by two judges (Weisskopf-Joelson & Money, 1953).

Weisskopf's work (to be discussed) indicates that increasing the ambiguity and incompleteness of the stimulus pictures did not increase, but instead decreased "projection," as defined by her. This finding was corroborated in a study by Weisskopf-Joelson and Lynn (1953), who varied the ambiguity of the pictures of the CAT.

There is some experimental verification for Rotter's criterion (see above) in the work of Terry (1952). Using a rating scale for level of response, she found that for female Ss those cards which have female figures in them elicited the highest level of response and that cards which had no human figures were particularly low in the average level of response elicited. This criterion, which was defined as "the degree to which the subject is judged to have become involved in his story," would seem to be more closely related to what clinicians mean by "projection" than is Weisskopf's "transcendence index."

In studies of the achievement motive it was found that the sex and activity of the figures in the cards were important in eliciting high or low achievement scores (Veroff, Wilcox, & Atkinson, 1953). For both male and female Ss there was a greater achievement-related response to pictures containing male characters than those containing female characters. Weisskopf (1950a), using her index of transcendence, tested the hypothesis that female Ss are more productive with female figures, and males with male figures. Her findings showed that although females, in general, had higher transcendence scores than males, males' responses to *male* figures did *not* have a higher transcendence index than to female figures, and vice-versa. Various modifications of TAT cards to approximate closer similarity to different groups have yielded similar findings: similarity of the central figure to S is apparently noneffective in increasing productivity, and may, in some instances, actually hinder productivity. Veroff (1961), for example, reported that more motivational content (n Achievement, in this instance) was produced to pictures where characters were *not* similar to S, presumably because of defensive anxiety reactions to revealing self.

One final point. There is widespread acceptance of TAT type stimuli as characteristically comprising an achromatic series, possibly because the standard version was such. Yet color (or lack of color) may be still another influence on the type of story told. This may be an important factor in accounting for the predominantly sad feeling tone of the stories. The effect of color on thematic material was investigated by Brackbill (1951), who administered six chromatic TAT cards followed by six achromatic cards to twenty-five psychoneurotics and twenty-five normal controls and, in the reverse order, to fifty other similar Ss. Color had a differential effect on these two groups of Ss since it seemed to change the patients' productions more than it did the productions of the normal Ss. The psychoneurotics told more depressed stories to the chromatic cards, had a significantly longer mean reaction time, and were more productive as measured by number of words. Thus, it seems, color has an effect on the quality and quantity of productions, at least for psychoneurotic patients; and the predominantly sad tone of TAT stories was not a function of their achromatic nature. Thompson and Bachrach (1951), in administering five achromatic and parallel chromatic cards of the standard Murray TAT and the Thompson adaptation of the TAT for Negro Ss to thirty Negro and eighty white normal Ss, found ambiguous results when they measured productivity and affective content. No difference was statistically significant when tests were based on the total study, but when based on the individual cards, there were more statistically significant differences than nonsignificant ones. Lubin(1955), on the other hand, presented four achromatic and four chromatic TAT cards to a group of mentally-retarded Ss. Verbal productivity and increased number of themes were found with respect to the chromatic series. The specific role of color or lack of color as a response determinant is still not clear.

*Picture Pull.* Research has shown that the subject is not left to his own resources completely in structuring the stimuli of the TAT, since the quality of the pictures exerts a strong influence on the kinds of stories told.[3] This notion was recognized some time ago by workers such as Eron (1948, 1950, 1953), Eron, Terry, and Callahan (1950), Bijou and Kenny (1951), and Weisskopf (1950a). These researchers recognized the differential capacity of the TAT cards to elicit projective material. More recently, Ullmann (1957), using number of emotional words as a criterion, also reported reliable differences between the cards.

In general, the early research focused on differences between the first half of the Murray TAT and the second "less-structured" half. These studies, utilizing as measures of productivity, transcendence, outcome, tone, etc., have tended to suggest that the less-structured cards are not associated with greater imaginal content or productivity (greater "fantasy" was the expression usually used). On the other hand, cards of medium ambiguity (see also Murstein, 1958b) were probably the most productive.

That the cards are not of equal stimulation-value was recognized by

---

[3] For an excellent discussion of the stimulus properties of the standard series of cards in terms of difficulty, form demand, frequency of plots, variations, etc., see Henry (1956).

Murray, when he designated those cards numbered 10 and below as more structured than those numbered 11 and above. This differentiation was based on a subjective evaluation of the physical characteristics and content of the cards as well as on their diagnostic value.

One of the earliest empirical studies of the differential stimulus value of the cards was carried out by Kutash (1943), who was interested in the responses of sixty psychopathic defective criminals and used fifteen cards of the second edition. He devised a classification scheme of sixty-eight "intrapsychic conflicts" and then determined the "stimulus value" of each card on the basis of the number of expressions of conflict by the whole group in response to that particular card. There is no indication, however, of the reliability of the differences in stimulus value among these cards.

A similar criticism limits the usefulness of a study by Bijou and Kenny (1951), who had fifty-one Ss rank twenty-one of the Murray cards designated for males in order of ambiguity, which they defined as "the number of possible interpretations." By combining the rankings of their Ss, they were able to assign each picture a median and mean ambiguity rank-order value. Although they demonstrated that the ranking was reliable on the basis of a split-half technique ($R = .80$), the standard deviations were so large as to make any real differentiation on this basis questionable. To test Murray's contention that the second ten cards were more ambiguous than the first, they computed the significance of the difference between the means of these two groups and, accepting the criterion of a P of .01, rejected Murray's claim.

Other researches have indicated that there is a significant difference between the two sets of cards: for example, Eron (1950) obtained many more significant differences in themes and levels of interpretation than could be expected by chance between the two halves of the test; a study by Kannenberg (1948) indicated that the differential effect of the two halves of the test was not a function of the order of presentation or special instructions to make the stories as imaginative as possible.

Eron, Terry, and Callahan (1950) have demonstrated that each of the TAT cards has a stimulus value of its own which determines very largely the emotional tone of the stories offered in response to it. The differences among the cards as to their affective pull were significant. Also, Eron (1950) found that the cards themselves were a more potent factor in determining the type and number of themes related than the psychiatric classification of the individual.

When stories were analyzed according to a need-press schema, as was done by Lindzey and Goldberg (1953), the same powerful influence of the pictures themselves is noted. Using eight cards and seven variables, for example, need sex, need achievement, need aggression, etc., rated for presence or absence on a five-point scale, they found that they could group the cards according to the ratings which they evoked for each of the variables, and that within each cluster it was possible to assume that the mean ratings for the cards could have been drawn from a common population. In addition to mean scores, they also ascertained differences in the variability of scores assigned to the stories and they found that for five of the seven variables the cards differ significantly in the variance of ratings assigned to the stories they evoke. Similarly, Terry (1952) found that there was a significant degree of heterogeneity among the cards in the level of response elicited by each one, which also reinforces the impression that each card has its own "picture pull." In a study by Garfield and Eron (1948), however, the outcomes of the stories and the activity of the central character showed much greater variability than did the emotional tone among Ss. Thus, outcome would seem to be more clearly a result of the individual's projection than of the "picture pull." Terry (1952) found that although the emotional tone of the stories and their outcomes were positively correlated, showing that happy endings tended to go with happy stories, there was significantly more interindividual variation among the outcomes, which would corroborate the findings of Garfield and Eron. The relationship between emotional tone and outcome was made more meaningful by considering it in the framework of drive theory, as did Wittenborn and Eron (1951), who employed the drive evocation –drive reduction paradigm to predict successfully how such TAT responses will correlate with one another.

The "picture pull" of different cards is to be viewed not only as a group phenomenon but as a variable which may yield different results with different Ss. There seem to be differential "meanings" of the pictures for different Ss, depending on S's initial categorization of the picture. Male Ss in an achievement situation may produce achievement content if the stimulus is recognized as relevant to an achievement situation. If this initial recognition does not occur, little or no achievement content may result. These considerations refer to *objectivity* (see Chapter 1). Veroff (1961) and Veroff, *et al.* (1960) handled this problem by an intensive program of selection of relevant pictures (through use of ratings by judges) which might reflect the motives in which they were interested, and which would not be biased for or against a given social group. In addition, because of sex differences in apperceptive responses, two sets for men and women were chosen.

Relevant to the foregoing considerations is the finding that various "cognitive qualities" of the stimulus are related to the material elicited by them, and should be a significant aspect of interpretation of this material. Newbigging (1955), for example, found that the happiness of stories told by Ss varied according to the "happiness" of the pictures as ranked by judges. As the happiness of the pictures decreased, words per story and response time increased.

Another approach to the stimulus cards is along lines already established with the more "objective" tests. Reznikoff (1961) explored the possibility that the social desirability (SD) of TAT cards could be related to variations in themes. Using Eron's most common themes (1950) and correlating their frequency with ratings by clinician judges along an SD scale (using a Q-sort technique) resulted in insignificant correlations, however, suggesting that SD is not related to TAT thema.

A different approach by Fisher and Shotwell (1961), however, yielded the finding that preference rankings of TAT cards by normals, delinquents, and mentally retarded Ss showed an agreement pattern as to preferred and nonpreferred cards. When unanimous agreement as to preferred status was found, the themes associated with these cards were those of peace, contentment, and happiness; cards unanimously disliked were associated with themes of evil, death, and conflict. These expressed preferences or lack of preference, it might be noted, closely parallel Eron's (1950) ratings of emotional tone.

*Ambiguity.* Kenny and Bijou (1953) explored the relationship of the "significance" of TAT stories to the ambiguity of the cards. They examined responses to TAT cards which had been classified into three groups according to their degree of ambiguity. However, the amount of overlap in the ranking of the pictures by the judges in their first study (described previously) would seem to cast doubt on the use of such a grouping as a criterion. The significance of the stories was judged by two clinical psychologists using a Q-sort technique, and it was found that with increasing stimulus ambiguity there is an initial increase in the extent of personality factors revealed in the stories and then a decrease. It would seem that the relationship between ambiguity and projection is curvilinear. For low values of ambiguity as well as for high values, projection is low, with an optimum point somewhere in between. Subsequent research, it should be noted, was directed toward defining the characteristics of pictures at this point on the continuum, so that pictures can then be derived which are maximally useful in eliciting information about whatever variable is under investigation.

A somewhat different attack on the ambiguity value of the cards was taken by Weisskopf (1950b), who used physical dimensions to define ambiguity rather than to define it in terms of psychological group judgments, as in the foregoing studies. She investigated the amount of "fantasy" elicited by TAT pictures as a function of stimulus brightness and ambiguity. She measured the quantity of "fantasy" by "transcendence" indices (Weisskopf, 1950a), which were defined in terms of the mean number of responses that go beyond pure description when the subject is asked merely to describe the stimulus. She conducted three experiments with three groups of college students, manipulating the stimulus ambiguity in three different ways. In the first experiment, she found no significant difference between the amount of "fantasy" elicited by pictures of reduced and normal intensity or brightness. In the second experiment, she found significantly less "fantasy" when Ss were presented with the incomplete drawings of the picture than when they were presented with the complete picture. In the third, she found significantly less "fantasy" when the pictures were exposed for .2 of a second than when exposed for five seconds. It would seem that the more ambiguous the picture is, when defined in physical terms, the less "fantasy" is elicited. This would explain, perhaps, her original findings (1950a) that the "pictures of the everyday series (1 to 10) have higher transcendence indices than the pictures of the fairy tale series (11 to 20)," since the latter are more ambiguous in a physical sense, although not in the sense of the term as employed by Bijou and Kenny (see above). Weisskopf-Joelson and Lynn (1953), working with a group of fifty nine-year-old children, used as stimuli pictures traced from the CAT, in which parts of contours had been eliminated in order to increase their ambiguity. These authors compared the "amount of projection" elicited by these incomplete (ambiguous) stimuli to that elicited by the fully traced pictures, finding that the stimuli which were more ambiguous elicited significantly less projection than the less ambiguous pictures. Kenny (1954), however, found a significant correlation between Weisskopf's transcendence index and his own indices of ambiguity based on raters' judgments. Although Weisskopf's work is important in any determination of "picture pull," her assumption that "transcendence indices" are "indicators of the amount of clinically interpretable material elicited by each picture, and thus of the clinical value of the picture" has in no way been proved by her work. Pictures with low transcendence indices may still be quite diagnostic. Renaud (1946), for example, found responses to picture 11 of critical importance in differentiating head-injury cases and psychoneurotics, primarily because the scene was so remote from the individual's overt behavior. Gurel and Ullmann (1958), on the basis of an investigation of TAT protocols of 100 male VA patients, concluded that transcendence, as defined by Weisskopf, and number of emotional words for each card are significantly correlated, and that both indices may be viewed as "measures of personal material introduced by the subject into the test."

Finally, Laskowitz (1960) reported a study in which ambiguity was introduced in two different ways: by progressively photographing the cards out-of-focus; and by a cumulative omission of contour lines so as to make more ambiguous identification of expression, age, and sex of the figures. He worked with ten cards from the standard series, from which two sets of five cards each were treated by either one or the other of the "ambiguity methods." His Ss, 227 college students, were asked to describe what they saw. Using as an index of "fantasy" Weisskopf's transcendence index, he discovered that maximum projection was not elicited by stimuli of medium ambiguity (as he had hypothesized) but by stimuli of *least* ambiguity, that is, of maximum structure. Both methods of producing ambiguity were, it might be noted, correlated at a significant level.

The findings thus far reviewed suggest that although several methods of creating ambiguity have been used, and although projection has been measured by different operational means, a common thread has run through the various results reported: pictures do differ in ambiguity and in "pull," in terms of content elicited; various measures of amount of projection seem to be related to each other; and projection is greatest not with respect to stimuli of greatest ambiguity but to either medium or minimum ambiguity (see also Murstein [1958a]; Veroff [1961]; and Veroff et al. [1960], for a similar conclusion).

Although pictures have differential capacity to elicit various types of content, there has been little attention, until recently, to the question of a methodology for picture selection by which "cue value" of pictures can be ascertained and controlled. The next sections will present some relevant material in this area, as well as some theoretical problems in interpreting the meaning of stimulus ambiguity and structure.

*Norms.* The most straightforward way of determining "picture pull" is through normative study of the specific cards—the actual responses that are modally elicited by the stimulus qualities of each card in the standard series. Norms, ideally, should be specific for males and females, for different age groups and, no doubt, also for social class and cultural and ethnic background. A number of authors, Bellak (1951), Rapaport et al. (1946), and Stein (1948) have described, in a general way, the common responses to each of the cards, but without furnishing any data to substantiate their assertions. Eron (1950, 1953), Rosenzweig and Fleming (1949), Valentine and Robin (1950a, 1950b), Wittenborn (1949), and Roquebrune (1959) substantiated their norms with frequency data. Rosenzweig, Roquebrune, and Wittenborn, however, did not include all the cards, and Wittenborn's procedure departed quite markedly from the standard procedure. His Ss (N of 100), all of whom had applied for counselling service at their university student health unit and thus cannot be termed a "normal" population, wrote their responses to selected cards, and their responses were then classified according to the roles ascribed the figures in ten pictures. There was no comparison to matched *other* college or clinical groups and therefore no way of evaluating the utility of these findings. Roquebrune (*Ibid.*) presented norms based on 256 boys and 117 girls, ages 8–17, but only for cards 5 and 6.

Rosenzweig and Fleming (1949) studied 50 men and 50 women, ages 20–40, with no history of psychiatric disturbance and representing a broad cross section of the adult population, although they were above average in education and probably intelligence. Responses were analyzed according to identification of figures and objects, and problems and outcomes. Separate norms for men and women were presented. They also investigated reaction time, total time, and total wordage for the same sample. Rosenzweig (1949) explained the necessity for such normative endeavors (at a time when TAT usage was essentially clinical and intuitive in nature) in terms of the importance of distinguishing cultural themes, common elements, and stimulus-provoked content from purely idiosyncratic elements. The former group of responses he labeled *apperceptive* norms (similar to Rorschach P); the latter group of subject-oriented responses, which presumably reflect S's needs and personality trends, he called *thematic* norms. He noted that both types of norms are required in projective testing, the former for scoring, and the latter for interpretive purposes.

Valentine and Robin (1950a, 1950b) have presented norms for the female series obtained in Great Britain on 15 depressed and 15 schizophrenic patients, and 15 normal controls matched for intelligence. Eron (1950) offered responses of 150 veterans (both a normal and psychiatric population, of at least normal intelligence and high school education although the sample is weighted heavily toward the upper end of these variables) to the male series, analyzed according to emotional tone, outcome, themes, identifications, and levels of interpertation. He also furnished similar data derived from the stories of 60 normal American young women (1953). A very direct approach to the problem of stimulus definition was made by Cohen and Adams (1952), who asked 50 men and 50 women to identify the characters in their stories. The percentage norms which they presented did not differ significantly from the norms obtained by Eron (1950) through an analysis of story content. They supplied additional information, however, such as age of characters, choice of main character, and number of additional characters introduced into the story.

Although these normative studies focus on slightly different aspects of the TAT productions, there is a considerable amount of overlap, and the agreement in these areas seems to be very high. Thus, it seems quite feasible to account for the stimulus qualities of the pictures and their influence on the stories by the establishing of norms. By determining how most people react to different aspects of the cards, we can designate those factors on which a clear majority of them agree as determined by the stimulus; whereas the factors that show wide intersubject differences can be designated as individually determined.

*Methodology for Determining Cue Characteristics of Pictures.* There has recently been some stress on specific methodological procedures for assessing the contribution a picture makes to a particular thematic score, other than through a normative approach in terms of actual story responses. This is important, especially in the light of findings that picture cues which seem to be "motive related" elicit higher scores on measures relevant to that motive.[4]

Jacobs (1958) has reported a method for determining the cue characteristics of pictures which is independent of S's responses. The cue value of a picture for a given motive is defined by Jacobs,

. . . as the probability that the picture will engage some or all of the family of perceptual response dispositions which have been associated with attainment of the aim or goal state of that motive. Thus, the greater the number of persons who give responses characteristic of a given motive to a picture, the higher the cue value of the picture for that motive (p. 618).

Jacobs' basic method is to obtain judgments from people as to the chief "concerns" (goals, needs, motives) of figures in a given picture. A list of fourteen goals, derived from Murray's list of needs and White's list of goals, was presented to these Ss for ranking in order of the importance of goals that seemed most appropriate for the content of each of twelve pictures. Specifically, Ss were asked to "decide what the person(s) in that situation is (are) most likely to be concerned about" (p. 621). The twelve pictures included situations such as men sitting around a conference table, a man looking out of a doorway, or a young boy sitting at a desk at school, as well as several cards from the Murray TAT. He also had Ss rank the pictures as to the extent to which they sug-

---

[4] Atkinson has maintained that knowledge and control over the *physical* stimulus is only a first step, since cognitive expectancies among different individuals may actually differ with respect to pictures which are physically the *same* ([1958b], p. 615; see also, our Chapter 9).

gested a particular concern. Four motives were used for this purpose: achievement, avoidance of failure, affiliation, and avoidance of rejection. Written stories to some of these pictures were also available for one group of Ss. By these procedures, Jacobs hoped to answer the following questions:

What is the relative cue value of each picture for each of the concerns in the list? Do the pictures differ in ambiguity, and can this difference be assessed? What is the relative strength of the picture cues for achievement and affiliation? And is the S's judgment of the pictures in this ranking task influenced by his own motivation? (p. 622)

In his discussion, Jacobs attempted to answer the first question by listing the mean rank assigned by his Ss to each picture for each concern. This "consensus" could thus be regarded as the operational definition of the cue value for each of the pictures. By regarding ambiguity as definable by the variability in interpretations given to a particular picture (on the assumption that ambiguity increases as variability or lack of consensus increases), Jacobs was able to answer his second question. He examined the agreement or nonagreement of responses (ranks assigned) to each picture, and defined as "ambiguous" the pictures at the lack-of-agreement end of the continuum. The agreement or nonagreement of judges was determined by a table containing the average intercorrelations between rankings of the same picture by all judges. These $r$'s ranged from .20 to .60. This independent measure of ambiguity serves many useful purposes, according to Jacobs. $E$ may wish to know if greater conformity in response to pictures is elicited after experimental treatment. Or, he may wish to work only with nonambiguous pictures so that *some* response to picture content, even on a minimum level, would be produced by all Ss. Jacobs' method, of course, does not rely on a physical examination of the stimulus. But an examination of his material revealed that the more ambiguous pictures as defined by him, showed an absence of physical cues in at least one of three classes: the environmental situation portrayed, the ongoing activity, and the facial and postural cues of persons in the pictures.

Jacobs answered his third question, as to the relative strength of picture cues for two motives, achievement and affiliation, by examining the second group of rankings by his Ss for four concerns. The mean rank for these concerns for each picture was used as an estimate of relative cue strength for these motives. His fourth and final question, does S's motivation influence the judgments of concerns suggested by the pictures, was answered by having judges rank Ss' responses (where written stories were available) for several motives. These ranks were compared to the average ranks assigned by S for each motive, on the assumption that "if the motivation of Ss had an effect on the cognitive judgments, this should be reflected in the rank assigned to the concern which represents that kind of motivation" (p. 628). Jacobs concluded after this analysis that his method of assessing the cue value of pictures is independent of individual differences in strength of motivation as measured by thematic material written in response to the same cues.

We have now presented in detail a method of assessing cue-value and ambiguity which utilizes judgments and ratings as well as variability in ratings (agreement or nonagreement). Birney (1958), continuing this methodological orientation, wondered whether or not one could determine the modal response to pictures for use in special problems of personality research. Can one select pictures in such a way as to obtain material with predictable projective content?

To answer these questions, Birney proposed to compare ratings (using a modification of Jacobs' method) of judges, with thematic content produced to the same pictures by a different group of Ss. Stated another way, Birney's question is, essentially, do the characteristics of a picture affect the content of written stories in response to that picture? Birney's hypotheses were:

There will be a positive correlation between the rank order of pictures determined by judges' ratings of achievement strength and the rank order of pictures determined by the percentage of stories scored for n Achievement. There will be a positive correlation between the rank order of pictures determined by judges' ratings of achievement-related affect and the rank order of pictures determined by the proportion of positive affect scores. . . . There will be positive correlations between the rank order of pictures as determined by judges' ratings of how suggestive the picture is of subcategories in the achievement scoring system and the corresponding rank orders of pictures determined by the percentage of such scores obtained from imagery counts in stories written to those pictures (pp. 634–635).

Raters were 150 male and female college students. With these rating procedures, pictures could be ordered on the basis of the median values of the ranks assigned to the "achievement statement" (one of many statements concerning various situations which S was asked to rank), as well as on the basis of median rank assigned to the achievement concern for the pictures. High agreement was obtained between these tasks. Projective material was elicited to several of the pictures through use of a group method under high-achievement arousal conditions; Ss were seventy-two college males (preliminary analysis had shown that there were no sex differences in ratings). After an extensive analysis of results, the author concluded that, "The actual prediction of thematic content from ratings made of the pictures is shown to be feasible" (p. 643).

Haber and Alpert (1958), in an analysis of the determinants of any particular score (they were specifically interested in n Achievement), have explored the various cues which might influence a given achievement response. First, within the testing situation itself, there are task instructions, the experimenter, the room used, and immediate past achievement experiences. Second, as for the stimuli themselves, it is already known how important variations of picture content can be in determining a response. The authors have stressed, however, that for both classes of cues, there are individual differences in *sensitivity:*

> Given such individual differences, in order to predict accurately a S's imagery score we have to have independent measures of the amount and intensity of motivating cues actually present in the situation, and we have to know how sensitive an individual is to situational motivation cues. . . . We need to know the amount or number or intensity of the achievement cues in each picture used and the sensitivity of each S to these achievement cues (p. 645).

Third, there are individual differences in S's disposition to make achievement-related responses, that is, fewer cues are needed to arouse the particular motive for some individuals. And fourth, another variable affecting the response is the anxiety or avoidance reaction "to the cues associated with achievement-related behaviors."

Although in this particular section we are primarily interested in the *second* class of variables, we will briefly describe their study which was focused on the interrelationships among these several kinds of influences on the final response. Their overall method involved the testing of each S (eighty male undergraduates were used) under both relaxed and achievement conditions, each time with a set of six matched pictures, three in each set being high in achievement cues, and three low. The authors have described in considerable detail the procedures which were used (similar to those of Jacobs and Birney, see earlier) to select pictures meeting their criteria of containing either high or low achievement-related cues. The results of their extensive pretesting, incidentally, have supported some of the findings already described previously: for example, the "average judgment of a group about the relevance of achievement in the pictures is related to the amount of imagery elicited by these pictures." Or, "there is very little relation between rankings and imagery for *individual* Ss or for *individual* pictures" (p. 651).

Although the analysis of results was oriented from several methodological points of view (including test reliability, experimenter differences, etc.), the finding most relevant to our purposes concerned the significant differences in imagery between the low- and high-cue groups (divided on the basis of pictures), and between the relaxed and aroused groups (divided on the basis of situational cues).

*General Discussion: Role of Stimulus.* Attention should be drawn to the fact that there is by no means agreement concerning the logic or validity of ascertaining or controlling ambiguity and cue value by the several methods noted previously.[5] Murstein (1961, 1963), for example, has suggested that the distinction between *structure* and *ambiguity* has often been overlooked. Structure can be viewed as a physical attribute of the stimulus, whereas ambiguity refers to the stimulus uncertainty of the picture, that is, the multiplicity of responses it may give rise to. A TAT picture, thus, may be highly structured (such as Card 13MF) but highly ambiguous, that is, capable of multiple interpretation. Lesser (1961), however, has raised some problems concerning this distinction. Is the term *multiple interpretation* used in the intra-individual or inter-individual sense? The former concerns aspects of reliability or stability, whereas the latter does not. Moreover, if the inter-individual approach is used to define stimulus ambiguity, the particular sample used to yield such measures must be specified, since a stimulus may be ambiguous for one population, but not for another.

Murstein (1959) made some additional observations on "ambiguity." Noting again the distinction between structure and ambiguity (see also Murstein [1958b]), he pointed out that although the structure of a stimulus may determine who are the characters and what they are doing, the consideration, *why* are they doing it, does not come from the structure. Ambiguity may thus reside in the identification of characters, description of actions, and the meaning of actions. The current notion that cards of medium ambiguity yield the most useful measures of personality description is itself an ambiguous notion, according to this worker. Does medium ambiguity refer to the characters' identities, physical actions, or the meaning attributed to their behavior? Statements about the ambiguity of a picture are confusing unless we can delineate more specifically the referents in terms of the foregoing qualities.

Following some of Kenny's reasoning (described earlier in Chapter 3) as to the distinction between the categorization process—essentially a perceptual event—and the schematic process ("imaginative sequences of thought"), Murstein (1963) has proposed that perceptual ambiguity

---

[5] One recent and important development not discussed in this section is the application of the concepts and techniques of scaling and scalogram analysis to TAT stimuli. A brief summary of some relevant studies is presented in Chapter 12.

refers essentially to the categorization process and *not* to the physical or structural properties of the card. He has described a research in which he had his Ss judge the TAT cards as to, "(*a*) *who* was in the picture, (*b*) their *age*, and (*c*) the *relationship* of any of the characters. The students further wrote (*d*) *what* was going on, (*e*) *why* this was happening, and (*f*) how the story would *end*" (p. 170). Ambiguity for the "who" categories (according to Murstein the various "who" categories reflect the categorization process and the other judgments reflect the thematic process) was determined by $\hat{H}$, the measure of uncertainty, which yields results similar to $A$, a measure of the overall ambiguity of a card based on proportion of cases in any specific category, used by Kenny (1961). In this way, Murstein was not only able to describe the ambiguity of the cards in terms of the various categorizations, but could ascertain the relationship of the uncertainty of these categorizations to the variability of the themes.

We have thus seen some of the problems of, and methodologies introduced into, the complex job of identifying the stimulus characteristics of the TAT cards. The significant feature of recent thinking in the field is that it is no longer felt necessary to stress the importance of such research; that is, it is commonly accepted that without knowledge of *what* S is responding to, evaluation of his responses is a shaky procedure. Rather, the problems currently raised are those relating to methodology; the precise procedures by which stimulus attributes can be identified, ranked, and related to S's responses; the isolation and control over specific stimulus attributes for particular purposes; and the concomitant concern as to whether or not response variations accompanying stimulus changes are meaningful in terms of actual behavior. Of course, the essence of the problem is the determination of how much of the S's response is due to subjective and internal factors, and how much to external (stimulus) factors.

*The Task and Its Administration.* Along with the recent swing toward exploration of the stimulus situation, there has been an underemphasis on the task itself, the conditions of administration of that task, and the surrounding situation. When we appreciate the fact that such factors, taken together with those variables previously discussed, as well as the subjective ones which are being studied (self-concept, motivation, personality, etc.), not to mention S's set, and his understanding of the nature of the test situation, all interact with each other, then it becomes apparent that the task of understanding the relationships between and among these variables is a complex one, indeed.

The task in the TAT is for S to make up stories about the twenty pictures with which he is presented.[6] Sometimes he is told that this is a test of imagination and that imagination is one form of intelligence. He is told to make up a plot about each picture, with a beginning, a middle, and an end; to tell what happened before, what is happening in the picture, and how it turns out; what the characters are thinking and feeling; and to speak his thoughts as they come to his mind. S is usually told that he should take about five minutes for each picture, and if the time is recorded at all, it is done very unobtrusively. If any of the elements, for example, antecedents or outcomes, are omitted, S can be prompted with a nonleading question. The authors of the test recommend that administration be carried over to two sessions with ten pictures being administered each time. The directions for the second set, which it will be remembered is "more unusual and dramatic," are to make the stories as imaginative as possible. Special instructions for the blank card, No. 16, are to imagine some kind of picture and then to make up a story about it.

There have been only rare attempts to discover just what psychological events occur when an individual is confronted with a representation of a social situation which he must interpret—few experiments which analyze the elements that comprise and determine the final apperception as it is reported to another individual.

Many early attempts to understand further the psychological process involved in the picture-interpretation response were based on the perception-personality approaches, which tended to oversimplify the situation. (See Chapters 2 and 3 for a detailed presentation of these considerations.) The response family involved in the TAT situation may well rest on the important building-block of what is perceived. We are taken beyond the direct perceptual act, however, as soon as S interprets, makes certain judgments, and then verbalizes to E all, but more likely only a part, of these cognitive acts. Even further removed from the "direct" perceptual response is the act of *writing* a story in response to a picture.

With these cautionary remarks as a general context, a study will be described, which, although generalizing from the experimental situation "as if" verbal responses and perceptual responses are equated, nevertheless does demonstrate a procedure by which further knowledge can be gained as to what is comprised in the act of responding to pictorial stimuli with a verbal description. Orbach (1952) was interested in studying the "perception of meaning" in schizophrenic pa-

---

[6] Chapter 9 presents some "departures" from this standard procedure.

tients, hypothesizing that the disturbance in affective social relations, which had been demonstrated in psychiatric observation, would be reflected in "perceptual" reports the patients make about tachistoscopically presented pictures depicting affective social interaction. His Ss included thirty acute and thirty chronic schizophrenic patients, and thirty normal individuals, matched for sex, age, and education. Six pictures (four of affective social interaction between two people, and two of an affective experience for a single person) were tachistoscopically presented for four exposures in succession in the uniform order of one hundredth, one twenty-fifth, one fifth, and one second. The reports of the Ss were rated on three dimensions: Omission, Addition, and Social Relations,[7] according to reliable eleven-point scales which had been constructed for each of the dimensions by a normalized transformation of ranked data, and which ranged from no response to the most complete and accurate response. The content of the responses was also considered by identifying all the details in each of the six pictures and determining how many of them were included by Ss in each group for each of the four exposure times.

Orbach found more variability among the "perceptual" reports of the schizophrenics, especially the chronic ones, than of the normal subjects, since many of the patients omitted the descriptive aspects on shorter exposures and the affective social content on longer exposures. With each increased exposure time, however, all groups made significantly more accurate and complete reports, indicating that cognitive factors operate with considerable adequacy even in the "perception" of chronic schizophrenic patients. Only the normal group, however, continued to gain significantly in the extent of social interaction reported after the third exposure, and at each exposure the normal group consistently reported more social interaction. The acute schizophrenics, however, reported more incongruent social interaction than the other groups. Although these results correspond to observations with chronic schizophrenics of withdrawal from affective relationships, and with acute schizophrenics of distorted evaluations of social interaction, they do not demonstrate unequivocally that these disturbances in schizophrenic responses are a function of the affective content of the stimuli, since no pictures depicting nonaffective relationships were presented. The specific roles of such factors as attention, motivation to cooperate, and verbal facility, are therefore not clear. This particular study, however, does offer a methodology (not unlike some of the "microgenetic"

---

[7] The dimension, Social Relations, refers to the presence and quality of the relationship ascribed between two or more people.

techniques—see Chapter 3) which might be quite relevant to the study of the "psychological events" which comprise a TAT response.

The relationship of TAT stories to memory is also an important consideration in the understanding of the psychological process involved in the picture-interpretation response. Loeblowitz-Lennard and Riessman (1945) reported on a brief study. Using eight of the standard TAT pictures in a group presentation, they had twenty-five college students write stories in response to the pictures. After this was completed and the pictures removed, the Ss were asked to describe in one or two sentences all the pictures they could remember. Then, three days later, they were again asked to describe them. Two types of recall responses were differentiated: subjective (in which recall was colored by the meaning which the picture had for the individual in terms of his response) and objective (in which recall was limited to the concrete facts of the picture). The bulk of the responses were of the subjective rather than the objective type, matching the material as developed in the story. There was a change in the second recall period (three days later), however, from subjective reporting to more objective reporting. A definite relationship was also found between order and frequency of recall—those pictures recalled earlier were also recalled more frequently.

Although limitations in the design, such as lack of statistical evaluation because of limited data and no systematic control of order of presentation of cards, make general conclusions dubious, it would appear that there are differences in the degree to which the pictures were remembered. For example, the picture of the older gray-haired woman turned away from a younger man who is looking downwards (6BM) was outstanding in the frequency of its recall, its high order in the recall, the high subjective/objective ratio, and the limited range of story material produced. Although this study strongly suggests that there is a relationship between recall of certain pictures and the meaning of these pictures to an individual, no further work has been done on the connection between TAT productions and such personality functions as memory and judgment. This would seem to be a fruitful area for further research.

The use of twenty cards in the original series apparently was not arbitrary; empirically this seemed an ideal number of cards to have as a representative sample of S's "fantasy." In practice, however, not many clinicians use all twenty cards, and much of the research that has appeared is based on less than twenty pictures. Usually clinicians select the pictures that they feel have some relationship to their patients' problems. For example, if the patient were having trouble with his employer, the clinician would select pictures with parent or authority figures to get at some of his dominant attitudes toward such symbols, or if there were difficulties in sexual adjustment, pictures would be used which are expected to provoke persistent reactions to such situations. This haphazard administration is unfortunate if the data are to be used for research purposes, since without standard administration there can be no comparability of results.

The procedure of selecting specific cards may not be justified because it is a way of "stacking the cards." If the clinician suspects there is trouble in the S's relationship to the mother and presents the usual mother-son card, naturally he will find something about which he can make a good deal of comment. The source of the trouble may also lie in his relationship to like-sexed peers, however, and this may be completely overlooked because no appropriate card was administered. A study by Bellak, Ekstein, and Braverman (1947) indicated that cards 6BM and 7BM elicited significantly more "Oedipal" themes than any of the other cards. Thus, it is to be expected that Ss will react to this stimulus with such themes, whereas they would not necessarily so respond to card 10. That clinicians tend to "stack the cards" might be concluded, incidentally, from Ullmann's study (1957), in which significant differences in the median number of emotional words for the different TAT cards were found. The frequency of clinicians' selection of TAT cards for clinical use was found to be significantly and positively related to this productivity variable. Is the clinician thus obtaining an "unrepresentative" picture of S? Would this picture change if the "unproductive" cards were used? Another reason for not selecting specific cards is that there is then no baseline of seemingly neutral cards against which to evaluate the coherence, length, logic, language use, etc., in the stories to the critical cards. Also, perhaps one of the most effective criteria for the significance of particular ideational content is its appearance on cards where it is not usually expected.

A study by Terry (1952) would indicate that differences in order of presentation are not too important, at least for emotional tone, outcome, and level of response. She set up an experiment in which four of the cards, 3GF, 13MF, 15, and 18GF, were systematically rearranged so that each one directly preceded the succeeding cards (4MF, 14, 16, and 19) in a 4 × 4 Latin Square design. She found that the effect of changing card order did not show up in the ratings of the stories to the succeeding cards. So it would seem that the effect of just one preceding card is negligible. Kannenberg's (1948) results, however, would suggest that the combined effect of several preceding cards might be a significant factor. She found that reversing the first and second halves of the test affected the expression of certain of the factors she analyzed; namely, needs for friends and social approval, as well as a general state of apprehensiveness. It might be noted that Morgan, Snider, and Sobel (1958) have reported a sizeable influence on TAT content as a result of material discussed preceding the TAT administration.

Recently, there has been some methodological attention to the precise nature of the effect that serial position of TAT cards has on the thematic response. Many investigators have "built-in" controls in their experimental design for this variable (e.g., Birney, 1958). Reitman and Atkinson (1958), in a report of an investigation concerned with this problem, called attention to an earlier report by Atkinson (1950), of findings based on the use of a Latin Square design in which the stimulus appeared only once in a particular serial position; the findings suggested that ordinal position did not affect achievement scores. Reitman and Atkinson reported, however, that subsequent analysis of these data revealed a "saw-toothed" effect: achievement scores based on stories written to pictures in even serial positions were higher than those written to pictures in odd serial positions. In addition, they reported that achievement scores of the *first* four stories were significantly higher than those for the *last* four stories.

The authors pursued these findings in a study which explored whether or not the same set of pictures in various serial positions would yield equally significant relationships when an outside behavioral criterion was used. Their interest was in the achievement motive, and their behavioral criterion involved the use of several simple arithmetic problems under achievement conditions. They found significant differences between Ss high or low in achievement scores, in terms of performance on the arithmetic tasks, when these achievement scores were based on pictures in the first four serial positions. This was not found when pictures in the last four serial positions were used to differentiate high and low achievement groups. (*Note:* Symonds [1949] concluded that pictures *later* in a given series yield more valid material.) The authors suggested that these findings are probably not limited to the study of achievement scores alone. They have stated, "The studies reviewed here suggest that these variables quite possibly may have one meaning when coded from stories written early on the TAT and quite another when coded from later stories, entirely apart from any effects of the cues of the specific pictures upon the stories they elicit" (p. 673). It should be noted, of course, that Reitman and Atkinson have based their conclusions on the significance of prediction to a relatively simple behavioral criterion. Moreover, they themselves have stated that they do not know what results would be obtained when sets of ten, twelve, or twenty pictures are used. (In this study they had used a form consisting of eight pictures.) On the premise that serial position effects would be even more drastic with longer series, they have proposed the use of a short series from which scores could be obtained for several motives.

Does the time exposure of a card affect the content elicited? Relevant findings suggest that only a brief period of time, a few minutes perhaps, is necessary for optimal results. Exposures which are too brief (e.g., a fraction of a second, or only one or two seconds) of course do not allow S to "take in" the entire stimulus situation. On the other hand, increasing exposure time beyond a certain point does not seem to add to the richness or relevance of the material elicited. Lindzey and Heinemann (1955), for example, reported that there seemed to be no superiority of a group procedure which exposed the stimulus for eight minutes over a procedure which exposed the stimulus for five minutes. Their criterion of superiority was the correlation between S's scores on the group procedure and on an individual procedure.

Are there differences between group and individual administration procedures? On a priori grounds it would seem that there should be a difference between individually and group administered protocols. For one thing, E must take a more active part in the individual administration than in the group procedure. Also, the means of expression are different, and in the written administration spontaneity is not necessary. A third important factor is the intragroup effect which may prevail because of the presence of other subjects.

Clark (1944) constructed a multiple choice group test based on fourteen of the TAT pictures. Three stories for each picture were chosen from 852 stories collected from Ss in several localities. A scoring key was built up for each story based on needs, the effect of the environment on the organism, the reactions of the organism to the environment, the adequacy of the principal character as shown by the general theme, and dominant tones of the stories and the endings. The scores were recorded on a specially developed tabulation sheet. Clark evaluated the test by administering it to fifty students at the University of Southern California. The results were compared with written stories secured in a group situation. A substantial relationship between the two tests was evident in four out of five categories; this relationship was improved when the clinical form of the test was administered first. The new test did not indicate "needs" as accurately as it did the other categories, and proved most nearly comparable to the clinical test in revealing the "ending" and the "adequacy of the leading character." The study, however, did not compare this group modification with the standard procedure.

Eron and Ritter (1951) made a direct comparison between stories told in the standard individually administered situation and a group situation in which Ss wrote their own stories. They found that in content, that is, actual thematic material elicited, the two methods were almost identical; however, there were differences in formal aspects of the stories. The stories given orally were significantly longer, contained more alternate themes, and more comments about the artistry of the pictures. The written method was more conducive to humorous stories and positive feeling tone. Similar results were obtained by Terry (1952). She found a significant difference in the level of response, which is defined as "the degree to which the subject is judged to have become involved in his story, as expressed through elaboration of plot and descriptions of emotional responses of the story characters," between the two types of administration. Although the difference was significant, its practical effect, however, is probably negligible since both means fall within the third category of the scale (the first level of the scale in which personal feelings are mentioned). Finally, Lindzey and Heinemann (1955) have indicated that their study, which compared group and individual procedures, suggested no essential differences between the two procedures.

Other studies have explored additional changes in administration procedure. Sumerwell, Campbell, and Sarason (1958), for example, measured the effects of four different instructions on Eron's scales of emotional tone and outcome. Murray's instructions, and instructions informing S that he was taking a personality test or an intelligence test, produced more depressive stories than the neutral instructions. Caglieris and Saraval (1960) found that musical stimuli significantly increased S's approach to the TAT in that he told more "fantastic" stories.

Indeed it has been amply demonstrated in a variety of ways that set, induced by the type of instructions given to S, has a significant influence on the response. Lubin (1960), for example, presented either two TAT cards with high sexual cue value or two TAT cards with high aggressive cue value to sixty male college freshmen who were divided into three groups, each receiving one of the following instructional sets: facilitated—normal, well-adjusted people tend to let their imagination go as it is stimulated by the cards; inhibited—normal, well-adjusted people are the master of their imagination and emotions;

neutral—innocuous instructions. Lubin found that responses elicited under the "facilitating" instructional set (suggestion which placed stress on spontaneity) contained significantly more sexual and aggressive content than responses elicited under the other two conditions. In a subsequent, related study, Lubin (1961) demonstrated further that the stories obtained under these conditions of instructional set influenced significantly "blind" ratings of adjustment made by several experts. Stories obtained under the facilitating condition (greater spontaneity) were rated significantly higher on a scale of adjustment (in the direction of greater pathology), or lower when derived from the inhibiting conditions. The author, in addition, demonstrated that the amount of sexual and aggressive content in the stories was an important determinant of these ratings.

Although other variations in administration of the TAT have been introduced, their effect on the resultant productions has thus far not been evaluated. These variations include such things as having the individual interpret his own "fantasy," questioning S as to source of story, giving the Ss the choice of pictures about which they wish to build their stories, asking for expressions of like or dislike, having the Ss describe the pictures, taking the card away after twenty seconds, asking S to choose a proper name for the chief character to facilitate identification, and having S outline as many plots as possible for each picture instead of asking for one long story.

It is entirely likely that certain aspects of S's responses in the TAT situation are influenced by E's verbal (or even nonverbal) responses during the test administration, whether these are planned or unplanned. There are a number of studies which have manipulated E's responses in interview situations in order to discover the nature of the resulting changes, if any, in the S's verbalizations. Since at least some parameters of the TAT situation are not unlike those of the interview, it would seem reasonable to expect that experimental manipulation and exploration of E's verbal and reinforcing responses in the TAT situation should provide some positive findings as to effects on S's verbal productions.

On the basis of studies by Salzinger and his associates in the experimental analysis of interview situations (see Salzinger, 1959), we know that in an interview situation using schizophrenic Ss the quantity of verbal affect responses can be modified by the questions E asks as well as by E's verbal indications of agreement (Salzinger & Pisoni [1958]; Suzanne Salzinger [1956]). Salzinger and Pisoni (1960) found that with normal Ss also, verbal reinforcement resulted in increases in S's verbal affect responses. In a recent report of a study designed to explore further aspects of the conditioning of verbal affect responses, the same authors (Salzinger & Pisoni, 1961) noted:

. . . The interviewer who uses verbal reinforcement influences the interviewee's behavior, but his delivery of reinforcement is influenced in turn by the patient's behavior. This implies that the amount of influence (bias) that a given interviewer exerts will vary differentially with the rate of acquisition of each particular subject. Before an investigator can say that two groups of subjects, whether patients or normals, differ from each other in terms of the information, opinion, or feeling he has elicited, he must be able to show not only that his reinforcement procedure is identical in both groups, but also that their reaction to reinforcement (rate of acquisition) is the same (p. 515).

Thus, it is very likely that $E$'s verbal behavior and certain characteristics of $S$'s verbal behavior are in interaction with each other, and that $E$'s influence on $S$'s verbal behavior will vary as a result of individual differences among the $Ss$. We can see that at least for interview situations (with schizophrenic $Ss$ for the most part) there is some explicit knowledge as to the influence of $E$'s verbal behavior on $S$'s productions. Extending this knowledge to test situations, especially to those of a projective nature, would seem to be an extremely appropriate area for research. This would seem particularly true for the TAT, where both the scoring and interpretation of the protocols are based, at least in part, on the quality and quantity of affect in $S$'s verbal products.

Finally, the reader is referred to Chapter 9 for further material concerning the influence of certain TAT administration procedures on the ultimate response; the section *Innovations and Modifications*, describes several changes in procedures, such as the "negation" method, which have produced significant changes in the content of the response.

*Acceptance of the Task.* The task is presented to $S$ as a test of imagination, one form of intelligence. Its author, in a Department of the Army and Air Force Training Manual, has stated:

If the pictures are presented as a test of imagination, the subject's interest, together with his need for approval, can be so involved in the task that he forgets his sensitive self and the necessity of defending it against the probing of the examiner and, before he knows it he has said things about an invented character that apply to himself, things which he would have been reluctant to answer to a direct question. As a rule the subject leaves the test happily unaware that he has presented the psychologist with what amounts to an X-ray picture of his inner self (1951, p. 55).

Many workers, it seems, do believe that the task is accepted by most $Ss$ as a test of imagination. Rosenzweig and Isham (1947) have stated that S is "unaware of the purpose of the instrument." Symonds (1949) mentioned that the purpose of the test is hidden from S. Combs noted, "Since the significance of the materials revealed is necessarily unknown to the subject and since he is purposely misled as to the reasons for administration of the device, he is stripped of his protective armor and is at the mercy of whatever individual or agency interprets the results" (1947, p. 74).

Are all Ss stripped of their protective armor however? Ordinarily, no doubt the task is accepted as a test of imagination, and S is not explicitly aware of how his stories will be analyzed or interpreted; but it cannot be assumed that this is always the case. The likelihood that it will be so accepted is probably a function of the sophistication of S. It is not good practice to assume that S is always taken in by the "cover story." This is important because, as has been demonstrated by Weisskopf and Dieppa (1951), TAT productions are undoubtedly susceptible to distortion when S makes a conscious effort to give a specific kind of picture of himself.

Twenty-four psychoneurotic patients took the test under three sets of instructions: first with the standard instructions and then with the instructions to make the worst possible and best possible pictures of themselves (the sequence of the latter two conditions was randomized). Three judges rated the protocols for nine characteristics and were then asked to mark each one as best, neutral, or worst protocol. Results were evaluated by analysis of variance. When the ratings were based on the worst stories, Ss were rated as less well adjusted, more hostile, less eager to conform, of stronger sexual impulse, and more spontaneous. The tendency was for the ratings of the neutral administration to fall between the worst and the best, but considerably closer to the best. Also the judges were able to label 79% of the worst protocols but only 58% of the neutral or best ones (significant beyond the .01 level of confidence). Thus, it would seem that Ss can influence the diagnosis of their personalities made by experienced TAT examiners. When trying to make a bad impression, they changed their stories to a more significant degree than when trying to make a good impression. This makes one suspect that individuals taking the TAT under ordinary conditions might be attempting to make a good impression on the examiner even if not explicitly instructed to do so. The authors used only three cards: 1, 8BM, and 13MF, and thus may have biased the results by their selection. But even if only these cards are susceptible to faking and not the others, it should be sufficient to make TAT analysts wary of their assumptions.

In Chapter 1 it was noted that the wide cultural variations in "acceptance" of the task, in attitude toward the testing situation and $E$, and in the "style" of expression in response to the task—cooperation, as it were—are significant features of projective test performance often overlooked by the cross-cultural worker. Such a discussion is relevant to our current purposes too. For even within our own culture, individuals and subgroups may be expected to vary along these lines. The specific influences of these determinants on TAT performance and subsequent interpretation of that performance in the light of these variables are crucial and significant areas for the research clinician.

One criterion of cooperativeness is the length of the stories. Murray (1943) suggested that "stories from a sane adult averaging less than 140 words per story indicate lack of rapport and cooperation, lack of self-involvement. As a rule they are not worth scoring." However, a number of investigators have claimed to have obtained very good results with stories of fewer than 100 words (Jacques [1945]; Rotter [1946]; Symonds [1949]). Thus, Murray's criterion of cooperation would seem to be too stringent.

A good indication of lack of cooperation on the part of $S$ is his failure to carry out the explicit instructions to make up a story with a definite plot—with a beginning, middle, and end—especially when this is done repeatedly. If $S$ eliminates any of the essential parts, for example, the outcome; if he gives only a description of the picture, or if, on the other hand, he cannot limit himself to one plot and must give a number of alternate themes; if he calls the picture unreal, describing it as a dream, a painting, a scene in a play, or if the central character is not in the picture; if he denies a theme which is usually given, or makes derogatory remarks about the picture or the artist; if he injects his conscious personal experiences, making the stories autobiographical, or if he makes up a story which is completely unrelated to the picture; if he rejects any of the cards or reifies the characters in the stories; if $S$ behaves in any of these ways, it is quite likely that he is not cooperating to the fullest extent, and allowances must be made in the interpretation. It should be emphasized that this lack of cooperation need not necessarily be deliberate but may be a mechanism of defense of which $S$ is unaware, serving to detach the storyteller from the content and thus avoid the anxiety which the implications of the picture produce. Or such lack of "cooperation" may be a manifestation of the personal "style" of $S$, his personality characteristics, and emotional organization.

*Carrying Out of the Task by the Subject.* Once $S$ has accepted the task and cooperates to the extent of making up stories in response to the stimuli with which he is presented, it is important to determine what takes place as his stories come into being. One way to approach this is to define as rigorously as possible the entire stimulus situation to which S is responding with the particular stories he produces. Obviously there is more in the situation than the twenty pictures about which he is instructed to make up stories. For one thing, there is the set with which he comes to the experiment. Is he a college boy trying to pick up extra credit in introductory psychology by being a subject for some graduate student, or is he doing his girl friend a favor by being a guinea pig for her? Is he a patient who feels he is being persecuted by E and that everything he says will be held against him, or is he very anxious to secure treatment, trying to make absolutely sure that E recognizes every last nuance of his symptoms?

Introductory statements concerning the nature of intelligence and imagination do not control and make uniform the individual sets with which Ss come to the experiment. S is very much aware that he is not playing "psychological games." He knows E wants to find out something about him; perhaps he does not know exactly what it is, but he is never completely off guard. The experiment by Weisskopf and Dieppa (1951) indicates that the individual to some extent can manipulate his answers in accordance with his purpose in taking the test. Verville (1946) also demonstrated the effect of the set toward the test situation on behavior in the situation. Some of her Ss were told that personality was being tested. These Ss manifested significantly slower response times than those Ss who performed under different instructional sets. (A previous section has already described some material supporting the notion that response sets, altered experimentally, do indeed influence performance.)

S need not be consciously aware, however, of any effort to distort his story; he may be set in such a way that it is inevitable that the stories will fit in with his predominant attitude. Leuba and Lucas (1945) investigated the effect of three attitudes, happiness, criticalness, and anxiety, on observation and thought. The attitudes were hypnotically induced in each of three Ss, and after each condition was induced, S was asked to describe six pictures, telling what he thought about the picture and of what it reminded him. They found that the induced attitude was influential in determining what S observed. Three judges rated whether each statement expressed happiness, criticalness, or anxiety. In every case the difference between the mean number of indications of the induced mood and the mean number of indications of each of the other two moods was statistically significant. The authors felt that, "the results seem to indicate that common sense and clinical insight are correct in assigning a major role to moods, feelings and attitudes in the determination of intellectual processes; and even very brief descriptions of suitably chosen pictures show clearly the effects of a dominant attitude" (1945, p. 524).

It has already been pointed out in our discussion of the relation of TAT stories to behavior how experimentally induced motivation can influence TAT productions. Physiological needs, such as hunger and sex (see Mussen & Scodel [1955], for example), and psychologically induced motivations, such as need for achievement, have been related to differences in the stories. Similarly, a number of experiments have shown that conditions directly antecedent to the test administration will effect the productions. Many of these studies have dealt with the effect of frustration.

Crandall (1951) investigated the relationship between induced frustration and punishment-reward expectancy reflected in thematic apperception stories, by developing two roughly equivalent sets of pictures which he used for pre- and postexperimental conditions, frustrating thirty Ss and using thirty controls. He found a statistically significant increased punishment expectancy in the stories of the frustrated Ss. Bellak (1944) found that after Ss had been criticized for the poor quality of their stories, their subsequent productions contained a significant increase in the number of verbs and nouns connoting aggression. Criticism had a differential effect on different individuals, however, since the standard deviation increased from 9.81 before criticism to 22.2 after criticism. Thus, it would seem that even though a recent event may change the nature of the TAT story, the amount of such change is subject to significant individual variations which would allow diagnostic differentiation. An important finding was that the effect of criticism on the stories was found only with certain cards and not with others. This emphasizes the importance of the stimuli themselves in eliciting the expression of predominant needs. Lindzey (1950) has also shown that after a social frustration the incidence of aggressive acts in TAT stories carried out by heroes against other figures increased more than the incidence of aggressive acts carried out by the other figures.

An important factor is the environmental conditions under which the experiment is performed. Is it in the dean's office, a hospital ward, a prison, an employment bureau? An experiment by Eron (1950) indicated that the restrictive environment of a mental hospital may be as important a factor in determining the quality of an individual's productions as the specific symptom syndrome with which he is diagnosed. Masserman and Balken (1938) also came to a similar conclusion.

Not just the immediate surroundings but even the spirit of the times will affect the stories. In 1943, Rautman and Brower (1945) analyzed stories of elementary school children in order to investigate the extent to which they were preoccupied with war and related activities. They found that approximately the same proportion of the children had as many war stories as other stories built around themes of death and killing and concluded that the children as a group did not seem unduly preoccupied with the war. However, in a parallel study (1951), which they conducted six years later in the same school and grade, they found that the percentage of war stories decreased from 6.47% in 1943 to 1.77% in 1950, although stories built around themes of death and killing remained the same. Also more stories had happy conclusions in the second study (51%, as opposed to 35% in the previous investigation).

In the picture-story method then, all these factors and their effect on S's response must be considered—his attitude toward the situation, what he is set for, the immediately preceding circumstances, the environmental setting, the general tenor of the times—before we can get to the heart of the experiment, what there is in S's persisting motivations, his organization of values, his early training and experience, his characteristic attitudes toward himself and others, etc., which are evoked by these very specific stimuli and which put the stamp of individuality on his stories.[8]

*Recording of Results.* The most generally followed procedure is for E to write down as much as he can of what S says. With some Ss, it is not too difficult to record everything that is said; but with others, something of what is said is lost even though it is permissible to ask S to talk more slowly so that everything can be written down. The ideal situation would be to make a tape recording. Although this has been done, there are few comparison studies between protocols obtained by longhand and various recording devices. Conceivably, the presence of a mechanical device, or, for that matter, an E who writes down everything, including asides, could have an unfavorable effect on some Ss.

A number of investigators have reported a type of administration whereby S writes his own stories. As noted previously, Eron and Ritter (1951) found, in comparing written and oral protocols, that there was no significant difference between the two methods in thematic content, but that there were some differences in certain formal aspects of the two types of records. It was their subjective impression that there was less emotional involvement in the stories which were written by the Ss.

---

[8] This assumes, of course, that we are familiar with the effect of S's age, sex, social status, and other such factors on TAT stories, as well as of the stimulus situation, and that we can eliminate from consideration elements of the productions which are a function of these factors, and concentrate on what is peculiar to S.

Terry (1952) has experimentally verified this with an empirically derived rating scale of level of response. If the written procedure is followed, it is recommended that pen and ink rather than pencil be used so that slips made by S will not be lost. Often these can be important features in an interpretation.

Sauer and Marcuse (1957) were concerned with exploring differences in TAT responses between high anxious and low anxious Ss to overt and covert recording procedures. The former involved the use of a microphone and apparatus in full view of S; in the latter procedure, these were concealed. Overt recording, in general, resulted in an increase of scores such as speed of response, rate of speech, and number of words used in the high-anxiety group.

Thus, although there are only a limited number of studies relevant to this consideration, it would seem that the method of recording results bears an important relationship to response variables, and in all probability, in unequal degrees for different Ss, depending on set, personality organization, level of anxiety, etc. The interested worker is cautioned to be aware of this variable in the design of his study, in the interpretation of his results, and in the generalizations which are made on the basis of his own as well as other studies.

*Analysis and Evaluation of the Responses.* As noted in Chapter 9, there is no standard method of analyzing TAT responses. It is not like the Rorschach, in which each response is scored for location, determinants, and content. Many clinicians and researchers have their own scoring schemes adapted for their own particular use, which often accounts for the lack of comparability among results reported in the literature.

Chapter 9, in the section *Innovations and Modifications*, contains a description of some of the many scoring systems found in the literature. In the same chapter, attention was also devoted to the question of reliability; it was noted at that time that fairly high scorer reliability has been reported for specific systems which are not too "global," and when there is some training period for the scorers beforehand. Some comments were made as to the increased attention to formal and stylistic aspects of the response. The reader is referred to these earlier sections for this material, which will not be summarized here. The importance of establishing the reliability and objectivity of any special system is stressed again. In the meantime, Murray's system, based on a "need-press" approach, and some derivatives from this system, will be presented.

The method recommended by the authors of the TAT is an analysis of content in accord with Murray's concept of personality as a system of needs and press (Murray, 1943). For each story a hero is determined according to specified criteria; the needs motivating this hero (Murray listed twelve primary viscerogenic needs and twelve secondary psychogenic needs) and the press impinging on him (twenty press were listed which, like the needs, have been culled from the autobiographies of college student Ss) are noted. The interaction of a need and press is called a thema, and the themas are tallied. It was assumed by Murray that the narrator identifies with the hero, that the needs expressed by the hero are in reality the needs of the narrator, and that the press impinging on the hero represent the narrator's own conception of his psychological environment. Thus, by analyzing each sentence according to need and press and assigning each need and press a rating for strength (based on the criteria of intensity, duration, frequency, and importance to the plot), a rank-order system of needs and press could then be tabulated and assigned to the narrator. Murray provided the average and range of scores among male college students for some of the needs and press. The outcomes of the stories were rated on a scale from $-2$ (very unpleasant ending: frustration, failure, death) to a $+2$ (very pleasant: success and happiness). An optimism index was obtained by summing algebraically the ratings on outcomes and dividing by the number of stories.

Although the Murray system lends itself well to an objective, psychometric scoring, it has not been widely used because it is so time consuming and also because many individuals do not subscribe to the theoretical formulation of personality according to need and press, or do not go along with the assumptions about identification of the narrator with the hero. This system, however, has the advantage of being based on an a priori classification which has general application, and this makes it possible to obtain comparative data on a number of samples exposed to differing experimental conditions without a *post hoc* determination of the relevant variables. The latter procedure of inspecting the data for meaningful relationships is subject to the subtle statistical error, pointed out by Cronbach (1949), of implicit testing of critical ratios. This makes reported confidence levels questionable since the level of significance of results finally quoted depends on the number of explicit and implicit comparisons made.

Many simplifications of the need-press system have been used in various researches, and it has been demonstrated by Pittluck (1950) and Mussen (1950) that good interexperimenter reliability can be obtained in scoring such categories. A modification which has had some circulation is that of Aron (1949), but, although it is comprehensive and carefully worked out, it is definitely not a simplification. Aron reports that a minimum of 10 minutes is required for scoring each story. It is thus very unlikely that it can be adapted for clinical practice. One complication is that she scores need and press for everybody in the story, not just the hero. Although this may eliminate the arbitrary judgment sometimes needed in selecting a hero, it makes the whole procedure that much more unwieldy. Furthermore, she presents very little normative and validational data. Her sample is not sufficiently large to make for statistical verification, and she overgeneralizes her results without considering statistical probabilities, since she uses raw scores alone as her basis of differentiation between groups. If the chi-square technique were appropriately applied to her data, it is doubtful whether many of the differences she quotes would be more significant than would be expected by chance.

Aron's method of demonstrating interinterpreter reliability is novel but of uncertain merit. Because there was a multiplicity of ways of scoring each item, she utilized a comparison method which would take into account "perfect or near perfect agreement," "partial agreement," and "no agreement." Some difference in scoring was permissible for "perfect or near-perfect agreement" (certain differences in character, hero identification, or press were not recognized as reducing agreement sufficiently). More marked differences between scores changed the rating to "partial agreement"; and "no agreement" was the result of pronounced differences in the scoring of need or press, or the failure of one of the raters to score where the other rater did. Although Aron gives examples for classifying the various types of agreement, this is so much a judgmental function that it would seem that her method cannot be accepted as an adequate test of reliability.

Because of the overgenerality and cumbersomeness of the Murray system and its derivatives for ordinary clinical use, other systems of analysis have been introduced.[9] In addition, research demands have created the need for a wide variety of scoring systems. A very good summary of the systems of Rotter, Henry, Tomkins, Rapaport, and Wyatt, along with Murray's need-press analysis, appeared in an article by Wyatt (1947), and by Shneidman, et al. (1951), who published a volume with a complete TAT protocol which had been presented to fifteen psychologists,[10] each of whom did a blind interpretation and

---

[9] Murray himself presented a more simplified version of his method in a Department of the Army and Air Force Training Manual (1951).

[10] The contributors included the following: M. Arnold, B. Aron, L. Bellak, L. Eron, R. Fine, A. A. Hartman, R. R. Holt, W. Joel and D. Shapiro, S. Klebanoff, S. Korchin, J. I. Lasaga, J. B. Rotter and S. Jessor, H. Sargent, P. M. Symonds, and R. K. White.

gave a practical demonstration of his own method of analysis. The editors synthesized and compared qualitatively the methods and results of each analyst. They found they could classify almost all the systems according to their main emphasis, into five categories: (a) normative; (b) hero-oriented; (c) intuitive; (d) interpersonal; and (e) perceptual. No method is exclusively one or the other of these, but all methods presented emphasized one approach and used some or all of the others secondarily.

Finally, the reader is referred to the system in wide use by workers such as Atkinson, McClelland, and their associates in their studies of n Achievement and other motives. It might be noted that these studies, viewed as a whole, illustrate the extent to which diligent and systematic application of research attention in a seemingly narrow area has yielded an astonishingly large number of significant issues and problems, applicable perhaps to all projective testing. Atkinson's book (1958a) is a good example of this last point.

In this book (Ibid.) can be found detailed manuals for the scoring of three motives, achievement, affiliation, and power; considerable attention has been devoted to increasing knowledge with respect to these motives, and much of this work had stemmed from the earlier studies of McClelland, Atkinson, and their co-workers and students. These researches comprise a related "program" of systematic exploration which offers, as one of its many advantages, numerous opportunities for exploring objectivity of the scoring systems, comparisons among and between various validity indices, and exploration of a number of important methodological considerations. The necessity of using fairly objective, similarly constructed scoring systems for the various motives, the need for uniformity of the picture stimuli if cross-comparisons are made, the importance of assessment of the cue-values of the stimuli, and the need to understand individual, age, sex, and subcultural differences in response to various stimuli, have been thoroughly recognized and implemented by these workers.

The manuals for the three motives noted earlier (Heyns, Veroff, & Atkinson [1958]—Affiliation; McClelland, Atkinson, Clark, & Lowell [1958]—Achievement; and Veroff [1958]—Power), are supplemented by a detailed appendix in Atkinson's book (Smith & Feld, 1958), which can be used to train and "test" scorers, and clarify scoring problems in all three systems. Objectivity and reliability of these systems had been demonstrated by Feld and Smith (1958).

These systems, which are partially derived from Murray's original notions, are quite similar in structure. They imply quite directly that needs, motives, and goals are manifested by the content of TAT stories

—which, incidentally, are directly translated into scoring details. The authors have been explicit in their manuals as to detailed and exhaustive delineation and definition of each scoring category and whether and when each is scored or not scored.

## SUMMARY AND CONCLUSIONS

In this chapter, an attempt was made to present the array of relevant factors and variables which are significant with respect to the TAT response and the interpretation of that response. As with the Rorschach, the general framework chosen for this attempt was to view the TAT as an experimental situation. As in any systematic research endeavor, the results obtained are a function of the variation in the experimental conditions. In this case, the results consist of stories told by Ss in response to certain pictures, and inferences about S which are made by E on the basis of these stories. The effect of variations in subject, experimenter, apparatus, and procedure on these results has been indicated. Our survey was organized into the following sections: (a) Hypothesis; (b) Experimenter and subject—variables discussed included sex, cultural and ethnic variables, intelligence, age, and experimenter's interpretation; (c) Apparatus and stimulus—variables included criteria for selection, picture pull, ambiguity, norms, and methodology for determining cue characteristics; (d) Task and its administration; (e) Acceptance of the task; (f) Carrying out of the task by S; (g) Recording of results; and (h) Analysis and evaluation of the responses.

As has been pointed out in the first section of this chapter, the principal hypotheses underlying the TAT are not unlike those underlying other projective techniques. Some of these were described. In addition, several assumptions more specifically associated with the TAT have been discussed. Attention was focused on three major TAT assumptions, which are that (a) TAT products are reflections of needs and motives; (b) the products themselves are "fantasies" or reflections of the fantasies of the Ss; and (c) somehow, there is a direct, or at least a predictable, relationship of these products to behavior. It has not been demonstrated thus far that "fantasy" and TAT products are identical; moreover, questions, inconsistencies, and lack of uniform evidence concerning all three assumptions exist. With respect to the first and third assumptions, because it is with respect to these that some positive evidence can be found, it might be said that the main problem for future research is to determine just how TAT responses are related to specific motivational systems and to behavior; moreover, future research can determine whether or not specific predictions can be made from these scores, derived from a controlled testing situation, to behavior on the job, in school, at home, with the opposite sex, with like-sexed peers, etc. The overall material suggests that in some situations responses seem to be compensational with regard to needs; in others, representational. At times, themes in the stories signify actual behavior; at other times, a fear, a wish, or a defense. Perhaps the most that can be expected is the drawing up of some limited generalizations which will have merit in making specific predictions possible, so that it can be stated, given an individual of a certain sex, age, education, or socioeconomic status, when he is placed in a certain kind of situation, the needs and defenses which we have seen operating in his TAT productions allow us to predict that he will react in a certain specific way. These predictions will differ according to S, the need, drive or attitude under consideration, and the situations in which the criterion behavior is evoked.

Just as we have suggested for the Rorschach technique, we must break down the TAT into its component parts in order to validate our hypotheses. In the TAT, these component parts have traditionally been motivational systems, primarily. They need not necessarily be the only component parts which should be investigated, however. We have seen that specific experiments have been set up in which sharply defined motivations are investigated: achievement, aggression, dependence, sex, affiliation, acquisition, etc. Once we have been able to validate limited generalizations about the relationship between expression of these motivations in behavior and in TAT stories, we can then set about validating more molar relationships of personality content as represented in TAT products and behavior. Other "components" might also be similarly handled, such as various "formal" and stylistic factors, as well as interrelationships and configurations of various components.

Although a method is offered in the next chapter for systematic exploration and quantification of the TAT response, we have learned, from our survey, that the complex TAT situation is comprised of many factors. From this material, it seems important to note that the questions of standardization of procedures, as well as of making explicit statements as to how variations and modifications influence a given set of results are of extreme importance. Moreover, the general consideration of actual clinical use poses a serious question. How effective and efficient is a clinical instrument, even in the hands of an experienced clinical psychologist, when it is subject to such an extreme number of influences, in the "extratest" sense? Controlling the variables noted and

562 AN EXPERIMENTAL APPROACH TO PROJECTIVE TECHNIQUES

developing methodologies for doing so seem to be an essential accompaniment to the task of systematically evaluating and assessing the *response* side of the picture.

REFERENCES

Abel, Theodora M. Responses of Negro and white morons to the Thematic Apperception Test. *Amer. J. ment. Defic.*, 1945, **49**, 463–468.
Amen, Elizabeth. Individual differences in apperceptive reactions: a study of the responses of pre-school children to pictures. *Genet. Psychol. Monogr.*, 1941, **23**, 319–385.
Angelini, A. L. Um novo método para avaliar a motivação humana. Unpublished doctoral dissertation, Univer. São Paulo, Brazil, 1955.
Aron, Betty. A manual for analysis of the Thematic Apperception Test. Berkeley, Calif.: Willis E. Berg, 1949.
Atkinson, J. W. Studies in projective measurement of achievement motivation. Unpublished doctoral dissertation, University of Michigan, 1950.
Atkinson, J. W. (Ed.) *Motives in fantasy, action, and society.* Princeton, N.J.: D. Van Nostrand, 1958. (*a*)
Atkinson, J. W. Thematic apperceptive measurement of motives within the context of a theory of motivation. In J. W. Atkinson (Ed.) *Motives in fantasy, action, and society.* Princeton, N.J.: D. Van Nostrand, 1958, 596–616. (*b*)
Balken, Eva R., & Vander Veer, A. H. Clinical application of the Thematic Apperception Test to neurotic children. *Amer. J. Orthopsychiat.*, 1944, **14**, 421–440.
Beier, E. G., Gorlow, L., & Stacey, C. L. The fantasy life of the mental defective. *Amer. J. ment. Defic.*, 1951, **55**, 582–589.
Bellak, L. The concept of projection: an experimental investigation and study of the concept. *Psychiat.*, 1944, **7**, 353–370.
Bellak, L. A guide to the interpretation of the Thematic Apperception Test. (Revised) New York: Psychological Corp., 1951.
Bellak, L., Ekstein, R., & Braverman, S. A preliminary study of norms for the Thematic Apperception Test. *Amer. Psychologist*, 1947, **2**, 271. (Abstract)
Bernstein, L. The examiner as an inhibiting factor in clinical testing. *J. consult. Psychol.*, 1956, **20**, 287–290.
Bijou, S. W., & Kenny, D. T. The ambiguity values of TAT cards. *J. consult. Psychol.*, 1951, **15**, 203–209.
Birney, R. C. Experimenter effect on the achievement motive. Unpublished manuscript, Amherst College, 1956.
Birney, R. C. Thematic content and the cue characteristics of pictures. In J. W. Atkinson (Ed.) *Motives in fantasy, action, and society.* Princeton, N.J.: D. Van Nostrand, 1958, 630–643.
Brackbill, G. A. Some effects of color on thematic fantasy. *J. consult. Psychol.*, 1951, **15**, 412–418.
Byrd, E., & Witherspoon, R. L. Responses of preschool children to the Children's Apperception Test. *Child Develpm.*, 1954, **25**, 35–44.
Caglieris, A. N., & Saraval, A. Alcune osservazioni sull'azione proiettiva della musica mediante stimoli musicali accoppiati al T.A.T. *Arch. Psicol. Neurol. Psichiat.*, 1960, **21**, 67–78.
Child, I., Storm, T., & Veroff, J. Achievement themes in folk tales related to so-

cialization practice. In J. W. Atkinson (Ed.) *Motives in fantasy, action, and society.* Princeton, N.J.: D. Van Nostrand, 1958, 479–492.

Clark, Ruth M. A method of administering and evaluating the Thematic Apperception Test in group situations. *Genet. Psychol. Monogr.,* 1944, **30**, 3–55.

Cohen, L. D., & Adams, H. Further studies on the apperceptive and thematic norms for the TAT. Unpublished paper, Duke University, 1952.

Coleman, W. The TAT: I. Effect of recent experience. II. Some quantitative observations. *J. clin. Psychol.,* 1947, **3**, 257–264.

Combs, A. W. A comparative study of motivations as revealed in thematic apperception stories and autobiography. *J. clin. Psychol.,* 1947, **3**, 65–75.

Crandall, V. J. Induced frustration and punishment-reward expectancy in thematic apperception stories. *J. consult. Psychol.,* 1951, **15**, 400–404.

Cronbach, L. Statistical methods applied to Rorschach scores: a review. *Psychol. Bull.,* 1949, **40**, 393–429.

Davenport, Beverly F. The semantic validity of the TAT interpretations. *J. consult. Psychol.,* 1952, **16**, 171–175.

Davenport, J. W. The projective expression of the achievement motive in relation to career orientation and social satisfaction in home economics freshmen. Unpublished master's thesis, University of Massachusetts, 1953.

Department of the Army and Air Force. Training manual 8-242, AFM 160-45. Military clinical psychology. Washington: U.S. Government Printing Office, 1951, 54–71.

Eron, L. D. Frequencies of themes and identifications in the stories of schizophrenic patients and non-hospitalized college students. *J. consult. Psychol.,* 1948, **12**, 387–395.

Eron, L. D. A normative study of the Thematic Apperception Test. *Psychol. Monogr.,* 1950, **64** (Whole No. 315).

Eron, L. D. Responses of women to the Thematic Apperception Test. *J. consult. Psychol.,* 1953, **17**, 269–282.

Eron, L. D., & Ritter, Anne M. A comparison of two methods of administration of the Thematic Apperception Test. *J. consult. Psychol.,* 1951, **15**, 55–61.

Eron, L. D., Terry, Dorothy, & Callahan, R. The use of rating scales for emotional tone of TAT stories. *J. consult. Psychol.,* 1950, **14**, 473–478.

Feld, Sheila, & Smith, C. P. An evaluation of the objectivity of the method of content analysis. In J. W. Atkinson (Ed.) *Motives in fantasy, action, and society.* Princeton, N.J.: D. Van Nostrand, 1958, 234–241.

Field, W. F. The effects of thematic apperception upon certain experimentally aroused needs. Unpublished doctoral dissertation, University of Maryland, 1951.

Fisher, G. M., & Shotwell, Anna M. Preference rankings of the Thematic Apperception Test cards by adolescent normals, delinquents and mental retardates. *J. proj. Tech.,* 1961, **25**, 41–43.

Garfield, S. L., Blek, L., & Melker, F. The influence of method of administration and sex differences on selected aspects of TAT stories. *J. consult. Psychol.,* 1952, **16**, 140–146.

Garfield, S. L., & Eron, L. D. Interpreting mood and activity in TAT stories. *J. abnorm. soc. Psychol.,* 1948, **43**, 338–345.

Gurel, L., & Ullmann, L. P. Quantitative differences in response to TAT cards: the relationship between transcendence score and number of emotional words. *J. proj. Tech.,* 1958, **22**, 399–401.

Haber, R. N., & Alpert, R. The role of situation and picture cues in projective measurement of the achievement motive. In J. W. Atkinson (Ed.) *Motives in fantasy, action, and society.* Princeton, N.J.: D. Van Nostrand, 1958, 644–663.

Harrison, R. Studies in the use and validity of the Thematic Apperception Test with mentally disordered patients. II. A quantitative validity study. III. Validation by the method of "blind analysis." *Charact. & Pers.,* 1940, 9, 122–138.

Henry, W. E. *The analysis of fantasy: The Thematic Apperception Technique in the study of personality.* New York: John Wiley and Sons, 1956.

Heppell, H. K., & Raimy, V. C. Projective pictures as interview devices. *J. consult. Psychol.,* 1951, 15, 405–411.

Heyns, R. W., Veroff, J., & Atkinson, J. W. A scoring manual for the affiliation motive. In J. W. Atkinson (Ed.) *Motives in fantasy, action, and society.* Princeton, N.J.: D. Van Nostrand, 1958, 205–218.

Jacobs, B., Jr. A method for investigating the cue characteristics of pictures. In J. W. Atkinson (Ed.) *Motives in fantasy, action, and society.* Princeton, N.J.: D. Van Nostrand, 1958, 617–629.

Jacques, E. The clinical use of the Thematic Apperception Test with soldiers. *J. abnorm. soc. Psychol.,* 1945, 40, 363–375.

Kannenberg, Katherine M. A comparison of results obtained from the Thematic Apperception Test under two conditions of administration. *Amer. Psychologist,* 1948, 3, 363. (Abstract)

Kenny, D. T. Transcendence indices, extent of personality factors in fantasy responses, and the ambiguity of TAT cards. *J. consult. Psychol.,* 1954, 18, 345–348.

Kenny, D. T. A theoretical and research reappraisal of stimulus factors in the TAT. In J. Kagan and G. Lesser (Eds.) *Contemporary issues in thematic apperceptive methods.* Springfield, Ill.: Charles C Thomas, 1961, 288–310.

Kenny, D. T., & Bijou, S. W. Ambiguity of pictures and extent of personality factors in fantasy responses. *J. consult. Psychol.,* 1953, 17, 283–288.

Korchin, S. J., Mitchell, H. E., & Meltzoff, J. A critical evaluation of the Thompson Thematic Apperception Test. *J. proj. Tech.,* 1950, 14, 445–452.

Kutash, S. B. Performance of psychopathic defective criminals on the Thematic Apperception Test. *J. crim. Psychopath.,* 1943, 5, 319–340.

Laskowitz, D. The effect of varied degrees of pictorial ambiguity on fantasy evocation: a comparative analysis of two techniques of producing gradated ambiguity with Thematic Apperception Test cards with respect to the amount of fantasy evoked. *Dissertation Abstr.,* 1960, 20, 3379–3380. (Abstract)

Lesser, G. S. Religion and the defensive responses in children's fantasy. *J. proj. Tech.,* 1959, 23, 64–68.

Lesser, G. S. Discussion of Dr. Murstein's paper. In J. Kagan and G. S. Lesser (Eds.) *Contemporary issues in thematic apperceptive methods.* Springfield, Ill.: Charles C Thomas, 1961, 274–287.

Leuba, C., & Lucas, C. The effects of attitudes on descriptions of pictures. *J. exp. Psychol.,* 1945, 35, 517–524.

Lindzey, G. An experimental examination of the scapegoat theory of prejudice. *J. abnorm. soc. Psychol.,* 1950, 45, 296–309.

Lindzey, G. Thematic Apperception Test: interpretative assumptions and related empirical evidence. *Psychol. Bull.,* 1952, 49, 1–25.

Lindzey, G., & Goldberg, M. Motivational differences between male and female as measured by the Thematic Apperception Test. *J. Pers.*, 1953, **22**, 101–117.

Lindzey, G., & Heinemann, Shirley H. Thematic Apperception Test: individual and group administration. *J. Pers.*, 1955, **24**, 34–55.

Lindzey, G., & Silverman, M. Thematic Apperception Test: techniques of group administration, sex differences, and the role of verbal productivity. *J. Pers.*, 1959, **27**, 311–323.

Little, K. B., & Shneidman, E. S. Congruencies among interpretations of psychological test and anamnestic data. *Psychol. Monogr.*, 1959, **73** (Whole No. 476).

Loeblowitz-Lennard, H., & Riessman, F., Jr. Recall in the Thematic Apperception Test: an experimental investigation into the meaning of recall of phantasy with reference to personality diagnosis. *J. Pers.*, 1945, **14**, 41–46.

Lubin, B. Some effects of set and stimulus properties on TAT stories. *J. proj. Tech.*, 1960, **24**, 11–16.

Lubin, B. Judgments of adjustment from TAT stories as a function of experimentally altered sets. *J. consult. Psychol.*, 1961, **25**, 249–252.

Lubin, N. M. The effect of color in the TAT on productions of mentally retarded subjects. *Amer. J. ment. Defic.*, 1955, **60**, 366–370.

Mason, Beth, & Ammons, R. B. Note on social class and the Thematic Apperception Test. *Percept. mot. Skills*, 1956, **6**, 88.

Masserman, J. H., & Balken, Eva R. The clinical application of phantasy studies. *J. Psychol.*, 1938, **6**, 81–88.

McArthur, C. Personality differences between middle and upper classes. *J. abnorm. soc. Psychol.*, 1955, **50**, 247–254.

McClelland, D. C., Atkinson, J. W., Clark, R. A., & Lowell, E. L. A scoring manual for the achievement motive. In J. W. Atkinson (Ed.) *Motives in fantasy, action, and society.* Princeton, N.J.: D. Van Nostrand, 1958, 179–204.

McClelland, D. C., Clark, R. A., Roby, T. B., & Atkinson, J. W. The projective expression of needs: IV. The effect of the need for achievement on thematic apperception. *J. exp. Psychol.*, 1949, **39**, 242–255.

McClelland, D. C., Sturr, J. F., Knapp, R. H., & Wendt, H. W. Obligations to self and society in the United States and Germany. *J. abnorm. soc. Psychol.*, 1958, **56**, 245–255.

Morgan, J. N., Snider, M., & Sobel, M. G. *Highlights from a study on lump sum redemption settlements and rehabilitation.* Ann Arbor, Mich.: Survey Research Center, 1958.

Morrison, H. W. Validity and behavioral correlates of female need for achievement. Unpublished master's thesis, Wesleyan University, 1954.

Murray, H. A. *Thematic Apperception Test.* Cambridge: Harvard University Press, 1943.

Murray, H. A. Uses of the Thematic Apperception Test. *Amer. J. Psychiat.*, 1951, **107**, 577–581.

Murstein, B. I. Nonprojective determinants of perception on the TAT. *J. consult. Psychol.*, 1958, **22**, 195–198. (*a*)

Murstein, B. I. The relationship of stimulus ambiguity on the TAT to the productivity of themes. *J. consult. Psychol.*, 1958, **22**, 348. (*b*)

Murstein, B. I. The measurement of ambiguity for thematic cards. Paper read at A.P.A. meeting, 1959.

Murstein, B. I. The role of the stimulus in the manifestation of fantasy. In J. Kagan and G. S. Lesser (Eds.) *Contemporary issues in thematic apperceptive methods*. Springfield, Ill.: Charles C Thomas, 1961, 229–273.

Murstein, B. I. *Theory and research in projective techniques (emphasizing the TAT)*. New York: John Wiley and Sons, 1963.

Mussen, P. H. Some personality and social factors related to changes in children's attitudes toward Negroes. *J. abnorm. soc. Psychol.*, 1950, 45, 423–441.

Mussen, P. H. Differences between the TAT responses of Negro and white boys. *J. consult. Psychol.*, 1953, 17, 373–376.

Mussen, P. H., & Scodel, A. The effects of sexual stimulation under varying conditions on TAT sexual responsiveness. *J. consult. Psychol.*, 1955, 19, 90.

Newbigging, P. L. Influence of a stimulus variable on stories told to certain TAT pictures. *Canad. J. Psychol.*, 1955, 9, 195–206.

Orbach, C. E. The perception of meaning in schizophrenia. Unpublished doctoral dissertation, Teachers College, Columbia University, 1952.

Pittluck, Patricia. The relation between aggressive fantasy and overt behavior. Unpublished doctoral dissertation, Yale University, 1950.

Rapaport, D., Gill, M. M., & Schafer, R. *Diagnostic psychological testing*. Vol. II. Chicago: Year Book Publishers, 1946.

Rautman, A. L., & Brower, Edna. War themes in children's stories. *J. Psychol.*, 1945, 19, 191–202.

Rautman, A. L., & Brower, Edna. War themes in children's stories: II. Six years later. *J. Psychol.*, 1951, 31, 263–270.

Reitman, W. R., & Atkinson, J. W. Some methodological problems in the use of thematic apperceptive measures of human motives. In J. W. Atkinson (Ed.) *Motives in fantasy, action, and society*. Princeton, N.J.: D. Von Nostrand, 1958, 664–683.

Renaud, H. Group differences in fantasies: head injuries, psychoneurotics, and brain diseases. *J. Psychol.*, 1946, 21, 327–346.

Reznikoff, M. Social desirability in TAT themes. *J. proj. Tech.*, 1961, 25, 87–89.

Ricciuti, H. N., & Sadacca, R. *The prediction of academic grades with a projective test of achievement motivation: II. Cross-validation at the high school level.* Princeton, N. J.: Educational Testing Service, 1955.

Riess, B. F., Schwartz, E. K., & Cottingham, Alice. An experimental critique of assumptions underlying the Negro version of the TAT. *J. abnorm. soc. Psychol.*, 1950, 45, 700–709.

Riessman, F., Jr., & Miller, S. M. Social class and projective tests. *J. proj. Tech.*, 1958, 22, 432–439.

Roquebrune, G. Aspects génétiques et typologiques des résultats obtenus à une épreuve projective. *Enfance*, 1959, No. 1, 29–47.

Rosen, B. C. The achievement syndrome: a psychocultural dimension of social stratification. In J. W. Atkinson (Ed.) *Motives in fantasy, action, and society*. Princeton, N.J.: D. Van Nostrand, 1958, 495–508.

Rosenzweig, S. Apperceptive norms for the Thematic Apperception Test. I. The problem of norms in projective methods. *J. Pers.*, 1949, 17, 475–482.

Rosenzweig, S., & Fleming, Edith. Apperceptive norms for the Thematic Apperception Test. II. An empirical investigation. *J. Pers.*, 1949, 17, 483–503.

Rosenzweig, S., & Isham, A. C. Complementary Thematic Apperception Test patterns in close kin. *Amer. J. Orthopsychiat.*, 1947, 17, 129–142.

Rotter, J. B. Thematic Apperception Tests: suggestions for administration and interpretation. *J. Pers.*, 1946, **15**, 70–92.

Ruess, A. L. Some cultural and personality aspects of mental retardation. *Amer. J. ment. Defic.*, 1958, **63**, 50–59.

Salzinger, K. The experimental approach to the interview. In J. Zubin (Ed.) *Experimental abnormal psychology.* New York: Columbia University Library, 1959, 1–46.

Salzinger, K., & Pisoni, Stephanie. Reinforcement of affect responses of schizophrenics during the clinical interview. *J. abnorm. soc. Psychol.*, 1958, **57**, 84–90.

Salzinger, K., & Pisoni, Stephanie. Reinforcement of verbal affect responses of normal subjects during the interview. *J. abnorm. soc. Psychol.*, 1960, **60**, 127–130.

Salzinger, K., & Pisoni, Stephanie. Some parameters of the conditioning of verbal affect responses in schizophrenic subjects. *J. abnorm. soc. Psychol.*, 1961, **63**, 511–516.

Salzinger, Suzanne. Rate of affect response in schizophrenics as a function of three types of interviewer verbal behavior. Paper read at the Eastern Psychological Association, Atlantic City, 1956.

Sanford, R. N. Personality patterns in school children. In R. G. Barker, J. S. Kounin, and H. F. Wright (Eds.) *Child behavior and development.* New York: McGraw-Hill, 1943, 567–589.

Sarason, Barbara R., & Sarason, I. G. The effect of type of administration and sex of subject on emotional tone and outcome ratings of TAT stories. *J. proj. Tech.*, 1958, **22**, 333–337.

Sarason, S. B. The use of the Thematic Apperception Test with mentally deficient children. I. A study of high grade girls. *Amer. J. ment. Defic.*, 1943, **47**, 414–421. (*a*)

Sarason, S. B. The use of the Thematic Apperception Test with mentally deficient children. II. A study of high grade boys. *Amer. J. ment. Defic.*, 1943, **48**, 169–173. (*b*)

Sarason, S. B. The TAT and subjective interpretation. *J. consult. Psychol.*, 1948, **12**, 285–299.

Sauer, R. E., & Marcuse, F. L. Overt and covert recording. *J. proj. Tech.*, 1957, **21**, 391–395.

Schwartz, E. K., Riess, B. F., & Cottingham, Alice. Further critical evaluations of the Negro version of the TAT. *J. proj. Tech.*, 1951, **15**, 394–400.

Shneidman, E. S., Joel, W., & Little, K. B. *Thematic test analysis.* New York: Grune and Stratton, 1951.

Singer, J. L. Projected familial attitudes as a function of socioeconomic status and psychopathology. *J. consult. Psychol.*, 1954, **18**, 99–104.

Singer, J. L., & Opler, M. K. Contrasting patterns of fantasy and motility in Irish and Italian schizophrenics. *J. abnorm. soc. Psychol.*, 1956, **53**, 42–47.

Smith, C. P., & Feld, Sheila. How to learn the method of content analysis for *n* achievement, *n* affiliation and *n* power. In J. W. Atkinson (Ed.) *Motives in fantasy, action, and society.* Princeton, N.J.: D. Van Nostrand, 1958, Appendix I, 685–818.

Stein, M. I. *The Thematic Apperception Test: an introductory manual for its clinical use with adult males.* Cambridge, Mass.: Addison-Wesley, 1948.

Sumerwell, Harriet C., Campbell, Mary M., & Sarason, I. G. The effect of differential motivating instructions on the emotional tone and outcome of TAT stories. *J. consult. Psychol.*, 1958, **22**, 385–388.

Symonds, P. M. Criteria for the selection of pictures for the investigation of adolescent phantasies. *J. abnorm. soc. Psychol.*, 1939, **34**, 271–274.

Symonds, P. M. *Adolescent fantasy.* New York: Columbia University Press, 1949.

Terry, Dorothy. The use of a rating scale of level of response in TAT stories. *J. abnorm. soc. Psychol.*, 1952, **47**, 507–511.

Thompson, C. E., & Bachrach, A. J. The use of color in the Thematic Apperception Test. *J. proj. Tech.*, 1951, **15**, 173–184.

Ullmann, L. P. Productivity and the clinical use of TAT cards. *J. proj. Tech.*, 1957, **21**, 399–403.

Valentine, M., & Robin, A. A. Aspects of Thematic Apperception testing: depression. *J. ment. Sci.*, 1950, **96**, 435–447. (*a*)

Valentine, M., & Robin, A. A. Aspects of Thematic Apperception testing: paranoid schizophrenia. *J. ment. Sci.*, 1950, **96**, 869–888. (*b*)

Veroff, J. A scoring manual for the power motive. In J. W. Atkinson (Ed.) *Motives in fantasy, action, and society.* Princeton, N.J.: D. Van Nostrand, 1958, 219–233.

Veroff, J. Thematic apperception in a nationwide sample survey. In J. Kagan and G. S. Lesser (Eds.) *Contemporary issues in thematic apperceptive methods.* Springfield, Ill.: Charles C Thomas, 1961, 83–111.

Veroff, J., Atkinson, J. W., Feld, Sheila, & Gurin, G. The use of thematic apperception to assess motivation in a nationwide interview study. *Psychol. Monogr.*, 1960, **74** (Whole No. 499).

Veroff, J., Wilcox, Sue, & Atkinson, J. W. The achievement motive in high school and college age women. *J. abnorm. soc. Psychol.*, 1953, **48**, 108–119.

Verville, Elinor. The effect of emotional and motivational sets on the perception of incomplete pictures. *J. genet. Psychol.*, 1946, **69**, 133–145.

Vogel, Margaret. An investigation of the affiliation motive in college age women using low cue strength pictures. Unpublished honor's thesis, University of Michigan, 1954.

Walker, E. L., & Atkinson, J. W. The expression of fear-related motivation in thematic apperception as a function of proximity to an atomic explosive. In J. W. Atkinson (Ed.) *Motives in fantasy, action, and society.* Princeton, N.J.: D. Van Nostrand, 1958, 143–159.

Webb, W. B., & Hilden, A. H. Verbal and intellectual ability as factors in projective test results, *J. proj. Tech.*, 1953, **17**, 102–103.

Webster, H. Derivation and use of the masculinity-femininity variable. *J. clin. Psychol.*, 1953, **9**, 33–36.

Weisskopf, Edith A. A transcendence index as a proposed measure in the TAT. *J. Psychol.*, 1950, **29**, 379–390. (*a*)

Weisskopf, Edith A. An experimental study of the effect of brightness and ambiguity on projection in the Thematic Apperception Test. *J. Psychol.*, 1950, **29**, 407–416. (*b*)

Weisskopf, Edith A., & Dieppa, J. Experimentally induced faking of TAT responses. *J. consult. Psychol.*, 1951, **15**, 469–474.

Weisskopf, Edith A., & Dunlevy, G. P., Jr. Bodily similarity between subject and central figure in the TAT as an influence on projection. *J. abnorm. soc. Psychol.*, 1952, **47**, 441–445.

Weisskopf-Joelson, Edith A., & Lynn, D. B. The effect of variations in ambiguity on projection in the Children's Apperception Test. *J. consult. Psychol.*, 1953, **17**, 67–70.

Weisskopf-Joelson, Edith A., & Money, L., Jr. Facial similarity between subject and central figure in the TAT as an influence on projection. *J. abnorm. soc. Psychol.*, 1953, **48**, 341–344.

Wittenborn, J. R. Some Thematic Apperception Test norms and a note on the use of the test cards in the guidance of college students. *J. clin. Psychol.*, 1949, **5**, 157–161.

Wittenborn, J. R. & Eron, L. D. An application of drive theory to TAT responses. *J. consult. Psychol.*, 1951, **15**, 45–50.

Wyatt, F. The scoring and analysis of the Thematic Apperception Test. *J. Psychol.*, 1947, **24**, 319–330.

# 12 A PSYCHOMETRIC APPROACH TO THE TAT

It has been pointed out in the previous chapter that there are about as many ways of analyzing the TAT as there are clinical psychologists who use the method. The most popular method among clinicians seems to be a subjective, intuitive approach in which the entire protocol is perused a number of times by the analyst and such things are noted as repetitive themes, the sequence of stories, peculiar verbalizations, perceptual distortions, slips of the tongue, the differential degree of emotion invested in the stories, the outcome, and unusual interpretations. These may or may not be written down by the analyst. They are then usually checked against a subjective kind of norm which the psychologist has built up in his experience by reading a large number and variety of TAT protocols submitted by patients and, it is hoped, by normal individuals. Then, on the basis of the total impression which remains with him, the psychologist writes up his interpretation of S's personality. This may very often be quite congruent with the impressions of the individual that the therapist, caseworker, or teacher may have. Also it may furnish them with new information of which they were previously unaware but which on further investigation they now see as true. It is difficult, if not impossible, however, to pin down the basis on which specific statements about S are generally made—what there is specifically in the story or series of stories which leads the analyst to a particular conclusion. It is for this reason that such methods of TAT analysis are generally uncommunicable and cannot be duplicated.

There is the danger with this kind of impressionistic analysis of the protocol, as has been pointed out in the discussion of the Rorschach, that all the evidence may not come under consideration. On the basis of the first two or three cards, sometimes even on the basis of the first card alone, certain impressions are gained about the S. All subsequent stories are then considered in the light of these initial impressions, negative evidence tends to be sloughed off, and only the evidence that reinforces the initial impression is retained. This is not necessarily a deliberate practice and may often be quite unconscious on the part of E. It has been pointed out by many that the TAT is very often as much a projective device for E as it is for the individual taking the test (Eron [1950]; Rosenzweig [1949]; and Rotter [1946]). To eliminate this kind of selective perception, it is necessary that a method be devised whereby the available evidence in a protocol may be noted and summarized consistently and objectively. Equally important is the need for adequate normative data against which the individual results can be checked. With such a method, however, there is the danger that important qualitative differences will be overlooked, since many clinicians claim that it is impossible to quantify, categorize, and standardize the subtle nuances of an individual's responses that often are the key to the interpretation.

*Scalability.* Before turning our attention to the chief purpose of this chapter—that is, the presentation and discussion of rating scales for use in the analysis of a TAT record—a brief summary of an important development in TAT research will be presented. This development has grown out of several attempts to apply Guttman's scaling techniques to TAT items. Guttman's research (see [1950] for a summary) had been based on a methodology relevant to the measurement of attitudes; a few workers, however, have felt that his work could probably be applied equally effectively to a projective instrument such as the TAT.

Chapter 11 has already presented material demonstrating various approaches to exploring systematically the stimulus dimensions of the TAT, for example, attempts to order and rank the stimuli according to a dimension such as "pull" or ambiguity. Using an approach more specifically based on Guttman's scaling techniques, Auld, Eron, and Laffal (1955) felt that answers to two problems could be appropriately handled. These questions were: "(1) When should one consider two responses as indicative of a single underlying trait (habit or motive) of the subject? and (2) Conceding that two or more responses both reveal the strength of the habit or motive, how can one combine the ratings obtained from the two responses into a single rating of the habit or motive?" (p. 423). These workers have suggested that the use of the Guttman technique would provide a method of "ordering" the Ss in such a way as to avoid the problem of having to weight responses. They worked with the Navy adaptation of the Group TAT (Briggs, 1954); their Ss were 100 sailors at a submarine base; and their general task was to scale the stimulus cards for the dimensions of sex and aggression. The general premise for the construction of this type of scale is that pictures vary in "pull," that is, in their ability to elicit material for a particular motivational content. Stated another way, some cards are more ambiguous than others, in terms of the degree to which they "pull" sex content or aggressive content. Moreover, Ss also differ with respect to the *strength* of a particular need. Presumably, Ss with strong aggressive needs should express these needs even in their responses to cards of high ambiguity with respect to that dimension, whereas Ss with low aggressive needs would express these needs only in response to cards of low ambiguity. If the stimulus properties of the cards are therefore known, the strength of S's needs could be easily determined; Ss could be "ordered" with respect to the particular dimension with which E is working. Cards, of course, should be specifically designed to tap only a given motive.

Auld, Eron, and Laffal were able to arrange four of the ten pictures of the series with which they worked into a Guttman-type scale of sexual reactivity (with a coefficient of reproducibility of .93 and a scale error of only 7%). However, an attempt to construct a reproducible scale of aggressive reactivity was not as successful, primarily, the authors felt, because there was an insufficient number of pictures in that series which consistently evoked a preponderance of aggressive themes.

Lesser (1958), noting the difficulty the foregoing authors had in extracting a scale for aggression, attempted to do so using a group of preadolescent boys. His Ss were seventy-two boys, ages 10-0 to 13-4, and an especially constructed series of cards were used. There were ten pictures, each designed to represent only the drive area of aggression, which were graded from extremely ambiguous to unambiguous. The author's score of "fantasy aggression" was based on a count of instances in each S's stories of aggressive acts such as injuring, assaulting, expressing contempt, and ridiculing. On the basis of a table which contained the percentage of Ss giving aggressive themes to each picture, the author decided to include seven of the ten cards to construct his scale. Criteria used to eliminate pictures included percentages lower than 20 and higher than 80. (Such pictures, apparently, were regarded as either irrelevant or too strongly "cued" in terms of the aggression drive.) Lesser felt, on the basis of his results, that the feasibility of utilizing Guttman's approach to scaling had been demonstrated with the TAT with respect to "fantasy aggression," thus making possible a quantified basis on which specific strength of an individual's needs along a single dimension could be assessed. This could mean that such a procedure, applied to *other* dimensions, would make possible a method by which several standardized scale series of TAT stimuli could yield for any given S a "profile" of "comparative strengths" of different drives. Lesser did suggest, however, that failure to incorporate some measure for assessing the strength of anxiety over the expression of aggression in this study (see Pittluck, 1950) was a decided limitation in terms of the usefulness of the scores obtained. Were this possible, he felt, prediction to overt behavior would be more accurate.

Scaling procedures as applied to TAT stimuli have not been extensively developed. Their feasibility has been demonstrated, however, as a result of a few studies such as those noted previously, essentially along lines of a unidimensional concept of the variables involved. In other words, it has been felt that by varying the ambiguity of a stimulus in terms of a single drive, we can assess the strength of that drive in terms of whether or not thematic content is elicited for all cards, no matter what their level of ambiguity, or only for strongly-cued, unambiguous cards.

Is it reasonable to assume that responses vary only along a *single* dimension, such as ambiguity of the stimulus? Might not there be several, simultaneously active dimensions along which the stimulus could vary? Is it possible to scale these simultaneously, that is, in the sense of a multidimensional scaling model? These are difficult questions, indeed, and the complex methodologies required to handle them are perhaps too involved for ordinary use.

One recent study concerned with scaling procedures does indeed suggest that the notion of unidimensionality of the stimulus variable in any scaling procedure is probably an oversimplification. Brayer, Craig, and Teichner (1960) were interested in applying equal interval scale procedures to TAT stimuli, and were faced with the fact that ambiguity, the usual dimension considered in past attempts to "order" the stimuli, was defined in a variety of ways (see Chapter 11). Some workers defined ambiguity in terms of the physical properties of the stimulus (brightness, intensity, or elimination of certain contours of the stimuli); others, in terms of number of different interpretations of a card or through methods of ranking and ratings. The authors have indicated that the picture is even more complicated as a result of the fact that *other* dimensions might coexist, so that even with cards of equal ambiguity the "ease of story construction might vary." One such dimension could be level of difficulty. Difficulty of interpreting a picture might increase with lack of familiarity with the situation portrayed. Is there a relationship between ambiguity and level of difficulty, or are these independent variables? Perhaps difficulty is an inverse function of ambiguity, that is, the less ambiguous a picture, the more difficult it would be to interpret because there are fewer alternative possibilities for interpretation. Brayer, Craig, and Teichner attempted to demonstrate the applicability of scaling procedures using an equal-interval method; and to determine whether or not judged difficulty of TAT pictures is a scalable dimension, independent of ambiguity.

The authors had twenty-six undergraduates rank each of ten cards from the standard series five times. The cards were selected to represent a wide range of ambiguity and level of difficulty, defined as, "the difficulty people would have in deciding what the picture is really about." The stimuli were randomly distributed on a table in front of S. The Ss then compared each picture with every other picture (forty-five judgments for each S) with the instruction to select which, in each pair, was more difficult. Each card was presented half of the time on the right and half on the left to control for position preferences. Rank-order comparisons were transformed into paired-comparison data and, following a procedure outlined by Thurstone, each set of data was transformed into scales with comparable units. An analysis of the data in this form indicated that not only was difficulty "scalable," but that each procedure yielded the same results, that is, both the rank-order and paired-comparisons methods, when transformed into scales, yielded similar positions along the scales for the cards used, in terms of difficulty.

The authors attempted to answer the second problem they posed, as to the relationship between difficulty and ambiguity in terms of a scaled series, by utilizing data from a study by Bijou and Kenny (1951), with eight of the ten cards used in the current study for their own research in ambiguity. Rank-order correlations, obtained for each of the authors' scales, and the ambiguity scale of Bijou and Kenny, were of a nonsignificant order. These workers thus concluded that difficulty level and ambiguity of cards are independent variables. Although their study was not designed to explore the influence of difficulty level on responses, their work does suggest that the stimulus cards may be better ordered along multi- rather than unidimensional models.

The problems involved in scaling procedures are complex, indeed. For example, even if scales for various specific single motives were developed, how would more complex interactions be inferred between two or among several motives? Problems such as these were raised and some of their implications discussed by Lesser (1961a, 1961b) and Murstein (1961).

## THE USE OF RATING SCALES FOR THE TAT

Sophisticated procedures such as unidimensional scaling, noted earlier, have been applied to adaptations of the TAT especially designed for specific research purposes, but not generally to the complete standard set of Murray cards which might be used in a clinical situation. Can objective psychometric procedures be utilized so as to make the TAT itself a more efficient clinical instrument?

The use of rating scales in the scoring and interpretation of a record affords an opportunity to combine qualitative, clinical judgments and a more or less rigorous quantification. It is possible for the ratings to be as subjective and wholistic as necessary, but it is essential that the criteria for rating be verbalized, so that the method can be communicated and subsequent raters can utilize the scales with comparable results. Pertinent quotations from protocols make communication of the criteria more objective. The scales should be derived empirically from the protocols themselves and not based on predetermined categories. The original ratings should be made on a continuum with no a priori subdivisions, so that they can be analyzed by statistical techniques suitable for continuous data.

Although there are many aspects of TAT stories which can be quantified by the use of rating scales, such as emotional tone of the stories, outcome, adequacy of central character, level of interpretation, and activity-passivity, and thus be made amenable to the most sophisticated statistical treatment, there are other factors which cannot be so ordered, primarily because little judgmental function is utilized in their definition. These are such things as actual themes, identification of characters and objects, distortions of the percepts, etc. More straightforward counting procedures can be used with these aspects of the stories. Of course, it might be possible to rate the degree of perceptual distortion or the strength of identification with various characters, etc., but designating the distortions, characters, themes, etc., is merely a matter of categorization and counting. Although such procedures may be more simple, they have somewhat limited utility because they yield discrete data with which most of the more discriminatory kinds of statistical techniques cannot be justifiably used. However, despite their limited statistical utility, frequency counts are often necessary, and there are respectable methods by which they can be evaluated, for example, chi square, tau, Mann-Whitney U test, and other nonparametric procedures (see McNemar [1949]; Mann & Whitney [1947]; Moses [1952]; and Siegel [1956]).

The use of these psychometric procedures with a projective technique like the TAT is not really as radical a procedure as some personologists, on the one hand, or psychometricians, on the other, may fear. The differences between the two types of procedures have been overemphasized (see Chapter 1 for a discussion of this point of view). The standardized projective technique, like the psychometric test, employs a standard set of stimulus materials but, like the free-association method, it is in some measure ambiguous or indeterminate. S responds as he wishes, but E must determine how much of his response is determined by the stimulus and how much by the personality of S. Since it is not known in advance, however, what an adequate response is, the external or internal determination of an individual's responses can only be evaluated by comparing them with a compilation of responses elicited from other Ss who are comparable to him in age, sex, social status, etc. When we use such a procedure, we are utilizing norms, and this is similar to what we do with responses in psychometric tests. As Rosenzweig (1949) has noted,

. . . In the psychometric tests a response is either right or wrong, partially or fully, according to its agreement with the conventional expectancy. The norms used in projective methods determine likewise whether agreement has occurred with the empirically popular or common modes of response. In other words, the correct response of the psychometric tests is roughly equivalent to the popular response of the projective technique (p. 478).

There are some differences, however. If S should fail to give the popular or common response on the projective tests, he is not necessarily penalized; but on the psychometric test, S is failed on such items, does not receive credit, and the incorrect response is discarded. In the projective test, lack of agreement between a given response and what is popularly expected can be an important diagnostic finding, since a determination of how the individual deviates from the group norm indicates what is peculiar about him as a person. These characteristic responses, rather than the popular ones, are the primary goal of the projective method. Norms on projective techniques, therefore, both define the person's agreement with the group and also delimit what is characteristic of him as an individual.

Quantification of TAT variables was attempted very early in the history of this method. Murray (1943) suggested a five-point rating scale for the intensity of needs and press and also for the relative optimism of the outcomes. The rating of needs according to Murray's criteria of strength is a procedure which has commonly been used in research (see Aron [1949]; and Mussen [1950]). Harrison and Rotter (1945) rated officer candidates, on the basis of blind analysis, for emotional maturity and stability on both a three-point and five-point scale and found the latter slightly more reliable (although no measure of significance is reported). Rautman and Brower (1945, 1951) rated the outcomes of stories as neutral, sad, or happy, as did Garfield and Eron (1948), who also used the three-point scales for mood of story and activity of central character. Coleman (1947) rated the level of response of the stories on a five-point scale from "no response" to second level of interpretation of feelings. Harrison (1940) rated the "significance" of the stories on a three-point scale and Garfield, Blek, and Melker (1952) used a three-point scale for rating "level of plot." Although it is encouraging that so many investigators have seen the necessity for such scaling of TAT responses, the scales thus far mentioned are gross, crudely devised, and not anchored to empirically derived criteria which are described by pertinent quotations from the protocols. Thus, either they are not amenable to clear-cut statistical evaluation, or they are not communicable, or both.

The rating scales for emotional tone and outcome of stories (to be described) have the advantages of: (*a*) being empirically derived from the actual protocols used for the rating; (*b*) covering a wide range of response which was actually measured, thus making the data appropriate for use with statistical techniques designed for continuous data only; and (*c*) having demonstrated consistently high reliability which is not inflated by the use of the contingency coefficient (see McNemar, 1949).

*Derivation of Rating Scales.* In the original derivation of these measures, all the stories in a sample of twenty-five protocols were independently rated by three judges on a 10-cm. line representing a scale which extended from sad on the left, to happy on the right. Each story of every protocol was judged as to where it ranked between the two extremes, and a mark was made at that point. All stories for the same card were rated at the same time. The resulting ratings were tabulated in centimeter intervals, and the average Pearson *r* computed among three raters was .76. The next step was to divide the 10-cm. line into five 2-cm. intervals. Each of these intervals was described according to the stories for which there was complete agreement among all raters, thus making a five-point scale. To check the reliability of these five-point scales, the protocols of thirty other Ss were rated by the same three judges, and the average $r$ computed by Fisher's transformation was .86 for emotional tone and .75 for outcome. Because of the great similarity among the outcome scales for the various cards, only one general scale of outcome was used, whereas specific scales were used for the emotional tone of each card. This may account for the seemingly higher reliability of the emotional tone scales.[1] A general scale for emotional tone is included, to be utilized when a given story cannot be suitably matched to the scale for the specific card. The emotional tone scales for each individual picture in the adult series are presented below together with the general rating scale for emotional tone of TAT stories and the scale for the outcome of the stories.

### General Rating Scale for Emotional Tone [2]

? Subject cannot make up a story

0. Complete failure, submission to fate, death, murder, suicide, illicit sex with violence, revenge, aggressive hostility, severe guilt, complete hopelessness
1. Conflict with attempt at adjustment, rebellion, fear, worry, departure, regret, illness, physical exhaustion, resignation toward death, loneliness
2. Description, lack of affect, balance of positive and negative feelings, routine activities, impersonal reflection
3. Aspiration, desire for success and doubt about outcome, compensation for limited endowment, description with cheerful feeling, reunion with friends, contentment with world, feeling of security
4. Justifiably high aspiration, complete satisfaction and happiness, reunion with loved ones

### General Rating Scale for Outcome

? Subject cannot give an outcome even when explicitly asked for, conditional (if) outcomes, alternative outcomes of different emotional value

---

[1] The significance of the difference in reliability was not calculated since the reliability of both scales was thought to be sufficiently high to warrant continued use.
[2] The designation of the categories has been changed from −2, −1, 0, +1, +2, to 0, 1, 2, 3, 4 to make it consistent with the designation of the Rorschach scales reported in this book.

X. No outcome, descriptive story

0. Complete failure, submission to fate, death, murder, suicide, extreme punishment, extreme remorse
1. Some frustration, incomplete success in attaining goal, goal attained at expense of happiness, disappointment to friends and family, acceptance of unsatisfactory situation or submission to authority
2. Continuation of ordinary situation, balance of happy and unhappy situations
3. Moderate success, reunion with friends, recovery from temporary disability or depression, happiness in success of others, tolerable resolution of conflict
4. Great success, discovery and/or happiness, extreme contentment, marital bliss, unusual good fortune, reunion with loved ones

*Rating Scales for Emotional Tone of Stories in Response to Specific Cards* [3]

(1)

0. Complete frustration and hopelessness with no resistance
1. Dejected, inadequacy with attempt to adjust, parental pressure
2. Frustration with no depression, aspirations balanced by conflict, lack of feeling tone
3. High aspirations with cooperation but some hindrance
4. High aspirations with approbation and no conflict

(2)

1. Conflict between ambition and duty to family, with some feelings of guilt or apprehension, disappointment with lot, jealousy, economic pressure
2. Description of picture, planning for future with no apparent affect
3. Optimistic future planning, description with cheerful feeling
4. Complete satisfaction with present status and life's accomplishments

(3BM)

0. Uncontrolled emotionality, murder, mentally ill, complete frustration, death of loved one, suicide
1. Self-pity, aggressive parental pressure, transitory depression, adolescent confusion over reality principles, physical incapacity

(3GF)

0. Death of close relative, suicide

---

[3] All five points are not described for each picture since, in the original work with 200 protocols, stories of certain emotional tone categories were not found for each picture.

1. Parental pressure, disappointment, frustration in love, frustration in job, personal slight, upset over interpersonal conflict, abandoned

(4)

0. Desire for revenge, murder, aggressive hostility
1. Disillusionment, occupational failure, conflict over extramarital relations, jealousy, pressure from mate, personal affront, economic pressure

(5)

0. Overdominant parent or mate, extreme parental or partner pressure, aggressive hostility, murder
1. Parental or partner pressure without aggression, loneliness, slight frustration
2. Checking on room or occupants, doing household duties
3. Unexpected gift, welcome guests, good news

(6BM)

0. Death, bad news, severe guilt, conflict over acceptance of sexual role
1. Parental pressure, filial obligation, conflict over desires and duties, departure from parental home

(6GF)

1. Crime (of murder-mystery type, without extreme grief), fear, guilt, marital discord, threatening male
2. Description, impersonal discussion
3. Happy marital situation, proposal, successful career, popularity with opposite sex

(7BM)

0. Disappointment of parents in child, guilt, repeated failure
1. Disagreement, recalcitrance, rebellion against parental authority, feelings of inadequacy
2. Parental advice, impersonal discussion, counselling
3. Aspiration with encouragement and/or advice

(7GF)

0. Extreme feelings of rejection, hatred for parents
1. Painful or shameful revelation
2. Disinterested explanation of facts of life, listens while daydreaming to neutral story, child growing up
3. Filial affection, aspiration, parental encouragement

## (8BM)

0. Murder, death, extreme guilt
1. Worry and concern about accident and operation, frustration of ambitions
2. Descriptive, perfunctory, lack of emotional involvement, impersonal reflection
3. Aspiration, hope and planning for future, adventurous daydreaming

## (8GF)

1. Economic deprivation, fatigue, frustration
2. Daydreaming, posing for artist, etc.
3. Aspiration, daydreaming with pleasant affect, pleasant anticipation

## (9BM)

1. Economic misfortune, physical exhaustion, danger of combat, social disapproval
2. Men at rest, pure description, no emotional involvement
3. Comradely feeling, contentment, carefree, happy-go-lucky, lack of concern for convention

## (9GF)

0. Suicide, death, murder
1. Sibling rivalry, marital triangle, escape from perilous or shameful situation, mental abnormality
2. Disinterested discussion of recreational activity

## (10)

0. Death, extreme sorrow, tragedy
1. Departure, leaving loved ones, personal failure, being comforted for minor misfortune
2. Lack of affect, balance of conflict
3. Reunion, happiness, acceptance, feelings of pleasure
4. Marital bliss, extreme contentment, satisfaction, good adjustment

## (11)

0. Life is futile or horrible, complete absence of hope, no avoidance of fate, death, destruction, war
1. Struggle against aggressive forces, animals fighting, story detached from reality
2. No emotional involvement, little interpersonal action, description
3. Vacation, pleasure trip, happy people

## (12M)

0. Death, suicide, malpractice (hypnotism) with aggression, rape, curse
1. Reconciliation to death, illness, parental pressure
2. Hypnosis with no harm involved (experimentation with or demonstration of hypnosis), being awakened from sleep
3. Reunion

## (12F)

0. Evil influence
1. Marital discord, fear of old age, retribution
2. Portrait, ordinary activity
3. Comfort, interest and advice

## (13MF)

0. Illicit sex with violence, rape, death, murder for infidelity
1. Disillusionment with sexual experience, regret for illicit sex, illness of wife

## (14)

1. Resignation to death of relative, reflection on worldly conflicts with or without appeal to religion, loneliness
2. Daydreaming without emotional involvement, any other theme with no emotional involvement, adolescent revery
3. Contentment with environment, appreciation of world around
4. Happy well-adjusted hero, vacation, planning for happiness

## (15)

0. Death of close relative, loneliness for deceased, mourning, hopelessness, hero rejected by society, suicide
1. Impersonal speculation on death, return of dead to cemetery, visiting grave of friend
2. Description of painting or picture, no affect

## (17BM)

1. Vindictiveness, revenge, trying to escape from unfavorable environment, fear, inadequacy
2. Vacillation in plot (balance of happy and sad themes), doing routine job of acrobatics
3. Compensation for limited endowment, desire for success with uncertainty about outcome
4. Hero happy and successful, display of physical prowess, adulation of crowd, winning of contest

(17GF)

0. Suicide
1. Loneliness, dissatisfaction with environment, economic deprivation, social or racial discriminaton
2. Ordinary activity, symbolism, contemplation
3. Prosperous commercial activity, homecoming, recovery from illness

(18BM)

0. Suicide, manslaughter, thwarted escape, hallucinations, delusions
1. Environmental frustration, accident, ordinary drunkenness, personal sorrow not of serious proportion
2. Description of poster or painting, no emotional involvement

(18GF)

0. Murder, death, psychosis
1. Discipline, coercion, comfort in face of sorrow, illness

(19)

0. Death due to forces of nature or war
1. Fear (child's fear of supernatural), bad storm with little or no emphasis on comfort of home
2. Description of picture
3. Comfort of home during storm, feeling of security

(20)

0. Death of loved one, suicide, murder
1. Disappointment in love, worry, feeling of rejection, economic pressure, disillusionment, loneliness
2. Out for a walk, description, no feeling tone

Three judges used the scales (Eron, 1953) with a population of sixty normal women. An average interrater correlation of .85 was obtained for emotional tone and .77 for outcome. Liccione (1955) obtained an average Pearson $r$ of .93 for emotional tone and .84 for outcome between two raters when the stories of 250 adolescent girls were analyzed according to these scales. Eron, Sultan, and Auld (1955) extended the methodology to a special set of TAT pictures drawn up for assessment of submarine personnel in the U.S. Navy, obtaining Pearson $r$'s between two judges of .89 for emotional tone and .81 for outcome. Bernstein (1956) applied the scales to stories obtained from sixty-seven female college sophomores in written and oral administration and achieved reliability coefficients of .88 for emotional tone and .82 for outcome when two raters were compared. Sarason and Sarason (1958), also working with college students, obtained interrater reliabilities of .87 for emotional tone and .79 for outcome. Waxenberg (1955) obtained comparable levels of reliability in a study comparing stories of psychosomatic patients and other physically ill persons. It would seem, then, that the order of reliability of the scales of emotional tone and outcome is sufficiently high to warrant their continued use.

*Applications of Rating Scales.* It was found through the use of these scales that each card had a specific emotional tone and that few cards elicited stories which varied more than two or three intervals. It was also apparent that the TAT pictures evoke primarily sad stories (Eron, 1950). Thus, the expected response to these stimuli is negatively toned, and for an individual to make up happy stories about the pictures constitutes a distortion of their stimulus properties. This is an important finding which has been made explicit only by the use of rating scales, since many investigators have stated, unwarrantedly, that people making up sad stories show depressive tendencies (Rapaport, Gill, & Schafer [1946]; and Rotter [1946]). It was found that the pictures could be arranged in rank order of the intensity of sadness of the stories which were given as responses to them. Also, the pictures differed significantly among themselves with respect to emotional tone (86% of 360 chi squares calculated separately for men and women between each card and every other card were significant beyond the 5% level of confidence.) Thus, it is obvious that each of the pictures has its own stimulus value which influences the emotional tone of the stories elicited by it in a manner different from other pictures. The outcomes for the stories when rated by these scales were found to be less determined by the stimulus properties of the cards, and were more a function of the individual's creativity (Eron [1950]; and Garfield & Eron [1948]). It was also determined by the use of these scales that it was characteristic of normal individuals to attach happy endings to sad stories, although such behavior had been characterized as singularly schizophrenic (Rotter, 1946). There is a difference in the emotional tone of stories told by men and women, with the latter giving significantly sadder stories on ten of the twenty cards. Also, the total frequency distribution for men and women differed significantly at the 1% level of confidence. Thus, male and female Ss seem to represent two different populations with respect to emotional tone of the TAT stories. This result is at variance with that of Garfield, Blek, and Melker (1952), who found little emotional tone difference between male and female stories. This discrepancy may be due to the difference in the derivation of the scales which were used. The scales presented here are more precise and more finely differentiated. A cross-validation (Eron,

1953) on a different population has corroborated the results with this experimentally derived rating scale. The rank order of the cards in terms of their sadness for men and women appears in Table 1 in the *Supplement,* Part VIII.[4] Those cards on which there is a significant difference between men and women are starred.

Although the predominant mood of these stories is sad, there are only a few individuals who consistently tell sad stories from one picture to the next. To evaluate the significance, then, of the number of sad stories any one individual contributes, it is necessary to compare the ratings on the total protocol with the number of stories of various degrees of sadness which most individuals contribute in a series of twenty stories in response to the standard pictures. Thus, Tables 2–5 in the *Supplement,* Part VIII, can be used to evaluate individual TAT records in two ways. Tables 2 and 3 give the percentage of stories of each degree of emotional tone and outcome contributed for each card by the kind of subject designated. From them we can tell what the modal response is for each card (Rosenzweig's apperceptive norms).[5] Tables 4 and 5 give the percentage of Ss who have any given number or more of stories of each degree of emotional tone or outcome value (Rosenzweig's thematic norms) in a total of twenty stories.

The scales described previously are among only a few thus far devised for the TAT on this kind of experimental basis with neither a priori categorization nor discrete intervals.[6] This methodology could conceivably be extended to many characteristics by which TAT stories are described and interpreted, for example, adequacy of central character; aggressiveness or passivity; realism; degree of various kinds of

---

[4] The interested reader is referred to the *Supplement,* an appendix to this book, which has been deposited as Document number 7955 with the ADI Auxiliary Publications Project, Photoduplication Service, Library of Congress, Washington 25, D.C. See Footnote 1, Chapter 6, for details as to ordering copies of the *Supplement,* in whole or in parts.

[5] In these and subsequent tables the groups of Ss referred to are as follows: Group I, 50 normal male college students, age 20–36; Group II, 40 normal female college students, age 19–34; Group III, 20 normal females, age 20–35, in third to fifth month of pregnancy.

[6] A rating scale for level of response which was derived in a manner similar to those for emotional tone and outcome has been published by Terry (1952). Level of response was defined by this author as the "degree to which the subject is judged to have become involved in his story; as expressed through elaboration of plot and descriptions of emotional responses of the story characters" (p. 507). Reliability of the scale (correlation between two raters) was reported to be high. Individual differences, card differences, and differences between oral and written stories (written stories show a significantly lower average level of response) were found.

tensions; attitudes toward love, authority, parents, peers, siblings, old age, youth, childhood, etc. Through the use of the scales, the stimulus can be defined and its effect on the response assessed. The scales also provide a convenient and reliable measure by which the effect of various treatments on TAT productions can be determined. For example, written and oral administrations have been compared (Eron & Ritter [1951]; Terry [1952]); the effect of differential placement of cards in the series has been assessed (Terry, 1952); sex differences have been noted (Eron [1953]; Eron, Terry, & Callahan [1950]); effect of hospitalization has been indicated (Eron, 1950); and use in diagnostic differentiation has been evaluated (Eron [1950]; Ritter & Eron [1952]). More recently, Murstein (1960) used the scales of emotional tone and outcome, among other measures, to explore differences between parents of leukemic and nonleukemic children. The only significant difference found was in terms of the emotional tone of the stories, with parents of nonleukemic children telling fewer unhappy stories. The scales have also been successfully applied in a study of the changing family relationships of adolescent girls (Liccione, 1955), in an investigation of the effects of extended duration of enclosure in a submarine on Navy personnel (Eron & Auld, 1954), and in a study of the effects of sleep deprivation on fantasy (Murray, 1959).

This methodology has clinical applicability also. Once the common responses to the cards have been determined, anything in a given protocol which is deviant from this objective standard can be noted. According to experienced TAT analysts (Rapaport et al. [1946]; Rotter [1946]; and Shneidman et al. [1951]), unusual responses loom large in interpretation; experimental evidence (Ritter & Eron, 1952) supports the belief that what is deviant in TAT content is important for personality diagnosis. If, for example, most Ss respond to a particular card with a story of a certain emotional tone and the S under consideration contributes a story which is of a grossly different mood, it is safe to assume that this stimulus has a particular, significant meaning for the S. In a similar way, if it is known that most Ss contribute a certain number of stories of given emotional tone in a series of twenty stories and if the S whose record is being interpreted has excessively more or less stories of this mood, there is some indication that the level of emotional reactivity is distorted in S. On the basis of these deviations, it is then possible to make an interpretation of S's personality. These are the building blocks for the interpretation. How they are assembled and organized and what stress is put on any one will depend on E's theoretical orientation toward personality. This method is merely a procedure for insuring that all the important elements are isolated from each protocol and that they are all brought to the attention of E without the danger of any of the elements being overlooked.

## THE USE OF FREQUENCY COUNTS

Although all TAT variables cannot be rated and thus made amenable to sophisticated statistical treatment, there are counting procedures by which we can at least estimate the frequency of occurrence of various features of the stories among normal Ss of different age, sex, education, etc. Reference can thus be made to norms to evaluate the individuality or communality of variables such as themes, perceptual distortions, identifications of characters and objects, and deviations from the instructions to make up a story about the pictures. The norms compiled by Rosenzweig and Fleming (1949), Wittenborn (1949), and Eron (1950, 1953) are valuable for this kind of an evaluation of responses. The norms compiled by Rosenzweig and Fleming, and Wittenborn, however, cannot be used to determine the significance of persistent responses throughout an entire protocol, because only selected cards were used. Eron presented norms for all the cards and utilized at least the same thematic analysis throughout, so that it is possible to combine results on all the cards to ascertain and evaluate the persistent themes.

*Themes.* A complete outline of the theme checklist follows. The list is divided into two parts, Equilibrium and Disequilibrium, referring to the state of tension or adjustment of the characters in the story. Each main heading is then broken down into the area of the relationships involved: interpersonal, intrapersonal, or impersonal. The interpersonal category is further broken down for the direction of the relationship: parent, partner (peer of opposite sex), peer (same sex), or sibling. Specific themes then appear under each subheading. Each theme is defined and the reference is to the central character in the story unless otherwise stated in the definition. Every story is analyzed for the presence of each theme. Every time a theme appears it is tallied, so that most stories will have more than one theme and occasionally there will be stories with no themes which appear on the checklist and thus are impossible to classify. Only the manifest content is considered—the actual behavior of the characters in the stories as narrated by S, regardless of its covert significance. The checklist was originally derived for the analysis of male protocols. In extending it to female protocols (Eron, 1953), some revisions were necessary because of the different cards which are used for women, thus making it necessary to include new themes and eliminate some of the old ones since the list was empirically derived from actual circumstances represented in the pictures. The checklist was further extended to make it applicable for use with the group administered Navy TAT (Eron & Auld, 1954). The complete check list of themes which can be used for either male or female protocols by those desiring to do an intensive analysis follows immediately.

### Revised Checklist of Themes

I. Disequilibrium (tension)
  A. Interpersonal
    1. Parent or parent figure
      a. *Pressure*—parent or parent figures are prohibitive, compelling, censuring, punishing, disapproving, interfering, checking up, disagreeing with, quarreling with, restraining, or unduly influencing child
      aa. Child is exerting pressure on parents
      b. *Succorance*—child seeks or receives aid, help, advice, consolation from parent
      c. *Nurturance*—child bestows or offers aid, advice, consolation to the parent
      d. *Aggression from*—physical harm inflicted on or intended for child by parent
      e. *Aggression to*—physical harm inflicted on or intended for parent by child
      f. *Departure*—child is taking leave of parental home, runs away from home
      g. *Concern*—parent is worried over physical or mental well-being of child
      gg. *Concern*—child is concerned over parent
      h. *Incest*—actual or contemplated
      i. *Death or illness* of parent
      j. *Death or illness* of child
      k. *Disappointment to*—parent is disappointed in child's behavior or accomplishments; parent rejects child
      l. *Disappointment in*—child is disappointed by parent, ashamed of parents, derogates parent, rejects parent; does not listen to advice of parents
      m. *Filial obligation*—child feels it is his duty to remain with, comply with, or support parents
      n. *Confession*—child tells parent of some misdemeanor or crime he has committed

nn. *Confession*—parent confesses to child
 o. *Bad news*—child brings sad tidings to parent (e.g., death of other parent, sibling, etc.)
oo. *Bad news*—parent brings sad tidings to child
 p. *Marriage*—child tells parent of past or impending marriage, parent objects to marriage, interferes with marriage
 q. *Collusion*—parent and child are planning or executing together some antisocial act
 r. *Parental conflict*—child is concerned over marital problems of parents; parents disagree over child care, etc.
 s. *Lost*—child has been abandoned by parents or is lost
 v. Facts of life explained to child by parent
 w. Parent tells child a sibling is coming
 x. Parent is jealous of child

2. Partner (spouse, sweetheart, peer of opposite sex)
 a. *Pressure*—hero or heroine and partner are quarreling, cannot agree; female exerting pressure on male
aa. Male is exerting pressure on female
 b. *Nurturance*—male character bestows or offers to partner aid, consolation, advice, etc., or these are being sought by female
 c. *Succorance*—male character receives or seeks aid, comfort, consolation, assistance from partner, advice from partner
 d. *Aggression from female character*—physical harm inflicted on or intended for partner by female
 e. *Aggression from male character*—physical harm inflicted on or intended for partner by male
 f. *Departure from*—male character leaves partner either temporarily or permanently
ff. *Departure from*—female character leaves partner either temporarily or permanently
 g. *Concern*—male character is worried over physical or mental well-being of partner
gg. *Concern*—female character is worried over physical or mental well-being of partner
 h. *Illicit sex*—extra- or premarital heterosexual relationship, nonincestuous, includes "petting"
 i. *Illicit sex with violence*—rape
 j. *Death or illness* of female partner
jj. *Death or illness* of male partner

k. *Disappointment*—male character is disappointed in female's behavior or accomplishments, rejects female, derogates female

l. *Disappointment*—female character is disappointed in male's behavior or accomplishments, derogates male, rejects male

m. *Jealousy*—female character is jealous of partner's attention to others or others' attention to partner

n. *Competition*—male character is jealous of partner's attention to others or others' attention to partner

o. *Unfaithful*—male character discovers partner has been having extramarital relations or finds her raped

oo. *Unfaithful*—female character discovers partner has been unfaithful

p. *Decision*—male character must choose between marriage and not, or between two partners, or whether to have sexual relations (if no moral struggle involved; if moral struggle, then scored IB6)

pp. *Decision*—female character must choose between marriage and not, or between two partners

q. *Pursuit*—male character is wooing or trying to get partner to submit, wants contact with other sex

r. *Seduction*—female character is actively pursuing or talking male into relationship, wants contact with other sex

s. *Unrequited*—male character's love is unreturned, impotence; waits for partner

ss. *Unrequited*—female character's love is unreturned, is "done in" by partner; waits for partner

t. *Restraint*—central character and partner cannot be married or have intercourse (because of economics, deformities, menstrual periods, etc.)

u. *Childbirth*—pregnancy, abortion

v. *Venereal Disease*

w. *Surprise*—female character surprised by partner

x. *Ulterior Motive*—contact established with opposite sex for extrasex reason, to gather some extrasex advantage for own personal gain; no love

3. Peer (same sex as central character)

a. *Pressure*—like-sexed peers are prohibitive, compelling, censuring, punishing, disapproving, interfering, restraining, etc.

    b. *Succorance*—central character seeks or receives aid, advice, consolation from peer

    c. *Nurturance*—central character bestows or offers aid, advice, consolation from peer

    d. *Aggression from*—physical harm inflicted on or intended for central character by peer

    e. *Aggression to*—physical harm inflicted on or intended for peer by central character

    f. *Desertion*—central character has been deserted by his companions or is lost from them

    g. *Concern*—central character is worried about physical or mental well-being of friends

  gg. *Concern*—friends are worried about central character

    h. *Homosexuality*—actual or contemplated

    i. *Death or illness* of friend

    j. *Belongingness*—desire expressed to be with or accepted by peers

    k. *Unappreciated by peers*—rejected by peers, peers not interested in welfare

    l. *Competition*—central character is competing with peer in game or contest, or professionally

    m. *Hypnotism*

    n. *Envy*—central character is envious of peer's accomplishments, capacities, belongings, etc.

  nn. Others envy central character

    o. *Revenge*—central character is anxious to extract revenge from a peer for some past deed or is taking the revenge

    p. *Disregard for*—central character is unconcerned over welfare of peers, deserts peers

    q. *Devaluation of peer*—derogation, rejection of peer by central character

4. Sibling

    a. *Pressure*—sibling is prohibitive, compelling, censuring, punishing, disapproving, interfering, restraining, etc.

    b. *Succorance*—central character seeks or receives aid, advice, consolation from sibling

    c. *Nurturance*—central character bestows or offers aid, advice, consolation on sibling, or such behavior is sought of him

    d. *Aggression from*—physical harm inflicted on or intended for central character by sibling

e. *Aggression to*—physical harm inflicted on or intended for sibling by central character

f. *Rivalry*—between two siblings; must be stated, not inferred; siblings are jealous of each other; striving for same goal

g. *Concern*—central character is worried about physical or mental well-being of sibling

h. *Incest*—actual or contemplated

i. *Death or illness* of sibling

B. Intrapersonal

1. *Aspiration*—dreaming of future, hoping for future, determination

2. *Inadequacy*—realization, whether justified or not, of lack of success; individual is at a loss to cope with situation

   b. Unrealized

3. *Curiosity*—wondering about construction of object, contents of room, etc., desire to observe, inquire, explore, investigate; to acquire facts

4. *Behavior disorder*—personal maladjustment of all sorts, neurosis, psychosis, sleeplessness, hallucination, withdrawal, eccentricity, morbid preoccupation, nightmare, excessive emotionality

5. *Suicide*—attempted or complete, preoccupation with

6. *Moral struggle*—concern over what is right and wrong, hesitancy in indulging in some act because of ethical proscriptions

7. *Guilt*—remorse, shame

8. *Drunkenness*

9. *Fear—worry*—central character is apprehensive, alarmed, terrified of some person, thing, force

10. *Rumination*—inability to understand world and its problems, adolescent reverie, man's insignificance, "What am I?" "What's it all about?"

11. *Occupational concern*—deciding between jobs, considering vocations, dissatisfied with present employment or present pastime; worried about job; emphasis on decision which must be made in choosing occupation

12. *Physical illness or death of central character*—(other than when in a peer, partner, sibling, or parent relationship, which are included in those specific categories)

13. *Retribution*—forced to atone or be punished for some antisocial act

14. *Reminiscence, sad*—individual is unhappy in his memories of the past or contemplation of the future, hopelessness
15. *Intra-aggression*—does physical harm to self (short of suicide which is carried under that heading) either accidentally or deliberately, looks forward to own death
16. *Religion*—prayer, seeking consolation from God, religious conflict, religious awakening
17. *Loneliness*—central character misses someone, is an outcast, friendless, homeless
18. *Compensation*—when individual has one characteristic or stroke of fortune to make up for another bad characteristic or misfortune
19. *Vacillation*—wasting time, putting off a distasteful task, procrastination, loitering, waiting for someone unspecified
20. *Acquisition*—desire expressed by central character to acquire material things, or is working greedily for possession of goods; miserliness
21. *Exhaustion*—characters completely "pooped" from overexertion, resting after hard work
22. *Revenge*—central character is preoccupied with wish to retaliate for some past wrong from unspecified individual (when peer, carried under that heading)
23. *Inconsequential sadness*—over death of dog, broken toy, loss of object, etc.
24. *"Hurt feelings"*—central character is upset over some happening, slight, insult, etc.
25. *Jealousy*—of unspecified individual (if specific person named, carried under appropriate heading)
26. *Self-pity*—central character feels sorry for self
27. *Supernatural*—return of the dead, ghosts
28. *Homesickness*—expressed by central character
29. *Physical illness or death* of unspecified character (not central character, partner, peer, sibling)
30. *Bored*—central character is bored, has nothing to do
31. *Regression*—central character is unwilling to grow up, assume adult responsibilities, grow old
32. *Posing*—central character posing for portrait, looking in mirror or at reflection
33. *Accusation*—central character accused, usually falsely, of some misdemeanor, crime, infidelity
34. *Grief*—central character is very sad; not inconsequential (see IB23).

35. *Hatred*—(no specific person mentioned as object)
36. *Concern*—for unspecified person (not partner, peer, sibling, or parent)

C. Impersonal

1. *Economic pressure*—individual is compelled to, or prohibited from, or limited in, doing something because of lack of money
2. *Legal restriction*—individual is incarcerated, arrested or detained against his will, or is worried about it; punishment; gets caught
3. *Generalized restriction*—environment is generally frustrating because of backwardness, danger, lack of opportunity, etc.; hopelessness of life
4. *Aggression toward environment*—robbery, accident, murder of unspecified individual (if individual named, carried under the proper heading); unspecified offenses
5. *Aggression from*—impersonal source, accident, animal, nature, disease, etc.
6. *War*
7. *Escape from perilous, restricting, or shameful environment*—individual is in the act of getting out (doesn't include rescue, which comes under II); "goofing off" from job; hiding; AWOL
8. *Obligation to society*
9. *Crime without punishment*

II. Equilibrium

A. Interpersonal

1. Parent
   a. *Cooperation*—parent is working with child toward his own goal
   b. *Resignation*—parent is resigned to child's activity
   c. *Idealization*—child idealizes parent, wants to be like parent
   d. *Reunion*—of child with parents
   e. *Fulfillment*—child lives up to expectations of parents
   f. *Contentment*—blissful home situation, stress security of home
   g. *Ordinary familial activity*—just talking, spending an evening, working, etc.

2. Partner
   a. *Admiration*—female character admires or looks up to male character

    aa.  *Admiration*—male character admires or looks up to female character

    b.  *Cooperation*—between mates, so that both are working for same end and are happy

    c.  *Contentment*—mutual love and affection

    d.  *Reunion*—of partners

    e.  *Ordinary activity*—doing routine things

    f.  *Proposal*—of marriage

    g.  *Anniversary*—celebration

    h.  *Dancing*—mutual enjoyment

    i.  *Sex*—satisfactory and sanctioned

  3.  Peer

    a.  *Cooperation*—working together for same goal

    b.  *Congeniality*—sociability, friendliness, satisfactory affiliation

    c.  *Reunion*—with friends

    d.  *Approbation*—central character is lauded, appreciated by friends and peers

    dd.  *Approbation*—central character is proud of his friends

    e.  *Exhibition*—central character is amusing, entertaining, attracting others

    f.  *Ordinary activity*—everyday association with nothing in particular happening

  4.  Sibling (No II themes found in sample of 300 cases)

B.  Intrapersonal

  1.  *Self-esteem*—confidence, belief in own superiority, conceit

  2.  *Tranquility*—peace of mind, content with environment and own accomplishments, enjoyment, esthetic appreciation

  3.  *Reminiscence, happy*—individual is content with his memories, or contemplation of future

  4.  *Retirement*—central character is asleep, resting, no physical exhaustion, relaxation

  5.  *Occupational satisfaction*

  6.  *Resignation to lot*—individual accepts situation without struggle

  7.  *Ordinary activity*—individual is going about his everyday activities

C.  Impersonal

  1.  *Favorable environment*—individual is being helped by favorable circumstances, is enjoying his surroundings

  2.  *Rescue*—successful escape from perilous environment or cessation of noxious stimuli (already accomplished)

Reliability studies of the checklist have been very encouraging. Liccione (1955) used the checklist with adolescent girls, and the agreement obtained between two judges in categorizing the themes in 310 stories was 88%. A repeat scoring of the stories by one rater, five months later, yielded 90% agreement with the original scoring by that rater. Eron, Sultan, and Auld (1955) obtained an index of agreement of 89% in the Navy study. The formula used to express agreement in these studies was the conventional one:

$$\frac{2 \times \text{number of agreements}}{\text{Total of Analyst A} + \text{total of Analyst B.}}$$

Card-by-card normative data for frequency of themes appearing in the checklist are presented according to group in Table 6 of the *Supplement*, Part VIII. These data correspond to Rosenzweig's apperceptive norms. The frequency among the individuals in these groups of various themes (Table 7) and combinations of themes (Table 8) in a complete series of twenty pictures is also presented. The reference here is to frequency of Ss, that is, the number of Ss having a given number or more of any specific theme in a total protocol. This corresponds to Rosenzweig's thematic norms.

*Other Frequency Counts.* In this method of TAT analysis, unusual formal characteristics such as symbolic or abstract stories, autobiographical stories, fairy tales, and stories in which the central character does not appear in the picture are noted according to the list appearing below. Both apperceptive and thematic norms are presented in the *Supplement*, Part VIII, for these characteristics (Tables 9 and 10).

Perceptual distortions and misidentifications, for example, misidentifying the sex of the characters in picture 10, or failing to recognize the object in card 3BM as a gun, are not uncommon among normal Ss. These have been similarly arranged in the *Supplement*, Part VIII, by card and for the total series of twenty pictures (Tables 11 and 12).

*Unusual Formal Characteristics*

A. Symbolic—depicting an idea or moral
B. Abstract—depicting a feeling
C. Descriptive—no action depicted, no story, mere description of picture
D. Unreal—"This is a picture," "This is someone's dream," etc.—cannot accept as a real situation
E. Fairy tale—legend, impossible happening
F. Central character is not in picture

G. Autobiographical—where narrator is character in the story, "like what happened to me," inserts reference to self
H. Continuations—refers to past stories
I. Alternate themes given for same picture
J. Comments about artistic merits of picture, recognition of artist or painting
K. Denial of a theme—"This is not—" when it is commonly given
L. Rejection—S refuses or is unable to make up story
M. Peculiar verbalizations
N. Confused, no single discernible plot, impossible conclusion, etc.
O. Includes examiner in story
P. Little or no connection of story to picture
Q. Humorous
R. Reification—makes characters real, gives them names, etc.

## USE OF A NORMATIVE APPROACH IN DIAGNOSTIC DIFFERENTIATION

As indicated previously, it has been demonstrated that it is possible to use this kind of approach to differentiate abnormal from normal groups according to the number of deviations each S has from the group norm, defined as a characteristic exhibited by 40% of the group. There are items of this nature which can be derived from the normative tables presented in the *Supplement* and described earlier; for example, if an individual fails to give a theme or an emotional tone which has been contributed by 40% of the group, or distorts the perceptions of a particular object or character, or fails to carry out the instructions in a way that is done by less than 40% of the Ss, these can be counted as deviations from the group norm. By the use of appropriate cutoff points, individuals who have an unusual number of total deviations or particular kinds of deviations can be separated out. The list of deviations which were used in the original study with male Ss (Ritter & Eron, 1952) appears below; the range of deviations of various kinds found in the normal group of fifty college men, Group I, can be found in the *Supplement*, Part VIII (Table 13).

To demonstrate how a psychometric method of analysis can be used to pick out the important items in a protocol and to insure consideration of all the elements in the final analysis, a protocol contributed by a patient is reproduced in the *Supplement*, Part IX, followed by a sample scoring sheet on which each of the stories is analyzed and apperceptive and instructional deviations are checked. There is also a summary sheet on which are collated the analyses for a total series of twenty stories with deviations from the thematic norm appropriately checked as to whether they are characteristic of less than 1%, less than 10%, or less than 20% of the corresponding normative group.[7] An interpretation is then made, based on these apperceptive and thematic characteristics which have been noted and are assumed to be peculiar to S, since they deviate from the norm. This, of course, is not the kind of interpretation that would be submitted in a psychological test report to a referring agency, but is primarily a technique for demonstrating this method of psychometric evaluation of a protocol.

### Usual Deviations for Each Card in the Adult Male Series

Card 1

1. failure to give either themes IA1a (parent or parent figures are prohibitive, compelling, censuring, punishing, disapproving, interfering, checking up, disagreeing with, quarreling with, restraining, or unduly influencing child) or IBI (dreaming of future, hoping for future, determination)
2. misidentification of boy, violin and/or music sheet
3. presence of an UFC other than IIIA, IIIB, IIIE, or IIIQ

Card 2

1. failure to give story of emotional tone of 1 (conflict between ambition and duty to family with some feelings of guilt or apprehension, disappointment with lot, jealousy, economic pressure)
2. distortion or misidentification of any object or character
3. presence of an UFC other than IIIA, IIIB, IIIE, or IIIQ

Card 3BM

1. failure to give story with emotional tone 1 (self-pity, aggressive parental pressure, transient depression, adolescent confusion over reality principles, physical incapacity) or 0 (uncontrolled emotionality, murder, mentally ill, complete frustration, death of loved one, suicide)
2. no immediate identification of sex of character (either male or female is OK, as long as there is no hesitation)
3. unusual comments about figure (hunchback, deformed, muscular, etc.)
4. distortion or misidentification of any object or character
5. presence of an UFC other than IIIA, IIIB, IIIE, or IIIQ
6. concern with gun (uncertain of what object is, dwells on it)

---

[7] This is a more rigorous criterion than the 40% cut off point for deviance used in the foregoing research (Ritter & Eron, 1952). It is felt that when applying this method to the individual clinical case, this more stringent criterion is desirable.

Card 4

1. failure to give story with emotional tone 1 (disillusionment, occupational failure, conflict over extramarital relations, jealousy, pressure from mate, personal affront, economic pressure)
2. fails to give theme IA2a (partner is prohibitive, compelling, censuring, punishing, quarreling with, etc.)
3. distorts or misidentifies any object or character
4. is credited with an UFC other than IIIA, IIIB, IIIE, or IIIQ

Card 5

1. failure to give story with emotional tone of 2 (checking on room or occupants, doing household duties) or 1 (parental or partner pressure without aggression, loneliness, slight frustration)
2. failure to give theme IA1a (parent or parent figures are prohibitive, compelling, censuring, punishing, disapproving, interfering, checking up, disagreeing with, quarreling with, restraining, or unduly influencing child)
3. distortion or misidentification of any object or character
4. Presence of an UFC other than IIIA, IIIB, IIIE, or IIIQ

Card 6BM

1. failure to give a story with emotional tone 1 (parental pressure, filial obligation, conflict over desires and duties, departure from parental home)
2. failure to give theme IA1a (parent or parent figures are prohibitive, compelling, censuring, punishing, disapproving, interfering, checking up, disagreeing with, quarreling with, restraining, or unduly influencing child)
3. interpretation of characters as other than mother and son
4. distortion or misidentification of any object or character
5. presence of an UFC other than IIIA, IIIB, IIIE, or IIIQ

Card 7BM

1. failure to give story of emotional tone 1 (disagreement, recalcitrance, rebellion against parental authority, feelings of inadequacy)
2. failure to give theme IA1b (child seeks or receives aid, help, advice, consolation, from parent)
3. interpretation of characters as other than father and son or father and son figures (e.g., if interpreted as contemporaries)
4. distortion or misidentification of any object or character
5. presence of an UFC other than IIIA, IIIB, IIIE, or IIIQ

Card 8BM

1. failure to give story of emotional tone 3 (aspiration, hope and planning for future; adventurous daydreaming)

2. failure to give theme IB1 (dreaming of future, hoping for future, determination)
3. interpretation of background as actual scene, not vision, dream, etc.
4. unusual interpretation of figure on table (sex)
5. distortion or misidentification of any object or character
6. presence of an UFC other than IIIA, IIIB, IIIE, or IIIQ

Card 9BM
1. failure to give story of emotional tone 2 (men at rest, pure description, no emotional involvement)
2. failure to give theme IIB4 (central character is asleep, resting, no physical exhaustion)
3. specification of more or less than four figures
4. identification of characters as Negroes
5. distortion or misidentification of any object or character
6. presence of an UFC other than IIIA, IIIB, IIIE, or IIIQ

Card 10
1. failure to give story of emotional tone 1 (departure, leaving loved ones, personal failure, being comforted for minor misfortune)
2. failure to give theme IIA2c (mutual love and affection)
3. unusual identification of central characters (mother and son, sister and brother, two males or two females, etc.)
4. distortion or misidentification of any object or character
5. presence of an UFC other than IIIA, IIIB, IIIE, or IIIQ

Card 11
1. failure to give story of emotional tone 1 (struggle against aggressive forces, animals fighting, story detached from reality)
2. distortion or misidentification of any object or character
3. presence of an UFC other than IIIA, IIIB, IIIE, or IIIQ

Card 12M
1. failure to give story of emotional tone 1 (reconciliation to death, illness, parental pressure)
2. failure to give theme IA3m (hypnotism)
3. misidentification of sex or age of characters
4. distortion or misidentification of any object or character
5. presence of an UFC other than IIIA, IIIB, IIIE, or IIIQ

Card 13MF
1. failure to give story of emotional tone 1 (disillusionment with sexual experience, regret for illicit sex, illness of wife) or 0 (illicit sex with violence, rape, death, murder for infidelity)
2. failure to give theme IB7 (guilt-remorse) or IA2h (illicit sex—

extra- or premarital heterosexual relationship, nonincestuous, includes "petting")

3. identification of characters as other than lovers or man and wife (e.g., mother-son, father-daughter, sister-brother, doctor-patient)
4. distortion or misidentification of any object or character
5. presence of an UFC other than IIIA, IIIB, IIIE, or IIIQ

### Card 14

1. distortion or misidentification of any object or character
2. presence of an UFC other than IIIA, IIIB, IIIE, or IIIQ

### Card 15

1. failure to give story of emotional tone 1 (impersonal speculation on death, return of dead to cemetery, visiting grave of friend) or 0 (death of close relative, loneliness for deceased, mourning, hopelessness, hero rejected by society, suicide)
2. distortion or misidentification of any object or character (includes sexual misidentification, manacled hands, identification as a Negro)
3. presence of an UFC other than IIIA, IIIB, IIIE, or IIIQ

### Card 16

1. presence of an UFC other than IIIA, IIIB, IIIE, or IIIQ

### Card 17BM

1. distortion or misidentification of any object or character
2. presence of an UFC other than IIIA, IIIB, IIIE, or IIIQ

### Card 18BM

1. failure to give story of emotional tone 1 (environmental frustration, accident, ordinary drunkenness, personal sorrow not of serious proportion)
2. failure to give theme IB8 (drunkenness)
3. emphasis on number of hands, etc.
4. distortion or misidentification of any object or character
5. presence of an UFC other than IIIA, IIIB, IIIE, or IIIQ

### Card 19

1. failure to give story of emotional tone 1 (fear, child's fear of supernatural, bad storm with little or no emphasis on comfort of home)
2. failure to give theme IC5 (aggression from impersonal source, accident, animal, nature, disease, etc.)
3. distortion or misidentification of any object or character
4. presence of an UFC other than IIIA, IIIB, IIIE, or IIIQ
5. interpretation of people in picture (usually in window)

### Card 20

1. failure to give story of emotional tone 1 (disappointment in love, worry, feeling of rejection, economic pressure, disillusionment, loneliness)

2. failure to give theme IB19 (vacillation, wasting time, putting off a distasteful task, procrastination, loitering)
3. distortion or misidentification of any object or character
4. presence of an UFC other than IIIA, IIIB, IIIE, or IIIQ

## SUMMARY AND CONCLUSIONS

The feasibility and applicability of a psychometric approach to the TAT has been demonstrated. The use of empirically derived rating scales which cover a wide range of response and which can demonstrate consistently high reliability uninflated by the use of the contingency coefficient was strongly recommended, since the most sophisticated statistical treatment can be applied to data obtained by the use of such measures. Scales of emotional tone and outcome of TAT stories which had been derived in the recommended manner were presented.

Although some important aspects of TAT stories cannot be scaled in this manner, it has been shown that frequency counts, which are appropriately evaluated by acceptable nonparametric techniques, have considerable utility. Such characteristics of TAT stories as themes, unusual formal characteristics, and perceptual distortions were thus included. Checklists are provided for determining the presence of these characteristics and the reader is referred to both apperceptive and thematic normative data which appear in the *Supplement*.

Through the use of these scales, checklists, and norms, it is possible to tabulate all the essential elements of a TAT protocol and to isolate those elements which are either deviant or peculiarly characteristic of the S. These items then furnish the basis for inferences to be made about the S in a personality interpretation. How the TAT interpreter fashions these elements into a meaningful description of the individual will depend on his own theoretical orientation. This psychometric methodology is a way of insuring that all the elements come into his purview and makes possible the use of both apperceptive and thematic norms in the evaluation of a given story or protocol.

Equally important is the usefulness of this psychometric approach in various research contexts—the wide number of areas discussed in preceding chapters, for example. Uniformity and objectivity of scoring responses would be of crucial importance in comparing results and generalizing from a vast number of different research approaches.

## REFERENCES

Aron, Betty. *A manual for analysis of the Thematic Apperception Test*. Berkeley, Calif.: Willis E. Berg, 1949.

Auld, F., Jr., Eron, L. D., & Laffal, J. Application of Guttman's scaling method to the TAT. *Educ. Psychol. Measmt.* 1955, 15, 422–435.

Bernstein, L. The examiner as an inhibiting factor in clinical testing. *J. consult. Psychol.*, 1956, 20, 287–290.

Bijou, S. W., & Kenny, D. T. The ambiguity values of TAT cards. *J. consult. Psychol.*, 1951, 15, 203–209.

Brayer, R., Craig, Grace, & Teichner, W. The difficulty value of TAT cards. Paper presented at Eastern Psychological Association Meeting, 1960.

Briggs, D. L. A modification of the Thematic Apperception Test for Naval enlisted personnel (N-TAT). *J. Psychol.*, 1954, 37, 233–241.

Coleman, W. The TAT. I. Effect of recent experience. II. Some quantitative observations. *J. clin. Psychol.*, 1947, 3, 257–264.

Eron, L. D. A normative study of the Thematic Apperception Test. *Psychol. Monogr.*, 1950, 64 (Whole No. 315).

Eron, L. D. Responses of women to the Thematic Apperception Test. *J. consult. Psychol.*, 1953, 17, 269–282.

Eron, L. D., & Auld, F., Jr. A study of the Thematic Apperception Test stories and sentence completions of subjects in Operation Hideout. *Bu. Med. Surg.*, Navy Dept. MRL Report, No. 243, Feb. 1954.

Eron, L. D., & Ritter, Anne M. A comparison of two methods of administration of the Thematic Apperception Test. *J. consult. Psychol.*, 1951, 15, 55–61.

Eron, L. D., Sultan, Florence, & Auld, F., Jr. The application of a psychometric scoring procedure to a group modification of the Thematic Apperception Test (N-TAT). *J. consult. Psychol.*, 1955, 19, 83–89.

Eron, L. D., Terry, Dorothy, & Callahan, R. The use of rating scales for emotional tone of TAT stories. *J. consult. Psychol.*, 1950, 14, 473–478.

Garfield, S. L., Blek, L., & Melker, F. The influence of method of administration and sex differences on selected aspects of TAT stories. *J. consult. Psychol.*, 1952, 16, 140–146.

Garfield, S. L., & Eron, L. D. Interpreting mood and activity in TAT stories. *J. abnorm. soc. Psychol.*, 1948, 43, 338–345.

Guttman, L. The basis for scalogram analysis. In S. A. Stauffer (Ed.) *Studies in social psychology in World War II. Volume IV. Measurement and prediction.* Princeton, N.J.: Princeton University Press, 1950, 60–90.

Harrison, R. Studies in the use and validity of the Thematic Apperception Test with mentally disordered patients. II. A quantitative validity study. III. Validation by the method of "blind analysis." *Charact. & Pers.*, 1940, 9, 122–138.

Harrison, R., & Rotter, J. B. A note on the reliability of the Thematic Apperception Test. *J. abnorm. soc. Psychol.*, 1945, 40, 97–99

Lesser, G. S. Application of Guttman's scaling method to aggressive fantasy in children. *Educ. Psychol. Measmt.*, 1958, 18, 543–551.

Lesser, G. S. Custom-making projective tests for research. *J. proj. Tech.*, 1961, 25, 21–31. (*a*)

Lesser, G. S. Discussion of Dr. Murstein's paper. In J. Kagan and G. S. Lesser (Eds.) *Contemporary issues in thematic apperceptive methods.* Springfield, Ill.: Charles C Thomas, 1961, 274–287. (*b*)

Liccione, J. V. The changing family relationships of adolescent girls. *J. abnorm. soc. Psychol.*, 1955, 51, 421–426.

Mann, H. B., & Whitney, D. R. On a test of whether one of two random variables is stochastically larger than the other. *Amer. math. Statist.*, 1947, 18, 50–60.

McNemar, Q. *Psychological statistics.* New York: John Wiley and Sons, 1949.

Moses, L. E. Non-parametric statistics for psychological research. *Psychol. Bull.*, 1952, **49**, 122–143.

Murray, E. J. Conflict and repression during sleep deprivation. *J. abnorm. soc. Psychol.*, 1959, **59**, 95–101.

Murray, H. A. *Thematic Apperception Test.* Cambridge: Harvard University Press, 1943.

Murstein, B. I. The effect of long-term illness of children on the emotional adjustment of parents. *Child Develpm.*, 1960, **31**, 157–171.

Murstein, B. I. The role of the stimulus in the manifestation of fantasy. In J. Kagan and G. S. Lesser (Eds.) *Contemporary issues in thematic apperceptive methods.* Springfield, Ill.: Charles C Thomas, 1961, 229–273.

Mussen, P. H. Some personality and social factors related to changes in children's attitudes toward Negroes. *J. abnorm. soc. Psychol.*, 1950, **45**, 423–441.

Pittluck, Patricia. The relation between aggressive fantasy and overt behavior. Unpublished doctoral dissertation, Yale University, 1950.

Rapaport, D., Gill, M. M., & Schafer, R. *Diagnostic psychological testing.* Vol. II. Chicago: Year Book Publishers, 1946.

Rautman, A. L., & Brower, Edna. War themes in children's stories. *J. Psychol.*, 1945, **19**, 191–202.

Rautman, A. L., & Brower, Edna. War themes in children's stories: II. Six years later. *J. Psychol.*, 1951, **31**, 263–270.

Ritter, Anne M., & Eron, L. D. The use of the Thematic Apperception Test to differentiate normal from abnormal groups. *J. abnorm. soc. Psychol.*, 1952, **47**, 147–158.

Rosenzweig, S. Apperceptive norms for the Thematic Apperception Test. I. The problem of norms in projective methods. *J. Pers.*, 1949, **17**, 475–482.

Rosenzweig, S., & Fleming, Edith. Apperceptive norms for the Thematic Apperception Test. II. An empirical investigation. *J. Pers.*, 1949, **17**, 483–503.

Rotter, J. B. Thematic Apperception Tests: suggestions for administration and interpretation. *J. Pers.*, 1946, **15**, 70–92.

Sarason, Barbara R., & Sarason, I. G. The effect of type of administration and sex of subject on emotional tone and outcome ratings of TAT stories. *J. proj. Tech.*, 1958, **22**, 333–337.

Shneidman, E. S., Joel, W., & Little, K. B. *Thematic test analysis.* New York: Grune and Stratton, 1951.

Siegel, S. *Nonparametric statistics for the behavioral sciences.* New York: McGraw-Hill, 1956.

Terry, Dorothy. The use of a rating scale of level of response in TAT stories. *J. abnorm. soc. Psychol.*, 1952, **47**, 507–511.

Waxenberg, S. E. Psychosomatic patients and other physically ill persons: a comparative study. *J. consult. Psychol.*, 1955, **19**, 163–169.

Wittenborn, J. R. Some Thematic Apperception Test norms and a note on the use of the test cards in the guidance of college students. *J. clin. Psychol.*, 1949, **5**, 157–161.

# 13 EPILOGUE

Projective techniques, like other innovations in psychology, developed as a rebellion against the status quo. Just as Wundt rebelled against philosophical arm-chair psychology, Binet against the brass instrument psychology of Wundt (although retaining a trace of it in the weight judgment test), and personality and trait psychology against the Binet global IQ, projective techniques rebelled against the entrenched approaches to the evaluation of personality which psychometricians had developed.

For, although the psychometric movement had gradually succeeded in providing tests for the measurement of intelligence, aptitudes, interests, and achievement, and had accomplished a great deal in distinguishing among these fields and providing tools for their measurement, there remained certain aspects of personality in which psychometrics had not made much progress. These included such areas as motivation, emotion, and such aspects of personality which reflect psychopathology. Projective techniques were born to fill the existing gap in personality measurement. But here, despite the expenditure of tremendous effort, science has not made as much progress as initially expected. Perhaps one of the reasons is the difficulty in isolating reliable external criteria for validating tests in the personality area, whereas in the other areas, simple, objective criteria were more easily found.

Needless to say, projective techniques, especially the Rorschach and the TAT, are as popular as ever, maintaining their lead over other tests in clinical practice. Why is this so? Perhaps social historians will supply a future answer.

The burden of our book has been to examine certain projective techniques (especially the Rorschach and the TAT), indicate their theoretical and practical bases, and evaluate their present-day achievements and failures. What have we learned? Have projective techniques outlived their usefulness, and are they ready to be replaced by more directly focused techniques?

Psychometric standards of reliability, objectivity, and validity have not been conventionally applied to projective techniques. Why not? Some of the historical factors in the growth of these techniques have been examined which may explain this paradox. For example, the special language of the Rorschach technique, or the need to construct a separate "projective theory" may have impeded progress. Projective techniques arose as a protest, and seemed to veer away from the rest of psychology in the attempt to establish their uniqueness. This was especially true of the Rorschach technique, preventing the more experimentally minded psychologists from entering the field. The TAT and its derivatives, however, received more attention from experimentalists. One of the reasons for this may be that the TAT was developed in this country from the very beginning, whereas the Rorschach was imported full-grown from abroad. Furthermore, the Rorschach grew up outside the main stream of psychology, both here and abroad, as a separate "medieval craftguild," whereas the TAT was developed at a university where experimental approaches to personality were part of the training program. As a result, experimentally oriented students were able to leave their impress on the TAT, but have not been able to dent the intuitive, subjective armor of the Rorschach. Another reason might be that the TAT is very much like an interview, and lent itself immediately to content analysis, and when the protocols were treated as interviews, results could be easily related to the results of other clinical evaluations.

Assumptions of projective techniques have by no means been made completely explicit, nor have they all been tested. One major assumption is that perception and personality are related through the mediation of projection. This is essentially known as the "projective hypothesis." Has the marriage between perception and personality been successful? The mere raising of this question reminds one of H. L. Mencken's observation that "whenever a husband and wife begin to discuss their marriage, they are giving evidence at a coroner's inquest." In fact, the experimental evidence for the connection between perception and personality is indeed tenuous.

We have come to believe that a study of the subject's *interpretative* process, rather than of his perception *per se* is of prime importance for the projective worker. For the projective response is *more than* or *other than* a strictly perceptual response, and is subject to the influence of many uncontrolled variables. Recent experimental attention to social-cultural-economic-ethnic factors in the formation of responses highlights our vast ignorance in understanding and interpreting projective material. It has been shown, for example, that concrete behavior is more often found in low socioeconomic groups, not because of higher incidence of pathology, but because of lesser exposure to the linguistic facilitation of abstract thinking. Additional factors to be further understood or eliminated before validity studies can be developed have to do with the subject's set, basic verbal "style," general ability, and the E-S interaction. The role of reinforcement in influencing the response is also beginning to receive some attention. It can be readily demonstrated that a properly placed "mhm" after a certain class of animal responses will tend to elicit more of them in the succeeding responses. Similar effects can be demonstrated on other types of responses. How many of our comparisons between patients and normals have been nullified by these effects, or by the differential nature of these effects, can only be guessed. Other situational factors have also been experimentally shown to affect the subject's responses—for example, instructional sets, hypnosis, activity during or prior to the testing situation, or the introduction of anxiety or other forms of stress.

Until fairly recently, the attributes of the stimuli of projective techniques have received little experimental attention. With respect to the TAT, Murstein has analyzed the role of ambiguity in eliciting projective responses and has adapted the $\hat{H}$ index from information theory to measure the degree of perceptual ambiguity of a picture. His ingenious use of this technique, following Kenny, to measure the dispersion of responses to questions regarding the age of the hero, his sex, his relationship to the other figures, etc., can be regarded as a milestone in the analysis of the ambiguity levels of the cards. By analyzing a TAT card into its elements, and the response into its components, the relationship between the uncertainty of the stimulus and the variability of the responses can be objectively determined. It is heartening to know that more than "fuzziness" is required in the stimulus in order to elicit projective material.

In the Rorschach technique, the work of Baughman and of Siipola in dissecting the stimulus properties which are tied in with a given response represents an endeavor which has not received sufficient attention. It is amazing to see how our built-in scoring prejudices crumble in the wake of this powerful method. By removing, one by one, the various stimulus properties of the Rorschach cards, Baughman demonstrated, for example, that the movement (M) response occurred with the significantly highest frequency in the silhouette version, indicating that it (M) is independent of color and shading. He similarly disproved color as an essential element in the stimulus for eliciting "color shock," and shading for eliciting "shading shock."

Another method for determining the stimulus correlates of Rorschach responses was suggested by Kendall, who had his Ss look at each blot and check one response category (from a list of fourteen which was provided) which they felt best described what they saw. The percentages of responses in each category were computed and indices of similarity for each of the possible pairs of cards were obtained. When these (cosine) correlations were subjected to factor analysis, four clusters of cards were found. A fifth cluster was found when Behn-Rorschach stimuli were also used. The categories of responses which were most characteristic of each cluster were then compared to the common physical attributes for each cluster of cards. In this way, the stimulus correlates of the common responses were determined. This is an indirect way for finding the determinants which give rise to the responses to Rorschach cards, and will help to eliminate subjectivity in scoring.

The wide variety of influences on the projective response, including that of the stimulus itself, contributes to the difficulty in establishing the validity and reliability of projective techniques. Methodological approaches to ascertaining validity and reliability are beset with difficulties; these have been described in detail in the preceding pages. As we begin to particularize the criteria for validation, a curious phenomenon appears. Some of the criteria are better served by non-projective tests. Thus, if hostility can be gauged more readily in a word association test, or by content analysis of interviews, why bother with more time-consuming, less-structured tests? If there is an advantage in using the latter, it should be demonstrable. The use of the Rorschach or other projective techniques to gauge intelligence is not justified unless something beyond measured intelligence is looked for, and if it is, the criterion for the measure sought should be spelled out. As a matter of fact, as the criteria for evaluating projective techniques begin to be spelled out, it becomes more and more apparent that projective techniques are not very efficient and that there are more direct techniques for eliciting the kind of material claimed to be unique to them. Prediction of total or global behavior is virtually impossible, it might be noted, but there is some success in predicting rigidly and narrowly defined "specific" behavior under certain types of experimental conditions. But projective techniques arose as the need for predicting "non-laboratory" behavior became greater—for example, prognosis in therapy. It is with respect to the latter types of prediction that the failures of projective techniques have been most glaring.

Attempts to explore further the components of the projective response have yielded new methods, for example, that of isolating a variable such as the seeing of movement on the Rorschach and constructing instruments concerned with that variable alone. The Levy Movement Blots are an example of such an instrument. Dissatisfaction with certain methodological and statistical inadequacies of the Rorschach technique has resulted in the development of a completely new instruments, for example, the Holtzman Inkblot Technique. Problems in connection with the Rorschach Inquiry have been handled by Baughman's ingenious techniques in conducting the Inquiry. And the low reliability of various conventional Rorschach scores has resulted in the construction of a large number of specific, focused scales, described in detail in this book. But the problem remains: have projective techniques fulfilled their promise? By being regarded essentially as interviews, are they better serving their purpose?

In general, we can summarize the present situation with regard to projective techniques by inquiring whether the concept they are based on is still useful, or whether it is time to give up. Many concepts have developed in science which eventually lost their appeal and good standing. Among them are phlogiston, in physical science, marasmus in medical science, and spontaneous generation in biology. In psychology, it is a little more difficult to point to rejected concepts, since we are never certain whether they might not come back to smite us. All the attempts of Watson to eliminate the unconscious, and of Dunlap to eliminate emotion, for example, have failed. Some have even tried to eliminate personality, but they too have failed.

What will be the fate of projective techniques? It is clear that any attempt to eliminate them today would only provide the need to smuggle them in through the back door. As experimentation in the field of perception progresses, we may be able to specify parameters which determine our responses to visual stimuli more rigorously through more exact specification of the physical characteristics of their component parts. The work of Gibson promises well in this direction. In this way, having specified the physical parameters, we can more directly attribute deviations in responses to the nature of the task imposed on the subject (the instructional variable), the state of the organism, and its history. If there is any systematic variance left after eliminating the influence of the known parameters, we may invoke personality traits

But these personality traits will remain independent, disembodied entities—constructs, if you will—so long as we are ignorant of their origin. Thus, if impulsivity is found to be dependent on some substance in the bloodstream, or on some experience during early development, it loses its status as an independent factor and is relegated to being a parameter of the state of the organism, or of its history. There will still be a need for the integrative concept of personality, but projection may play no part in this integration. While waiting for this millennium, we must bend every effort to objectify our tools, if not for the sake of science, at least for the sake of our patients who may be subjected to needless hazards because of the poor quality of our tools, on the one hand, and our stereotyped interpretations, on the other hand.

Have we established the usefulness of projective techniques? The answer to this question must be qualified. For some limited purposes, perhaps yes. For the general purpose of evaluating personality, the answer must be very tentative and probably negative. Have we made progress in recent years? Here the answer is definitely yes. When we measure our progress against our ultimate aims, the distance we have traveled is infinitesimal. When we measure our present position against our starting point, we have indeed gone far, for even the longest journey must have a first step, and this we have indeed accomplished.

Projective techniques were once young and promising. Today they are only promising. How long can they continue to promise without delivering? Is it not time to collect on the promissory note? These are questions which are decided by practice rather than by science. Even if projective techniques were to disappear, scientists will probably continue to explore the relation between perception and personality. Clinicians, however, would give up their interest if we provided them with better tools. Until these better tools appear, the Rorschach, TAT, and their cognate techniques will flourish despite our warnings. The only safeguard against the harm they may cause is to educate the novice about the limitations of these techniques and to further research to improve them.

We can foresee the day when future scientists will read the historical accounts of our own efforts in the same way that we read the historical accounts of the past, not with disparagement and superior airs, but with humility and wonder as to how—given our ignorance and primitive approach—we were able to persist at all in our search. Furthermore, some of the claims and clinical hunches which the experimentalists now disdain may become the cornerstones of new, objective findings when the more powerful tools of the future become available.

# Author Index

(Boldface numbers indicate pages where full references are given)

# Subject Index